Managing Apple Devices

THIRD EDITION

Arek Dreyer and Adam Karneboge

Managing Apple Devices, Third Edition
Arek Dreyer and Adam Karneboge
Copyright © 2016 by Peachpit Press

Peachpit Press
www.peachpit.com

To report errors, please send a note to errata@peachpit.com.
Peachpit Press is a division of Pearson Education.

Executive Editors: Lisa McClain and Nancy Davis
Production Editor: Maureen Forys, Happenstance Type-O-Rama
Project Editor and Copy Editor: Kim Wimpsett
Technical Editor: Craig Cohen
Proofreader: Darren Meiss
Compositor: Cody Gates, Happenstance Type-O-Rama
Indexer: Jack Lewis
Cover Production: Happenstance Type-O-Rama
Cover Design: Mimi Heft

Notice of Rights
All rights reserved. No part of this book may be reproduced or transmitted in any form by any means, electronic, mechanical, photocopying, recording, or otherwise, without the prior written permission of the publisher. For information on getting permission for reprints and excerpts, contact permissions@peachpit.com.

Notice of Liability
The information in this book is distributed on an "As Is" basis, without warranty. While every precaution has been taken in the preparation of the book, neither the authors nor Peachpit shall have any liability to any person or entity with respect to any loss or damage caused or alleged to be caused directly or indirectly by the instructions contained in this book or by the computer software and hardware products described in it.

Trademarks
Many of the designations used by manufacturers and sellers to distinguish their products are claimed as trademarks. Where those designations appear in this book, and Peachpit was aware of a trademark claim, the designations appear as requested by the owner of the trademark. All other product names and services identified throughout this book are used in editorial fashion only and for the benefit of such companies with no intention of infringement of the trademark. No such use, or the use of any trade name, is intended to convey endorsement or other affiliation with this book.

ISBN-13: 978-0-13-430185-3
ISBN-10: 0-13-430185-4

Thanks to Heather Jagman for her love, support, and encouragement.
—Arek Dreyer

Thanks to Dr. Nasser Hanna and the amazing staff at Indiana University Health. I would have never been able to embark on this journey without them.

This book is dedicated to my parents, Monica and Brian Karneboge.
—Adam Karneboge

Acknowledgments Thanks to you, dear reader, for staying on top of what's new, while keeping your users' needs as the root of what you do.

Thank you to Tim Cook and everyone at Apple for always innovating.

Thanks to Craig Cohen for insightful technical editing.

Thanks to Schoun Regan for his help and guidance, and to his team for setting an example of great documentation.

Thank you to the amazingly capable Nancy Davis and Lisa McClain for gently making sure these materials made it into your hands, and to Kim Wimpsett, Darren Meiss, and Maureen Forys and her team at Happenstance Type-O-Rama for working their editorial and production magic.

Thank you to the following people. Without your help, guidance, suggestions, and feedback, this guide would be much less than what it is.

Jeremy Agostino

Mike Boylan

Weldon Dodd

Josh Durham

Charles Edge

John Filardo

Patrick Gallagher

Erik Gomez

Richard Goon

Christopher Holmes

Andrew MacKenzie

Keith Mitnick

John Poynor

Owen Pragel

Maurits Sanders

Sal Soghoian

Sam Valencia

Kevin White

Joan Work

Table of Contents

Lesson 1	About This Guide 1
	Prerequisites.. 1
	Learning Methodology................................ 2
	Lesson Structure 3
	Exercise Setup 4
Lesson 2	**Apple Management Concepts 9**
Reference 2.1	Understanding Apple's Goals 10
Reference 2.2	Device Management and Supervision 12
Reference 2.3	Apple ID Considerations 17
Reference 2.4	iCloud in Managed Environments...................... 26
Reference 2.5	Apple Deployment Programs 35
Reference 2.6	Deployment Scenarios 39
Exercise 2.1	Configure Your Client Mac 41
Exercise 2.2	Create Apple IDs.................................... 52
Exercise 2.3	Verify Administrator Apple ID Access 58
Exercise 2.4	Configure Your iOS Device........................... 62
Lesson 3	**Infrastructure Considerations 67**
Reference 3.1	Network Considerations 67
Reference 3.2	Security Considerations.............................. 75
Reference 3.3	Physical Logistics 83
Reference 3.4	Support Options 88
Exercise 3.1	Verify Network Service Availability..................... 90
Lesson 4	**OS X Server 5 on El Capitan 99**
Reference 4.1	OS X Server Benefits 99
Reference 4.2	OS X Server Setup................................... 101
Reference 4.3	TLS/SSL Certificates................................. 107
Exercise 4.1	Prepare Your Mac to Install OS X Server for El Capitan 115
Exercise 4.2	Install OS X Server for El Capitan 130
Exercise 4.3	Configure OS X Server for El Capitan.................. 133
Exercise 4.4	Configure Server on Your Client Computer (Optional)..... 143

Lesson 5	Caching Service	147
Reference 5.1	Caching Service Architecture	147
Reference 5.2	Caching Service Setup	152
Reference 5.3	Caching Service Troubleshooting	159
Exercise 5.1	Turn On and Verify the Caching Service	164
Lesson 6	Configuration and Profiles	171
Reference 6.1	Understanding Profiles	171
Reference 6.2	Setting Up Profile Manager	176
Reference 6.3	Creating Profiles via Profile Manager	181
Reference 6.4	Manually Installing Profiles	187
Exercise 6.1	Turn On Profile Manager	192
Exercise 6.2	Create, Download, and Install Profiles for Users and Groups	193
Exercise 6.3	Inspect the Effects of Signing	205
Exercise 6.4	Clean Up Profiles	213
Lesson 7	Mobile Device Management	215
Reference 7.1	Mobile Device Management Architecture	215
Reference 7.2	Profile Manager Device Management	219
Reference 7.3	User-Initiated Enrollment	222
Reference 7.4	Profile Manager Inventory and Organization	231
Reference 7.5	Profile Manager Administrative Tasks	239
Reference 7.6	Automatically Pushing Profiles	243
Exercise 7.1	Enable Device Management	247
Exercise 7.2	Enroll Over the Air	250
Exercise 7.3	Deploy Management Settings	258
Exercise 7.4	Unenroll Over the Air	265
Lesson 8	Out-of-the-Box Management via Apple Programs for Device Enrollment	273
Reference 8.1	Introduction to Apple Programs for Device Enrollment	274
Reference 8.2	Integrate the DEP with Profile Manager	282
Reference 8.3	Configure DEP and Apple School Manager Assignments in Profile Manager	292
Reference 8.4	Troubleshooting the Enrollment Process	303
Exercise 8.1	Enroll with the Apple Deployment Programs (Optional)	305
Exercise 8.2	Configure Profile Manager for the Device Enrollment Program	318
Exercise 8.3	Assign Devices to an MDM Service	326
Exercise 8.4	Create and Manage Device Enrollments	329

Lesson 9	Activation Lock Management 339
Reference 9.1	Activation Lock Introduction 339
Reference 9.2	Manage Activation Lock 343
Exercise 9.1	Observe Activation Lock on an Unsupervised Device 351
Exercise 9.2	Control Activation Lock on a Supervised Device 359
Lesson 10	VPP-Managed Apps and Books. 373
Reference 10.1	Volume Purchase Program Essentials 374
Reference 10.2	VPP Service Enrollment and Administration 383
Reference 10.3	Integrate VPP with Profile Manager 387
Reference 10.4	Purchasing VPP Apps and Books. 390
Reference 10.5	VPP Managed Distribution Assignments 396
Reference 10.6	VPP Managed Distribution User Enrollment. 402
Reference 10.7	Installing VPP Managed Distribution Apps and Books Assigned via Apple ID 409
Exercise 10.1	Configure Profile Manager for the Volume Purchase Program. 410
Exercise 10.2	Purchase and Assign Licensed Apps to Devices. 418
Exercise 10.3	Deploy Licensed Apps to Devices 428
Exercise 10.4	Assign Apps and Books to Users and Invite Participants for VPP Managed Distribution. 432
Exercise 10.5	Inspect the Effects of App Assignment and Remove VPP Managed Distribution Services 449
Lesson 11	In-House Apps and Books 459
Reference 11.1	Deploy In-House Apps and Books. 459
Reference 11.2	Manage In-House Apps and Books via Profile Manager 467
Exercise 11.1	Deploy In-House Apps via Profile Manager (Optional). 474
Exercise 11.2	Deploy In-House Books via Profile Manager 489
Lesson 12	Apple Configurator 2: Planning and Setup 495
Reference 12.1	About Apple Configurator 2 496
Reference 12.2	Apple Configurator 2 Planning. 498
Reference 12.3	Apple Configurator 2 Installation and Setup 505
Exercise 12.1	Get Apple Configurator 2 516
Lesson 13	Apple Configurator 2: Preparing, Configuring, and Managing iOS Devices 525
Reference 13.1	Use Configuration Profiles 526
Reference 13.2	Prepare iOS Devices. 530

Reference 13.3	Create and Use Blueprints	545
Reference 13.4	Organize Devices	547
Reference 13.5	Back Up and Restore iOS Devices	551
Reference 13.6	Automate Device Management	556
Exercise 13.1	Create Configuration Profiles with Apple Configurator 2	560
Exercise 13.2	Prepare an iOS Device Using Automated Enrollment via the DEP	566
Exercise 13.3	Create and Apply Blueprints	576
Exercise 13.4	Back Up and Restore an iOS Device	599

Lesson 14	**Apple Configurator 2: App and Document Management**	**605**
Reference 14.1	Considerations for Managing Apps with Apple Configurator 2	606
Reference 14.2	Manage Apps and Documents via Apple Configurator 2	608
Reference 14.3	Update Apps Deployed via Apple Configurator 2	618
Reference 14.4	Single App Mode	621
Exercise 14.1	Distribute Volume Purchase Program Apps via Apple Configurator 2	625
Exercise 14.2	Distribute In-House Apps via Apple Configurator 2 (Optional)	638

Lesson 15	**User Data and Services**	**645**
Reference 15.1	User Content Considerations	645

Lesson 16	**Managing Access**	**659**
Reference 16.1	Managed Open In	659
Reference 16.2	Limit Access to Content and Services	661
Exercise 16.1	Manage Open In	667
Exercise 16.2	Restrict Access to Services via Profile	693

Lesson 17	**Develop a Management Plan**	**701**
Reference 17.1	Define Requirements	701
Reference 17.2	Consider Third-Party Solutions	704
Exercise 17.1	Develop a Management Plan	706

Index	**713**

Lesson 1
About This Guide

This guide covers a wide range of technologies that help you manage both iOS and OS X devices and provides an intense and in-depth exploration of how to deploy and maintain iOS 9 and OS X El Capitan systems. This guide is for both self-paced learners working independently and those participating in an instructor-led course.

The primary goal of this guide is to help you formulate an effective plan for deploying and maintaining groups of Apple devices. You will be introduced to a variety of Apple management technologies, including Mobile Device Management, the Volume Purchase Program, and the Device Enrollment Program. To help you become truly proficient, this guide covers the theory behind the tools you will use. For example, not only will you learn how to use Profile Manager—the Apple implementation of Mobile Device Management—but you will also learn about the ideas behind profile management, which makes configuration easier for both administrators and users while maintaining a highly secure environment.

GOALS

▶ Understand how this guide is organized to facilitate learning

▶ Set up an environment for self-paced exercises

Prerequisites

This guide assumes you have some knowledge of Apple devices. Specifically, you should be comfortable with basic navigation, troubleshooting, and networking for both iOS and OS X. When working through this guide, a more comprehensive understanding of OS X is preferred, including knowledge of how to troubleshoot the operating system. Refer to *Apple Pro Training Series: OS X Support Essentials 10.11: Supporting and Troubleshooting OS X El Capitan* (Peachpit Press, 2016) if you need to develop a solid working knowledge of OS X.

Further, a more comprehensive understanding of OS X Server is preferred, including knowledge of how to set up and maintain services configured in the Server app.

> **NOTE** ► OS X Server can provide the NetInstall service, which allows you to quickly deploy OS X system software and configuration to multiple Mac computers. Thus, the NetInstall service is often a key component for many OS X deployment workflows. Refer to *Apple Pro Training Series: OS X Server 5.0 Essentials: Using and Supporting OS X Server on El Capitan* (Peachpit Press, 2016) if you need to develop a solid working knowledge of OS X Server and NetInstall.

Unless otherwise specified, all references to systems are the most current versions available at the time of this writing. Because of subsequent upgrades, some screenshots, features, and procedures may be slightly different from those presented on these pages. The minimum referenced versions are as follows:

- iOS version 9.3
- OS X version 10.11.4
- OS X Server version 5.1

Using the Apple Deployment Programs and Apple School Manager

The exercises in this guide illustrate how to enroll with either the Apple Deployment Programs for businesses or Apple School Manager for schools, including the Device Enrollment Program (DEP) and the Volume Purchase Program (VPP). Of course, some of these programs are not available in all countries.

Exercise 8.1, "Enroll with the Apple Deployment Programs," lists many of the reasons why you might not be able to complete that exercise; if this is the case for you, simply read along with the exercise.

> **MORE INFO** ► For more information about the Apple Deployment Programs, see https://help.apple.com/deployment/business/. For more information about Apple School Manager, see https://help.apple.com/schoolmanager/.

Learning Methodology

Each lesson in this guide is designed to give technical coordinators and system administrators the skills, tools, and knowledge to deploy and maintain Apple devices by doing the following:

- Providing knowledge of how Apple deployment technologies work
- Showing how to use specific deployment tools
- Explaining deployment procedures and best practices

The exercises contained within this guide are designed to let you explore and learn the tools provided by Apple for deploying and managing iOS and OS X systems. These exercises move along in a somewhat linear fashion, starting with verification of access to necessary services, moving on to the configuration of those services, and finally testing the results of those services on client devices. Each subsequent lesson and exercise builds on previous topics, with more advanced topics toward the end of the guide.

The exercises in this guide assume you are starting with a Mac that is not yet running OS X Server and that you do not use this server as a production server. This guide also assumes you have one client iOS device and one client Mac computer with OS X. Again, it is recommended that these test client devices are not also being used for production purposes. This is because several of the exercises require that the client devices be erased or reset to their original software state.

This guide serves as an overview of Apple deployment technologies and is not meant to be a definitive reference. The technologies covered in this guide offer many different workflow implementations; it is impossible to include all the possibilities and permutations here. Administrators who are new to managing Apple devices have the most to gain from this guide; still, others who have more experience will also find value in this guide because it covers the latest updates and features for managing iOS and OS X devices.

Lesson Structure

Most lessons in this guide contain a reference section followed by an exercise section.

> **NOTE ▶** "Note" resources, like this one, offer important information to help clarify a subject. For example, to avoid confusion, you should know that this first lesson is the only one in the guide without an exercise section.

The reference sections contain initial explanatory material that teaches essential concepts. The exercise sections augment your understanding of concepts and develop your skills through step-by-step instruction for both self-paced learners and the hands-on portions of an instructor-led course.

> **TIP ▶** "Tip" resources, like this one, provide helpful hints, tricks, or shortcuts. For example, each lesson begins with an opening page that lists the learning goals and necessary resources for the lesson.

MORE INFO ▶ The "More Info" resources, like this one, provide ancillary information. These resources are merely for your edification and are not considered essential for the coursework.

Throughout this guide you'll find references to Apple Support articles. You can find these articles at the Apple Support website (www.apple.com/support), a free online resource containing the latest technical information for Apple products. This guide also references the free online Apple help documentation. You can reach this documentation via specific web addresses or within many applications' Help menus. We strongly encourage you to read the suggested documents and search the Apple Support website for answers to any problems you encounter.

Lesson files and bonus materials are available online when you register your book on www.peachpit.com. Detailed instructions for downloading files are provided in Exercise 2.1, "Configure Your Client Mac." The "Updates & Errata" document contains updates and corrections to the guide (if any).

Exercise Setup

This guide was written so that both the self-paced learner and a student attending an instructor-led class can complete most of the exercises using the same techniques. Those attending an instructor-led course may have the exercise setup provided as part of the training experience; self-paced learners attempting these exercises will have to set up an appropriate environment using their own equipment.

Most exercises contain the following sections:

- ▶ Challenge—Gives you an opportunity to try to complete the exercise without using the detailed steps
- ▶ Considerations—Includes information that might help you complete the exercise
- ▶ Solution—Includes the detailed steps you can use to complete the exercise

NOTE ▶ Some of these exercises, if performed incorrectly, could result in data loss or damage to files. As such, it's recommended that you perform these exercises on an isolated network, using iOS and OS X devices that are not critical to your daily productivity. Peachpit Press is not responsible for any data loss or damage to equipment that occurs as a direct or indirect result of following the procedures described in this guide.

Mandatory Requirements

Here's what you will need to complete the lessons in the guide:

- You need one Mac computer with OS X El Capitan. On this Mac you will install OS X Server, and in this guide it is referred to as your "server computer" or, more simply, your "server." After you are done using your server computer with this guide, you should erase and reinstall OS X on its startup volume before using it again in a production environment.

    NOTE ▶ OS X Server does not require the use of an Ethernet network interface, except to provide Caching and NetInstall services; therefore, if you do not want to perform the Caching service exercise, you can use Mac systems that do not have built-in Ethernet interfaces. Alternatively, on Mac systems lacking built-in Ethernet, you can complete the Caching service exercises by using an Apple USB to Ethernet adapter or an Apple Thunderbolt to Gigabit Ethernet adapter.

- You need an iOS "client" device, running iOS 9.3 or later, and a Mac "client" device, running OS X El Capitan or later. Ideally, you should have one of each type of device since parts of an exercise may focus more heavily on one type over the other. It's also recommended that you test similar technologies on the two client platforms to observe any differences. After you are done using your client devices with this guide, you should reset the devices before using them again in a production environment. Mac computers should be erased and have OS X reinstalled on startup volumes, and iOS devices should have all content and settings erased via the General settings.

    NOTE ▶ Using a virtualized OS X client system is not recommended because virtualized systems are not fully compatible with Apple push services. Using a simulated iOS client system is also not recommended because many deployment techniques are not supported during simulation.

- You need several email addresses you can access, for use in creating and verifying new Apple IDs. You will need multiple Apple IDs that are associated with verified email addresses so you can sign in to a variety of Apple services as required for testing. You'll find specific details about the required Apple IDs in Lesson 2, "Apple Management Concepts."

- For setting up two-step verification for an Apple ID, you need a trusted device that you control that can receive four-digit verification codes using either SMS or Find My iPhone.

- You need a valid licensed copy of OS X Server. Exercise 4.1, "Prepare Your Mac to Install OS X Server for El Capitan," includes more information about purchasing or redeeming a code for OS X Server.

  NOTE ▶ Apple Developer Program members have access to prerelease versions of iOS, OS X, and OS X Server. See https://developer.apple.com/programs/ for more information.

- An Internet connection is required. You'll find specific details about the required Internet access in Lesson 3, "Infrastructure Considerations."
- You need an isolated network or subnet with an exercise-specific configuration. This can be facilitated with something as simple as a small network Wi-Fi router with multiple Ethernet interfaces. For example, an Apple AirPort Extreme is a good choice. You can find instructions for the general setup of an exercise network and specific instructions for configuring AirPort Extreme at www.apple.com/support/airport.

  NOTE ▶ Mac computers can use both Ethernet and Wi-Fi; however, all iOS devices rely solely on Wi-Fi (and optionally cellular). Thus, a Wi-Fi network is required to test iOS deployments.

- You need a router (such as AirPort Extreme) to connect the small isolated network to the Internet.
- To complete the Caching service exercise, you need an Ethernet network cable to connect your server computer to the Ethernet switch.
- You need the student materials demonstration files, which you can download after registering your guide with Peachpit. You'll find instructions for registration and download in Exercise 4.1, "Prepare Your Mac to Install OS X Server for El Capitan."

If you lack the equipment necessary to complete a given exercise, you are still encouraged to read the step-by-step instructions and examine the screenshots to understand the procedures demonstrated.

Network Infrastructure

As previously stated, the exercises require an isolated network. You should replicate the instructor-led classroom environment, which is described in the next sections, as closely as possible so that you do not need to translate between the exercise instructions and your situation.

IPv4 Addresses

The instructor-led environment provides an Internet Protocol version 4 (IPv4) network with a gateway of 10.0.0.1 and a subnet mask of 255.255.255.0; if possible, configure your internal network with the same parameters.

Many consumer-level routers are configured with a gateway of 192.168.1.1 and a subnet mask of 255.255.255.0. You might not be able to change this on your router; in many cases, you will be able to replace the "10.0.0" portion of an IPv4 address in the exercise with a value appropriate for your isolated network (for example, 192.168.1.171 instead of 10.0.0.171 for a server address for student 17). You will need to remember to substitute your network prefix throughout the exercises.

DHCP

The classroom Dynamic Host Control Protocol (DHCP) service provides IPv4 addresses in the range of 10.0.0.180 to 10.0.0.254; if possible, configure your internal network's DHCP service with the same parameters.

If DHCP service is available on your isolated network, your Mac computers will use DHCP during the initial setup, but you will then configure your server to use a manually assigned IPv4 address.

If you can configure your isolated network's DHCP service, configure it to use a similar range of IPv4 addresses. If you are unable to change the range of IPv4 addresses, the DHCP service may assign to a device an IPv4 address already in use by your server computer or your administrator computer. This is another reason to keep your network isolated; do not introduce new devices to it.

Domain Names

The exercises in this guide use the Bonjour .local domain so that your devices can use Bonjour to quickly find the services necessary to complete the exercises. You do not need to set up an infrastructure to ensure that your client devices and your services use the same Domain Name System (DNS) service. Using the .local domain, your devices will be able to find your services only if they are on the same subnet.

This Bonjour .local configuration is recommended for this learning environment only; in a production environment, you should use a fully qualified domain name for your server.

> **NOTE ▶** If your test environment provides a DNS record that provides a fully qualified domain name for your server's primary IPv4 address, when you perform the exercises, use your server's fully qualified domain name instead of its Bonjour.local name.

Advanced Administrators

If you already have advanced server administration skills, you may choose to use different settings, including your organization's Internet domain (instead of .local), your organization's DNS service, and a different IPv4 address scheme, but be warned that this introduces a high level of variability that the exercises cannot address in the given space, and be prepared to modify the exercises on your own as necessary.

Exercise Order

The exercises in this guide are designed to be relatively independent of each other so that you can perform them out of order or skip exercises you are not interested in. However, some exercises you must perform in the correct order, and where appropriate, an exercise lists the prerequisites for that exercise.

- ▶ You must perform all the exercises in Lesson 4, "OS X Server 5 on El Capitan," to install and provide basic configuration for OS X Server before performing exercises in later lessons.
- ▶ You must perform Exercise 6.1, "Turn On Profile Manager," and Exercise 7.1, "Enable Device Management," to complete any additional exercise that relies on Mobile Device Management (MDM) services. Many exercises after Lesson 7 in this guide assume that an MDM service is available.

Apple Online Documentation

Apple's online documentation and support pages are a great source for up-to-date information. Useful resources include the following:

https://help.apple.com/deployment/ios/ (also available in the iBooks Store with the title "iOS Deployment Reference")

https://help.apple.com/deployment/osx/ (also available in the iBooks Store with the title "OS X Deployment Reference")

https://help.apple.com/deployment/education/ (also available in the iBooks Store with the title "Education Deployment Guide")

https://help.apple.com/deployment/business/

Lesson 2
Apple Management Concepts

In 1997 Apple famously affirmed its corporate philosophy by introducing the highly successful "Think different" advertising campaign. Through the years, this motto has continued to ring true as Apple has introduced products that have dominated new categories in personal computing. The iPhone redefined the concept of a smartphone. Then a few years later, Apple thought differently again by creating the iPad and becoming the standard-bearer of tablet devices. Even Apple's mainstay, the Macintosh computer line, continues to sell better year after year despite the fact that the overall portable computer market has been shrinking.

These successes clearly illustrate that Apple's "Think different" design philosophy has worked exceedingly well. Given this record, it should come as no surprise that Apple's interpretation of how to best manage information technology (commonly abbreviated as IT) is significantly different than the approach of its competitors. This lesson, and much of this guide, intends to explain how Apple believes IT administrators should manage iOS and OS X devices.

The lesson begins by defining Apple's goals because understanding them will clarify the reasoning behind the technology design. Then, you will be introduced to the key iOS and OS X features and services you will use when managing Apple devices. Finally, you will explore the most common deployment scenarios, or models, to provide a framework on which to build your specific deployment plans.

GOALS

▶ Understand Apple's design goals and methodologies for device management

▶ Describe the various technologies provided by Apple for deploying and maintaining iOS and OS X devices

▶ Consider which deployment scenario may best meet your needs

Reference 2.1
Understanding Apple's Goals

Like any publicly held corporation, Apple's primary goal is to make a profit and return value to its shareholders. To accomplish this goal, Apple sells only a few categories of products, but those product categories are supported by countless interconnected technologies and services. Despite this complexity, everything Apple produces shares a single common goal: to provide the best possible customer experience.

Apple's Customer

Attempting to create great customer experiences sounds like an obviously good idea, but it raises the question, "Who is Apple's customer?" The hard truth is that the end user, not the IT administrator, is the "customer" that Apple is trying to please. It's the employee crafting a message using the built-in Mail application on her Mac, not the Exchange administrator. It's the student downloading an ebook on his iPad, not the network administrator who installed the Wi-Fi. It's the chief executive officer (CEO) sending a secure chat message to her assistant via iMessage, the contents of which cannot be decrypted by anyone else, even Apple.

Apple considers ease of use, access to content, and strong personal privacy as the primary elements of a great customer experience. Everything Apple creates is in the service of the person using the device, not the people managing it. Understanding this point of view is essential to understanding Apple's view of IT administration.

How Apple Sees IT

Although Apple's overall philosophy is user-centric, don't think that Apple doesn't care about the needs of IT administrators. Even a cursory look at the management technology provided for iOS and OS X devices shows that great care was taken in its design. In fact, Apple views the IT administrator's role much as it views its own: as a provider of technology that is primarily in service of the user.

In many ways, Apple's focus on the needs of the end user goes against many traditional IT administration goals. Traditionally, IT focuses on the needs of the organization by placing an emphasis on uniformity, restricting access, and organizational security. In contrast, Apple technology enables IT administrators to focus on the needs of individual users by placing an emphasis on personalization, easy access, and user privacy.

This emphasis can understandably frustrate IT administrators when their organizations require more restricted device configuration. Apple is listening to these complaints, and as iOS and OS X management techniques have matured, Apple has increased control for IT administrators.

However, even as Apple gives more power to IT administrators, it's important to remember that management of Apple devices is always going to be on Apple's terms. Apple famously holds tight control of all aspects of its products, from hardware to software to services. Therefore, organizations that deploy Apple products are inevitably choosing to embrace Apple's management philosophy and tools. In other words, any organization or IT administrators who try to work in opposition to Apple's technologies and strategies are not going to find success managing Apple devices.

> **MORE INFO** ▶ You can find more about Apple's IT initiatives at www.apple.com/ipad/business/it/ or www.apple.com/iphone/business/it/ (for business customers) or www.apple.com/education/it/ (for education customers).

Keeping Up with What's New

The tools, features, and programs available to us as administrators keep evolving and changing. What you learn in this guide today is a good foundation for what is now available, but your continued success as an administrator relies on your willingness to remain flexible and adapt to new tools, features, and programs. This guide does not cover in detail all the programs recently released as part of Apple School Manager, such as Shared iPad, which allows students to log in to any iPad and then have their content ready on that device, or Classroom, which allows an instructor to guide students' experience with their iPad by helping them open an app, keep a specific app open, open a webpage or iBook chapter, view an iPad, lock an iPad, AirPlay an iPad to Apple TV for all students, and more. In fact, at the time of this writing, a new kind of Apple ID for education, created and assigned by a school, called a Managed Apple ID, is still in preview. These are exciting times, especially if your organization is eligible to take advantage of these features and programs.

> **MORE INFO** ▶ For more information about Shared iPad, search for Shared iPad in the iOS Deployment Reference at https://help.apple.com/deployment/ios/. For more information about Classroom, see Classroom Help at https://help.apple.com/classroom/ipad/1.0/.

This Guide's Goal

In summary, understanding Apple's design goal will help you understand Apple's technology management philosophy and thus the tools provided. Always remember that Apple's goal is to provide the best possible end-user experience for its products. Ergo, the goal of this guide is to help you learn the tools and techniques that will become part of your plan to provide the best possible experience for users in your organization.

Reference 2.2
Device Management and Supervision

Configuring a single Apple device is easy, even for novice administrators, because most settings can be found in the iOS Settings app or OS X System Preferences. Configuring each device individually, however, doesn't scale to meet the needs of even the most modest IT organization. Quickly deploying configuration across multiple devices is best practice for most management tasks. This section describes the core Apple technologies for configuring iOS and OS X devices en masse.

Management via Profiles

Profiles were originally created to provide an easy setup method for iOS devices but are now also available in OS X. A *profile* is a document that includes instructions for specific system settings, such as Internet Accounts or Network preferences. An administrator can create a profile that contains settings that would otherwise be difficult for a user to configure. Profile documents can be identified on OS X computers by an icon and the filename extension .mobileconfig.

Wi-Fi.mobileconfig

Opening a profile in OS X or selecting a profile in iOS will install its configuration settings (after you answer affirmatively that you want to proceed with the installation). You can inspect installed profiles on an OS X computer in System Preferences > Profiles. If there is no profile installed, the Profiles preferences icon does not appear.

Reference 2.2 Device Management and Supervision **13**

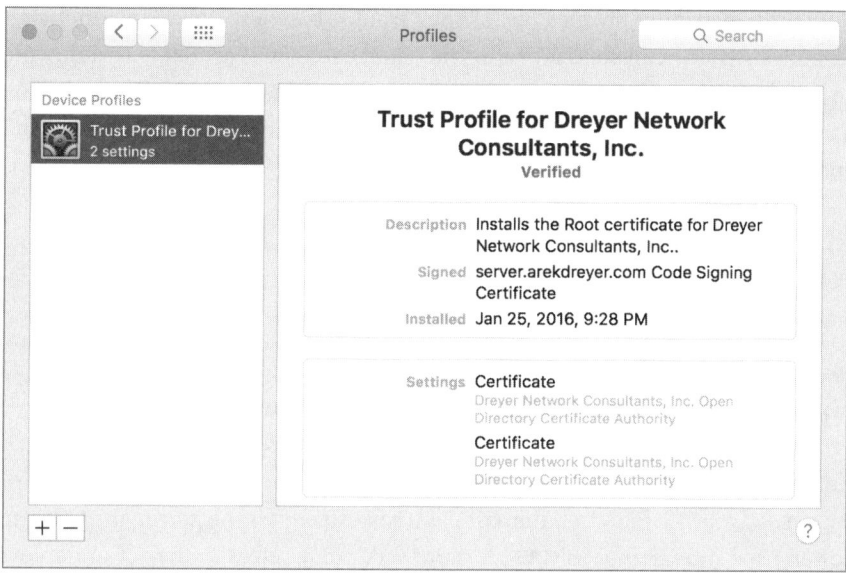

For an iOS device, open Settings > General > Profiles to inspect the installed profiles.

> **NOTE ▶** Depending on what is installed on the iOS device, Settings > General displays either nothing, Profile, Profiles, Device Management, or Profiles & Device Management.

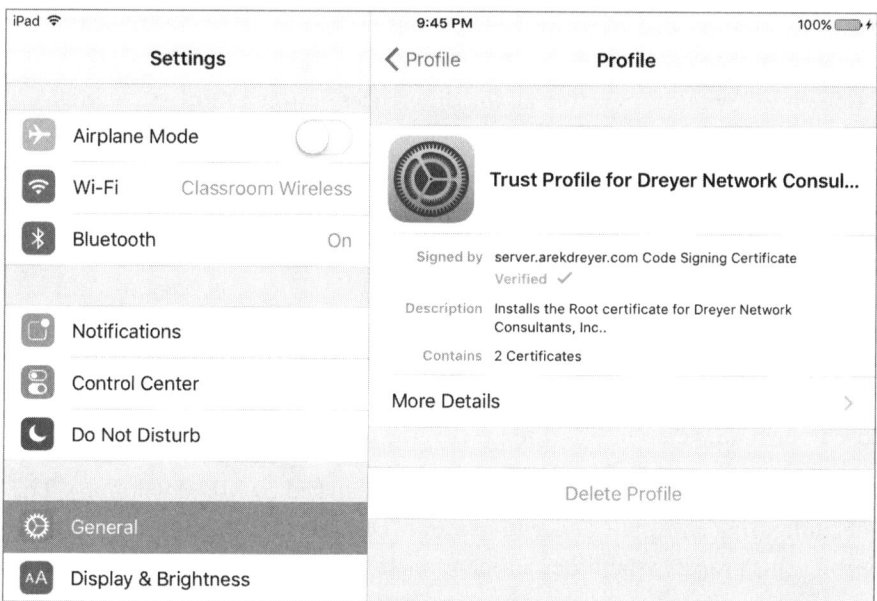

Administrators can distribute profiles just as they would share any other document. For example, an administrator can send a profile via email or make it available as a downloadable link on a website. Alternatively, administrators can automatically push profiles to Apple devices that are enrolled in a Mobile Device Management (MDM) service such as Profile Manager on OS X Server.

> **MORE INFO** ▶ For more information about profiles, see Lesson 6, "Configuration and Profiles."

Mobile Device Management

Mobile Device Management is an umbrella term for any technologies that allow an administrator to remotely manage devices. MDM is also referred to as over-the-air (OTA) management because MDM functions are delivered over network connections that are commonly accessed via Wi-Fi or cellular connections. Although the acronyms OTA and MDM are often used interchangeably, OTA more accurately refers to the act of deploying something remotely, whereas MDM describes the underlying technology that makes that deployment possible.

From an Apple perspective, MDM is the specific implementation used for remotely managing iOS and OS X devices. Using the developer documentation of MDM implementation, any vendor can create an MDM service to manage Apple devices.

> **NOTE** ▶ Dozens of third-party MDM solutions are also available for managing Apple devices. While the specific features of each will vary, they all support core MDM functionality. Obviously, covering all the differences between third-party MDM solutions is beyond the scope of this (or any) guide.

> **MORE INFO** ▶ The web site http://enterpriseios.com offers a comparison of MDM providers in a table format that community members and vendors can update.

> **NOTE** ▶ This guide focuses on the Apple Profile Manager service that is part of OS X Server, but keep in mind that nearly all the technologies covered in this guide are shared between MDM solutions. In other words, even if you choose to use a third-party MDM, you will still find great value in this guide.

Out of the box, Apple devices are not automatically managed by MDM solutions. The process of configuring an Apple device to use an MDM service is commonly referred to as *enrollment*. This process establishes a secure relationship between the device and the

MDM service. After enrollment, most MDM functions are performed automatically, usually with no interruption of the user's experience.

As covered later in this guide, you'll learn that you have a variety of MDM enrollment methods to choose from. Enrollment methods vary from requiring a great deal of user interaction to fully automated workflows. In fact, you can use multiple different enrollment methods based on your specific organizational needs. The specific MDM enrollment workflows you choose are among the most important aspects of your device management plan.

> **MORE INFO** ▶ For more information on MDM, see Lesson 7, "Mobile Device Management."

Device Supervision

Fundamentally, device supervision is a mechanism through which an organization proves its ownership of an iOS device. When an iOS device is supervised, administrators can activate additional management features. In other words, administrators are allowed to perform the most restrictive management actions only on supervised devices that are verifiably owned by their organization.

> **NOTE** ▶ OS X systems have no equivalent to device supervision. Instead, OS X supports multiple user accounts with the ability to define administrator accounts that have more control over the system than standard user accounts.

You can supervise an iOS device using either Apple Configurator (including legacy Apple Configurator or Apple Configurator 2) or the Apple Device Enrollment Program, as detailed later in this guide. There are two ways you can identity whether an iOS device is supervised. One way is to open Settings > General > About. The organization providing device supervision will appear directly below the device's name.

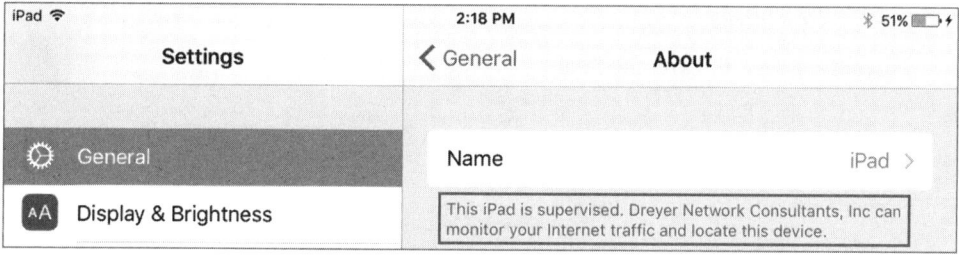

The other way to tell whether an iOS device is supervised is to look at the bottom of the lock screen. There will be a supervision message underneath the "slide to unlock" text if it's supervised.

The following are some of the popular management functions that can be activated only on supervised iOS devices:

- Restricting iOS device pairing (and syncing) with other Mac computers and PCs
- Automatically installing apps (via Configurator or MDM)
- Engaging (and locking a device to) single app mode
- Delivering settings via MDM to prevent the installation of profiles outside of your MDM
- Delivering settings via MDM to configure a global Hypertext Transfer Protocol (HTTP) proxy
- Delivering settings via MDM to restrict iBooks content
- Delivering settings via MDM to disable app removal, AirDrop, and the iMessage service
- Delivering settings via MDM to prevent modification of Siri, Internet Accounts, Find My Friends, and cellular service settings

The following are restrictions that are available only for supervised devices with iOS 9 or later; some of these are perfect to apply for students taking an exam:

- Prevent installing apps using App Store
- Prevent downloading apps automatically
- Prevent using keyboard shortcuts
- Prevent using Define
- Prevent modifying the device name
- Prevent modifying the wallpaper
- Hide the News app
- Prevent pairing with Apple Watch

NOTE ▶ Remember that device supervision is not the same as device management. An iOS device can be enrolled in an MDM service but not supervised. Conversely, an iOS device can be supervised but not enrolled in an MDM server. Obviously, an iOS device that is both supervised and managed gives administrators the most options for managing that device.

Given this list of management functions, choosing whether to supervise iOS devices has a huge influence on your management plans. Put another way, if your organization requires that IT control these features, your plans must include a workflow that will supervise any iOS devices you intend to manage.

MORE INFO ▶ You can turn on device supervision on iOS devices only via the Device Enrollment Program, as described in Lesson 8, "Out-of-the-Box Management via Apple Programs for Device Enrollment," or through Apple Configurator, as described in Lesson 13, "Apple Configurator 2: Preparing, Configuring, and Managing iOS Devices."

Reference 2.3
Apple ID Considerations

An Apple ID is how Apple services identify you as an individual. Apple doesn't care about the personal identification number (PIN) you use to lock your iOS device or even the separate password you may use to log in to your OS X computer. From Apple's point of view, those other identifiers are all secondary to your Apple ID.

Case in point: When setting up a new iOS or OS X device, Setup Assistant asks for your Apple ID before any other personal or security settings. In fact, signing in with your Apple ID during Setup Assistant affects all the first-time configuration steps that follow.

If you tap "Don't have an Apple ID or forgot it?" in Setup Assistant, you get another chance to create an Apple ID.

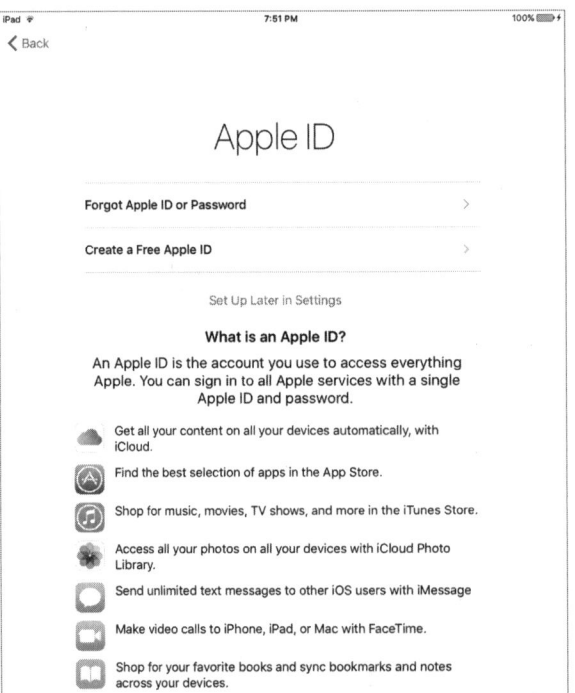

Make no mistake, you don't need to sign in with your Apple ID to set up an iOS or OS X device, but you do need to sign in if you expect to use any of the Apple services that integrate so well with these devices, including the App Store, iCloud, and Apple Deployment Programs.

> **MORE INFO** ▶ The complete list of services that authenticate with an Apple ID is long and constantly changing as Apple adds new capabilities. For the latest list, refer to Apple Support article HT202659, "Where can I use my Apple ID?"

Unfortunately, many IT administrators are confused about the best methods for organizing the usage of Apple IDs or, worse, try to circumvent proper Apple ID usage as part of their management plans. In this section, you'll learn the best practices for creating and using Apple IDs in managed environments.

> **MORE INFO** ▶ This guide focuses on the management aspects of Apple IDs as they relate to deploying Apple devices. A full exploration of Apple ID is beyond the scope of this guide. For more information about Apple IDs, visit the Apple ID support website at www.apple.com/support/appleid.

Creating Apple IDs

You can create as many Apple IDs as you need, and in the case of an administrator trying to manage Apple devices, you will need multiple Apple IDs for various administrative tasks. Your users will also need Apple IDs if they intend to access any online Apple service, including the App Store.

> **TIP** ▶ Later in this lesson you'll find specific instructions for verifying or creating Apple IDs necessary for completing the exercises in this guide.

You can set up a new Apple ID using any verifiable email address that isn't already tied to an existing Apple ID and isn't using an email domain owned by Apple, such as @apple.com. Alternatively, you can set up an Apple ID without an email address by applying for a free email address hosted by iCloud. Any non-iCloud email address must be verified by opening a web link embedded in an automated email sent to the specified email address.

> **NOTE** ▶ Active email accounts that use Apple's legacy domains mac.com or me.com are already set up as Apple IDs. Further, these accounts can also use the icloud.com domain.

Additional information required to create an Apple ID includes entering a secure password, a birth date, and a mailing address, as well as setting up three security questions and answers. The security questions are used to verify users during password changes or after forgetting their Apple IDs.

> **NOTE ▶** Individuals younger than 13 are not allowed to create their own Apple IDs because they are too young to legally engage in a license agreement. However, as covered later in this lesson, parents can create Apple IDs for their children via iCloud Family Sharing, and administrators at educational institutions can set up Apple IDs for their students.

The most common methods for initiating the creation of a new Apple ID are as follows:

▶ When signing in to an Apple website—To access certain Apple websites, you need an Apple ID. Examples include the Apple Support site and Developer site. For the creation of a new Apple ID, these pages link to the website https://appleid.apple.com. You can also manually navigate to this website at any time to create new Apple IDs or manage existing Apple IDs.

▶ When signing in to iCloud during Setup Assistant—On an iOS or OS X device, you can create a new Apple ID when signing in using Setup Assistant or the iCloud account settings. Signing in to iCloud on an Apple device is the only way to enable iCloud services for an Apple ID. It is also the only way to request an email address using the icloud.com domain.

▶ When signing in to an Apple store—To facilitate purchases, you must associate billing information with your Apple ID. When creating a new Apple ID within an Apple store, such as the App Store or iTunes Store, you will also be required to select a billing address and payment method. When acquiring a free item, you are allowed to select None as the billing method, but you must still select a billing address associated with your Apple ID.

> **MORE INFO ▶** See Apple Support article HT204034, "Create an iTunes Store, App Store, or iBooks Store account without a credit card or other payment method," for more information.

Managing Apple IDs

Once you've created an Apple ID, you can modify it by signing in at https://appleid.apple.com. There you can change most aspects of an Apple ID, including the password, the security settings, and even the email address associated with it. Assuming that two-step verification (discussed later in this lesson) has not been turned on for this Apple ID, you can sign in with only the email and password to manage most settings. To edit password and security settings of an Apple ID that does not have two-step verification turned on, you must also answer two of the three security questions that were set during the ID creation.

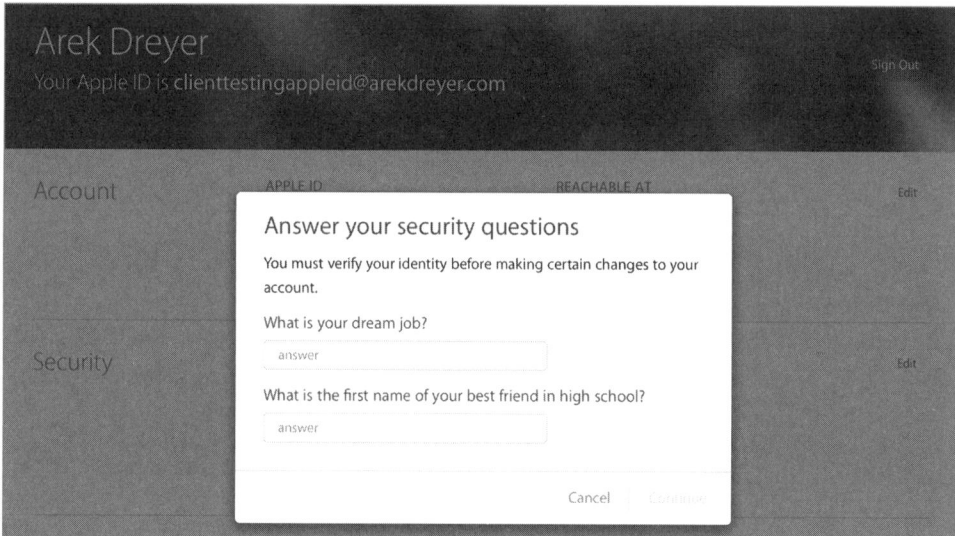

NOTE ▶ Apple IDs cannot be combined. In other words, access to content and services from one Apple ID cannot be merged with another Apple ID. Instead, users are allowed to change the email associated with an Apple ID, and Family Sharing allows up to six people in a family to share each other's purchases (see the "Family Sharing" section).

As a convenience to the user, multiple email addresses can be associated with an Apple ID as long as those addresses aren't associated with another Apple ID. Again, any additional email address must be verified by opening a web link embedded in an automated email sent to the new email address.

With the exception of Apple IDs that use Apple domains (mac.com, me.com, or icloud.com), any email associated with an Apple ID can also be changed as long as the email address is verified, including the primary address used to create the Apple ID. This process is obviously convenient for a user who wants to change an Apple ID, but it also creates a problem for any administrator who tries to use shared Apple IDs for management tasks.

For example, a school administrator could set up a single Apple ID for use by all the teachers who share school-owned iPads. Any teacher who wants to install additional apps would need to know the Apple ID username and password. However, by default, anyone with access to that Apple ID could sign in to https://appleid.apple.com and change the primary email to another email unbeknownst to the other individuals using that Apple ID. Doing so would prevent all others from accessing the Apple ID and its associated services. Fortunately, you can avoid this problem by setting up two-step verification for shared Apple IDs.

Apple ID Two-Step Verification

To enhance the security of any Apple ID, including the ability to prevent other users from modifying shared Apple IDs, you can configure two-step verification. As you've learned, most aspects of an Apple ID can be modified by anyone who knows the email and password. The only additional verification is answering the three security questions set during the creation of the Apple ID. Unfortunately, this form of verification is known to be easily circumvented using social hacking techniques.

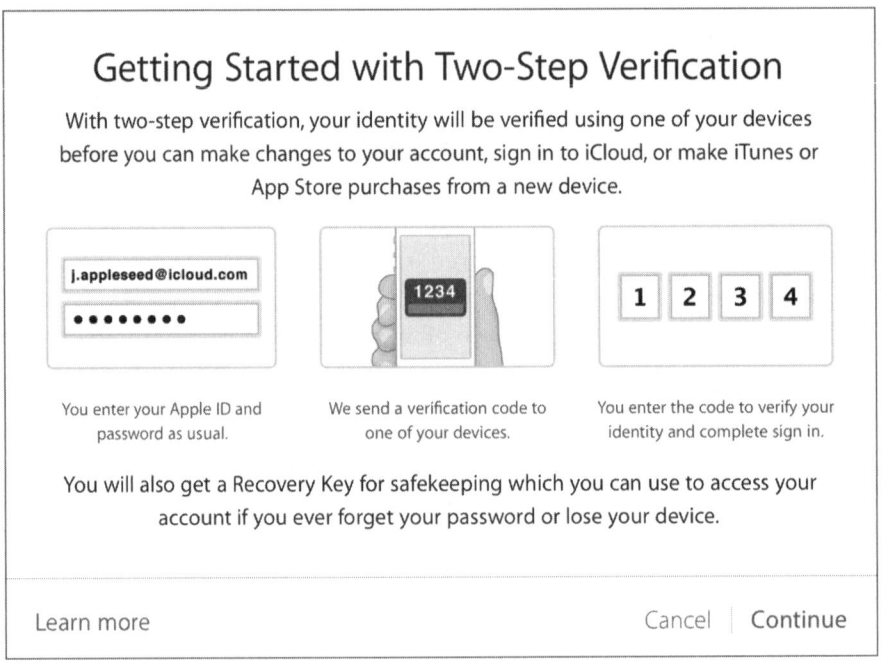

Setting up two-step verification disables the security questions in favor of more robust verification methods. Currently, to turn on two-step verification for an Apple ID, you must use the password and security settings at the Apple ID management website (https://appleid.apple.com). The process involves adding an Apple device or short message service (SMS)–capable mobile phone as a verified "trusted" device.

After a device is identified as a trusted device, it's used for the second step (password creation being the first step) of authenticating an Apple ID. If a user attempts to sign in to an Apple ID service that requires two-step verification, a random security code will be sent to the trusted device. The random code received by the trusted device must be entered to the authenticated service for access to be granted. At the time of this writing, only a few Apple websites require two-step verification, including the Apple ID management site and the Apple Deployment Programs site.

Turning on two-step verification also generates a complex Recovery Key that can be used in lieu of the old security questions should the trusted device be lost or unable to receive the random verification codes. In other words, the Recovery Key is a "backup second step." Apple does not provide a method for securely storing your Apple ID Recovery Key. That is left up to you.

Maintaining the trusted devices and Recovery Key is important. Once two-step verification is turned on, you must always provide two steps of verification to access an Apple ID. If you cannot provide at least two of the three verification methods (random code via trusted device, Recovery Key, and password), the Apple ID will not be accessible, even with Apple's help. Assuming you can successfully sign in to the Apple ID management website, you can modify both the trusted devices and the Recovery Key from the password and security settings.

> **MORE INFO** ▶ You can find out more about two-step verification in Apple Support article HT204152, "Frequently asked questions about two-step verification for Apple ID."

> **MORE INFO** ▶ Two-step verification is different from two-factor authentication, the improved security method built into iOS 9 and OS X El Capitan. See Apple Support article HT204915, "Two-factor authentication for Apple ID," for more information.

Shared Apple IDs

When considering how Apple ID fits into your deployment plans, think of two general categories of Apple ID: those used solely by individuals and those shared by individuals on the behalf of an organization.

Technically, every Apple ID should be accessed by only a single user. In fact, the Apple Support FAQ for Apple ID states in plain language that "Your Apple ID should not be shared with anyone else. It provides access to personal information including contacts, photos, device backups, and more. Sharing your Apple ID with someone else means you are giving them access to all your personal content and may lead to confusion over who actually owns the account." Clearly, Apple expects every user in your organization to have a unique Apple ID. Historically, this precedent has been a source of contention for organizations trying to manage groups of Apple devices.

> **MORE INFO** ▶ The Apple ID support page at www.apple.com/support/appleid/ includes even more information about Apple IDs.

The terms and conditions for Apple ID require the creator to be 13 years and older, and there are currently two ways to create an Apple ID for children younger than 13 (the age may vary by country or region):

- You can create an Apple ID for a child via Family Sharing (see Apple Support article HT201084, "Family Sharing and Apple ID for your child").
- Educational organizations can use Apple School Manager to create Managed Apple IDs for students who are not yet 13 years old; search for Managed Apple ID at https://help.apple.com/schoolmanager for more information about Managed Apple IDs, which are owned and controlled by your school or district.

> **NOTE** ▶ Previously, educational organizations requested Apple IDs for students who are not yet 13 years old via the Apple ID for Students program. Educational institutions can no longer sign up for the Apple ID for Students program, which has been replaced by Apple School Manager.

The other primary reason organizations have resorted to sharing Apple IDs is to work around the App Store authorization mechanism. In short, prior to iOS 9, any item acquired from the App Store (including free items) had to be authenticated with an Apple ID. This presented a significant licensing issue for some organizations, especially for devices that were shared among multiple users.

This issue can be resolved by using managed licenses as part of the Apple Volume Purchase Program and with the feature that appeared with iOS 9, the ability to assign apps to a device rather than to an Apple ID. This is covered later in this lesson.

In other cases, administrators may simply not understand how to properly deploy assets to individual users and are using shared Apple IDs because they haven't learned best practices. Ideally, guides like this one will help alleviate this practice because using shared Apple IDs is often not the best method for managing iOS and OS X devices.

Institutional Apple IDs

In some specific cases, it is desirable for an organization to create Apple IDs that are shared among administrators. This is true for any important organizational resource managed by individuals—a backup individual should always be in place. In these cases, the resources accessed by an Apple ID may be difficult to recover should the primary responsible individual be unable to access the resource.

> **NOTE ▶** Sharing the username and password for an Apple ID without two-step verification turned on is extremely risky. Standard Apple IDs that lack two-step verification can be modified at https://appleid.apple.com by anyone who knows the sign-in information, which allows them to change the primary Apple ID email address to one that may be unknown to the organization.

The simplest method for sharing an Apple ID is to securely communicate the Apple ID and password to another responsible individual in the organization. The other responsible individuals should also have knowledge of any additional security information associated with the Apple ID, such as information about the two-step verification process. Another best practice is to associate a group email address or multiple email addresses with a shared institutional Apple ID.

The following is a list of example services with which an institutionally shared Apple ID may be best for your organization:

- Apple ID used for legacy Apple Configurator systems and, for limited cases, for Apple Configurator 2
- Apple Push Notification service certificate creation
- For businesses and nonprofit organizations: Apple Deployment Programs (Volume Purchase Program and Device Enrollment Program) program agent account and administrator accounts
- For schools: Apple School Manager (Volume Purchase Program and Device Enrollment Program) Managed Apple IDs
- Apple Developer Program, Apple Developer Enterprise Program, or iOS Developer University Program team agents
- GSX program facilitators

Reference 2.4
iCloud in Managed Environments

For your users, iCloud may very well become the single most important service accessed by your Apple deployment. After all, it's the personal documents and settings that are most important to each user. If you don't have a plan for some form of off-device user document storage, at best you're doing your users a disservice by not providing an easy method for sharing content. At worst, if you're not providing some form of backup, you're potentially setting up your users for tragic failure should a device be lost or become irreparably damaged.

Many third-party storage solutions have excellent implementations for iOS and OS X, and there are many great backup solutions for OS X. However, because of the security design in iOS, iCloud is the only solution that provides both cloud-based document sharing and cloud-based system backup for iOS.

It's unfortunate that many organizations prevent iCloud use because of a lack of understanding of how to properly manage iCloud services. This section explores some best practices for setting up iCloud in managed environments.

> **MORE INFO** ▶ This guide focuses on the management aspects of iCloud as it relates to deploying Apple devices. Full details about iCloud are beyond the scope of this guide. For more information about iCloud, visit the iCloud support website at www.apple.com/support/icloud.

iCloud Setup

Strictly speaking, iCloud services aren't free; they are included as part of the purchase of an Apple device. Any Apple ID can gain free iCloud services by signing in on an iOS or OS X device within Setup Assistant or via iCloud settings. Users can sign in with an existing Apple ID, and it will be "upgraded" to include iCloud services, or they can create a new Apple ID with iCloud services.

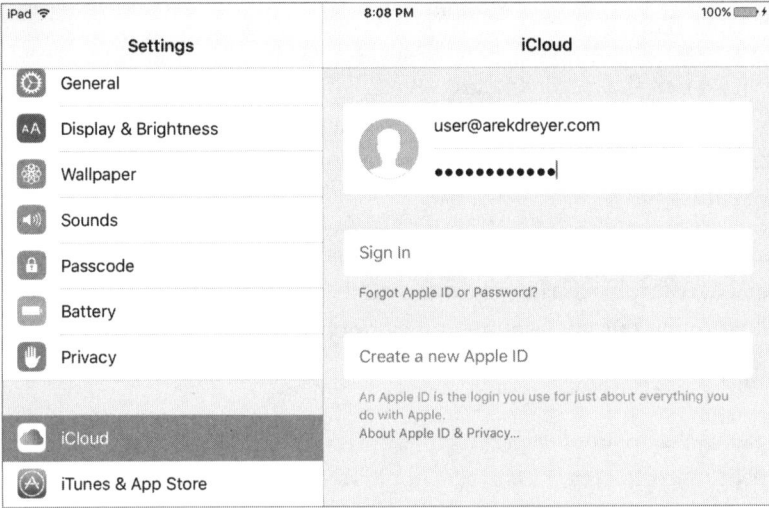

NOTE ▶ Only Apple IDs that use an Apple-owned domain, such as http://icloud.com, can access iCloud mail services with email addresses ending in that Apple-owned domain. Signing in with a non-Apple domain Apple ID will not permit use of iCloud mail services. In other words, if you sign in with an Apple ID like arekd@example.com, it will enable iCloud services for everything except Mail.

MORE INFO ▶ For more information about iCloud Mail, see Apple Support article PH2620, "iCloud: Set up an @icloud.com email address."

An important caveat is that a single Apple device can add iCloud services to only a specific number of Apple IDs. Every time an Apple ID is upgraded or created during iCloud setup, the specific Apple device is verified by Apple's iCloud service. This is not documented by Apple, but at the time of this writing, it's our experience that an Apple device can add iCloud services to an Apple ID three times during the device's life span. That is, a single Apple device can add iCloud services for three Apple IDs. If you attempt to add iCloud services to a fourth Apple ID on the device, the system will report an error.

NOTE ▶ If you sign in to a device using an Apple ID that already includes iCloud services, it does not count toward the device's maximum number of iCloud upgrades.

You should consider this iCloud setup limitation when planning your deployment. If you are planning to give each user her own Apple device, it's recommended that each user set up her iCloud service when first receiving the device. The best practice is to have the user sign in while using Setup Assistant. This will set up iCloud services and also configure the user's Apple ID for other Apple services on the device, including the App Store, iTunes, iMessage, and FaceTime.

On the other hand, if you are planning to deploy and share Apple devices among multiple users, you need to carefully consider how to add iCloud services. Depending on the number of individual Apple IDs you require, it may not be possible to give all your users iCloud access using standard methods.

> **TIP** ▶ This per-device iCloud upgrade limitation is one of the key reasons for educational institutions to create Managed Apple IDs using Apple School Manager. Managed Apple IDs allow some iCloud services but do not allow other services such as iTunes Store, Apple Pay, and iCloud Mail.

iCloud Content and Backup

A key feature of iCloud is the ability to save user documents to Apple's servers and automatically push those documents to other Apple devices. Documents saved in iCloud are also available by going to www.icloud.com using any modern web browser. For iOS devices, iCloud also offers the ability to back up app and system configuration.

At the time of this writing, the basic iCloud service includes 5 GB of storage. Many users may easily fill this storage allotment, especially when using iCloud for data backup. Apple makes more iCloud storage available for a monthly subscription price (if you already have a yearly subscription and select a new monthly plan, your original annual plan will no longer be available). iCloud storage settings, including the ability to purchase more storage, can be managed from the iCloud settings on an iOS or OS X device.

> **MORE INFO** ▶ iCloud service storage upgrades vary by country and may change over time to remain competitive with other cloud storage services. You can find the current upgrade options listed in Apple Support article HT201238, "iCloud storage pricing."

If you are going to rely on iCloud for your users' storage needs, your deployment plans must include methods for dealing with storage limitations. If the budget is available, you can plan for the monthly (or legacy annual) purchase of more storage. Regardless of the amount of storage, though, you should always budget some time to train your users on how to manage storage using the iCloud settings.

If you are concerned about the unintentional leakage of organizational information via iCloud, evaluate the following restrictions for managed devices. For iOS devices, you can restrict the following:

- Allowing iCloud backup
- Allowing iCloud documents and data
- Allowing iCloud keychain
- Allowing managed apps to store data in iCloud
- Allowing iCloud Photo Sharing

For OS X, the following restrictions are available:

- Allowing iCloud documents and data
- Allowing use of iCloud password for local accounts

    MORE INFO ▶ See Lesson 16, "Managed Access," for more information about preventing the unintentional leakage of organizational information.

    MORE INFO ▶ Lesson 15, "User Data and Services," covers techniques for managing user backups in greater detail.

iCloud Security

Your organization may have legitimate security concerns that information could leak through iCloud services. This concern is valid for any sharing service, including legacy services that have been in use for years such as simple email. When security is a concern for your organization, your deployment plans must address that concern.

To start, the iCloud service itself employs an array of security technologies. All iCloud data is encrypted in transit, and nearly all data stored in iCloud remains encrypted on Apple's servers. Only the iCloud mail service (hosted on mac.com, me.com, or icloud.com domains) stores email messages in an unencrypted format on the server, but this is a standard practice that permits interoperation with other email services. In this case, a common practice is to use optional S/MIME encryption to protect email messages.

    MORE INFO ▶ You can find more details regarding the security mechanisms used by iCloud in Apple Support article HT202303, "iCloud security and privacy overview."

As an administrator, you have additional management options for controlling iCloud access on iOS devices. Using a profile, you can restrict the ability to save documents or backups to iCloud. For more specific control, an administrator can also manage the ability of individual apps to share documents with other apps and services. Doing so limits an app's ability to interact with iCloud or any other document-sharing service.

In addition to these management features, Apple has engineered iOS to always enforce strict segregation between services. For example, email hosted by your organization is stored in its own encrypted container on iOS, separate from other email services. In this case, iCloud services are also stored separately from other services. This security architecture allows your organizational services to live alongside personal services such as iCloud.

Given the advanced security architecture built into iOS and an administrator's ability to further control what is shared through iCloud, you may consider the advantages of allowing iCloud for personal use. By encouraging your users to take advantage of iCloud for personal use, they will keep their personal information away from your organizational services. Consider this a win-win for both sides because users can use an organizational device for occasional personal communications and administrators can keep those personal communications off their services.

To help users with more than one device on the network sync their iCloud data faster, the Caching service for OS X Server 5.0 and later can cache iCloud data (photos and documents) for devices with iOS 9 or El Capitan or later. The iCloud data is encrypted in transit over the network, as well as on the Caching server's storage.

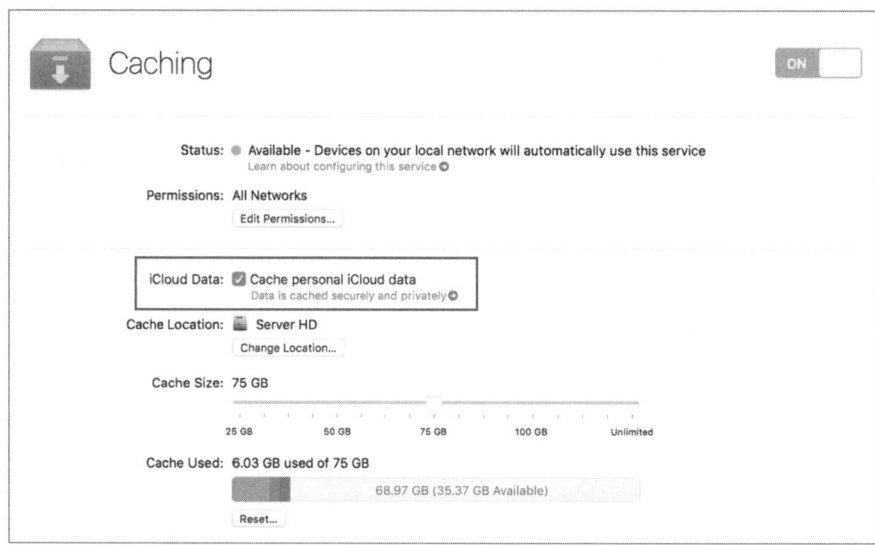

MORE INFO ▶ Lesson 15, "User Data and Services," covers techniques for managing user documents in greater detail.

Find My Device and Activation Lock

One of the most useful features of iCloud is the Find My Device service (also known as Find My iPad, Find My iPhone, or Find My Mac), which allows you to remotely locate a lost iOS or OS X device. This service uses the device's built-in wireless capabilities to pinpoint the misplaced or stolen device.

The first time an Apple ID is signed in to iCloud on a device, the system will prompt the user to turn on the Find My Device service. This service can also be turned on or modified in the iCloud settings.

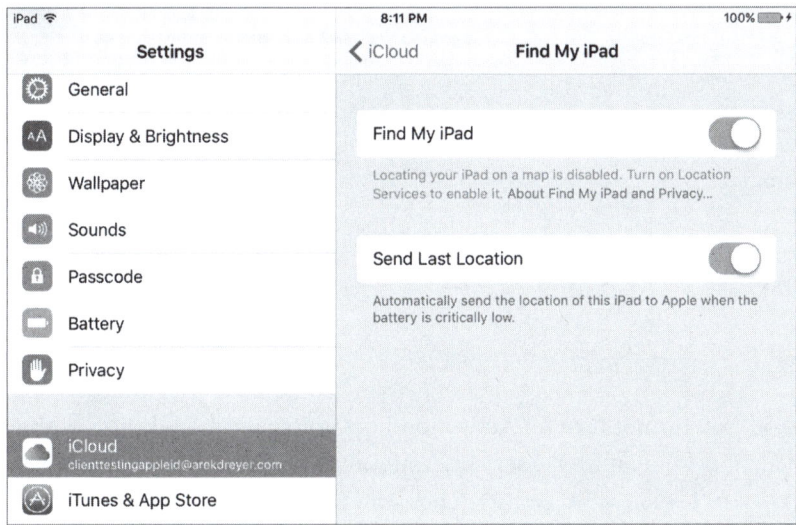

TIP ▶ The Send Last Location setting is off by default.

You can find lost devices by signing in to the Find My iPhone app for iOS or by using any modern web browser to sign in to www.icloud.com and then selecting Find iPhone. This will allow you to locate any lost iOS or OS X device that has Find My Device turned on. Within this interface, you can also remotely force the device to make a sound, to lock and display a message, or to completely wipe the system contents.

Normally, turning on Find My Device will also turn on another security feature known as Activation Lock. Should a lost device with Activation Lock turned on be wiped and reset, the subsequent Setup Assistant process will not proceed unless a user enters the password associated with the Apple ID that originally turned on Find My Device. Activation Lock is a theft-deterrent measure that prevents another user from completing Setup Assistant without knowing the previously used Apple ID. The following figure is an example of the Activate iPad screen for an iPad that has Activation Lock enabled.

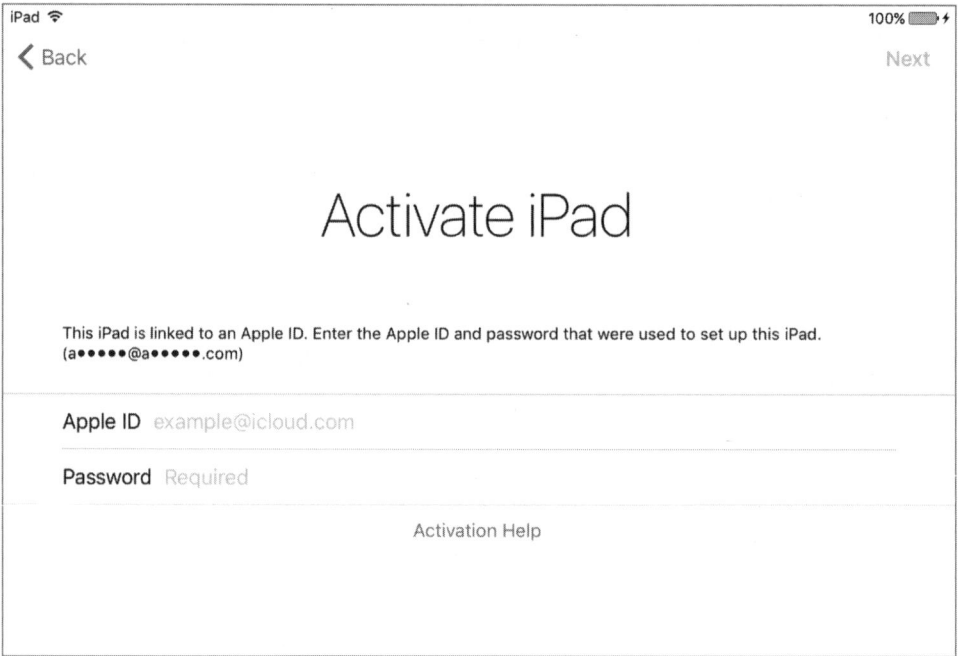

MORE INFO ▶ You cannot turn on Activation Lock for supervised devices without further instruction from an MDM service. You can find techniques for managing Activation Lock in Lesson 9, "Activation Lock Management."

A single Apple ID can turn on Find My Device and Activation Lock for multiple devices, but on each device you can configure only one Apple ID for these services. In other words, after activating Find My Device and Activation Lock on an iOS device, you cannot add additional Apple IDs for these services. On OS X, attempting to sign in with another Apple ID for these services will require that the user authenticate using the password for the previously used Apple ID. These implementations effectively prevent someone from surreptitiously changing the Apple ID used for Find My Device and Activation Lock.

> **NOTE** ▶ Again, Apple regards personal privacy as more important than administrative needs. This is why only a single Apple ID can be used to track an Apple device (with the exception of Lost Mode for supervised iOS devices). Apple intends that Apple ID to belong to the user, not to an administrator trying to track device usage.

However, the fact that only one Apple ID can be used for Find My Device and Activation Lock presents a problem for some organization-owned devices. Specifically, your deployment plan needs to consider which Apple ID will be used to turn on these security features. In some organizations, sharing an Apple ID among trusted administrators may be best. In other situations, individuals may be required to use their own Apple IDs and then work with an organization's administrators if they need to use Find My Device.

> **MORE INFO** ▶ See Apple Support article PH2700, "iCloud: Use Lost Mode" for more information about using Lost Mode.

> **MORE INFO** ▶ See Reference 3.2, "Security Considerations" for more information about the new feature for iOS 9, MDM Lost Mode, which requires a supervised iOS device, and does not require iCloud.

iCloud Family Sharing

iOS 8 and OS X Yosemite introduced iCloud Family Sharing, allowing families of up to six people to share each other's photos, calendars, Find My Device, iTunes, iBooks, and Mac App Store purchases without sharing account information. In other words, family members can sign in with their own personal Apple ID and share iCloud-based services and purchases with up to five other people in the Family Sharing group.

An adult user who is signed in to iCloud on an Apple device can start and organize a Family Sharing group from the iCloud settings. This first Apple ID is designated the "organizer" of the Family Sharing group. The organizer account must be set up with credit card payment information because all other family members can be allowed to purchase using this payment information. The organizer can invite other adults via their Apple ID to the Family Sharing group and also create new iCloud accounts for children younger than 13.

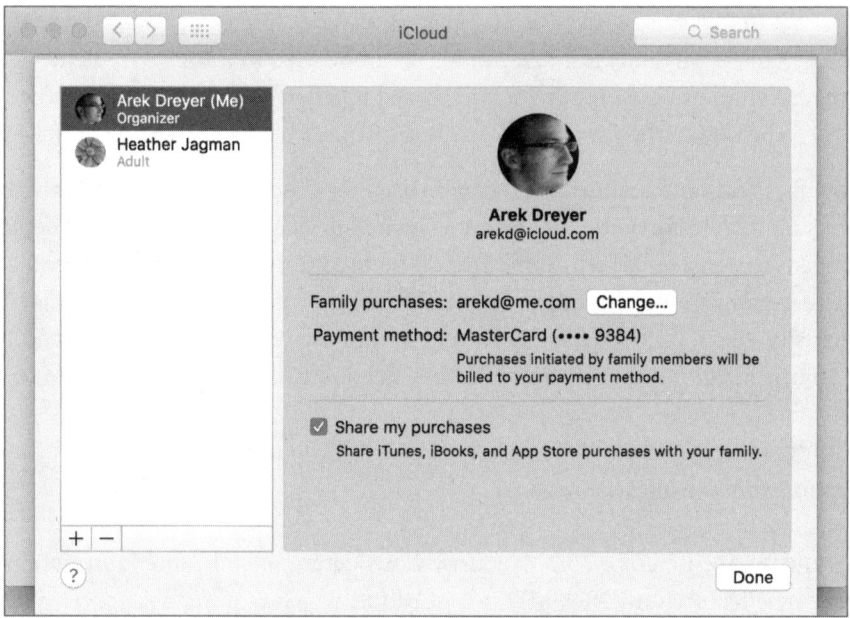

While extremely convenient for managing a family of personal devices, it's important to recognize that iCloud Family Sharing is not designed for institutional use. There are many intentionally designed features of iCloud Family Sharing that make it ideal for families but extremely limited for organizational management. On the other hand, users in your organization can still join an iCloud Family Sharing group without interrupting your management plans.

For example, Apple IDs created by an educational institution via the legacy Apple IDs for Students program (replaced by Apple School Manager) can participate in their parents' iCloud Family Sharing group; however, at the time of this writing, it is not documented whether Managed Apple IDs created with Apple School Manager can participate in iCloud Family Sharing. Also, assets purchased on the behalf of your organization via the Volume Purchase Program (also covered later in this lesson) are prevented from being shared to the other members of an iCloud Family Sharing group. Finally, while device location information may be shared to other members in an iCloud Family Sharing group, they cannot lock or wipe a device unless they authenticate as the Apple ID used to turn on Find My Device.

> **MORE INFO** ▸ You can find out more about iCloud Family Sharing at https://www.apple.com/icloud/family-sharing/.

Reference 2.5
Apple Deployment Programs

The Volume Purchase Program (VPP) and the Device Enrollment Program (DEP) are two integral deployment programs available to schools and businesses. In March 2016, Apple introduced Apple School Manager, available at https://school.apple.com, as a starting point for schools to use the VPP, the DEP, Managed Apple ID, and more. Businesses and nonprofits should continue to use https://deploy.apple.com as a starting point for the VPP and the DEP. For many organizations, regardless of the type, these programs are indispensable because managing certain aspects of their Apple deployment without them would be impossible.

> **MORE INFO** ▶ At the time of this writing, Apple Deployment Programs and Apple School Manager are available in many regions but not all regions where Apple devices are sold. Check https://deploy.apple.com/enroll/selectcountry to see whether your country or region has availability for Apple Deployment Programs; for Apple School Manager, search for Overview at https://help.apple.com/schoolmanager/.

Device Enrollment Program

The Apple Device Enrollment Program (DEP) allows administrators to manage the initial activation and setup of iOS and OS X devices. Only devices that are purchased directly from Apple or through participating Apple Authorized Resellers and carriers can be managed via the DEP service. This ensures that only those devices belonging to an organization are affected by the DEP management settings. As a result, a personally purchased Apple device can never be affected by an organization's DEP settings.

Devices in the DEP service will automatically be redirected to your MDM service during activation and setup. Within your MDM service, you can specify a variety of enrollment and Setup Assistant options. The most significant options include the ability to enforce automatic MDM enrollment and device supervision during the setup process.

This means that individual users, instead of administrative staff, can easily complete the steps needed to enable management for an Apple device. Setup Assistant displays the name of the organization that will configure the device.

If the user taps About Configuration, she can verify the configuration information.

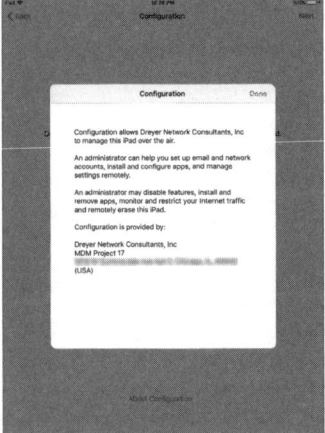

As an administrator, you can optionally require that users provide credentials using your organization's directory services. Note that in the following there is no Skip button, and users cannot tap Next until they enter credentials.

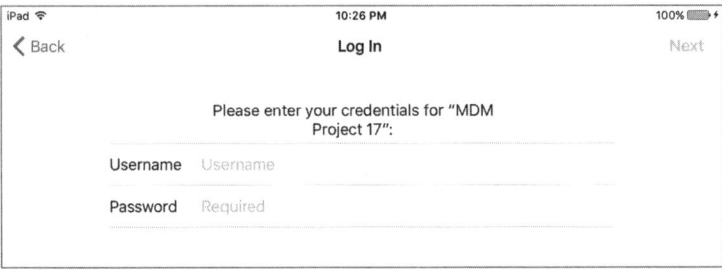

The DEP is also the only means to turn on device supervision over the air and to prevent the removal of an MDM enrollment profile. Further, devices that are reset will conform to your enrollment and Setup Assistant options as long as they are still part of the DEP. This situation not only makes reprovisioning devices a snap but also acts as a strong theft deterrent by preventing unauthorized users from completing the device setup.

MORE INFO ▶ Lesson 8, "Out-of-the-Box Management via Apple Programs for Device Enrollment," explores how to use the Device Enrollment Program.

Volume Purchase Program

The Apple Volume Purchase Program (VPP) allows administrators in an organization to manage the purchase and licensing of content from the iOS App Store, the Mac App Store, and the iBooks Store. From the VPP website, administrators can purchase new content and manage existing purchases. There are two primary methods for distributing the VPP content: legacy redemption codes and managed license distribution (also referred to as *managed distribution*). Managed distribution requires iOS 7 or later or OS X Mavericks v10.9 or later.

The legacy method involves distributing redemption codes for purchased apps. These codes can be deployed locally to iOS devices via the legacy version of Apple Configurator or distributed remotely using a supported MDM service. (Apple Configurator 2 and Profile Manager do not support distribution of redemption codes.) Unfortunately, redemption codes deployed to an individual are fully transferred to that user's Apple ID. Thus, an organization could lose the license upon redeeming the code.

This drawback of redemption codes is the primary reason that most deployments now rely on managed license distribution.

> **NOTE** ▶ See Apple Support article HT202863, "Migrate from redemption codes to managed distribution with the Volume Purchase Program."

With managed distribution, a supported MDM service or Apple Configurator 2 facilitates the relationship between an organization's licensed purchase and devices or users:

- You can assign apps and books to employees, contractors, teachers, or students.
- For iOS 9 or later or OS X El Capitan or later, you can distribute apps to devices. This new feature, called *device-based app assignment*, is particularly exciting for organizations whose users share devices among multiple people.

After you assign an app or book to a person, they must agree to join your organization's VPP program and provide their Apple ID. Your MDM keeps track of the relationship between the user's directory record and the user's Apple ID (which you do not know; after all, an Apple ID is personal).

VPP licenses for apps can be assigned to individuals or devices as appropriate and later recovered by the organization for use by another individual or device. Keep in mind, though, that even with managed license distribution, iBooks Store content cannot be revoked from a user's Apple ID or otherwise reassigned.

> **MORE INFO** ▶ Lesson 10, "VPP-Managed Apps and Books," describes the Volume Purchase Program.

Apple School Manager

Among other features, Apple School Manager gives school administrators the ability to create Apple IDs en masse for their students. Through this program, an administrator can upload lists of students and their associated email addresses, or connect to a supported Student Information System (SIS), for the creation of new Managed Apple IDs.

This program also provides a workflow that allows individuals younger than 13 to have a Managed Apple ID, which is limited for the student's protection. Services and features that shouldn't be made available to children are turned off for Managed Apple IDs.

MORE INFO ▶ Apple School Manager serves only a specific audience and is well understood by reading Apple's own documentation. Details regarding this program are beyond the scope of this guide. For more information, please refer to http://help.apple.com/schoolmanager/.

Reference 2.6
Deployment Scenarios

An administrator has many significant decisions to make when formulating an Apple deployment plan. This process is further complicated by the interconnected nature of the many available technologies because one technology choice often affects other choices.

Despite this complexity, you can find a management solution by framing your deployment plans around three common deployment scenarios. These three scenarios weren't arrived at by accident because Apple has specifically designed the management technologies in iOS and OS X to support them.

User-Owned Device

This scenario reflects a workflow in which the user personally owns the Apple device but administrators need to allow access to organizational assets and services. Other common terms used to describe this scenario include "bring your own device" (BYOD) in enterprise environments and "student-owned device" in educational environments.

- ▶ Administrative oversight in this scenario is light to moderate because the device is ultimately under the control of the user.
- ▶ Users can self-enroll the device into an MDM service.
- ▶ Supervision is not an option because the device is owned by the user.
- ▶ The user will almost certainly use a personal Apple ID to access services such as the App Store and iCloud.
- ▶ Administrators can use MDM profiles to grant access to specific resources and enforce security requirements.
- ▶ Administrators can purchase apps and books via VPP and then grant access to apps and books to users and groups and grant access to apps to eligible devices or device groups.

Organization-Owned, Personally Enabled Device

This scenario reflects a workflow in which the organization owns the Apple device and it is used by one individual. Other common terms used to describe this scenario include "corporate-owned personal device" in enterprise environments and "one-to-one device" in educational environments.

- ▶ Administrative oversight in this scenario is moderate to high because the device control is shared between the user and administrators.
- ▶ The user can provide the initial configuration by completing Setup Assistant. The DEP can be used to enforce supervision and MDM enrollment during the device setup.
- ▶ Each user will have a unique Apple ID. This can be the user's personal Apple ID or an Apple ID provided by the organization; for schools, this could be a Managed Apple ID.
- ▶ Administrators can use MDM profiles to grant access to specific resources and enforce security requirements. Supervision will allow for more restrictive management options.
- ▶ Administrators can purchase apps and books via the VPP and then grant access to apps and books to users and groups and grant access to apps to eligible devices or device groups.

Organization-Owned, Nonpersonalized Device

This scenario reflects a workflow in which the organization owns the Apple device and it is shared by multiple users. Other common terms used to describe this scenario include "single-use device" or "kiosk device" in enterprise environments and "shared device" or "cart device" in educational environments.

- ▶ Administrative oversight in this scenario is moderate to heavy because the device is largely controlled by administrators.
- ▶ Administrators will fully control the initial configuration, including device supervision and MDM enrollment. This can be managed via the DEP or Apple Configurator.
- ▶ Users will not use a personal Apple ID on these devices; instead, administrators can create and use institutionally shared Apple IDs. In most cases, each Apple ID will be used for multiple devices that share a similar location, such as those stored nightly in a charging cart; schools will use Managed Apple IDs.

- Administrators can use the full breadth of MDM configuration and control features because the devices will also be supervised.
- Administrators can use device-based app assignment to install apps on devices. Another option, at least for iOS devices, is to deploy apps and documents using Apple Configurator 2, which will ensure that all devices have the same configuration.
- Administrators can assign in-house books to devices.

  NOTE ▶ Search for Shared iPad at https://help.apple.com/deployment/ios/ for more information about the Shared iPad program for schools.

Exercise 2.1
Configure Your Client Mac

▶ **Prerequisite**

   ▶ A Mac with OS X El Capitan on its startup volume that has never had OS X Server installed and configured on its startup volume

NOTE ▶ Before you use a dedicated server Mac to run OS X Server, you can use a client Mac to perform the exercises in this lesson and in Lesson 3, "Infrastructure Considerations." This client Mac will be a client for Profile Manager, and you can optionally use the Server app or screen sharing to remotely administer your server.

In this exercise, you will configure your client Mac in preparation to remotely manage your server and to be managed by your server's Profile Manager service.

To match your experience with the exercise instructions, you'll use one of two options to configure a local administrator account, depending on whether you are performing these exercises independently or are in an instructor-led environment.

In both situations, you'll use Sharing preferences and apply any necessary system software updates.

Challenge

Set up your client computer with a unique computer name. Download the student materials.

Considerations

The exercises in this guide are written so that the individual reader and the student in the instructor-led environment have similar experiences.

Solution

Establish Your Student Number

In this exercise, you will use a student number to provide unique names and addresses for your computers.

1. If you are in an instructor-led environment, obtain your student number from the instructor.

    If you are performing these exercises independently, you can use any number from 1 to 17. Because the following steps use student number 17 in its examples, you might consider choosing 17 as your student number.

If your client computer has not yet been set up and is at the Welcome pane, perform the steps in the Option 1 section. Otherwise, skip to "Option 2: Configure an Existing OS X System for Your Client Computer."

Option 1: Configure OS X on Your Client Computer Using Setup Assistant

As previously noted, these steps are necessary only if your client computer has not already been set up, which is the situation in an instructor-led environment.

Ensure that you have El Capitan installed on your client computer. If it isn't already installed, install it now using the Mac App Store, OS X Recovery, or a method specified by your instructor; then continue when you reach the Welcome pane.

In this section, you'll step through the OS X Setup Assistant for the initial system configuration of your client computer.

1. Ensure that your client computer is connected to a valid network, unless you plan to use Wi-Fi as your primary network connection.

2. If necessary, turn on your client computer.

3. At the Welcome screen, select the appropriate region, and click Continue.

4. Select the appropriate keyboard layout, and click Continue.

   Setup Assistant evaluates your network environment and tries to determine whether you are connected to the Internet. This can take a few moments.

5. If you plan to use Ethernet for your primary network connection and are not asked about your Internet connection, your computer's network settings have already been configured via DHCP, and you may skip to step 8.

   If you plan to use Wi-Fi for your primary network connection and are at the Select Your Wi-Fi Network screen, select an appropriate Wi-Fi network, provide the Wi-Fi network's password if necessary, click Continue, and skip to step 8.

   If you plan to use Ethernet for your primary network connection and you see the Select Your Wi-Fi Network screen, this could indicate any number of conditions, including the following:

   ▶ Your Mac does not have a built-in Ethernet port.
   ▶ Your Mac is connected via Ethernet to a network that does not supply the DHCP service.
   ▶ Your Mac has not yet received DHCP configuration.
   ▶ Your Mac is connected via Ethernet to a network that offers DHCP service, but the network is not connected to the Internet.
   ▶ Your Mac is not connected to a network via Ethernet.

   If you are performing the exercises in an instructor-led environment, ask your instructor how you should configure your computer; it is possible that the classroom DHCP service is not turned on or that your computer is not connected to the classroom network.

   To configure your Mac to use an Ethernet port, click Other Network Options.

6. If you are at the How Do You Connect? screen, select Local network (Ethernet), and click Continue.

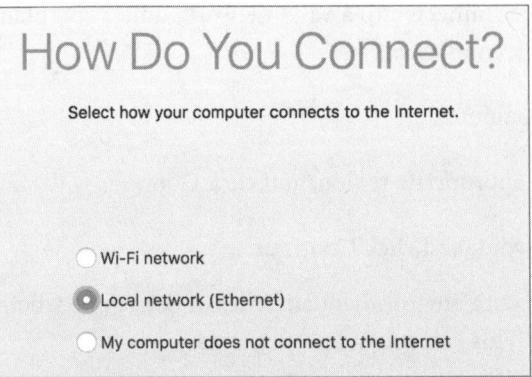

7   If you are at the Your Internet Connection screen, leave the settings at their defaults, and click Continue.

   NOTE ▶ If no DHCP service is available or your network is not connected to the Internet, you will see the warning message "Your Mac isn't connected to the internet." In this case, click Try Again, configure your router to provide DHCP service, and make sure your network is connected to the Internet. Then click Continue in the Your Internet Connection pane. For advanced users on a network without DHCP, you can set your TCP/IP connection type to Manually, configure settings appropriate for your network, and then click Continue in the Your Internet Connection pane.

8   At the Transfer Information to This Mac screen, select "Don't transfer any information now," and click Continue.

9   If the Enable Location Services screen appears, select "Enable Location Services on this Mac," and click Continue.

10 At the "Sign in with Your Apple ID" screen, select "Don't sign in," click Continue, and then click Skip to confirm that you want to skip signing in with an Apple ID. If you do enter an Apple ID, some of the following figures may look slightly different from your results, and you may need to perform extra steps.

11 At the Terms and Conditions screen, read the terms and conditions, and click Agree; then in the dialog to confirm that you have read and agree to the OS X software license agreement, click Agree.

Create Your Local Administrator Account

Creating the local administrator account as specified in the following steps is essential. If you do not, future exercises may not work as written. Highlighted text is used throughout this guide to identify text you should enter exactly as shown.

1   At the Create Your Computer Account screen, enter the following information:

▸   Full Name: Local Admin

▸   Account Name: ladmin

▸   Password: ladminpw

▸   (verify field): ladminpw

▸   Hint: Leave blank.

▸   Deselect the checkbox "Set time zone based on current location."

> **NOTE ▸** In a production environment, always use a strong password.

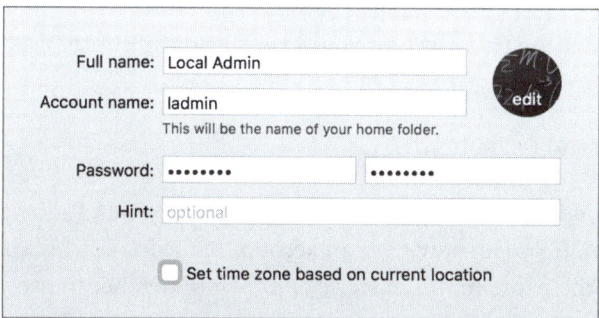

2   Click Continue to create the local administrator account.

3   At the Select Your Time Zone screen, click your time zone in the map or choose the nearest location in the Closest City pop-up menu, and then click Continue.

4   At the Diagnostics & Usage screen, leave selected "Send diagnostics & usage data to Apple" and "Share crash data with app developers," and then click Continue.

Please skip the Option 2 section, and continue with the "Set the Computer Name and Turn On Remote Management" section.

Option 2: Configure an Existing OS X System for Your Client Computer

This option is designed only for those who are performing the exercises independently and who have a computer that is already set up with an existing administrator account.

> **NOTE ▶** If your computer has not been set up (that is, if the initial administrator account has not been created), perform the steps in "Option 1: Configure OS X on Your Client Computer Using Setup Assistant" instead.

Create a New Administrator Account in System Preferences

1   If necessary, log in with your existing administrator account.

2   Open System Preferences.

3   In System Preferences, open Users & Groups.

4   In the lower-left corner, click the lock icon.

5   In the dialog that appears, enter the password for your existing administrator account, and click Unlock.

6   Under the user list, click the Add (+) button.

> **NOTE ▶** Creating this account as specified here is essential. If you do not, future exercises may not work as written. If you already have an account named Local Admin or ladmin, you will have to use the name in this exercise and then remember to use your substitute name throughout the rest of the exercises. Highlighted text is used throughout this guide to indicate text you should enter exactly as shown.

7   In the dialog that appears, use the following settings:

▶   New Account: Choose Administrator.

▶   Full Name: Local Admin

▶   Account Name: ladmin

8   Select "Use separate password."

9   If you are performing the exercises in an instructor-led environment, enter ladminpw in the Password and Verify fields.

If you are performing the exercises independently, you can select a more secure password for the Local Admin account. Be sure to remember the password you have chosen because you will need to reenter it periodically as you use this computer.

You may provide a password hint if you want.

NOTE ▶ In a production environment, always use a strong password.

10 Click Create User.

11 At the bottom of the user list, click Login Options.

12 If an account is selected for Automatic Login, in the pop-up menu, choose Off.

13 Quit System Preferences, and log out.

14 At the login screen, select the Local Admin account, and enter its password (ladminpw, or whatever you specified earlier).

15 Press Return to log in.

This concludes Option 2; everyone should continue with the following section.

Set the Computer Name

Specify a computer name associated with your student number. If you are performing the exercises independently, you can choose to skip this section.

1 Open System Preferences.

2 Open Sharing.

3 Set Computer Name to client*n*, replacing *n* with your student number.

   For example, if your student number is 17, the computer name should be client17 (all lowercase with no spaces). If you are working through the exercises on your own, you may select your "student number." (Remember that 17 is used in the examples throughout the book.)

4 Press Return.

   Notice that the name listed beneath the Computer Name field, which is the local host name, updates to match your new computer name.

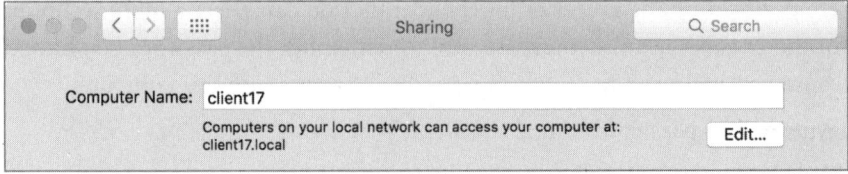

Turn On Remote Management

Allow the instructor to observe your computer, control your keyboard and mouse, gather information, copy items to your computer, and otherwise help you if necessary; this also allows you to use screen sharing from another Mac. If you are performing the exercises independently, you can choose to skip this section.

1   Click somewhere over the phrase "Remote Management," but don't select the checkbox yet.

2   For "Allow Access for," select "Only these users."

3   Click the Add (+) button, select Local Admin, and click Select.

4   In the dialog that appears, Option-click the Observe checkbox to automatically select all the checkboxes.

5   Click OK.

6   Select the checkbox Remote Management.

7   Confirm that Sharing preferences displays the text "Remote Management: On" and displays a green status indicator next to the text.

8   Click the Show All (looks like a grid of icons) button to return to the main System Preferences pane.

Update Software

To take advantage of possible fixes and improvements, be sure you're running the most recent versions of OS X and iTunes. If a local Caching service is available, your Mac will automatically use it.

1   While still in System Preferences, open App Store preferences.

2   Select the checkbox "Install app updates."

3   Select the checkbox "Install OS X updates."

   MORE INFO ▶ By default, the App Store preference "Install system data files and security updates" is selected, so updates for important system and security software are installed automatically; however, if the update requires a restart, you will be presented with a notification stating "Updates Available." See Reference 4.1, "Understand Automatic Software Update," in *Apple Pro Training Series: OS X Support Essentials 10.11: Supporting and Troubleshooting OS X El Capitan* (Peachpit Press, 2016) for more information.

4   If the button at the bottom of the window is Check Now, click Check Now.

   If the button at the bottom of the window is Show Updates, click Show Updates.

5   If you are in an instructor-led environment, ask your instructor what updates are appropriate to install; otherwise, if there are any updates, click Update All.

   If there are no updates available, press Command-Q to quit the App Store, quit System Preferences, skip the rest of this section, and continue with the section "Download the Student Materials."

6   If the "Some updates need to finish downloading before they are installed" dialog appears, click Download & Restart.

   If the Restarting Your Computer notification appears, click Restart; after your Mac restarts, you will be automatically logged back in.

7   Quit the App Store.

8   Quit System Preferences.

Download the Student Materials

Some files are necessary for the completion of some of these exercises. In some instructor-led environments, you may be prompted to follow the steps in the Option 1 section to download them. Otherwise, skip to Option 2, and perform those steps.

Option 1: Download the Student Materials in an Instructor-Led Environment

> **NOTE ▶** If you are performing the exercises independently, skip to "Option 2: Download the Student Materials for the Independent Reader."

If you are in an instructor-led environment, you will connect to the classroom server and download the student materials used for this course. To copy the files, you'll drag the StudentMaterials folder to your Documents folder.

1   In the Finder, choose File > New Finder Window (or press Command-N).

2   In the Finder window sidebar, click mainserver.

    If mainserver does not appear in the Finder sidebar, in the Shared list, click All, and then double-click the mainserver icon in the Finder window.

    Because mainserver allows guest access, your client computer logs in automatically as Guest and displays the available share points.

3   Open the Public folder.

4   Drag the StudentMaterials folder to the Documents folder in the Finder window sidebar.

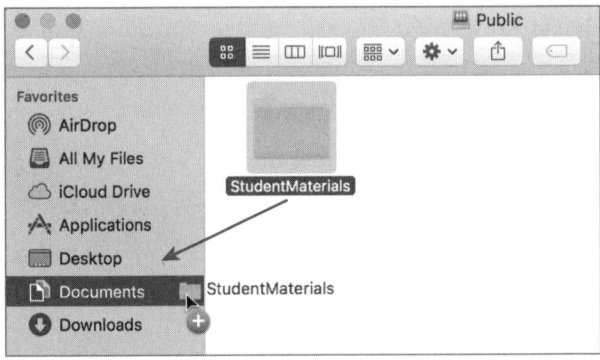

5   Once the copy is completed, disconnect from mainserver by clicking Eject next to the mainserver listing.

In this exercise, you configured your client Mac and downloaded the student materials. You have completed this exercise; skip the Option 2 section that follows.

Option 2: Download the Student Materials for the Independent Reader

> **NOTE ▶** If you are in an instructor-led environment and have followed the steps in Option 1, skip this section.

If you are performing the exercises independently, you will download the materials from Peachpit's website, place them in your Documents folder, and then run Software Update.

You may access the files by registering your product on www.peachpit.com.

1   Using Safari, go to www.peachpit.com.

2   Enter the book's ISBN-13, 9780134301853, in the Search field at the top right of the home page.

3   Click the "Register your product" link located above the description on the book's page.

4   If necessary, sign in to your existing Peachpit account or create one as prompted.

5   On the Register a Product page, enter the ISBN-13, 9780134301853, in the ISBN field if necessary, and click Submit.

6   The book along with an Access Bonus Content link will be listed on the Registered Products tab of your Peachpit account.

7   Click the Access Bonus Content link to access the student materials.

8   Click the Student Materials link to download the appropriate files to the Downloads folder (or whichever location you have selected in Safari Preferences) on your computer.

9   In the Finder, choose File > New Finder Window (or press Command-N).

10 Choose Go > Downloads.

11 Double-click the StudentMaterials.zip file to decompress it if necessary.

12 Drag the StudentMaterials folder from your Downloads folder to your Documents folder in the Finder window sidebar. If you want, you can also place StudentMaterials in your Dock for easy access.

13 Drag the StudentMaterials.zip file from your Downloads folder to the Trash in the Dock if necessary.

In this exercise, you configured your client Mac and downloaded the student materials.

Exercise 2.2
Create Apple IDs

> **Prerequisites**
> - Four email addresses that you can check during this exercise
> - Exercise 2.1, "Configure Your Client Mac"

Challenge

Create two Apple IDs:

- Create what this guide refers to as an "administrator Apple ID" that you will use to purchase OS X Server (or redeem a code for OS X Server) in the App Store. You will also supply the credentials for this administrator Apple ID in the Server app to enable push notifications.
- Create what this guide refers to as a "client testing Apple ID," without a credit card.

Considerations

It's best practice to use an Apple ID that's associated with an organization, rather than a personal Apple ID, for purchasing OS X Server and enabling Apple push notifications with the Server app. If you already have access to an Apple ID that has purchased OS X Server, you do not need to create another Apple ID for the following exercises.

Although you could use iCloud preferences in OS X to create an Apple ID for use with iCloud, there is a per-device limit, so you might want to use the App Store or iTunes instead.

Solution

Create and Verify Your Administrator Apple ID

If you already have access to an Apple ID that has purchased OS X Server and want to use that Apple ID for these exercises, you can skip this section and continue with the section "Create Your Client Testing Apple ID."

1 On your client Mac, open the App Store (it's available in the Dock or from the Apple menu).

2 From the Store menu, choose Create Account.

3 At the Welcome to the App Store window, click Continue.

4 Read the terms and conditions and Apple privacy policy, select the checkbox to agree to the terms and conditions, and then click Agree.

5 Provide the appropriate details to set up your administrator Apple ID.

   In the Email field, enter an email address you have access to that is not yet associated with an Apple ID.

   NOTE ▶ Use a secure password that you will remember because this Apple ID will be associated with your credit card or PayPal account.

   You may want to make a record of your security questions to help you recall them later.

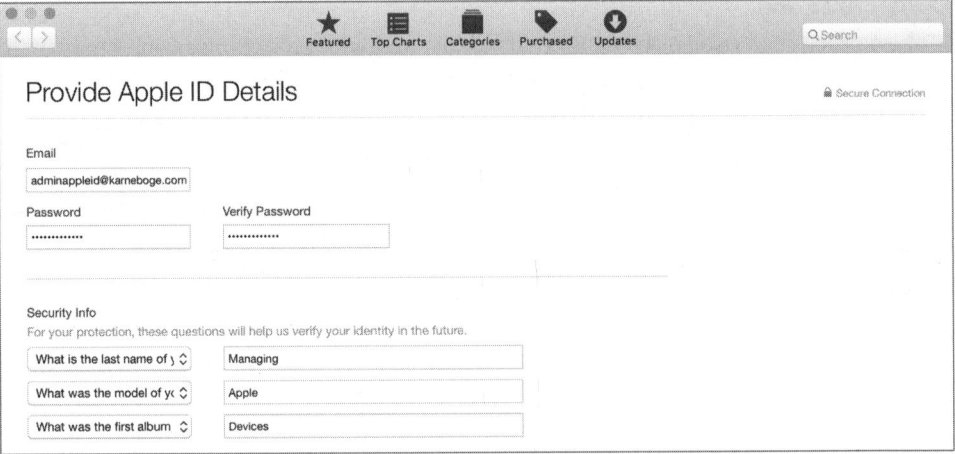

6   Click Continue.

7   In the Provide a Payment Method window, enter the appropriate information, and click Create Apple ID.

> **NOTE ▶** See "Apple Management Concepts" in the reference section of this lesson for more information about the limitations on creating Apple IDs.

8   Check your inbox for the email address associated with the new Apple ID.

9   Click the Verify Now link included in the message from Apple.

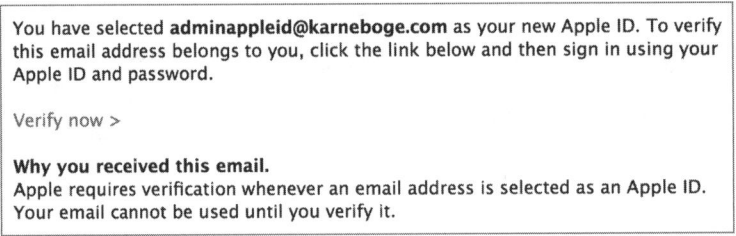

The Apple ID site opens.

10 Enter the Apple ID and password you just created, and click Verify Address.

11 If Safari asks to save this password, click Never for This Website.

12 After the My Apple ID website informs you "Email address verified," close the Safari window.

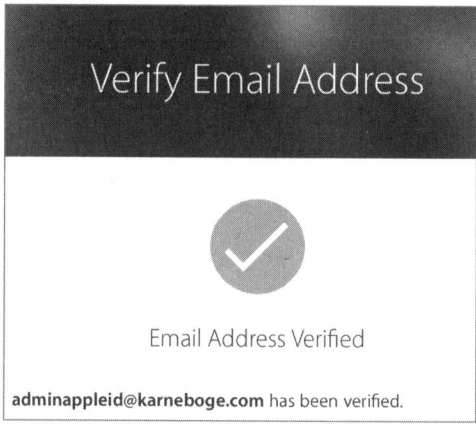

13 In the App Store, in the Verify Apple ID pane, click OK.

14 In the App Store, in the Congratulations pane, close the App Store window.

Create Your Client Testing Apple ID

Be sure that you log out of your administrator Apple ID before creating your client testing Apple ID.

1   On your client Mac, open the App Store if necessary.

2   From the Store menu, choose Sign Out.

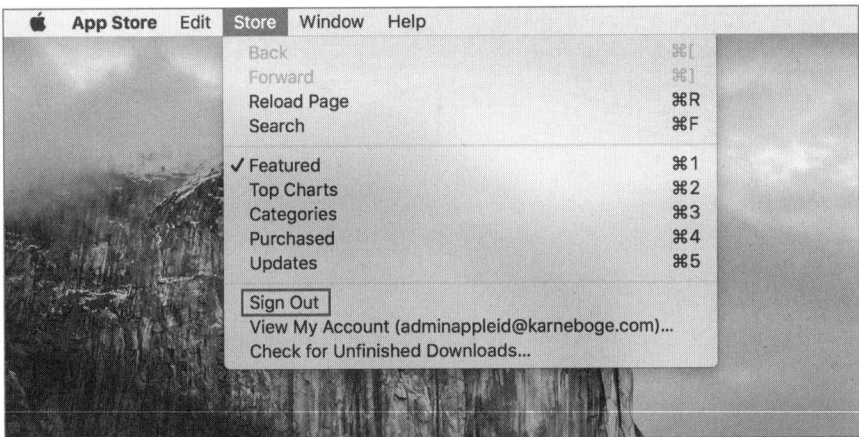

3   In the Search field, enter TextWrangler, and then press Return.

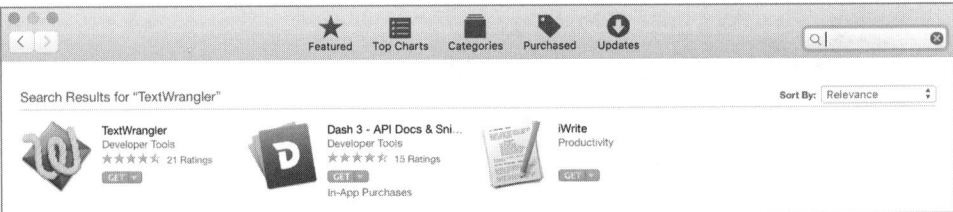

4   In the search results, select TextWrangler, and inspect the details of the app.

   NOTE ▶ Be sure to select the free app. You can search for and select any free app. If TextWrangler is already installed or not available, find and select another free app.

5   Click Get.

6   Click Install App.

   NOTE ▶ Do not enter the Apple ID you just created in the previous section.

7   In the "Sign in" pane, click Create Apple ID.

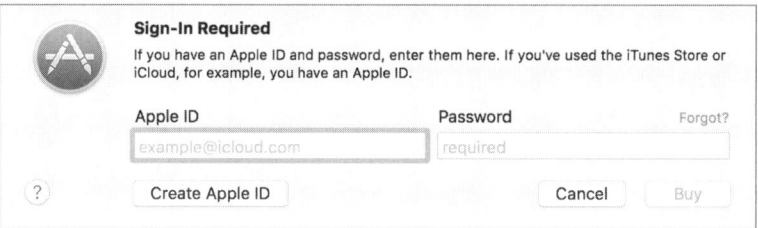

8   In the Welcome to the App Store pane, click Continue.

9   Read the terms and conditions and Apple privacy policy, select the checkbox to agree to the terms and conditions, and then click Agree.

10 Enter the appropriate details to set up your client testing Apple ID.

    For the Email field, use an email address you have access to that is not yet associated with an Apple ID.

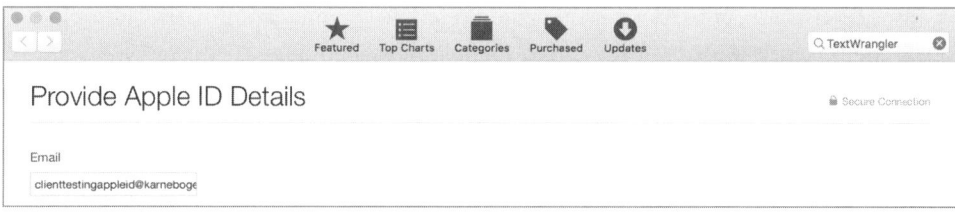

    NOTE ▶ Use a secure password that you will remember.

    You may want to make a record of your security questions to help you remember them later.

11 Click Continue.

12 In the Provide a Payment Method window, confirm that Payment Type is None.

13 Enter your Billing Address information, and click Create Apple ID.

14 Check the email client that receives email for the address associated with the new Apple ID.

15 In the confirmation email you receive from Apple, click the Verify Now link.

The My Apple ID site opens.

16 Enter the Apple ID and password you just created, and click Verify Address.

The My Apple ID website informs you "Email address verified."

17 Close the Safari window.

18 In the App Store, in the Verify Apple ID pane, click OK.

19 In the App Store, in the Congratulations pane, click Start Shopping.

20 Quit the App Store.

You just used the App Store to create an Apple ID that is not connected to any payment information.

> **NOTE** ▶ You have not yet installed the free app you selected, which is fine for the purposes of this exercise.

In this exercise, you created what this guide refers to as your "administrator Apple ID" and your "client testing Apple ID" for use in the rest of this guide.

Exercise 2.3
Verify Administrator Apple ID Access

▶ **Prerequisite**

- Exercise 2.2, "Create Apple IDs"

Challenge

Use the site https://appleid.apple.com to confirm that you know your administrator Apple ID credentials. Confirm that you've verified this Apple ID.

Optionally, add an alternate email address for this Apple ID.

Solution

Verify Your Administrator Apple ID

1 In Safari, open https://appleid.apple.com.

2 Enter your administrator Apple ID credentials, and press Return.

3 If Safari asks to save this password, click Never for This Website.

4 If Safari prompts you to verify your email address, your Apple ID is not verified. If Safari displays your account information, your Apple ID is verified.

> **Verify Email Address**
> Your Apple ID email address must be verified before you can sign in. Verify the address below or choose a different address.

Add an Alternate Email Address (Optional)

If you are in an instructor-led environment, close the Safari window, and skip the rest of this exercise.

1 In Safari, Click Edit in the Account area of your account information for your administrator Apple ID.

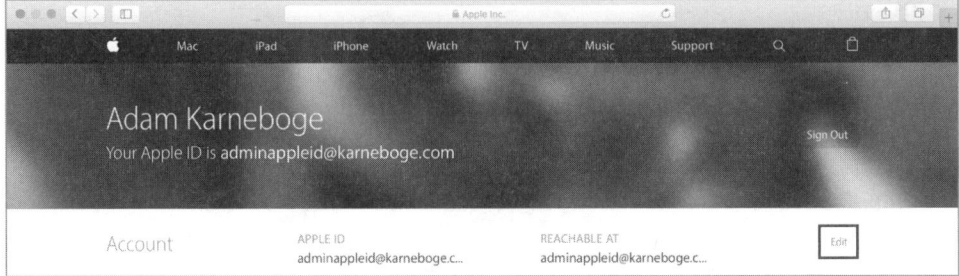

2 Click Add an Email Address under the Reachable At area of your account information, and enter a new email address that is not associated with an existing Apple ID.

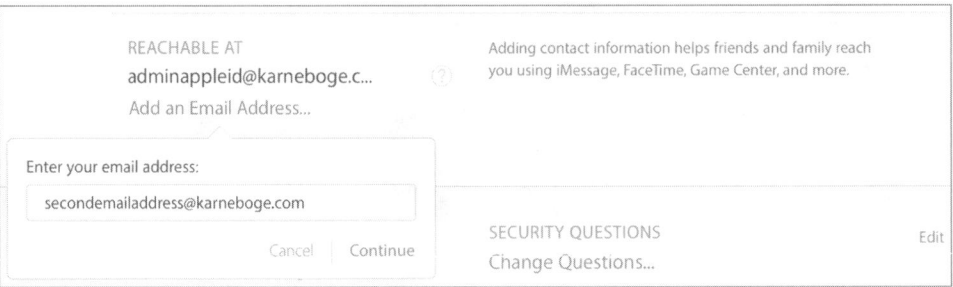

3 Click Continue. You will see an area to enter a six-digit verification code.

4 Check the email client that receives mail for the alternate address you just associated with your administrator Apple ID.

5 In the confirmation email you receive from Apple, there will be a six-digit verification code.

> You recently added **secondemailaddress@karneboge.com** as a new alternate email address for your Apple ID. To verify this email address belongs to you, enter the code below on the email verification page:
>
> **053342**
>
> **Why you received this email.**
> Apple requires verification whenever an email address is selected for your Apple ID. Your email cannot be used until you verify it.
>
> If you did not make this change or you believe an unauthorized person has accessed your account, you should change your password as soon as possible from your Apple ID account page at https://appleid.apple.com.

6 Enter the six-digit verification code, and click Verify.

You will now see the alternate email address listed in the Reachable At area of your account information.

7 Click Done in the Account area of your account information for your administrator Apple ID.

8 Click Sign Out.

9 Close the Safari window.

In this exercise, you confirmed that your administrator Apple ID is accessible and verified and confirmed that you can add an alternate email address to your administrator Apple ID. You will later use this administrator Apple ID to purchase software that will allow you to verify connectivity to the Apple Push Notification service (APNs) in Exercise 3.1, "Verify Network Service Availability," and to purchase OS X Server in Exercise 4.2, "Install OS X Server for El Capitan."

Exercise 2.4
Configure Your iOS Device

> **Prerequisite**
> - An iOS device for testing

Challenge
Set your iOS device to have an out-of-the-box configuration.

Considerations
Not everyone has a spare iOS device for testing, so make a backup of your iOS device before using it for the exercises in this guide.

Choose Settings > General > Reset > Erase All Content and Settings to return your iOS device to its factory default configuration.

Solution
If your iOS device is fresh out of the box, you don't need to do anything else, and you can skip to the section "Set Up Your iOS Device."

Optional: Make an iCloud Backup of Your Production iOS Device
If this iOS device is just for testing and you do not need to create a system backup, skip to the next section, "Reset Your iOS Device."

1 On your iOS device, press the Home button to return to your Home screen.

2 Open Settings.

3 Tap iCloud.

4 If you are not already signed in with iCloud, enter your personal iCloud credentials, and tap Sign In.

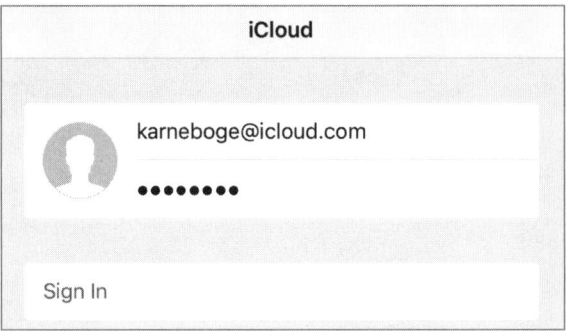

5   If you see the Verify Your Identity dialog, choose a device to receive a verification code, and then tap Send.

    After the verification code is sent to the other device, enter the code.

6   If you see the Merge with iCloud dialog, for the purposes of this exercise, tap Don't Merge.

7   If you see the Allow iCloud to Use the Location dialog, for the purposes of this exercise, tap Don't Allow.

8   If you see a notification that Find My iPad is enabled, tap OK.

9   Tap Backup.

10 Tap Back Up Now.

11 Wait until the iOS device backup process is complete.

12 Confirm that the backup has completed by looking at the Last Backup time.

Reset Your iOS Device

1   If the Settings app is not already open, press the Home button to return to your Home screen, and then open Settings.

2   Tap General.

    ⚙ General

3   Tap Reset. You may need to scroll down if Reset is not visible.

4   Tap Erase All Content and Settings.

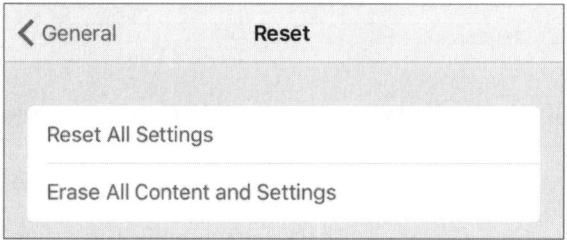

5   At the confirmation dialog, tap Erase.

6   At the second confirmation dialog, tap Erase.

7   If your iOS device still has Find My iPad turned on (the name Find My iPad may vary by device), enter your Apple ID credentials, and tap Erase.

Set Up Your iOS Device

Setup Assistant opens and walks you through the steps to set up your iOS device.

1   Ensure that your iOS device is not connected to a computer.

2   If necessary, turn on your iOS device.

3   At the Hello screen, slide to set up the device.

4   Tap your language.

5   Tap your country or region.

6   At the Choose a Wi-Fi Network screen, tap the name of the network. In an instructor-led environment, this may be Classroom Wireless.

7   If necessary, enter the Wi-Fi password, and then tap Join.

    In an instructor-led environment, the password may be student!.

8   In the Location Services screen, tap Enable Location Services.

9   If you see the Touch ID screen, tap Set Up Touch ID Later, and then tap Continue.

10 At the Create a Passcode screen, for the purposes of this exercise, tap Passcode Options, tap Don't Add Passcode, and then tap Continue.

    NOTE ▶ In production it is best practice to have a passcode for your iOS device.

11 At the Apps & Data screen, tap Set Up as New iPad (this screen may vary by device).

12 At the Apple ID screen, tap "Don't have an Apple ID or forgot it."

13 At the next Apple ID screen, tap Set Up Later in Settings.

14 In the confirmation dialog, tap Don't Use.

15 Read the terms and conditions, and then tap Agree.

16 If necessary, in the confirmation dialog, tap Agree.

17 If you see the Siri screen, tap Turn On Siri.

18 At the Diagnostics screen, tap Send to Apple.

19 At the App Analytics screen, tap Share with App Developers.

20 At the Welcome screen, tap Get Started.

In this exercise, you optionally made an iCloud backup of your iOS device, reset your iOS device, and used the device Setup Assistant.

Lesson 3
Infrastructure Considerations

The previous lesson focused specifically on core Apple technologies and how they will fit in your organization's management plans. This lesson explores other technologies, services, and workflow issues that will also greatly affect your management plans.

Because some topics may require a great deal of resources and configuration or require products from vendors other than Apple, the full exploration of these topics is beyond the scope of this guide. Even if a specific solution isn't provided for every topic, this lesson includes recommendations that will help guide your decision-making process.

When possible, this lesson presents specific steps for verifying deployment requirements. For example, one of the primary goals of this lesson is to show you how to test for specific network services required for managing Apple devices.

GOALS

▶ Consider the infrastructure requirements for your deployment plan

▶ Verify the availability of Apple-specific network and Internet services

▶ Explore Apple Support options for help dealing with problematic software and devices

Reference 3.1
Network Considerations

Scoping an appropriate network infrastructure is a book unto itself; nevertheless, this section explores topics related to network infrastructure and services as they apply to the deployment of Apple devices. Network and Internet access is so fundamental to modern computing that if any problems arise, it will likely directly affect every user and device in your organization. Quite simply, poor network infrastructure planning can make or break any deployment plan.

Network Infrastructure

At the least, you need to estimate the network link and bandwidth requirements for new devices. You should also consider the bandwidth and architecture required by any network-based management tools you plan to use. Some of the deployment methodologies covered in this book can require a lot of network bandwidth. You will be well served to do some preliminary bandwidth testing using your chosen deployment tools. Other specific network infrastructure considerations are as follows:

- Ethernet infrastructure—From a network link perspective, estimating Ethernet network requirements is simple. Generally, you need as many available Ethernet ports as you have desktop computers or immobile network devices to deploy. Gigabit Ethernet equipment is now fairly common and inexpensive, so any new ports you're planning to install should meet or exceed this performance standard.

- Physical Wi-Fi infrastructure—Planning an appropriate Wi-Fi network is much more complicated. The availability of these networks is affected by interference variables you have little control over. You will need to define a few primary specifications for your Wi-Fi network, including the expected number of simultaneous users, the required coverage area, and the minimum required bandwidth. Most new Apple devices support the latest 802.11ac technology for the highest performance and 802.11k, 802.11r, and 802.11v to improve access point roaming transitions. In short, you'd be wise to invest in access points that support these advanced technologies.

    MORE INFO ▶ See Apple Support article HT202628, "Wi-Fi network roaming with 802.11k, 802.11r, and 802.11v on iOS," and for more information about how iOS improves client roaming, see Apple Support article HT203068, "Wireless roaming reference for enterprise customers."

    NOTE ▶ Although the latest Apple AirPort Extreme access points offer 802.11ac performance, they are not recommended for enterprise use. This is because both the AirPort hardware and the management software are designed specifically for consumer needs. Many excellent third-party vendors will be glad to help you design a robust Wi-Fi network.

- Wi-Fi SSIDs—You may also consider using multiple Wi-Fi network identifiers (service set identifiers [SSIDs]) to segregate Wi-Fi access based on need. For example, you may have a guest network that is unauthenticated but allows only for external Internet access. In this case, access to your internal network would be available through a separate Wi-Fi network with secure authentication. You may also want to consider an unauthenticated Wi-Fi network that will allow users to enroll their own device in your Mobile Device Management (MDM) service. After enrollment, the MDM service could then push a configuration profile that provides authentication to the internal network.

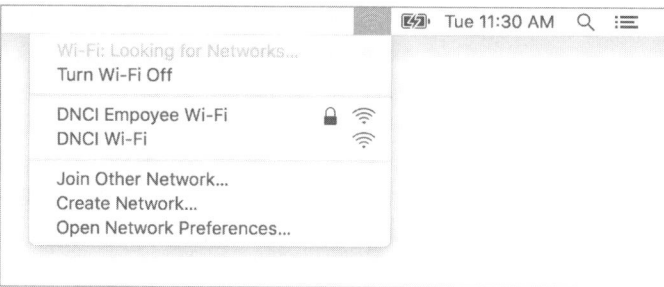

▶ Wi-Fi authentication—Beyond the physical aspects of your Wi-Fi network, you must also consider how devices and users will join these networks. Most enterprise-grade Wi-Fi equipment supports WPA2 Enterprise encryption, which allows for user- or device-specific authentication.

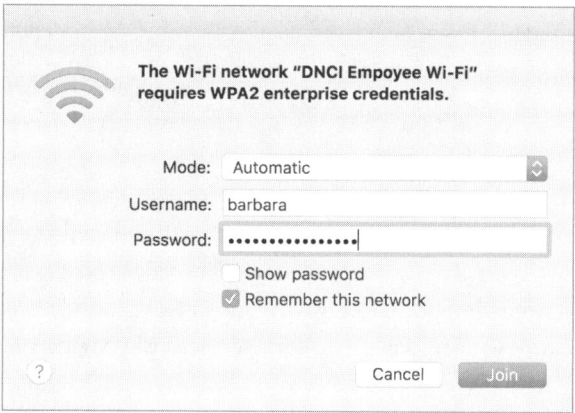

▶ Subnet planning—In most cases, subnet planning is based around physical location. However, many network planners have also historically separated Ethernet subnets from Wi-Fi subnets. This may cause an issue if you plan on using any network services that rely on Bonjour or mDNS. For example, both AirPlay and AirPrint devices are discovered automatically via local-area Bonjour. This would, for example, complicate your deployment if a wireless iOS device needed to access an AppleTV connected only via Ethernet to a different subnet.

> **MORE INFO** ▶ You can find out more about Bonjour from Apple's dedicated Bonjour support website at www.apple.com/support/bonjour/.

> **MORE INFO** ▶ Apple TV (third generation or later) with software version 7.0 or later supports peer-to-peer AirPlay, which allows for direct wireless AirPlay discovery on iOS 8 or later and OS X Yosemite or later. This feature is supported only on Apple devices that support the Bluetooth 4.0 standard.

- Port access—Make sure that your devices can access the appropriate network ports.
- Internet access—If there is any resource that users can't get enough of, it's Internet access. Deploying fancy new Apple devices will only make it worse as users will discover new apps and tools to further devour Internet bandwidth. Beyond entertainment, if your management plans rely heavily on Internet or cloud services, providing fast and reliable Internet access is a necessity. Further, deployments and updates of Apple software and App Store apps will place a heavy burden on Internet access. Simply put, you can never have enough.

> **TIP** ▶ The Caching service as part of OS X Server can save gigabytes of Internet bandwidth every day by hosting Apple software locally. You can find out more about setting up the Caching service in Lesson 5, "Caching Service."

Network Service Integration

It's not the network; it's the services on the network that your users are interested in. When planning a deployment of new Apple hardware, especially if it's a new platform for your organization, ensure that the systems integrate well with your network services. In some cases, you may have to establish new or updated network services to provide the necessary support. This is especially true if your organization is considering iOS devices for the first time. The following are some network services that are common in larger organizations:

- Directory Services—The most popular directory service is Microsoft's Active Directory, but it's not the only Lightweight Directory Access Protocol (LDAP)–based directory service. Apple has its own Open Directory service, and many other organizations are served by variations of Open LDAP. OS X includes built-in support for Active Directory, Open Directory, and other LDAP-based directory services. On the other hand, iOS devices can only indirectly access these services through other network services. For example, iOS devices can be managed by an MDM service that is integrated with your organization's directory service. The OS X Server MDM service, Profile Manager, includes such directory service integration.

- Email—Both iOS and OS X include support for industry-standard email protocols (POP, IMAP, and SMTP). Various authentication and encryption standards are supported, along with S/MIME certificate-based validation and encryption. Users can manually set up their own accounts; on OS X they can open Internet Accounts preferences, and on iOS they can open Settings > Mail, Contacts, Calendars. Most email settings can be easily managed via configuration profiles.

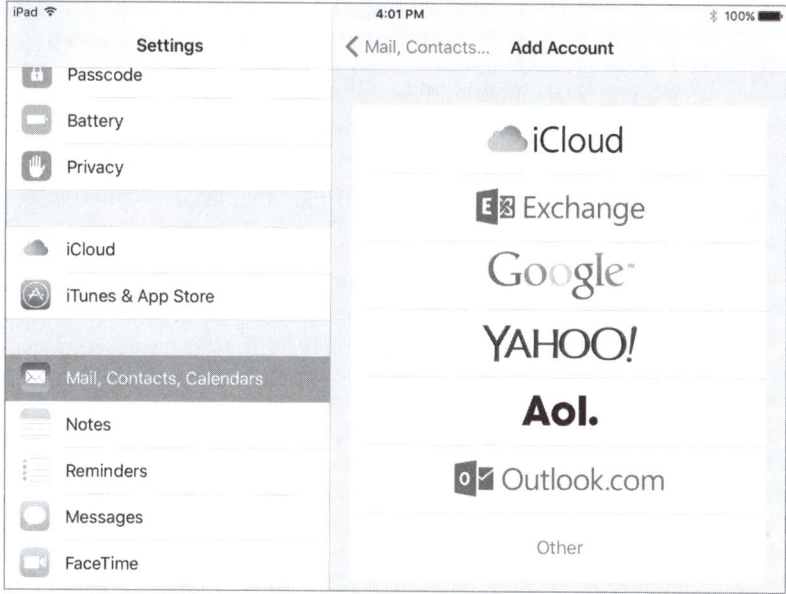

- Calendars and Contacts—Both iOS and OS X include support for the industry-standard CalDAV calendar service and CardDAV contacts service. Both platforms also support contacts searching via LDAP. Most calendar and contacts service settings can be easily managed via configuration profiles.

- Exchange ActiveSync—Both iOS and OS X include support for Microsoft's Exchange Server 2007 and later. iOS communicates to Exchange via the Exchange ActiveSync (EAS) protocol, whereas OS X communicates via the Exchange Web Services (EWS) protocol. iOS 9 offers improved integration with Exchange ActiveSync v16. Exchange settings can be easily configured locally and managed via configuration profiles.

    MORE INFO ▶ See the section "Microsoft Exchange Server" in the iOS Deployment Reference at http://help.apple.com/deployment/ios/ and the OS X Deployment Reference at http://help.apple.com/deployment/osx/.

- ▶ File Services—OS X includes support for many legacy file-sharing services, including Server Message Block (SMB) (up to SMB3), Apple Filing Protocol (AFP), Network File system (NFS), WebDAV, and File Transfer Protocol (FTP). iOS includes WebDAV access through a few supported apps. For example, the iOS versions of Pages, Numbers, and Keynote can access files from a WebDAV share.

- ▶ Personal folders for iOS use—A new feature of OS X Server 5 is the option in the File Sharing pane called "Create personal folders when users connect on iOS." To use this feature on an iOS device, choose Settings > Mail, Contacts, Calendars > Add Account > Other > Add OS X Server Account, and ensure that the File Sharing feature is turned on for that account. Then users can use apps such as Keynote, Numbers, and Pages that have been written to support the appropriate app extensions to store and access documents stored on your server in their personal folder. Note that this personal folder location is not related to a user's network home folder.

  MORE INFO ▶ For more information about app extensions, see https://developer.apple.com/app-extensions/.

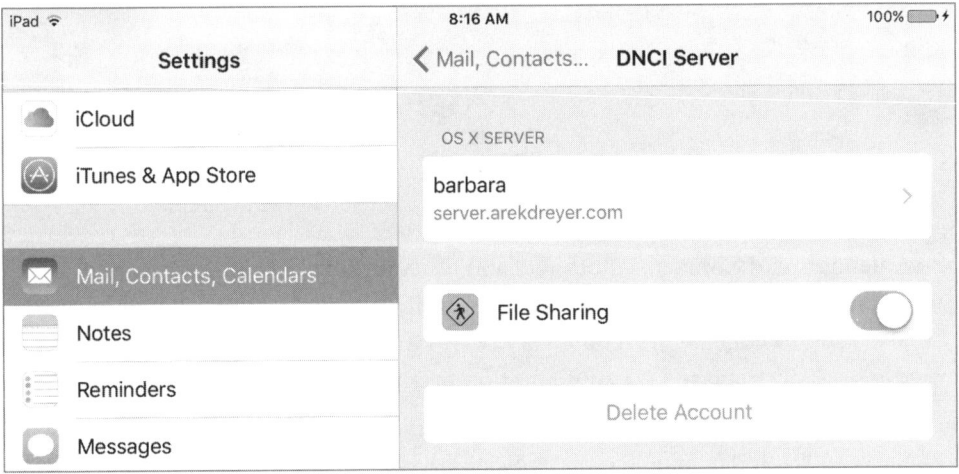

- ▶ Cloud services—The explosion of cloud-based file sharing has largely replaced the need for legacy file-sharing services. iOS and OS X obviously include tight integration with Apple iCloud. On a Mac, iCloud Drive appears in the sidebar of Finder windows. On an iOS device, documents that are stored in iCloud Drive are available within each app, and you can use Settings > iCloud > iCloud Drive > Show on Home Screen to view all the documents in iCloud Drive. Many other third-party cloud services support both iOS and OS X. However, you should thoroughly test to make sure that any cloud service is compatible with all the iOS and OS X apps you intend to use. You may find that certain combinations of apps and cloud services do not work well together.

MORE INFO ▶ See www.apple.com/icloud/icloud-drive/ for more information about iCloud Drive.

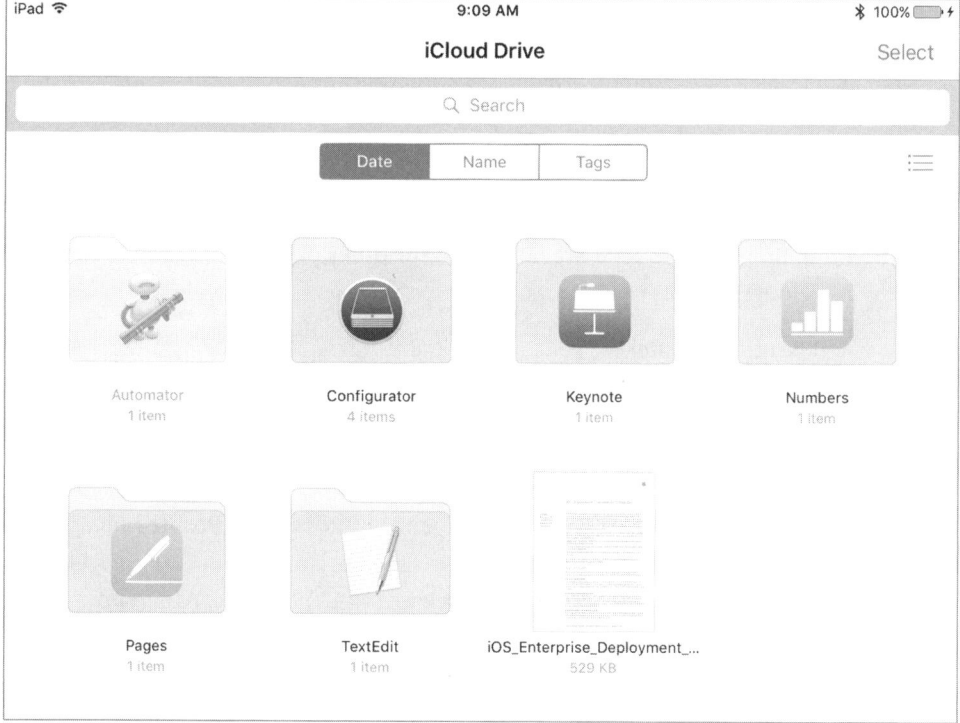

▶ Print services—Through the installation of third-party print drivers, OS X supports a vast array of network printers and print servers. Conversely, iOS apps can directly print using only the AirPrint protocol. Solutions to this limitation include resharing legacy printers using AirPrint servers and installing third-party apps that can accept documents and then send them to legacy printers. Note that this latter technique may not work with documents created by every app, and you may have to use an intermediary format such as PDF. For example, a third-party printing app may not be able to accept a Pages document, so you will first have to export the document as a PDF before you can open it with the printing app.

Network Service Availability

Part of a network administrator's job is to prevent Internet access that would be detrimental to the organization. Almost all networks use a firewall to block unwanted traffic into their network from the Internet. Some network administrators, especially those in primary education environments, must also restrict outbound Internet access.

Most network firewalls can restrict both inbound and outbound traffic without any additional configuration of client devices. Ideally, any sort of additional network traffic filtering, such as web content filtering, should also be accomplished using "transparent" methods that don't require additional client configuration.

If, however, your organization requires filtering that involves client configuration, make sure to choose a filtering solution that includes support for both iOS and OS X devices. Even better are filtering solutions where the client can be set up via configuration profiles. Too often filtering solutions are optimized for other platforms and leave much to be desired when integrating Apple devices.

Finally, when limiting or filtering your network and Internet service, you must make sure to always allow services required for managing your Apple devices. The following are the Apple management services you need to make sure are always unrestricted on your network:

- ▶ MDM services—For your Apple devices to enroll into Apple's Profile Manager, the devices must be able to access Transmission Control Protocol (TCP) port 443 for secure website access and TCP port 1640 for enrollment access. After enrollment is complete, devices need to access only TCP port 443 for management updates. If your MDM service is hosted on an internal network and you want to manage devices off your network, you must forward these two ports to the device hosting your MDM service.

- ▶ Apple Push Notification service—The Apple Push Notification service (APNs) is responsible for initiating MDM service actions and updates. The MDM service must have unrestricted inbound and outbound access to the APNs servers on TCP ports 2195. All managed devices must have unrestricted inbound and outbound access to APNs servers on TCP port 5223.

- ▶ Apple Internet services—Beyond APNs, several other Apple services are responsible for various parts of the deployment and management of Apple devices. Apple doesn't publish a definitive list of all the Domain Name System (DNS) names and Internet Protocol (IP) addresses its services use. However, in multiple locations, Apple documentation plainly states this: "The entire 17.0.0.0/8 address block is assigned to Apple, so it's best to allow this range in your firewall settings." In short, it's easier to just allow any traffic going to Apple's network than to try to pinpoint specific services.

MORE INFO ▶ You'll find detailed step-by-step instructions for verifying and troubleshooting access to Apple services in the exercises later in this lesson.

Reference 3.2
Security Considerations

It's no secret that Apple devices are valuable and often highly portable objects, thus making them high-priority targets for thieves. Beyond the value of the device itself, there may be considerably more value in the information contained within the device and transmitted by the device. Now that more and more employees are relying on mobile devices for access to organizational resources, the threat of an information breach may be an even greater concern. Consequently, protecting your Apple devices, their content, and their communication should be a fundamental part of your deployment plan.

Physical Security

The physical security required will vary based on the location, mobility, and purpose of your managed devices. Office environments and equipment rooms are already generally secure and probably don't require any additional security measures. Additional security should always be considered in open environments such as computer labs and conference areas. Mobile devices pose a more complex security problem because physical security is often left to the device's user.

In cases where the devices remain within the confines of a single location, administrators have a variety of options to increase physical security. Solutions start with any method you would normally use to secure a room, including quality door locks, alarm systems, and surveillance systems. For open lab environments, simply having full-time lab attendant staff in the area is usually a pretty good theft deterrent.

If you don't have an adequately secure location, you should consider a third-party locking mechanism to physically secure your devices. Some Mac computers feature a Kensington security slot as part of their external housing. This is a small slot that allows you to attach a compatible security lock without having to modify the computer's case. Kensington and other third-party manufacturers sell a wide range of security solutions that work with the built-in security slot, but even for Mac computers that lack this slot, there are other creative products that will work.

If you need to secure smaller devices when they aren't in use, such as Mac notebooks or iOS devices, you should consider storage cabinets or carts. These security solutions come in many shapes and sizes, and many of these carts also include electronics designed to meet the charging and syncing needs of Apple devices. One vendor, Bretford, has partnered with Apple for many years to create storage cabinets and carts are specifically optimized to support iOS and OS X devices.

For devices that are always on the go, physical security also means simply protecting the device from everyday accidents. The word *variety* doesn't even begin to accurately describe the vast selection of enclosures designed to protect mobile Apple devices. Even Apple sells a line of stylish, simple protective cases. However, many third-party options offer superior protection for your Apple devices. In any case, taking the time to research and select an appropriate protective covering for your portable Apple devices may also be an important part of your management plans.

Securing Data at Rest

For some organizations, securing the data stored on the Apple device is much more important than securing the device itself. With the majority of Apple devices being mobile, a great deal of thought has gone into securing the data on these devices. The technologies and options for securing data on iOS and OS X differ quite a bit because the two platforms serve different purposes.

Any device capable of running a recent version of iOS always uses multiple levels of data encryption for every aspect of the system. As long as the user sets a personal identification number (PIN) or passcode, the data on an iOS device that has not been unlocked with the PIN or passcode is effectively unreachable. Ultimately, the encryption used for iOS devices is so good that a device is much more likely to be compromised by a poorly selected PIN than by the technology encrypting the data. For iOS devices that have Touch ID, the minimum passcode length during Setup Assistant is six digits. For other devices, the minimum length is four digits. By default, users can opt out of setting a PIN or passcode. Fortunately, an administrator can specify that the user select a stronger PIN or passcode via profile management.

> **MORE INFO** ▶ Apple has gone to great lengths to build advanced security mechanisms into iOS. A detailed analysis of the security technology built in to iOS is documented in Apple's iOS Security white paper (available at www.apple.com/ipad/business/it/security.html).

OS X computers do not use any form of local data encryption by default. This behavior is a historical standard for traditional computer systems because it provides the most flexibility when initially deploying a system. For example, it's much more difficult to deploy a custom system image to a drive that is already encrypted.

After an OS X computer has completed its initial setup, you can turn on Apple's FileVault system partition encryption. This technology provides strong encryption for the entire system partition, which typically also includes all application and user data. Through profile management an administrator can require that FileVault be turned on after at least one user logs in to the system.

Once it's turned on, only users who have been granted FileVault unlock access will be able to start up the system and access the system's content. Users are granted access by authenticating with their account passwords. Again, the quality of the user's password will greatly affect the likelihood that a system can be compromised. The password policy for OS X user accounts can be managed via profile management or via a directory service for network-based accounts.

> **MORE INFO** ▶ You can find more details regarding FileVault encryption in Apple Support article HT204837, "Use FileVault to encrypt the startup disk on your Mac," or from Lesson 10, "Manage FileVault," in *Apple Pro Training Series: OS X Support Essentials 10.11: Supporting and Troubleshooting OS X El Capitan* (Peachpit Press, 2016).

Securing Data in Transit

As more and more work gets done on the road or at home via the Internet, you must also consider the security of the data transmitted to and from an Apple device. iOS and OS X share support for many of the same network security technologies. In fact, many of the profile management settings for network features are identical for both platforms. If your organization requires stringent network security, you should evaluate the following network security topics:

- Network access—Both iOS and OS X support industry-standard Wi-Fi authentication including the most secure options, WPA2 Personal and WPA2 Enterprise. Both protocols use strong encryption, but WPA2 Enterprise adds support for 802.1X authentication, which facilitates the use of individual unique passwords or certificates. On OS X computers, you can also take advantage of 802.1X for securing Ethernet connections. iOS 9 or later and OS X El Capitan or later add support for TLS v1.2 in 802.1X authentication. Settings for network access can be easily managed through configuration profiles for both platforms.

- Virtual private network (VPN)—Both iOS and OS X support industry-standard VPN remote access protocols. Both platforms include built-in support for the following VPN standards, which can be configured manually or via configuration profiles: IKEv2, Cisco IPSec, L2TP over IPSec, and PPTP. iOS and OS X also support SSL VPN from various VPN providers, using apps available from the App Store. Both platforms support VPN features such as IPv6, proxy servers, and split-tunneling, and they support various authentication methods, including password, two-factor token, digital certificates, and for OS X, Kerberos. Both platforms support VPN On Demand for networks that use certificate-based authentication; this allows devices to automatically connect to VPN services for specific domains that you specify in a configuration profile. For iOS 7 or later and OS X Yosemite or later, you can configure individual apps to use the VPN connection independent from other apps (Per App VPN) to ensure that only network traffic related to organizational data (as opposed to personal data) uses the VPN. For iOS devices that are supervised using Apple Configurator 2 or the Device Enrollment Program, you can configure Always-On VPN, which prevents network traffic unless the device is connected to the VPN. Settings for VPN access can be easily managed through configuration profiles. However, some nonstandard VPN implementations may require additional third-party software. Check with your VPN vendor for information regarding iOS and OS X compatibility. If you're planning for a new VPN solution, you should strongly consider a vendor that integrates with the built-in VPN support on iOS and OS X.

MORE INFO ▶ For more information about VPN for iOS, see the iOS Security document (at http://www.apple.com/ipad/business/it/), the virtual private networks sections of the iOS Deployment Reference (at http://help.apple.com/deployment/ios/), and the OS X Deployment Reference (at http://help.apple.com/deployment/osx/).

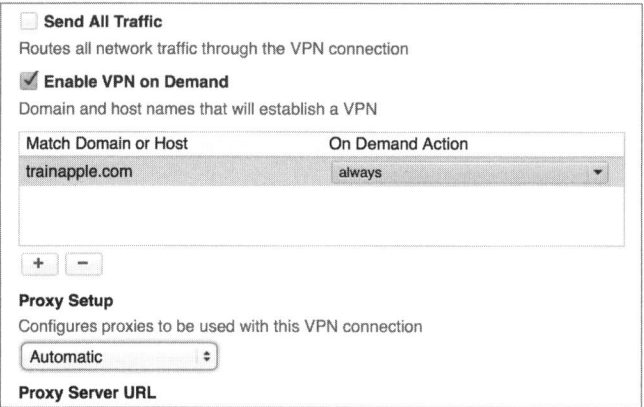

▶ Secure Sockets Layer (SSL), Transport Layer Security (TLS), and Datagram Transport Layer Security (DTLS)—Both iOS and OS X support up to SSLv3 and TLSv1.2 to encrypt data in transit between servers and clients. Internet applications such as Safari, Calendar, and Mail will automatically take advantage of secure SSL or TLS connections when possible. Further, all MDM services use SSL encryption to protect management communications. Both SSL and TLS connections establish trust via associated public key infrastructure (PKI) certificates. iOS and OS X include support for most third-party certificate signing authorities. You can also deploy your own organizational certificates via trust profiles.

NOTE ▶ iOS 9 or later and OS X El Capitan or later require a 1,024-bit or larger bit group when negotiating a TLS/SSL connection with Diffie-Hellman key exchange.

- Single sign-on—iOS and OS X support Kerberos-based single sign-on (SSO) through different mechanisms. OS X computers support a more traditional SSO approach through integration with a directory service, such as Microsoft's Active Directory. Further, because OS X supports multiple users, SSO authentication can be established at user login. Configuring OS X to use a directory service can be facilitated through a variety of methods, including binding to a directory service (including via NetInstall workflows) or applying configuration profiles. Devices with iOS 7.0 or later support SSO only through the application of configuration profiles, which can be installed manually or managed with MDM. Safari and specifically built third-party apps (those that use the NSURLConnection or NSURLSession class) support SSO on iOS; on Mac computers, many third-party apps, apps built in to OS X (including Safari, Mail, Calendar, Messages), and services such as file sharing, screen sharing, and secure shell [SSH]) support Kerberos.

- AirDrop—At the time of this writing, there are two discovery methods used by AirDrop. The legacy AirDrop discovery method is available only to OS X and uses Wi-Fi exclusively. The newer AirDrop discovery method is available to both iOS and OS X devices and uses a combination of Bluetooth and Wi-Fi. Further, the newer AirDrop discovery method is available only to iOS 7 or later and OS X Yosemite. However, both implementations use TLS to securely encrypt data in transfer. Also, if this type of ad hoc file sharing presents a security risk for your organization, you can turn off AirDrop via configuration profiles.

- Apple services—Apple has designed all its Internet services with security in mind. iMessage and FaceTime take advantage of the Apple Push Notification service, which utilizes end-to-end encryption that allows access only by the sender and receiver. Not even Apple can decrypt iMessage and FaceTime traffic. Apple's speech recognition, Siri, sends all communication through encrypted HTTP Secure (HTTPS), and any saved voice recordings on Apple's servers are stored anonymously. If your organization thinks any of these services present a security risk, you can easily turn them off via configuration profiles.

MORE INFO ▶ Lesson 2, "Apple Management Concepts," covered iCloud security. Further, you can find more details regarding the security mechanisms used by iCloud in Apple Support article HT202303, "iCloud security and privacy overview."

▶ Managed Open In—This feature of iOS doesn't directly secure data in transit; instead, it prevents data from being transferred using nonapproved apps. Specifically, Managed Open In restricts data moving in and out of your managed applications. For example, this would prevent a user from sending an email attachment that contains a document from one of your managed apps. Managed Open In settings are deployed via configuration profiles.

MORE INFO ▶ Lesson 16, "Managing Access," covers taking advantage of Managed Open In.

Recovery Solutions

In the case that an Apple device is lost, stolen, or otherwise unrecoverable, you will have to devise a method for dealing with this issue. Both iOS and OS X include several mechanisms that will help you recover a lost device. Further, if recovery isn't an option, both platforms include mechanisms for securely wiping the device. You should consider the following recovery solutions in case of the worst:

▶ Microsoft's Exchange ActiveSync—Although primarily used for integration with the mail, calendar, and contacts services, the ActiveSync protocol also includes the ability to remotely lock and wipe iOS devices.

▶ MDM lock—Most MDM solutions feature the ability to remotely lock managed Apple devices. For any iOS devices that do not have a PIN or passcode, the screen will be locked, but the user can easily unlock the iOS device because no passcode is present. For this reason alone, it would be wise to require passcodes for managed iOS devices. Since OS X computers don't normally use a device PIN or passcode, you must always specify a temporary code when sending a remote lock command to an OS X computer; the OS X computer immediately reboots when it receives the lock command.

▶ MDM wipe—Most MDM solutions also feature the ability to remotely wipe managed Apple devices. Wiping an iOS device results in an immediate restart of the device back to a "like new" state. After wiping, all user and app data on the iOS device is unrecoverable. Wiping an OS X computer also results in an immediate restart, but instead the device's system volume will be erased so it will restart into OS X Recovery. Note that only when you wipe OS X systems with FileVault 2 turned on will the data be truly unrecoverable.

▶ iCloud Find My Device—As covered in the previous lesson, the Find My Device service has the ability to remotely lock, send a message, make a sound, wipe, or report the location of an Apple device. Find My Device is the only solution that can report the location of an Apple device without requiring the user to unlock the device or open a third-party app. Turning on Find My Device is also the only method for enabling the Activation Lock feature to prevent another user from attempting to reactivate the device. In short, this is the most comprehensive recovery solution for Apple devices.

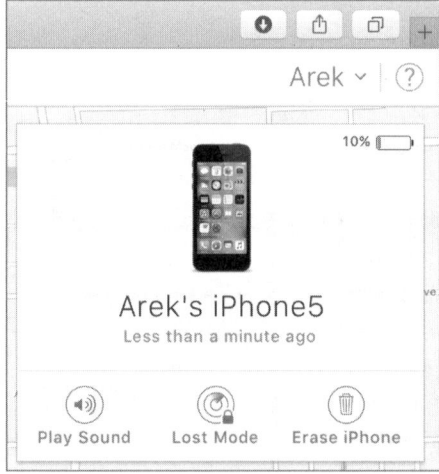

▶ MDM Lost Mode—A new feature for iOS 9.3 is the ability to send an Enable Lost Mode command to a stolen or lost iOS device that is supervised and enrolled in an MDM service that supports that feature (such as Profile Manager in OS X Server 5.1). Once a device is in MDM lost mode, an administrator can send a command to query its location (specifically its longitude and latitude). MDM Lost Mode does not allow an administrator to surreptitiously monitor the location of iOS devices. An administrator cannot query for a device's location until the device is in lost mode, and in lost mode, the device displays a clear message that the device is lost, along with contact information; this message prevents the user from using the device. After an administrator sends a command to disable lost mode for the device, if an administrator sent the Fetch Device Location command, the device displays an alert that an administrator located the device. Because this requires the device to be supervised, it is not available for Mac computers with OS X.

▶ Third-party solutions—Third-party theft recovery solutions include Computrace LoJack for Laptops by Absolute Software, GadgetTrak Mac, and Undercover by Orbicule. These third-party solutions must install proprietary software on your Apple devices to provide tracking. Note that third-party iOS apps are not allowed to track the device's location without the user first opening the vendor's app. This makes most third-party recovery solutions less than ideal. However, these solutions may also include insurance that will pay out should the service not recover the device.

Reference 3.3
Physical Logistics

Physical logistics may be a simple issue for some, but for larger deployments the logistics of handling the physical hardware can be a major undertaking. This section explores the physical ramifications of deploying new devices.

Delivery is just one part of the physical deployment. You must also consider whether your physical infrastructure is equipped to handle the new or additional devices you intend to deploy. Along with the deployment of new devices, this section also covers planning for the disposal of your old equipment.

Power Infrastructure

Apple has made great strides toward minimizing the power requirements for their devices. Nevertheless, the demand for higher-performance devices and multiple devices per user is driving power requirements for technology even higher. Adding new devices also drives the adoption of additional new peripherals that will also draw from your power infrastructure. Further, the electrical systems of many older buildings were not designed for modern computing environments. Even if you're using infrastructure that supported your previous computing resources, you should double-check the power requirements for your new hardware and make sure that your infrastructure can handle the load.

> **NOTE ▶** If you overload a power circuit, in most cases a safety breaker will cut the power to prevent the wiring from overheating and starting a fire. Other times, your equipment may experience low power situations commonly referred to as *brownouts*. Both situations are generally bad for your electronic equipment and should be avoided. Shorts and brownouts are common causes of damaged power supplies and logic boards.

The most accurate method for making sure that your infrastructure meets the power needs of your new system is to test one of your new devices using a pass-through electric monitor. These devices accurately measure the electric usage of your equipment. It's important to understand that the power draw of a computer varies widely between sitting idle and crunching numbers. Also, iOS and mobile Mac charging stations reduce their power consumption as the devices become fully charged. In either case, you should consider an electric monitor that can track peak usage and averages.

Estimating Power Needs

You can also estimate the power requirements of your new equipment by gathering information from Apple's websites and then using simple calculations. Apple rates all its devices by the maximum amount of power (watts) that is used during operation or charging. Most electric outlets and circuits, on the other hand, are rated by the amount of current that runs through the wiring (amps).

If you know the proper equation, you can calculate the amperage based on given wattage and voltage. However, a better practice is to simply add up your total wattage needs and then let an expert electrician figure out what kind of amperage to supply. In this case, you will need to estimate the total wattage of your systems.

At the time of this writing, the power consumption for Apple devices is as follows:

- iPod and iPhone—All standard iPod and iPhone power adapters draw a maximum of 5 watts (W) of power.
- iPad—Standard iPad power adapters range from 5 W to 12 W depending on configuration. For specific power information, see Apple Support article HT202105, "Using iPad power adapters with your iPhone, iPad, and iPod."
- Mac notebooks—Standard Mac notebook power adapters range from 29 W to 85 W depending on configuration. For specific power information, see Apple Support article HT201700, "Find the right power adapter and cord for your Mac notebook."
- Mac mini—The Mac mini line of computers includes power supplies that range from 85 W to 110 W depending on configuration. For specific power information, see Apple Support article HT201897, "Mac mini: Power consumption and thermal output (BTU) information."
- iMac—The iMac line of computers includes power supplies that range from 58 W to 365 W depending on configuration. For specific power information, see Apple Support article HT201918, "Power consumption and thermal output information for iMac computers."

- Mac Pro—The Mac Pro line of computers includes power supplies that range from 205 W to 318 W depending on configuration. For specific power information, see Apple Support article HT201796, "Mac Pro: Power consumption and thermal output (BTU/h) information."

Note that these are maximum-rated loads; in typical use, a Mac desktop computer rarely draws this level of power. On the other hand, power adapters for Mac notebooks and iOS devices almost always operate at their highest power rating when charging the device but then drop significantly when the device is fully charged.

When calculating the total system power, don't forget to include other high-power items. Peripheral equipment such as external displays, projectors, networking equipment, and printers can all add significant load. If you are considering a third-party multiple-device charging station or cart, make sure to research the maximum possible power load. Many such products will completely max out a common power outlet circuit.

Considering power outlets, another factor you may need to research is how many of your power outlets are configured as shared circuits. Especially in older buildings or areas not designed for high power loads, multiple individual wall outlets (even in separate rooms) may be part of a single circuit and may even be tied into the lights. Ultimately, you will need to verify the capacity of your power infrastructure with someone who understands the issues, such as an electrician who specializes in infrastructure for computer systems.

> **TIP** Ideally, your equipment should be supplied power from sources behind power conditioners or uninterruptible power supplies that provide a steady stream of power. These solutions range from support for a single computer to support for entire office complexes, and they are available from a variety of vendors.

Cooling Infrastructure

Electronic devices, like humans, prefer to operate within a comfortable temperature range. If you navigate to the Apple Technical Specifications webpages, you'll find that most Mac computers are designed to operate in an environment with ambient temperatures from 50° to 95° F (10° to 35° C). Apple-engineered iOS devices, which tend to travel outside more often, have a bit more leeway, supporting operational temperatures from 32° to 95° F (0° to 35° C). Generally, keeping the ambient temperature cool enough is the focus for most administrators because modern computer hardware can give off quite a bit of heat.

All Apple devices have thermostats and cooling systems that will try to prevent them from overheating. Nevertheless, if the ambient temperature is too high, the device may fail and even be seriously damaged. In some cases, the device may go into a forced sleep mode as a fail-safe to prevent further operation at high temperatures.

With the popularity of lower-powered devices such as Mac notebooks and iOS devices, the additional heat generated may not be enough to warrant cooling upgrades. However, if you are deploying high-power Mac computers (Mac Pro or high-end iMac) or your environment is especially dense, like that found in a computer lab, you should evaluate your cooling infrastructure.

The Mac power consumption Apple Support articles referenced in the previous section also include thermal output measured in British thermal units per hour (BTU/h). This is a standard heat output measurement that can be directly compared to the cooling ability of an air-conditioning system. In this case, you should calculate the total estimated BTU/h for your computing systems and then consult a heating, ventilation, and air conditioning (HVAC) specialist.

Handling Logistics

The delivery person is here with a truck full of new devices. Now what? If your deployment plan includes detailed handling logistics, you will be prepared for this moment.

For most technophiles, unboxing new hardware is a joyous occasion, but if you have a building or campus full of new devices to deploy, it becomes another logistical hurdle you must overcome. You should plan a workflow that takes into account all the stages from delivery to deployment. While planning these stages, it's important to recognize that your new (valuable, densely packed, and easily movable) equipment may be at its most vulnerable for theft. Typical installation workflows include these steps:

- ▶ Receive delivery—Make sure your receiving staff is ready for your order and that the location is equipped to securely receive and temporarily store your new equipment in packaging.
- ▶ Unbox equipment—Large deployments usually require a staging area where the equipment is unboxed and sorted. The packing materials will also need to be stored and moved to the proper location for disposal or recycling. You may want to save some of the packaging in case you need to store or return equipment.
- ▶ Record asset information—Most organizations require that physical assets, such as portable computers, be tracked and possibly tagged for accounting purposes. More sophisticated techniques include the creation of custom asset tags with barcodes or even the physical application of an engraved identifier.

▶ Perform the initial configuration—Your plan may include administrative setup prior to deployment. For example, you may plan to re-image OS X computers or prepare iOS devices with Apple Configurator. If this is the case, you'll need to set up a specific preparation area where you can re-image or prepare the devices.

▶ Deploy equipment to user or location—Eventually you will hand off the equipment to the user or deliver it to the location where it will be used. Part of this may involve connecting cables or security devices to a computer. For portable devices, this may also involve placing the device in a protective case before handing it over to the user. In some environments, several bureaucratic steps may be required, such as the user signing a legal document or recording the transaction in an asset management tool.

> **TIP** Avoid a lot of this physical work for your staff by simply having the user be the first person to unbox and set up a new device. This guide covers such deployment scenarios in Lesson 8, "Out-of-the-Box Management via Apple Programs for Device Enrollment."

To properly manage these deployment tasks, you will need to estimate the amount of time, workspace, and effort required for each stage. Everyone involved will want to know when the new devices will be ready, so you should try to stick to a schedule. However, to successfully meet that schedule, you will need to procure an appropriate amount of deployment workspace and staff to complete the job.

Disposal and Recycling

What are you going to do with all your old devices? Your deployment plan should also include handling logistics regarding moving or disposing of old equipment. There are many logistical similarities between disposing of obsolete devices and setting up new ones. Both require adequate planning and accurate estimation of time, workspace, and effort to be successful. A typical disposal workflow includes these steps:

▶ Verify inventory—Identify the equipment slated for replacement or disposal. This inventory may be required both for internal accounting and for the records of anyone who may be collecting your equipment.

▶ Back up or transfer user data—There is a good chance that your users will have data they want to save or move to the new devices. Your current management plans should already include some sort of backup, but there may be faster methods to consider. Migration Assistant for OS X allows for a direct transfer between devices. Also, if you rely on cloud-based services, such as iCloud, you may not need to transfer any additional data.

- Securely erase data—Some of your devices may store sensitive data that needs to be destroyed before disposal. iOS devices feature an easy option to quickly erase all content and settings, but many OS X computers still store data in an unencrypted format. You may need to plan for time to securely wipe these older systems.

- Collect the equipment—Someone will have to collect the old devices and transport them to the disposal destination. Often this task coincides with the delivery of a new device and can be handled by the same staff.

- Dispose of equipment—In a best-case scenario, whoever is picking up your equipment will be ready when you are to hand it off. However, you may have to find a location to temporarily store old equipment until it leaves your facility.

  NOTE ▶ All local waste or recycling services require special handling for most electronics. You should always check with your waste service provider or local municipality when disposing of any electronic equipment.

Reference 3.4
Support Options

It's inevitable that at some point hardware equipment will either malfunction or break from misuse. The more equipment you have, the more likely you will have to deal with repair or replacement issues. Beyond hardware, there are also "soft" issues to deal with. These issues can range from helping a user with a simple setup question to solving complex network service integration issues.

Your management plans need to include solutions that provide support for when you and your users experience issues. Since you're reading this guide, you or someone from your team will likely be the first line of defense to resolve any issues. Sometimes, though, even the best administrators need additional help. This section explores various support options available for both Apple hardware and software.

AppleCare

Apple offers a variety of support options through AppleCare. These solutions range from the complimentary hardware warranty and software support included with every Apple device to the support options for complex enterprise customers. As an administrator, you need to be aware of the standard AppleCare coverage included with your devices, but you may also want to consider expanded AppleCare options. AppleCare services include the following:

- Standard AppleCare limited warranty—Apple devices include 90 days of basic software support and one year of hardware repair coverage.

- AppleCare+ and AppleCare Protection Plan—These optional plans allow you to extend basic software support and hardware repair coverage for iOS devices and Apple TV for a total of two years, for Mac computers for a total of three years, and for Apple Watch for a total of two or three years. The AppleCare+ plan also includes up to two incidents of accidental damage for iOS devices (each subject to an additional service fee). You can find out more about these support options at www.apple.com/support/products.

    NOTE ▶ AppleCare does not offer any plans that cover accidental damage of OS X computers or the theft or loss of any Apple device. If you suspect that your organization may require additional coverage, you should seek out third-party insurance options.

- AppleCare Help Desk Support—This optional support program can be purchased annually and includes dedicated phone support access for two contacts at your organization. These two contacts can directly call an unlimited number of times during the subscription for help with diagnosing and troubleshooting both software and hardware issues. Of note, this program also provides graphic user interface–level support for OS X Server. You can find out more about this support option at www.apple.com/support/products/enterprise/help.html.

- AppleCare OS Support—This optional support program can be purchased annually. This program includes the Help Desk Support program and supersedes it by adding support for enterprise-level issues. For example, this program can help you troubleshoot Microsoft Active Directory integration issues or complex configuration that may require use of the command line. You can find out more about this support option at www.apple.com/support/professional/it-departments/.

- AppleCare for Enterprise—This optional 24/7 support program includes comprehensive hardware and software support. An AppleCare Account Manager helps review your IT infrastructure, track issues, and provides monthly activity reports for support calls and repairs. Up to six members of your IT department can use phone or email for this support option, including support for MDM, Active Directory, and IBM MobileFirst for iOS apps. Your employees can contact Apple directly over the phone, which helps to reduce the load on your internal help desk. For hardware issues, IBM Global Technology Services provides onsite service within the next business day. To minimize downtime, AppleCare for Enterprise can be combined with the AppleCare iOS Direct Service Program, so you can replace your hardware without waiting for a technician. You can replace up to 10 percent of your covered iPad or iPhone devices for any reason. You can find out more about this support option at www.apple.com/support/enterprise/.

Self-Service

If you are deploying a large number of devices, relying solely on an outside source for your equipment repair may not be the best solution. Many Apple customers with large numbers of devices are better served by implementing local repair and replacement techniques. This allows your organization to receive a much quicker turnaround for hardware repair and replacement procedures than through an outside servicer. As part of your management plan, consider implementing the following techniques for dealing with hardware repair and replacement:

- iOS Direct Service Program—This program allows customers to screen their own iOS devices and accessories for hardware issues and directly order replacements through Apple's online service system. You can find out more about this program at www.apple.com/support/programs/ids.

- Apple's Self-Servicing Account Program—As the name implies, this allows customers to perform their own repairs for in- or out-of-warranty Apple hardware. This program also includes access to Apple's online service system and next-day shipment for many replacement parts. You can find out more about this program at www.apple.com/support/programs/ssa.

- Purchasing spare accessories or devices for immediate replacement—Budgeting for this varies widely based on need and size of deployment, but the best solution for your users is to simply have another device available when they need it. For smaller deployments, you may be able to get by with only spare accessories such as power adapters, cable adapters, and protective cases. For larger deployments, however, you should carry several spare devices because you are likely to have a large number of failures or accidents over time.

- Stocking replacement parts through third-party vendors if your equipment includes older and out-of-warranty Apple hardware—Common hardware parts supplied by third-party vendors include batteries, system memory, storage drives, and even some touch screens.

Exercise 3.1
Verify Network Service Availability

▶ **Prerequisite**

- Exercise 2.1, "Configure Your Client Mac"

Challenge

Confirm that your client Mac and your iOS device can reach the appropriate Apple services and that no firewall rules block access to the Apple Push Notification service (APNs).

Considerations

In the command-line environment, you can use the telnet command to test whether your Mac can connect to APNs. Apple Technical Note TN2265 specifies the following host names and ports to use:

- 1-courier.push.apple.com 5223
- gateway.sandbox.push.apple.com 2195
- gateway.push.apple.com 2195

You need an app to test push notifications. If you have the ability, you could write one yourself. If not, you can use your administrator Apple ID to purchase and download various apps for OS X and iOS to test connectivity to APNs.

You may find that push notifications do not work well in a virtualized or simulated environment.

Solution

Use telnet to Confirm Connectivity to APNs

1 On your client Mac, press Command–Space bar (or click the Spotlight icon in the upper-right corner of the screen) to reveal the Spotlight search field.

2 In the Spotlight Search field, enter Terminal.

3 Press Return to open the top hit of your Spotlight search, which is the Terminal app.

4. In Terminal, enter the following command, and then press Return. Note that the host name starts with the number 1, not the letter *l*.

   telnet 1-courier.push.apple.com 5223

   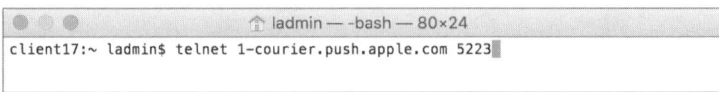

5. If you are able to make a successful connection, you will see something similar to the following:

   Trying 17.149.36.91...

   Connected to us-courier.push-apple.com.akadns.net.

   Escape character is '^]'.

6. If you have made a successful connection, start to close the connection by pressing Control-] (for a standard U.S. keyboard the right bracket key is above and to the left of the Return key); then at the telnet prompt, type quit, and press Return.

   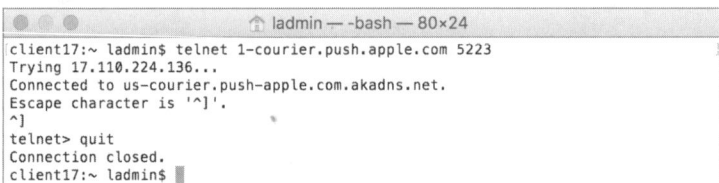

7. If you are unable to make a connection and see Operation timed out, press Control-C to stop attempting to connect.

   If you are unable to make a connection, confirm that you have an active Internet connection and that no firewall is blocking the connection; then try starting with step 4 again.

8. Confirm that the IPv4 address you connected to starts with 17. If it does not, check the DNS service your Mac uses.

9 Use the procedure starting at step 3 to test two more connections:

   telnet gateway.sandbox.push.apple.com 2195

   telnet gateway.push.apple.com 2195

10 Press Command-Q to quit Terminal.

You just used the telnet command to confirm basic connectivity to the Apple Push Notification service.

Purchase and Run the Push Diagnostics App (Optional)
Install Push Diagnostics via the App Store.

> **NOTE** ▶ Push Diagnostics notifies you of success or failure with an audio notification. You may want to turn down your volume before running the test because test results initiate audio cues.

1 On your client Mac, from the Apple menu, choose App Store.

2 From the Store menu, choose Sign Out.

3 In the Search field, enter push diagnostics, and then press Return.

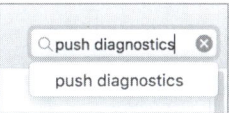

4 In the search results, click Push Diagnostics (do not click Get).

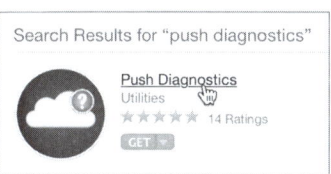

5 Confirm that the app is from Twocanoes Software, Inc.

6 Click Get.

7 Click Install App.

8. Provide your administrator Apple ID credentials, and then click Sign In.

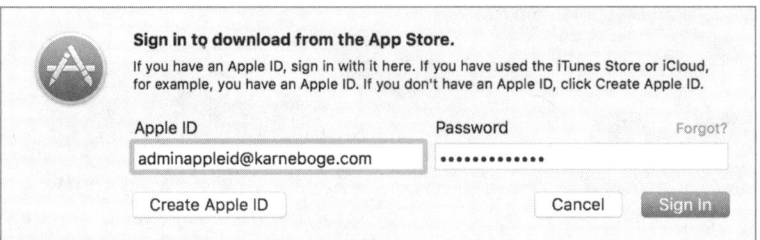

9. If you see the Verification Required dialog, enter your password, click OK, answer the security questions, and click Continue.

10. If you see the "Require a password when making purchases on this computer" dialog, click Require After 15 Minutes.

11. If you see the "Verification is required" dialog, click Billing Info. If you do not see this dialog, skip to step 17.

12. In the Edit Payment Information window, click Done.

13. In the "iTunes Terms & Conditions have changed" dialog, click OK.

14. Read the terms and conditions, click the checkbox to agree, and then click Agree.

15. In the Congratulations window, click Start Shopping.

16. Repeat steps 4 through 10.

17. In the Confirmation Required dialog, click Buy. Note that the status changes from Install App to Installing.

18. When the status changes to Open, click Open.

19. Click the text at the bottom of the window to start the tests.

NOTE ▸ The Push Diagnostics app provides audible feedback.

20 If the test push fails, click the text at the bottom of the Push Diagnostics window to run the test again.

21 Hover the pointer over the Courier, Gateway, Feedback, and Test Push icons to show the details of each test.

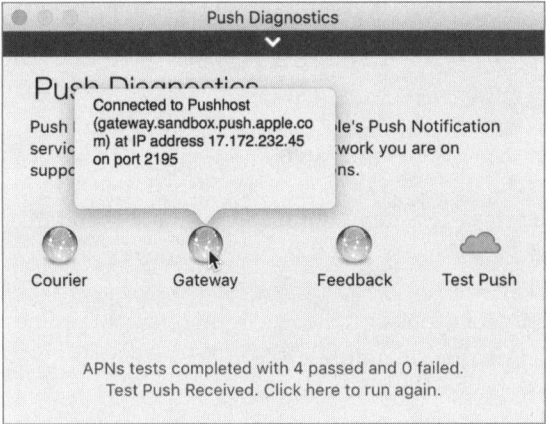

Inspect the log.

1 Click the arrow just beneath the toolbar to display the contents of the log.

Note the steps to resolve the DNS name, check for a proxy, and then make a connection to a network address (including a specific port).

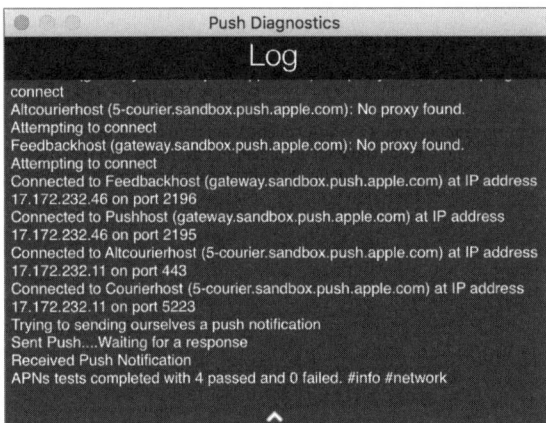

2   Click the arrow at the bottom of the log contents to hide the contents of the log.

3   Quit Push Diagnostics.

Install and Run Services Test from Amsys plc (Optional)
On your iOS device, purchase and run Services Test.

1   On your iOS device, open the App Store.

2   If your iOS device is an iPod touch or an iPhone, tap Search at the bottom of the App Store.

3   Enter services test in the Search field, and then tap Search.

4   If you do not see the Amsys plc Services Test item, tap iPad Only, and then tap iPhone Only.

   NOTE ► Some Apps are written only for types of iOS devices that have a specific resolution. However, they will still function on a different iOS device with a different resolution or larger screen.

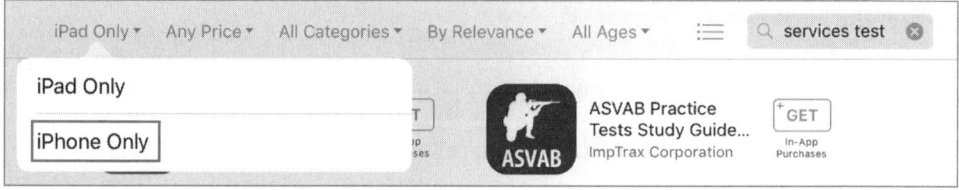

5   If necessary, swipe through the results until you see Services Test from Amsys plc.

6   Tap the price, and then tap Buy.

7   In the Sign In to iTunes Store dialog, tap Use Existing Apple ID.

8   Enter your administrator Apple ID credentials, and then tap OK.

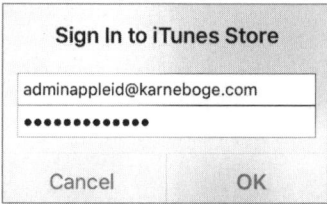

9 If you see the Apple ID Verification dialog, tap Settings.

10 If necessary, click Continue in the Verification Required dialog to verify your payment information. Enter the security code for the method of payment associated with this Apple ID, tap Done, and then in the Confirmation Required dialog tap Buy.

11 If necessary, reenter your password.

12 If you see the "Require password for additional purchase on this device" dialog, click Require After 15 Minutes.

13 Tap Open next to Services Test.

14 Confirm that General Test is selected at the bottom of the screen.

15 In the upper-right corner, tap Play to start the tests.

16 Confirm that all the tests have green status indicators. Note that you need to swipe up to see all the tests and their status indicators.

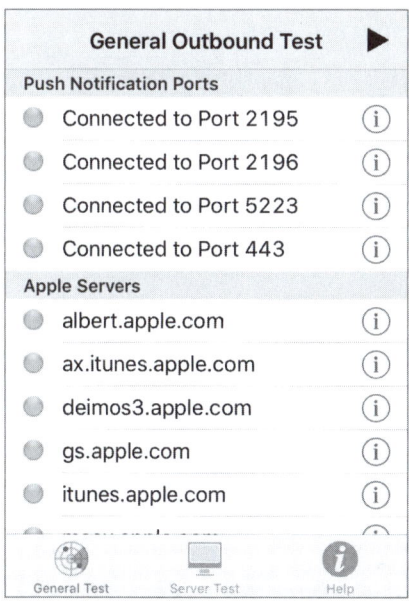

Demonstrate what happens if no network is available.

1   On your iOS device, swipe up from the bottom of the screen to access Control Center.

2   Tap the airplane icon to turn on Airplane mode.

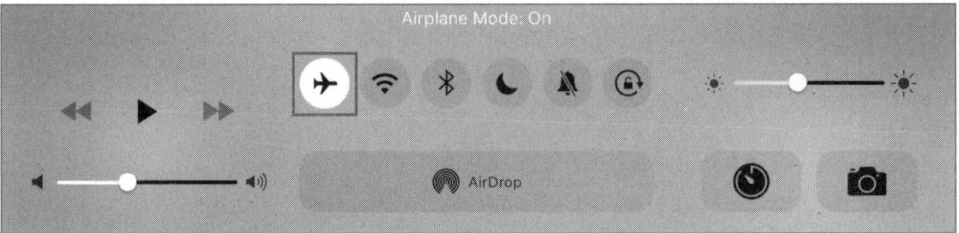

3   Swipe down to close Control Center and return to Services Test.

4   In Services Test, tap Play.

5   Confirm that all the tests start with a yellow status indicator and then change to red as each test times out.

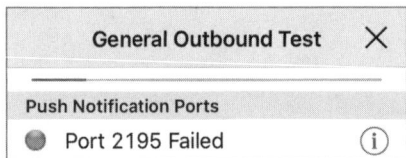

6   Tap Stop (X) in the upper-right corner.

Turn off Airplane mode, and run the tests again.

1   Swipe up from the bottom of the screen to access Control Center.

2   Tap the airplane to turn off Airplane mode.

3   Swipe down to close Control Center and return to Services Test.

4   In Services Test, tap Play.

5   Confirm that all the tests have green status indicators.

In this exercise, you demonstrated a few of the ways to confirm connectivity to the Apple Push Notification service.

Lesson 4
OS X Server 5 on El Capitan

OS X Server 5 helps your users collaborate, communicate, share information, and access the resources they need to get their work done. While OS X Server indeed provides a variety of services, the aim of this guide is to focus on the services that facilitate the management of Apple devices.

This lesson begins with a brief introduction of OS X Server before moving into the requirements and initial setup of OS X Server. This lesson also covers selecting and configuring Secure Sockets Layer (SSL) certificates required for Apple device management.

GOALS

▶ Perform the initial installation and configuration of OS X Server

▶ Consider TLS/SSL certificate requirements and best practices

NOTE ▶ Although you can install OS X Server 5.0 on OS X Yosemite, the version available from the Mac App Store at the time of this writing is OS X Server 5.1, which requires OS X El Capitan 10.11.4. Server 5.1 provides additional support for new features in iOS 9.3.

Reference 4.1
OS X Server Benefits

Other solutions are capable of providing management for Apple devices, but at only $19.99 (US), not many of them are as inexpensive as OS X Server. Also, despite the price, because Apple develops OS X Server, it's often the first management solution that supports the latest Apple management features and operating systems.

Further, even if you intend to use a third-party Mobile Device Management (MDM) solution, other services in OS X Server are still clearly the best solution. For example, the Caching service has no supported alternative. The NetInstall service that provides network system disk access for OS X computers is available from other servers, but the implementation in OS X Server is supported by Apple.

Services Covered in This Guide

Again, this guide focuses on the OS X services that are most responsible for helping administrators manage their Apple deployments:

▶ Caching service—As introduced previously, the Caching service greatly reduces Internet bandwidth used for the installation of Apple-sourced software and media. Lesson 5, "Caching Service," focuses on the architecture, setup, and troubleshooting of this service.

> **NOTE** ▶ OS X Server 5 still offers the legacy Software Update service. However, this older service is limited to providing updates for OS X system software and Apple software installed from outside the Mac App Store. Because of this service's limited use in contemporary Apple deployments, it's not covered in this guide.

▶ Profile Manager—This is the name given to the MDM service provided by OS X Server. The vast majority of material in this guide deals directly with or is designed around MDM management workflows. Both Lesson 6, "Configuration and Profiles," and Lesson 7, "Mobile Device Management," cover Profile Manager specifically. In addition, nearly all lessons that follow these two deal with topics related to MDM services.

▶ NetInstall—This service makes OS X systems available for startup via a network connection. NetInstall is often used as a platform for installing or re-imaging Mac computers en masse. Coverage of this service is beyond the scope of this guide, but you can find out more from *Apple Pro Training Series: OS X Server 5.0 Essentials on El Capitan* (Peachpit Press, 2016).

▶ File Sharing—The local file-sharing service provided by OS X Server supports both iOS and OS X devices. The new option in Server 5, "Create personal folders when users connect on iOS," is available for supported iOS apps (at the time of this writing: Keynote, Numbers, and Pages) with Server 5 on El Capitan (not available with Server 5 on Yosemite). Additionally, in the File Sharing pane, you can configure each shared folder to support WebDAV, and some iOS apps support WebDAV.

▶ Wiki—The OS X Server Wiki service not only provides a browser-based interface for collaborative document creation but serves as an alternative for local file sharing.

> **MORE INFO** ▶ For more detailed coverage of OS X Server setup and services outside the scope of this guide, check out *Apple Pro Training Series: OS X Server 5.0 Essentials on El Capitan* (Peachpit Press, 2016).

Reference 4.2
OS X Server Setup

This section outlines the system requirements for OS X Server and presents suggestions for scoping server hardware. It also gives recommendations for network configuration of an OS X Server.

> **MORE INFO ▶** You'll find more detailed step-by-step instructions for installing and configuring OS X Server in the exercises later in this lesson.

Verifying Server Hardware Requirements

OS X Server 5.1 is an app that runs on any Mac running El Capitan 10.11.4 with 10 GB of free disk space. Before you install OS X Server, confirm that your system meets at least the minimum hardware requirements. You can find this information on the label attached to the box of every Mac sold, or you can find it with the About This Mac and System Information applications.

To run El Capitan, your Mac must be one of the following models or later:

- ▶ iMac (mid-2007 or later)
- ▶ MacBook (13-inch Aluminum, late 2008; 13-inch, early 2009 or later)
- ▶ MacBook Pro (13-inch, mid-2009 or later; 15-inch or 17-inch, mid/late 2007 or later)

- MacBook Air (late 2008 or later)
- Mac mini (early 2009 or later)
- Mac Pro (early 2008 or later)
- Xserve (early 2009)

Some features of OS X Server require an Apple ID, and some features require a compatible Internet service provider.

Server Hardware Considerations

For the purposes of the exercises in this guide or any other deployment testing, you can run OS X Server on just about any contemporary Mac. In practice, however, consider the size of your Apple deployment and select hardware appropriate for your production needs:

- Memory—In general, more system memory results in better system performance, but exactly how much memory is ideal for your situation is impossible for this guide to prescribe. You can, however, get a good idea of system memory usage for an existing server from the Memory Usage and Memory Pressure statistics available in the Stats pane of the Server app. Obviously, if you observe extremely high memory usage, upgrading the Mac computer's system memory is a good idea.

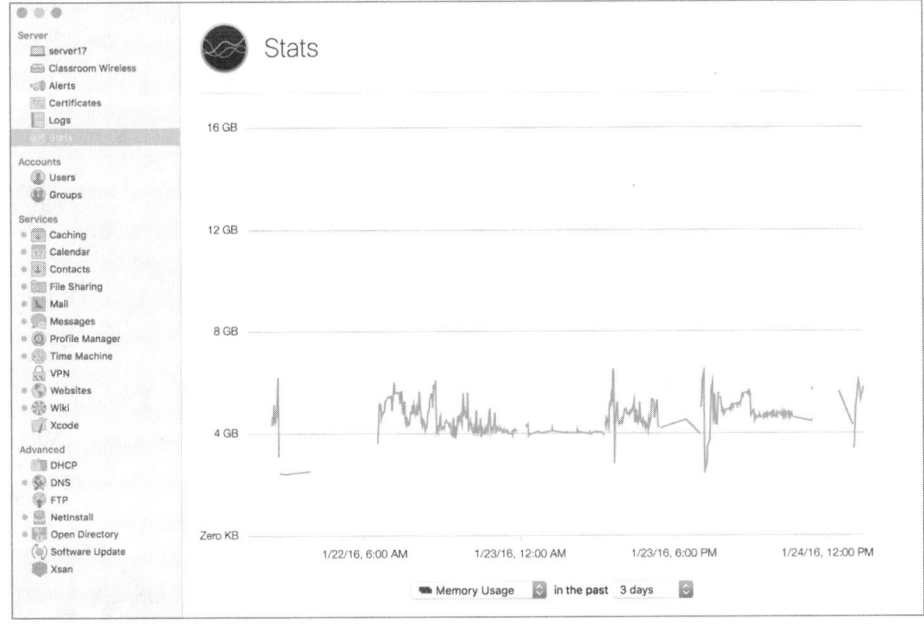

- Storage—Be sure you have enough disk space to hold the data for the services you plan to offer. If the services you plan to offer are disk intensive (for example, the Wiki service with a high volume of user content), consider using a faster physical disk or even an external disk system. An external disk is especially useful for the Caching service since it can potentially fill an entire disk, and the more items that are cached, the more effective the service.
- Backup—You cannot re-create a lost MDM database because of the security architecture of the MDM service. Thus, if the data store for Profile Manager is lost, you will lose the ability to manage your Apple devices. The devices will retain existing management settings but will accept new management only when enrolled into a new MDM service. In short, you really need to back up your management server. OS X Server is fully supported by the Time Machine backup built in to OS X.
- Network interfaces—Be sure to consider the speed of the network interface when making a server hardware decision. Most Mac computers support Gigabit Ethernet. All Mac computers capable of running OS X Yosemite or El Capitan that include built-in Ethernet interfaces support Gigabit Ethernet. If your Mac is equipped with Thunderbolt interfaces, you can use Apple Thunderbolt to Gigabit Ethernet adapters to add Ethernet interfaces. All services, except for Caching and NetInstall, can operate from the Mac system's Wi-Fi interface. But for performance reasons, it's not recommended that you provide services via a Wi-Fi interface.
- Availability—To help ensure that OS X Server stays up and running, you can turn on the Energy Saver system preference "Start up automatically after a power failure" (not available on all Mac systems). It's also recommended that you use an uninterruptible power supply (UPS) for your server, including any external volumes, to keep your server up and running in the case of a brief power outage.

Server Network Considerations

Again, for the purposes of completing exercises in this guide or for general testing, you can configure your server using whatever Internet Protocol (IP) address was set via Dynamic Host Control Protocol (DHCP) and even use the computer's local Bonjour name. However, some services may be negatively affected if the server's IP address or host name is changed.

> **TIP** If you absolutely must change the name of your server, do so only via the server Overview settings in the Server app. On a computer running OS X Server, you should never change the name via Sharing preferences.

For example, your MDM service must be resolvable on all managed devices to a single Domain Name System (DNS) host name. Managed devices communicate with the MDM service only via the single host name used during enrollment. In other words, if you want to change the DNS host name clients use to resolve the MDM service, you will have to reenroll all your devices with the new host name.

Given that changes to a server configuration can dramatically affect device management, it's obviously best to select network settings that will remain appropriate throughout the duration of your deployment. Consider the following factors when configuring network access for your management server:

- IP address—Configuring a static IP address for your production OS X Server is highly recommended. The primary reason for this is to prevent accidental changes that would prevent the DNS host name of the server to become unreachable.

- Subnets—With the exception of two specific issues, most OS X Server services aren't affected by subnet settings. First, if you don't use a DNS host name and instead rely on the Bonjour local host name (often defined as something like computername.local), only devices on the local subnet will recognize your server's local host name. Obviously, this issue can be resolved by configuring a "real" DNS host name. Second, the NetInstall discovery service broadcast doesn't travel beyond the local subnet by default. Resolving this issue is detailed in Apple Support article PH15509, "Set up NetInstall service across subnets."

- Computer name—The server's computer name affects access to the server only from the local subnet. The computer name is often used to define the Bonjour local host name, which again is resolvable only on the server's local subnet. For any server that needs to be reachable beyond the local subnet (that is, most servers), the computer name doesn't really matter.

- DNS host name—A server's DNS host name is how most clients will resolve access to almost all the services hosted on your server. You must coordinate with your DNS network administrator to make sure the server's DNS host name is properly configured. Remember that OS X Server requires both a forward and reverse DNS host name record for proper setup.

- Network ports—The variety of services offered by your server use a range of both User Datagram Protocol (UDP) and Transmission Control Protocol (TCP) network ports. A properly configured firewall should allow traffic only for the necessary network ports. Thus, newly configured services often require changes to established network firewalls. You will likely have to work with the network firewall administrator to open additional ports for managing Apple devices. Throughout this guide, when a specific service's architecture is detailed, the required network ports will be included with the documentation.

> **MORE INFO** ▶ Apple maintains a list of all the well-known network ports used by Apple products in Apple Support article HT202944, "TCP and UDP ports used by Apple software products."

▶ Simple Mail Transfer Protocol (SMTP) relay—A variety of services in OS X Server will send email messages as part of their function. If your organization relies on an SMTP relay service for sending email messages, then you need to configure OS X Server to take advantage of this service.

> **MORE INFO** ▶ For information about configuring OS X Server to use an SMTP relay, see Apple Support article HT202962, "OS X Server: Sending email invitations, notifications and alerts when an SMTP relay is required."

External Access and Reachability Testing

Managed devices can receive management changes only if they can access your MDM service. Thus, if you require that devices are able to receive management changes when they are outside your network or on the Internet, your network infrastructure will have to be properly configured to allow connections from outside your network to reach your server.

If your server is on an internal network that uses private IP addresses, as is the most common case, your network routing will need to be configured so that it forwards traffic from a public Internet IP address to your server. If this is the case, only the required specific TCP ports will likely be forwarded to your server. Obviously, coordinating with a network administrator will be required to properly configure network routing and firewall rules.

Another consideration if your server is to be accessed from the Internet is that the DNS host name must be resolvable to any host on the Internet. As covered previously, in most of these cases, your server will be accessible via an external public IP address that forwards to an internal private IP address. This type of IP forwarding also requires a DNS configuration—commonly known as *split DNS*—where a single host name resolves to the proper IP address both externally and internally.

In other words, even though your server uses a single DNS host name, devices in your network will resolve this host name to a private IP address; devices outside your network will resolve the same host name to a public IP address. Again, coordinating with a network administrator is required to properly set up this type of DNS configuration.

Properly testing external service reachability can be tricky because it requires that you have access to a test external network. Fortunately, reachability testing will help you determine whether your server is accessible to Internet clients. This testing service is turned on by default, and you can find the results in the server Overview tab in the Server app.

You can further verify reachability for specific services by clicking the Details button to the right of the reachability information. The reachability service works by instructing automated servers at Apple to try to contact your server. In the reachability detailed view, you can see what external IP address, public host name, and specific services are available. This information will be valuable for any network administrator who is trying to help you facilitate external access for your server.

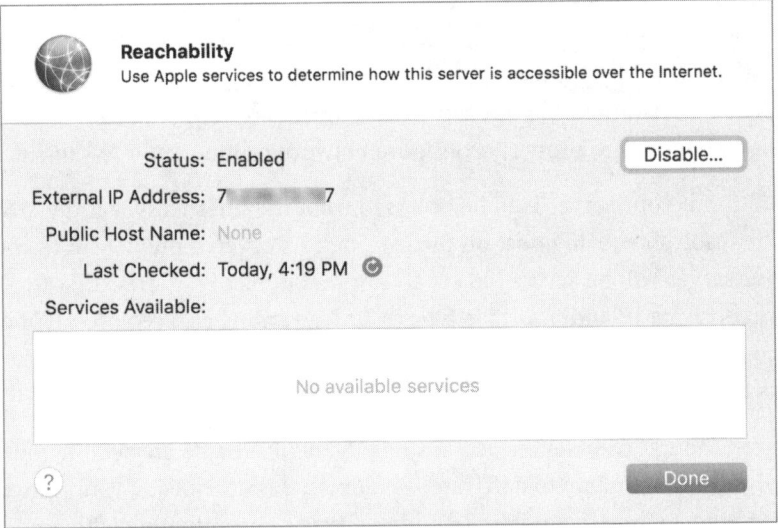

Reference 4.3
TLS/SSL Certificates

Transport Layer Security (TLS) and its predecessor, SSL, are protocols for the secure transmission of data between hosts. More specifically, TLS/SSL technology is used to prove your server's identity to client devices and to encrypt communication between your server and client devices. This encryption isn't just recommended to secure OS X Server services; it's required for any MDM service including Profile Manager. This section starts with the basics of TLS/SSL certificates and then provides recommendations for certificate best practices in regard to managing Apple devices.

Understanding Certificates

To enable TLS/SSL communications, you must configure your server with a TLS/SSL certificate (also referred to as simply a *certificate*). A certificate is a file that identifies the certificate holder. A certificate specifies the permitted use of the certificate and has an expiration date. This is why certificates must be renewed on a regular basis (most often annually).

Importantly, a TLS/SSL certificate also includes a public key infrastructure (PKI) public key. This public key is mathematically tied to a private key that is securely stored on the server. Data encrypted with one key can be decrypted only by using the other key. Thus, if you can decrypt data with one key, it proves that the data was encrypted with the other key.

To initiate secure TLS/SSL connections, client devices download the certificate (containing the public key) from your server. If a client can successfully verify the identity of the server from the certificate, it will use the public key to begin secure communications with the server. This raises the question, how exactly does a client device verify, or trust, a certificate?

The answer is that a certificate is verified by its digital signature. A certificate is either self-signed or signed by a certification authority (also known as a certificate authority or, more simply, a CA). A self-signed certificate, as the name implies, doesn't require the involvement of other CAs; thus, OS X Server will automatically create a self-signed certificate during the setup process. You can use a self-signed certificate for most TLS/SSL services, but self-signed certificates created by OS X Server (and most other servers) are not trusted by Apple devices for MDM services.

In other words, if you need to manage Apple devices, you will need to configure a certificate that has been signed by a verifiable CA. Certificates used by servers are most often signed by an intermediate CA, which is a CA whose certificate is signed by another CA.

The PKI infrastructure allows for a hierarchical chain of certificates, commonly known as a *chain of trust*. For example, the following figure shows the chain of trust for https://www.apple.com, which can be revealed in Safari by clicking the lock to the left of a web address:

The certificate for www.apple.com is signed by an intermediate CA with the name of Symantec Class 3 EV SSL CA–G3, and that intermediate CA is signed by a CA with the name of VeriSign Class 3 Public Primary Certification Authority–G5. You can follow a chain of certificates, starting with a signed certificate, up to the intermediate CA and ending at the top of the chain. The certificate chain ends with a CA that signs its own certificate, which is called a *root CA*. But how does a device know whether it can trust a CA?

The answer is that trust has to start somewhere. iOS and OS X include a collection of root and intermediate CAs that Apple has determined are worthy of trust out of the box. By extension, your Apple devices also trust any certificate or intermediate CA whose certificate chain ends with one of these CAs.

Although you can't directly inspect the list of root certificates included on iOS devices, you can on an OS X computer from the Keychain Access application. Open Keychain Access (in the Utilities folder). In the upper-left Keychains column, select System Roots. Note that in the following figure the bottom of the window states that, at the time of this writing, there are more than 180 trusted CAs or intermediate CAs by default in El Capitan.

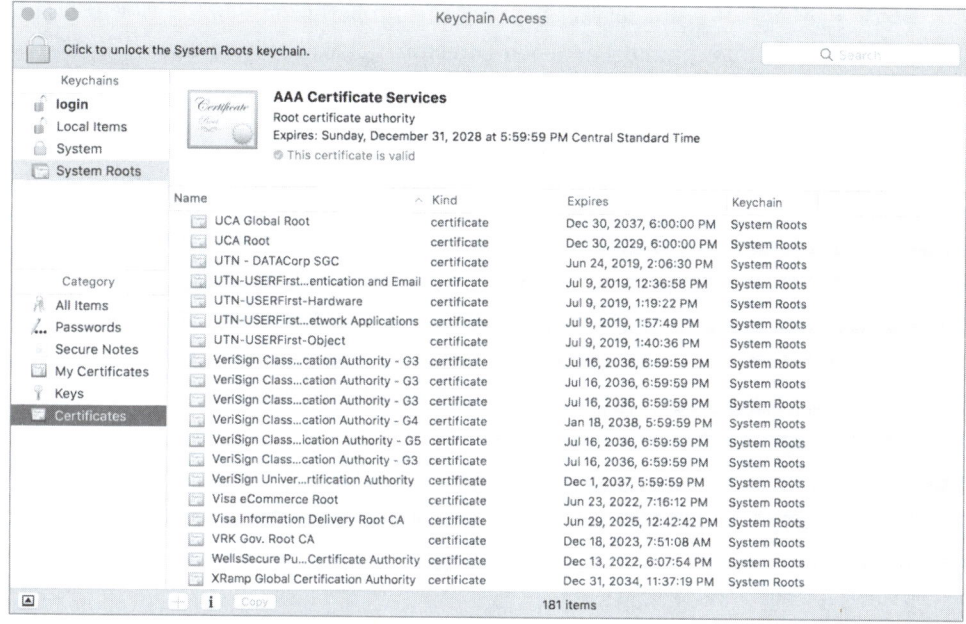

MORE INFO ▶ The Apple PKI website (https://www.apple.com/certificateauthority/) contains more information about the root certificates included with Apple devices. You can also find a complete list of trusted root certificates for iOS in Apple Support article HT204132, "Lists of available trusted root certificates in iOS," and for OS X in article HT202858, "Lists of available trusted root certificates in OS X."

Certificate Signed by an Open Directory CA

Again, any MDM service must use a TLS/SSL certificate signed by a trusted CA. This limits you to one of two choices if using Profile Manager as your MDM service: a certificate signed by a widely trusted CA (as covered in the next section) or a certificate signed by your own local Open Directory CA. Fortunately, OS X Server makes this latter choice an easy option by automatically creating an Open Directory CA and signing your server's TLS/SSL certificate during the creation of an Open Directory master.

NOTE ▶ Creating an Open Directory master is required to enable device management for Profile Manager. In other words, you're probably going to end up with an Open Directory CA even if you don't use it to sign the server's certificate.

NOTE ▶ Make sure your server's host name is properly configured prior to creating an Open Directory master. The Open Directory CA will only automatically sign the certificate with a name that matches the host name of the server.

When creating an Open Directory master from the Server app, Setup Assistant will guide you through several screens. One of the setup screens allows you to enter organizational information. This information will be used to create an Open Directory CA that will then be used to sign an intermediate CA, which is then used to sign your server's TLS/SSL certificate. This process will also create a code-signing certificate that will come in handy for verifying profiles, as covered in Lesson 6, "Configuration and Profiles."

Organization Information

Enter the name of your organization. This information will be shown to users to help them identify your server.

Organization Name: Dreyer Network Consultants, Inc.

Provide an email address that users can use to contact you. This will be used to verify your server's authenticity as well as for support.

Admin Email Address: ladmin@arekdreyer.com

Cancel   Previous   Next

MORE INFO ▶ You can find detailed step-by-step instructions for creating an Open Directory master in the exercises later in this lesson.

Assuming you completed the Open Directory master creation before acquiring other certificates, the Server app will automatically configure all supported services to use the certificate signed by the Open Directory CA. You can verify this by simply navigating to your server's default secure website, https://hostname, where "hostname" is the name of your server. You will still see a default web services page and can inspect the certificate used to protect the site (as of this writing, configuring your server as an Open Directory master starts the Websites service).

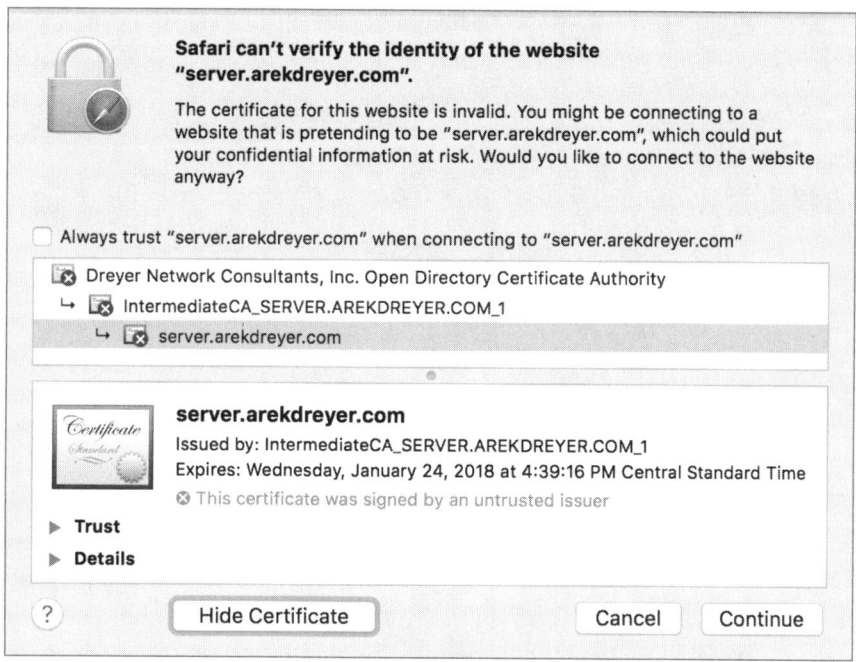

You'll note that even though a chain of trust has been created, you still have the fundamental problem that Apple devices, by default, do not trust your server's Open Directory CA. In a managed environment, you can easily solve this problem by using a trust profile, also covered in Lesson 6, "Configuration and Profiles."

In fact, deploying a trust profile is required for the enrollment of most MDM services, including Profile Manager. Thus, if you or your staff is going to be directly responsible for managing the enrollment of Apple devices, using a certificate signed by the Open Directory CA is a perfectly acceptable solution for most deployments.

Issues with an Untrusted Certificate

In some environments, using a certificate signed by an Open Directory CA is not the recommended solution. For example, your organization may require that all TLS/SSL services use certificates that meet a certain specification or are provided by a specific vendor.

Alternately, if your environment relies upon users self-enrolling their own devices, you don't want the first user experience of your management solution to be a warning message. The following warning message appears on an unmanaged iOS device when connecting for the first time to an MDM service using a certificate signed by an untrusted Open Directory CA:

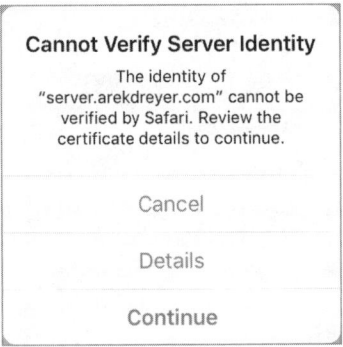

Not only does this type of warning message make your management solution look sketchy, it means that you (and your users) can't trust any connection made to your management server. In other words, when connecting from an unmanaged device, you will have no way of identifying a legitimate connection to your server from an illegitimate server acting as your server or a server that is attempting a man-in-the-middle attack.

Further, you don't want to establish that it's OK for your users to click Continue when presented with this warning. Quite to the contrary, you should be instructing them that accepting connections to unverified servers is extremely dangerous.

> **NOTE** ▶ You can use a configuration profile to prevent the user of an iOS device from trusting an untrusted TLS certificate.

Certificate Signed by a Widely Trusted CA

If you determine that your server needs a certificate signed by a widely trusted CA, the Certificates pane of the Server app provides two main methods for configuration: getting a trusted certificate by generating a certificate-signing request (CSR) or importing an existing certificate identity.

> **NOTE** ▶ At this point, when configuring OS X Server for managing Apple devices, you only need to acquire a standard TLS/SSL certificate, the kind that is commonly used to protect websites. Although a code-signing certificate can be used with an MDM service, it is not required to set up and use the service.

Get a Trusted Certificate

It all starts in the Certificates pane of the Server app; the Add (+) button reveals a pop-up menu.

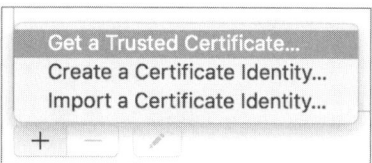

The Get a Trusted Certificate assistant will create a new certificate identity consisting of an unsigned certificate and a private/public key pair. After you enter contact information for the certificate, the system will present a CSR. You will need to copy and paste (or save to a text file) the CSR content. The act of providing a CSR to a CA vendor is the most common method for acquiring a certificate signed by a widely trusted CA.

At this point, you will need to identify a CA vendor. Your organization may already work with a CA vendor, so that will likely be your first choice. Otherwise, the only recommendation is choosing a CA vendor that works with Apple devices. When selecting a CA vendor, an obvious quick test is that an Apple device can establish a secure connection to the vendor's website.

After acquiring a TLS/SSL certificate subscription from a CA vendor, you will need to give the vendor your server's CSR. Most CA vendors will accept the CSR content via a simple paste into a website. After the CA vendor has validated and signed your certificate, the vendor will return it to you as a download. The download will often include the CA vendor's intermediate and root certificates. Double-click the pending certificate in the Server app, and drag all certificates provided by the CA vendor into the appropriate area.

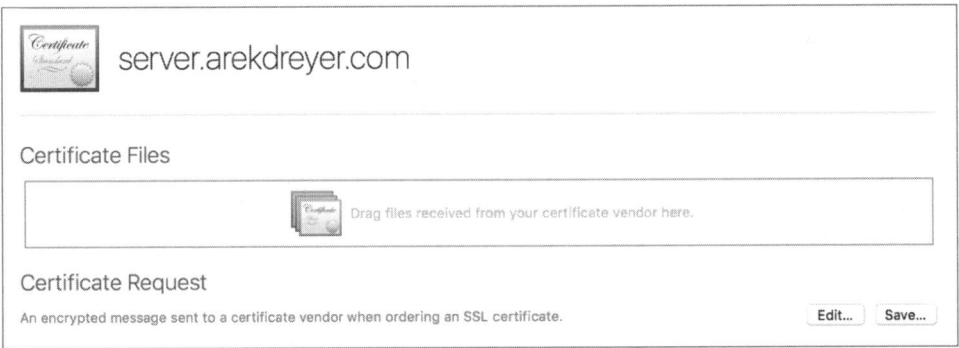

Import a Certificate Identity

The Add (+) button reveals a pop-up menu. From this menu, you can select the option to import a certificate identity. This option assumes you already have a valid certificate identity consisting of a signed certificate and a private/public key pair. This is often the case if your organization uses a centralized certificate repository or if your organization has a wildcard certificate that can be used for multiple services. The term *wildcard* means the certificate can be used with any host name inside a specific domain.

If this is the case, someone else has already done all the hard work for you and will provide you with the appropriate certificates and private/public key pair. Transporting a private key in the clear is dangerous, so the key is often stored in an encrypted document. Further, to make certificate identities easier to transport, this encrypted document will also contain all the appropriate certificates. The most common file types are .pfx and .p12, both of which share a similar encrypted format.

The person providing you with the certificate identity will also have to provide you with the encryption key used to protect the document containing the private key. Once you have all the certificate identity documents, simply drag them to the certificate import window in the Server app and then provide the encryption key.

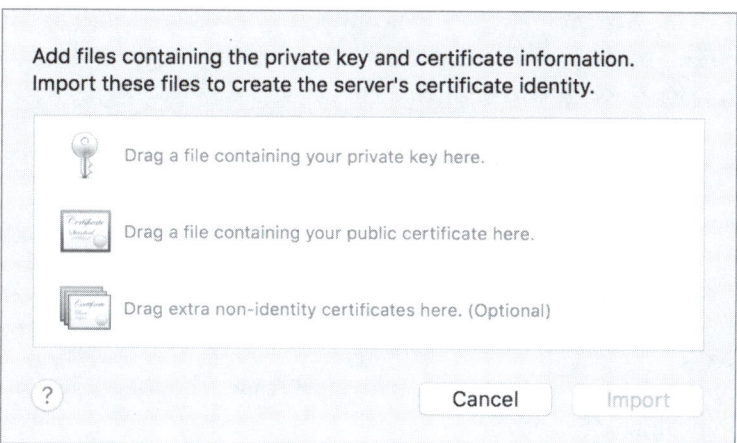

Exercise 4.1
Prepare Your Mac to Install OS X Server for El Capitan

▶ **Prerequisites**

- ▶ You'll need a Mac computer that is qualified to run OS X Server, that has OS X El Capitan on its startup volume, and that does not yet have OS X Server installed and configured on its startup volume.

- ▶ Your own administrator Apple ID or the administrator Apple ID from Exercise 2.2, "Create Apple IDs."

- ▶ Even though best practice calls for a PTR DNS record (reverse DNS record) to exist for the IPv4 address of your server computer, the exercises in this guide are written for use in a test network with Bonjour .local names, so there should be no PTR record for the primary IPv4 address of your server.

In this exercise, you will configure your server computer in preparation to install OS X Server on it.

You'll use one of two options to configure a local administrator account, depending on whether you are performing these exercises independently or are in an instructor-led environment with a Mac computer that has already been set up.

In both situations, you'll use System Preferences to configure Network and Sharing preferences. You will also download the student materials that you'll use throughout this class. Finally, you will apply any necessary system software updates.

Challenge

Set up your server computer with a unique computer name. Download the student materials.

Considerations

The exercises in this guide are written so that the individual reader and the student in the instructor-led environment have a similar experience.

In a production environment, it is best practice to use your server's fully qualified domain name. However, to make the exercises possible for those who cannot provide appropriate DNS records to computers and devices on their test network, the exercises in this guide use your server's Bonjour .local name instead of a fully qualified domain name.

Solution

Use Your Client Computer to Confirm Lack of PTR Records

Before you configure your server Mac, use your client Mac to confirm that your DNS service does not provide a PTR record defining a host name for the primary IPv4 address your server will use.

1   On your client Mac, press Command–Space bar (or click the Spotlight icon in the upper-right corner of the screen) to reveal the Spotlight Search field.

2   In the Spotlight Search field, enter Network Utility.

3   Confirm that Network Utility is listed in the Top Hit section of the search results, and then press Return to open it.

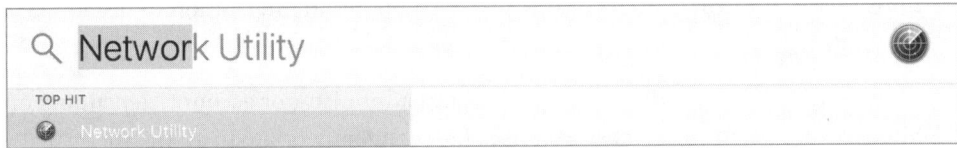

4 Click the Lookup tab.

5 In the "Enter an internet address to lookup" field, enter 10.0.0.*n*1 (where *n* is your student number; for example, student1 uses 10.0.0.11, student 6 uses 10.0.0.61, and student 15 uses 10.0.0.151).

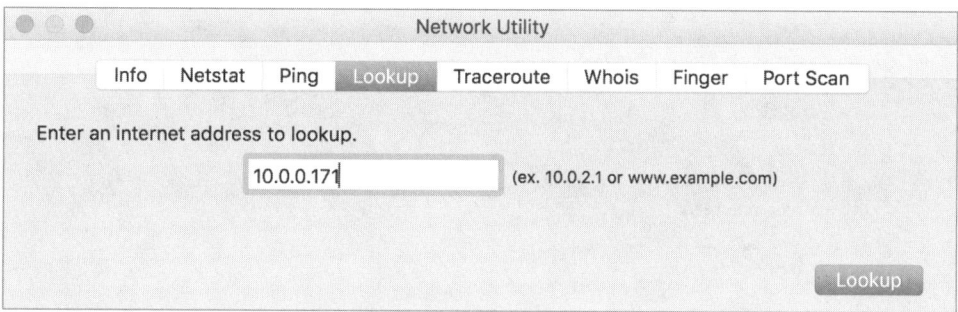

6 Click Lookup.

7 If the result field contains the text "The operation couldn't be completed," there is no PTR record for your server's primary IPv4 address. You can continue with the next section, "Configure OS X on Your Server Computer."

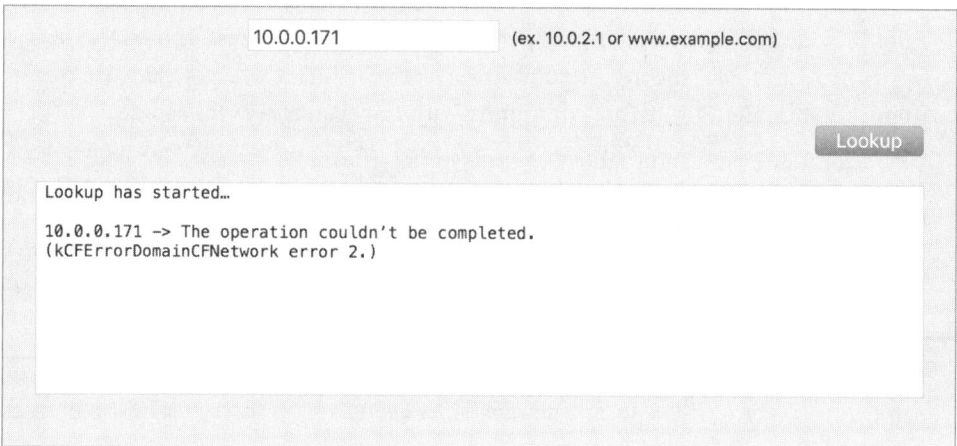

8   If the result field contains a DNS name such as "server*n*.trainapple.com" (where *n* is your student number), the DNS server that you are using provides PTR records for your server's primary IPv4 address. In an instructor-led environment, check with your instructor. If you are performing these exercises independently, check your DNS server entries.

```
                    10.0.0.171              (ex. 10.0.2.1 or www.example.com)

                                                                      Lookup

Lookup has started…
10.0.0.171 -> server17.trainapple.com
```

For best results when you perform the exercises on your test network, the DNS service for your server computer, your client computer, and your iOS device should not provide a PTR record for your server's primary IPv4 address. If the DNS service does provide a PTR record for your server's primary IPv4 address, here are two options you might try before continuing with the exercises in this guide:

▶ Configure your internal DNS server to not offer a PTR record for your server's primary IPv4 address.

▶ Configure your test network's DHCP service to use an external DNS service that does not offer a PTR record for your server's primary IPv4 addresses.

After you make one of the suggested changes, perform the previous step 5 again.

If you cannot perform either of the previous options, perform the following to configure your server to use a .local Bonjour name even though there is a PTR record available for its primary IPv4 address:

▶ After you install OS X Server, select your server in the Server app sidebar, click the Overview tab, click Edit next to the Host Name field, click Next to start Change Host Name Assistant, and select Local Network in the Accessing Your Server pane. Click Next, enter server*n*.local in the Host Name field, and then click Finish.

For experienced administrators, if you must use your server's fully qualified domain name instead of its Bonjour .local name, replace every instance of a Bonjour .local name with your server's fully qualified domain name throughout all the exercises in this guide.

Configure OS X on Your Server Computer

Starting with a fresh installation of OS X is most convenient. If your Mac is at the Welcome pane when you turn it on, you can use the Option 1 section that follows. If you need to use an existing OS X system, skip to Option 2 so your Mac will be configured as expected for the rest of the exercises.

Option 1: Configure OS X on Your Server Computer with Setup Assistant

This option is necessary if your server computer has not already been set up, which is the situation in an instructor-led environment. If you are using a Mac with existing accounts, perform the steps in "Option 2: Configure an Existing OS X System for Your Server Computer" instead.

Ensure that you have OS X El Capitan installed on your server computer. If it isn't already installed, install it now using the App Store, the Recovery HD, or a method specified by your instructor, and then continue when you reach the Welcome pane.

In this section, you'll step through the OS X Setup Assistant for the initial system configuration of your server computer.

1   Ensure that your computer is connected to a valid network connection, unless you plan to use Wi-Fi as your primary network connection.

2   If necessary, turn on the Mac that will run OS X Server.

3   At the Welcome screen, select the appropriate region, and click Continue.

4   Select the appropriate keyboard layout, and click Continue.

    Setup Assistant evaluates your network environment and tries to determine whether you are connected to the Internet. This can take a few moments.

5   If you plan to use Ethernet for your primary network connection and are not asked about your Internet connection, your computer's network settings have already been configured via DHCP, and you may skip to step 8.

If you plan to use Wi-Fi for your primary network connection and are at the Select Your Wi-Fi Network screen, select an appropriate Wi-Fi network, provide the Wi-Fi network's password if necessary, click Continue, and skip to step 8.

6   If you are at the How Do You Connect screen, select Local network (Ethernet), and click Continue.

7   If you are at the Your Internet Connection screen, leave the settings at their defaults, and click Continue.

NOTE ▶ If no DHCP service is available or your network is not connected to the Internet, you will see the warning message "Your Mac isn't connected to the internet." In this case, click Try Again, configure your router to provide DHCP service, and make sure your network is connected to the Internet. Then click Continue in the Your Internet Connection pane. For advanced users on a network without DHCP, you can set your TCP/IP connection type to Manually, configure settings appropriate for your network, and then click Continue in the Your Internet Connection pane.

8   When asked about transferring information to this Mac, select "Don't transfer any information now," and click Continue.

9   If the Enable Location Services screen appears, select "Enable Location Services on this Mac," and click Continue.

10 At the Sign in with Your Apple ID screen, select "Don't sign in," click Continue, and then click Skip to confirm that you want to skip signing in with an Apple ID.

Note that if you do provide Apple ID credentials, some figures in upcoming exercises may look slightly different, and there may be extra steps. In an instructor-led environment, entering an Apple ID at this time is not recommended.

11 At the Terms and Conditions screen, read the terms and conditions, and click Agree; then in the dialog to confirm that you have read and agree to the OS X software license agreement, click Agree.

Create your local administrator account.

NOTE ▶ Make sure you create this account as specified here. If you do not, future exercises may not work as written. Highlighted text is used throughout this guide to indicate text you should enter exactly as shown.

1 At the Create Your Computer Account screen, enter the following information:

- Full Name: Local Admin
- Account Name: ladmin
- Password: ladminpw
- (verify field): ladminpw
- Hint: Leave blank.
- Deselect the checkbox "Set time zone based on current location."

  If you are performing the exercises independently and if your server is accessible from the Internet, you can select a more secure password for the Local Admin account. Be sure to remember the password you have chosen because you will need to reenter it periodically as you use this computer.

  If you are performing the exercises independently, you may provide a password hint if you want.

  If you entered your Apple ID, you can select or deselect the checkbox "Allow my Apple ID to reset this user's password"; it does not have a major effect on the exercises.

  NOTE ▸ In a production environment, always use a strong password.

2 Click Continue to create the local administrator account.

3 At the Select Time Zone screen, click your time zone in the map or choose the nearest location in the Closest City pop-up menu, and then click Continue.

4 At the Diagnostics & Usage screen, leave selected "Send diagnostics & usage data to Apple" and "Share crash data with app developers," and then click Continue.

Please skip the Option 2 section, and continue at the section "Set the Computer Name."

Option 2: Configure an Existing OS X System for Your Server Computer

This option is designed only for those who are performing the exercises independently and who have a computer that is already set up with an existing administrator account.

NOTE ▸ You may not use a Mac whose startup volume has already had OS X Server installed.

If your computer has not been set up (that is, if the initial administrator account has not been created), perform the steps in "Option 1: Configure OS X on Your Server Computer with Setup Assistant" instead.

Create a new administrator account in System Preferences.

1   If necessary, log in with your existing administrator account.

2   Open System Preferences.

3   In System Preferences, open Users & Groups.

4   In the lower-left corner, click the lock icon.

5   In the dialog that appears, enter the password for your existing administrator account, and then click Unlock.

6   Click the Add (+) button under the user list.

7   In the dialog that appears, use the following settings:

   NOTE ▶ Make sure you create this account as specified here. If you do not, future exercises may not work as written. If you already have an account named Local Admin or ladmin, you will have to use a different name here and then remember to use your substitute name throughout the rest of the exercises. Highlighted text is used throughout this guide to indicate text you should enter exactly as shown.

   ▶   New Account: Choose Administrator.
   ▶   Full Name: Local Admin
   ▶   Account Name: ladmin

8   If necessary, select "Use separate password."

9   If your server is not accessible from the Internet, enter ladminpw in the Password and Verify fields.

   If you are performing the exercises independently, you can select a more secure password for the Local Admin account. Be sure to remember the password you have chosen because you will need to reenter it periodically as you use this computer.

   You may provide a password hint if you want.

If you entered your Apple ID, you can select or deselect the checkbox "Allow my Apple ID to reset this user's password"; it does not have a major effect on the exercises.

NOTE ▶ In a production environment, always use a strong password.

10 Click Create User.

11 At the bottom of the user list, click Login Options.

12 If an account is selected for Automatic Login, use the pop-up menu to switch it to Off.

13 Quit System Preferences, and log out.

14 At the login screen, select the Local Admin account, and enter its password (ladminpw, or whatever you specified earlier).

15 Press Return to log in.

This is the end of Option 2; everyone should continue with the next section.

Set the Computer Name

You will specify a computer name associated with your student number. If you are performing the exercises independently, you can choose to skip this section.

1 Open System Preferences.

2 Open Sharing.

3 Set Computer Name to servern, replacing *n* with your student number.

    For example, if your student number is 17, the computer name should be server17 (all lowercase and no spaces).

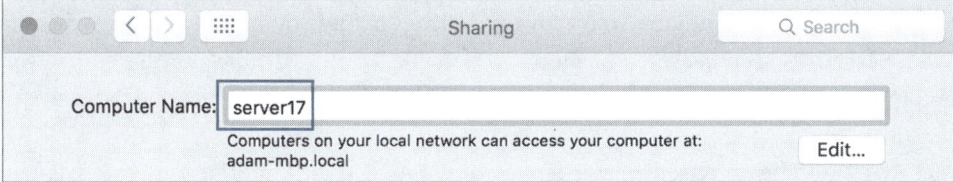

4 Press Return.

Notice that the name listed under the Computer Name field, which is the local host name, updates to match your new computer name.

Turn On Remote Management

Enable Remote Management, which will allow the instructor to observe your computer, control your keyboard and mouse, gather information, copy items to your computer, and otherwise help you if necessary.

> **NOTE ▶** Even though you know administrator credentials for other students' computers and have the technical ability to remotely control their computers, please do not use that ability to interfere with their classroom experience.

1 Click somewhere over the phrase "Remote Management," but don't select the checkbox yet.

2 For "Allow Access for," select "Only these users."

3 Click the Add (+) button, select Local Admin, and click Select.

4 In the dialog that appears, hold down the Option key while selecting the Observe checkbox, which selects all the checkboxes.

5 Click OK.

6 Select the checkbox Remote Management.

7 Confirm that the Sharing pane displays the text "Remote Management: On" and displays a green status indicator next to the text.

8 Click Show All (looks like a grid) to return to the main System Preferences pane.

Configure Network Interfaces

It is best practice to configure your network settings before you initially install and configure OS X Server. To keep the setup as simple as possible for all situations, for this course your Apple devices will access your server's services via Bonjour, rather than via DNS names.

> **NOTE ▶** The exercises are written for only one network interface to be active, but using multiple network interfaces will not significantly impact your ability to complete the exercises.

1   In System Preferences, click Network.

2   In the instructor-led environment, configure your Mac computer's built-in Ethernet port (or its Thunderbolt to Ethernet adapter port) to be the only active network service.

    If you are performing the exercises independently, you may leave additional interfaces active, but be aware that this may cause differences between the way the exercises describe the windows and what you actually see.

    In the list of network interfaces, select each network interface that you will not use in the exercise (which should be all interfaces except one Ethernet port), click the Action (gear icon) pop-up menu, and choose Make Service Inactive.

3   If you will use multiple network interfaces, click the Action (gear icon) pop-up menu, choose Set Service Order, drag the services to an appropriate order so that your primary interface is at the top of the list, and click OK.

4   Select the network interface you chose earlier in this exercise.

5   Click Advanced.

6   Click the TCP/IP tab.

7   In the Configure IPv4 pop-up menu, choose Manually.

8   In the instructor-led environment, enter the following information to manually configure the Ethernet interface (IPv4) for the classroom environment:

    IP Address: 10.0.0.*n*1 (where *n* is your student number; for example, student1 uses 10.0.0.11, student 6 uses 10.0.0.61, and student 15 uses 10.0.0.151)

    Subnet Mask: 255.255.255.0

    Router: 10.0.0.1

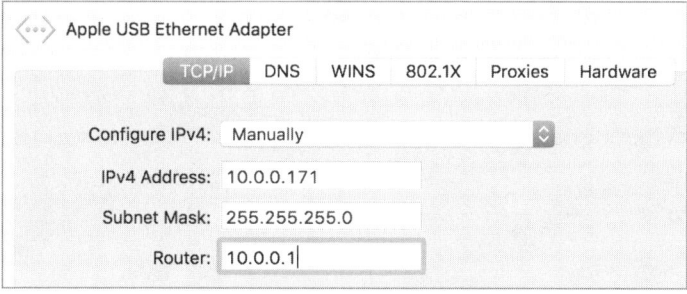

If you are performing the exercises independently and choose to use different network settings, see the "Exercise Setup" section in Lesson 1.

9 Click the DNS tab.

Even though you just switched Configure IPv4 from DHCP to Manually, you did not yet apply the change. Values assigned by DHCP are listed, but once you click Apply, those values will not remain unless you deliberately add them.

10 In the DNS Servers field, click Add (+).

11 In the instructor-led environment, enter 10.0.0.1.

If you are performing the exercises independently, enter the value or values appropriate for your environment.

12 If there are any other values in the DNS Servers field, select another value, and then click Delete (-) to delete the value; do this until 10.0.0.1 (or your desired values if you are performing the exercises independently) is the only value in the DNS Servers field.

13 Click OK to save the change and return to the list of network interfaces.

14 Review the settings, and then click Apply to accept the network configuration.

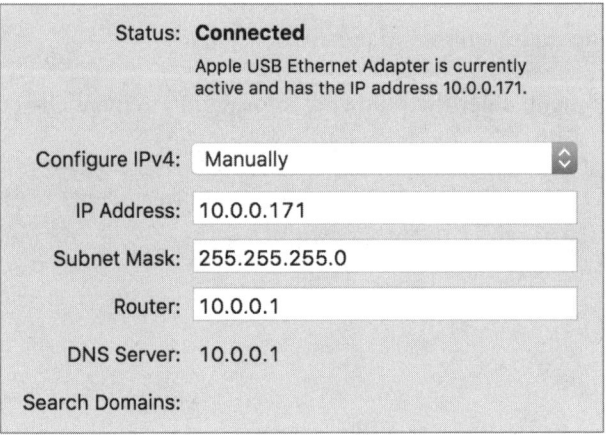

15 Click Show All (looks like a grid) to return to the main System Preferences pane.

Update Software

To take advantage of possible fixes and improvements, be sure that you're running the most recent version of OS X. If a local Caching service is available, your Mac will automatically use it.

1   While still in System Preferences, open App Store preferences.

2   Select the checkbox "Install app updates."

3   Select the checkbox "Install OS X updates."

4   If the button at the bottom of the window is Check Now, click Check Now.

    If the button at the bottom of the window is Show Updates, click Show Updates.

5   If you are in an instructor-led environment, ask your instructor what updates are appropriate to install; otherwise, if there are any updates, click Update All.

    If there are no updates available, press Command-Q to quit the App Store, quit System Preferences, skip the rest of this section, and continue with the section "Download the Student Materials."

6   If the "Some updates need to finish downloading before they are installed" dialog appears, click Download & Restart.

    If the Restarting Your Computer notification appears, click Restart; after your Mac restarts, you will be automatically logged back in.

7   Quit the App Store.

8   Quit System Preferences.

Download the Student Materials

Some files are necessary for the completion of some of the exercises. You have already downloaded them to your client computer, but you should also have them available on your server computer. If you are in an instructor-led environment, you can use the Option 1 section that follows. Otherwise, skip to Option 2.

Option 1: Download the Student Materials in the Instructor-Led Environment

If you are performing the exercises independently, skip to "Option 2: Download the Student Materials for the Independent Reader."

If you are in an instructor-led environment, you will connect to the classroom server and download the student materials used for the course. To copy the files, you'll drag the folder to your Documents folder.

1   In the Finder, choose File > New Finder Window (or press Command-N).

2   In the Finder window sidebar, click mainserver.

    If Mainserver does not appear in the Finder sidebar, in the Shared list, click All, and then double-click the mainserver icon in the Finder window.

    Because mainserver allows guest access, your client computer logs in automatically as Guest and displays the available share points.

3   Open the Public folder.

4   Drag the StudentMaterials folder to the Documents folder in the sidebar.

5   Once the copy is complete, disconnect from mainserver by clicking Eject next to the Mainserver listing.

Skip the Option 2 section that follows, and resume with the section "Install the Server App."

Option 2: Download the Student Materials for the Independent Reader

If you are in the instructor-led environment, skip this section.

If you are performing the exercises independently, copy the student materials from your client or download the materials from Peachpit's site, and place them in your Documents folder.

If both of your Mac systems have AirDrop enabled, you can use AirDrop to copy the StudentMaterials folder from your client to your server computer. Click AirDrop in a Finder window on each Mac. On your client computer, open a new Finder window, open your Documents folder, drag the StudentMaterials folder to the picture for your server computer in the AirDrop window, and then click Send. On your server computer, click Save. When the transfer has completed, open the Downloads folder, and drag StudentMaterials to your Documents folder in the Finder window sidebar. Finally, close the AirDrop window on your client computer and on your server computer.

Another option is to use a removable disk. If you have a USB, FireWire, or Thunderbolt disk, you can connect it to your client, copy the StudentMaterials folder from your local administrator's Documents folder to the volume, eject the volume, connect the volume to your server computer, and drag the StudentMaterials folder to your Documents folder in the Finder window sidebar.

Alternatively, you can download the files from Peachpit again using the following steps:

> **NOTE ▶** You registered this guide for the lesson files in Exercise 2.1, "Configure Your Client Mac." If you have not already done so, see the section "Option 2: Download the Student Materials for the Independent Reader" in that exercise for details.

1. Using Safari, open www.peachpit.com, and click the Account link or Account Sign In link at the top right of the home page to access your Peachpit account.

2. Click the Registered Products tab and locate Managing Apple Devices: Deploying and Maintaining iOS 9 and OS X El Capitan Devices.

3. Click the Access Bonus Content link to access the student materials.

4. Click the Student Materials link to download the appropriate files to the Downloads folder (or whichever location you have selected in Safari Preferences) on your computer.

5. In the Finder, choose File > New Finder Window (or press Command-N).

6. Choose Go > Downloads.

7. Double-click the StudentMaterials.zip file to decompress the file.

8. Drag the StudentMaterials folder from your Downloads folder to your Documents folder in the Finder window sidebar. If you want, you can also place StudentMaterials in your Dock for easy access.

9. Drag the StudentMaterials.zip file from your Downloads folder to the Trash in the Dock if necessary.

In this exercise, you used System Preferences and the Finder to configure OS X on your server computer in preparation to install OS X Server.

Exercise 4.2
Install OS X Server for El Capitan

> **Prerequisite**
>
> ► Exercise 4.1, "Prepare Your Mac to Install OS X Server for El Capitan"

Challenge

Now that you have OS X configured on your server computer, install OS X Server on your server computer and configure it so you can administer it remotely.

Considerations

Your server computer isn't a server until you run and configure the Server app.

If you are a member of the Mac Developer Program or iOS Developer Program (available at https://developer.apple.com), you may obtain a free redemption code for OS X Server.

Solution

Install Server

In a production environment, it's recommended to download the latest version of OS X Server from the App Store.

> **TIP** ► If you've already purchased OS X Server, you must use the same Apple ID used for the original purchase to avoid being charged again.

If you are in an instructor-led environment, use the Option 1 section that follows. Otherwise, you should skip to Option 2.

Option 1: In the Instructor-Led Environment, Copy Server

In the instructor-led environment, the classroom server has the Server app available in the StudentMaterials folder; move the Server app to the Applications folder on your server computer with the following steps:

1   In the Finder on your server computer, open a new Finder window, click Documents in the sidebar, open the StudentMaterials folder you downloaded, and then open the Lesson4 folder.

2   Drag the Server app into the Applications folder in the sidebar.

Please skip the Option 2 section, and continue at the "Open Server" section that follows.

Option 2: For the Independent Reader, Download or Purchase Server in the App Store

If you are performing the exercises independently, use your own administrator Apple ID or the administrator Apple ID from Exercise 2.2, "Create Apple IDs," to purchase or redeem a code for OS X Server from the App Store. This automatically places the Server app in your Applications folder. If you have already purchased the Server app, download it again from the Purchased tab in the App Store. If you have the Server app available on a removable volume, drag the Server app from your removable volume into your Applications folder.

Open Server

Once you have the Server app installed in the Applications folder, open the Server app.

1   In your Dock, click Launchpad.

2   You may need to swipe to the next page in Launchpad to see the Server app (hold down the Command key and press the Right Arrow key, or if you have a trackpad, swipe to the left with two fingers to get to the next page in Launchpad).

3   Click Server to open the Server app.

4   Keep the Server app in the Dock. Click and hold Server in the Dock, and then choose Options > Keep in Dock from the menu that appears.

5 In the "To set up OS X Server on this Mac, click Continue" pane, click Continue.

6 Read and agree to the terms of the software license agreement.

7 Ensure that "Use Apple services to determine this server's Internet reachability" is selected, and click Agree.

8 Provide local administrator credentials (User Name: Local Admin, Administrator Password: ladminpw), and click Allow.

9 Wait while OS X Server for El Capitan configures itself.

10 Close the Server Tutorials window.

After its initial installation, the Server app displays the Overview tab in the Server pane.

NOTE ▶ The public IPv4 address in the following figure is obscured intentionally.

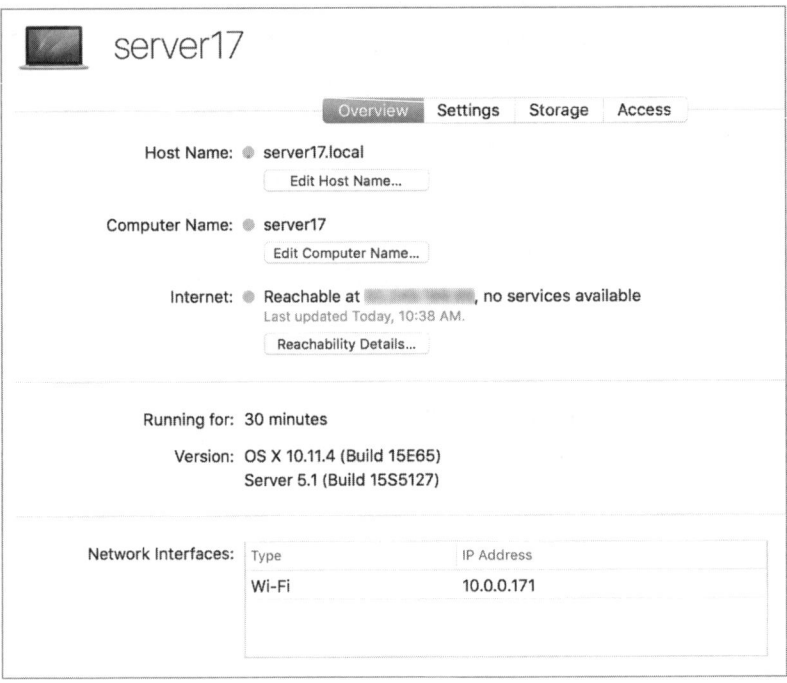

You have successfully installed OS X Server.

Configure Your Server to Allow Remote Access via the Server App

Configure your server so that you can administer it with the Server app on your client computer.

1 In the Server app, click the Settings tab.

2 Select the checkbox "Using Server app on a remote Mac."

It's recommended that you administer your server with only one instance of the Server app at a time; if you have the Server app open while logged in on your server, quit the Server app before opening the Server app on your client computer.

In this exercise, you used the Server app to configure your server with OS X Server, and you turned on remote access using the Server app.

Exercise 4.3
Configure OS X Server for El Capitan

▶ **Prerequisites**

- ▶ Exercise 4.2, "Install OS X Server for El Capitan"
- ▶ Text files from the student materials, which you obtained as part of Exercise 4.1, "Prepare Your Mac to Install OS X Server for El Capitan"

Challenge

Configure Apple Push Notifications. Configure and start services you will use for the rest of the course:

- ▶ Open Directory, including importing users and groups
- ▶ Mail
- ▶ Calendar
- ▶ Contacts
- ▶ Wiki

Considerations

In the Server app's list of services, Open Directory is hidden by default in a section of advanced services. The downloadable student materials contain user import files with eight users and a group import file with two groups.

Solution

Enable Apple Push Notifications

1 If necessary, open the Server app, authenticate to your server, select your server in the Server app sidebar, and then click the Settings tab.

2 If the Apple Push Notifications (APN) checkbox is not already selected, select it now.

3 Enter your administrator Apple ID credentials.

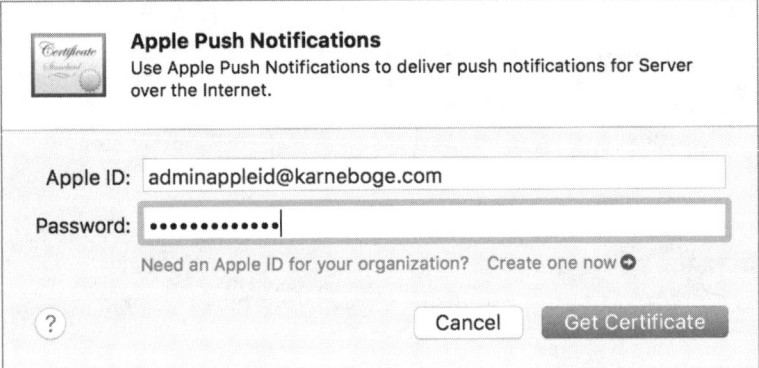

4 Click Get Certificate.

5 After the Server app successfully creates and processes the Apple Push Notification service certificates and displays their shared expiration date, click Done.

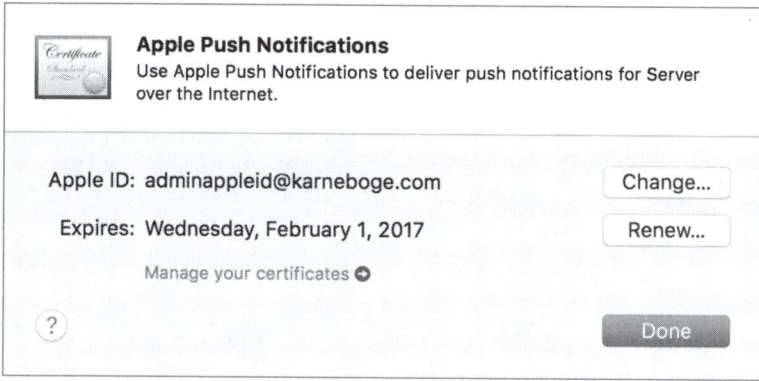

Configure Your Server as an Open Directory Master

In a production environment, you would definitely confirm or verify DNS records before configuring your server as an Open Directory master. However, because this environment uses Bonjour names, you can skip the usual DNS verification step.

1   If the Server app does not display the list of advanced services, hover the pointer above "Advanced" in the sidebar, and then click Show.

2   Click Open Directory.

3   Click the On/Off switch to turn on the Open Directory service.

4   Select "Create a new Open Directory domain," and click Next.

5   Configure a password; you can leave the "Remember this password in my keychain" option selected.

    If your server is not accessible from the Internet, in the Directory Administrator pane, enter diradminpw in the Password and Verify fields, and click Next.

    Of course, in a production environment, you should use a secure password.

6   In the Organization Information pane, enter the appropriate information.

    If the following fields do not already contain the information shown, enter it, and click Next:

    ▶   Organization Name: MDM Project *n* (where *n* is your student number)
    ▶   Admin Email Address: ladmin@server*n*.local (where *n* is your student number)

7 View the Confirm Settings pane, and click Set Up.

The Server app displays its progress in the lower-left corner of the Confirm Settings pane.

When the configuration is complete, the Server app displays the Servers section of the Open Directory pane, with your server listed as the master. It also displays any additional IPv4 addresses your Mac has in addition to your server's primary IPv4 address (such as Wi-Fi).

Inspect the SSL Configuration

One of the benefits of configuring your server to be an Open Directory master is that it automatically creates a code-signing certificate for Profile Manager to use. Use the following steps to inspect your server's Secure Sockets Layer configuration:

1 In the Server app sidebar, select Certificates.

Note that all the services are set to use the same certificate: server*n*.local certificate (where *n* is your student number), which is signed by your server's OD intermediate CA.

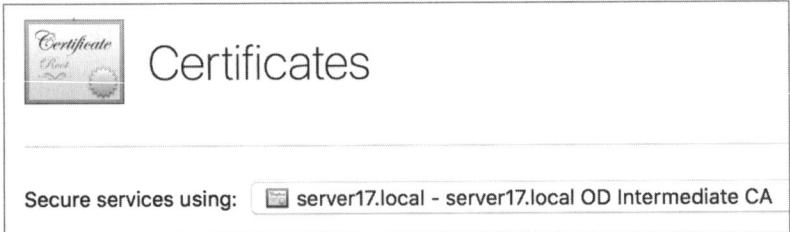

2 Double-click the server*n*.local certificate (where *n* is your student number).

3 Inspect the details of the certificate.

4 Scroll to the end of the certificate information, and note that Purpose is Server Authentication.

Note the Renew button for the certificate. When the renewal date approaches, the Server app automatically generates an expiration alert for the certificate, and the alert offers a Renew button. You don't have to wait for the alert; you can use this button to renew the certificate at any time.

5 Click OK to return to the list of certificates.

6   Double-click Code Signing Certificate.

7   Scroll to the end of the certificate information, and note that Purpose is Code Signing.

8   Click OK to return to the list of certificates.

Import Users into Your Server's Shared Directory Node

To expedite the exercise, in the StudentMaterials folder is a text file with user accounts. This import file defines these users with a "net" password. Of course, in a production environment, each user should have a unique password or passphrase that is secret and secure.

Import the accounts into your server's shared directory node.

1   In the Server app sidebar, select Users.

2   Click the Action (gear icon) pop-up menu, and choose Import Users.

3   In the sidebar, click Documents. Open StudentMaterials, and then open the Lesson4 folder.

4   Select the users.txt file.

5   Click the Directory pop-up menu, and choose Local Network Directory.

6   If directory administrator credentials are not automatically provided thanks to the keychain item, provide directory administrator credentials in the Admin Name and Password fields.

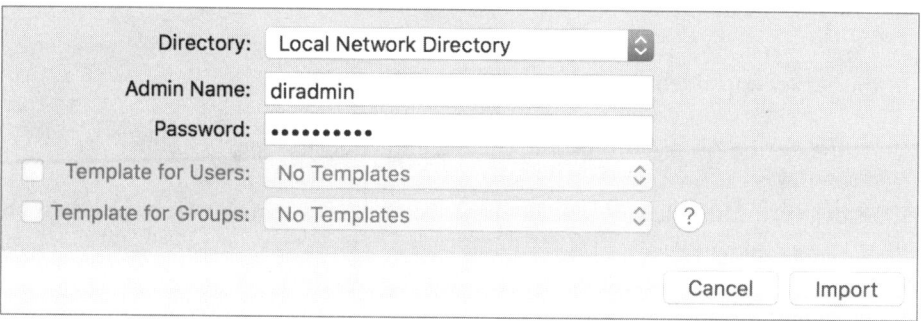

7   Click Import.

8 At the "Importing users and groups may take several minutes. Are you sure you want to continue?" dialog, click Continue.

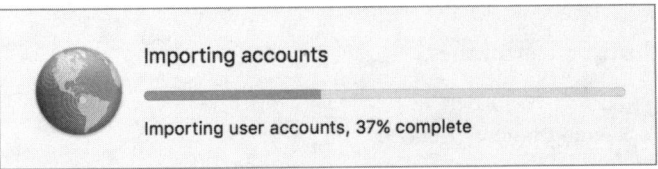

9 After the import has completed, select Local Network Users from the pop-up menu, and confirm that there are eight new local network users.

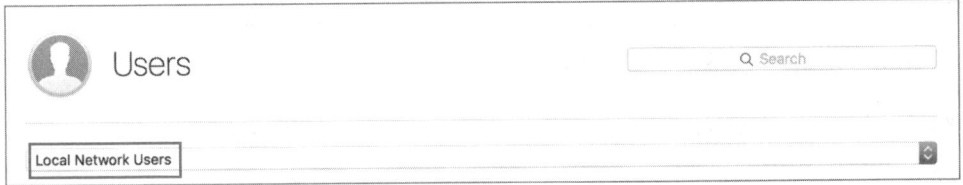

NOTE ▶ If any of the users are listed as Limited or No Access, after the import has completed, choose View > Refresh.

You now have added eight local network user accounts.

Import Groups into Your Server's Shared Directory Node

To expedite the exercise, you have two import files: one that defines some of the imported users as members of the Marketing group and another that defines users as members of the Engineering group.

1 In the Server app sidebar, select Groups.

2 Click the Action (gear icon) pop-up menu, and choose Import Groups.

3 If necessary, in the sidebar, click Documents. Open StudentMaterials, and then open the Lesson4 folder.

4 If necessary, select Local Network Directory from the Directory pop-up menu, and provide directory administrator credentials in the Admin Name and Password fields.

5 Double-click the groups.txt file to start importing the file.

6   At the "Importing users and groups may take several minutes. Are you sure you want to continue?" dialog, click Continue.

7   After the import has completed, select Local Network Groups from the pop-up menu, and confirm that there are two new local network groups, each containing four members.

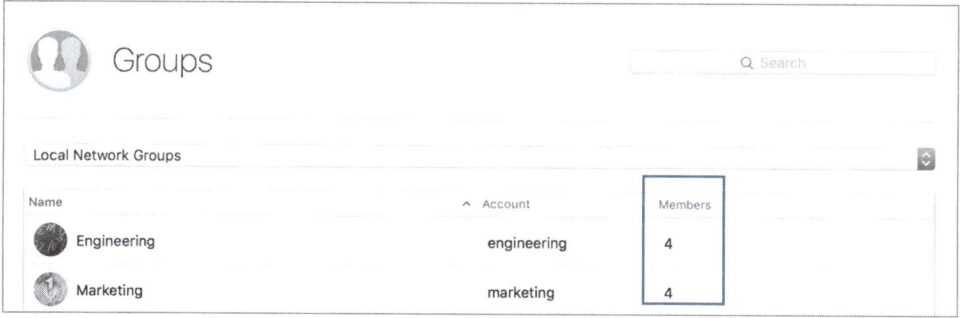

You now have two new local network groups populated with the local network users you previously imported.

Configure and Start the Mail Service

Once you've configured the Mail service, you can use it in other parts of this guide for configuration profile examples and to mail VPP notification invitations. This is not a production server, so to expedite the setup, you will disable virus and junk mail filtering.

1   In the Server app sidebar, select Mail.

2   Click Filtering Settings.

3   Deselect the "Enable virus filtering" checkbox.

4   Deselect the "Enable junk mail filtering" checkbox.

5   Click OK to close the Mail Filtering pane.

6   Under the Domains field, click the Add (+) button.

7   In the Domain field, enter servern.local (where *n* is your student number).

8   Press Command-B to display the accounts browser window.

9   Select an account in the accounts browser, and then press Command-A to select all users and groups.

10 Drag the accounts to the field that lists the Members and Email columns.

11 Press Command-B to hide the accounts browser window.

12 Click Create.

13 Click the On/Off switch to start the Mail service.

14 Wait for the Mail service to become available (green status indicator in the Status field).

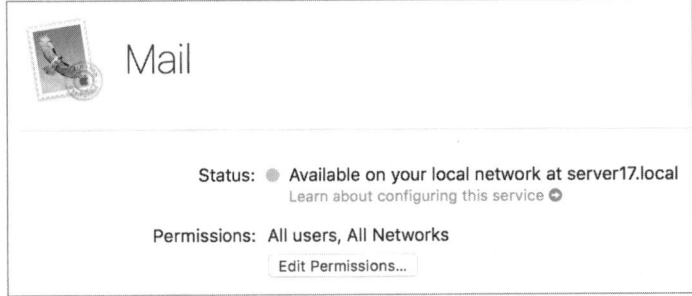

Verify the Mail Service

1   Open Mail on either your server Mac or your client Mac.

2   In the "Choose a Mail account provider" pane, select Other Mail Account, and click Continue.

3   In the Add a Mail Account pane, confirm that the import file includes an email address for your server, for example:

▶   Name: Barbara Green
▶   Email Address: barbara@server*n*.local (where *n* is your student number)
▶   Password: net

4   Click Sign In. The pane will display the message "Unable to verify account name or password."

5   In the Incoming Mail Server and Outgoing Mail Server fields, enter server*n*.local (where *n* is your student number).

    The User Name and Password fields should already be populated.

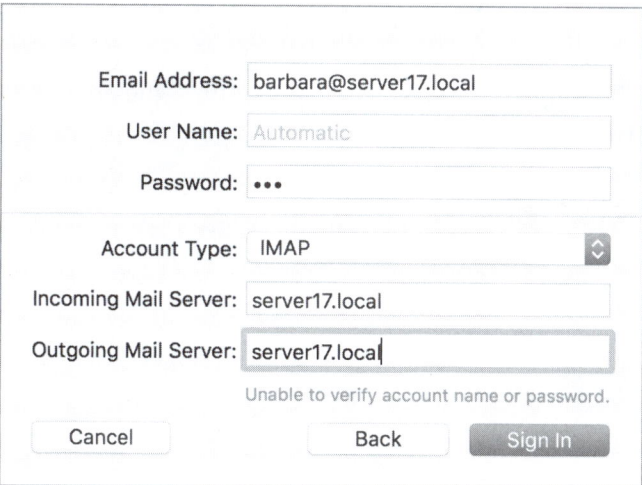

6   Click Sign In.

7   If you see the Verify Certificate window, click Show Certificate, select the "Always trust" checkbox, and click Connect.

8   If necessary, enter the local administrator credentials, and then click Update Settings.

9   In the "Select the apps you want to use with this account" pane, deselect Notes, and click Done.

Send and Receive a Test Message

1. Choose File > New Message.

2. In the To field, enter barbara@server*n*.local (where *n* is your student number).

3. Enter Test Message in the Subject field.

4. Enter some text in the main body field.

5. Click the Send button in the upper-left corner of the message.

6. Confirm that the message is delivered. If necessary, choose Window > Message Viewer.

7. Quit Mail.

Turn On the Calendar Service

To have another service available for the Settings for Everyone configuration profile, you can turn on the Calendar service.

1. In the Server app sidebar, select Calendar.

2. Click the On/Off switch to start the service.

    You can leave all the settings at their defaults.

Turn On the Contacts Service

Using the Contacts service allows you to quickly look up information, such as email addresses, for the users hosted by your server.

1. In the Server app sidebar, select Contacts.

2. Select the checkbox "Allow users to search the directory using the Contacts application."

3. Click the On/Off switch to start the service.

    You can leave all the other settings at their defaults.

Turn On the Wiki Service

By default, the Wiki service allows iOS users to edit files on the wiki using iWork.

1   In the Server app sidebar, select Wiki.

2   Click the On/Off switch to start the service.

    You can leave all the other settings at their defaults.

3   Quit Server.

In this exercise, you turned on Apple Push Notifications on your server computer, configured the server as an Open Directory master, imported users and groups, and turned on a few key services.

Exercise 4.4
Configure Server on Your Client Computer (Optional)

▶ **Prerequisites**

   ▶ Exercise 4.3, "Configure OS X Server for El Capitan"

   ▶ Text files from the student materials, which you obtained as part of Exercise 4.1, "Prepare Your Mac to Install OS X Server for El Capitan"

Challenge

Install the Server app on your client computer, and prepare it to remotely administer your server computer.

Considerations

Your server does not allow remote administration by default.

If you attempt to remotely administer your server, you will get a message that your client computer does not trust the identity of the SSL certificate used by the server.

Solution

Install the Server App

On your server computer, you ran the Server app to configure your server computer as a server. However, on your client computer, you can run the Server app to remotely administer your server.

Option 1: In the Instructor-Led Environment, Copy the Server App

In the instructor-led environment, the classroom server has the Server app available in the StudentMaterials folder; move the Server app to the Applications folder on your client Mac with the following steps:

1   In the Finder on your client Mac, open a new Finder window, click Documents in the sidebar, open the StudentMaterials folder you downloaded, and then open the Lesson4 folder.

2   Drag the Server app into the Applications folder in the Finder window sidebar.

Option 2: For the Independent Reader, Download or Purchase OS X Server in the App Store

If you are performing the exercises independently, you should have already purchased OS X Server by the time you completed Exercise 4.1. If this is the case, open the App Store from the Dock or from Recent Items under the Apple menu, sign in with the Apple ID you used to purchase OS X Server, and download OS X Server, which automatically places the Server app in your Applications folder. If you have already purchased the Server app and have it available on a removable volume, drag the Server app from your removable volume into your Applications folder.

Use the Server App to Administer Your Server

Using your client computer, open the Server app, connect to your server, and accept its SSL certificate.

1   On your client computer, open the Server app.

> **NOTE** ▶ Do not click Continue; otherwise, you will configure your client Mac to be a server.

2   Click and hold Server in the Dock, and then choose Options > Keep in Dock from the menu that appears.

3   Click Other Mac.

4   In the Choose a Mac window, select your server, and click Continue.

5   Provide the administrator credentials (Administrator Name: ladmin, Administrator Password: ladminpw).

6   Select the "Remember this password in my keychain" checkbox so the credentials you provide will be saved in your keychain (a secure store of passwords) and so you will not need to provide credentials again.

7   Click Connect.

Because your server is using a self-signed SSL certificate that has not been signed by a certificate authority your client computer is configured to trust, you'll see a warning message that you are connecting to a server whose identity certificate is not verified.

NOTE ▶ In a production environment, you might want to address this situation as soon as possible by using Keychain Access on your server computer to configure your server to use a valid SSL certificate for the com.apple.servermgrd identity, which is used to communicate with a remote instance of the Server app. This is outside the scope of this guide.

8   Click Show Certificate.

9   Select the checkbox to always trust com.apple.servermgrd when connecting to your server.

10 Click Continue.

11 You must provide your login credentials to modify your keychain.

Enter your password (ladminpw), and click Update Settings.

After you click Update Settings, the Server app connects to your server.

12 Quit Server.

In this optional exercise, you configured your client computer to remotely configure your server with the Server app.

Lesson 5
Caching Service

This lesson focuses on the OS X Server Caching service, which can greatly reduce the Internet bandwidth used for deployments of Apple devices. This is the first service covered in this guide so that future lessons can take advantage of the performance boost provided by the Caching service.

GOALS

▶ Understand the Caching service benefits and architecture

▶ Understand the options for modifying the permissions for the Caching service

▶ Set up and troubleshoot the Caching service

Reference 5.1
Caching Service Architecture

The Caching service speeds up the download and distribution of software and other content provided by Apple. It caches the first download of various items distributed by Apple and makes these items available to Apple devices on your local network, which means you can offer fast downloads of items distributed by Apple to clients on your network.

Further, the Caching service works transparently with zero client configuration needed, which saves time by reducing the wait for deployed items and dramatically decreases the Internet bandwidth required for deployment services. In fact, the reason this guide suggests turning on the Caching service before other management services is so you can take advantage of its benefits while working through the rest of the exercises in this guide.

Caching Service Requirements

The Caching service supports Mac systems with OS X 10.8.4 or later, iOS devices with iOS 7 or later, and Apple TV. It also supports iBooks Store content for iOS 6 or later and OS X Mavericks 10.9 or later, and it supports Windows computers. Finally, the Caching service supports iTunes content for Mac systems and Windows computers with iTunes 11.0.2 or later.

By default, the Caching service supports clients that share the same public Internet Protocol (IP) address behind a Network Address Translation (NAT) device, but Server 5 and later offer the ability to serve a wider variety of network configurations.

For eligible devices, the Caching service transparently caches many items from Apple, including the following:

- iOS and OS X software updates (iOS updates downloaded with iTunes are not cached; they must be delivered "over the air")
- iOS and OS X App Store purchases and downloads
- iTunes purchases and downloads
- iBooks Store purchases and downloads
- iTunes U items
- Apple TV updates and Apple TV apps
- OS X Internet Recovery (OS X Mavericks or later)
- iCloud data (photos and documents) (OS X El Capitan 10.11 or later, and iOS 9 and later)

  MORE INFO ▶ For a full list of content types supported by the Caching service, including region-specific restrictions, see Apple Support article HT204675, "Content types supported by the Caching service in OS X Server."

The server requirements to use the Caching service are as follows:

- The server must be running OS X Server.
- The server needs an Internet connection; if it's on a portable Mac, it must be connected via Ethernet to your network.
- The server must have at least 50 GB of free space dedicated to caching content. Any disk can be specified for the Caching service, including the system volume.
- If the Caching service is going to support a network of clients with public IP addresses or if the Caching service does not have the same public IP address as your clients, you must also set up additional local Domain Name System (DNS) entries with descriptive text (TXT records) that helps clients discover your Caching service.

  NOTE ▶ The Caching service caches only items distributed by servers that are under Apple's control (including items from a content distribution network partner); it does not cache content from third parties.

NOTE ▶ OS X computers that have been configured to use a legacy Software Update service will not receive software updates or App Store content from the Caching service. This intentional design gives administrators who want to restrict updates via the legacy Software Update service the power to trump the unfiltered updates provided by the Caching service.

Caching Service Automatic Discovery

A key feature of the Caching service is that eligible clients will automatically discover and use the local Caching services. Otherwise, the client will use servers operated by Apple or a content distribution network partner (just like clients did before the Caching service was introduced as a feature). This allows an organization to provide the benefits of a Caching service on their network without having to manage any Apple devices. The Caching service is discovered by clients using one of two methods:

▶ If the clients and the server that provides the Caching service share the same public IP address behind a NAT device, the clients will automatically discover local caching services. This is the most common network configuration; thus, it is the most common used by the Caching service.

▶ If the clients and the server that provides the Caching service use public addressing (which is rare with IPv4 but becoming more common with IPv6) or if the server has a different public IP address than clients behind a NAT device, you must provide additional DNS service configuration so clients can discover local caching services.

Caching Service on a Private Network

On a private network, the automatic client configuration of the Caching service assumes that your clients and the caching server (or servers) share an Internet connection behind a NAT router. Both server and client traffic from your private network to the Internet must have the same source IP address. (This applies even if the client and the caching server are on different subnets, as long as they have the same public IP source address.) Fortunately, this is a common configuration for many networks that use private IP addressing.

In the following figure, a network router performs NAT, and the organization has two subnets. The clients and the caching servers in both subnets have the same IP source address on the public Internet side of the NAT router, even though they are in different subnets. The clients in both subnets automatically use one of the caching servers in their organization's network (in the following figure, one subnet has two servers to illustrate that you don't need a Caching service for each subnet behind NAT). Once the clients leave the local network, they automatically use servers operated by Apple on the Internet.

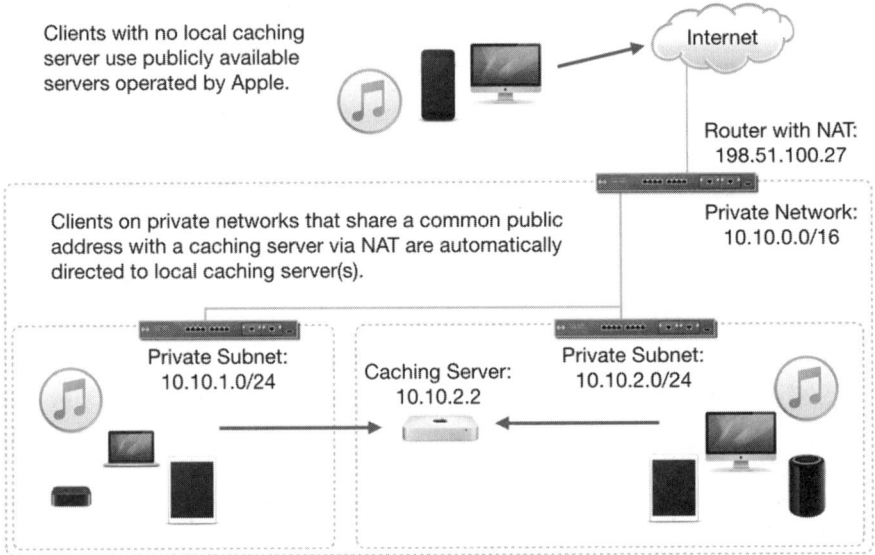

When starting up, the server running the Caching service automatically sends a request for registration to Apple servers. This request includes the following:

- The server's local address
- The speed of the server's network connections and whether they are wired
- If applicable, the ranges of private IP addresses to serve (by default, this range is based on the subnet mask configured for each of the server's wired Ethernet network connections)
- If applicable, the ranges of public IP addresses to serve
- Whether the server has alternating-current (AC) power
- The cache size
- A list of capabilities

If the request with Apple's registration service succeeds, it returns the server's public IP address (and a list of caching server peers, if any).

When a client communicates with Apple servers to download an item, the following happens:

- If the client's public IP address matches your caching server's public IP address, the Apple servers instruct the client to get the content from the local caching server (or servers).

▶ As covered in the next section, if the client can access a DNS TXT record for ._aaplcache._tcp, then the client will attempt to use the Caching service specified by the DNS TXT record.

▶ The client downloads the item from the caching server (if the caching server doesn't have the item yet, the caching server first downloads it from servers operated by Apple on the Internet).

If the client cannot communicate with its local caching server, it automatically downloads the content from servers operated by Apple on the Internet.

If you change the Caching service permissions, the Caching service updates its registration to reflect the new permissions.

To prevent stale registrations, the Caching service updates its registration with Apple every 55 minutes. Imagine a Mac with OS X Server with a private IP address, with a connection from an Internet service provider (ISP) that doesn't provide a static public IP address. If the public IP address provided by the ISP changes, the periodic update of the Caching service registration updates the public IP address.

When you stop the Caching service, it deregisters (with lcdn-registration.apple.com) so clients will no longer attempt to download items from it.

Caching Service with Complex Networks

The first implementation of the Caching service, with earlier versions of OS X Server, served the most common networking scenario: Client devices and servers share the same public IPv4 address behind a NAT device. However, the Caching service for OS X Server 4 (on OS X Yosemite) and later supports more complex networks. For example, your client devices may be behind NAT with one public IP address, and your servers may use a different public IP address. Or perhaps all your devices use a public IP address (because your organization claimed a large class of IPv4 addresses many years earlier or because IPv6 removes the problem of IPv4 address exhaustion).

Whatever the case may be, if you can add the appropriate DNS TXT records to the DNS service that the devices on your network use, your devices can find the appropriate Caching service.

The following figure may look similar to the previous example but with a fundamental difference. In this case, the organization's local networks use public IP addressing, thus necessitating DNS records for the Caching service. Again, once the clients leave the local network, they automatically use servers operated by Apple on the Internet.

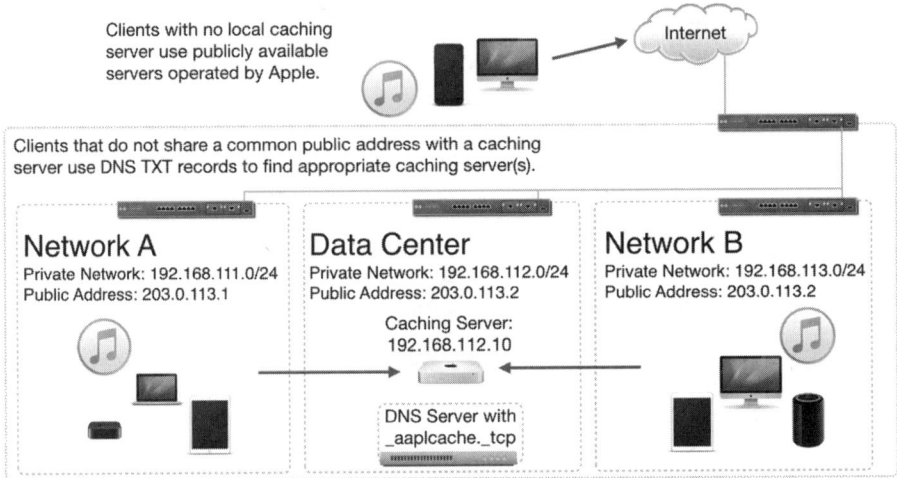

Reference 5.2
Caching Service Setup

Configuring the Caching service can be really simple. If you're on a local private network that shares an Internet connection, you can simply click the On/Off switch in the Caching pane of the Server app to turn on the service. Again, because Caching service–compatible clients don't need configuration, turning on the service on your local network is all that's required.

TIP ▸ Configuring multiple caching servers (or peers) on a local network provides a performance boost in two ways. Not only will clients load-balance across multiple caching servers, peer caching servers can download content from each other rather than from the Internet.

Editing Caching Service Permissions

By default, the Caching service offers service to "local subnets," which are based on the subnet mask of any Ethernet interfaces providing the Caching service. Click Edit Permissions to modify the Caching service's network availability. Again, the default configuration assumes a local private network sharing an Internet connection.

When you click Edit Permissions, you can access two pop-up menus.

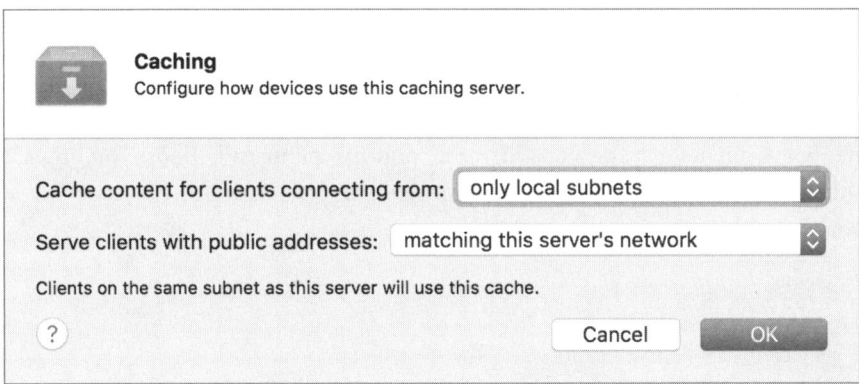

The "Cache content for clients connecting from" pop-up menu has three options:

▸ "all networks" (use this if you have multiple internal subnets, with fast interconnections between subnets)

▸ "only local subnets" (default; use this if you don't want Caching server traffic over slow links between internal subnets)

▸ "only some networks" (use this if you have complex network needs)

If you choose "only some networks," the default is Private Networks, which includes the loopback address (127.0.0.1), RFC 1918 private networks (10.0.0.0/8, 172.16.0.0/12, and 192.168.0.0/16), and RFC 3927 link-local networks (169.254.0.0/16). To customize this range, click Add (+) and either choose "Create a new network" or choose a custom network range if it has already been defined in the Server app (from configuring access for various services).

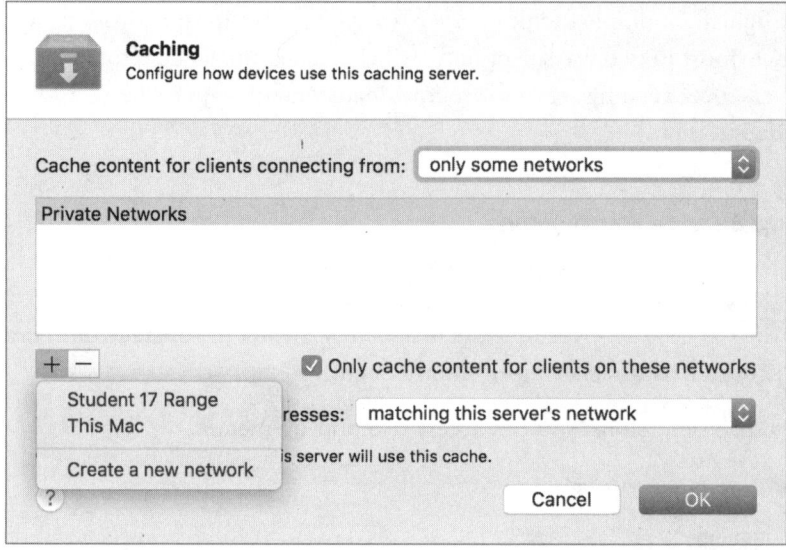

To serve clients that don't have the same public IP address as your server, you will need to click the "Serve clients with public addresses" pop-up menu and choose "on other networks." Then click the Add (+) button and choose either an existing network or "Create a new network."

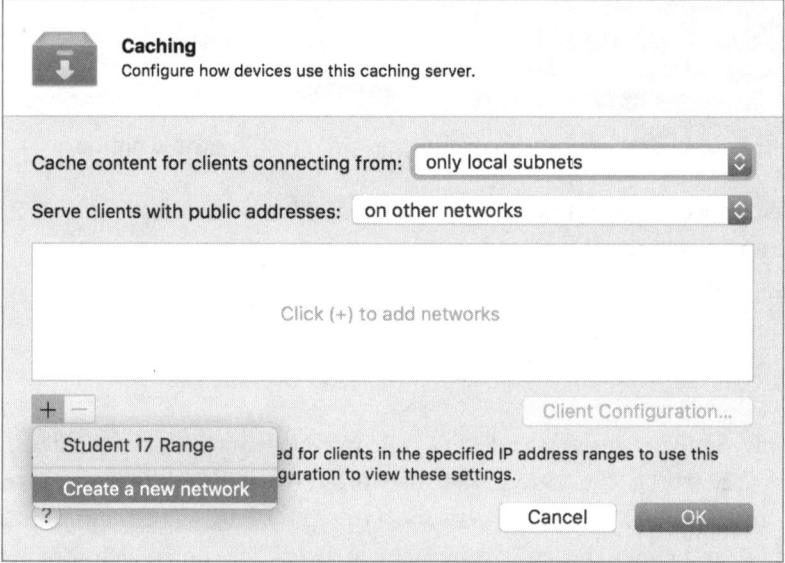

When creating a new network, give the network a name, define the range, and then click Create.

TIP ▶ Rather than entering both the Starting IP Address and Ending IP Address values, you can enter a Classless Inter-Domain Routing (CIDR) address in the Starting IP Address field (for example, 192.151.100.0/24) and then press Tab; the correct Starting IP Address and Ending IP Address fields will be automatically populated.

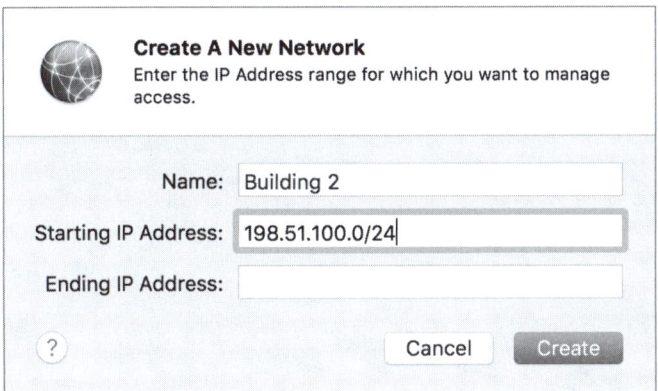

TIP ▶ To update the name or range of a network after you've created it, select your server in the Server app sidebar, click the Access tab, click the Action (gear) menu, and choose Edit Networks.

Once you've added the IP network ranges you desire, click Client Configuration.

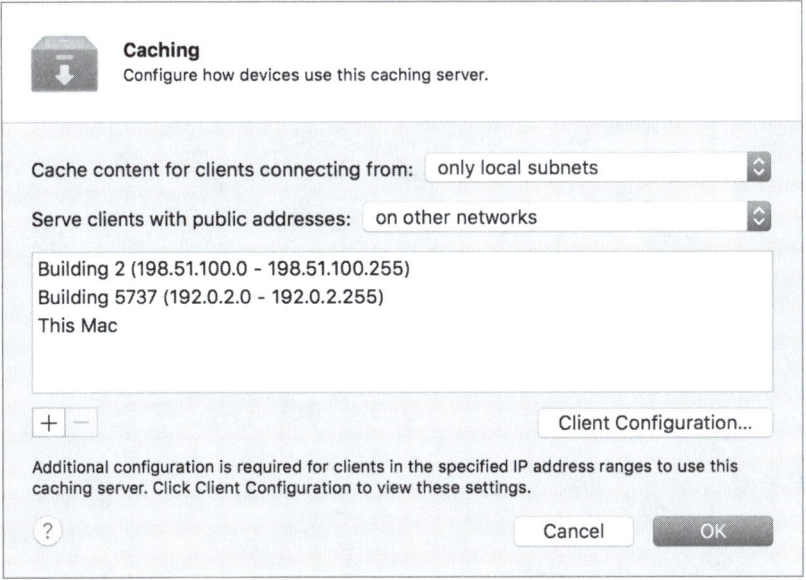

By default the Client Configuration pane displays the TXT record to copy into a Berkeley Internet Name Domain (BIND) DNS service.

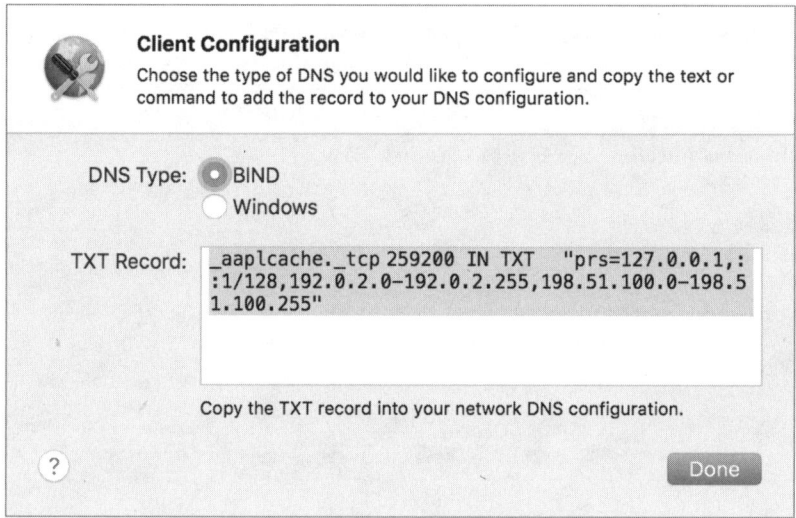

If your network uses a Windows-based DNS service, select Windows. You can copy this command, modify it with the appropriate zone name, and run it on the Windows server.

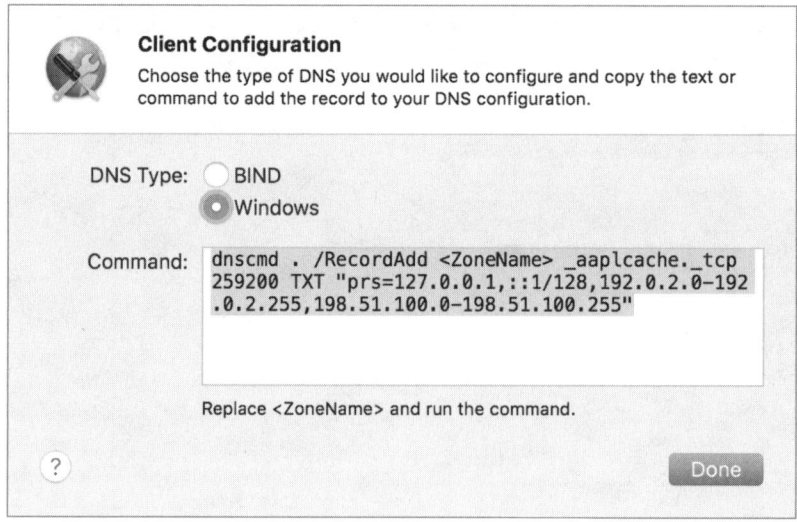

After you've configured the permissions, double-check the Permissions section in the Caching pane.

> Permissions: Only Local Subnets on Building 2, Building 5737, This Mac
> Edit Permissions...

If your clients have access to the appropriate DNS TXT record, they will attempt to use your server's Caching service. Once the clients leave the local network and no longer have access to the DNS TXT record, they automatically use servers operated by Apple on the Internet.

Additional Caching Service Configuration

The Caching pane of the Server app allows for additional Caching service configuration, including the following:

▶ Click the "Learn about configuring this service" link, which opens the OS X Server help documentation, to reveal detailed configuration instructions. You can also access this by opening the following uniform resource locator (URL) and searching for "Provide caching service": https://help.apple.com/serverapp/mac/5.1/.

▶ The "Cache personal iCloud data" option checkbox appeared with Server 5.1. Starting with Server 5.0, this option was automatically turned on, and you had to use the command line to turn the option off. Newly created personal iCloud data will always be uploaded to Apple's iCloud servers first, and if it is cached on your server, it will always be encrypted. If users have multiple devices on your network, leaving this option on will save you bandwidth when devices download personal iCloud data from local caching servers instead of from Apple's servers. This option is especially useful if the following three are true: you use Shared iPad, your users don't always use the same iPad, and your users' apps use iCloud.

▶ Click Change Location to select a different volume for Caching service content. By default, the Caching service uses the startup volume for the cached content. The volume you select to use for the Caching service must have at least 50 GB free (even if you set the Cache Size slider to 25 GB). If your users download a large variety of different content, consider using a volume large enough to cache as much content as you can. If you do change the volume used for the Caching service, the existing cached content will be copied to the newly selected volume.

▶ Use the slider to set the cache size. Even though the maximum is unlimited, the Caching service is smart enough to not fill up the entire volume; when only 25 GB is left on the Caching service volume, your server deletes the least recently used cached content (not necessarily the oldest content) to make space for new content.

Monitoring the Caching Service

The Usage section of the Caching pane shows you at a glance the kind of content your caching server has downloaded. Simply move the pointer over any of the colors in the usage bar to reveal specific cached content usage. You can also reset the cached content if the need arises.

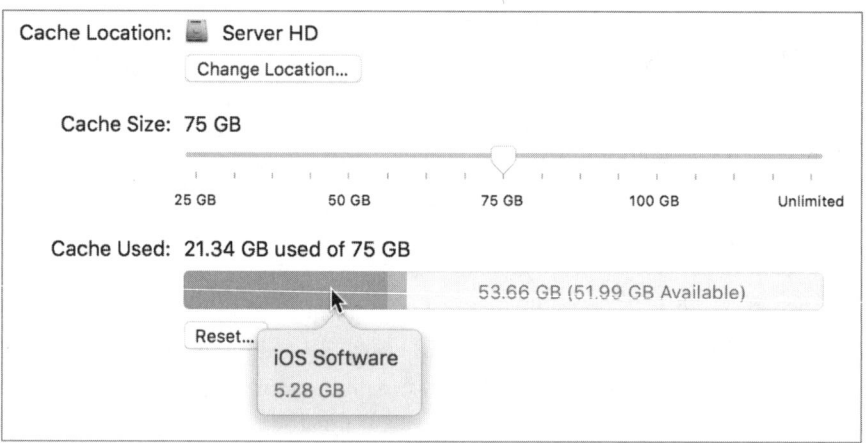

TIP If you set the Cache Size slider to Unlimited, the usage bar no longer has a scale, and the colors will take up the entire usage bar.

Additionally, the Stats pane of the Server app has one graph dedicated to the Caching service. Start by selecting the Stats pane in the Server app sidebar. Use the pop-up menus to choose Bytes Served as the type of activity and then choose a time period. The graph shows how much data the Caching service has downloaded from the Internet and from other peer servers and how much it has served to clients from its cache.

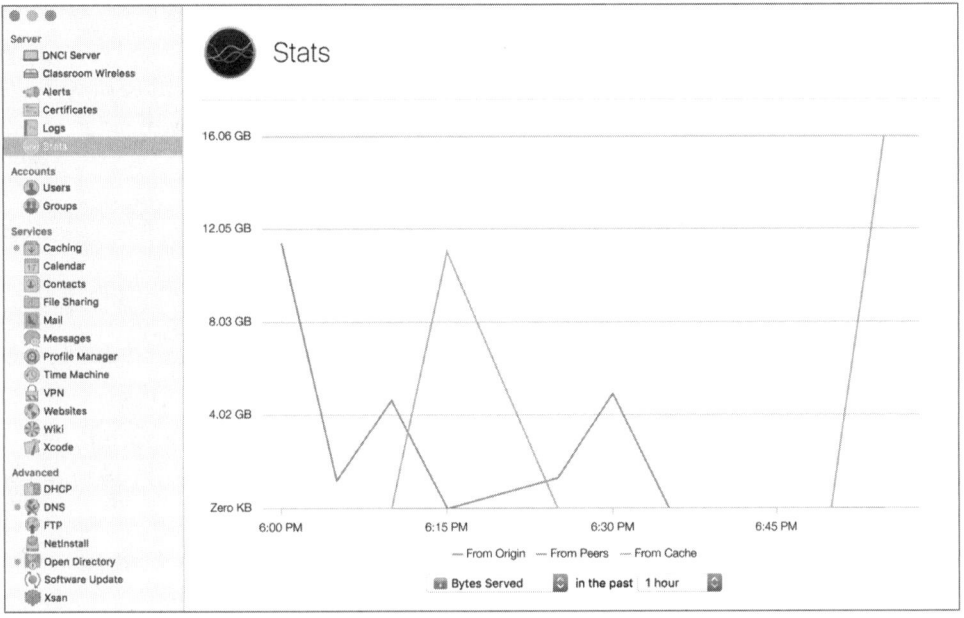

Reference 5.3
Caching Service Troubleshooting

The Caching service operation is largely transparent, so there often isn't much troubleshooting necessary. The first time a client downloads an item that isn't already cached, that initial download isn't any faster. However, subsequent downloads of the same item, whether from the same client or from a different client, are limited only by the speed of the client and server disks or the bandwidth of the local network.

Test the Caching Service

To test downloading items, you can use a computer that's an eligible client of the caching server to download an item from iTunes (11.0.2 or later), the Mac App Store, the App Store, or the iBooks Store. After the item is installed, delete it, and download it again (or download the same item from multiple eligible clients). Confirm that the subsequent download speeds are appropriate for downloading items locally as opposed to across the Internet.

Remember that you can use your server that's running the Caching service to perform the first download of an item; it is automatically a Caching service client as well as a server. Also, remember that downloading an iOS app in iTunes is the equivalent of downloading the app from the iOS App Store. Thus, you can "prime" an iOS app download in the caching server by downloading it using iTunes on the caching server.

Confirm Caching Service Basics

If you still suspect problems with the Caching service, here are some strategies:

- For iTunes, confirm that iTunes is version 11.0.2 or later. On a Mac, choose iTunes > About iTunes. On a PC with Windows and iTunes, choose Help > About iTunes.
- Confirm that devices are using a local network configured for your Caching service. In other words, confirm that devices are using local Ethernet or Wi-Fi and not using a cellular network or a neighboring Wi-Fi network.
- Confirm that the OS X clients are not configured to use a Software Update server.
- Confirm that the Caching service is turned on in the Server app. The Caching service status indicator in the Server app sidebar list of services is green when the service is turned on. If for some reason the Caching service cannot turn on, check the Caching service logs for error messages, as covered later in this lesson.
- If you have a more complex network, double-check your Caching service configuration. Are all relevant subnets configured? Is your network configured so the server shares the same Internet connection as your clients? For networks with public IP addresses, did you properly configure the Caching service DNS records?

Examine Caching Service via Activity Monitor

Use Activity Monitor to confirm that your server is downloading items from the Internet and then serving items to clients. On your server, open Activity Monitor, choose View > All Processes, click the Network tab, set the pop-up menu at the bottom to Data, and monitor the graph. When any process (the Caching service included) is downloading an item, this is reflected in a purple "Data received/sec" line. When any process is sending data, like that of a client downloading content from your Caching service, this is reflected in a red "Data sent/sec" line.

Packets in:	35,284,171	DATA	Data received:	80.23 GB
Packets out:	28,173,692		Data sent:	55.91 GB
Packets in/sec:	4,972		Data received/sec:	6.97 MB
Packets out/sec:	3,124		Data sent/sec:	1.13 MB

The data statistics at the bottom of Activity Monitor reflect all data moving in and out of your server regardless of source. To be sure the Caching service is responsible for the data activity, make sure to first enable the viewing of all processes by choosing All Processes from the menu. Then sort the process listing by Sent Bytes. If the Caching service is doing its job, you will see the AssetCache process move to the top of the Sent Bytes list.

A single caching server can handle hundreds of clients simultaneously and can saturate a Gigabit Ethernet network interface. The theoretical maximum for a single Gigabit Ethernet network interface is 120 MB/sec. In other words, if your caching server is reporting anywhere above 100 MB/sec with a single Gigabit Ethernet connection, it's performing admirably and fully utilizing the interface. If your caching server maintains consistently high data rates, your client's draw could possibly be even greater, and you should consider additional servers for the Caching service.

Examine Caching Service Logs

You can use the Logs pane of the Server app to check the Caching service log for basic functionality. From the Logs pop-up menu, choose Service Log under the Caching menu item. This view filters out any line in the generic system log that does not contain the AssetCache string. However, if the system log has been automatically rotated as part of daily system maintenance tasks, the Caching service Logs field may simply contain "No contents to display."

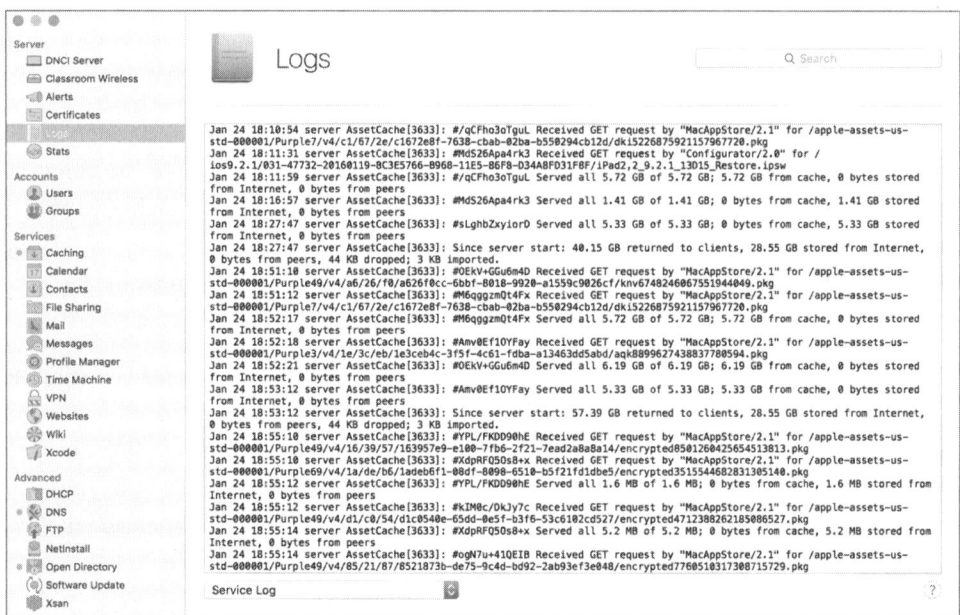

In general, a functioning Caching service should show quite a few entries in this log. Most of the information output by the AssetCache process is transactional in nature, showing things such as requested file URLs and data transfer totals. Although this log shows how busy your Caching service is, it doesn't help with much if you're trying to verify network configuration issues.

For more detailed Caching service configuration information, you can examine the Caching service debug log from the Console app on your server. In the Console app, choose File > Open, and navigate to and select /Library/Server/Caching/Logs/Debug.log. You can click Hide Log List in the Console app toolbar to devote more room to displaying the log contents.

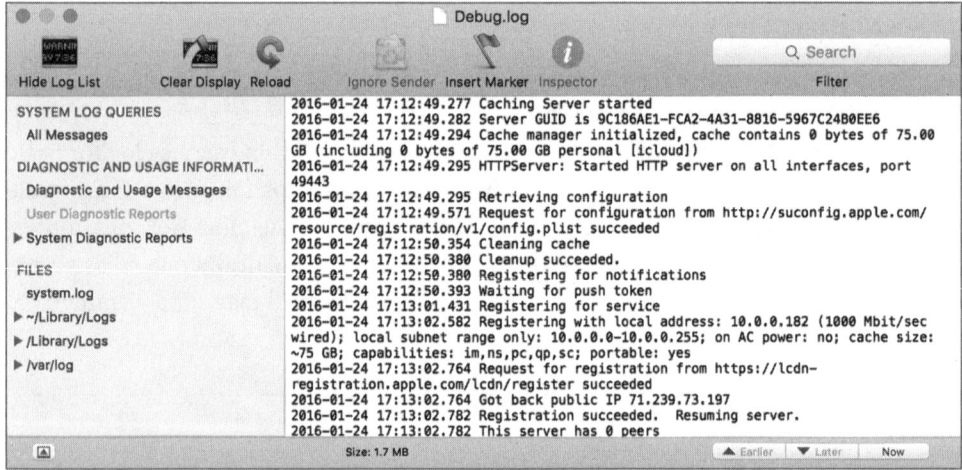

The Caching service Debug.log often includes messages regarding the service's network configuration and ability to register with Apple's servers. From here you can verify whether the Caching service local and public network configuration matches your actual network arrangement. Also, you may find errors if the Caching service is unable to successfully register with Apple's servers. Obviously, your caching server must be able to reach Apple's servers to access resources it will be caching.

For troubleshooting with an iOS device, you can use the Console in Apple Configurator 2 (which is covered in more detail in Lesson 12, "Apple Configurator 2: Planning and Setup," Lesson 13, "Apple Configurator 2: Preparing, Configuring, and Managing iOS Devices," and Lesson 14, "Apple Configurator 2: App and Document Management"). In the following example, searching for the string "AssetCache" helps locate the log message that contains the IPv4 address of the caching server.

For more advanced information, see the section "Configure advanced cache settings" in Server Help at https://help.apple.com/serverapp/mac/5.1/. For example, if you set the LogClientIdentity key to "true," the server logs the IP address and port number of the client requesting each asset.

MORE INFO ▶ The open source project Cacher parses the Caching service log and presents it in an easy-to-read format. See https://github.com/erikng/Cacher for more information.

MORE INFO ▶ CacheWarmer instructs your Caching service to download system software and other assets in anticipation of a device request so that the first device that requests an item doesn't have to wait for your server to download it from Apple's servers. You can use it for free for a single model of an iOS device; you can purchase a license to use additional iOS device models and to use it for OS X updates as well. You can find more information at http://assetcache.io/cachewarmer/.

MORE INFO ▶ If your server has enough memory to hold frequently requested items in memory, it can serve these items more quickly. See the article "The effect of RAM on Caching" at https://assetcache.io/blog/the-effect-of-ram.html for more information.

Exercise 5.1
Turn On and Verify the Caching Service

> **Prerequisites**
>
> ▸ Exercise 4.1, "Prepare Your Mac to Install OS X Server for El Capitan"
>
> ▸ Exercise 4.2, "Install OS X Server for El Capitan"
>
> ▸ Exercise 4.3, "Configure OS X Server for El Capitan"
>
> ▸ A wired Ethernet connection for your server (if your server is not a desktop Mac (Mac mini, iMac, or Mac Pro)

Challenge

Turn on the Caching service with its defaults. Verify that the Caching service successfully registered with Apple. Verify that the client sees a caching server, download something that is cached, and confirm that the content is cached on a caching server. Delete and download it again, and confirm that the item is delivered from the Caching service.

> **NOTE ▸** If there are multiple servers running the Caching service on your local network, it's possible that when you download an item using the App Store, you will use another server, not your own server. If you are in an instructor-led environment, the instructor should turn off the Caching service for the local network, and only one student at a time should perform this exercise.

Considerations

In the Logs pane on your server, the Service Log for the Caching service displays entries in the system log that contain the string "AssetCache["; for more information, look in /Library/Server/Caching/Logs/Debug.log.

The Caching service will serve your server itself. You can use the App Store to get a free app and then use the Caching pane of the Server app to confirm that the Caching service cached the app. You can delete that app and get it again and use the Logs pane to confirm that the Caching service provided the app to your server.

Solution

Turn On the Caching Service

As a reminder, you need an Ethernet connection to successfully run the Caching service. If your server has Wi-Fi only and you turn on the Caching service, the service will appear to start, but you will get a message that you need Ethernet.

1 On your server, open the Server app from the Dock.

2 In the Server app sidebar, select Caching.

3 Click the On/Off switch to start the service.

   You can leave all the settings at their defaults.

The Usage bar graph of cached content will not change until the caching server has had a chance to cache at least one item.

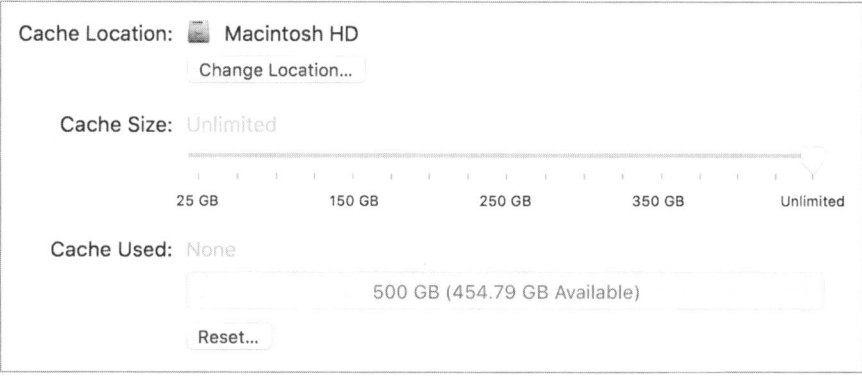

Verify the Caching Service Started via Logs

1 In the Server app sidebar, select Logs.

2 Click the pop-up menu, and then in the Caching section, choose Service Log.

3 Verify that the log contains the entry "Caching Server version 149.1 started."

   NOTE ▶ The version number of the caching server may be different than the version number shown in step 3. As of the time of writing, version 149.1 was the latest version of the Caching service.

Confirm the Caching Service Successfully Registered with Apple

1. On your server, press Command–Space bar (or click the Spotlight icon in the upper-right corner of the screen) to reveal the Spotlight search field.

2. In the Spotlight search field, enter Console.

3. Press Return to open the top hit of your Spotlight search, which is the Console app.

4. Choose File > Open.

5. Press Command-Shift-G to display the "Go to the folder" dialog.

6. Enter /Library/Server/Caching/Logs/.

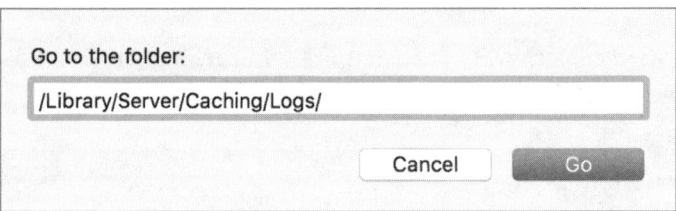

7. Click Go.

8. Select Debug.log, and then click Open.

9. Confirm that the string "Registration succeeded" appears in the log.

```
2016-02-04 10:38:15.270 Registering for notifications
2016-02-04 10:38:15.288 Waiting for push token
2016-02-04 10:38:25.396 Registering for service
2016-02-04 10:38:32.127 Registering with local address: 10.0.0.171 (100 Mbit/sec wired); local subnet range only: 10.0.0.0-10.0.0.255; on AC power: no; cache size: ~454 GB; capabilities: im,ns,pc,qp,sc; portable: yes
2016-02-04 10:38:32.322 Request for registration from https://lcdn-registration.apple.com/lcdn/register succeeded
2016-02-04 10:38:32.322 Got back public IP
2016-02-04 10:38:32.347 Registration succeeded. Resuming server.
2016-02-04 10:38:32.347 This server has 0 peers
```

10. Quit Console.

Download a Free App from the App Store

You can download any app, but this exercise suggests a small free app. You can use any OS X computer on your local network, but for the purposes of this exercise, use the server itself.

1   On your server, open the App Store.

2   In the Search field, enter Local Path, and then press Return.

3   Click the icon for the app to reveal more information about the app.

4   In the Information column for the app, note its size. At the time of this writing, Local Path is listed at 0.9 MB.

5   Click Get.

6   Click Install App.

7   If necessary, enter your administrator Apple ID credentials, and then click Sign In.

8   If you see the "Require a password when making purchases on this computer" dialog, click Require After 15 Minutes.

9   If necessary, in the Save Password for Free Items pane, click Yes.

10 In the Confirmation Required dialog, click Buy. Note that the status changes from Install App to Installing.

Leave the App Store running while you continue with this exercise.

Verify the Caching Service via the Caching Service Pane

> **NOTE ▶** If there is another caching server available to the App Store, it may use that instead of your server's Caching service, and you will not see any usage.

1   On your server, in the Server app sidebar, select Caching.

2   Press Command-R if the Usage bar graph does not indicate any content.

Note that the graph now shows that the Caching service downloaded some OS X software, about the same amount as the size of the app you just downloaded. In the following figure, the Cache Used field is 863 KB, which with rounding corresponds to the App Store information of 0.9 MB for the Local Path app.

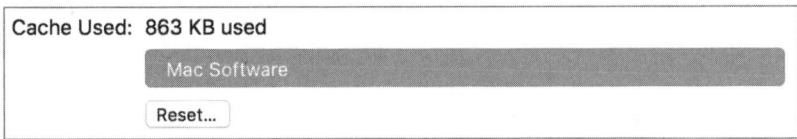

Verify the Caching Service via Logs

1   In the Server app sidebar, select Logs.

2   If necessary, click the pop-up menu, and then in the Caching section, choose Service Log.

```
Feb  4 10:38:08 server17 AssetCache[9462]: Caching Server version 145 started
Feb  4 10:38:32 server17 AssetCache[9462]: Registration succeeded.  Resuming server.
d to act on a ping it dequeued before timing out.
Feb  4 10:48:18 server17 AssetCache[9462]: #0C+b8vD60+CD Received GET request by "MacAppStore/2.1" for /apple-assets-us-std-000001/Purple49/v4/a2/44/d4/a244d4c0-af45-2fbb-5634-16875662a89b/encrypted8996036593995228261.pkg
Feb  4 10:48:19 server17 AssetCache[9462]: #0C+b8vD60+CD Served all 862 KB of 862 KB; 0 bytes from cache, 862 KB stored from Internet, 0 bytes from peers
Feb  4 10:48:19 server17 AssetCache[9462]: Since server start: 862 KB returned to clients, 862 KB stored from Internet, 0 bytes from peers; 0 bytes imported.
```

The entry that begins with "Received GET request by 'MacAppStore/2.1'" represents the request for the app.

You may see another entry with statistics, as shown in the previous figure. The entry with "Served all 862 KB of 862 KB" represents that the Caching service provided the app to your Mac (which happens to also be running the Caching service, but it could be any eligible Mac). "0 bytes from cache, 862 KB stored from Internet, 0 bytes from peers" means that the app was not yet cached. In a classroom environment, you may see the app delivered from a peer.

Delete the App and Install the App Again

1   Click Launchpad in the Dock.

2   Drag the app you just downloaded (Local Path) to Trash.

3   At the dialog asking if you're sure you want to delete the app, click Delete.

4 Click App Store in the Dock (or in the list of apps in Launchpad).

5 In the App Store, press Command-R to reload the page.

If the App Store is not still displaying the Local Path app information, enter Local Path in the Search field, and press Return.

6 Click Install.

7 Quit the App Store.

Verify the Caching Service via Logs Again

1 In the Server app, press Command-R to refresh the view of the log.

```
Feb  4 10:48:18 server17 AssetCache[9462]: #OC+b8vD6O+CD Received GET request by "MacAppStore/2.1" for /apple-assets-us-
std-000001/Purple49/v4/a2/44/d4/a244d4c0-af45-2fbb-5634-16875662a89b/encrypted8996036593995228261.pkg
Feb  4 10:48:19 server17 AssetCache[9462]: #OC+b8vD6O+CD Served all 862 KB of 862 KB; 0 bytes from cache, 862 KB stored
from Internet, 0 bytes from peers
Feb  4 10:48:19 server17 AssetCache[9462]: Since server start: 862 KB returned to clients, 862 KB stored from Internet, 0
bytes from peers; 0 bytes imported.
Feb  4 10:53:45 server17 AssetCache[9462]: #PIR0TpJP6loD Received GET request by "MacAppStore/2.1" for /apple-assets-us-
std-000001/Purple49/v4/a2/44/d4/a244d4c0-af45-2fbb-5634-16875662a89b/encrypted8996036593995228261.pkg
Feb  4 10:53:45 server17 AssetCache[9462]: #PIR0TpJP6loD Served all 862 KB of 862 KB; 862 KB from cache, 0 bytes stored
from Internet, 0 bytes from peers
Feb  4 10:53:45 server17 AssetCache[9462]: Since server start: 1.7 MB returned to clients, 862 KB stored from Internet, 0
bytes from peers; 0 bytes imported.
```

The log contains a second entry of "Received GET request by 'MacAppStore/2.1'" for the app.

The entry that starts with "Served all 862 KB of 862 KB; 862 KB from cache" indicates that the Caching service didn't have to download the app; it had the app in its cache.

The entry that starts with "Since server start: 1.7 MB returned to clients" represents two times the app was delivered to your Mac (862 KB + 862 KB = 1724 KB = 1.7 MB).

In this exercise, you turned on the Caching service and used the Caching service pane and the Logs pane to confirm that it served cached content.

Verify the Caching Service on Your Client Mac (Optional)

1 On your client Mac, open the App Store.

2 If necessary, choose Store > Sign In, enter your administrator Apple ID credentials, and then click Sign In.

3 Click Purchased, and then click Install to install the Local Path app.

4   If necessary, in the Save Password for Free Items pane, click Yes.

5   After Local Path is installed, choose App Store > Quit App Store to close the App Store.

6   Press Command–Space bar (or click the Spotlight icon in the upper-right corner of the screen) to reveal the Spotlight search field.

7   In the Spotlight search field, enter `Console`.

8   Press Return to open the top hit of your Spotlight search, which is the Console app.

9   If necessary, in the Console app sidebar, select All Messages.

10 In the Filter, type `AssetCacheLocator`, and press Return.

11 Click the disclosure triangle.

```
▼ 11:28:15 AM AssetCacheLocatorService:
  #14ebe98f [I:AssetCacheLocatorService.queue] found caching server on 10.0.0.171:4
  9356
```

The entry that contains "found caching server on 10.0.0.171:49356" shows that the client downloaded the Local Path app from your caching server.

12 Quit Console.

13 Click Launchpad in the Dock.

14 Drag the app you just downloaded (Local Path) to Trash.

15 At the dialog asking if you're sure you want to delete the app, click Delete.

> **NOTE ▶** If there is another caching server available to the App Store, it may use that instead of your server's Caching service. You may also see a different port number, which is the number that immediately follows the IP address.

Lesson 6
Configuration and Profiles

Profiles will serve as a fundamental part of your Apple management plans. Simply, the more configuration you can accomplish via profiles, the less manual setup you will have to complete. With every new release of iOS and OS X, Apple includes greater functionality for managing with profiles. At this point, you can manage hundreds of different settings and restrictions via profiles.

This lesson introduces the profile architecture and the Profile Manager service in OS X Server. Although Profile Manager appears as a single service in the Server app, its complexity goes well beyond what can be covered in a single lesson. As such, this lesson specifically focuses on the creation and manual installation of user-based profiles via Profile Manager and serves as a foundation for additional Profile Manager features covered in later lessons.

GOALS

▶ Understand managing with profiles

▶ Configure and turn on Profile Manager

▶ Create and manually install profiles

Reference 6.1
Understanding Profiles

As covered previously, profiles were originally created to provide easy setup for iOS devices but are now also used in OS X. A profile is a document that includes instructions for specific user and system settings. Profiles can be deployed using a variety of methods, including both manual and automatic installation.

This section introduces the general types of profiles used for managing Apple devices. You will also learn how to examine profile content and how profiles are protected to prevent tampering.

> **MORE INFO** ▶ You'll find detailed step-by-step instructions for creating profiles with Profile Manager and examining profile content in the exercises later in this lesson.

Profile Types

There are several general types of profiles, depending on purpose. Note that these general types are not mutually exclusive; a single profile can contain multiple types of content. The most common profile types are as follows:

- Configuration profile—This most common type of profile contains user or system settings. A wide variety of settings can be contained within a single configuration profile. Importantly, this allows an administrator to include both access to content and security restrictions within the same configuration profile. For example, a single configuration profile can automatically configure the user's email but also require that she set a device passcode meeting your organization's security standards. Because these two settings are within a single profile, they are inseparable, and if the user wants to keep her email automatically configured on her device, she must also set a passcode.

- Trust profile—This type of profile contains one or more digital certificates, which are most often used to validate and secure service connections. Apple devices can use certificates for a variety of purposes, including Mobile Device Management (MDM) enrollment, network configuration, virtual private network (VPN) configuration, and general authentication. Profiles containing certificates can also contain configuration. For example, a single profile could contain both the certificates and the configuration settings required for joining a network that uses 802.1X authentication.

- Enrollment profile—Enrollment profiles are used to establish a relationship with an MDM service. Often enrollment profiles also contain certificates that may be required by the MDM service. You can use an enrollment profile in conjunction with Apple Configurator 2 or NetInstall to automate the enrollment of Apple devices.

- Provisioning profile—A provisioning profile is used specifically for deploying iOS apps outside of the App Store. If a developer or organization wants to deploy a custom-built in-house app to iOS devices, an appropriate provisioning profile is required (members of the Apple Developer Enterprise Program can distribute iOS apps without a separate provisioning profile). These profiles are created exclusively with Apple's developer tools. iOS apps built for iOS 8 or later can include the profile in the app file. However, previous versions of iOS required the provisioning profile to be installed separately.

Profile Document Inspection

For the vast majority of profile creation and editing, you will be using a graphical tool such as Apple Configurator 2 or the Profile Manager administration portal. These tools provide easy-to-use interfaces for modifying profiles. However, understanding the underlying format of profile documents is also important should the need arise to create your own custom profiles or troubleshoot existing profiles.

> **NOTE ▶** Although you can create configuration profiles in Apple Configurator 2, these profiles are designed to be installed exclusively on iOS devices and are not supported to be installed on OS X computers. As covered later in this lesson, the Profile Manager administration portal provides an interface for creating profiles that are compatible with both OS X and iOS.

Profile documents can be identified on OS X computers by their icon and the filename extension of .mobileconfig.

Settings_for_Marketing
.mobileconfig

Profile documents are text files written in Extensible Markup Language (XML). They are similar in format to property list (.plist) files also used by OS X for storing configuration information. You can inspect and edit profiles using any text editor, including the built-in OS X application TextEdit.

```
● ● ●                    Settings_for_Marketing.mobileconfig
<?xml version="1.0" encoding="UTF-8"?>
<!DOCTYPE plist PUBLIC "-//Apple//DTD PLIST 1.0//EN" "http://www.apple.com/DTDs/
PropertyList-1.0.dtd">
<plist version="1.0"><dict><key>PayloadIdentifier</
key><string>com.apple.mdm.server.arekdreyer.com.1a6eddb0-
b107-0133-1a76-32001355f020.alacarte</string><key>PayloadRemovalDisallowed</
key><false/><key>PayloadScope</key><string>User</string><key>PayloadType</
key><string>Configuration</string><key>PayloadUUID</key><string>1a6eddb0-
b107-0133-1a76-32001355f020</string><key>PayloadOrganization</key><string>Dreyer
Network Consultants, Inc.</string><key>PayloadVersion</key><integer>1</
integer><key>PayloadDisplayName</key><string>Settings for Marketing</
string><key>PayloadDescription</key><string>Settings for Marketing</
string><key>PayloadContent</key><array><dict><key>PayloadType</
key><string>com.apple.webClip.managed</string><key>PayloadVersion</key><integer>1</
integer><key>PayloadIdentifier</key><string>com.apple.mdm.server.arekdreyer.com.
1a6eddb0-b107-0133-1a76-32001355f020.alacarte.webclip.1a6b7030-
b107-0133-1a75-32001355f020</string><key>PayloadUUID</key><string>1a6b7030-
b107-0133-1a75-32001355f020</string><key>PayloadEnabled</key><true/
><key>PayloadDisplayName</key><string>Web Clip (iPad in Business)</
string><key>IsRemovable</key><true/><key>Label</key><string>iPad in Business</
string><key>URL</key><string>https://www.apple.com/ipad/business/</string></dict></
array></dict></plist>
```

The XML format of a profile may be a bit difficult to read at first, but it's essentially a list of keys (or settings) and strings (or values) surrounded by the XML code, which appears in brackets (< >). Think of the key as the name of the setting and the string as the value of the setting. For example, at the bottom of the profile code in the figure, you can see the website address that defines the destination for one of the web clips defined in this profile.

> **MORE INFO** ▶ Apple maintains a list of standard configuration profile keys in the Configuration Profile Key Reference document at https://developer.apple.com/library/ios/featuredarticles/iphoneconfigurationprofileref/.

You can easily modify an unsigned profile by simply editing the text and saving the document. However, if the profile contains a code signature, your manual edits will not be trusted by Apple devices and subsequently will not be allowed to install.

Profile Code Signing

Accepting the installation of a profile implies that you trust the profile's content. As you just learned, anyone with access to a profile can modify its contents with a simple text editor. To prevent the installation of a profile that has been corrupted or tampered with, profiles can be code signed. A signed profile contains a cryptographic hash used to validate the profile's content. An Apple device will not allow the installation of a signed profile that can't be validated.

> **NOTE** ▶ When profiles are delivered over the air via an MDM service, the network traffic is encrypted to prevent interception or tampering by third parties, but you can also take advantage of code signing to provide an additional layer of verification.

The process of code signing requires a certificate that has been specified as capable of signing code. In other words, a code-signing certificate is used to digitally sign profiles. Fortunately, the setup of an Open Directory master on OS X Server automatically creates a code-signing certificate. This certificate can be configured to automatically sign all profiles created with Profile Manager. You also have the option of purchasing a code-signing certificate from a third-party certificate authority (CA), but this will incur an additional cost.

Apple devices will always check for code signing during the installation of a profile. This will result in one of several circumstances:

- ▶ Unsigned—In this case, the profile was not digitally signed. You are still allowed to install the profile, but there is no way for the system to validate the profile's content.

- Unverified or Not Verified—In this case, the profile was digitally signed but with a certificate the device doesn't trust, such as if you used the Open Directory–generated signing certificate but you neglected to install a trust profile to force the Apple device to trust the Open Directory–generated CA. Again, you are still allowed to install the profile, and while the system can confirm the profile's content, it doesn't trust the signing certificate.

- Verified—In this case, the profile was digitally signed by a certificate trusted by the device, and the content of the profile appears valid. This scenario should be your goal since it provides the safest configuration.

▶ Could not open profile—In this case, the profile was digitally signed, but the system has detected that it has been altered or corrupted from its original state. The system will not allow this type of profile to be installed.

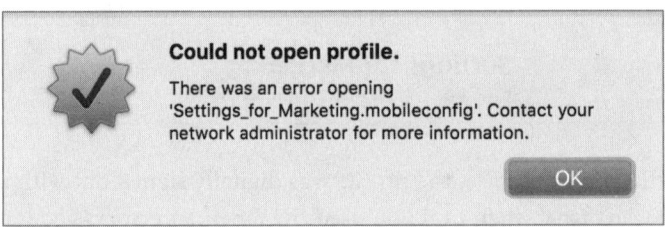

Reference 6.2
Setting Up Profile Manager

Profile Manager is the Apple device management service included with OS X Server. Now in its fifth major revision, Profile Manager has matured into a relatively robust and feature-rich MDM service. For example, Profile Manager was one of the first MDM services to support both the Apple Device Enrollment Program (DEP) and the Apple Volume Purchase Program (VPP) managed license distribution.

Because Profile Manager facilitates a variety of management technologies, this specific lesson focuses only on the most basic Profile Manager setup. Here you will learn how to turn on Profile Manager for creating user-based configuration profiles. Again, this lesson lays the foundation for later lessons that focus on other aspects of Profile Manager.

Profile Manager Components

Profile Manager allows for the management of Apple devices via three primary components:

▶ Profile Manager administration portal—Administrators use this web-based interface to create and modify management settings for both users and devices. Administrators with access to the Profile Manager administration portal can create profiles, perform management actions, inspect device inventory, distribute licensed VPP apps and books, and distribute in-house created apps and books. When it's configured, you can reach the Profile Manager administration portal at https://server.domain.com/profilemanager/.

▶ My Devices user portal—This web-based interface is designed to be accessed by your users. From here users can manually download profiles, enroll their devices into the MDM service, and perform some basic management actions. When configured, the My Devices user portal is reached at https://server.domain.com/mydevices/.

▶ Mobile Device Management service—When device management has been enabled for Profile Manager, it allows devices to be enrolled for automatic over-the-air (OTA) management of devices. This specific feature of Profile Manager is the focus of Lesson 7, "Mobile Device Management."

Profile Manager Service Configuration

Assuming you have already completed the initial setup of OS X Server, as covered in the previous lesson, turning on Profile Manager is as simple as flipping a switch. In the Server app sidebar, select Profile Manager, and then click the On/Off switch.

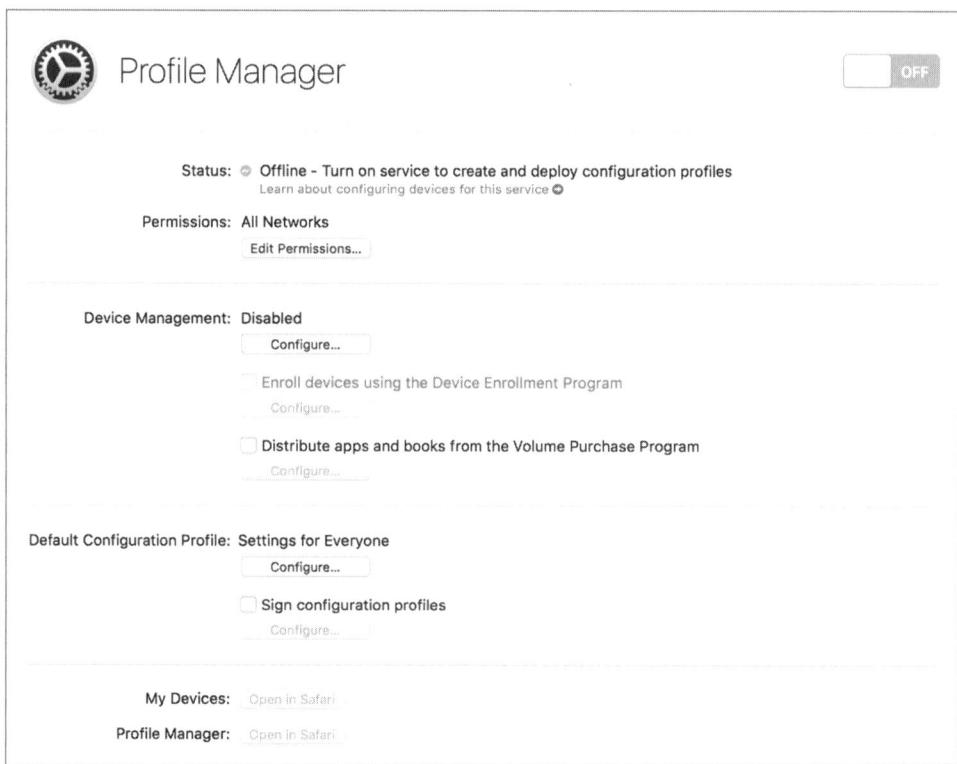

With only the default settings, turning on Profile Manager will allow the administration portal and the My Devices user portal. These websites will default to using the self-signed Transport Layer Security (TLS)/Secure Sockets Layer (SSL) certificate created during OS X Server setup or the Open Directory CA–signed certificate if available. You can also specify a TLS/SSL certificate signed by a third-party CA for Profile Manager. As covered previously, the Certificates pane of the Server app allows you to manage these certificates.

NOTE ▸ Again, if you plan on having users access Profile Manager via the My Devices user portal, configuring a TLS/SSL certificate signed by a third-party CA is strongly recommended.

Default Configuration Profile

A default configuration profile is automatically created for each user if your OS X Server also hosts a variety of other services, including Calendar, Contacts, File Sharing, Mail, Messages, and VPN. If any of these services are turned on, the default configuration profile will appear in the My Devices user portal. It's named "Settings for Everyone" by default. Installing this default configuration profile is optional for the user, but it makes for easy, no-hassle configuration of OS X Server–hosted services.

NOTE ▸ The default configuration profile is available for the user only in the My Devices user portal and will never be automatically pushed to a user's device.

MORE INFO ▸ The OS X Server Account icon represents the services from the File Sharing service available for iOS devices.

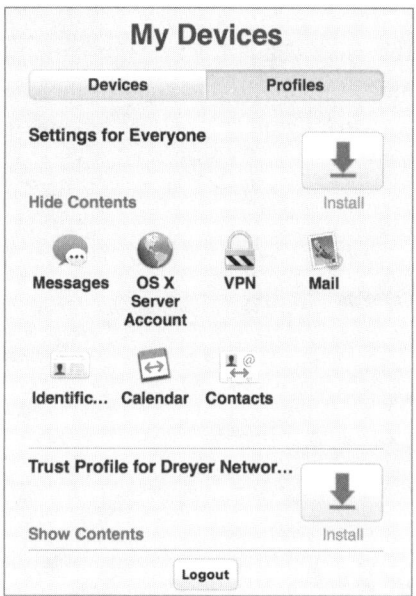

As you can see in the following figure, this default configuration profile contains user identification settings. When installed, these apps will be automatically configured with the user's accounts for OS X Server services. In the Profile Manager pane of the Server app, you'll find settings for the default configuration profile by clicking the Configure button under the name of the default configuration profile.

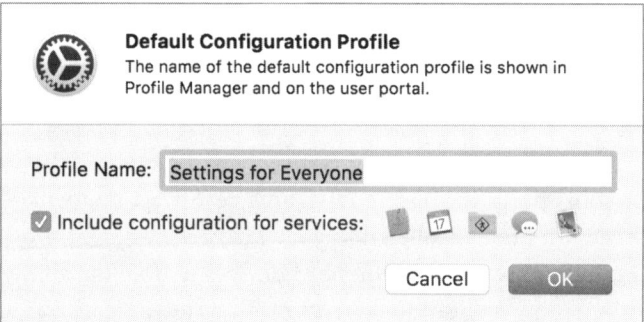

The default configuration profile name will appear both in the My Devices user portal and on the device when inspecting installed profiles. Note that icons will appear representing the OS X Server services that will be automatically configured should a user install the default configuration profile. Deselecting the checkbox here will turn off the default configuration profile should you not want to make it available even when you are offering other OS X Server services.

Turn On Profile Code Signing

As covered previously in this lesson, code signing provides validation for your configuration profiles. As such, turning on profile code signing at the bottom of the Profile Manager pane in the Server app is highly recommended. Turning on this feature for the first time will require that you select a code-signing certificate.

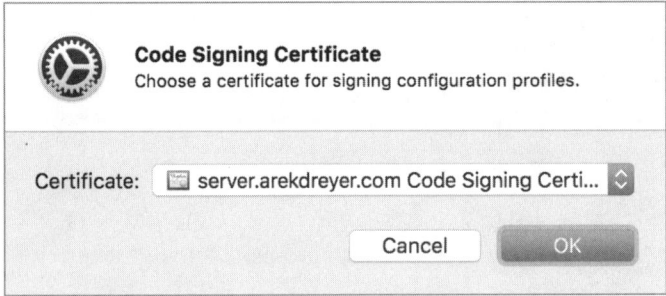

Again, if you have already promoted your OS X Server computer to an Open Directory (OD) master, that process automatically creates a code-signing certificate. Although this certificate is a great "free" choice, you must also remember that it was signed by the OD CA. Thus, as a default, your Apple devices do not trust it and will not fully verify any profiles signed by this certificate.

In other words, if you are using the OD-provided code-signing certificate, you must also deploy the OD CA trust profile to your Apple devices. The OD CA trust profile is also required for MDM service enrollment with Profile Manager. Thus, your managed devices will already have the required OD CA trust profile installed by the time they download any additional signed profiles from your server. In summary, as long as you plan to enroll your devices into the Profile Manager MDM service, selecting the OD code-signing certificate is an easy and safe choice.

Alternatively, you can obtain a third-party verified code-signing certificate that will be trusted by any Apple device, even if it's not enrolled into your MDM service. A third-party verified code-signing certificate is required only if you need devices to have the ability to verify a signed profile without installing an additional trust profile. However, as was just covered, purchasing a relatively expensive third-party verified code-signing certificate is probably not necessary if you plan to enroll devices into an MDM service such as Profile Manager.

Reference 6.3
Creating Profiles via Profile Manager

Any user who has administrator privileges on your server can access the Profile Manager administration portal to create and edit profiles. In this section, you will explore how to create user-based profiles that will allow you to personalize or restrict Apple devices.

Manual Profile Installation Workflows

Assuming you have stuck with the Profile Manager defaults and not enabled device management or configured Volume Purchase Program (VPP)–managed distribution, you will be allowed only to modify user and user group profiles to be used for download and manual profile installation.

While this basic Profile Manager configuration may seem limited, some administrators may need to use this service only for creating user profiles. For simple user-based configuration, there may be no need to complicate deployments by requiring enrollment into an MDM service. In this case, the administrator or the user will download the profile and install it manually.

In other cases, an organization may choose to deploy user profiles separately from device profiles. For example, an organization may choose to enroll their devices into a third-party MDM service that is also integrated with their web content filtering solution. While this solution may work great for managing device-level settings, through testing they discover that this third-party MDM doesn't handle user-based profiles well. In this case, an administrator may choose to use Profile Manager for creating and deploying user-based profiles to personalize the devices.

In other words, Apple devices can install multiple profiles from different sources. You may find that a third-party source for profiles handles certain situations better than Profile Manager but still use Profile Manager for situations where it provides a better solution. Using multiple management systems may complicate your deployment, but it may also provide the best overall solution.

> **NOTE** ▶ Although you can manually install multiple profiles from different sources on a single device, a device can be enrolled into only a single MDM service.

User and User Group Profiles

Profile Manager can create user-based or user group–based profiles for any local or network accounts known by the OS X Server system. This includes any accounts hosted by a third-party directory service such as Active Directory, assuming the OS X Server system has been properly configured.

> **MORE INFO** ▶ Integrating OS X Server with Active Directory is beyond the scope of this guide. Refer to *Apple Pro Training Series: OS X Server 5.0 Essentials on El Capitan* (Peachpit Press, 2016) if you need to develop a solid working knowledge of OS X Server.

Selecting Users or Groups from the Profile Manager administration portal Library reveals the list of users or groups known by the OS X Server system.

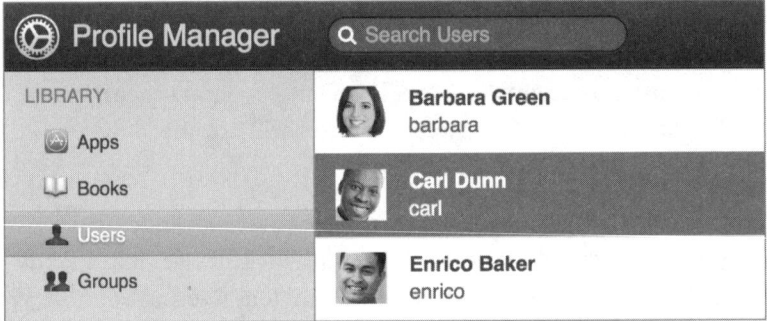

If you have a large organization with more than 200 users, you will need to use the search function at the top of the users list. Alternatively, in large organizations, managing user-based profiles via user groups is often a better approach. Any profile you configure for a group automatically appears for associated users in the My Devices user portal.

By default, the Everyone user group gives all users known by the server system access to the My Devices user portal and the ability to download configuration profiles. If you need to restrict these abilities to only specific users or user groups, you can turn off access to the My Devices user portal for the Everyone group and then turn it on per user or per user group. In the Profile Manager administration portal, select the account you want to manage, and then click the About tab to reveal these restrictions.

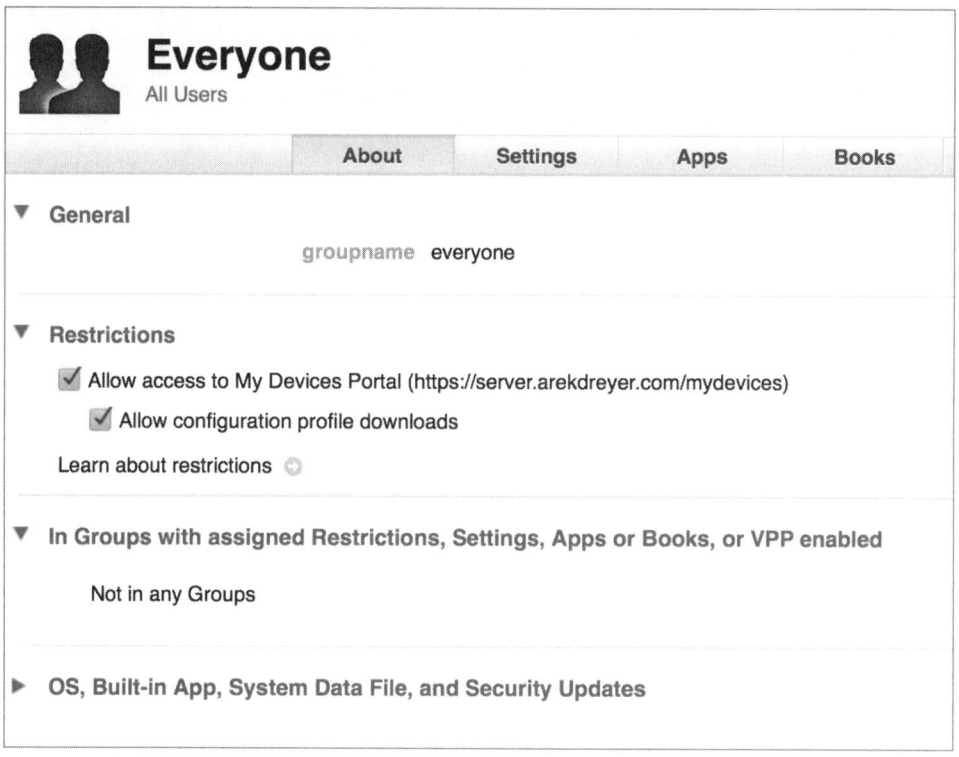

As for managing the configuration profile content, again start by selecting the user or user group, and then click the Settings tab to reveal the account's current profile settings. Click the Edit button to modify the profile content.

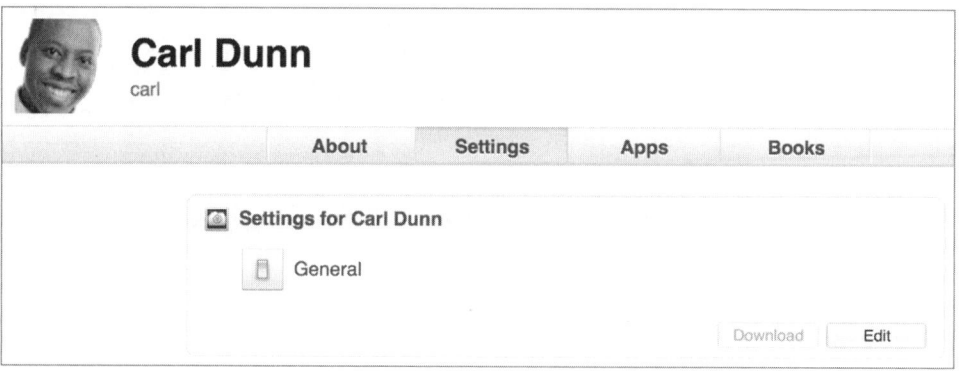

General Profile Settings

When editing in the Profile Manager administration portal, you are first presented with the General settings for the configuration profile. The General settings are the only mandatory settings required for a profile.

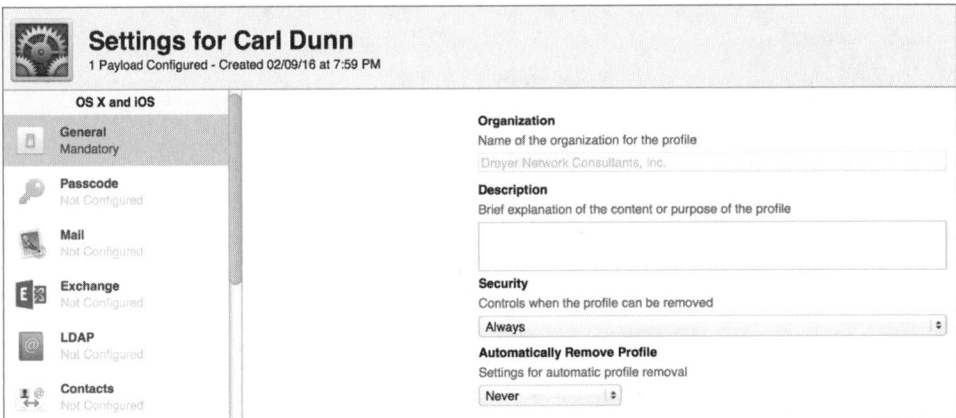

Profile documents are obviously identified by their names, but other general settings are available to all profiles:

- Delivery method—In Profile Manager, profiles are either manually downloaded or automatically pushed over the air via the MDM service. Note that you will see the Automatic Push option only if you have enabled device management with the Server app in the Profile Manager pane. This lesson focuses on manually downloading and installing profiles; Lesson 7, "Mobile Device Management," focuses on automatic push installation via the MDM service. Also note that if a profile is to be installed via an automation tool such as Apple Configurator 2 or NetInstall, the profile is first manually downloaded from Profile Manager before it's installed by the automated tool.

- Organization—This information will be visible to the user and should help him identify the origin of the profile. If you have turned on profile signing, you will not be allowed to change the Organization information because it will be automatically populated by the signing certificate information. On the other hand, when creating unsigned profiles, you can specify any value, but it should obviously reflect an identifier for your organization.

- Description—This optional field allows an administrator to enter any text she would find useful to describe the profile's content. Keep in mind the user can see the description, so choose your words accordingly.

▶ Security—When profiles are installed, you can choose whether the user has the ability to remove the profile. You can turn off the ability to remove a profile, or you can set an authorization password for removing the profile.

NOTE ▶ The setting to never allow the user to remove a profile doesn't apply to OS X systems unless the profile is installed via an MDM server and the Mac is running OS X Yosemite or later.

NOTE ▶ You cannot prevent the removal of an enrollment profile. Only if a device is enrolled using one of the Apple programs for device enrollment (the Apple Device Enrollment Program for businesses or Apple School Manager for schools) or enrolled and supervised with Apple Configurator 2 can you prevent the removal of device enrollment.

▶ Automatic removal—A profile can be set to be automatically removed after a specified interval or date. The interval time can be specified in both days and hours. This is especially useful for temporary settings that may be needed only for the device's initial setup. For example, during setup you can install a temporary profile that grants access to a limited Wi-Fi network used to facilitate device enrollment. Once the device is enrolled into the MDM service, this service can automatically push a new profile, granting permanent access to one or more secured Wi-Fi networks.

Profile Payloads

Configuration settings are categorized into a list presented on the left side of the editing pane of the Profile Manager administration portal. You'll note that when editing user or user group profiles, the categorized list starts with items that are shared by both OS X and iOS; then you'll see items for iOS only, and finally items for OS X only. Select a settings category from the list, click the Configure button, and then start editing the configuration payload.

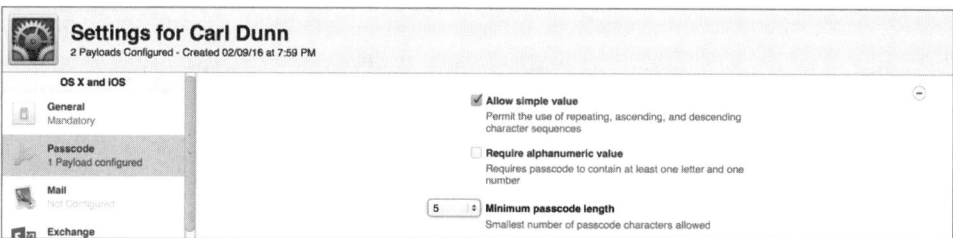

A *payload* is a collection of settings that will be included in the profile once you save the changes. You do not have to define all the settings in a payload, but the implication is that as soon as you click the Save button, those settings will be made available in the profile. Use caution when configuring payloads, especially if the profile is to be delivered automatically via the MDM service. It's certainly possible to deliver a payload of settings that aren't properly configured.

Profile Manager assumes that if you start to configure a payload, you will take the time to accurately specify the settings before you save the changes. If you are simply browsing through the possible settings or you're otherwise unprepared to specify definitive settings, you can delete a payload by clicking the Delete (–) button in the top-right corner of the editing pane.

In the following figure, the "1 Payload configured" text under the category name lets you know that a single collection of settings will be saved to the profile. The number here also implies that multiple payloads per category are allowed. For example, you may need to configure multiple Mail accounts or Wi-Fi networks in a single profile. Categories that allow for multiple payloads will feature a small Add (+) button in the top-right corner of the editing pane.

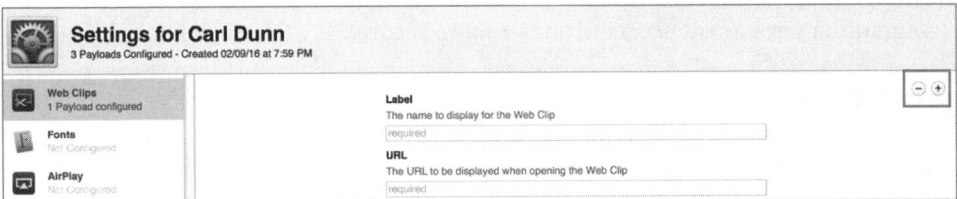

TIP ▶ When you are done editing a profile, make sure to click the OK button in the bottom-right corner to dismiss the editing pane; then click the Save button in the bottom-right corner to apply the changes.

Profiles can contain a wide variety of configuration information, the full scope of which is beyond any guide. Ultimately, the profile format is designed to be extensible. Apple adds new features to both iOS and OS X on a regular basis. You can also add custom settings to manage compatible third-party apps via profiles. Support for app settings management via profiles is a relatively recent addition, so compatibility will vary widely between different applications.

MORE INFO ▶ Although this guide doesn't contain documentation for all profile settings, some profile configurations are covered in future lessons should they pertain to a topic that is particularly unique or difficult to set up. You can also refer to Apple's online help documentation for Profile Manager at https://help.apple.com/profilemanager/mac/5.1/.

MORE INFO ▶ The open source project mcxToProfile is a command-line tool to generate configuration profiles. Among its varied utility, you can use the --defaults option to create a .mobileconfig file with an application's default preferences. See https://github.com/timsutton/mcxToProfile/. MCX is a legacy term and is not required for using this tool.

Reference 6.4
Manually Installing Profiles

Immediately after an administrator has created and saved a profile in Profile Manager, it's ready for download and installation. This section covers workflows for manually downloading and installing configuration profiles.

NOTE ▶ After a profile has been manually installed, changes made in Profile Manager do not automatically apply to devices. In other words, if an administrator makes a change to a manually installed profile, devices will realize changes only if the profile is downloaded and installed again.

Download Profiles via Administrator

As an administrator, you can manually download a profile and then distribute it using whatever method you choose. Because a configuration profile is simply a text document, you can deploy it to your users as you would any other document. For example, you can download a profile and send it as an email attachment, save it to a file server, or post it on an internal support website.

In the Profile Manager administration portal, an administrator can manually download any user or user group profile. You can download this profile on iOS or any other mobile platform, but these systems may be able to easily redistribute a downloaded profile. Thus, if you plan to redistribute a profile, you should use a desktop OS where you have more flexibility for managing documents. To download a profile in the Profile Manager administration portal, simply select the user or user group, click the Settings tab, and then click the Download button.

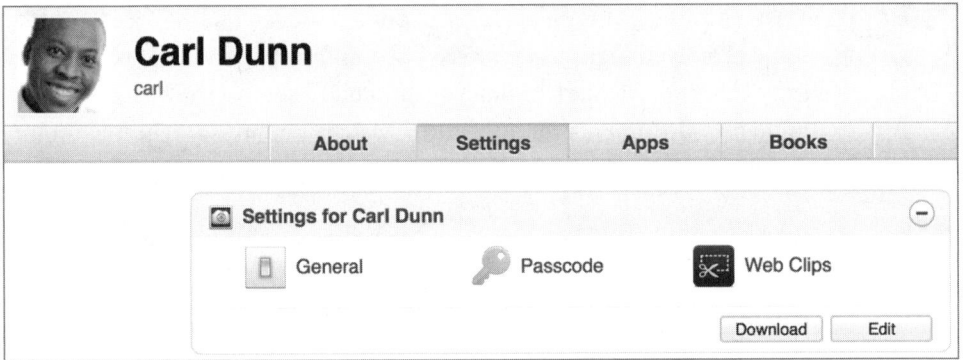

TIP ▶ The Download button will be available only if the profile has not been set to Automatic Download and changes have been saved. Again, make sure to click the Save button in the bottom-right corner to apply the profile settings.

TIP ▶ When downloading profiles on OS X computers, they may attempt to install immediately after download. Simply click Cancel at the confirmation dialog to prevent your Mac from being configured by the profile.

Download Profiles via User Portal

The most convenient method for manually installing profiles is to direct your users to the My Devices user portal. From here users can download and install any profiles scoped to their user accounts or associated user groups.

When a user authenticates, Profile Manager will automatically resolve any profiles associated with the user and present only those profiles. The user can click the Show Contents button to view icons representing categories with payloads configured in the profile (the figure displays the Hide Contents button to reflect that a user clicked Show Contents). When a user taps or clicks the Install button, the profile will download and immediately attempt to install on an iOS or OS X device.

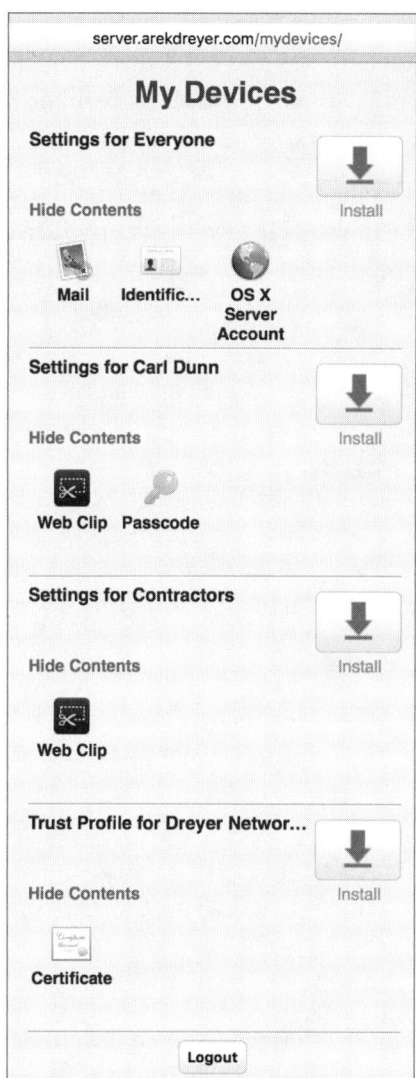

NOTE ▶ After you have enabled device management, profiles that are configured with a profile distribution type of Automatic Push instead of Manually Download do not appear in the user portal; enrollment profiles appear only for users who are administrators.

NOTE ▶ If your server has an Open Directory–generated CA, the user will also be allowed to download a trust profile for this CA.

Manual Profile Installation

If a user opens or downloads a profile, by default on both iOS and OS X the system will attempt to install the profile. On an iOS device, profile installation takes place in the Settings app, and on OS X, it takes place in Profiles preferences.

Before installing a profile, the user will be allowed to view general and configuration details about the profile, including whether the system was able to verify the profile via code signing. To finalize the install on an iOS device, the user must start by tapping Install.

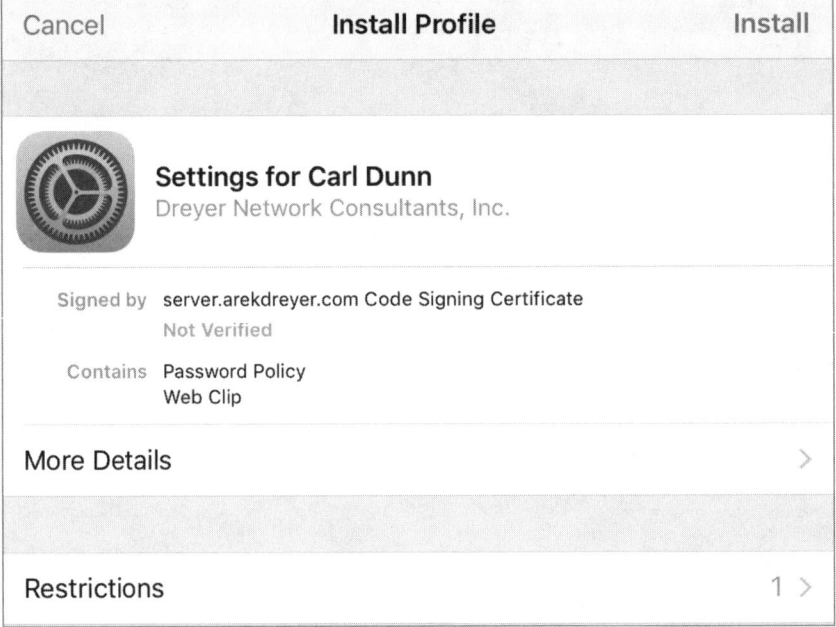

On a Mac, the user can click Show Profile to view more information about the profile or click Continue to start the process of installing the profile.

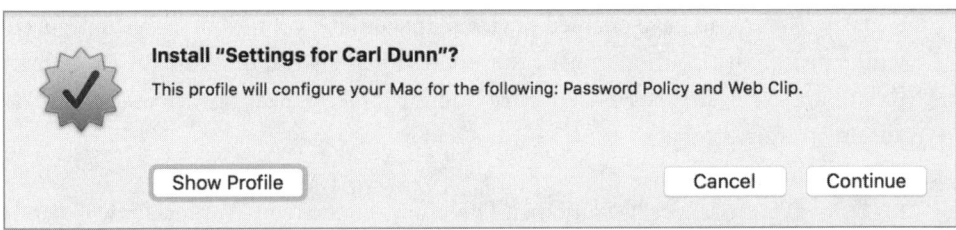

> **NOTE ▶** To complete the installation of a profile on an iOS device with a lock passcode set, the user must reenter the passcode. iOS devices without a lock passcode don't require authentication.

> **NOTE ▶** To complete the installation of any profile containing settings that could affect the operating system or other users on an OS X computer, the user must authenticate using an account with local administrator privileges. In other words, if an OS X user doesn't have administrator privileges, he will not be allowed to install profiles that can modify system settings.

> **NOTE ▶** Devices that are supervised and managed via an MDM solution can be prevented from manually installing additional profiles.

Upon installation, the profile's payload configuration will be applied immediately. The only exception is that for some OS X system-wide configurations, such as Energy Saver settings, the computer may need to be restarted for the settings to apply. Depending on the profile payload, the user may notice that some settings managed by the profile can no longer be modified locally. This is especially true if the profile contains restrictions that limit the availability of system features.

After installation, the user can verify the list of manually installed profiles from the appropriate interface: on OS X, System Preferences > Profiles, and on iOS, Settings > General > Profile (this may appear as Profile, Profiles, Device Management, or Profiles & Device Management). Depending on the profile settings, users may be able to remove the profile. Further, the local authentication rules that apply for installing a profile also apply for removing a profile.

If a profile is removed, any accounts or restrictions that were configured via the profile are immediately removed. In cases where the profile configured specific settings, the settings may still remain after the profile is removed, but the user will now be able to change the setting locally.

> **NOTE ▶** If you remove a profile that specifies passcode restrictions, the device's existing passcode does not get removed.

Exercise 6.1
Turn On Profile Manager

> **Prerequisites**
>
> ▶ Exercise 4.1, "Prepare Your Mac to Install OS X Server for El Capitan"
>
> ▶ Exercise 4.2, "Install OS X Server for El Capitan"
>
> ▶ Exercise 4.3, "Configure OS X Server for El Capitan"

Challenge
Turn on Profile Manager with its defaults.

Considerations
Do not enable device management yet because this lesson focuses on user and group management first.

Solution

1   On your server computer, if necessary, open the Server app, and connect to your server.

2   In the Server app sidebar, select Profile Manager.

3   Leave the default settings; click the On/Off switch to turn on the Profile Manager service.

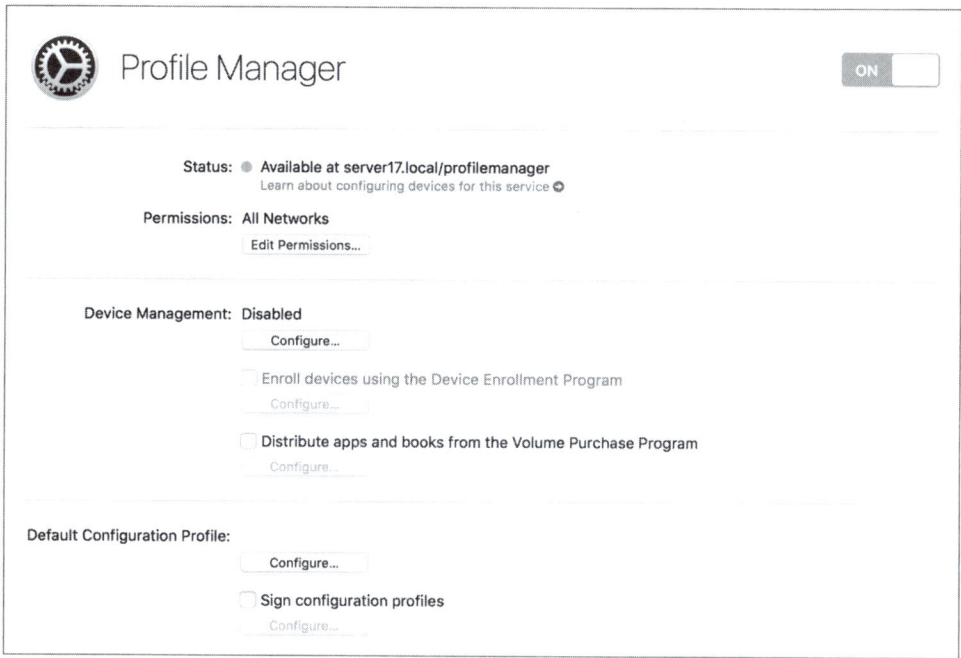

In this short exercise, you turned on the Profile Manager service with the default settings. The rest of this lesson's exercises have enough to explore without even turning on device management, which you will do in the next lesson.

Exercise 6.2
Create, Download, and Install Profiles for Users and Groups

▶ **Prerequisite**

▶ Exercise 6.1, "Turn On Profile Manager"

Challenge

Create a configuration profile for the user Barbara Green that contains a web clip for http://developer.apple.com/enterprise. Download the configuration profile, and demonstrate the effects; remove the configuration profile, and demonstrate the effects.

Create a configuration profile for the group Marketing that contains a web clip for http://www.apple.com/ipad/business. Download the configuration profile, and demonstrate the effects.

Change the Marketing configuration profile by adding another web clip for http://www.apple.com/education/ipad. Confirm that the settings do not take effect until you download and reinstall the configuration profile again. Remove the configuration profile, and demonstrate the effects.

Considerations

Use the Profile Manager administration portal. A link is available from the Profile Manager pane in the Server app.

If you're logged in to the Profile Manager administration portal (https://server*n*.local/profilemanager) as a local administrator, you must log out of that site before logging in to the user portal (https://server*n*.local/mydevices) as a regular user. Use your server Mac for the Profile Manager administration portal and your client Mac for the My Devices site so you do not need to frequently log in and out.

Solution

Create the configuration profile for the user.

1. At the bottom of the Profile Manager pane of the Server app, click the Open in Safari button for Profile Manager (or in Safari, open https://server*n*.local/profilemanager, where *n* is your student number).

2. Provide your local administrator credentials, and then click Log In.

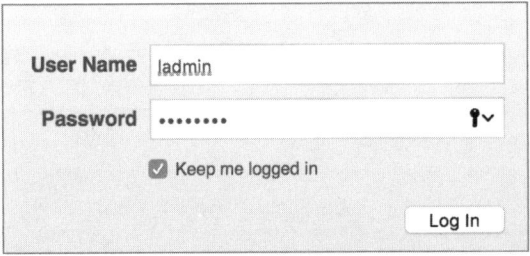

3. At the "Would you like to save this password?" dialog, click Never for This Website.

4. In the left column of the Profile Manager administration portal, select Users.

5   Select Barbara Green.

6   Click the Settings tab.

7   In the Settings for Barbara Green section, click Edit to begin creating a profile.

8   In the Description field for the general payload, enter descriptive text such as Contains a Web Clip.

9   Leave the other settings at their defaults.

10 Select Web Clips in the payload sidebar.

11 Click Configure.

12 Enter Apple in Enterprise in the Label field.

13 Enter http://developer.apple.com/enterprise in the URL field.

    NOTE ▶ Capitalization in URLs matters—all characters should be lowercase.

    Label
    The name to display for the Web Clip
    Apple in Enterprise
    URL
    The URL to be displayed when opening the Web Clip
    http://developer.apple.com/enterprise

14 Leave the other settings at their defaults.

15 Click OK.

16 Click Save in the Profile Manager administration portal.

17 Confirm that Settings for Barbara Green contains General and Web Clips payloads.

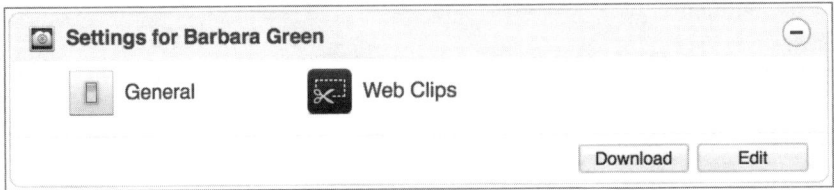

Download and Confirm the Configuration Profile on Your Client Mac

Be sure you are logged in as a local administrator on your client Mac.

1   On your client Mac, in Safari, open the user portal (https://server*n*.local/mydevices, where *n* is your student number).

2   If you see the message "Safari can't verify the identity of the website server*n*.local" (where *n* is your student number), click Continue.

3   Deselect the checkbox "Keep me logged in."

4   Provide the following credentials:

▶   User Name: barbara

▶   Password: net

5   Click Log In.

6   If you are asked "Would you like to save this password?" click Never for This Website.

7   Confirm that you can see the settings for Barbara Green. If that item does not appear, confirm that you clicked Save at the end of the preceding exercise and that you are logged in to the site as Barbara Green.

8   Click Show Contents for each of the profiles.

9   Confirm the following:

▶   Settings for Everyone displays icons for various OS X Server services

▶   Settings for Barbara Green displays a Web Clip icon

▶   The Trust Profile displays a Certificate icon

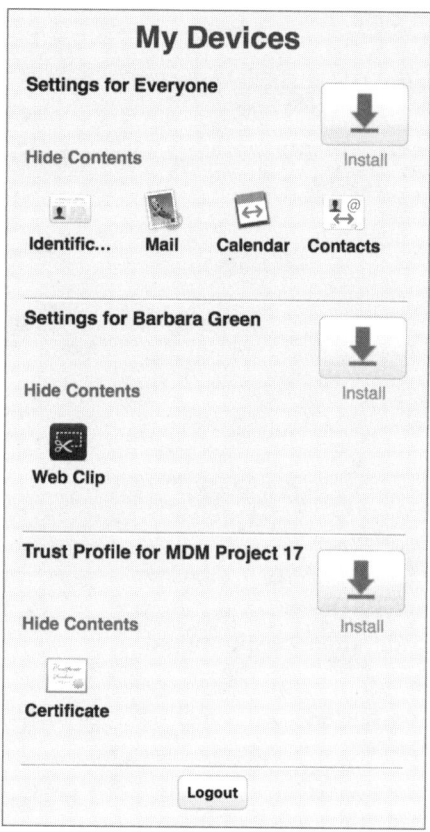

10 Click Install next to Settings for Barbara Green.

This automatically downloads the Settings_for_Barbara_Green.mobileconfig file and opens Profiles preferences.

11 Before installing the profile, inspect it. Click Show Profile.

12 Inspect the details of the configuration profile.

13 To install the profile, click Continue, and then click Install.

14 To confirm that the web clip was installed, in the Dock, click Apple in Enterprise.

15 Confirm that Safari opens to the expected page.

16 If necessary, refresh Safari to open the expected page.

17 Close the Safari window that just opened.

Download and Confirm the Configuration Profile on Your iOS Device

If your iOS device has a passcode, enter the passcode whenever prompted.

1 On your iOS device, in Safari, open the user portal (https://servern.local/mydevices, where *n* is your student number).

2 If you see the message "Cannot Verify Server Identity," tap Continue.

3 Deselect the checkbox "Keep me logged in."

4 Provide the following credentials:

- User Name: barbara
- Password: net

5 Tap Log In.

6 Confirm that you can see the settings for Barbara Green.

7 Tap Show Contents for each of the profiles.

8 Confirm the following:

   Settings for Everyone displays icons for various OS X Server services

   Settings for Barbara Green displays a Web Clip icon

   The Trust Profile displays a Certificate icon

9 Tap Install next to Settings for Barbara Green.

10 Before installing the profile, inspect it; tap More Details.

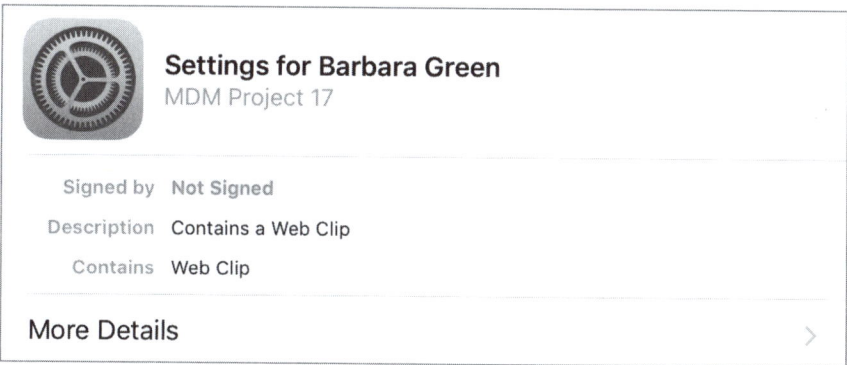

11 Tap the right arrow in the web clip.

Review the details of the web clip.

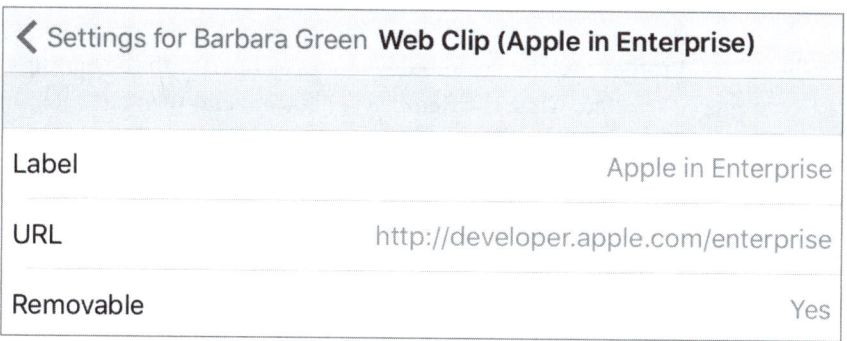

12 To install the profile, tap Settings for Barbara Green in the upper-left corner of the pane, and then tap Install Profile in the upper-left corner of the pane to return to the Install Profile pane.

13 Tap Install.

14 In the warning pane, tap Install, and then at the dialog tap Install.

15 At the "Profile Installed" message, tap Done.

Confirm that the web clip was installed.

1 Press the Home button.

2 Swipe to the next Home screen if necessary to see the Apple in Enterprise web link.

3 Tap the Apple in Enterprise web clip.

4 Confirm that Safari opens to the expected page.

5 If necessary, refresh Safari to open the expected page.

Remove the Configuration Profile and Confirm That the Web Location Disappears

1 On your iOS device, press the Home button.

2 Open Settings.

3 If you are not already in the Profile section, navigate to Settings > General > Profile.

4 Tap Settings for Barbara Green. Tap Delete Profile, and then tap Delete to confirm.

5 On your client Mac, Profiles preferences should already be open with the Settings for Barbara Green profile selected. Click the Remove (–) button, and then click Remove to confirm.

6 Confirm that removing the configuration profile had an effect.

   On your iOS device, press the Home button, and confirm that the Apple in Enterprise icon no longer appears.

   On your client Mac, confirm that the item Apple in Enterprise.webloc is no longer in the Dock.

Create a Configuration Profile for a Group

1. On your server computer, if necessary, open a Safari connection to the Profile Manager administration portal (https://server*n*.local/profilemanager, where *n* is your student number), and then authenticate with local administrator credentials.

2. In the left column of the Profile Manager administration portal, select Groups.

3. Select the Marketing group.

4. Click the Settings tab.

5. In Settings for Marketing, click Edit.

6. In the Description field for the general payload, enter Web Clips for Marketing group.

7. In the payload sidebar, select Web Clips.

8. Click Configure.

9. Enter iPad in Business in the Label field.

10. Enter http://www.apple.com/ipad/business in the URL field.

11. Leave the other fields at their defaults.

12. Click OK.

13. Click Save.

Use the following steps to download the configuration profile. Note that Barbara Green is not a member of the Marketing group, so that profile is not listed for her, even after a refresh of the user portal. You'll authenticate as a user who is a member of the Marketing group, install the profile for the Marketing group, and confirm that it took effect.

1. On your iOS device or on your client Mac, open the user portal (https://server*n*.local/mydevices, where *n* is your student number).

2. If you're still authenticated as Barbara Green, click or tap the Refresh button.

3. Confirm that there is no item for the Marketing group.

4 Click or tap Logout.

5 Deselect the checkbox "Keep me logged in."

6 Provide the following credentials:

▶ User Name: carl

▶ Password: net

7 Click or tap Log In.

8 Install the Settings for Marketing configuration profile.

9 Confirm that the iPad in Business item is available on your iOS device or your Mac.

Update the Marketing Configuration Profile

1 On your server computer, if necessary, open a Safari connection to the Profile Manager administration portal (https://servern.local/profilemanager, where *n* is your student number), and then authenticate with local administrator credentials.

2 In the left column of the Profile Manager administration portal, select Groups.

3 Select the Marketing group.

4 Click the Settings tab.

5 Click Edit.

6 In the payload sidebar, select Web Clips.

7 Click Add (+) in the upper-right corner.

8 Enter iPad in Education in the Label field.

9 Enter http://www.apple.com/education/ipad in the URL field.

Observe that in payload sidebar, there are now two payloads configured for Web Clips.

10 Leave the other fields at their defaults.

11 Click OK.

12 Click Save.

Download and Install the Updated Configuration Profile

1 To confirm that the changes did not automatically take effect, on your iOS device or client Mac, confirm that the iPad in Education web link is not available yet.

2 Open the user portal (https://server*n*.local/mydevices, where *n* is your student number).

   You should still be authenticated as Carl Dunn.

   If your browser is already at the mydevices site, click or tap the Refresh button.

3 For the Settings for Marketing configuration profile, click or tap Install.

   If you are on your client Mac, click Show Profile, and confirm that two web clips are listed.

If you are on your iOS device, tap More Details, and confirm that two web clips are listed.

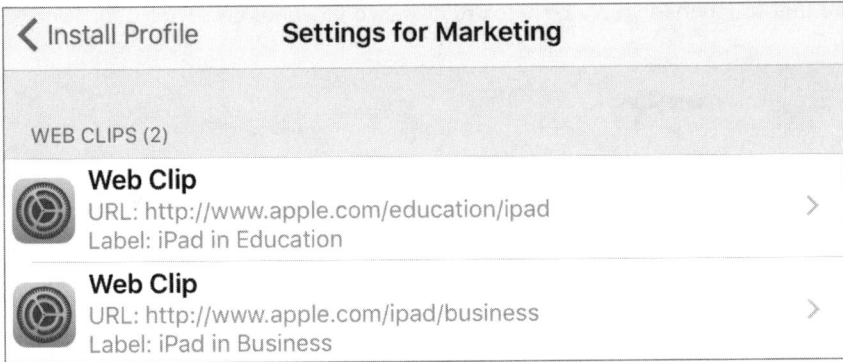

4   Continue installing the updated configuration profile.

5   Confirm that both web clips are available on your iOS device or in the Dock of your client Mac.

Remove the Marketing Configuration Profile

1   If you performed the exercise on your iOS device, press the Home button. If necessary, navigate to Settings > General > Profile. Tap Settings for Marketing. Tap Delete Profile, and then tap Delete to confirm.

If you performed the exercise on your client Mac, Profiles preferences should already be open with the Settings for Marketing profile selected. Click the Remove (–) button, and then click Remove to confirm.

2   Confirm that removing the configuration profile had an effect.

If you performed the exercise on your iOS device, press the Home button, and confirm that the two web clips no longer appear.

If you performed the exercise on your client Mac, confirm that the two web links are no longer in the Dock.

In this exercise, you created two configuration profiles: one for a user and another for a group. You manually downloaded and installed the profiles. You confirmed that after you made changes to a configuration profile, the changes were not automatically delivered; you had to download and install the configuration profile again.

Exercise 6.3
Inspect the Effects of Signing

▶ **Prerequisite**

▶ Exercise 6.2, "Create, Download, and Install Profiles for Users and Groups"

Challenge

Sign your configuration profiles with a code-signing certificate. Compare an unsigned profile with a signed profile.

Attempt to install a configuration profile that was modified after it was signed.

Considerations

Use the Server app to specify the code-signing certificate that was automatically created when you configured your server as an Open Directory master.

Use a text editor such as TextEdit to modify a signed configuration profile. OS X keeps the configuration profiles in your Downloads folder. If you download a file with the same name more than once, Safari simply appends a dash and a number at the end of the base of the filename.

Solution

Inspect an Unsigned Configuration Profile on a Mac

1   On your client Mac, open the user portal (https://servern.local/mydevices, where *n* is your student number).

2   If necessary, authenticate as Carl Dunn.

3   For the Settings for Marketing configuration profile, click Install to install.

4   Inspect the configuration profile without installing it:

    Click Show Profile, and confirm that the configuration profile is listed in red as Unsigned.

Settings for Marketing
MDM Project 17 Unsigned

Description Web Clips for Marketing group

5 Click Cancel.

   Don't remove the profile from your Downloads folder; you will use it again in the section "Modify and Install a Signed Configuration Profile."

Inspect an Unsigned Configuration Profile on an iOS Device

1 On your iOS device, open the user portal (https://servern.local/mydevices, where *n* is your student number).

   You should still be authenticated as Carl Dunn.

2 For the Settings for Marketing configuration profile, tap Install to install.

3 Inspect the configuration profile without installing it; confirm that the configuration profile is listed in red as Not Signed.

4 To cancel installing the configuration profile, tap Cancel.

Configure Profile Manager to Sign Configuration Profiles

1 If necessary, on your server computer, open the Server app, and connect to your server.

2 In the Server app sidebar, select Profile Manager.

3 Select the checkbox "Sign configuration profiles."

4   Click the Certificate pop-up menu, and choose the certificate signed by your OD intermediate CA.

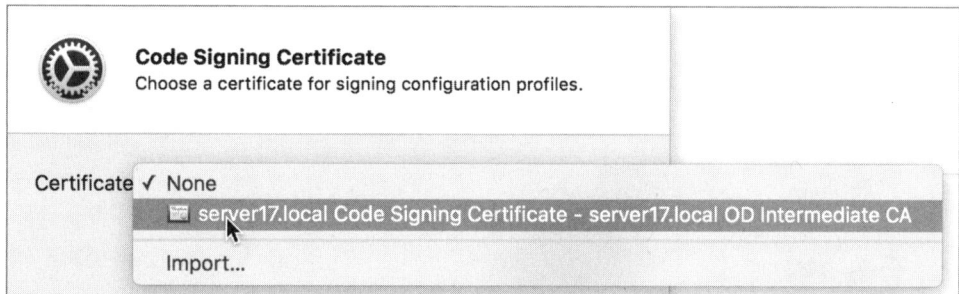

5   Click OK to save the change.

6   Confirm that the "Sign configuration profiles" checkbox is still selected.

Compare an Unsigned Profile with a Signed Profile on a Mac

Now that you've configured your server's Profile Manager service to sign configuration profiles, download one again, and confirm that it is listed as unverified.

1   On your client Mac, in the user portal, for the Settings for Marketing configuration profile, click Install.

2   Inspect the configuration profile without installing it; click Show Profile, and confirm that the configuration profile is listed in red as Unverified and that there is a Signed field.

   NOTE ▶ If your Mac is configured to trust your server's Open Directory CA, the profile will be listed in green as Verified.

3   To cancel installing the configuration profile, click Cancel.

Keep the profile in your Downloads folder; you will use it again in the section "Modify and Install a Signed Configuration Profile."

Compare an Unsigned Profile with a Signed Profile on an iOS Device

1   On your iOS device, in the user portal, for the Settings for Marketing configuration profile, tap Install.

2   Confirm that the configuration profile is listed in red as Not Verified and that there is a Signed field.

NOTE ▶ If your iOS device is configured to trust your server's Open Directory CA, the profile will be listed in green as Verified.

3   To cancel installing the configuration profile, tap Cancel.

Modify and Install an Unsigned Configuration Profile

You should have at least two configuration profiles for the Marketing group in your Downloads folder. The first one you downloaded was unsigned; the second one was signed and has a number appended in the filename.

Open the file in TextEdit.

1   On your client Mac, open TextEdit (use Spotlight; or click Launchpad in the Dock, click Other, and then click TextEdit).

2   Choose File > Open.

3   In the Open window sidebar, select Downloads.

4   Select the Settings_for_Marketing.mobileconfig file.

5   Click Open.

6   Inspect the contents of the file.

```
Settings_for_Marketing.mobileconfig
<?xml version="1.0" encoding="UTF-8"?>
<!DOCTYPE plist PUBLIC "-//Apple//DTD PLIST 1.0//EN" "http://www.apple.com/DTDs/
PropertyList-1.0.dtd">
<plist version="1.0"><dict><key>PayloadIdentifier</
key><string>com.apple.mdm.server17.local.63bbc760-b0f5-0133-
f57d-28667f011246.alacarte</string><key>PayloadRemovalDisallowed</key><false/
><key>PayloadScope</key><string>User</string><key>PayloadType</
key><string>Configuration</string><key>PayloadUUID</key><string>63bbc760-b0f5-0133-
f57d-28667f011246</string><key>PayloadOrganization</key><string>MDM Project 17</
string><key>PayloadVersion</key><integer>1</integer><key>PayloadDisplayName</
key><string>Settings for Marketing</string><key>PayloadDescription</key><string>Web
Clips for Marketing group</string><key>PayloadContent</
key><array><dict><key>PayloadType</key><string>com.apple.webClip.managed</
string><key>PayloadVersion</key><integer>1</integer><key>PayloadIdentifier</
key><string>com.apple.mdm.server17.local.63bbc760-b0f5-0133-
f57d-28667f011246.alacarte.webclip.92fc8b90-b0f6-0133-f57e-28667f011246</
string><key>PayloadUUID</key><string>92fc8b90-b0f6-0133-f57e-28667f011246</
string><key>PayloadEnabled</key><true/><key>PayloadDisplayName</key><string>Web Clip
(iPad in Education)</string><key>IsRemovable</key><true/><key>Label</key><string>iPad
in Education</string><key>URL</key><string>http://www.apple.com/education/ipad</
string></dict><dict><key>PayloadType</key><string>com.apple.webClip.managed</
string><key>PayloadVersion</key><integer>1</integer><key>PayloadIdentifier</
key><string>com.apple.mdm.server17.local.63bbc760-b0f5-0133-
f57d-28667f011246.alacarte.webclip.63b8a960-b0f5-0133-f57c-28667f011246</
string><key>PayloadUUID</key><string>63b8a960-b0f5-0133-f57c-28667f011246</
string><key>PayloadEnabled</key><true/><key>PayloadDisplayName</key><string>Web Clip
(iPad in Business)</string><key>IsRemovable</key><true/><key>Label</key><string>iPad
in Business</string><key>URL</key><string>http://www.apple.com/ipad/business</
string></dict></array></dict></plist>
```

Modify the URL in the file.

1   Choose Edit > Find > Find and Replace.

2   In the Find field, enter apple.com/ipad/business.

3   Click the right arrow next to the Find field.

4   In the Replace field, enter apple.com/appletv.

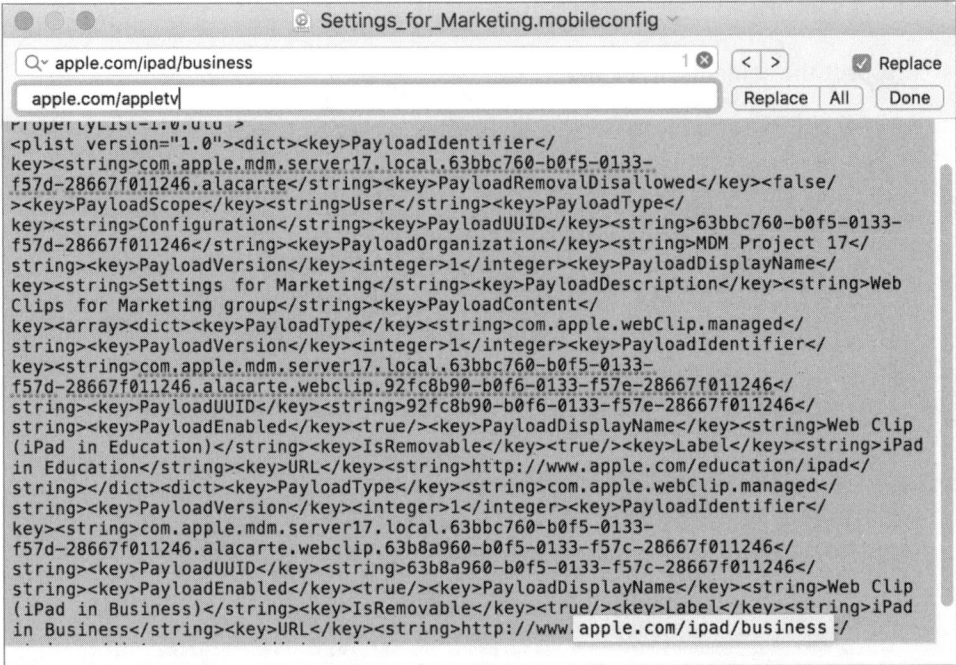

5 Click Replace.

6 Choose File > Save.

7 Choose File > Close.

Install the configuration profile you just modified.

1 While still using your client Mac, in the Finder, choose File > New Finder Window.

2 In the Finder window sidebar, click Downloads.

3 Open Settings_for_Marketing.mobileconfig.

4 Click Show Profile to preview the contents of the configuration profile.

5 Confirm that the URL change you made is in effect.

6 Continue installing this modified configuration profile.

Confirm that the change took effect.

1 In the Dock, hover the pointer above iPad in Business.

Note that since you did not change that name in the .mobileconfig file, that original name is still displayed.

2 Click iPad in Business.webloc.

3 Confirm that Safari opens to the URL you specified with TextEdit.

4 Close the Safari window.

5 If System Preferences is not still open, open System Preferences, and select Profiles.

6 Select Settings for Marketing, click the Remove (–) button, and then click Remove to confirm.

Modify and Install a Signed Configuration Profile

1 On your client Mac, open TextEdit if it is not already open.

2 Choose File > Open.

3 In the Open window sidebar, select Downloads.

4 Select the Settings for Marketing file with the highest number appended to it.

If more than two files start with *Settings_for_Marketing-*, select the file with the largest number.

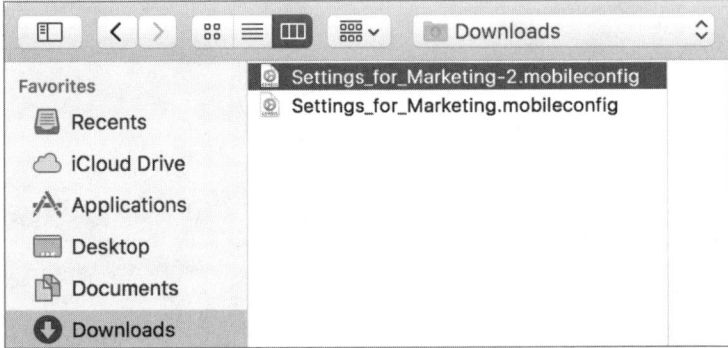

5 Click Open.

6 Inspect the contents of the file. Scroll through, and note that there are more than just plain text characters.

```
0A        *UHU~
†Ä0Ä1
0       +0Ä      *ÜHÜ~
†Ä$ÄÇĬ<?xml version="1.0" encoding="UTF-8"?>
<!DOCTYPE plist PUBLIC "-//Apple//DTD PLIST 1.0//EN" "http://www.apple.com/DTDs/
```

Modify the URL in the file.

1 Choose Edit > Find > Find and Replace.

2 If necessary, in the Find field, enter apple.com/ipad/business.

3 Click the right arrow next to the Find field.

4 In the Replace field, enter apple.com/support.

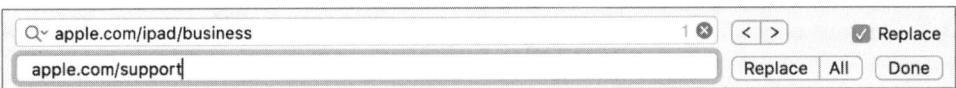

5 Click All to replace all instances.

6 Choose File > Save.

7   Choose File > Close.

8   Quit TextEdit.

Attempt to install the file.

1   Open your Downloads folder.

2   Open the file you just modified.

3   Confirm that you cannot open the file.

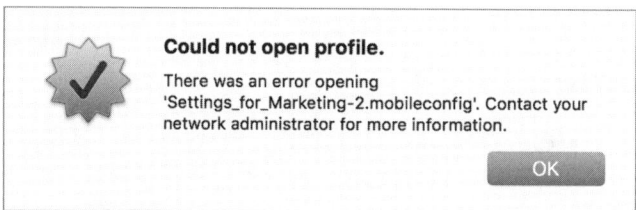

4   Click OK.

In this exercise, you configured your server's Profile Manager service to sign configuration profiles, and you demonstrated that if the contents of a signed configuration profile are modified, you cannot install it.

Exercise 6.4
Clean Up Profiles

▶ **Prerequisite**

  ▶ Exercise 6.3, "Inspect the Effects of Signing"

Challenge
Remove all manually downloaded profiles.

Considerations
Remove the profiles from OS X and from iOS, and remove the .mobileconfig files in OS X.

Solution

Remove Manually Downloaded Profiles: Mac

1. On your client Mac, open System Preferences.

2. If the Profiles preferences pane appears, click it.

3. Select each profile, click the Remove (–) button, and then click Remove to confirm removing the profile.

4. After all the profiles have been removed, System Preferences returns to a view of all the available preferences.

5. In the Finder, choose Go > Downloads.

6. Drag all the files that start with *Settings_for* to the Trash.

7. In the Finder, choose Finder > Empty Trash, and then click Empty Trash.

Remove Manually Downloaded Profiles: iOS

Remove any profiles if there are any still installed.

1. On your iOS device, press the Home button.

2. Open Settings.

3. Open General.

4. Tap Profile or Profiles.

5. If any profiles are listed, for each profile, tap Delete Profile, and then tap Remove to confirm removing the profile.

You are now ready to continue with the next lesson.

Lesson 7
Mobile Device Management

A Mobile Device Management (MDM) service gives administrators the ability to remotely manage Apple devices. The administrative flexibility afforded by over-the-air (OTA) management puts MDM services at the center of most deployment plans. Beyond pushing configuration profiles, most MDM services can also remotely collect device information and send various management tasks such as remote lock and wipe.

This lesson expands upon the introduction of the Profile Manager service from the previous lesson. You will first learn about the MDM service architecture and then turn on this service for Profile Manager. Once device management is enabled, you will learn how users can self-enroll their own devices. You will see how Profile Manager can collect device information and facilitate common administrative tasks. Finally, you will push profiles to managed Apple devices, thus providing remote setup and configuration for your users.

GOALS

▶ Understand the Mobile Device Management architecture

▶ Configure device management for Profile Manager

▶ Enroll a device into management via the My Devices user portal

▶ Inspect device information and remote management tasks

▶ Automatically push configuration profiles to managed devices

Reference 7.1
Mobile Device Management Architecture

This section introduces MDM, also referred to as Enterprise Mobility Management (EMM). MDM is an umbrella term that references the collection of technologies that allow for remote administration of mobile devices. Apple's initial implementation of MDM services originally supported only iOS devices. Apple's MDM service is extensible, so later versions have grown to support OS X as well. Obviously, the latest versions of iOS and OS X include the most MDM service functionality. However, MDM services are still supported as far back as iOS 4 and OS X v10.7.

Apple's MDM implementation is well documented, so developers can create their own MDM services. Indeed, dozens of different third-party MDM solutions support Apple devices. This guide focuses on what many consider to be the standard bearer for Apple MDM services, Profile Manager in OS X Server.

That being said, the core technologies that make up the MDM architecture remain the same even between different MDM service implementations. Thus, even if your organization chooses to use another MDM service, the concepts covered in this guide still apply.

MDM Features

Although there may be differences between specific MDM implementations, most MDM services offer the following primary features:

- Managed configuration profiles—An MDM service can automatically push configuration profiles to managed devices. As covered in the previous lesson, these profiles can contain a wide variety of configuration information. Profile Manager can be used to create and distribute configuration profiles via the Settings tab.

- Device queries—An MDM service can automatically collect device information to help administrators keep inventory of their managed devices. An administrator can inspect a device's information from the About tab in Profile Manager.

- Security commands—An MDM service can push a security command to a managed device in case immediate action is required. The most common examples include remotely locking or wiping a lost or stolen device. Profile Manager refers to these operations as *tasks*, which are found by clicking the Action (gear icon) pop-up menu at the bottom of the Profile Manager administration portal.

- Managed apps and books—An MDM service can automatically push or prompt the user to install, configure, or remove apps and books. This includes both App Store items and custom-built, in-house items. Using Profile Manager to deploy items is detailed in Lesson 10, "VPP-Managed Apps and Books," and Lesson 11, "In-House Apps and Books."

MDM Push

The Apple Push Notification service (APNs) allows an MDM service to automatically push configurations and tasks. APNs is hosted for free by Apple on the Internet and is provided to allow secure push notification to client devices. In other words, an MDM service must use APNs to provide automatic configuration to clients.

NOTE ▶ Even if both the managed devices and the MDM service are on the same local network, Internet access is still required to facilitate push notification via APNs.

Apple devices configured for an MDM service check in with APNs and wait for notification signals. The execution of security commands; the installation of profiles, apps, and books; and the return of device query information rely on direct communication between the managed device and the MDM service. APNs is simply used to inform managed devices that they need to contact their MDM service for updates.

In other words, no data is transferred via APNs beyond informing the managed device that the MDM service has something for it. This keeps data secure between the MDM service and the managed device.

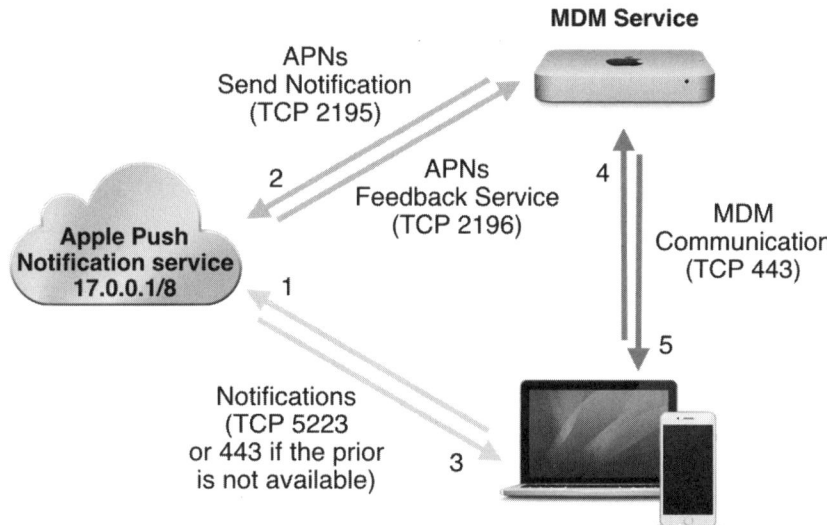

The APNs process works like this:

1. Managed devices establish an outbound connection to APNs on TCP port 5223 or 443 if the prior port isn't available. The devices attempt to maintain a lightweight persistent connection to APNs at all times. The APNs connection is reestablished whenever a managed device experiences a network state change, as would occur when being restarted, changing networks, or switching network interfaces.

2. The MDM service contacts APNs when it needs to notify managed devices of any change or task. To initiate these notifications, the MDM service establishes an

outbound connection to APNs on TCP port 2195. APNs also can send feedback to the MDM service via TCP port 2196.

3. The APNs notifies the managed devices to get in touch with the associated MDM service.

4. After the managed devices are notified to check in with the MDM service, the devices establish a direct connection to the MDM service, most often over TCP port 443. MDM services can provide management over any port number, but most services, including Profile Manager, use TCP port 443.

5. Upon connecting to the MDM service, managed devices may be instructed to download new or updated profiles. Alternatively, managed devices may be instructed to return query information, perform a task such as lock or wipe, or install a book or an app.

> **NOTE** ▶ Per Apple Support article HT203609, "If you're not getting Apple push notifications," if you want to use APNs, your network must not block, proxy, or otherwise inhibit connections required by this service. This includes inbound and outbound access for APNs over TCP ports 2195, 2196, and 5223. This article documents that the entire 17.0.0.0/8 network block is assigned to Apple, so you should allow access to these ports on that network.

MDM Enrollment

The act of configuring an Apple device to be managed by an MDM service is known as *enrollment*. Enrolling establishes trust between a managed device and the MDM service, which allows the MDM service to create profiles that can be accessed only by the managed device. The enrollment process also configures the managed device to receive MDM tasks and configuration via APNs.

After enrollment, most MDM services will request system information to build an inventory record of the managed device. Also, many MDM services will tell managed devices to automatically install any profiles that are already associated with the device or the user of the device. Profile Manager does both immediately after enrollment is complete.

Three main methods can be used to enroll a device into an MDM service:

▶ User-initiated enrollment—Users complete the enrollment process, often through a web-based user portal. This type of enrollment is most often used for managing devices not owned by the organization. User-initiated enrollment via Profile Manager is covered later in this lesson.

▶ Enrollment profile—Configuration profiles are created containing the information necessary to complete an enrollment without further user interaction. This type of enrollment is most often used for managing devices owned by the organization and configured by administrative staff prior to handoff to the user. Lesson 13, "Apple Configurator 2: Preparing, Configuring, and Managing iOS Devices," covers enrollment for iOS devices via profiles.

▶ Streamlined enrollment—Devices are enrolled automatically during activation and set up via Apple School Manager for schools, or via the Device Enrollment Program (DEP) for businesses. This type of enrollment is an option only for managing devices owned by the organization. With streamlined enrollment, user interaction is optional, so initial setup could be completed by administrative staff or the user. You'll learn how to take advantage of streamlined enrollment in Lesson 8, "Out-of-the-Box Management via Apple Programs for Device Enrollment."

Reference 7.2
Profile Manager Device Management

OS X Server can provide MDM services by enabling device management as part of the Profile Manager service. This section explores the service requirements and configuration steps to enable device management for Profile Manager.

> **MORE INFO** ▶ You'll find detailed step-by-step instructions for enabling device management with Profile Manager, enrolling devices, and managing devices via MDM services in the exercises later in this lesson.

Device Management Requirements

Aside from the general OS X Server requirements and suggestions outlined previously in Lesson 4, "OS X Server 5 on El Capitan," device management requires that you also turn on and configure the Profile Manager service as covered in Lesson 6, "Configuration and Profiles." The following are the other two final requirements for enabling device management for Profile Manager:

▶ Open Directory master—OS X Server must be configured as an Open Directory master to provide MDM services because enrollment into the MDM service requires the creation of device-specific certificates. The certificate authority (CA) created during the configuration of the Open Directory master is used to generate these device-specific certificates. As covered previously, you can promote your server to an Open Directory master from the Open Directory pane of the Server app.

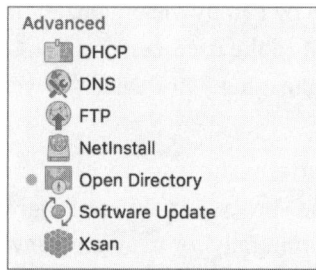

- Apple Push Notification service—As covered previously, MDM services use APNs to contact managed devices. You must authenticate with a verified Apple ID to configure your server for APNs. Also covered previously, you can enable APNs from the Server app Settings pane.

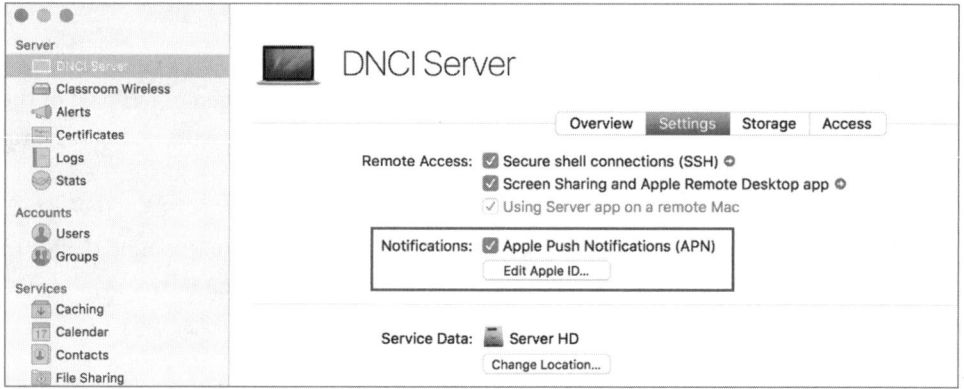

NOTE ▶ APNs configuration must be renewed annually. You can renew the APNs configuration at any time by selecting your server in the Server app sidebar, clicking the Settings tab, clicking the Edit Apple ID button for "Apple Push Notifications (APN)," and then clicking the Renew button. Both the Server app alerts mechanism and APNs portal will notify you in advance if your APNs configuration is about to expire.

Enable Device Management for Profile Manager

To enable MDM services for Profile Manager, you must complete the device management Setup Assistant. To open it, click the Configure button in the Server app's Profile Manager pane.

```
Device Management:  Disabled
                    [ Configure… ]

                    ☐ Enroll devices using the Device Enrollment Program
                    [ Configure… ]

                    ☐ Distribute apps and books from the Volume Purchase Program
                    [ Configure… ]
```

The device management Setup Assistant will determine whether any prerequisites for turning on MDM services aren't configured, including verifying the following items: the server is configured as an Open Directory master, you have entered organizational contact information, a valid Transport Layer Security (TLS)/Secure Sockets Layer (SSL) certificate is selected, and the server is configured for APNs. If the device management Setup Assistant discovers that any of these configurations are missing, it will prompt you to set up the appropriate services.

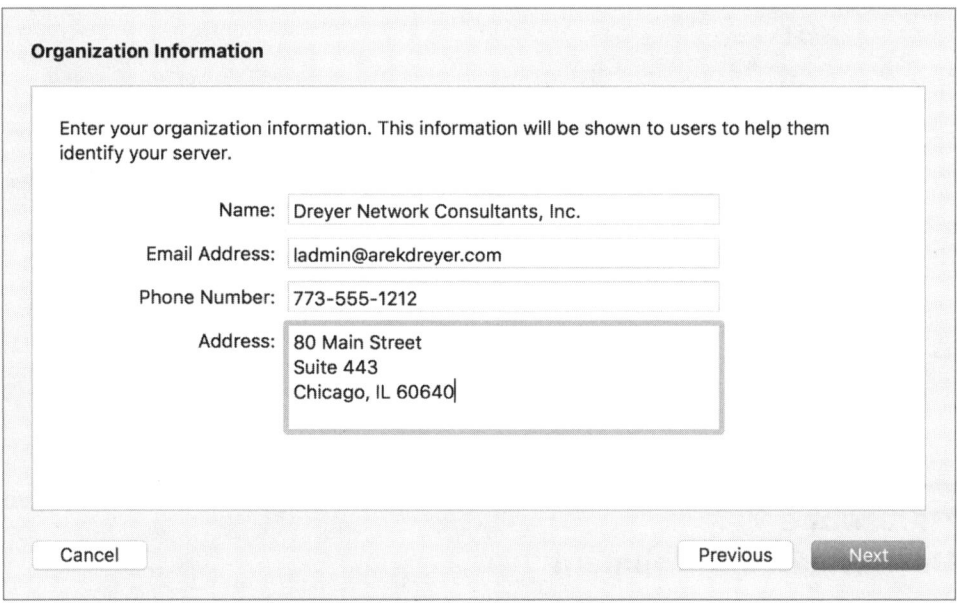

Once device management is enabled, the Server app will show Device Management: Enabled in the Profile Manager pane. You can also verify that device management is enabled from the Profile Manager administration portal. When device management is enabled, the Library section of the Profile Manager administration portal sidebar displays Devices and Device Groups directly above Users and Groups. Once you have confirmed that device management is enabled, you are ready to start enrolling devices for management, as covered in the next section.

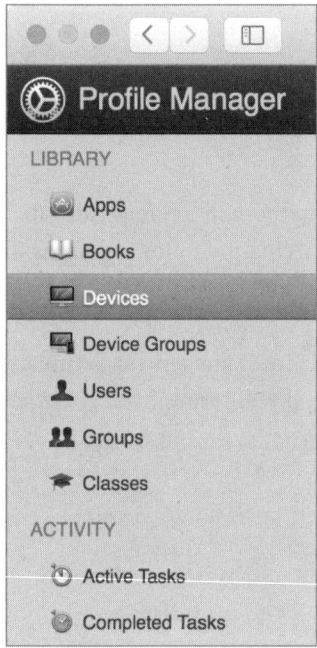

NOTE ▶ After you enable device management, Apps, Books, and Classes also appear along with Devices, Device Groups, Users, and Groups. You can use Apps and Books for in-house enterprise apps and in-house enterprise books before you configure Profile Manager for the VPP. You can create Classes for use with the Classroom app; search for Classroom at http://help.apple.com/deployment/education for more information.

Reference 7.3
User-Initiated Enrollment

User-initiated enrollment works best for environments where the device is owned by the user and administrative overhead is to be kept at a minimum. This section explores workflows where users enroll their own devices into management remotely, or *over the air*. Again, although this guide focuses on Profile Manager as the MDM service, the concepts and workflows associated with user-initiated enrollment apply to other Apple-compatible MDM services as well.

Encouraging User Enrollment

The primary administrative hurdle to overcome with user-initiated enrollment is that it's always optional for the user's device. Assuming the device is not owned by the organization, you can't force a device to enroll into management OTA. Further, users can always remove this type of OTA enrollment and effectively remove device management from their devices. As such, if you need users to enroll their own devices, your deployment workflow should include methods to encourage device enrollment and maintain device management.

> **NOTE** ▶ OS X computers can be enrolled (or unenrolled) into an MDM service only by a user with administrative credentials. On the other hand, iOS devices can be enrolled (or unenrolled) by any user as long as they know the unlock code, if one is set on the iOS device.

Deploy the Enrollment Website

The process for enrolling devices OTA always starts with a website address. In the case of Profile Manager, the address is the My Devices user portal located at https://*servername*/mydevices/, where *servername* is the server's Domain Name System (DNS) host name. This address isn't obvious for most users to enter, so you should try to make accessing this specific site easier for the user.

Consider the following methods for sending users a message containing a link to your MDM service enrollment website:

- iMessage—This method requires that both the administrator sending the message and the user's device are configured for iMessage.
- Email—This method obviously works only if the user's device is already set up to receive email.
- Email via text message—For iPhone users, include a link to the enrollment website in a short email sent to their text messaging service. This method provides an alternative for iPhone users if you aren't sure whether they are able to check their email on the device. Addressing the email will be a bit more difficult because each cellular service provider uses a different email domain for text messaging. For example, customers of AT&T Wireless can be reached at their ten-digit wireless phone number, followed by @txt.att.net.

TIP ▶ Some third-party MDM services include automated tools that can send enrollment messages to a large number of users' devices via an email. If you have a large number of enrollment emails to generate, you may be best served by a third-party MDM service.

Redirect to the Enrollment Website

If you're in need of a "stronger" form of encouragement, consider a method to automatically redirect the user's device to the enrollment website:

▶ Support website link—If your organization maintains a support website often accessed by users seeking help, consider including an enrollment website link. To encourage device enrollment, include reasons why users would benefit from having their devices managed.

▶ Host name alias redirect—If your server's host name or enrollment website address is particularly difficult to enter correctly, consider a DNS host name alias combined with a website redirect. The first step is to create an easy-to-remember DNS alias for your server, such as enroll.mydomain. Then configure a website for the new name that automatically redirects to the enrollment page. The Websites service in OS X Server can be easily configured to provide a website redirect.

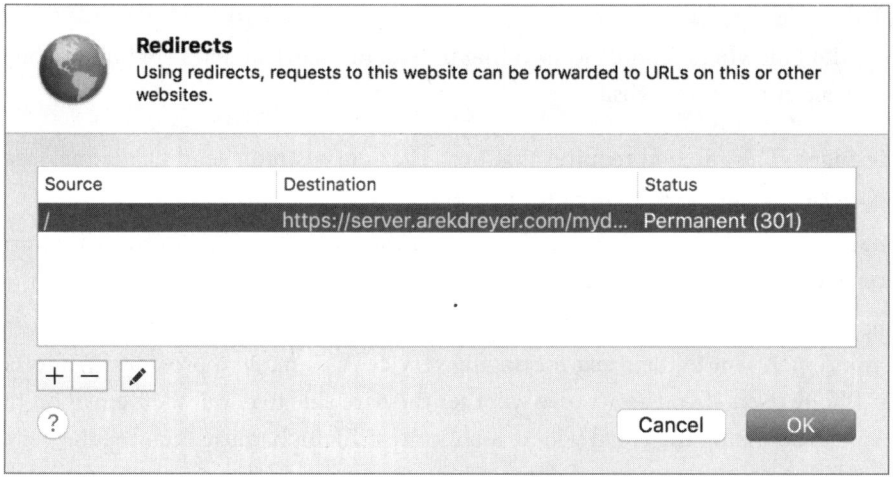

▶ Captive portal redirect—If your Wi-Fi equipment can create a captive portal when new devices connect, you can automatically redirect those devices to the enrollment website. Alternatively, you can set up a guest-accessible "enrollment-only" Wi-Fi network that is limited to only allowing connections to your MDM service and thus redirects all connections to the enrollment website. In either case, after the device is enrolled, the MDM service can immediately push a configuration profile that allows the device to automatically connect to a secured less-restricted network. Implementing these kinds of network-based redirects is beyond the scope of this guide. Work with your network administrator or a Wi-Fi equipment vendor to find a solution that works best with your enrollment workflow.

NOTE ▶ At the time of this writing, an iOS device in Setup Assistant will automatically connect to a Wi-Fi network if it has an SSID of Apple Store, but the device will disconnect from that network after Setup Assistant has completed.

Keeping Devices Managed

Ultimately, if users are going to voluntarily keep their devices enrolled into your MDM service, you will need to make it worth their while. In short, you need to entice them with a carrot instead of forcing them by threatening to use a stick.

The most important feature you have is combining configuration payloads in a profile. As covered in the previous lesson, a single payload can contain multiple types of profile configurations. For example, a profile that allows users to check organizational email on their devices can also include specific requirements for setting a strong device passcode. Thus, if users want to use email automatically configured and provided by the organization, they must also adhere to the device passcode requirements.

Also, keep in mind that all profiles pushed via an MDM service are tied to the enrollment profile. A user cannot delete an individual profile pushed by an MDM service, but they can delete the MDM enrollment profile. In other words, as soon as a user removes the MDM enrollment profile, all other profiles pushed via the MDM service will also be immediately removed. Removing management will also result in the immediate removal of all managed accounts and apps pushed by the MDM service.

In summary, the following items that can be pushed down via an MDM service may encourage users to keep their devices enrolled:

▶ Network access—You can limit the ability to access network resources by providing access only via network configuration profiles pushed by the MDM service. The most common method is to allow access to your secured Wi-Fi network only via a profile. You can also use a combination of firewall and proxy services to restrict access and then allow for access via proxy configuration in a profile pushed by the MDM service.

▶ Account configuration—You can limit the ability to access network services such as corporate email by providing access only via configuration profiles pushed by an MDM service.

▶ Managed apps and books—Apps and books deployed via an MDM service are considered "managed" apps and books. Managed items can be restricted or even removed if a device is unenrolled from management. You'll learn how to deploy managed apps and books in Lesson 10, "VPP-Managed Apps and Books," and in Lesson 11, "In-House Apps and Books."

Enrolling via the My Devices User Portal

Upon navigating to the Profile Manager My Devices user portal, https://servername/mydevices, the user will be first prompted to enter a user name and password. Once authenticated, the user sees a nice large Enroll button encouraging him to enroll the device.

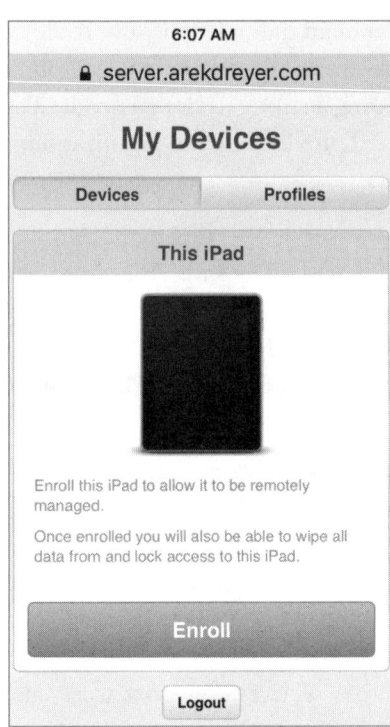

NOTE ▶ If you aren't using a TLS/SSL certificate signed by a widely trusted CA, the user will first be prompted with a dialog stating that the server can't be trusted. As covered in Lesson 4, "OS X Server 5 on El Capitan," if you want users to self-enroll, you should obtain and configure a TLS/SSL certificate signed by a widely trusted CA.

NOTE ▶ To complete the installation of an enrollment profile on an OS X computer, the user must authenticate using an account with local administrator privileges. In other words, if the user doesn't have local administrator privileges, he will not be allowed to enroll the computer into management.

Clicking Enroll will download an enrollment profile with the title Remote Management. The current version of Profile Manager creates a single enrollment profile containing everything necessary to complete the enrollment. Once the enrollment profile is downloaded, the system should automatically attempt to install the profile. On iOS devices, the Settings app opens.

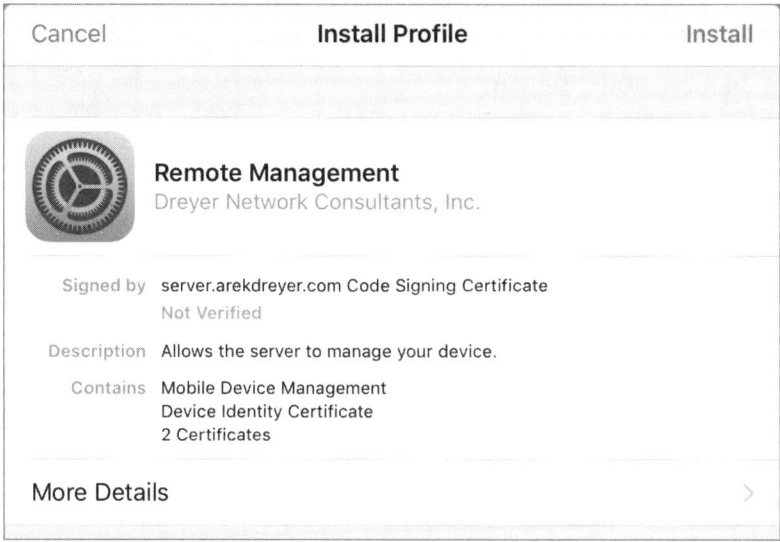

On OS X computers, Profiles preferences opens.

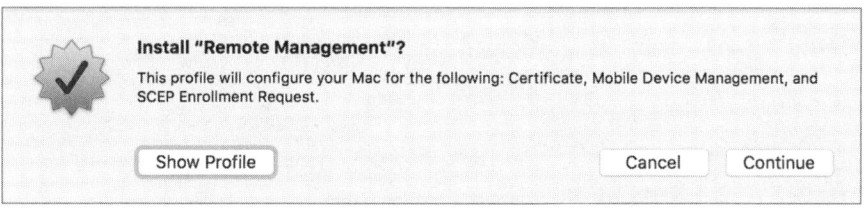

TIP ▶ Simple Certificate Enrollment Protocol (SCEP) is the mechanism through which trust is created between the managed device and the MDM service.

The user will have to tap or click through several installation dialogs to verify the enrollment. Several of these dialogs may be a bit scary looking to users, so you may want to educate your users that these dialogs are expected as part of the normal enrollment process. After the enrollment is complete, the user can inspect the management configuration by returning to the enrollment profile. On iOS devices you can find this in the Settings app by tapping General > Device Management, and on OS X computers you open Profiles preferences. Again, Profile Manager gives the enrollment profile the title Remote Management (other MDM services may provide a different name).

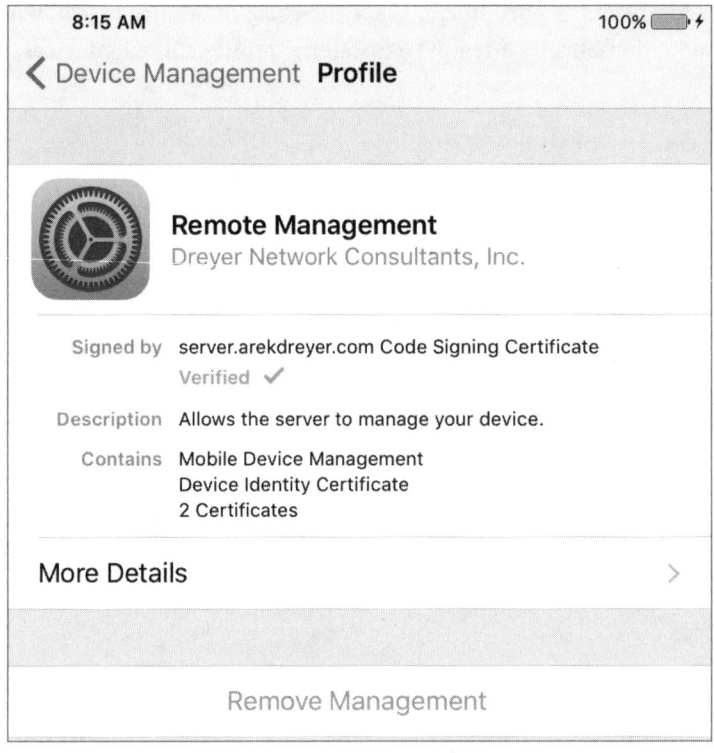

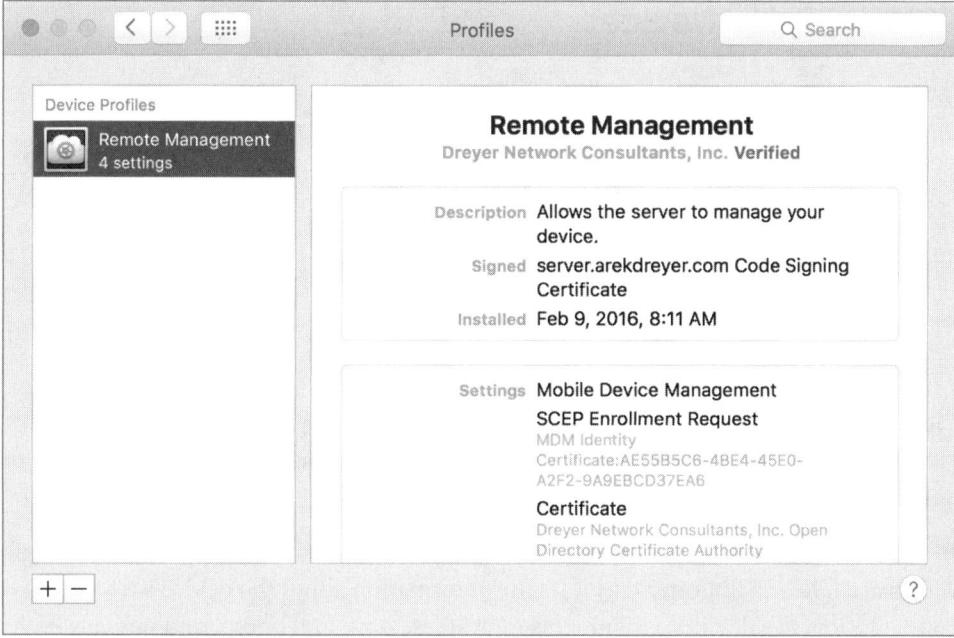

User-Initiated Unenrollment

As you can see from the previous iOS screenshot, the Settings app Profiles interface features a big red Remove Management button to remove the enrollment profile, thus unenrolling the device from management. Less obvious is the small Remove (–) button at the bottom-left corner of the OS X Profiles preferences, which can also be used to remove an enrollment profile.

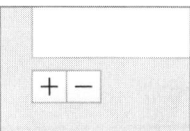

A user can also unenroll her device from the My Devices user portal by authenticating and then clicking the blue Remove text next to the name of the device.

Either method of unenrolling a device, locally or via the My Devices user portal, will remove all management from the device, including the removal of configuration profiles and in-house enterprise apps and books.

In Profile Manager, devices that were previously enrolled will leave behind a "placeholder." This placeholder is important, as it retains information about the device such as its owner; configuration; the device's assignments of profiles, apps, and books; and possibly its Activation Lock Bypass Code (see Lesson 9, "Activation Lock Management").

From the Profile Manager administrative portal, an administrator can easily identify device placeholders because they feature a small prohibitory icon (circle with a strikethrough) to the right of the device's name in the Devices list. You can use the administrative portal to create placeholders for devices that have yet to be enrolled, so you can preconfigure a device before it enrolls, including assigning it to a user, adding it to device groups, editing its configuration profile, and assigning it apps and books. However, devices that have reported inventory information but are now showing as placeholders indicate that the device was once managed but is not currently enrolled.

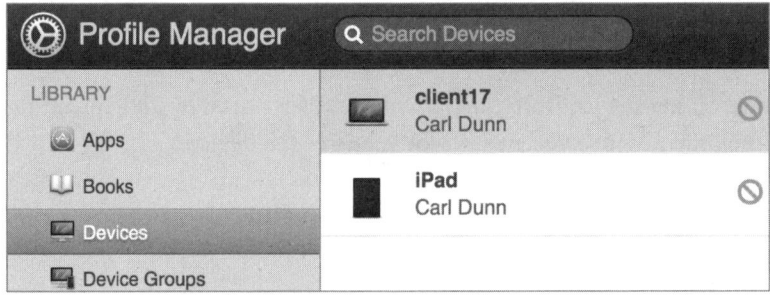

Reference 7.4
Profile Manager Inventory and Organization

As you have just seen, enrolling a device into Profile Manager automatically creates a record of the device and gathers a variety of device information. In the previous lesson, you saw how Profile Manager also keeps track of user management. In this section, you will explore device inventory and organization options in Profile Manager.

Inspect Devices

In the Profile Manager administration portal, you'll find all the currently managed devices in the Devices list. If you are looking for a specific device among a long list of managed devices, use the Search Devices field to narrow down the search results. For example, you can search for a specific user name to narrow the list to devices belonging to that user.

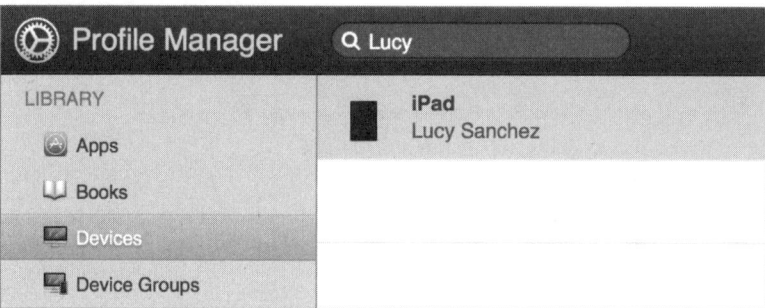

Selecting a specific device will reveal information about the device. Information collected from the device itself will appear when you select the About tab. The device inventory information is categorized into sections. Click the disclosure triangle to the left of each category to expand that section and reveal the device details.

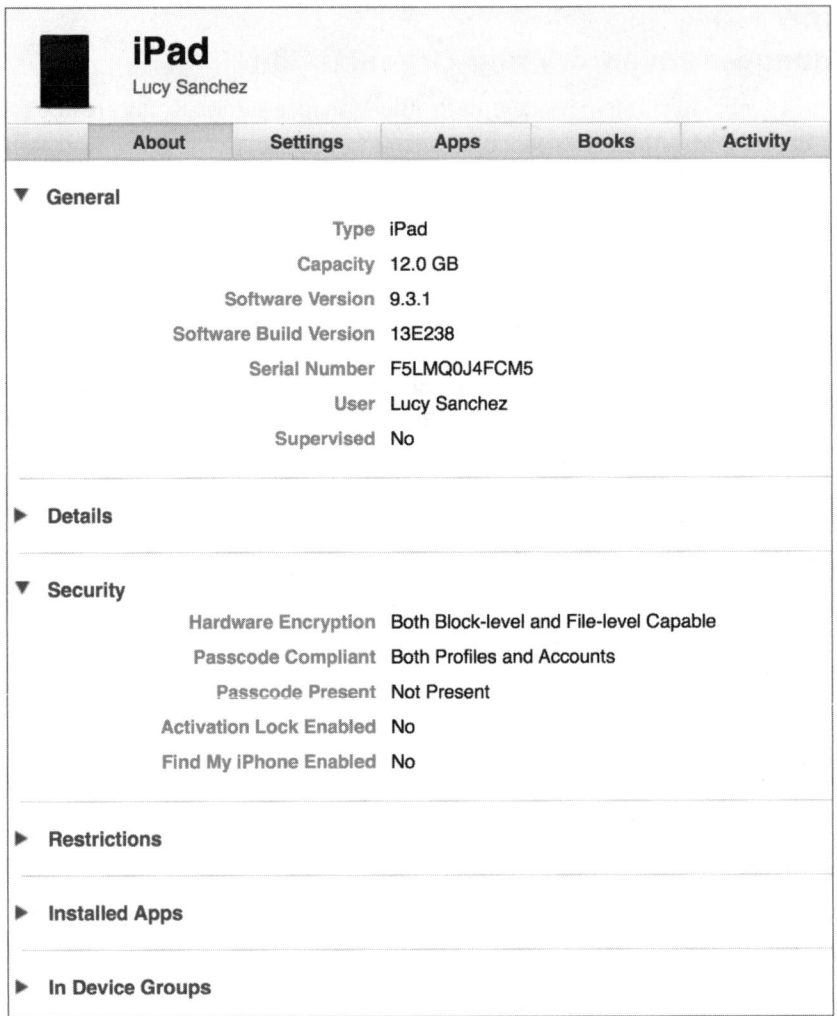

> **TIP** ▶ Profile Manager doesn't update the device information on a regular basis. You can request updated information by issuing an Update Inventory task, as covered later in this lesson.

As covered in the previous lesson, the Settings tab has a full interface for configuring profiles to be automatically pushed or manually downloaded to managed devices or users.

The Apps and Books tabs allow you to push or prompt for the installation of apps and books on managed devices or users. You'll learn how to manage apps and books in Lesson 10, "VPP-Managed Apps and Books," and Lesson 11, "In-House Apps and Books."

The Activity tab shows any current or past push-based actions for the selected device. Every time the MDM service performs any activity that requires a push to the device, that activity will appear in the Activity history.

iPad Lucy Sanchez						
	About	Settings	Apps	Books	**Activity**	
Clear Passcode: iPad					1 succeeded	02/09/16 at 8:27 AM
Lock: iPad					1 succeeded	02/09/16 at 8:26 AM
Update Info: iPad					1 succeeded	02/09/16 at 8:26 AM
Enroll Device: iPad					1 succeeded	02/09/16 at 8:24 AM

Associating Devices with Users

In Profile Manager, you can associate managed devices with a user account, which obviously makes keeping track of who is using each device easier. But, as you'll see later in this lesson, this association also allows Profile Manager to automatically push configuration profiles, apps, and books to devices based on the associated user.

In the previous screenshots, the example iPad is associated with the Lucy Sanchez user. When a user enrolls a device via the My Devices user portal, the device is automatically associated with the user account that the user used to log in to the user portal. When a user enrolls a device using Apple School Manager (for schools) or the Device Enrollment Program (for businesses), an administrator can choose whether or not to require credentials for enrollment; if the user supplies credentials, the device is automatically associated with the user's account. If you install an enrollment profile that isn't specific to any particular device (as opposed to one that was automatically generated as part of an enrollment process), the device will not be associated with a user.

You can easily determine whether a managed device is associated with a user account by looking at the Devices list. Devices that are associated with a user account will have the user's name listed directly below the device's name, whereas devices that aren't associated with a user account will have the device's serial number listed directly below the device's name.

As you saw previously, you can also search the Devices list by associated user names. Further, in the Profile Manager administrative portal you can select a user account in the users list and then click the Devices tab to reveal the list of devices associated with a specific user.

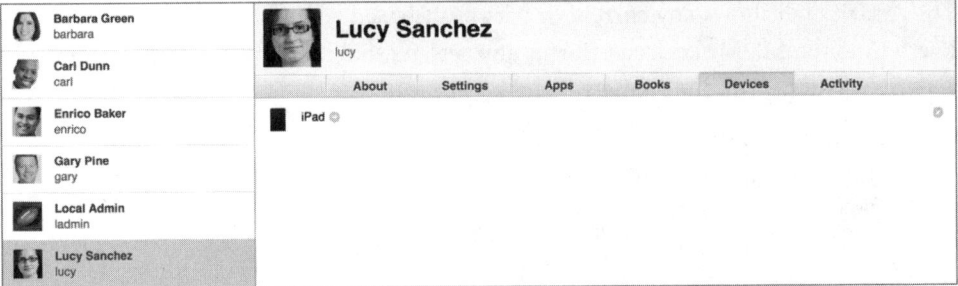

TIP If users or user groups appear to be missing in Profile Manager, click the small Refresh button (circular line with an arrow) at the bottom of the users or groups list to requery directory services.

In the user account devices list, you can click the small arrow to the right of the device's name to inspect the individual device. The small *x* to the far right of a device's name allows you to disassociate the device with the user. Finally, at the bottom of the user devices list, you can click the Add (+) button and then select Add Devices from the pop-up menu to associate additional managed devices to this user account.

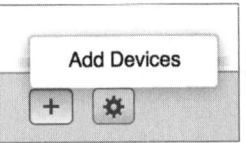

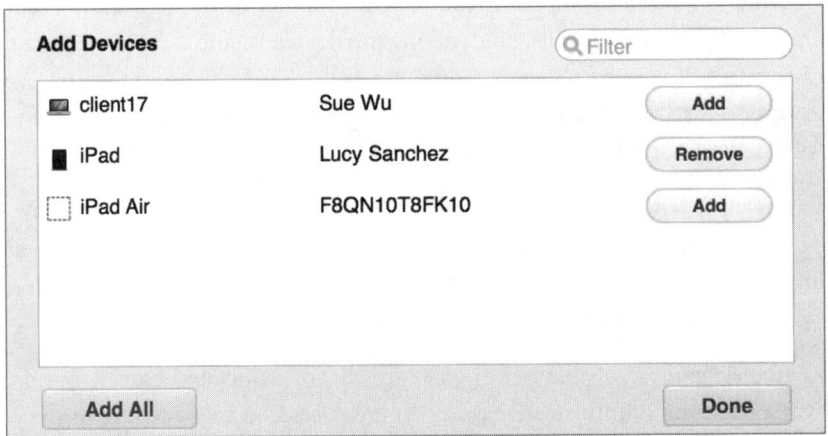

TIP ▶ If you have a long list of devices, use the search filter to limit the device list. Possible device search criteria includes a device's name, serial number, and network address.

Remember that associating or disassociating a managed device with a user may result in significant management changes being pushed to the devices. Associating a managed device to a user account will push down any user-based configuration, apps, and books to the device. On the other hand, disassociating a managed device from a user account may remove user-based configuration, managed apps, and managed books that are currently on the device.

Thus, when you click the Done button in the Add Devices dialog, you must also click the Save button in the Profile Manager administration portal to commit the changes.

NOTE ▶ Previous versions of OS X Server prompted one more time before saving to initiate the settings push; OS X Server 5.0 and later immediately make the changes once you click Save.

Device Groups

Administrators have long used groups to organize user accounts into manageable categories. Profile Manager recognizes users and user groups based on what's available from your directory service. In addition, Profile Manager maintains device and device group information and management. Keep in mind, though, devices and device groups are maintained only within the Profile Manager inventory database.

NOTE ▶ Although you can modify user and user group management settings in Profile Manager, you cannot edit user account attributes or user group membership. This is because Profile Manager uses the directory service as the authoritative source for user and user group membership.

As covered previously, device entries are created automatically for managed devices. Administrators can place devices into device groups to facilitate the categorization of devices. You can create any number of device groups based on your organizational needs. Just like OS X supports nested user-based groups or groups within groups, device groups can also contain devices along with other device groups.

TIP ▶ Although you're allowed a great deal of flexibility when creating device groups, you should always strive to create the simplest possible organization that meets your needs.

To create a new device group in Profile Manager, simply click the Add (+) button at the bottom of the Device Groups list. Enter a name for the device group and then make sure the device Group Members tab is selected. New device groups won't have any device members.

Managing device group membership is similar to managing a user's device associations. At the bottom of the device members list, you can click the Add (+) button and then select Add Devices or Add Device Groups from the pop-up menu to manage the devices in this device group.

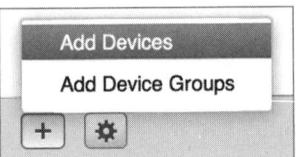

Remember that modifying device group membership may result in significant management changes to the devices. Adding a device to a device group will push down any configuration, apps, and books associated with the device group. On the other hand, removing a device from a device group will remove configuration, managed apps, and managed books associated with the device group that are currently on the device.

Again, this is why when you click the Done button in the Add Devices dialog, you must also click the Save button in the Profile Manager administration portal to commit the changes.

Device Placeholders

Devices that have a record in Profile Manager but are not currently managed are known as *device placeholders*. They exist for several reasons. As you've seen earlier, when a device is unenrolled, it leaves behind a placeholder so an administrator can recognize the device as being no longer managed.

Device placeholders also allow administrators to preconfigure settings for a device that will eventually be managed. The idea is that an administrator can create or import a list of devices that will be enrolled at some future point. If the administrator preconfigures the device placeholders, Profile Manager will immediately push down the settings as soon as the device is enrolled in management.

Add an Individual Placeholder

An administrator can create individual device placeholders in Profile Manager by clicking the Add (+) button at the bottom of the Devices list and selecting Add Placeholder. To create a device placeholder, you must define a device name and then specify a unique identifier for the device. The unique identifier is what will match the device's placeholder to the actual device once it's enrolled in management. Unique identifiers include a device's serial number, IMEI, MEID, or UDID. The easiest number to locate is often a device's serial number.

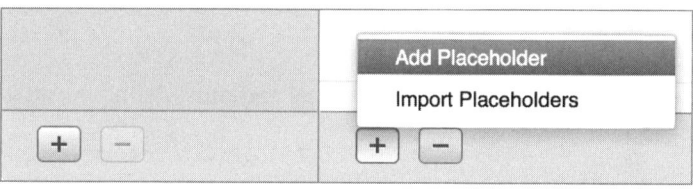

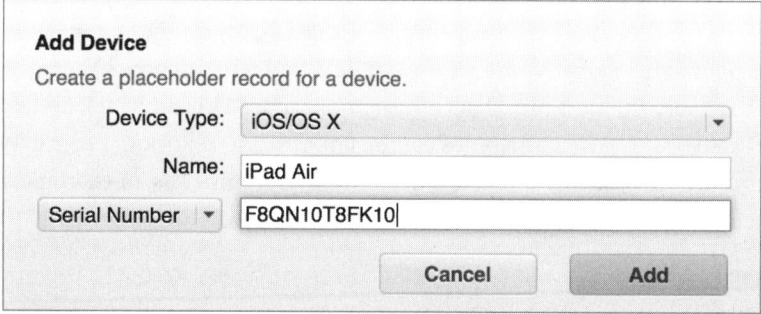

Once a placeholder is created, you can configure it just like any other device record, including the ability to manage settings, apps, and books for the specific device placeholder, or you can associate the device placeholder with a user or device group. Once the matching device is enrolled, it will take over the placeholder and automatically receive the management settings as defined by the device, associated user (and that user's groups), and associated device groups.

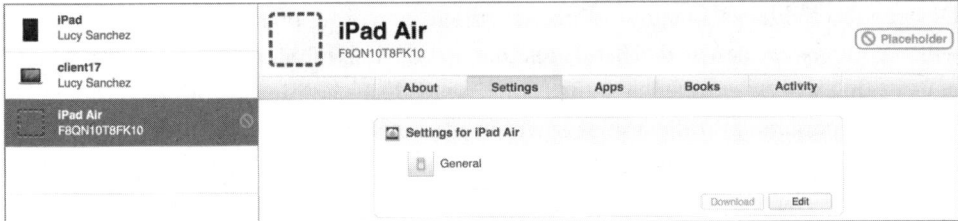

Import a Device List

Creating a single device placeholder at a time doesn't scale well. Administrators also have the option of importing a list of devices from a properly formatted comma-separated values (CSV) text file. You can create this text file in any application you like, but the end result needs to follow a specific format.

> **TIP** You can create a spreadsheet in an application like Numbers and then export it as a CSV text file, but you should still double-check the output in a text-editing application such as TextEdit.

The first line of the device list text file cannot contain spaces and must define the attributes that will be used.

Each line after that represents a device placeholder to be created and must define a device's name and at least one additional attribute. For iOS devices, eligible attributes include the following: DeviceName, SerialNumber, IMEI, MEID, and UDID; for OS X computers: DeviceName and SerialNumber; for Apple TV devices: DeviceName, DeviceID (which is actually the Bonjour Device ID, similar to a MAC address), and, optionally, AirPlayPassword. Unused attributes can be left out, and additional commas at the end of a record can be omitted. Using the device's serial number as an example, a device record in the import document could read exactly as follows:

`iPad Air,F8QN10T8FK10`

Notice that the device's name can contain spaces and special characters, but the device's unique identifier cannot.

After you have created the device list import file, return to Profile Manager, click the Add (+) button at the bottom of the Devices list, and choose Import Placeholders.

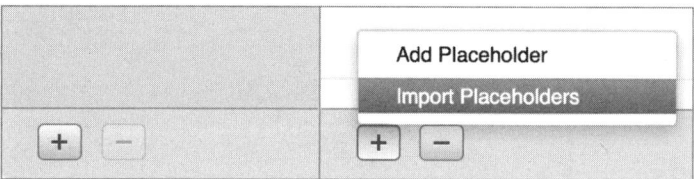

In the Open dialog, you can select the device list CSV text file. Select the appropriate file, and click the Choose button.

Upon successful creation of the placeholders, Profile Manager will automatically prompt to create a new device group containing the imported device placeholders. Managing a single device group record rather than potentially hundreds of individual device records is much easier, which can be a huge time-saver.

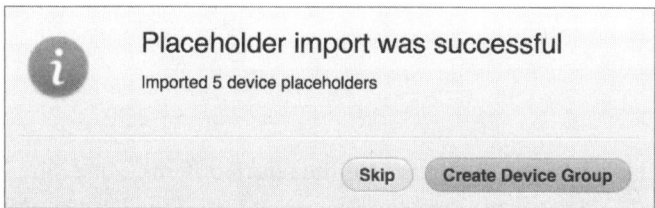

Reference 7.5
Profile Manager Administrative Tasks

Before you create the first configuration profile or define the first managed app or book, you can use some fundamental administrative tasks any time a device is managed. In this section, you will explore the available Profile Manager administrative tasks. Again, other MDM services offer similar features, so you'll find similar administrative tasks if you use a third-party MDM service.

Profile Manager Tasks

Because APNs is so efficient, the time between activating a task and the execution of the task on the managed device usually takes only a few seconds. Even if the device you're trying to manage isn't currently online, an MDM server working with APNs will queue the task and wait for the device to come back online.

To initiate a task, you can select a device, device group, user, or user group in Profile Manager and then click the Action (gear icon) menu to reveal a pop-up menu of administrative tasks.

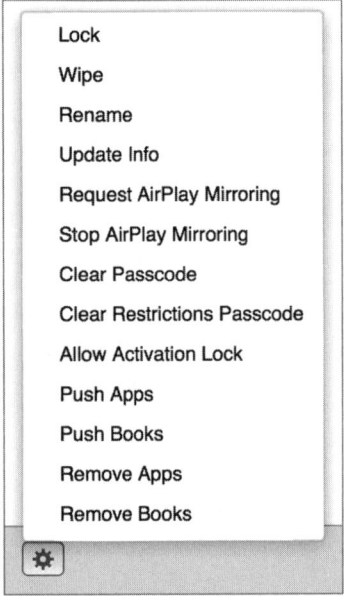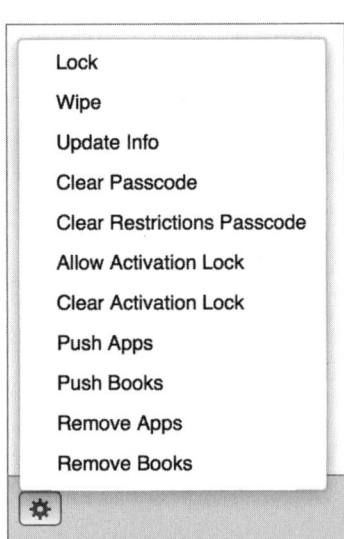

This pop-up menu will vary based on the capabilities of the selected items. For example, the Push VPP Apps task is available only to users and user groups, and the Request AirPlay Mirroring task is available only to individually selected devices.

The following is a brief description of available Profile Manager tasks:

- Lock—This immediately locks the selected devices. iOS devices will simply return to the lock screen, and if a local passcode is set, it will be required to unlock the device. For OS X computers, you will have to specify a passcode that will be used to unlock the device. When the lock task is sent to an OS X computer, it will restart immediately and require the specified lock passcode to fully start up again.

    NOTE ▶ OS X computers must have the local Recovery HD system present to perform a remote lock or wipe. The local Recovery HD system is standard on Mac computers running OS X v10.7 or later.

- Wipe—This task immediately wipes the selected devices. iOS devices will erase all content and data and then immediately restart to Setup Assistant as if they were new devices. For OS X computers, you will have to specify a passcode that will be used to unlock the device after the wipe. When the wipe task is sent to an OS X computer, it will restart immediately, delete the system volume, and require entering the specified lock passcode to fully start up again. Entering the passcode will start the Mac into the local OS X Recovery system.

- Rename—Available only to supervised iOS devices and to OS X computers, this task immediately renames the selected devices. Selecting this task in Profile Manager will prompt the administrator to enter a new name for the selected devices.
- Update Info—This task immediately queries new system information from the selected devices. This task may take a few minutes to complete as the devices rebuild their inventory information and then send it back to the MDM service. Also, this is the only task that requires that the managed devices have direct access to the MDM service.
- Request/Stop AirPlay Mirroring—Available only to devices capable of AirPlay Mirroring, this task immediately prompts the user to mirror the display to a specified AirPlay device. Supervised iOS devices will automatically mirror their display without user intervention and can be made to automatically stop AirPlay mirroring as well. Selecting this task in Profile Manager will prompt the administrator to select an AirPlay destination. AirPlay destinations must be configured in Profile Manager as either an enrolled Apple TV or a manually configured Apple TV placeholder.
- Clear Passcode—Available only to iOS devices, this task immediately clears the local lock passcode for the selected devices. If the device has passcode requirements, the user will be automatically prompted to set a new passcode.
- Clear Restrictions Passcode—Available only to supervised iOS devices, this task immediately clears the local restrictions passcode for the selected devices. The restrictions passcode is used to set and lock local iOS device restrictions. Local restrictions are an alternative to setting profile-based restrictions and can sometimes interfere with profiles delivered via an MDM service. Once the restrictions passcode is cleared, all local restrictions are disabled, thus making way for profile-based settings.
- Allow/Clear Activation Lock—This immediately allows or clears activation lock for the selected devices. You'll learn how to manage activation lock in Lesson 9, "Activation Lock Management."
- Push/Remove Apps—This opens a Choose Apps pane, in which you can choose App Store apps or enterprise apps to push or remove.
- Push/Remove Books—This opens a pane in which you can choose enterprise books to push or remove.

Lesson 10, "VPP-Managed Apps and Books," covers managing VPP items, and Lesson 11, "In-House Apps and Books," covers managing in-house enterprise apps.

My Devices User Portal Tasks

You may have noticed that the My Devices user portal makes a few of the administration tasks available to users. The idea is that if users self-enroll their own devices, being able to perform some of these basic administrative tasks on the devices would be helpful.

As you can see from the screenshot, users can lock or wipe their own devices from the My Devices user portal. For iOS devices, the user can also clear the current device passcode.

Reference 7.6
Automatically Pushing Profiles

Perhaps the most powerful feature of an MDM service is being able to automatically push profiles over the air to managed devices. This feature allows administrators to provide automatic configuration for users and to ensure devices adhere to organizational security requirements.

In the previous lesson, you learned how to create and manually download profiles using Profile Manager. The ultimate goal of this lesson is to show you how to automatically push profiles to users and their devices.

Management Organization

Profile Manager is flexible because you can create settings for each of the four types of records: user, user group, device, and device group. Although you can configure preferences individually for users, managing preferences for the user groups to which they belong is more efficient. Likewise, managing preferences for device groups rather than individual devices is more efficient.

As you saw earlier in this lesson, you can also associate users with devices, thus forming a union between user and device settings. Therefore, when a user is associated with a device, the resulting management may be a combination of all four record types.

For example, if Barbara is in the Engineering users group and she is associated with an iPad in the Group C devices group, her iPad could end up with profile settings defined by each record type. This situation could be made even worse if you consider that both users and devices can belong to multiple groups and those groups can even be nested into other groups. Obviously, the ability to create settings for any record type can lead to confusing management outcomes.

The solution to all this potential confusion is to simply avoid it with proper planning. A good start is to recognize that not all record types make sense for all management purposes, so when setting policy, you have to decide what is appropriate.

For example, you might want to define printers by device groups because a typical situation has a group of devices located geographically close to a specific printer. You may want to set virtual private network (VPN) access via a group of users such as remote salespeople. And individuals might have specific application access rights granted to them as well.

Another recommendation is to configure default settings via groups and then custom settings via individual users or devices. Also, avoid mixing and layering profiles with conflicting settings; the resulting settings may not be what you expected.

Automatic Profile Push

To have a profile automatically pushed to managed devices, you need only select the Automatic Push option in the General settings for one of the record types. For example, the following screenshot shows that the settings for the Engineering group will be automatically pushed. So, any device associated with a user in the Engineering group will automatically get these settings.

In this case, once the administrator clicks the Save button, Profile Manager will resolve which devices match the criteria for the Engineering group and then push down the profile to those devices. This is why making changes to group memberships and user device associations can have a huge effect on managed devices.

Inspecting Automatically Pushed Profiles

As covered previously in this lesson, you can inspect the device management enrollment in the Settings app on iOS and in Profiles preferences on OS X. From there you can also inspect any profile configuration that was automatically pushed to the managed device.

To view this on an iOS device, you would open the Settings app and navigate to General > Device Management > "MDM profile," where "MDM profile" is the name of the MDM enrollment profile. In the case of Profile Manager, the enrollment profile name defaults to Remote Management.

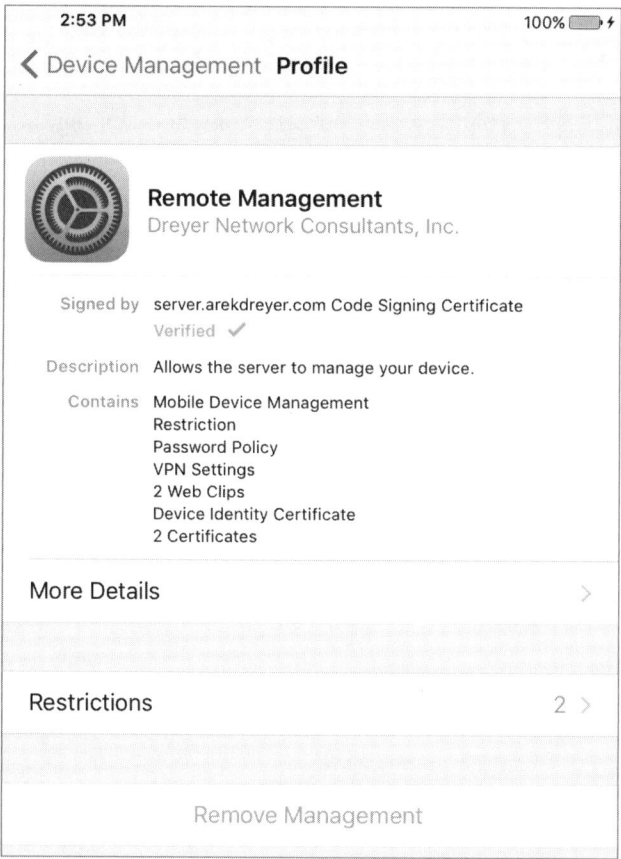

In this example screenshot, the device was automatically pushed settings for the user Carl Dunn that included two web clips and settings for the Engineering group that included a VPN configuration and password restrictions. As you can see, the Profile view in iOS 9 combines all device management settings into either the Contains listing or a separate Restrictions view.

The rationale behind separate views is to differentiate between settings that add functionality (the Contains listing) from settings that limit functionality (Restrictions). Unfortunately, this makes it difficult to determine exactly where a specific setting originates. In other words, from this view you can't determine which settings are from the Carl Dunn user or the Engineering group.

Tapping the Restrictions button lists the resulting device restrictions, and tapping the More Details button reveals additional information about the Contains listing.

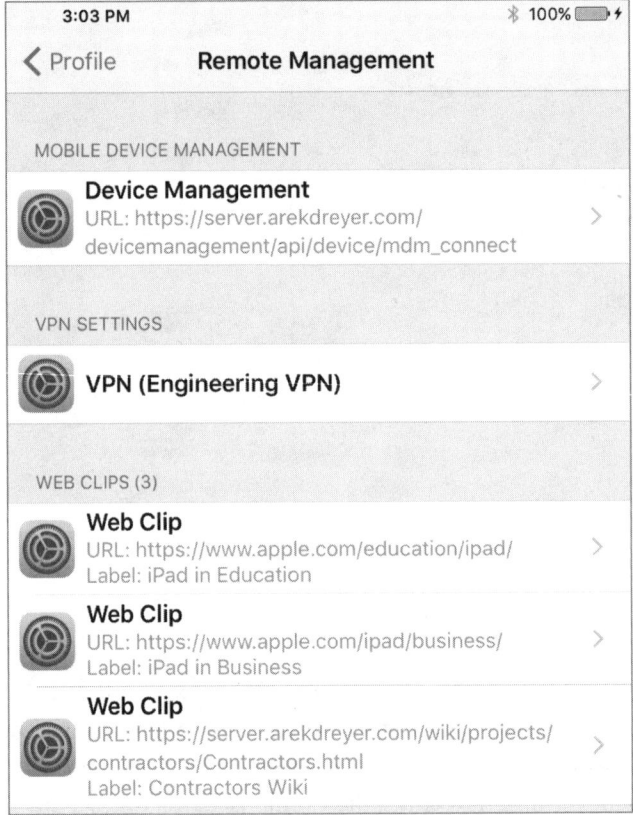

Unfortunately, even when viewing the profile details, as illustrated in the previous screenshot, you still cannot determine the origin of specific settings. For example, there is no indication that two of the web clips are from the Engineering group settings, and the only reason the VPN settings are named Engineering VPN is because the administrator entered that for the profile's name. If there is anything to be learned from this, it's to always choose descriptive names for your profiles in Profile Manager.

The story is better on OS X computers; you'll find both the enrollment profile and automatically pushed profiles in System Preferences > Profiles.

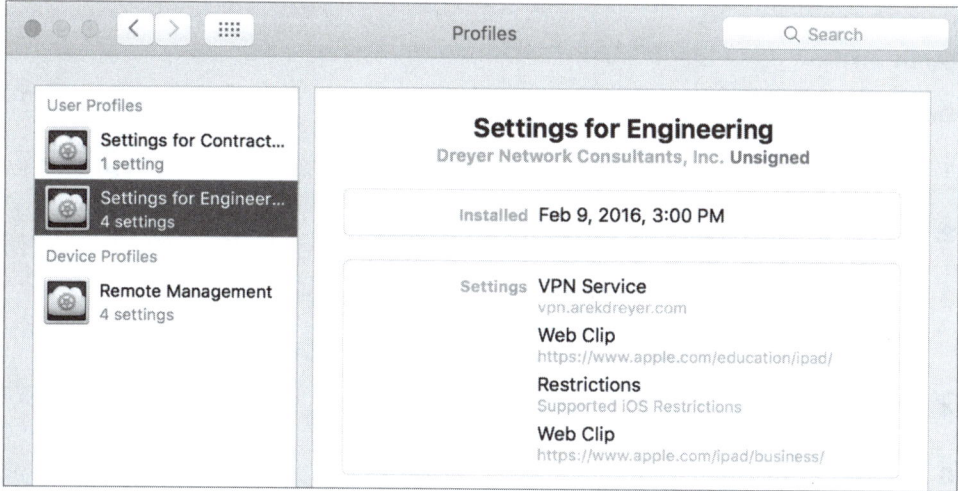

You cannot tell in the previous screenshot of Profiles preferences that this device is associated with Carl Dunn. The device automatically received profiles containing settings for both groups (Contractors and Engineering) that Carl Dunn is a member of. Selecting a profile from the list will reveal more detail about the configured settings.

Exercise 7.1
Enable Device Management

▶ **Prerequisites**

- ▸ Exercise 4.1, "Prepare Your Mac to Install OS X Server for El Capitan"
- ▸ Exercise 4.2, "Install OS X Server for El Capitan"
- ▸ Exercise 4.3, "Configure OS X Server for El Capitan"
- ▸ Exercise 6.1, "Turn On Profile Manager"
- ▸ Exercise 6.4, "Clean Up Profiles"

Challenge

Use the Server app to enable device management. Describe the changes in the Profile Manager administration portal.

Solution

Enable Device Management

1. On your server computer, if necessary, open the Server app, and connect to your server.

2. In the Server app sidebar, select Profile Manager.

3. Click the Configure button next to Device Management.

   The service gathers some data and gives a description of its capabilities.

4. In the Configure Device Management pane, click Next.

5. In the Organization Information pane, leave the default information for the Name and Email Address fields; the Server app automatically uses the information you provided when you set up your server as an Open Directory master.

6. Enter demonstration information in the Phone Number and Address fields, and then click Next.

7. In the Configure an SSL Certificate pane, click the Certificate pop-up menu, choose your Open Directory CA–created SSL certificate, and click Next.

8 Click Finish.

Wait until the Server app returns you to the Profile Manager pane.

NOTE ▶ Device Management requires the Apple Push Notification service (APNs) to be turned on, which you did in Exercise 4.3, "Configure OS X Server for El Capitan."

9 At the bottom of the Profile Manager pane of the Server app, click the Open in Safari button for Profile Manager; or in Safari, open the Profile Manager administration portal (https://server*n*.local/profilemanager, where *n* is your student number), and authenticate with local administrator credentials.

10 Confirm that Devices and Device Groups appear in the sidebar.

11 In the sidebar, select Users.

12 Select a user.

13 Click the Devices tab; this is where the Profile Manager app displays devices associated with the user.

Of course, no devices are associated with the user at this time, but the Devices tab was not available until you configured the Profile Manager service to enable device enrollment.

Enable Automatic Push for the Marketing Group Configuration Profile

When you created the web clips for the Marketing group, device management was not enabled, and manual installation was the only way to distribute a configuration profile. Now that device management is enabled, you should enable automatic push for the marketing group web clips configuration profile so that in future exercises distribution happens automatically.

1   In the sidebar of the Profile Manager administration portal, select Groups.

2   Select the Marketing group, and then click the Settings tab.

3   Under Settings for Marketing, click Edit.

4   In the General payload, for Profile Distribution Type, select Automatic Push.

    This option is available only when device management is enabled.

    > **Profile Distribution Type**
    > The manner in which the profile is distributed to devices
    > ● Automatic Push ○ Manual Download

5   Click OK.

6   Click Save.

Exercise 7.2
Enroll Over the Air

> ▶ **Prerequisites**
>
> ▶ Exercise 6.4, "Clean Up Profiles"
>
> ▶ Exercise 7.1, "Enable Device Management"

Challenge

Use the user portal as Gary Pine to enroll an iOS device and a Mac computer. Confirm enrollment in Profile Manager.

Considerations

If you're already logged in to the Profile Manager administration portal as an administrator, first log out, and then log back in as a different user.

Solution

Enroll an iOS Device Using the User Portal

This exercise flows best if you start by using your iOS device to enroll itself and then use your client Mac computer to enroll itself.

1 On your iOS device, in Safari, open the user portal (https://server*n*.local/mydevices, where *n* is your student number).

2 If necessary, tap Logout to make sure you're not logged in as an administrator.

3 In the Please Log In window, deselect the checkbox "Keep me logged in.", enter the following credentials, and tap Log In:

▶ User Name: gary
▶ Password: net

4 Note that because you turned on device management, you see both a Devices tab and a Profiles tab; previously you saw only the available profiles.

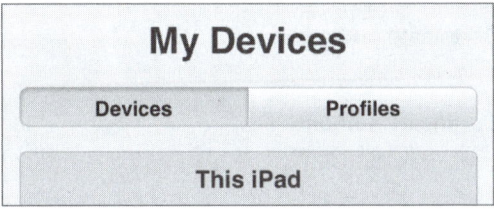

5 Tap Enroll.

252   Mobile Device Management

6   Tap More Details.

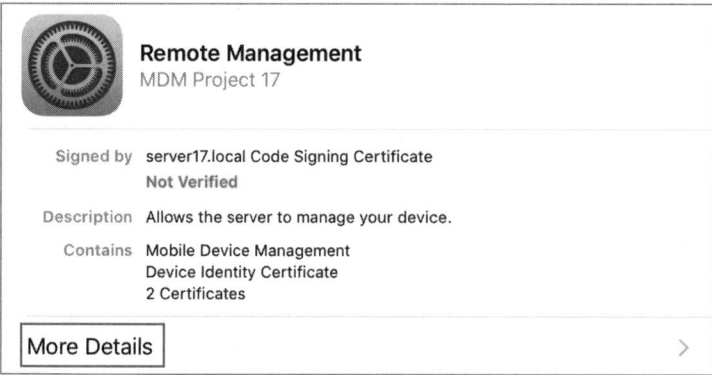

7   Inspect the contents of the profile.

Note that it contains several profiles.

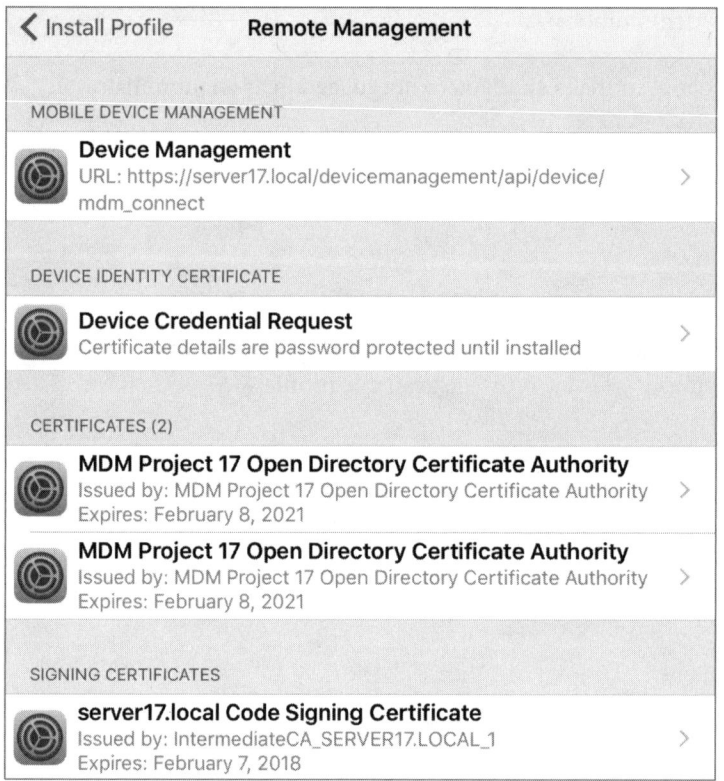

8   Tap the Device Management profile, and inspect its contents.

< Remote Management	**Device Management**
Server URL	https://server17.local/devicemanagement/api/device/mdm_connect
Topic	com.apple.mgmt.XServer.c2f8114d-a622-4924-874e-44a3ef068607
Check-in URL	https://server17.local/devicemanagement/api/device/mdm_checkin

9   Tap Remote Management in the upper-left corner of the pane, and then tap Install Profile in the upper-left corner of the pane to return to the Install Profile pane.

10 Tap Install.

11 In the Warning pane, tap Install.

    Installing this has serious implications for the user of this device.

12 In the Remote Management dialog, tap Trust.

13 Note that the Remote Management profile is listed as Not Verified.

14 Tap Done.

    You are returned to Safari.

15 Wait a few moments for the My Devices page to update. This may take up to 30 seconds. Optionally, you can choose to refresh the user portal.

    The updated page includes your iOS device's serial number; the Lock, Wipe, and Clear Passcode buttons; and a button to remove the device from management.

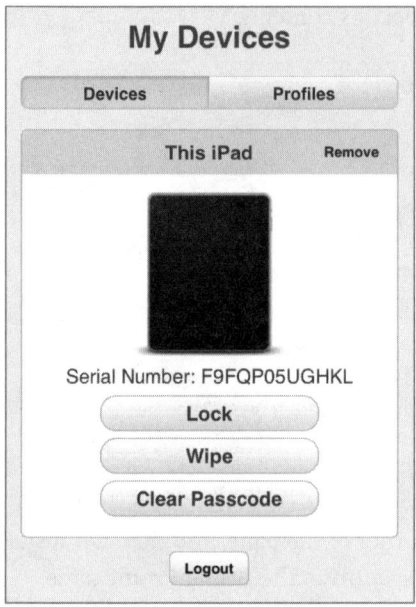

Enroll Your Client Mac Computer Using the User Portal

1   On your client Mac computer, in Safari, open the user portal (https://server*n*.local/mydevices, where *n* is your student number).

2   Click Logout to make sure you're not logged in as an administrator.

3   In the Please Log In window, deselect the checkbox "Keep me logged in," enter the following credentials, and click Log In:

▶   User Name: gary

▶   Password: net

4   Note that because you turned on device management, you see both a Devices tab and a Profiles tab; previously you saw only the available profiles.

    If you already enrolled an iOS device, you see that device in the list.

5   Click Enroll.

6   On your client Mac, click Show Profile.

    Inspect the contents of the profile.

7   Click Continue.

8   Click Show Details.

9   Scroll through the information, and note the warning text in red.

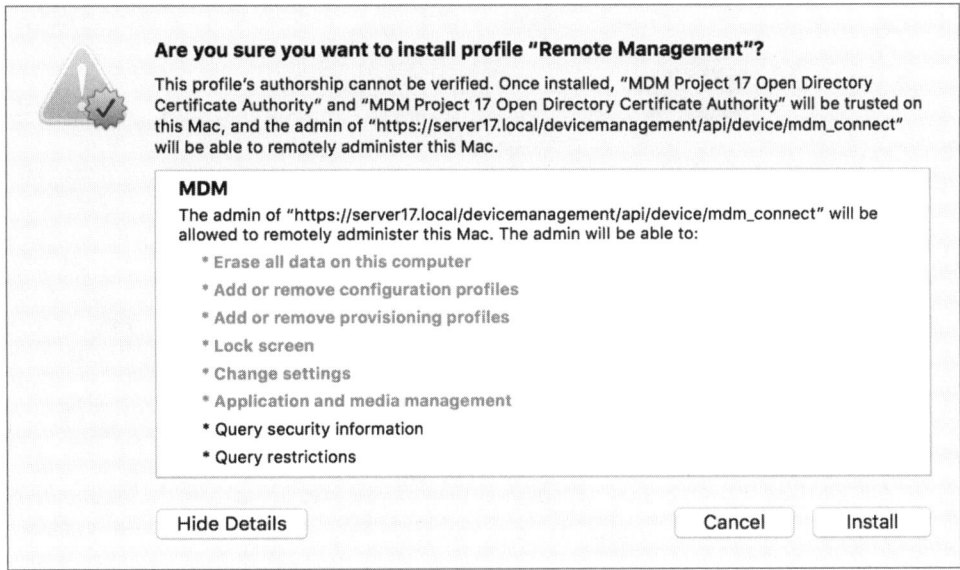

10 Click Install.

11 Enter the local administrator password, and click OK.

12 Inspect the contents of the profile, shown in the right column of Profiles preferences.

    Observe that the profile is now verified. When you entered your administrator credentials, your MDM server certificate trust settings were modified.

13 Quit System Preferences.

14 Wait a few moments for the user portal page to update. This may take up to 30 seconds. Optionally, you can choose to refresh the user portal.

    The updated page includes your Mac computer's serial number, the Lock and Wipe buttons, and a button to remove the device from management.

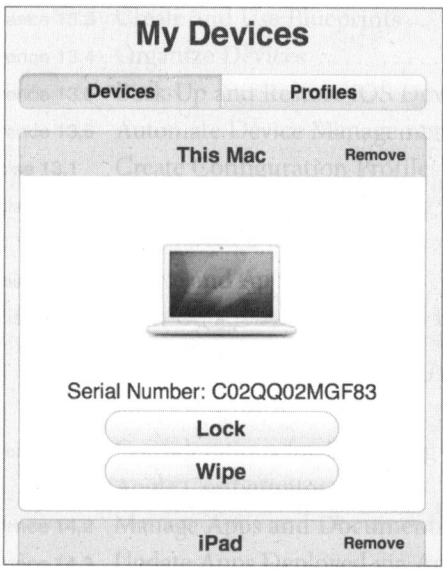

On the Server, Confirm That the Devices Are Enrolled

Even though the My Devices portal showed that the devices are enrolled, double-check with the Profile Manager administration portal.

1 If necessary, on your server, log in to the Profile Manager administration portal using local administrator credentials.

2 In the sidebar, select Devices.

   Confirm that the newly enrolled devices are in the list and are associated with the user who was logged in to the user portal when you enrolled the devices.

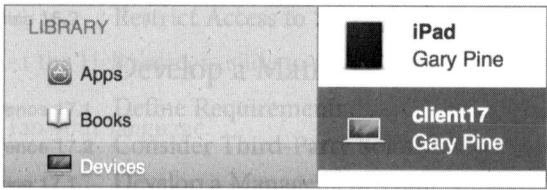

3 In the sidebar, select Users.

4 Select Gary Pine.

5   Click the Devices tab.

    Confirm that the newly enrolled devices are in the list.

    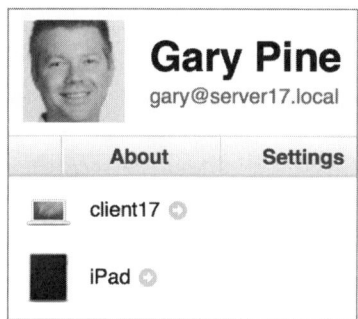

6   In the sidebar, select Completed Tasks.

7   Confirm that an Enroll Device task has completed for the iOS device and for the client Mac computer.

On the Devices, Confirm That the Devices Are Enrolled

When your iOS device is enrolled with device management and doesn't have any other profiles, the entry in the General portion of the Settings app is listed as Device Management instead of Profile or Profiles.

1   On your iOS device, press the Home button, and then open Settings > General > Device Management.

2   Confirm that the Remote Management profile is displayed.

    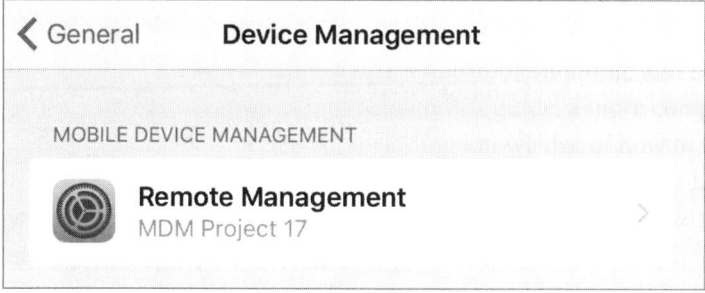

3   Tap the Remote Management profile.

4   Confirm that the profile is listed as Verified with a checkmark.

5   On your client Mac computer, open System Preferences, and then open Profiles preferences.

6   Confirm that the Remote Management profile is displayed.

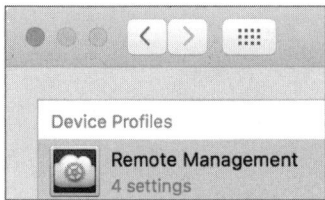

7   Confirm that the preference is listed in green as Verified (the last time you inspected this profile, it was listed in red as Unverified).

8   Quit System Preferences.

In this exercise, you used network user credentials at the user portal to enroll your client Mac computer and your iOS device over the air.

Exercise 7.3
Deploy Management Settings

▶ **Prerequisite**

   ▸ Exercise 7.2, "Enroll Over the Air"

Challenge
Now that you have a device enrolled as a user (Gary Pine), create a configuration profile for a group the user is a member of (Engineering) that contains a web link to a wiki page for that group. Confirm that the configuration profile is automatically installed on the enrolled device.

Make another set of changes to the Engineering configuration profile (force a minimum passcode length, and configure Safari for OS X so that windows open to the Apple Support page), and confirm that the changes are automatically applied over the air.

Considerations

Remember that you use the Server app to manage users and groups; when editing a group, you have access to a button to create a wiki for the group. Changes you make with the Server app should appear immediately in the Profile Manager administration portal; if not, try refreshing the webpage.

Passcode payload settings apply to iOS and OS X, but you notice the OS X changes only when local users change their passwords. You notice passcode requirements immediately on an iOS device.

You can use the Custom Settings payload to set key-value pairs. Inspecting an app's property list (plist file) can help you figure out which key-value pairs to specify, but you can discover many commonly used settings with an Internet search.

Solution

Create a Wiki Page for the Engineering Group

1   On your server computer, open the Server app, and authenticate as a local administrator.

2   In the Server app sidebar, select Groups.

3   Click the pop-up menu, and choose Local Network Groups.

   NOTE ▶ If the bottom of the Groups pane displays a locked lock icon, it is possible that you do not have directory administrator credentials in your keychain. If this is the case, click the lock icon, provide directory administrator credentials (it may be Administrator Name: diradmin, Administrator Password: diradminpw), select the checkbox "Remember this password in my keychain," and then click Authenticate.

4   Control-click the Engineering group, and then choose Edit Group.

5 Click Create Group Wiki.

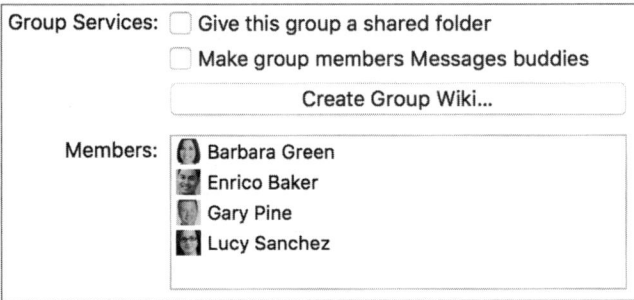

6 Enter Engineering wiki in the Description field. Leave the Name field as Engineering.

7 Click Continue.

8 In the Permissions field, start typing Engineering, and then choose Engineering (engineering). Note that you must actually click the choice that appears.

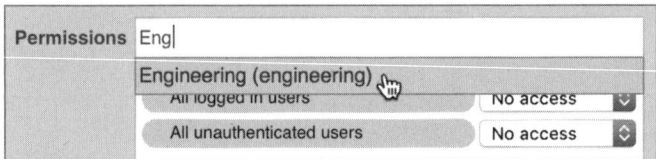

9 For the Engineering entry, set the permissions to Read & write.

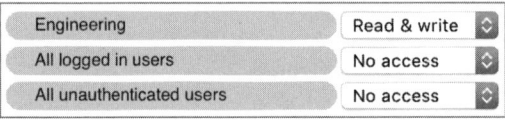

10 Click Continue.

11 Optionally select a different color scheme, and then click Create.

12 In the "Setup complete" pane, click Go to Wiki.

13 In Safari, choose File > Open Location (or press Command-L), which selects the URL.

14 Choose Edit > Copy (or press Command-C) to copy the URL.

You will paste this text in a configuration profile in the next section.

15 Close the Engineering wiki Safari window.

16 The Server app still displays the details of the Engineering group.

Click OK to return to the Groups pane.

Create a Configuration Profile for a Group the User Is a Member Of

1 If you do not already have the Profile Manager administration portal open on your server Mac, in Safari, open https://servern.local/profilemanager (where *n* is your student number), and then authenticate with local administrator credentials.

2 In the Profile Manager administration portal, select Groups.

3 Select Engineering.

4 Click the Settings tab.

5 Click Edit.

6 Leave Profile Distribution Type set to Automatic Push.

7 Enter Engineering group settings in the Description field.

8 Leave the other settings at their defaults.

9 In the payload sidebar, select Web Clips.

10 Click Configure.

11 In the Label field, enter Engineering wiki.

12 Click in the URL field, and then choose Edit > Paste (or press Command-V) to paste the URL you previously copied. The URL is https://servern.local/wiki/projects/engineering/Engineering.html (where *n* is your student number).

Label
The name to display for the Web Clip
Engineering wiki

URL
The URL to be displayed when opening the Web Clip
https://server17.local/wiki/projects/engineering/Engineering.html

13 Click OK.

14 Click Save.

15 Click the Members tab, and confirm that Gary Pine is listed as a member.

Confirm That the Configuration Profile Is Automatically Installed on the Enrolled Devices

1 On your iOS device, press the Home button, and if your iOS device is locked, swipe to unlock.

2 Look for the Engineering wiki web clip.

   On your client Mac, look for the Engineering wiki item in the Dock. Hover the pointer over the web link in the Dock to display the name of the file.

3 Optionally, tap or click the Engineering wiki item, and confirm that it opens to the wiki page.

4 On your server, in the Profile Manager administration portal sidebar, select Completed Tasks.

5 Confirm that the Push Settings: Engineering task is listed as Succeeded.

Add a Passcode Requirement to the Engineering Group Configuration Profile

1   On your server Mac, in the Profile Manager administration portal sidebar, click Groups, select Engineering, and then click the Settings tab.

2   In the Settings for Engineering field, click Edit.

3   In the payload sidebar, select Passcode.

4   Click Configure.

5   Click the "Minimum passcode length" pop-up menu, and choose 5.

Configure New Safari Windows to Open to Apple Support

1   In the payload sidebar, select Custom Settings.

    You may need to scroll because it is the last item in the list of settings.

2   Click Configure.

3   Enter com.apple.Safari in the Preference Domain field.

    Be sure to capitalize Safari, as custom settings are case sensitive.

4   Below the Property List Values field, click Add Item.

5   Double-click New Item, and then enter HomePage in the Key field.

6   Leave Type as String.

7   In the Value field, enter help.apple.com/profilemanager/mac.

Create a key NewWindowBehavior with the value of 0. This affects what happens when you open a new Safari window; 0 indicates that Safari will open a new window with whatever your home page is set to be.

1   Click Add Item.

2   Enter NewWindowBehavior in the Key field.

3   Set Type to Number.

4   Leave 0 (zero) in the Value field.

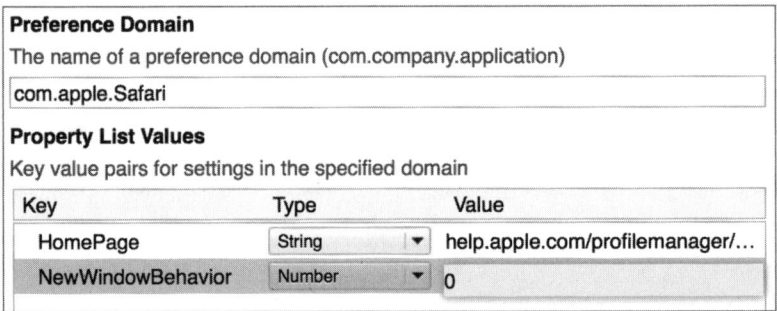

5   Confirm that your settings are correct.

6   Click OK.

7   Confirm that Settings for Engineering contains settings for Passcode, Web Clips, and Custom Settings.

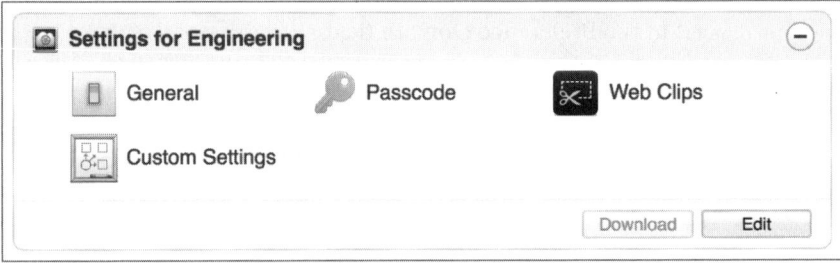

8   Click Save.

Confirm That the New Passcode Requirement Takes Effect on Your iOS Device

1   On your iOS device, press the Home button, and if your iOS device is locked, swipe to unlock.

2   If necessary, press the Home button, and in the Passcode Requirement dialog, tap Continue.

3   Attempt to set a three-character passcode by entering 123 and tapping Continue.

4   At the message that the passcode must be longer, enter the longer passcode 12345, and tap Continue.

   NOTE ▶ In a production environment, use a secure passcode.

5   Reenter 12345 as your new passcode, and tap Save.

Confirm That the New Safari Behavior Takes Effect on Your Client Mac

1   On your client Mac, quit Safari. Be sure to fully quit the application by going to Safari > Quit.

2   Open Safari, and confirm that the new window opens to the Profile Manager Help page.

3   Confirm that the new window opens to the Profile Manager Help page.

4   Press Command-W to close the Profile Manager Help page.

In this exercise, you created a wiki for the Engineering group, and you demonstrated that changes to configuration profiles were automatically applied over the air to your enrolled Mac and to your enrolled iOS device.

Exercise 7.4
Unenroll Over the Air

▶ **Prerequisite**

   ▶   Exercise 7.3, "Deploy Management Settings"

Challenge
Use the user portal to remove the device from management, and confirm that all the configuration profiles that were automatically installed are automatically removed. Use your iOS device to remove your client Mac, while watching Profiles preferences on your client Mac. Use your client Mac to remove your iOS device, while watching the Profiles setting on your iOS device.

Confirm that the settings from the configuration profiles are no longer in effect on the unenrolled devices.

Confirm that after you unenroll, a placeholder is left for the device in the Profile Manager list of devices.

Remove all configuration profiles from the Downloads folder on your client Mac.

Solution

Use the User Portal from Your Client Mac to Remove Your iOS Device from Management
On your iOS device, display the installed profiles, and then watch the profiles automatically disappear immediately after you use the user portal to remove the iOS device from management.

1   On your client Mac, open the user portal (https://server*n*.local/mydevices, where *n* is your student number) in Safari.

    Note that you can access this page from any modern browser on any platform; you do not need to use the enrolled computer or device.

2   If you do not see your two devices listed, click Logout, and log back in as Gary Pine (User Name: gary, Password: net).

3   On your iOS device, open Settings, and then navigate to General > Device Management.

4   Tap the Remote Management profile.

5   Tap Restrictions.

6   Confirm that the Passcode restriction for five or more characters is present.

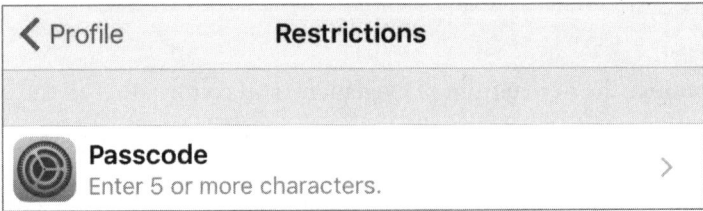

7   Tap Profile in the upper-left corner to return to the Remote Management pane of the profile.

8   Tap More Details.

9   Confirm that both the web clip with the label of Engineering wiki and the custom payload for com.apple.Safari are displayed.

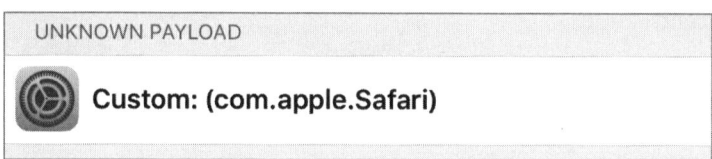

10 Return to the main General settings by tapping General.

11 On your client Mac, in the user portal, click Remove for your iOS device.

If nothing happens, choose View > Refresh, and try again.

12 At the confirmation dialog, click OK.

After you click OK on your client Mac, look at your iOS device, and watch as the Device Management button changes to Profile.

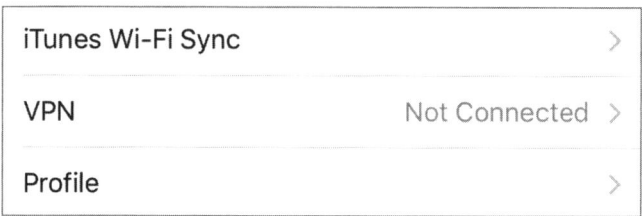

13 On your client Mac, confirm that the iOS device no longer appears in the My Devices portal.

14 On your iOS device, open Safari.

15 If Safari already displays the user portal, tap Refresh; otherwise, open https://servern.local/mydevices (where *n* is your student number), and authenticate as gary with the password net if necessary.

16 Confirm that your iOS device is displayed with an Enroll button, but do not tap Enroll.

Use the User Portal from Your iOS Device to Remove Your Client Mac from Management

On your client Mac, display the installed profiles, and then watch the profiles automatically disappear immediately after you use the user portal from your iOS device to remove the Mac from management.

1 On your client Mac, open System Preferences.

2 Open Profiles preferences.

3 Confirm that in the User Profiles section, Settings for Engineers is displayed, and confirm that in the Device Profiles section, Remote Management is displayed.

4 On your iOS device, for your enrolled client Mac, tap Remove.

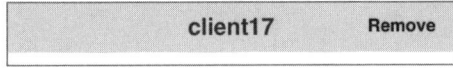

5 In the confirmation dialog, tap OK, and then watch your client Mac computer's screen.

After you confirm, the Settings for Engineering profile disappears, the Remote Management profile disappears, and then Profiles preferences close.

System Preferences displays all the preferences.

6   Quit System Preferences.

Confirm That the Effects of Management Are Removed

Removing management does not remove the passcode; this is an expected security feature. If you want to remove the passcode or set a shorter passcode, you can do that now.

1   On your iOS device, press the Home button, and confirm that the Engineering wiki web clip is gone.

2   On your client Mac, confirm that the Engineering wiki web link is no longer in the Dock.

    You already confirmed that System Preferences does not display the Profiles pane.

3   On your server, in the Profile Manager administration portal sidebar, select Completed Tasks.

4   Confirm that the Remove Device tasks for your client Mac computer and your iOS device are listed as Succeeded.

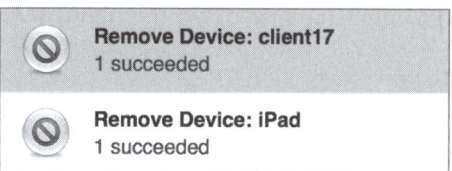

5   On your iOS device, open Settings, and then open Touch ID & Passcode, or Passcode, depending on the model of your iOS device.

6   Enter the existing five-character passcode (12345), and tap Done.

7 Tap Turn Passcode Off.

8 Enter the existing passcode, and tap Done.

9 Press the Home button.

Inspect the Placeholders

1 On your server Mac, open the Profile Manager administration portal.

2 In the Profile Manager administration portal sidebar, select Devices.

3 Confirm that an iOS device and a Mac computer are displayed, each with the name of the user last associated with the device and a prohibitory icon.

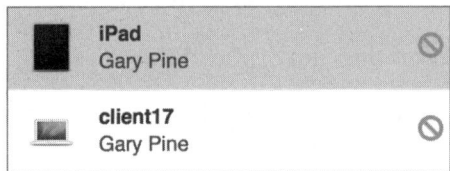

4 In the list of devices, select your client Mac computer.

5 Confirm that Placeholder is displayed in the upper-right corner of the right column.

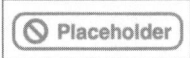

Cleanup: Remove the Placeholders

1 With the placeholder record for your client Mac computer still selected, click Remove (–) near the bottom of the Profile Manager administration portal window.

2 In the confirmation dialog, click Remove Placeholder.

3 Select the placeholder record for your iOS device, and then click Remove (–).

4 In the confirmation dialog, click Remove Placeholder.

Cleanup: Remove Configuration Profiles from Your Downloads Folder

1 On your client Mac, in the Finder, choose Go > Downloads.

2 Drag all the files that end with *mobileconfig* to the Trash.

3 Choose Finder > Empty Trash.

In this exercise, you watched as profiles were removed automatically after you unenrolled. You inspected the placeholders. You removed the profiles from your Downloads folder.

Lesson 8
Out-of-the-Box Management via Apple Programs for Device Enrollment

NOTE ▶ Prior to April 2016, both businesses and schools used the Device Enrollment Program through the Apple Deployment Programs website. However, after Apple introduced Apple School Manager in April 2016, schools can upgrade to using Apple School Manager instead of Apple Deployment Programs. These two programs are similar, but this guide focuses on the DEP, and the exercises are written for the DEP. For more information about Apple School Manager, see https://help.apple.com/schoolmanager/.

GOALS

▶ Understand how Apple School for Manager (for schools) and the Device Enrollment Program (DEP), which is part of Apple Deployment Programs (for business), can be used to manage the deployment of institutionally owned devices

▶ Configure Profile Manager to take advantage of the DEP service

It takes only one trip to an Apple store and one time opening a new Apple device to see how much attention to detail goes into the experience of using a new Apple device. The designers at Apple spend countless hours crafting the details of the box that every device comes in. Software engineers also carefully design the series of screens, called Setup Assistant, you first see when you turn on a new Apple device.

In short, Apple really cares about the user experience, and it wants the user's first experience with an Apple product to be great. Ideally, when users first experience an Apple device owned and managed by your organization, it should be just as good as, if not better than, setting up a personally owned device. In fact, with good planning and the proper implementation, you can give users a similar out-of-the box Apple experience and then some.

This lesson explores a deployment workflow where the administrator never needs to physically touch a user's device. Instead, the user will set up the device and during Setup Assistant enroll the device into management. After that, your Mobile Device Management (MDM) service will take over to make sure the device receives the appropriate configuration. Specifically, this lesson details how to use the Apple Device Enrollment Program to manage Setup Assistant.

Reference 8.1
Introduction to Apple Programs for Device Enrollment

The Apple programs for device enrollment (which consist of the Device Enrollment Program [DEP], part of Apple Deployment Programs for businesses, and Apple School Manager for schools) provide a streamlined mechanism for organizations to quickly enroll organizationally owned OS X and iOS devices into their organization's MDM service. Further, an administrator can use the DEP service or Apple School Manager to enforce management requirements for both iOS and OS X devices and prevent unauthorized use of iOS devices that have been reset.

This section provides an overview of the DEP service and Apple School Manager, including both the requirements and limitations of the services.

DEP Service and Apple School Manager Overview

From a technical perspective, the DEP service and Apple School Manager use a combination of web-based services and local system software to manage the setup and activation process on Apple devices. The DEP service and Apple School Manager rely upon the fact that during the Setup Assistant process of both iOS and OS X, once a device is connected to a network, it will attempt to communicate with Apple's activation servers.

For devices not taking part in the DEP service or Apple School Manager, device activation completes silently in the background. However, devices in these enrollment programs can be redirected to your MDM service during setup. If the MDM service is configured for the appropriate enrollment program, assigned devices will connect with the MDM service during the Setup Assistant process. This allows administrators to customize the setup experience and enforce management, with all of it delivered automatically over the air the first time a device is turned on.

Devices in the DEP or Apple School Manager benefit from the following administrative features, which are available only for devices that are in the DEP or Apple School Manager:

- ▶ Setup Assistant customization—For both iOS devices and OS X computers, administrators can configure Setup Assistant to skip specific setup screens. You can also configure Setup Assistant to facilitate user-based MDM enrollment by prompting the user to authenticate and complete the enrollment.

- ▶ Pause Setup Assistant—A new feature for iOS 9 or later and OS X 10.11 or later, an MDM that supports this feature can pause Setup Assistant until the device has completed installing apps and is otherwise configured and ready for the user. Note that if there are a large number of apps to be installed, this can take a considerable amount of time and negatively impact the user experience.

- Updates—The MDM can send a command to a device with iOS 9 or later that's enrolled in your MDM via the DEP or Apple School Manager to download and install software updates.

- User-based enrollment enforcement—Administrators can require that user-based MDM enrollment be completed during Setup Assistant. In other words, a user must perform an MDM enrollment to complete Setup Assistant. After setup, unless the device is erased, device management cannot be removed from Mac computers (with OS X Yosemite or later) or devices with iOS 7.1 or later, which means that enrolling via the DEP or Apple School Manager is the only method to permanently enforce MDM service enrollment. And you can prevent a user from wiping her supervised iOS device with iOS 9.3 or later by restricting the device from pairing with computers, disallowing the option Erase All Content and Settings, and not allowing the user access to the My Devices user portal.

    NOTE ▶ At the time of this writing, if an OS X computer is not able to connect to the appropriate enrollment service during Setup Assistant, the user can choose to skip the enrollment, which means that you are not technically able to enforce the enrollment.

- Theft deterrence—An administrator can require that iOS devices in the DEP or Apple School Manager must be enrolled during setup, which prevents unauthorized users from completing Setup Assistant. This enrollment renders an organizationally owned device that has been erased and reset useless for anyone who is not in your organization. Administrators should let users know that if a device goes missing, it can be remotely wiped and rendered useless.

- Remote supervision—For iOS devices, administrators can remotely enable supervised mode during Setup Assistant when the device enrolls. As covered previously, supervision is a method to prove ownership of a device, thus allowing greater administrative control. Remote supervision is allowed via DEP or Apple School Manager because they are the only methods where an organization can prove ownership of Apple devices without using Apple Configurator or Apple Configurator 2.

You can use the DEP and Apple School Manager in conjunction with Apple Configurator 2 to automatically enroll shared iOS devices with your MDM solution with minimal interaction on the iOS devices. See Lesson 13, "Apple Configurator 2: Preparing, Configuring, and Managing iOS Devices," for more information.

Finally, recognize that these enrollment programs are designed only to manage the initial configuration and enrollment of a device. After setup is complete, devices will effectively be like new, and a significant amount of additional configuration may be necessary. Other workflows, such as that available via Apple Configurator 2 (as covered in Lessons 12 through 14), provide a more complete method for deploying similarly configured devices.

> **TIP** ▸ If for some reason your organization cannot take advantage of the DEP service or Apple School Manager, you can still take advantage of Activation Lock to prevent unauthorized access to reset Apple devices. Activation Lock is covered in Lesson 9, "Activation Lock Management."

DEP Service Requirements

If you are considering taking advantage of the DEP service or Apple School Manager, you should be aware of the requirements. Because these services require that Apple validate organizational ownership, there are several technical and procedural requirements.

Technical requirements for DEP include the following:

▸ Device eligibility—To be eligible for the appropriate enrollment program, devices must be purchased either directly from Apple using your organization's Apple customer number after March 1, 2011, or from a participating Apple Authorized Reseller or carrier that linked the order to that reseller's DEP Reseller ID. (The actual date of device eligibility for orders from the participating reseller or carrier is determined by the sales history of that reseller or carrier, but the earliest ordered date is March 1, 2011.)

> **MORE INFO** ▸ Contact your Apple sales representative to inquire how to purchase devices eligible for the DEP or Apple School Manager. At the time of this writing, for example, any device that you purchase from an Apple Store must be shipped to you for it to be eligible for these enrollment programs; you cannot walk into an Apple Store, purchase a new iPad, walk out of the store with it, and have it be eligible for the DEP or Apple School Manager enrollment programs.

> **NOTE** ▸ See Apple Support article HT204401, "Device Enrollment Program: Understanding Apple Customer Numbers, DEP Reseller IDs, and DEP Customer IDs."

▸ System version—iOS devices must be running iOS 7.1 or later, and OS X devices must be running OS X 10.9 Mavericks or later.

- Internet connection—Both the MDM service and managed devices must have Internet access. This Internet access must not block, proxy, or otherwise filter outbound connections to Apple services.
- MDM service compatibility—Not every MDM service has been updated to support the DEP service and Apple School Manager. For example, OS X Server must be updated to version 3.1 or later for Profile Manager to support the DEP service or Apple School Manager. Check with your MDM service vendor to verify support for the DEP service and Apple School Manager.
- MDM service availability—Devices in the DEP and Apple School Manager must be able to connect to your MDM service to complete Setup Assistant. Your MDM service doesn't have to be available on the Internet, but if it isn't, iOS devices in the DEP that are off your network and cannot connect to your MDM service will not be able to complete Setup Assistant.
- Browser version—The Apple Deployment Programs site and Apple School Manager site are supported only by modern browsers: Safari 6.0.3 or later on OS X, Internet Explorer 9.0.8 or later on Windows, and Google Chrome 27.0.1 or later.

Program requirements for the DEP include the following:

- Regional availability—At the time of this writing, the DEP service and Apple School Manager are available in many regions but not in all regions where Apple devices are sold. To see whether the appropriate Apple enrollment program is available for your country or region, for businesses check https://deploy.apple.com/enroll/selectcountry/, and for schools, search for "Manage devices overview" at https://help.apple.com/schoolmanager/.
- Organization requirements for businesses—To take advantage of the DEP as a business, your organization must exist as a legal entity and have a direct sales agreement with Apple or an Apple authorized reseller that participates in the DEP service. An organization with direct sales access will already have an Apple customer number. If your organization purchases through a reseller, you will need to coordinate with your reseller for access to the appropriate enrollment program. Your business must also have a registered Data Universal Numbering System (D-U-N-S) number, which must match your organization's legal name and address. If you don't know this information, contact your organization's purchasing agent or finance department.
- Organization requirement for schools—To take advantage of Apple School Manager, your organization can be a K–12 institution or district, or any accredited, degree-granting higher education institution.

▶ Administrative requirements—For you to personally enroll an organization in the DEP service or Apple School Manager, you must have the legal authority to bind your organization to the DEP agreement. Further, someone else in your organization cannot have already enrolled for the DEP or Apple School Manager using the same Apple Customer Number. Apple will verify these details during the enrollment process.

DEP Service Enrollment

> **NOTE** ▶ This section focuses on the DEP service for businesses. See https://school.apple.com for detailed information about the process for Apple School Manager.

If you think your organization meets the requirements to take advantage of the DEP service, you can begin the enrollment process at https://deploy.apple.com. Click the Enroll Now link to set up your organization for DEP or the other available Apple deployment program: the Volume Purchase Program (VPP).

When you enroll in the DEP service, you must use an email address that has not been used by any other Apple services outside of the other Apple deployment programs; in other words, you must use an email address that has never been associated with an Apple ID, and which is associated with your organization. In other words, you should not use an email address that ends with your organization's domain, and not an email address that ends with @gmail.com or @yahoo.com, for example. Further, after Apple creates the Apple ID, you will need to enable two-step verification for this Apple ID. These Apple ID requirements are for security reasons. The individual who enrolls the organization for the DEP service will be known as the *program agent*. The program agent Apple ID must be associated with an appropriate individual at your organization.

> **NOTE** ▶ If the program agent wants to use the same Apple ID for both VPP and DEP, she must complete the enrollment for one of the two programs first. Once the enrollment is complete for one of the programs, she should sign in to the Apple Deployment Programs site before enrolling into the other program. In other words, if she attempts to enroll into another program from the start page before signing in, she will have to enroll with a different email address.

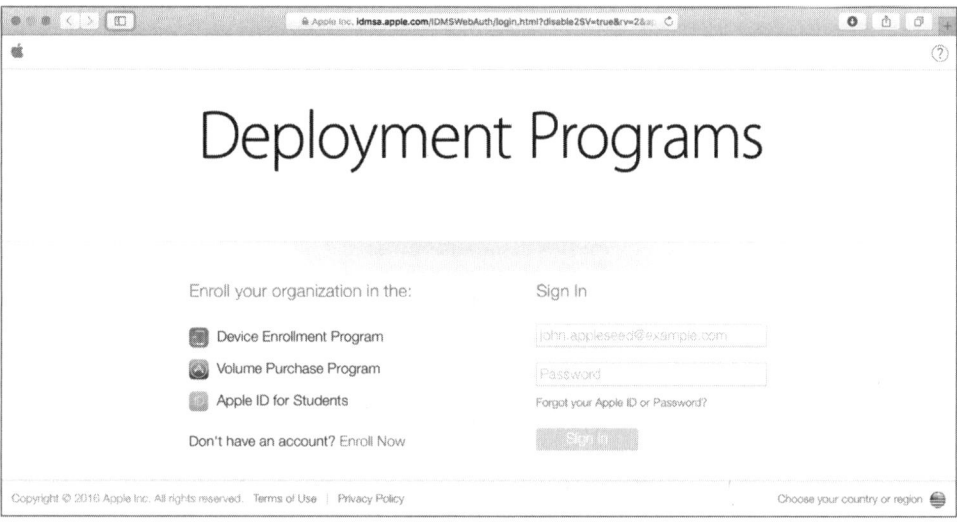

During enrollment for the DEP service, the program agent will provide organizational information along with a verification contact. This verification contact, usually a senior manager, will be personally contacted by Apple to verify the program agent's authority to bind the organization to the DEP agreement.

Once the program agent has completed the DEP service enrollment process and Apple has verified the organization information, Apple creates the program agent Apple ID using the email address used in the enrollment process. The program agent's Apple ID will be granted access to the DEP portion of the Apple Deployment Programs site. From the Apple Deployment Programs site, the program agent can be the sole administrator for the program or she can grant other Apple IDs with the ability to manage DEP, as covered in the next section of this lesson.

> **MORE INFO** ▶ For additional information regarding the process involved with Apple programs for device enrollment, visit the help documentation at https://help.apple.com/deployment/business/ or https://help.apple.com/deployment/education/.

Managing DEP Administrators

Upon initial registration in the DEP service, only the program agent will have access to the Apple Deployment Programs site (https://deploy.apple.com). However, this person can assign additional administrators from the Apple Deployment Programs site by clicking the Admins on the left and then Add Admin Account to the right.

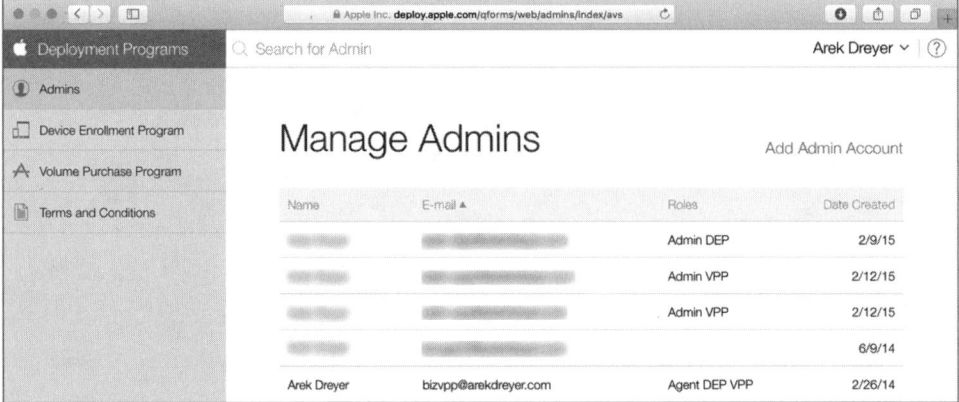

NOTE ▶ At the time of this writing, the Apple ID that you use to enroll your school for Apple School Manager is referred to as the administrator, and you can use the administrator to create one or more manager, which is similar to the Apple Deployment Programs program agent role.

To add another administrator, you must specify a first name and a last name along with a verifiable email address. You'll note that the email address for additional administrators doesn't have to match your organization's domain, which allows you to grant DEP administrative ability to consultants or nonemployee service agents. Also, it's important that the email address not have been used as an Apple ID for any other Apple services or websites.

The Apple Deployment Programs site will automatically generate an email invitation message for the new administrator. She will have to use the temporary password in the email invitation message to sign in at https://appleid.apple.com/; then she must enable two-step verification and agree to the DEP administrator terms at the Apple Deployment Programs site.

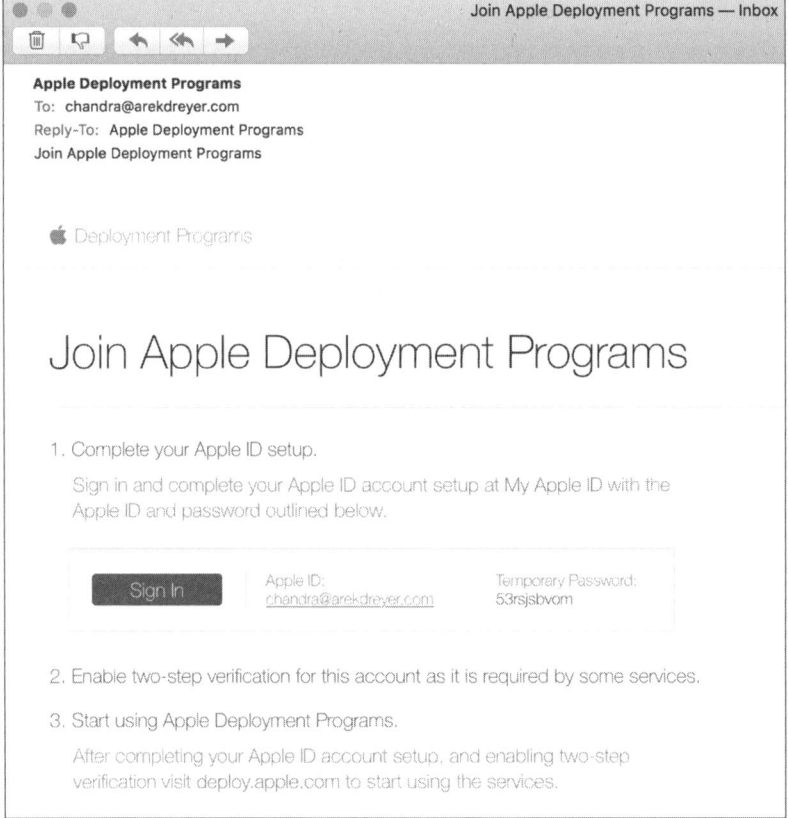

After she has completed these steps, she will be added as an administrator. The program agent can grant an administrator the ability to manage the DEP service, other Apple Deployment Services such as the Volume Purchase Program (VPP), and the ability to create other administrators.

> **NOTE** ▶ The DEP server token must be replaced annually by repeating the same process used to install the server token. Also, making changes to the Apple ID password that was used to set up the DEP server requires a server token replacement.

Reference 8.2
Integrate the DEP with Profile Manager

> **NOTE ▶** The information in this section applies to businesses using the DEP service. Schools can use Apple School Manager instead. Although the core concepts are similar, implementation details differ. See https://help.apple.com/schoolmanager/ for more information.

In this section, you will see how to use the DEP service with Apple's Profile Manager service. That being said, the core technologies behind the DEP service remain the same even between different MDM service implementations. Thus, even if your organization chooses to use another MDM service, the concepts covered in this guide still apply.

> **MORE INFO ▶** Detailed step-by-step instructions for using the DEP with Profile Manager are presented in the exercises found later in this lesson.

Assuming your organization's DEP account is active and you have access to the Apple Deployment Programs site, there are three general steps for integrating the DEP service with your MDM service:

1. Configure the service trusts between the DEP service and your MDM service. This step is required only one time for each server configured. However, at a minimum, the DEP server token must be replaced annually by repeating the same process used to install the server token.
2. From the Apple Deployment Programs site, assign Apple devices to your MDM service. It's likely that you will return to the Apple Deployment Programs site on occasion to verify and manage device assignments.
3. From your MDM service, configure device records from DEP assignments to customize the Setup Assistant behavior. As DEP device assignments change, it's likely that you'll also need to verify and manage the device enrollment settings on your MDM service.

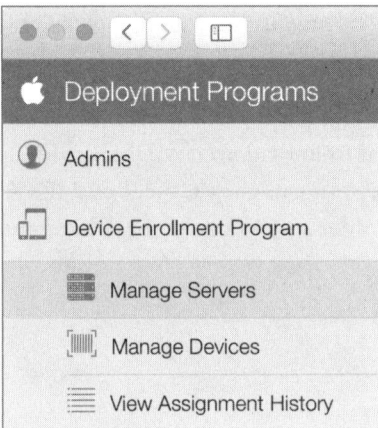

Add Servers in DEP

The first step to using the DEP service is to create a trust relationship between the DEP service and your MDM service. This involves a two-step process. First you will upload your MDM service's public key to the DEP service, and then you will download a server token from the DEP service to install into your MDM service.

Start by signing in to the Apple Deployment Programs site. In the sidebar, select Device Enrollment Program, and then select Manage Servers. Click the Add MDM Server text to the right. A dialog will appear where you can give your server a descriptive name. The name you enter here does not have to match the MDM service host name, but that would probably be a good idea.

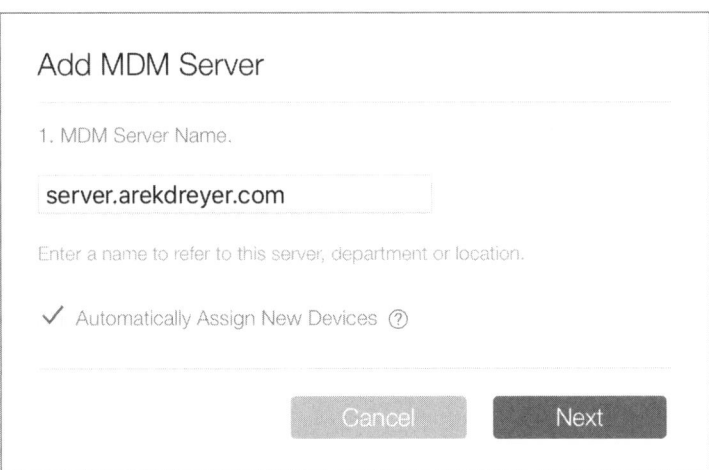

TIP ▶ The option Automatically Assign New Devices can be a huge time-saver when you purchase future Apple devices. However, devices purchased prior to the configuration of this MDM server cannot be automatically assigned.

After you've named your server, you will be prompted to upload your MDM service's public key. If you don't have a public key readily available, you can click Cancel, and the Apple Deployment Programs site will make a server placeholder so you can go back later and upload your public key when ready.

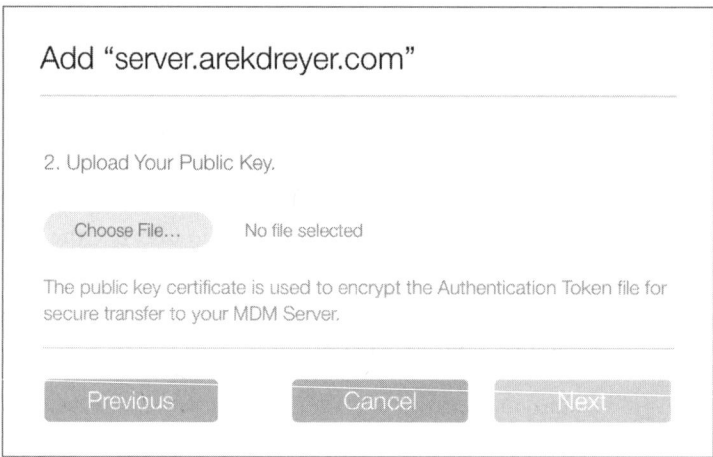

If you're using Profile Manager and device management is enabled, you can acquire the public key from the Profile Manager pane of the Server app. Selecting the option to enroll devices using the Device Enrollment Program opens an assistant that eventually allows you to export (or save) your public key to the local Mac computer. The default name of the file will be DeviceEnrollmentPublicKey.pem; a good temporary location for this file is your Downloads folder.

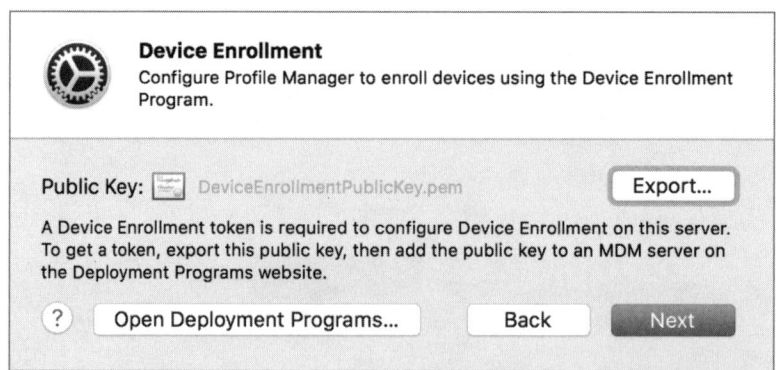

Return to the Apple Deployment Programs site to upload the MDM service public key by clicking the "Choose file" button. Once the public key is uploaded and you click Next, you will be allowed to download a server token by clicking the Your Server Token link. Click Done, and the server setup will be complete on the Apple Deployment Programs site.

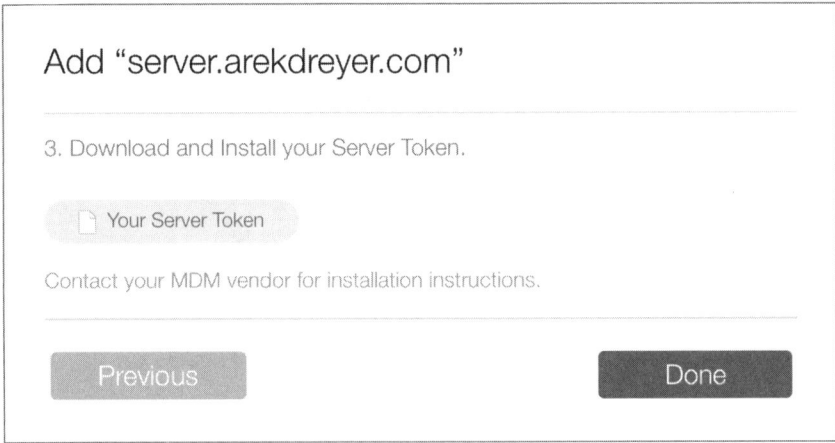

Head back to the Server app one more time, and you can click Choose to select the server token. As you can see in the following screenshot, the server token will have a long name that starts with the name of your server followed by "_Token_" and some other information. You can find it in your default Downloads folder.

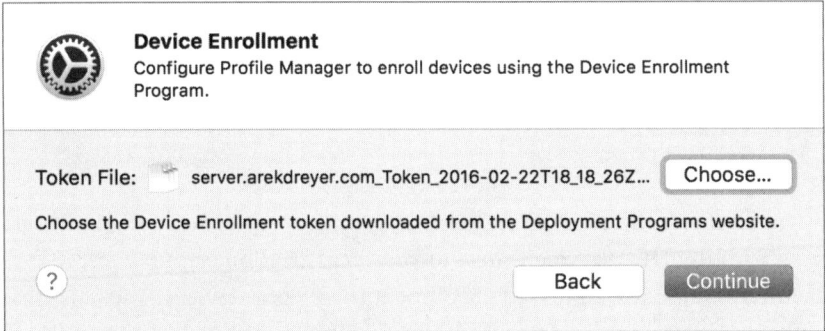

After you specify the token file and click Continue, the Server app imports the server, and Profile Manager is now set up for the DEP service as well. The Server app displays information about the token, including its expiration date. If you do not have Apple Configurator 2 installed and configured yet, you can leave the "Use Apple Configurator to configure enrolled devices" checkbox unselected at this time and click Done; you can return to this later.

NOTE ▶ Again, the DEP server token must be replaced annually by repeating the same process used to install the server token. Also, making changes to the Apple ID password that was used to set up the DEP server requires a server token replacement.

NOTE ▶ Occasionally the DEP service terms and conditions will change. The DEP program agent will be informed of these changes via an email message. In this case, your organization's DEP program agent will need to log in to the Apple Deployment Programs site and agree to the new terms. The DEP service may be unavailable until the new terms are accepted.

Manage Servers in DEP

You can always add servers or edit existing servers from the Apple Deployment Programs site. If managing with the DEP service is new to your organization, set up a test MDM service first before rolling out DEP-based enrollment to all your devices. You can create an unlimited number of servers in the Apple Deployment Programs site, but just make sure to properly assign your devices between servers.

NOTE ▶ Profile Manager supports only a single DEP server configuration. If you have a more complex organization with multiple DEP instances or a need to segregate DEP device assignments, you should consider a third-party MDM service capable of handling more complex DEP configurations.

Server Name	Number of Devices	Last Connected ▼	Last Connected IP
server.arekdreyer.com	1	Today	71.239.73.197
SimpleMDM	0	Today	52.10.146.89
Arekdreyer jamfcloud	1	Today	54.208.14.206
Meraki	0	2/3/2016	108.161.147.67
Bushel	0	1/20/2016	54.164.201.227
ElCapVM.local	0	11/22/2015	71.239.73.197

In the previous screenshot, the illuminated (green) device icon next to the server name indicates that all new devices will be automatically assigned to that server. To change this option to another server in the list, simply click the dimmed device icon next to the server's name. The server list will also show a full tally of the number of Apple devices assigned to your MDM servers.

Clicking a server's name will reveal more information about the server. The Server Details dialog allows you to download a comma-separated values (CSV) file of serial numbers assigned to this server, change the server's name, replace the server's public key, download a new server token, or delete the server configuration altogether. Deleting a server will require that you reassign or unassign all devices associated with that server.

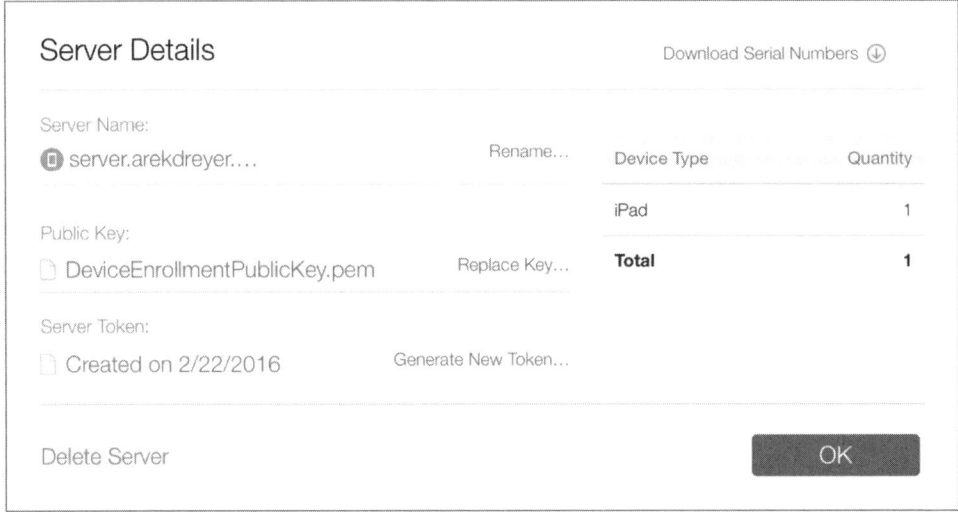

Assign Devices in the DEP

Once your organization is enrolled in the DEP service, any Apple devices associated with your organization can be assigned to an MDM server from the Apple Deployment Programs site. As covered previously, new purchases of Apple devices can be automatically assigned to an MDM server, but you will have to manually assign devices from past purchases.

In the Apple Deployment Programs site, you can assign devices to MDM servers en masse or individually. Assignment en masse is typically the most efficient method because a list of serial numbers or a single purchase order number can assign thousands of your devices in one step. On the other hand, managing assignment by individual serial number offers per-device granularity, so you will likely find both methods useful in your organization.

TIP ▸ You can view the full assignment history of every DEP action by clicking the View Assignment History link.

Manage Multiple DEP Devices

To assign multiple Apple devices at once, sign in to the Apple Deployment Programs site, and click the Manage Devices link. As you can see in the following screenshot, you can choose devices to manage by manually entering serial numbers, by looking up order numbers, or by uploading a CSV file containing serial numbers.

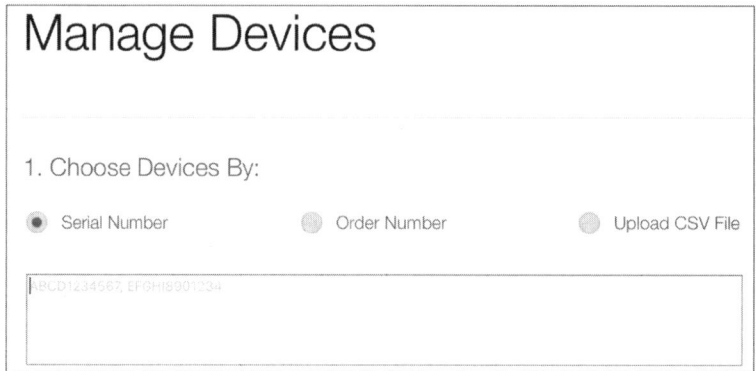

NOTE ▸ Only serial numbers verified by previous Apple orders can be managed in the DEP service. Thus, entering serial numbers from unverified orders will result in errors.

If you don't have lists of serial numbers handy, the quickest method is to look up previous order numbers. Select the Order Number radio button, and then enter a numeric

Apple order number in the field. Your organization's past orders will appear. As you type in more digits, the list of past order numbers should narrow. Alternatively, if you want all past orders to be assigned, simply select the "All available" option.

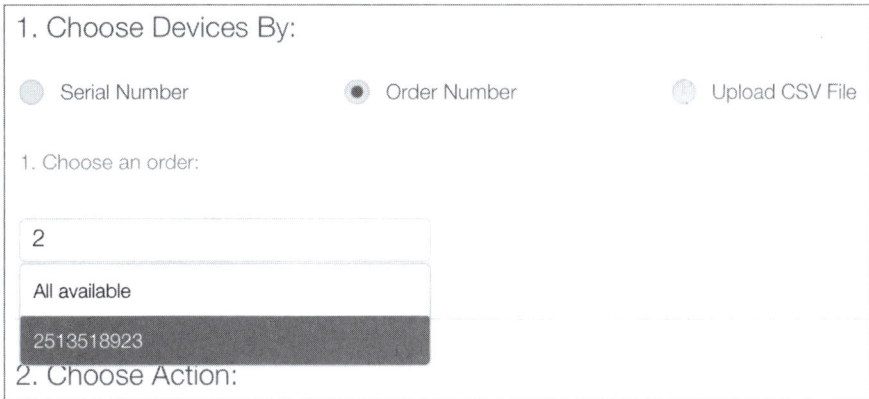

TIP ▶ If you are unsure of your specific Apple order numbers, you can search through the order history by simply entering the first digit and then selecting an order from the list. Remember to start with zero and work your way through nine to see all the possible order numbers.

Upon entering serial numbers or selecting an order number, you then move on to choosing an action. The default action is to assign the selected devices to a server. In this case, select a server from the Choose MDM Server pop-up menu. This list reflects the MDM servers you configured earlier. Once you've selected a server, simply click the OK button to assign the selected devices to the MDM server.

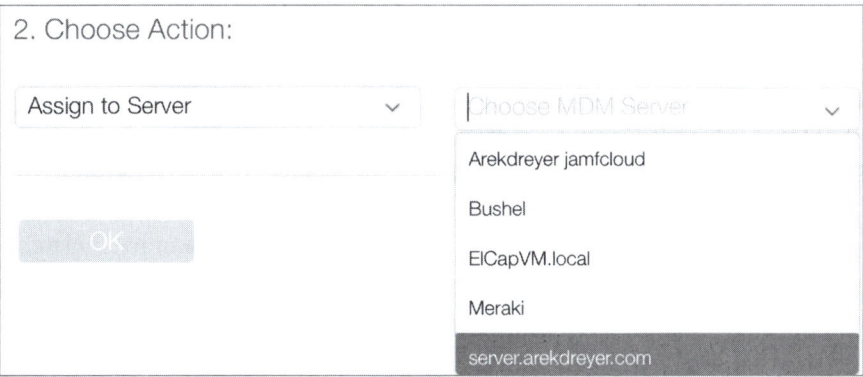

TIP ▶ Alternately, the Choose MDM Server pop-up menu also behaves as a text search field. If you have a long list of MDM servers, you can start entering the name of a server to filter the list.

While assigning devices to a server is the default action, if you click the Assign to Server pop-up menu, you will be allowed to choose another action. Whether you selected serial numbers or an order number will determine the options you have in the Choose Action menu.

If you have selected devices by serial number, you can choose the Unassign Devices action, which will make the devices behave as normal during Setup Assistant. In other words, unassigned devices will behave like a personally owned Apple device during Setup Assistant.

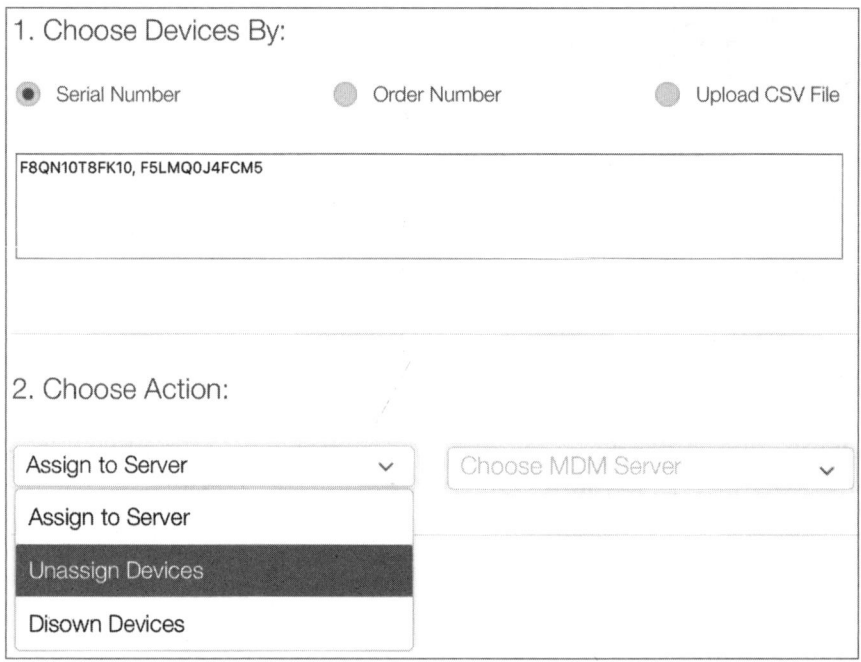

If you have selected devices by order number, you can choose the Download CSV action, which will download a CSV-formatted text file listing the serial numbers included in the selected order. This is an extremely convenient feature that may come in handy later.

In either case, you also have the ability to choose the Disown Devices action. This action will permanently remove the selected devices from your DEP service. Once removed, these devices will always behave like a personally owned Apple device during Setup Assistant and can never again be reassigned to an MDM service.

NOTE ▶ Again, it's important to remember that disowning devices will permanently remove those devices from your DEP service forever.

Manage Individual DEP Devices

In the Apple Deployment Programs site, you can assign or reassign specific Apple devices by serial number. To assign or reassign a single device, sign in to the Apple Deployment Programs site, and enter the serial number in the Search for Serial Number field at the top of the Apple Deployment Programs site interface. Make sure to input a full device serial number; then press the Enter key to initiate the search.

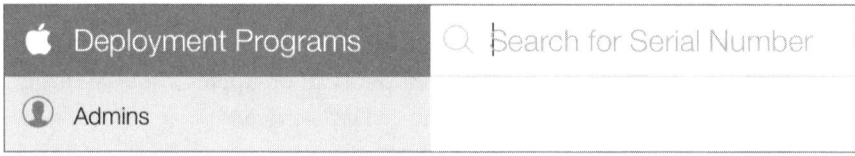

This will reveal an overview of the specific device and allow you to assign or reassign an MDM server from the pop-up menu. This interface also allows you to specifically unassign a device, thus preventing the device from seeking out an MDM server during Setup Assistant. Again, this is useful for testing different MDM services or reverting to the default Setup Assistant behavior that allows for management via Apple Configurator 2.

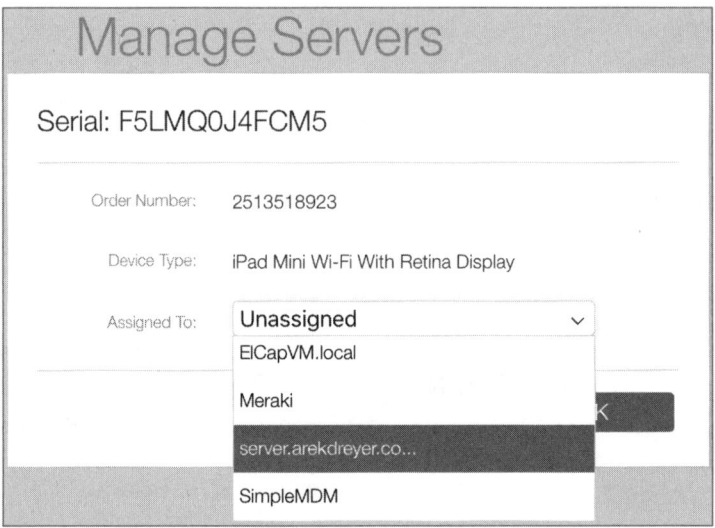

Reference 8.3
Configure DEP and Apple School Manager Assignments in Profile Manager

Immediately after you assign your Apple devices in the Apple Deployment Programs site or in the Apple School Manager site, they should be available for management by your MDM service. However, just because your MDM service now automatically recognizes your devices courtesy of the DEP or Apple School Manager assignment doesn't mean it will do anything to them. In fact, by default no changes are made to a DEP-assigned or Apple School Manager–assigned device's behavior during Setup Assistant. To customize the Setup Assistant process for devices assigned in the DEP or Apple School Manager, you must configure device enrollment settings in your MDM service.

Assignment Placeholders

In the case of Profile Manager, sign in to the administration portal, and your assigned DEP or Apple School Manager–managed devices automatically show up as placeholders in the Devices list. If your assigned devices don't appear, simply click the Refresh (circular arrow icon) button at the bottom of the Devices list to make Profile Manager requery the appropriate enrollment program assignments.

The following figure shows the selected placeholder for a device assigned to this server via the DEP service. Note that the name for the DEP placeholder is the specific model type of the device.

The previous figure also shows three other types of device records you will find in the Profile Manager administration portal:

▶ The first device is a currently managed device. Note the lack of an adjacent prohibitory symbol (circle with a strikethrough).

▶ The second device is a placeholder for a previously managed computer. Note the unique computer device name and associated user account name (Todd's MacBook Pro and Todd Porter).

▶ The third device is a manually created placeholder for a computer that has yet to be enrolled. Note the lack of a specific device icon.

Create Device Groups from Enrollment Program Assignments

You could define settings for individual DEP or Apple School Manager placeholders, but that certainly doesn't scale well. If you have a large number of devices to manage, you're better served by configuring device groups for the enrollment program placeholders and then applying the enrollment settings to the device group.

Start by creating a new device group in Profile Manager by selecting Device Groups from the Library and clicking the Add (+) button at the bottom of the Device Groups list. To define the group members, click the Members tab at the right and then the Add (+) button at the bottom of the Members list. This opens a window allowing you to add device group members.

Now here is the tricky part: If you have potentially hundreds of new devices to add as members of this device group, how do you do it efficiently? The answer is search filtering.

In the simple example that follows, the first screenshot shows the default list unfiltered. In the second screenshot, the list is filtered for a string of characters that would show up only on devices with placeholders named via the DEP service or Apple School Manager. In this case, the filter string is "16GB."

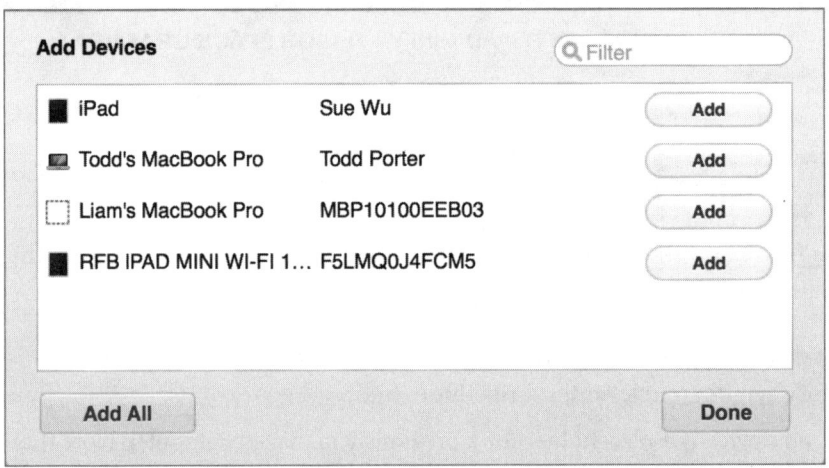

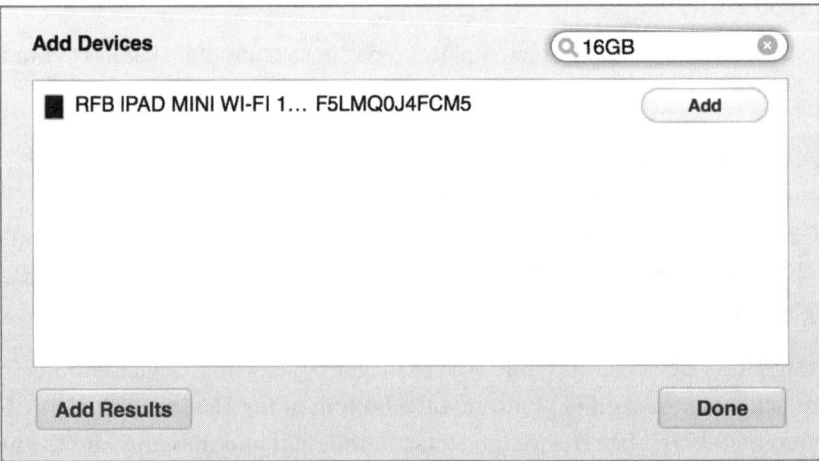

Once the list is filtered for your search criteria, simply click Add Results to add the appropriate enrollment program-assigned devices to the device group. You will have to click Done here and then click Save in the Profile Manager interface to apply the group membership changes.

Define Enrollment Settings for Enrollment Program Assignments

Once you have selected a specific device or device group of enrollment program-assigned devices, you can configure the enrollment settings in the Settings tab. First you must select the Prompt User to Enroll Device checkbox to activate the rest of the enrollment settings. Also, don't forget to click Save to apply these settings in Profile Manager.

The next three figures illustrate that you can configure the following enrollment settings for DEP-assigned or Apple School Manager–assigned devices.

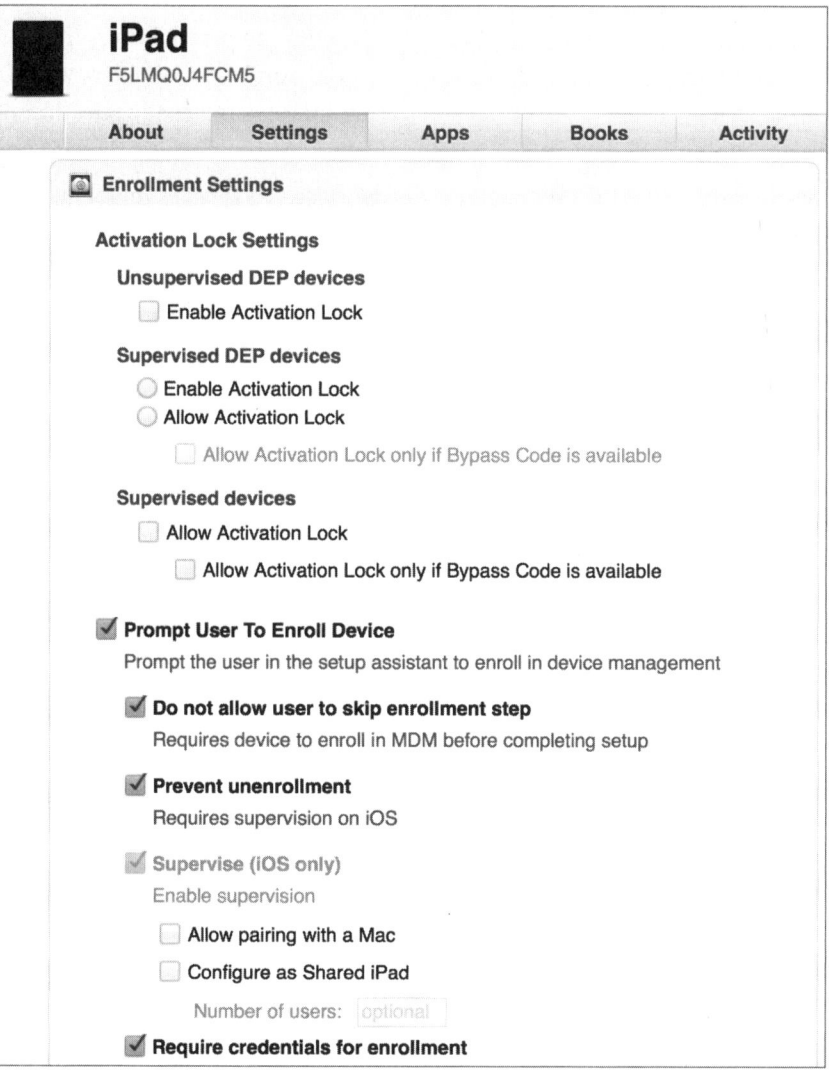

- Activation Lock Settings—See Lesson 9, "Activation Lock Management," for more information.
- Prompt User to Enroll Device—The user will be prompted during Setup Assistant to enroll the device for management.
- Do not allow user to skip enrollment step—This is probably the most important setting; it forces the user to complete the enrollment to continue. However, this enforcement applies to OS X computers only if they can contact the DEP service or the Apple School Manager service during Setup Assistant.
- Prevent unenrollment—Selecting this is the only method to prevent users from removing device management. This feature works only on Mac computers with OS X Yosemite or devices with iOS 7.1 or later. Selecting this also forces the selection of the Supervise setting for iOS devices.
- Supervise—Again, this is the only method to supervise iOS devices remotely, without having physical access to the device.
- Allow pairing with a Mac—This is the same supervised iOS device locking mechanism that can be turned on by Apple Configurator or Apple Configurator 2. Also covered previously, this allows for pairing with PCs as well as Mac computers.
- Configure as Shared iPad—This lets multiple students use the same iPad; see "Shared iPad" in the iOS Deployment Reference at https://help.apple.com/deployment/ios/.
- Require credentials for enrollment—This setting is definitely recommended because it will automatically associate the user with the managed device, which allows Profile Manager to automatically apply profiles based on user and user group settings along with device and device group settings. This setting also prevents unauthorized access to devices during Setup Assistant, thus rendering a wiped device useless to unauthorized users.

  NOTE ▶ Deselecting "Require credentials for enrollment" prevents OS X computers from being able to enroll during Setup Assistant. An iOS device without this option turned on can be enrolled, and then an administrator can associate that device with any user.

> **Setup Assistant Options**
> Choose which options to hide in Setup Assistant. Hidden options keep their most private setting.
>
> **iOS and OS X**
> ☑ Location Services
> ☐ Set Up as New or Restore
> ☑ Apple ID
> ☐ Terms and Conditions
> ☐ App Analytics
>
> **iOS**
> ☐ Move from Android
> ☐ Touch ID
> ☑ Passcode Lock
> ☐ Apple Pay
> ☐ Siri
> ☐ Display Zoom
>
> **OS X**
> ☑ FileVault
> ☑ Registration

▶ Setup Assistant Options—Similar to the options found in Apple Configurator 2, the default setting for a skipped option is the more secure or more private option. In most cases, this means turning off the service or feature. One of the options not available in Apple Configurator 2 is to skip the Terms and Conditions screen.

> **NOTE** ▶ The checkbox behavior is the opposite of the behavior in the legacy Apple Configurator. In the Profile Manager administration portal and in Apple Configurator 2, the selected checkboxes are the only options that will appear during Setup Assistant, and in the legacy Apple Configurator selected checkboxes will be skipped.

> **MORE INFO** ▶ You can find detailed descriptions and suggestions regarding the results of skipping the Setup Assistant screens in Lesson 13, "Apple Configurator 2: Preparing, Configuring, and Managing iOS Devices."

A new feature of Server 5 is the ability to specify the automatic creation of an administrator account for a Mac computer with OS X El Capitan or later.

OS X Account Setup Assistant Options
☑ Prompt user to create an account of type:
● Standard
○ Administrator
Managed OS X Administrator Account
☑ Create managed OS X administrator account
Full Name: Local Administrator
Account Name: ladmin
Password: ••••••••
Verify: ••••••••
☑ Show managed administrator account in Users & Groups
[Revert] [Save]

The following are some things you should know about the OS X account Setup Assistant options:

- Require credentials for enrollment (not shown in the previous screenshot)—Remember that if this option is not selected, then the OS X computer will not enroll during Setup Assistant. When a user is prompted to enroll with your MDM, the user must supply credentials for a directory user (a user that your MDM service knows about). If you configure Setup Assistant to prompt the user to create a computer account (see the next three bullet points), Setup Assistant automatically uses the Account Name attribute and password of the directory account that user provides for enrollment, but the user can configure different values when creating the computer account.

- Prompt user to create an account of type—If you deselect this option, the user must log in to the Mac with their directory username and password, and you must select the option to create a managed OS X administrator account. See the next two bullet points.

  - Standard—When a user creates a new account as part of Setup Assistant, that account will not be an administrator account. This might be more appropriate for a tightly managed Mac computer that is not mobile than for a user who has responsibility for his own computer and might need administrator credentials from time to time. You must specify the details of an administrator account in the Managed OS X Administrator Account section. However, you cannot edit that section when Standard is selected; first select Administrator, then configure the administrator account section, and then select Standard again.

▶ Administrator—When a user creates a new account as part of Setup Assistant, that account will be an administrator account.

▶ Managed OS X Administrator Account—As of the current writing, the User ID attribute of an account that a user creates during Setup Assistant is 502, and the User ID attribute of this managed administrator account is 501. You can use a task to remotely change a managed administrator account's password, which is something you cannot do with a normal administrator account.

▶ Show managed administrator account in Users & Groups—Deselecting this option hides the managed administrator account in Users & Groups preferences.

Verify DEP or Apple School Manager Functionality

Once you have completed the required steps to manage device enrollment via the appropriate enrollment program and Profile Manager, you should verify enrollment functionality by stepping through Setup Assistant on a new or like-new Apple device assigned via the enrollment program service. Take a new Apple device out of its box, or reset an existing device as if it were just out of the box.

Assuming a normal Setup Assistant workflow, the user will first select a language and region or country code. She will then connect the device to an Ethernet or Wi-Fi network. For organizations that require complex Wi-Fi security, this is where having an easily connected limited guest network comes in handy.

Assuming the device can connect to Apple's activation servers, the device will be redirected to your MDM service. Assuming the device can reach your MDM service, it will enforce your Setup Assistant settings. The process may take a few seconds to complete, but when it does, the user will be presented with a screen that states something along the lines of "*Your organization* will automatically configure your *device*."

Here's what it might look like for an iOS device and for an OS X computer:

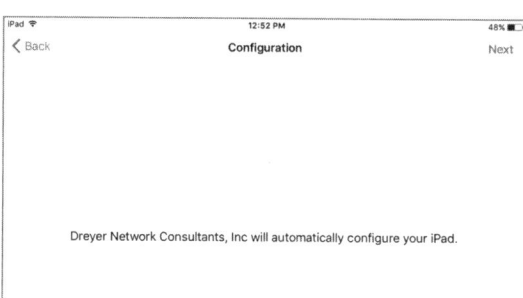
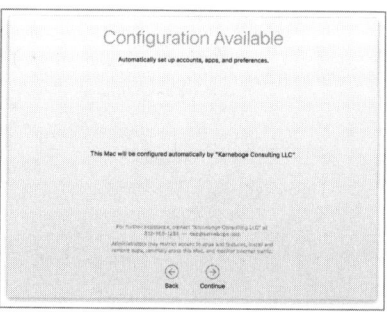

If you have defined user-based enrollment settings, the user will be prompted to authenticate with her user name and password. Upon successful authentication, the device will be enrolled into your MDM service and for iOS devices optionally supervised. The remainder of Setup Assistant should proceed as you have defined for the rest of the screens.

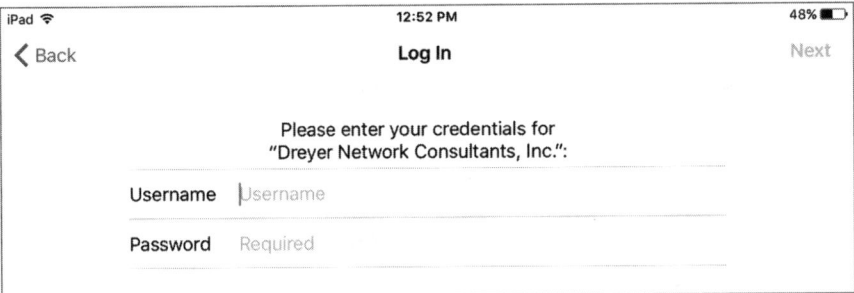

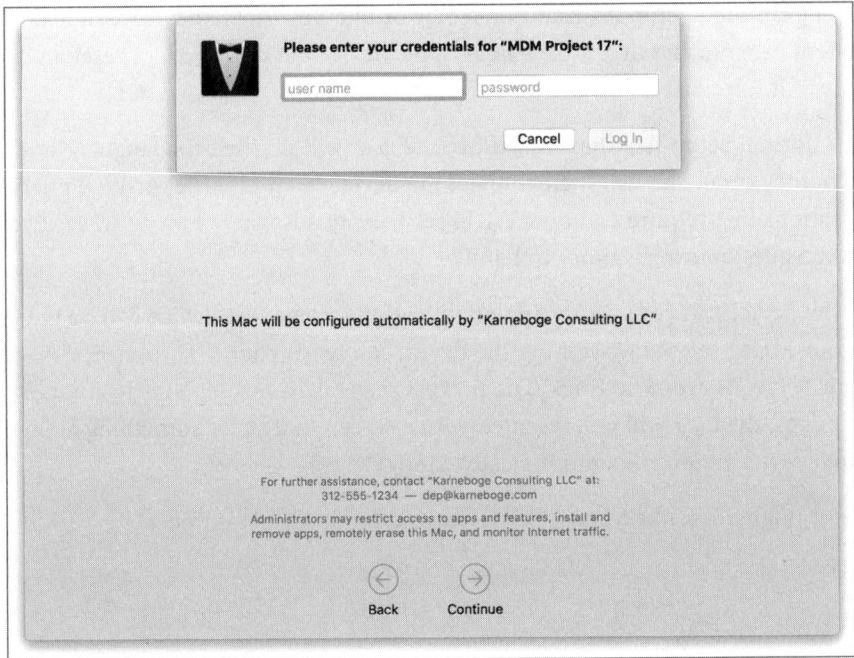

Once the device has completed Setup Assistant, you can verify the supervision and management settings from the Settings app on iOS and in Profiles preferences on OS X. The following screenshots show a device that has been supervised and managed via assignment in the DEP. At the lock screen, the device displays the text "This iPad is managed by your organization" (the description of the device will vary by device type).

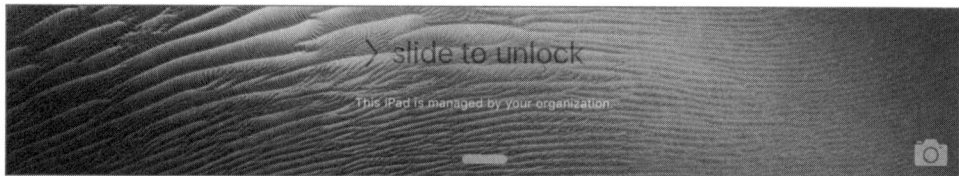

In the Settings app, navigating to General > About shows that the iOS device is supervised and that your organization "can monitor your Internet traffic and locate this device."

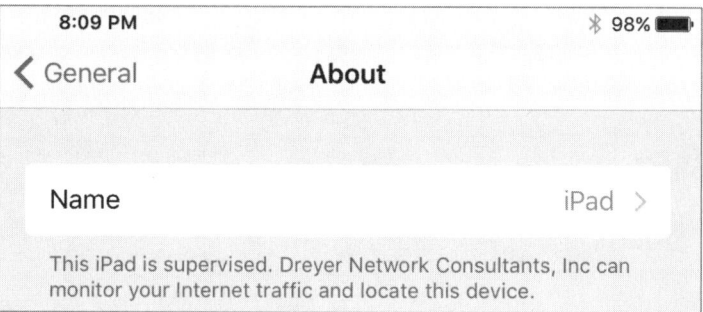

You can also verify the Remote Management enrollment on iOS in the Settings app by navigating to General > Device Management and by using Profiles preferences on OS X. The following figure shows the Remote Management profile on an iOS device; this profile looks similar to the Remote Management profile demonstrated in Lesson 7, "Mobile Device Management." In fact, you'll see the same settings for the Barbara user and Engineering group as demonstrated in the previous lesson. The one significant difference here is that you can't remove the enrollment profile because it is prevented by the enrollment settings from the MDM service.

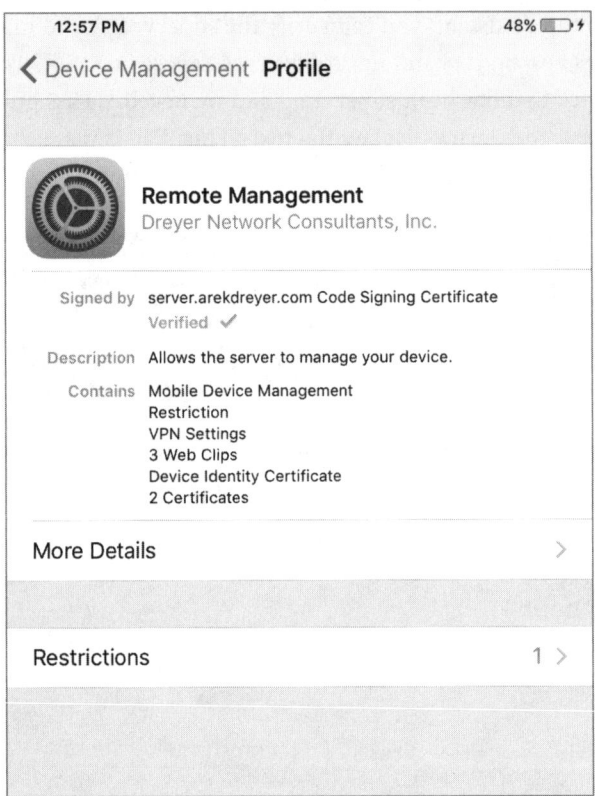

DEP and Apple School Manager Enforcement Limitations

iOS devices must successfully complete the device activation process to be used. In other words, if an iOS device is assigned to your server in the appropriate enrollment program and it cannot reach Apple's activation servers or your MDM service, the user will not be allowed to set up and use the device. Thus, for iOS devices assigned in the DEP or Apple School Manager, either Setup Assistant will successfully enforce your enrollment settings or the user will not be allowed to use the iOS device. This is what makes these enrollment programs an effective enforcement and theft-deterrent solution for iOS devices.

On the other hand, OS X computers are not required to connect to Apple's activation servers during the Setup Assistant process. If the OS X system can't establish a network connection, Setup Assistant will prompt the user to define network settings. However, if the user chooses to not set up networking, the OS X Setup Assistant process will continue without connecting to the appropriate enrollment service or your MDM service.

For OS X Yosemite and later, the situation is improved a bit courtesy of Notification Center. In cases where an OS X computer assigned in the DEP or Apple School Manager was supposed to enroll but it was skipped during Setup Assistant, the user will receive a notification encouraging enrollment. However, as you can see from the screenshot, the notification can be easily skipped and ignored.

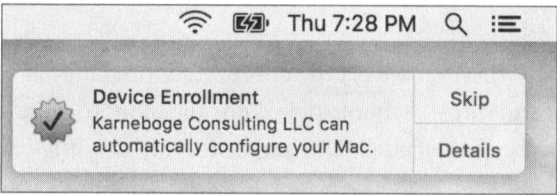

Further, the flexible nature of Mac computers makes it extremely easy to circumvent starting up from the built-in system volume. The ability of the Mac computer's firmware to start up from an external system volume easily allows someone to circumvent any management requirements imposed by the Setup Assistant process.

You could set firmware passwords on your Mac computers to protect them from this vulnerability, but at the time of this writing, you can't have this set at the factory. Thus, administrative staff would have to handle each Mac computer before giving it to the user, which defeats a significant advantage to deployments that use the DEP or Apple School Manager.

> **MORE INFO** ▶ You can find out more about setting up firmware passwords in Apple Support article HT204455, "Use a firmware password on your Mac."

In short, at the time of this writing, you cannot enforce Setup Assistant enrollment on OS X devices in the same way as possible for iOS devices.

Reference 8.4
Troubleshooting the Enrollment Process

For both iOS and OS X devices, be sure that your device can connect to your MDM service. Be sure that the appropriate DNS records for your MDM server are valid both inside your organization's internal network and outside it.

Overall, there are several things that must be true for a device to prompt a user to enroll with the MDM of your choice:

- Your organization must be enrolled in the appropriate Apple device enrollment program (the DEP for businesses or Apple School Manager for schools).
- The device must be purchased with your organization's Apple Customer Number or a DEP Reseller ID.
- The device must be assigned to an MDM server via the appropriate site, https://deploy.apple.com/ for businesses and https://school.apple.com/ for schools. Note that you can assign an MDM server to be the default MDM server for any new eligible devices that you purchase.
- The device must be configured in the MDM service to prompt the user to enroll. This is a step that is often overlooked by administrators who are new to the DEP.
- The device must be able to connect to Apple's activation servers and to its assigned MDM server.
- On an iOS device, the user must use Setup Assistant on the device.
- On a Mac computer, the user must either use Setup Assistant or reply to the notification to enroll.

For an iOS device, there is no way to cause Setup Assistant to run once it has already been completed, without wiping the device. Luckily, wiping iOS is simple. Open Settings > General > Reset, tap Erase All Content and Settings, enter the device PIN or passphrase if one exists, and then confirm twice.

On a Mac computer, during Setup Assistant you can skip enrolling with your MDM service. Then you can turn on additional logging by issuing the following commands with root privileges and then rebooting:

- defaults write /Library/Preferences/com.apple.MCXDebug debugOutput -2
- defaults write /Library/Preferences/com.apple.MCXDebug collateLogs 1
- touch /var/db/MDM_EnableDebug

Additional information will be logged to the following files:

- /Library/Logs/ManagedClient/ManagedClient.log
- /var/log/system.log

To turn off the additional logging, run the following commands with root privileges:

rm -f /var/db/MDM_EnableDebug

rm -f /Library/Preferences/com.apple.MCXDebug.plist

But what about Mac computers that have been assigned an MDM service via the appropriate Apple enrollment program? At the time of this writing, for Mac computers, there is no quick equivalent of Erase All Content and Settings. Although you can force Setup Assistant to run again by removing the file /var/db/.AppleSetupDone and logging out or rebooting, this is not enough to cause a user to be prompted to enroll with your MDM service.

You can force a Mac computer to be prompted to enroll with your MDM server, even if it has already been set up, by issuing the following commands with root permissions and then rebooting:

rm /var/db/.AppleSetupDone

rm -rf /var/db/ConfigurationProfiles/

rm /Library/Keychains/apsd.keychain

> **NOTE ▶** This process is not documented by Apple. Do not use these commands on Mac computers used in a production environment.

Exercise 8.1
Enroll with the Apple Deployment Programs (Optional)

Challenge

If you do not already have your Apple Deployment Programs (ADP) "program agent account," then create it.

If you do not already have your ADP "administrator account" dedicated for the Device Enrollment Program, then create one.

> **WARNING ▶** Your organization can enroll in the DEP only once, so if your organization is already enrolled in the Volume Purchase Program (VPP) and in the DEP, do not attempt to enroll with a new Apple ID, and do not attempt to change the details of the Apple ID used for the VPP or the DEP.

Considerations

NOTE ▶ The ADP Apple ID must be unique to programs listed on the ADP site and cannot be used to log in to the iTunes Store or any other Apple service.

NOTE ▶ If you're already using your email address for an existing Apple ID, you'll be asked to provide a new email address.

NOTE ▶ If your organization does not have a D-U-N-S number, it can take up to five business days to obtain one. See developer.apple.com/support/D-U-N-S/ for more information as well as to obtain one. Your D-U-N-S number is used by Apple to check the identity and legal entity status of your organization and is part of Apple's enrollment verification process for joining the Apple Deployment Programs, the Apple Developer Program, or the Apple Developer Enterprise Program.

You cannot use an Apple ID that has been used with iCloud as an ADP agent account or administrator account.

Solution

Create and Verify a New ADP Agent Account

There are plenty of reasons you might not be able to complete the rest of this exercise, including the following:

- ▶ The VPP is not available in your country
- ▶ The DEP is not available in your country
- ▶ Your organization has already enrolled with the DEP
- ▶ Your organization has already enrolled with the VPP
- ▶ Your organization does not have a D-U-N-S number
- ▶ Your organization does not have an Apple Customer Number or your Apple Authorized Reseller's DEP Reseller ID
- ▶ You do not have authority to sign legal documents on behalf of your organization

If any of these apply to you, read and follow along for the rest of the exercise, but do not actually perform the steps.

Create Your ADP Agent Account

NOTE ▸ Perform these steps using the Server app on your server computer, not on a remote Mac. You could use screen sharing from a remote Mac to control your server Mac.

1 On your server Mac, open the Server app, and if necessary, connect to your server.

2 In the Server app sidebar, select Profile Manager.

3 Select the checkbox "Enroll devices using the Device Enrollment Program."

4 Click Create an Account.

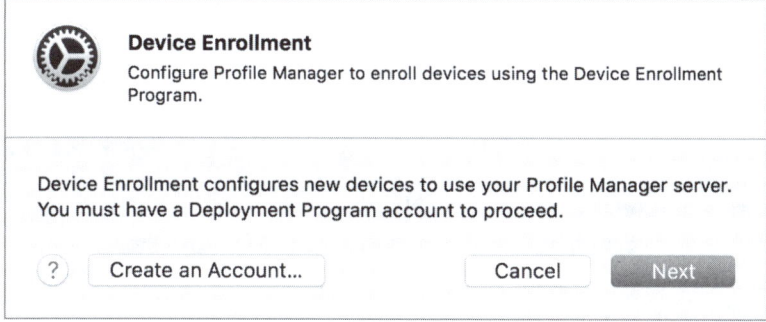

The Apple Deployment Programs site (https://deploy.apple.com) opens in Safari.

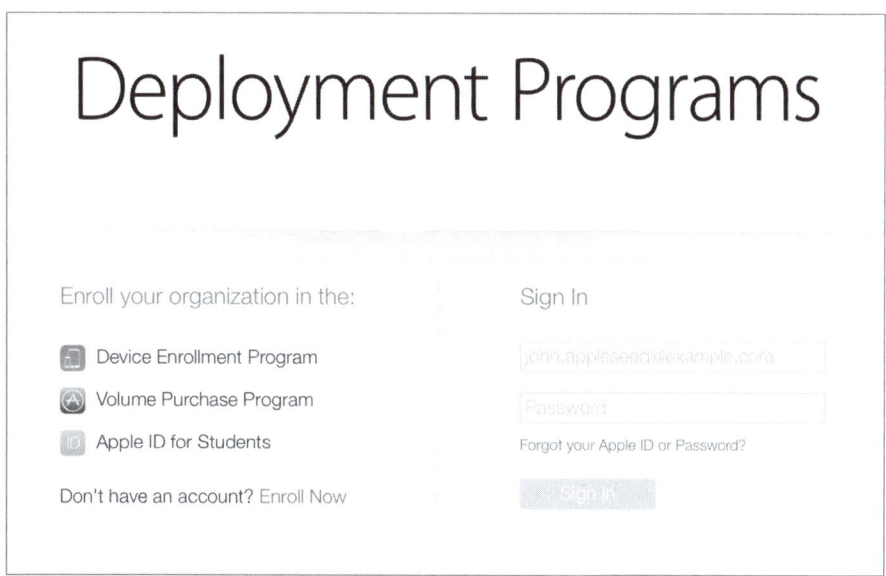

NOTE ▶ The URL in the location bar is different from https://deploy.apple.com, and the Apple ID field may already be populated. Ignore this for now, as you will be creating a new Apple ID.

5 If necessary, click the flag in the lower-right corner to change your country, and then choose your country on the next page.

NOTE ▶ The DEP is only available to organizations in certain countries. See Apple Support article HT204142 for more information.

6 Click Enroll Now.

7 Next to the Device Enrollment Program, click Enroll.

8 In the Your Details section, enter your first and last names in the appropriate fields.

9 In the Work Email field, enter an email address to use as your ADP agent account.

This email address cannot already be an Apple ID, be associated with a current Apple ID as an alternate email, or have been used for the Mac App Store, iTunes Store, or iCloud.

10 Enter appropriate information in the rest of the fields, and then click Next.

Verify and Update the Password for the New Account

1 Check your email for the email address associated with the new Apple ID.

2 Make a note of the temporary password contained in the email message.

3 Click the Sign In link included in the message from Apple.

The Apple ID site opens.

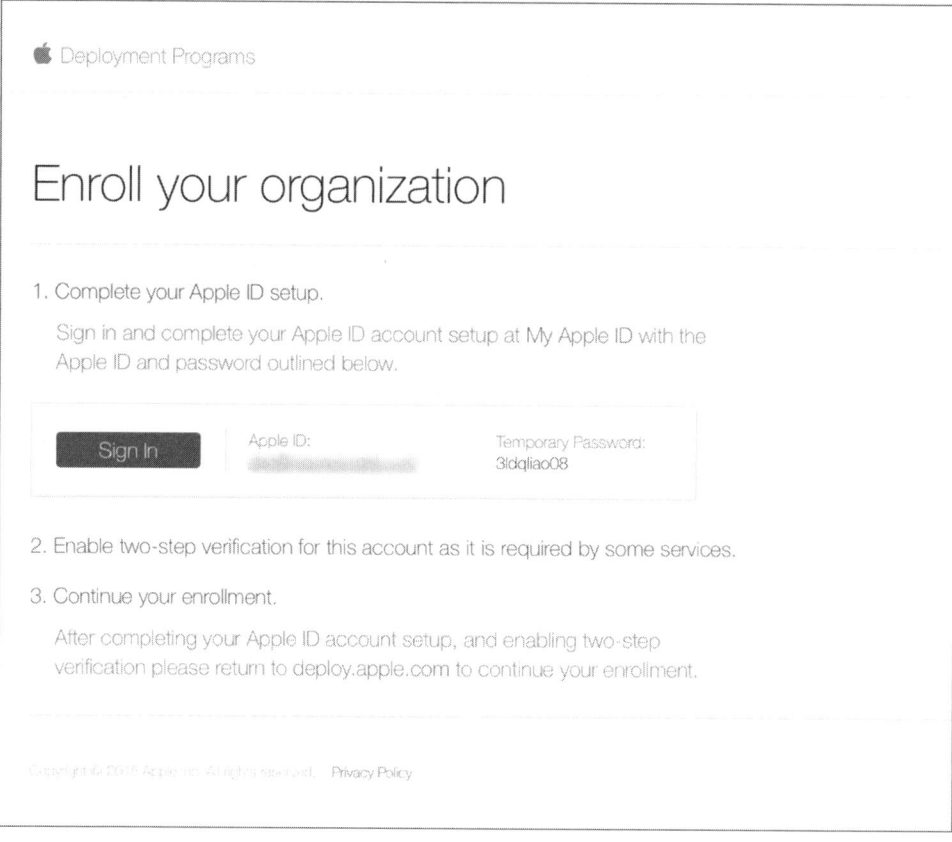

4   Enter the credentials for the ADP agent account you just created, with the temporary password contained in the email message from Apple.

5   Click Sign In.

6   At the Update Apple ID screen, enter the temporary password in the current password field.

7   Enter a new secure password in the New Password and Confirm New Password fields.

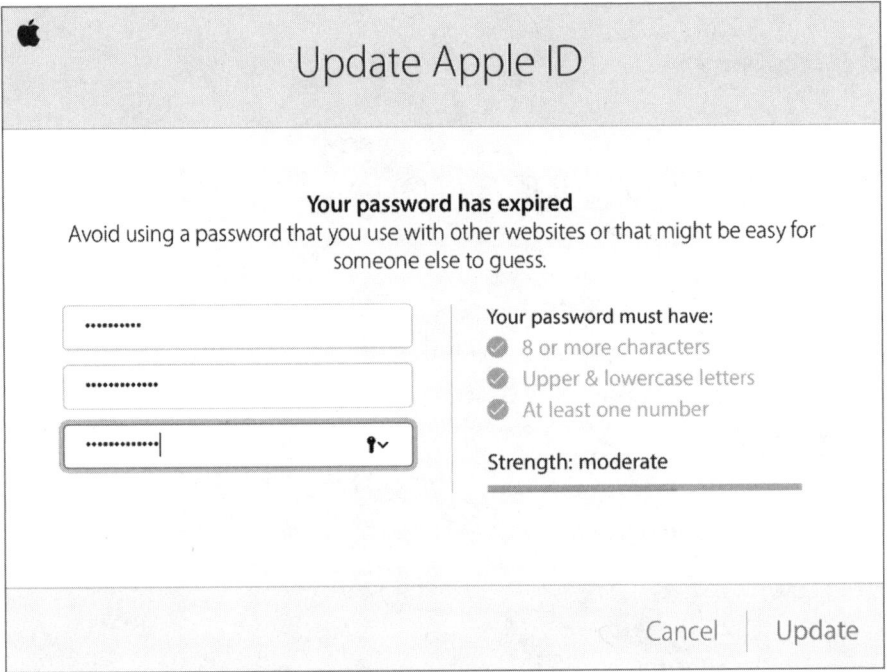

NOTE ▶ Use a secure password you will remember.

8 Click Update. The Apple ID site will now ask you to verify your new ADP agent Apple ID.

> **Verify Email Address**
> Your Apple ID email address must be verified before you can sign in. Verify the address below or choose a different address.

9 Click Continue to send a verification email. You will see an area to enter a six-digit verification code.

10 Check the email client that receives mail for the ADP agent Apple ID.

11 In the confirmation email you receive from Apple, there will be a six-digit verification code.

12 Enter the six-digit verification code, and click Verify.

13 Enter a birthday, choose three security questions, and then click Update.

    The Apple ID webpage informs you, "Apple ID Updated Successfully."

14 Click Continue.

Set Up Two-Step Verification for Your ADP Agent Account

1   If necessary, in Safari, open https://appleid.apple.com.

2   Enter your ADP agent Apple ID credentials, and press Return.

3   If Safari asks to save this password, click Never for This Website.

4   Under Two-Step Verification, click Get Started.

5   Answer the security questions, and then click Continue.

6   In the "Getting Started with Two-Step Verification" pane, click Continue.

7   In the "Add a trusted phone number" pane, click the Country pop-up menu, and choose the country associated with your phone that can receive SMS messages.

8   Enter the area code and phone number.

9   Click Continue.

10 Enter the verification code that was sent to your phone.

11 Click Verify.

12 In the Verify Trusted Devices pane, click Continue.

13 In the Print Your Recovery Key pane, write down the recovery key, or print the page in Safari.

NOTE ▶ You cannot continue with the process without entering the recovery key information in the next page.

14 Click Continue.

15 Enter the recovery key.

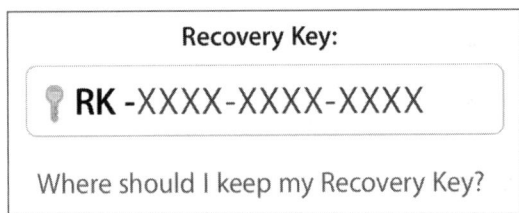

16 Click Confirm.

17 Carefully read the conditions to the two-step verification.

18 Select the checkbox to agree.

19 Click Enable Two-Step Verification.

The Apple ID webpage informs you, "Two-Step Verification Enabled."

20 Click Done.

21 In the upper-right corner of the Safari window, click Sign Out.

22 Close the Safari window.

Enroll in the DEP (Optional)
If you are going to enroll in the VPP and not the DEP, skip to the next section, "Enroll in VPP (Optional)."

1 In Safari, open https://deploy.apple.com.

2 Enter your ADP agent account credentials, and then click Sign In.

3 At the "Verify your identity" screen, if necessary, select your phone number, and then click Continue.

4 Enter your verification code that you received, and then click Continue.

5 In the Add Verification Contact Details window, enter the appropriate information for a person who can verify that you have the legal authority to sign and bind your organization to the Apple Device Enrollment Program agreement, and then click Next.

6 In the Add Institution Details window, enter the appropriate information, and then click Next.

   You will need your D-U-N-S number as well as your Apple Customer Number or DEP Reseller ID from your Apple Authorized Reseller.

7 At the Review Your Enrollment Details window, carefully review the information, and then click Submit.

8 At the Welcome back webpage, you will notice that your Device Enrollment Program application is In Review.

Now it's time to wait for your DEP application to be approved by Apple, which includes waiting for a phone call from Apple. This could take as little as an hour, or days, so in the meantime, move on with the VPP enrollment part of the exercise.

Enroll in the VPP (Optional)

If you are not going to enroll in VPP, skip to the next section, "Add a DEP Administrator Account."

Note that if you start with the VPP enrollment instead of the DEP enrollment, the order will be slightly different.

1 If necessary, in Safari, open https://deploy.apple.com.

2 Enter your ADP agent account credentials, and click Sign In.

   Note that if you've already started the process of enrolling in DEP, the site will display "In Review" in the Device Enrollment Program section.

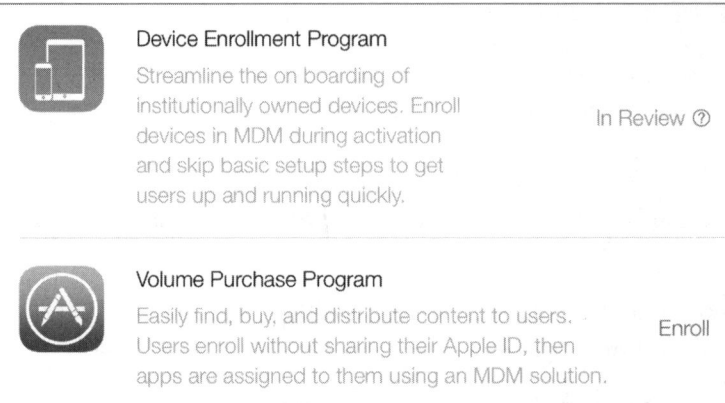

3   Next to Volume Purchase Program, click Enroll.

4   In the Add Organization Details window, enter the appropriate information, and then click Next.

    You will need your organization's D-U-N-S number.

5   In the Review Your Information window, carefully review the information, and then click Submit.

Now it's time to wait for your VPP application to be approved by Apple. Even though both the DEP and VPP applications may be in review, you can still continue with this exercise, or if you are in an instructor-led environment, you can move ahead to Exercise 8.2, "Configure Profile Manager for the Device Enrollment Program."

Add a DEP Administrator Account (Optional)
You'll create an ADP administrator account that you will use to administer the Deployment Enrollment Program. This guide refers to this as your "DEP administrator account."

1   In Safari, open https://deploy.apple.com.

2   Enter your ADP agent account credentials, and click Sign In.

3   In the sidebar, select Admins.

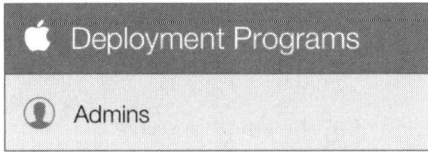

4   Click Add Admin Account.

5   Select the checkbox Device Enrollment Program.

6   Enter information in the First Name and Last Name fields.

7   Enter an email address that has not been associated with iTunes Store or iCloud (which will be your DEP administrator account).

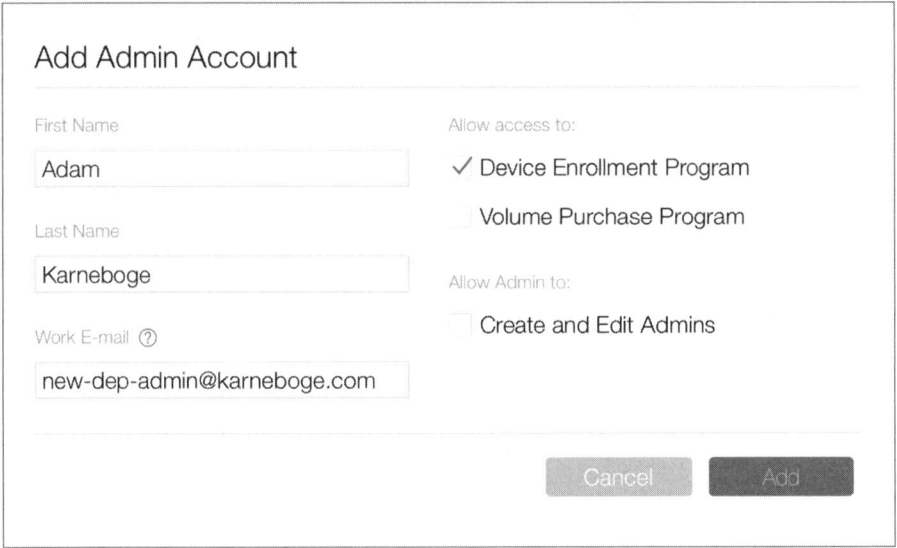

NOTE ▶ You may not see the Create and Edit Admins option.

8   Click Add.

9   Review the list of your agent and admins.

Activate Your DEP Administrator Account

1. Check your email for the email address associated with the new Apple ID.

2. Make a note of the temporary password contained in the email message.

3. Click the Sign In link included in the message from Apple.

   The Apple ID site opens.

4. Enter the credentials for the ADP agent account you just created, with the temporary password contained in the email message from Apple.

5. Press Return.

6. At the Update Apple ID screen, enter the temporary password in the current password field.

7. Enter a new secure password in the New Password and Confirm New Password fields.

   NOTE ▶ Use a secure password you will remember.

8. Click Update. The Apple ID site will now ask you to verify your new ADP agent Apple ID.

9. Click Continue to send a verification email. You will see an area to enter a six-digit verification code.

10. Check the email client that receives mail for the ADP agent Apple ID.

11. In the confirmation email you receive from Apple, there will be a six-digit verification code.

12. Enter the six-digit verification code, and click Verify.

13. Enter a birthday, choose three security questions, and then click Update.

    The Apple ID webpage informs you, "Apple ID Updated Successfully."

14. Click Continue.

Set Up Two-Step Verification for Your DEP Administrator Account

1 If necessary, in Safari, open the Apple ID site (https://appleid.apple.com).

2 Enter your ADP agent Apple ID credentials, and press Return.

3 If Safari asks to save this password, click Never for This Website.

4 Under Two-Step Verification, click Get Started.

5 Answer the security questions, and then click Continue.

6 In the Getting Started with Two-Step Verification pane, click Continue.

7 In the "Add a trusted phone number" pane, click the Country pop-up menu, and choose the country associated with your phone that can receive SMS messages.

8 Enter the area code and phone number.

9 Click Continue.

10 Enter the verification code that was sent to your phone.

11 Click Verify.

12 In the Verify Trusted Devices pane, click Continue.

13 In the Print Your Recovery Key pane, write down the recovery key, or print the page in Safari.

   NOTE ▶ You cannot continue with the process without entering the recovery key information in the next page.

14 Click Continue.

15 Enter the recovery key.

16 Click Confirm.

17 Carefully read the conditions to the two-step verification.

18 Select the checkbox to agree.

19 Click Enable Two-Step Verification.

   The Apple ID webpage informs you, "Two-Step Verification Enabled."

20 Click Done.

21 In the upper-right corner of the Safari window, click Sign Out.

22 Close the Safari window.

In this exercise, you created an ADP administrator account and enrolled your organization. You added an administrator account for the DEP. You turned on two-step verification for your DEP administrator account.

Exercise 8.2
Configure Profile Manager for the Device Enrollment Program

> **Prerequisites**
> - Exercise 4.1, "Prepare Your Mac to Install OS X Server for El Capitan"
> - Exercise 4.2, "Install OS X Server for El Capitan"
> - Exercise 4.3, "Configure OS X Server for El Capitan"
> - Exercise 6.1, "Turn On Profile Manager"
> - Exercise 7.1, "Enable Device Management"
> - A DEP Agent or Admin for your organization, or Exercise 8.1, "Enroll with the Apple Deployment Programs"

Challenge

Use your administrator account for Device Enrollment Program to add a Mobile Device Management server configuration to the Apple Deployment Programs website.

Create a device group for DEP devices, and update the enrollment settings so that devices in the device group force a user to enroll with credentials at activation yet are allowed to pair with other computers.

Solution

Add an MDM Server

1. On your server computer, in Safari, open the ADP site (https://deploy.apple.com), enter your DEP administrator account credentials, and then click Sign In.

2. At the "Verify your identity" page, select the appropriate phone number for two-step verification, and then click Continue.

3. Wait for your phone to receive the verification code, enter your verification code, and then click Continue.

4. If necessary, read the terms and conditions, select the checkbox "I have read and agree to the Administrator Terms and Conditions," and then click Agree.

5. In the sidebar, select Device Enrollment Program.

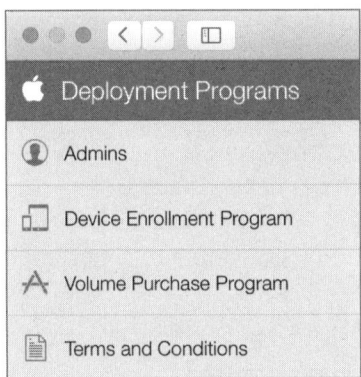

6. Click Add MDM Server.

7. For MDM Server Name, enter MDM Project *n* (where *n* is your student number), and then click Next.

   Do not select Automatically Assign New Devices.

8. A window with "2. Upload Your Public Key" is displayed. Keep this Safari window open; you will return to it after exporting your server's public key.

Export Your Server's Public Key

1. If necessary, on your server computer, open the Server app, select Profile Manager in the Server app sidebar, and then select the checkbox "Enroll devices using the Device Enrollment Program."

2. Otherwise, return to the Server app, and in the Device Enrollment dialog, click Next.

3. Enter a phone number for your organization, and then click Next.

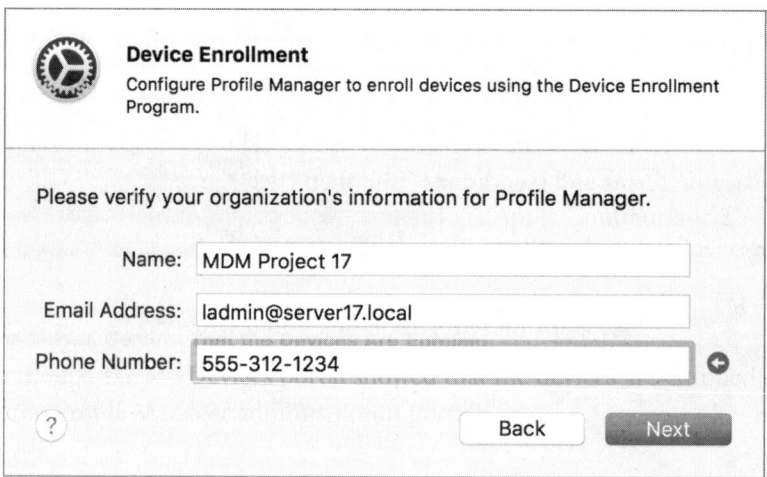

4. Next to the public key, click Export.

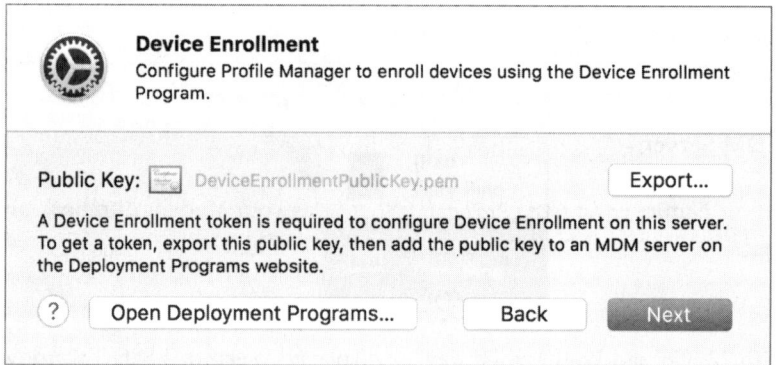

5. In the Save As pane, press Command-D to change your location to the Desktop, and then click Save.

Add the Public Key to Your MDM Server on the DEP Site

1 Keep the Server app open, and switch to Safari.

2 In Safari, click Choose File.

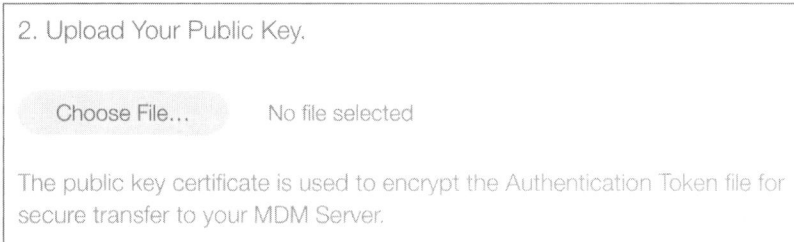

3 If necessary, select Desktop in the sidebar, and then select the DeviceEnrollmentPublicKey.pem file.

4 Click Choose.

5 Click Next.

   WARNING ▶ Do not click Done yet!

Download Your Server Token

1 Click Your Server Token.

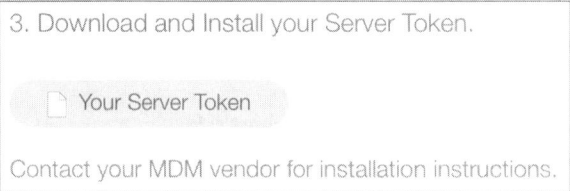

Your server token downloads to your Downloads folder, which takes only a moment.

2 Click Done.

Import Your Server Token

1 In the Server app, click Choose.

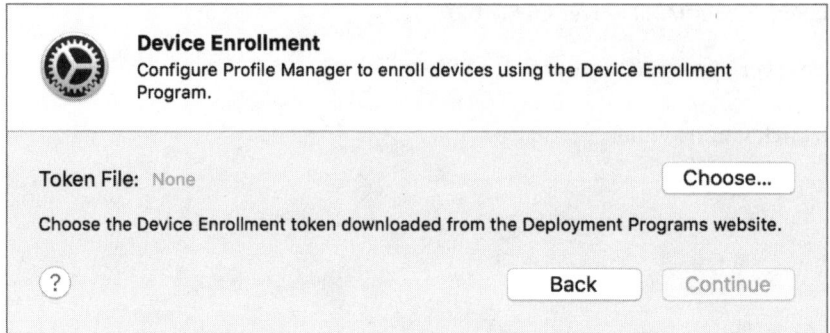

2. If necessary, select Downloads in the sidebar, and then click the List View (looks like a series of horizontal lines) button in the toolbar.

3. Click the Date Added column header so that the triangle points down, indicating that the last-added files are listed first.

4. Select your token file. Its name is the one you assigned when you created the new MDM server in the Device Programs site, followed by a string representing the date and time, and it has the suffix p7m.

5. Click Choose.

6. Click Continue.

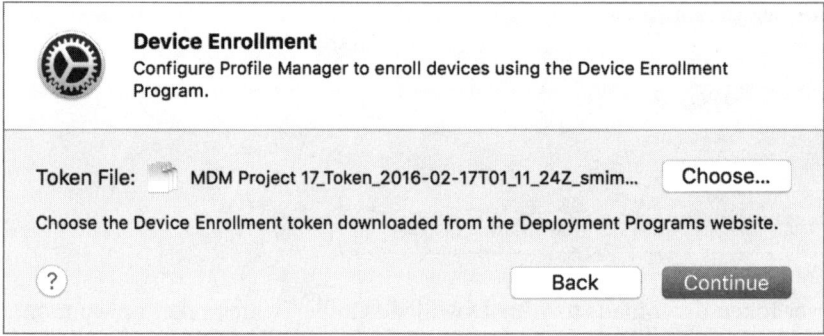

7. Click Done.

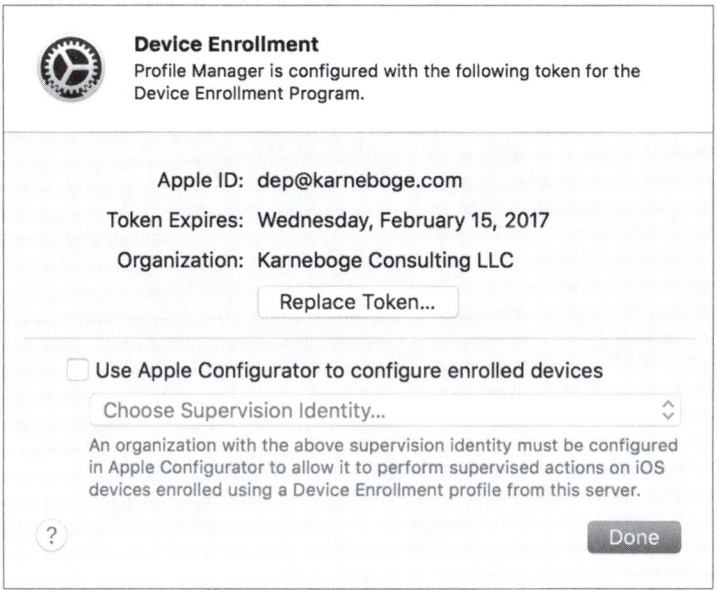

Create a Device Group for New DEP Placeholder Records

1 On your server Mac, in Safari, open the Profile Manager administration portal (https://server*n*.local/profilemanager, where *n* is your student number), and then authenticate with your server's local administrator credentials.

2 In the Profile Manager sidebar, select Device Groups.

3 If you do not yet have any device groups, click Add Device Group.

   If you already have device groups, click the Add (+) button at the bottom of the Devices column in the Profile Manager window.

4 Replace the default name, New Device Group, with a more descriptive name, such as DEP Devices.

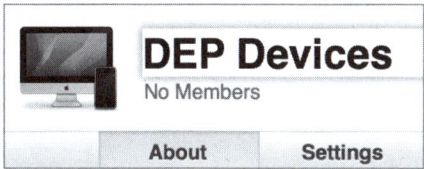

5   Click the Settings tab.

6   Select the checkbox Prompt User To Enroll Device.

7   Select the checkbox "Do not allow user to skip enrollment step."

8   Select the checkbox "Prevent unenrollment."

> **NOTE ▶** Preventing unenrollment requires supervision for iOS devices; when you select "Prevent unenrollment," the option "Supervise (iOS only)" is automatically selected and cannot be deselected. For more information, see Reference 8.3, "Configure DEP and Apple School Manager Assignments in Profile Manager."

9   Leave the checkboxes selected for Allow Pairing and "Require credentials for enrollment."

Enrollment Settings

Activation Lock Settings
  Unsupervised DEP devices
  ☐ Enable Activation Lock

  Supervised DEP devices
  ○ Enable Activation Lock
  ○ Allow Activation Lock
    ☐ Allow Activation Lock only if Bypass Code is available

  Supervised devices
  ☐ Allow Activation Lock
    ☐ Allow Activation Lock only if Bypass Code is available

☑ **Prompt User To Enroll Device**
  Prompt the user in the setup assistant to enroll in device management

  ☑ **Do not allow user to skip enrollment step**
    Requires device to enroll in MDM before completing setup

  ☑ **Prevent unenrollment**
    Requires supervision on iOS

  ☑ **Supervise (iOS only)**
    Enable supervision
    ☑ Allow pairing with a Mac
    ☐ Configure as Shared iPad
      Number of users: [optional]

☑ **Require credentials for enrollment**

10 Scroll to the Setup Assistant Options section, leave Location Services selected, and then deselect every other checkbox in the section, including those that apply only to OS X.

NOTE ▶ If you are in an instructor-led environment, your instructor may choose to demonstrate how to enroll a Mac computer with your MDM using the DEP. In this case, the OS X–only options will apply. If you are performing these exercises independently and you choose to enroll a DEP-eligible Mac computer, the OS X–only options will apply.

Setup Assistant Options
Choose which options to hide in Setup Assistant. Hidden options keep their most private setting.

iOS and OS X
- ☑ Location Services
- ☐ Set Up as New or Restore
- ☐ Apple ID
- ☐ Terms and Conditions
- ☐ App Analytics

iOS
- ☐ Move from Android
- ☐ Touch ID
- ☐ Passcode Lock
- ☐ Apple Pay
- ☐ Siri
- ☐ Display Zoom

OS X
- ☐ FileVault
- ☐ Registration

NOTE ▶ It is best practice to always turn on Location Services. Otherwise, the clock on your iOS device will be set to US/Pacific time (UTC-8).

11 Click Save.

In this exercise, you created a new MDM server on the Apple Deployment Programs site, exported your server's public key with the Server app, uploaded it to the site, downloaded a server token, and imported it with the Server app. Finally, you created a device group for DEP devices and forced enrollment for devices you will eventually add to the group.

Exercise 8.3
Assign Devices to an MDM Service

> **Prerequisites**
>
> ▸ A DEP Agent or Admin for your organization, or Exercise 8.1, "Enroll with the Apple Deployment Programs"
>
> ▸ Exercise 8.2, "Configure Profile Manager for the DEP"
>
> ▸ An iOS device that is eligible for the DEP (if you do not have one, read along with the exercise)

Challenge

Assign an iOS device to automatically enroll with your MDM server at activation time.

Add the iOS device to the DEP Devices group you created in the previous exercise.

Confirm that Setup Assistant requires the user to enroll in your server's MDM service.

Unassign the iOS device, and confirm that the Setup Assistant no longer requires the user to enroll.

Considerations

You can choose devices by order number or serial number, or you can upload a CSV file. For the purposes of this exercise, use the serial number instead of the order number.

Solution

Assign the Device

1 If necessary, use your server computer to log in to the Apple Deployment Programs site in Safari (https://deploy.apple.com) using your DEP administrator account with two-step verification.

2 In the sidebar, select Device Enrollment Program, and then select Manage Devices.

3 For step 1, select Choose Devices By: Serial Number.

4   Enter the serial number of your iOS device (the iOS device must be eligible for DEP).

You could enter multiple serial numbers, separated by a comma, but for the purposes of this exercise, enter one serial number only.

To identify the serial number, look at the back of the iOS device, or if your iOS device is on and accessible, choose Settings > General > About.

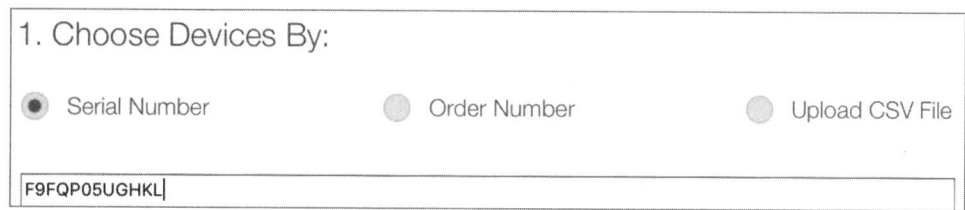

5   For step 2, Choose Action, leave the pop-up menu at Assign to Server.

6   Click the Choose MDM Server pop-up menu, and choose your server.

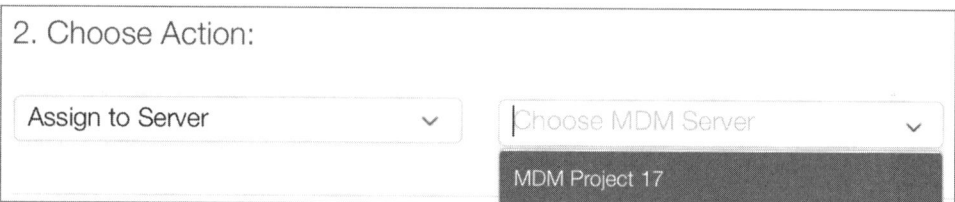

7   Click OK.

8   In the Assignment Complete pane, click OK.

Add the New DEP Placeholder Record to the DEP Device Group

1   If you do not have a Safari tab or window open to your Profile Manager administration portal, on your server Mac, in Safari, open https://servern.local/profilemanager (where *n* is your student number), and then authenticate with your server's local administrator credentials.

2   In the Profile Manager sidebar, select Devices.

3   At the bottom of the Devices section, click the Refresh button.

Note that the Refresh button appeared after you successfully linked your server to the Device Enrollment Program.

4   Confirm that there is a new placeholder record for the iOS device you just assigned to your server. The name of the placeholder will vary based on the type of iOS device you assigned to your MDM server in the Apple Deployment Programs site.

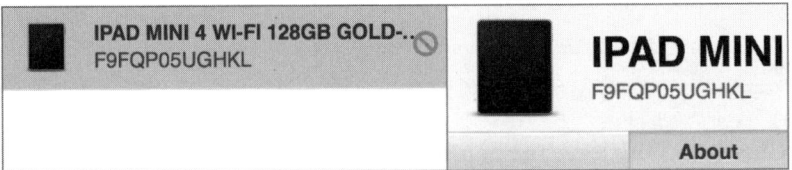

5   In the Profile Manager sidebar, select Device Groups, and then select DEP Devices.

6   Click the Add (+) button, and choose Add Devices.

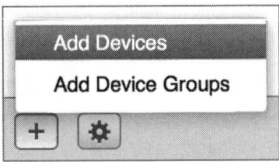

7   For the iOS device you just assigned to your MDM server, click Add.

8   Click Done.

9   Click Save.

In this exercise, you assigned an iOS device to your MDM server, and you added the placeholder record for that device to a device group that forces a user to enroll at activation.

Exercise 8.4
Create and Manage Device Enrollments

▶ **Prerequisites**

- Exercise 6.2, "Create, Download, and Install Profiles for Users and Groups"
- Exercise 8.3, "Assign Devices to an MDM Service"

Challenge

Wipe an iOS device, and confirm that the device Setup Assistant requires you to enroll with your server's Profile Manager service.

Unassign your device, and then wipe the iOS device, and confirm it is not required to enroll in any MDM service.

Considerations

Once a device is disowned (or removed) from the DEP, it is removed forever. Instead of disowning the device, use the Apple Deployment Programs site to unassign the device.

> **WARNING** ▶ If you are in an instructor-led environment, NEVER disown a device.

Solution

Reset Your DEP-Enrolled iOS Device

Use your DEP-eligible iOS device you assigned to your Profile Manager service.

Erase All Content and Settings

If your iOS device is at the Welcome screen, skip to the next section.

1 Press the Home button.

2 Open Settings.

3   Navigate to General > Reset.

4   Tap Erase All Content and Settings.

5   If your iOS device has a passcode, enter the passcode.

6   In the confirmation dialog, tap Erase.

7   In the extra confirmation dialog, tap Erase.

Wait while the iOS device erases all content and settings.

Prepare the iOS Device with Setup Assistant

1   Slide at the "slide to set up" screen.

2   Tap your language.

3   Tap your country or region.

4   Tap your Wi-Fi network. In an instructor-led environment, this may be Classroom Wireless.

5   If necessary, enter the Wi-Fi password, and then tap Join.

   In an instructor-led environment, the password may be student!.

6   At the Location Services screen, tap Enable Location Services.

7   At the Configuration screen, tap Next.

   Note that there is no option to skip.

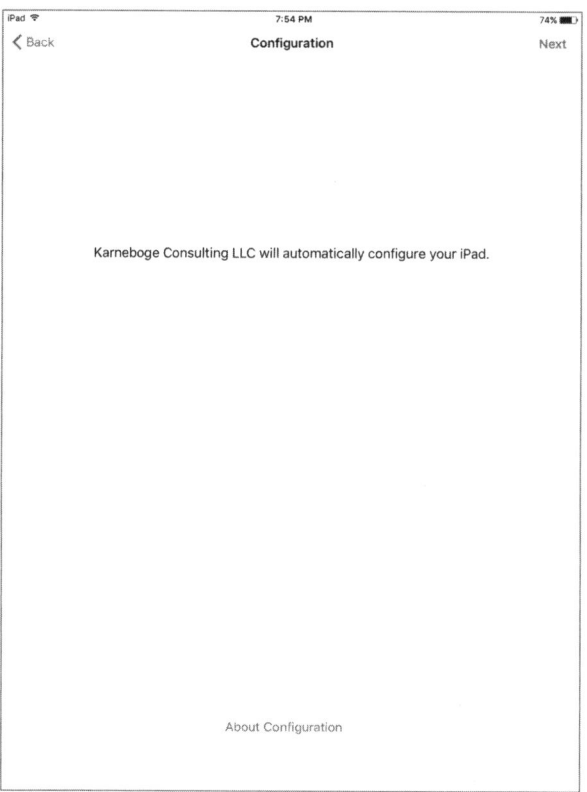

8. Enter credentials for a network user (Username: maria, Password: net).

9. Tap Next, and wait while your device enrolls with your organization and applies any applicable configuration profiles.

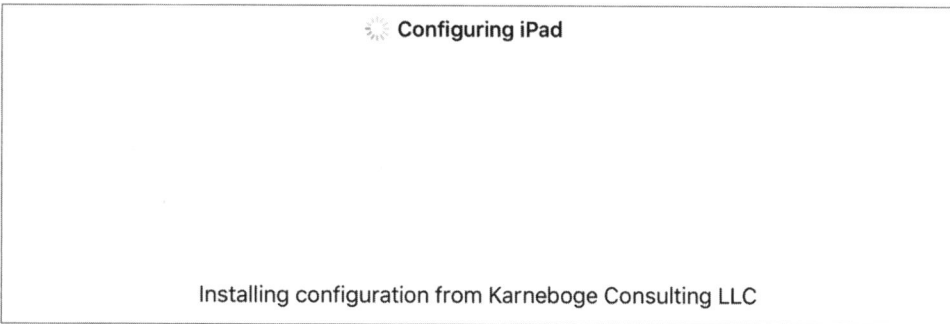

10 At the Welcome screen, tap Get Started.

Note that you did not see all the normal setup screens for the iOS, as you elected to skip them in your Profile Manager enrollment settings for the DEP Devices group.

Confirm the Device Is Associated with Maria Miller

1 If you do not have a Safari tab or window open to your Profile Manager administration portal, on your server Mac, in Safari, open https://servern.local/profilemanager (where *n* is your student number), and then authenticate with your server's local administrator credentials.

2 In the Profile Manager sidebar, select Devices.

3 At the bottom of the Devices section, click the Refresh button.

4 Select your iOS device.

5 Confirm that your device appears in the devices list as associated with Maria Miller and that Supervised is set to Yes.

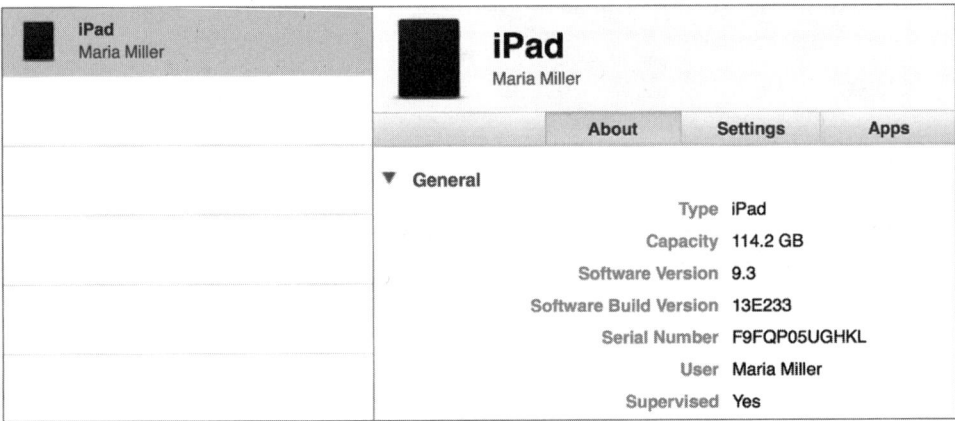

Inspect the Setup Profile That Your MDM Server Installed on Your iOS Device

1 On your iOS device, open Settings > General > Device Management.

2 Confirm that the Remote Management profile appears.

3 Tap the Remote Management profile.

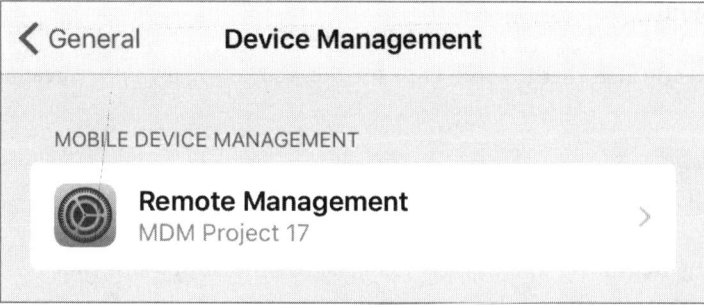

4 Confirm that there is no Remove button for the Remote Management profile.

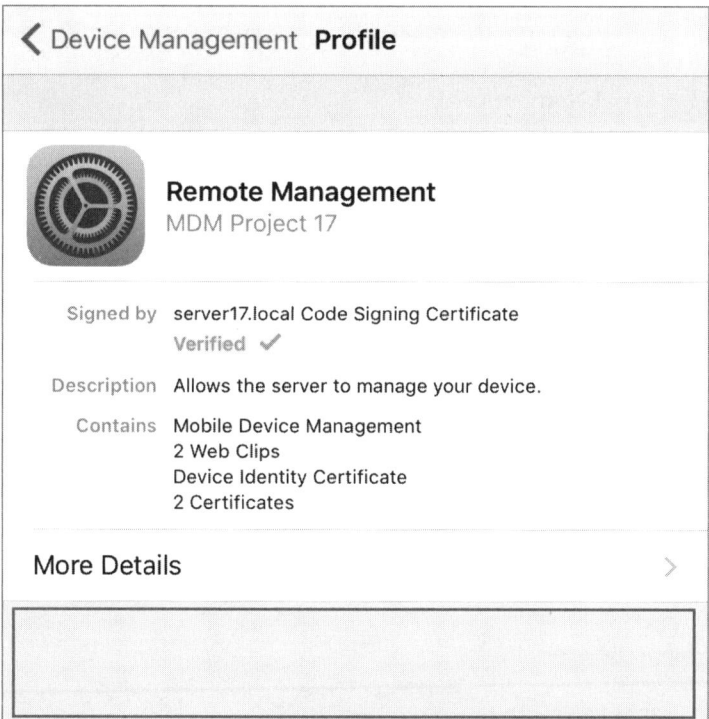

5 Confirm that the Contains field lists "2 Web Clips."

These web clips were automatically pushed because the user you enrolled, and thus associated with your iOS device, is a member of the Marketing group; in Exercise 6.2, "Create, Download, and Install Profiles for Users and Groups," you created web clips for iPad in Business and iPad in Education.

6   Press the Home button.

7   If necessary, slide to confirm that the web clips for the Marketing group are available.

Unassign the iOS Device

Remove the iOS device from being assigned to your MDM server.

1   If your Apple Deployment Programs session in Safari has timed out, use your server computer to log in to the Apple Deployment Programs site in Safari (https://deploy.apple.com) using your DEP administrator account with two-step verification.

2   Select Device Enrollment Program in the sidebar.

3   Click in the Search for Serial Number field.

4   Enter your iOS device's serial number in the Search field.

5   Press Return to search.

6   Click the Assigned To pop-up menu, and then choose Unassigned.

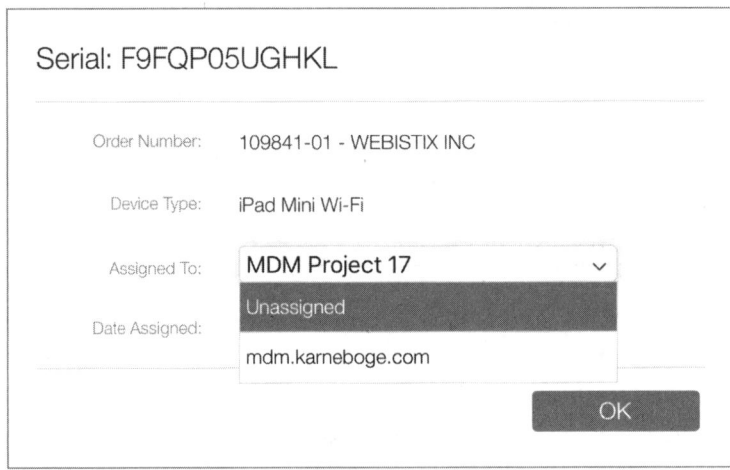

7   Click Reassign to unassign your iOS device.

Wipe Your iOS Device

1   In the Profile Manager administration portal sidebar, select Devices.

2   Select the iOS device you just unassigned.

3   Click the Action (gear icon) pop-menu, and choose Wipe.

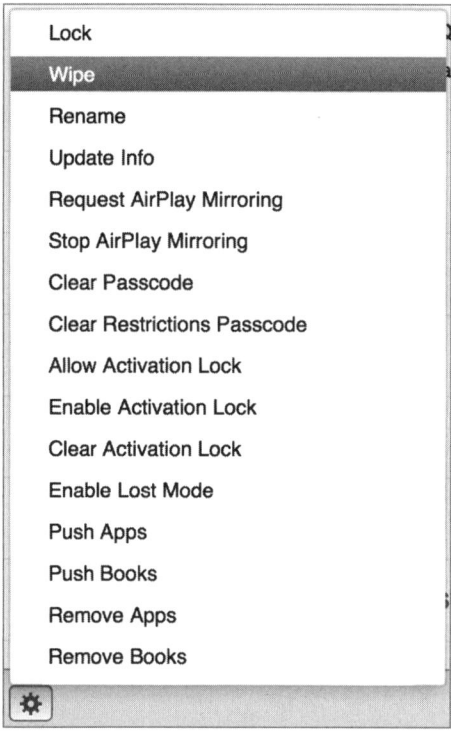

4   In the Wipe dialog, click Wipe.

Remove the Placeholder

1   In the Profile Manager administration portal sidebar, if necessary, click Devices and select the placeholder for the iOS device you just wiped.

2   At the bottom of the devices column, click Refresh.

3   Click the Remove (–) button.

4   At the Remove the placeholder record warning dialog, click Remove.

Prepare the iOS Device with Setup Assistant

Prepare to confirm that your iOS device is no longer forced to enroll with your server's Profile Manager service.

1 Slide at the "slide to set up" screen.

2 Tap your language.

3 Tap your country or region.

4 Tap your Wi-Fi network. In an instructor-led environment; this may be Classroom Wireless.

5 Enter the Wi-Fi password, and then tap Join.

   In an instructor-led environment, the password may be student!.

6 Tap Enable Location Services.

7 If you see the Touch ID screen, tap Set Up Touch ID Later, and then tap Continue.

8 At the Create a Passcode screen, for the purposes of this exercise, tap Passcode Options, tap Don't Add Passcode, and then tap Continue.

   NOTE ▶ In production it is best practice to have a passcode for your iOS device.

9 At the Apps & Data screen, tap Set Up as New iPad (this screen may vary by device).

10 At the Apple ID screen, tap "Don't have an Apple ID or forgot it."

11 At the next Apple ID screen, tap Set Up Later in Settings.

12 In the confirmation dialog, tap Don't Use.

13 Read the terms and conditions, tap Agree, and then tap Agree to confirm.

14 If you see the Siri screen, tap Turn On Siri.

15 At the Diagnostics screen, tap Send to Apple.

16 At the App Analytics screen, tap Share with App Developers.

17 At the Welcome screen, tap Get Started.

Confirm That the iOS Device Is Not Enrolled

1   In the Profile Manager administration portal sidebar, if necessary, select Devices.

2   Click the Refresh button at the bottom of the devices column.

3   Confirm that your iOS device is not listed.

In this exercise, you confirmed that when you assign an iOS device to your MDM server, you must enroll that iOS device with your MDM server to complete the device Setup Assistant. Similarly, when you unassign an iOS device, the device Setup Assistant for that iOS device does not prompt you to enroll with any MDM service.

Lesson 9
Activation Lock Management

In this lesson, you will see how Profile Manager can help administrators control and manage access to Activation Lock on iOS 7 or later devices. That being said, the core technologies behind Activation Lock remain the same even between different Mobile Device Management (MDM) service implementations. Thus, even if your organization chooses to use another MDM service, the concepts covered in this guide still apply.

GOALS

▶ Understand how Activation Lock affects the deployment and recovery of institutionally owned devices

▶ Manage Activation Lock via Profile Manager

Reference 9.1
Activation Lock Introduction

Activation Lock is a security mechanism that prevents unauthorized activation of erased and reset (*wiped*) iOS 7 or later devices. Activation Lock is automatically turned on for unsupervised iOS devices as part of the iCloud Find My Device feature. Activation Lock can also be turned on for supervised devices when managed properly. In other words, Activation Lock is available to all iOS 7 or later devices (and Apple Watch with watchOS2 or later), managed or unmanaged and supervised or unsupervised.

> **NOTE** ▶ Enable Activation Lock is a new task in Profile Manager available only for devices with iOS 9.3 or later that are supervised and enrolled with Apple School Manager. This allows an Apple School Manager administrator to force Activation Lock to be turned on, even if there is no Apple ID associated with the device. Search for Lost Mode and Activation Lock at https://help.apple.com/profilemanager/mac/5.1 for more information.

How Activation Lock Affects Administration

For administrators, Activation Lock is a double-edged sword; it can prevent administrators as well as unauthorized users from activating iOS devices. For this reason, administrators should be aware of the options available for properly managing Activation Lock.

Further, Activation Lock is such an effective theft deterrent that your deployment plan should include workflows for turning on this service and making sure that users understand its capabilities. In fact, the more people who know about Activation Lock, the more effective it is as a theft deterrent.

Find My Device and Activation Lock

Again, Activation Lock prevents unauthorized access to iOS 7 or later devices by requiring authentication during the Setup Assistant process. Activation Lock works in conjunction with the iCloud Find My Device service and is turned on by default when Find My Device is turned on. The combination of setting a device passcode and turning on Find My Device with Activation Lock makes it impossible for an unauthorized user to access an iOS 7 or later device.

> **MORE INFO** ▶ For more information about the "Find" part of Find My Device, please see Apple Support article PH2696, "iCloud: Find My iPhone overview."

Be aware that this combination of security features is effective both before a device is erased and reset (or *wiped*) and after. On iOS 7 or later devices with the Find My Device service turned on, an unauthorized user is not allowed to locally erase and reset an iOS device. In this case, if a user attempts to erase and reset an iOS device from the Settings app, he will be prompted for both the local device passcode and the iCloud password used to set up Find My Device.

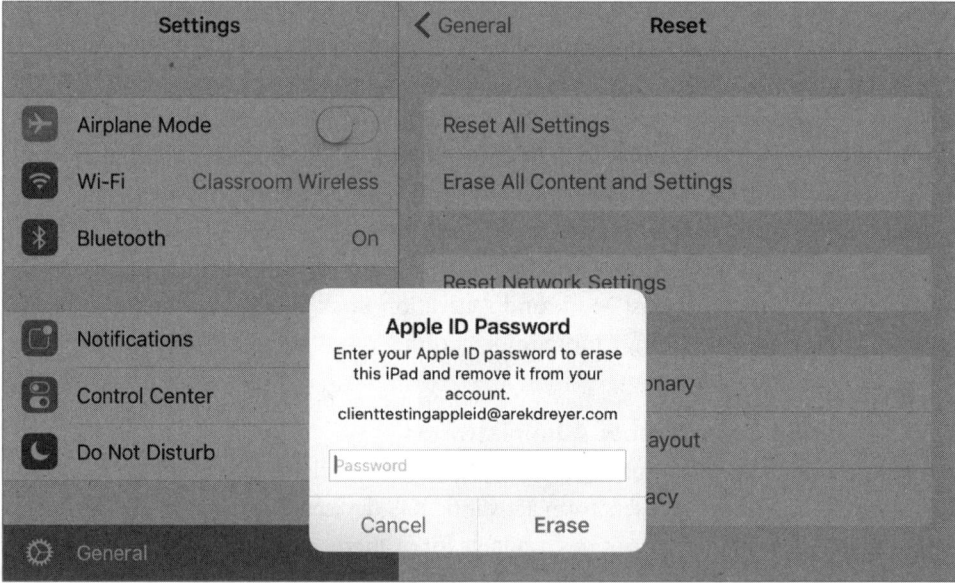

Both users and administrators can still choose to remotely wipe an iOS device with the Find My Device service turned on. As covered previously in this guide, users can wipe the device via the iCloud website or, if you're using Profile Manager, via the user portal. Administrators can also wipe the device via the Profile Manager administration portal. Further, devices supervised via Apple Configurator or Apple Configurator 2 can be erased and reset. However, in all these cases, upon reset after the wipe, an iOS device with Activation Lock turned on will have to be authorized in order to complete device setup or preparation.

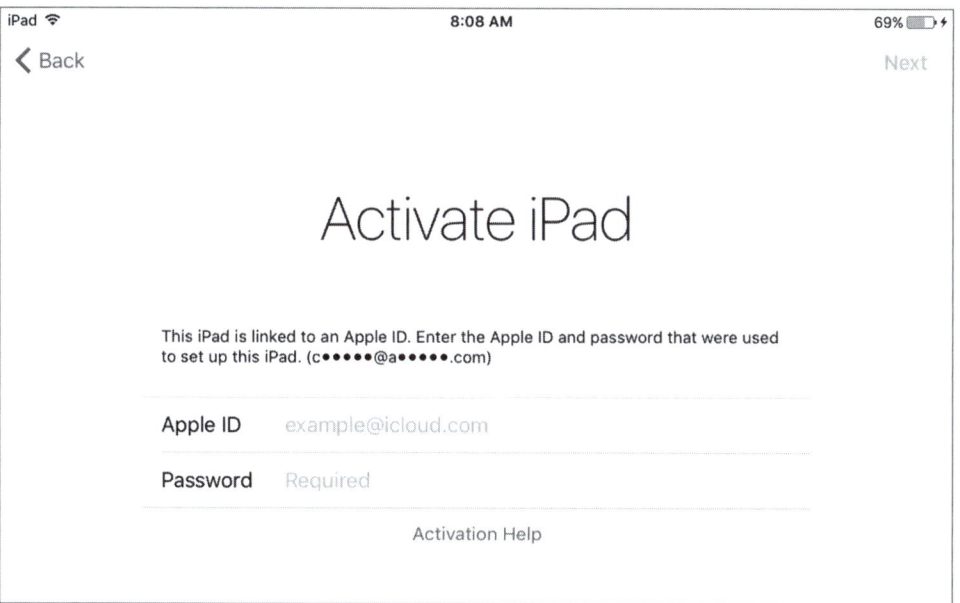

TIP ▶ A user can also clear a device's Activation Lock by releasing it from the Find My Device service. A user can release a device from the Find My Device interface when signed in to the iCloud website. Of course, this requires the cooperation of a person who has access to the credentials for the Apple ID used to turn on Find My Device.

NOTE ▶ Apple Configurator cannot prepare or refresh a device that has Find My Device enabled, even if Activation Lock is not enabled (the device is supervised and MDM wasn't used to allow Activation Lock). See Apple Support article HT202804, "Use Mobile Device Management and Find My iPhone Activation Lock," for more information.

Activation Lock Behavior

Aside from acting as a theft deterrent, Activation Lock can just as easily prevent administrators from being able to prepare or manage institutionally owned devices. With Activation Lock turned on, iOS 7 or later devices are prevented from activation and setup in all possible situations:

- Setup Assistant activation—As shown in the previous screenshot, a device with Activation Lock turned on cannot be activated during Setup Assistant until authenticated. Successful authentication of the iCloud account will clear the Activation Lock and allow Setup Assistant to continue.

- Managed Setup Assistant—Activation Lock also prevents managed Setup Assistant configuration for devices assigned in the Device Enrollment Program (DEP) service (for businesses) or in Apple School Manager (for schools). In other words, the Activation Lock must be cleared to proceed with the remainder of the Setup Assistant process, including any managed enrollment configuration.

- iTunes activation—A device with Activation Lock turned on cannot be activated via iTunes; thus, it cannot be set up or restored from a backup via iTunes. Older versions of iTunes simply cannot activate the device, but newer versions will prompt for iCloud credentials to clear the Activation Lock and proceed.

▶ Apple Configurator activation—A device with Activation Lock turned on cannot be activated via Apple Configurator or Apple Configurator 2; thus, it cannot be prepared by Apple Configurator or Apple Configurator 2.

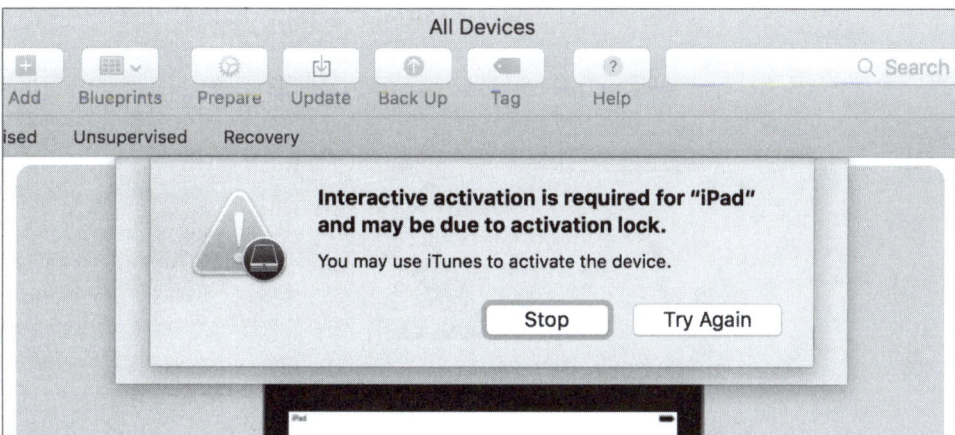

Reference 9.2
Manage Activation Lock

Profile Manager supports the management of Activation Lock through a variety of mechanisms. First, an administrator can use Profile Manager to *enable* (in other words, turn on) Activation Lock for supervised devices with iOS 9.3 or later that are enrolled with Apple School Manager. Second, an administrator can use Profile Manager to *allow* Activation Lock for supervised iOS devices after a user turns on Find My Device. Finally, Profile Manager provides several methods for allowing administrators to clear Activation Lock without users having to enter their iCloud authentication.

If an iOS device is enrolled with your Profile Manager service, you can use the administration portal to check whether Activation Lock is enabled. Select the device, click the About tab, and then click the disclosure triangle to open the Security section. Here's an example of an iOS device that is enrolled but isn't Supervised. Because the user enabled Find My Device, Activation Lock is automatically enabled.

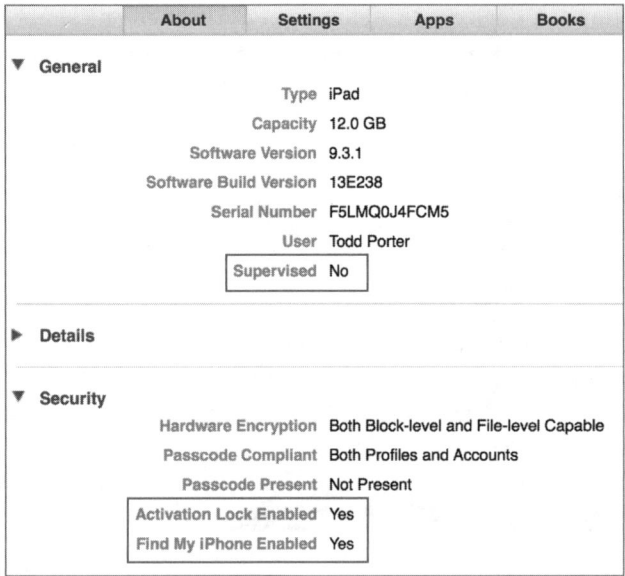

Allowing Activation Lock via Profile Manager

Again, as a default, supervised iOS devices are not allowed to turn on Activation Lock. This can result in Activation Lock not being enabled even though Find My Device is enabled.

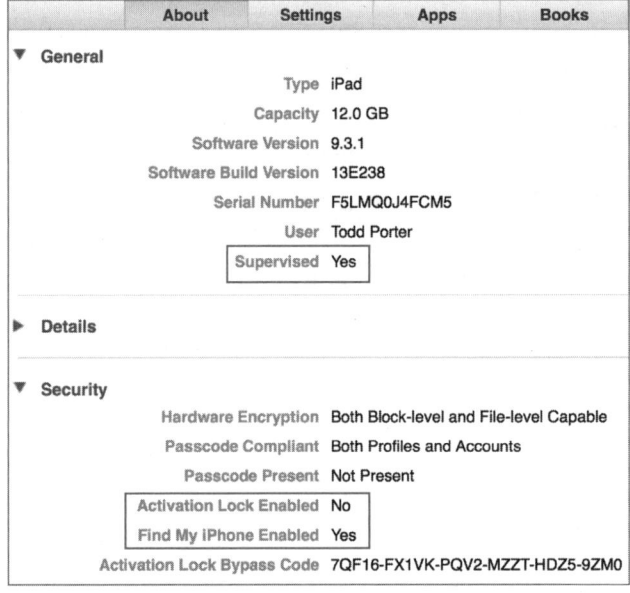

NOTE ▶ If you use Profile Manager, you may need to send the Update task to the device to get an updated report of whether Activation Lock and Find My Device are enabled.

However, if the iOS devices are going to be used outside a controlled environment, turning on Activation Lock is strongly suggested.

To manually allow a user to enable Activation Lock for supervised iOS devices, simply select a device, device group, user, or user group, and then from the Action (gear icon) menu, choose the Allow Activation Lock task. Keep in mind that if you select a user or user group, you will be allowing Activation Lock only for devices associated with the selected users. The Allow Activation Lock task uses the Apple Push Notification service (APNs) to allow users to turn on Activation Lock on the selected devices.

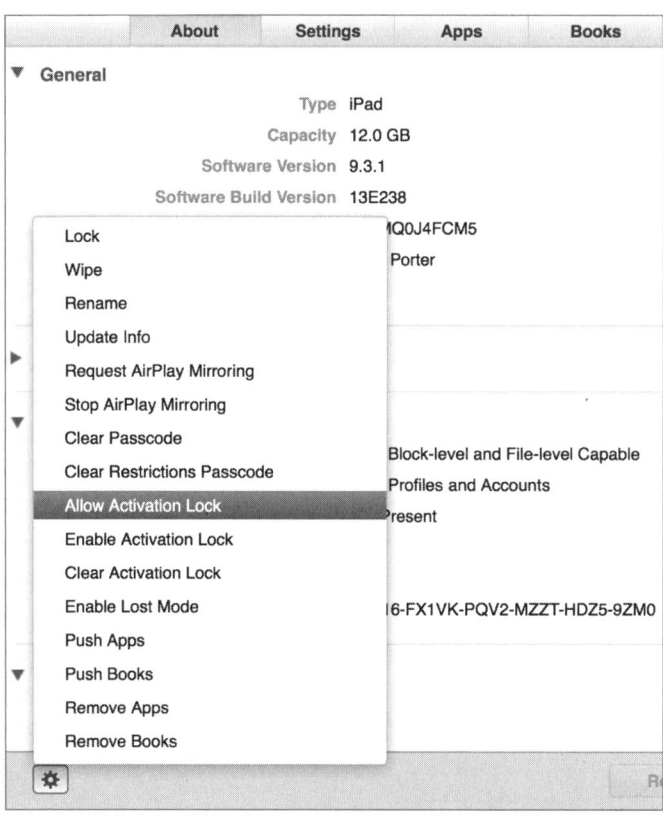

However, after you choose Allow Activation Lock, Activation Lock isn't actually enabled until the user turns on Find My Device. If Find My Device is turned on, the user must first turn it off (with Settings > iCloud > Find My Device) and provide his Apple ID password.

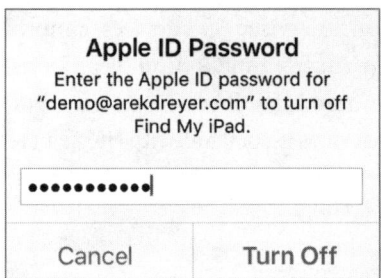

Then he can turn on Find My Device again.

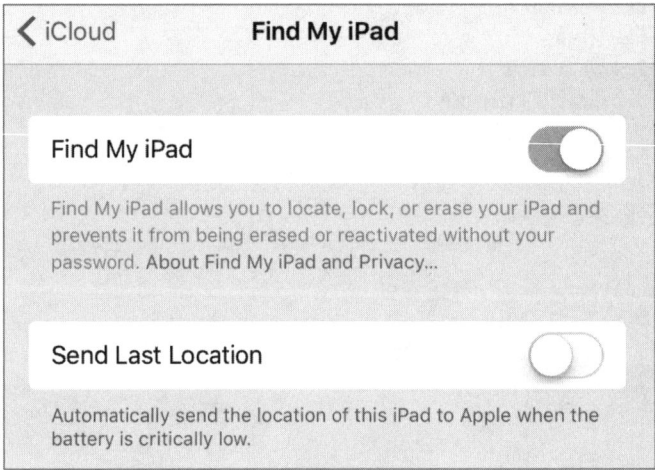

If you update the information for the device, you'll see that Activation Lock is now enabled.

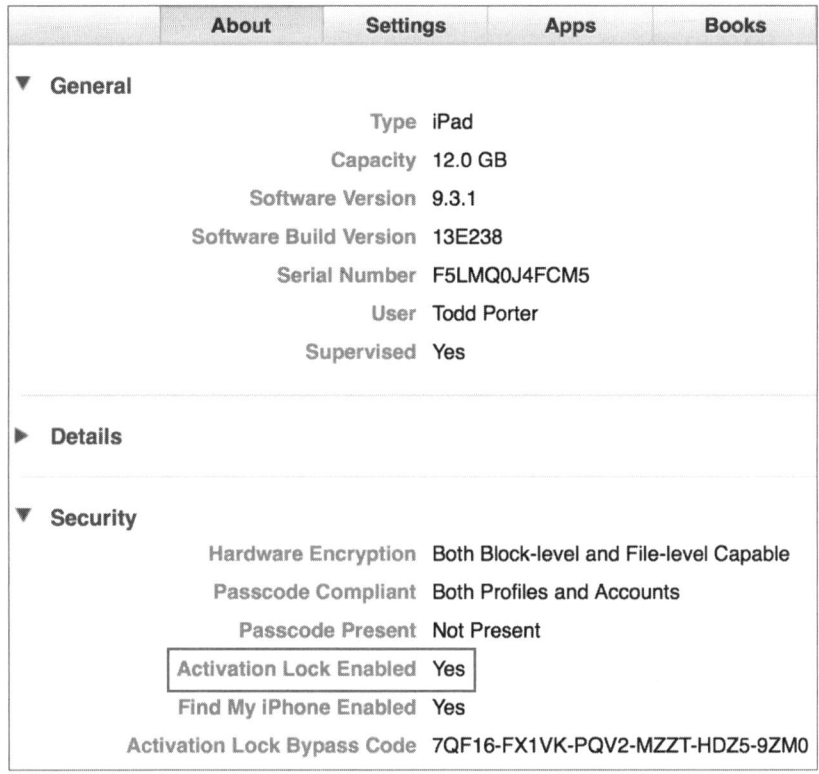

NOTE ▶ You may need to click the Action (gear) menu and choose Update Info to update the status of Activation Lock.

If users are allowed to enroll their own supervised iOS devices, Profile Manager can automatically allow Activation Lock after enrollment so that administrators don't have to remember to allow Activation Lock. To turn this on in Profile Manager, select a user or user group, and then click the Settings tab to reveal the user-based enrollment settings. If you want to automatically allow Activation Lock for all users, you can specify this by managing the Activation Lock enrollment settings for the Everyone group.

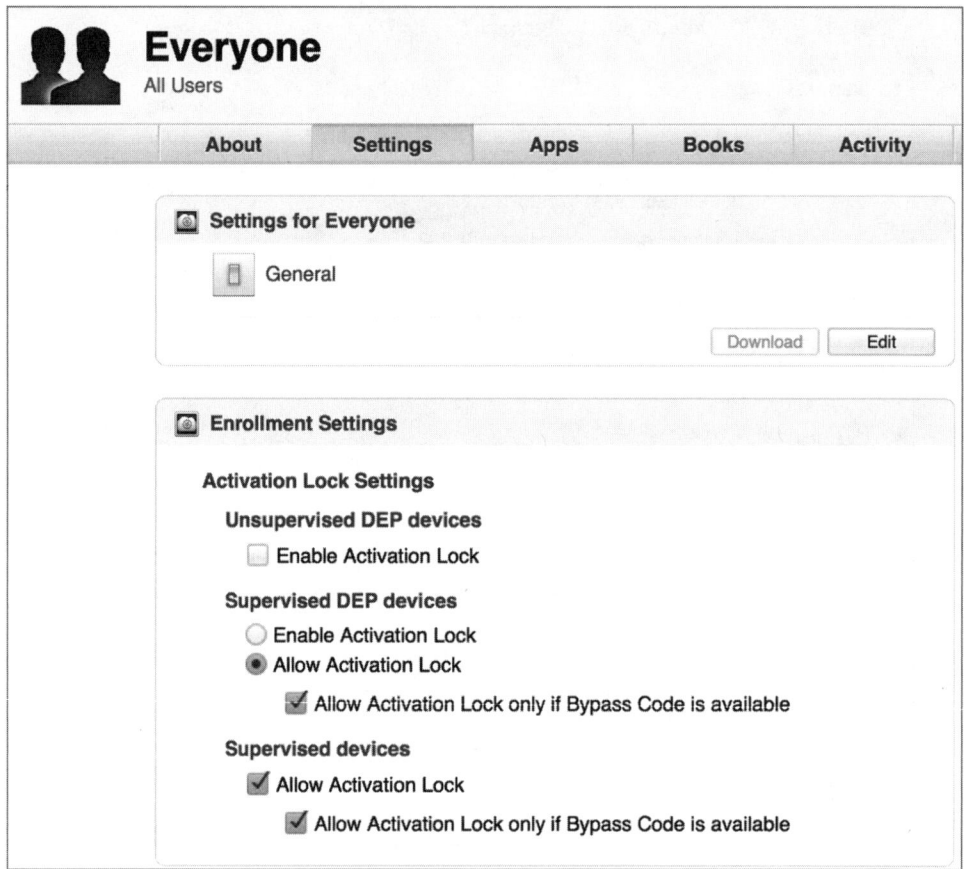

Selecting the option to automatically send the Allow Activation Lock command activates a suboption to send the command only if the Activation Lock bypass code has been obtained. This code can be used by an administrator to clear Activation Lock on a managed device, as covered in the next section.

> **NOTE ▶** The Enable Activation Lock option is applicable only to iOS devices with iOS 9.3 or later, supervised, and enrolled with Apple School Manager. If this does not apply to your devices, select Allow Activation Lock instead.

> **NOTE ▶** There are two categories for the Allow Activation Lock option under "Supervised devices": for devices supervised via the DEP and for devices supervised via Apple Configurator 2.

Clearing Activation Lock via Profile Manager

As covered previously, a user can clear an iOS device's Activation Lock by entering his iCloud credentials. However, this doesn't help administrators (or a user who has forgotten his iCloud password) in clearing Activation Lock. As such, Profile Manager provides two methods for clearing a device's Activation Lock.

Both methods for clearing a device's Activation Lock require that the MDM service has collected the device's Activation Lock bypass code. This code is generated automatically for supervised iOS 7 or later devices during setup. Profile Manager will always attempt to collect the Activation Lock bypass code when available.

> **NOTE ▶** If you are in a situation where an institutionally owned device has Activation Lock turned on and you don't have access to the iCloud authentication or the Activation Lock bypass code, you will need to contact AppleCare directly by phone to disable Activation Lock. Be prepared to present proof of institutional purchase along with the device's serial number to the AppleCare attendant.

Manually Enter Bypass Code

Assuming you have access to the Activation Lock bypass code, the first method to clear a device's Activation Lock is to enter it as the password when prompted for the iCloud credentials. In other words, when prompted to clear the Activation Lock during Setup Assistant or in iTunes, you can leave the iCloud user name blank and then enter the Activation Lock bypass code for the password. This combination will clear Activation Lock.

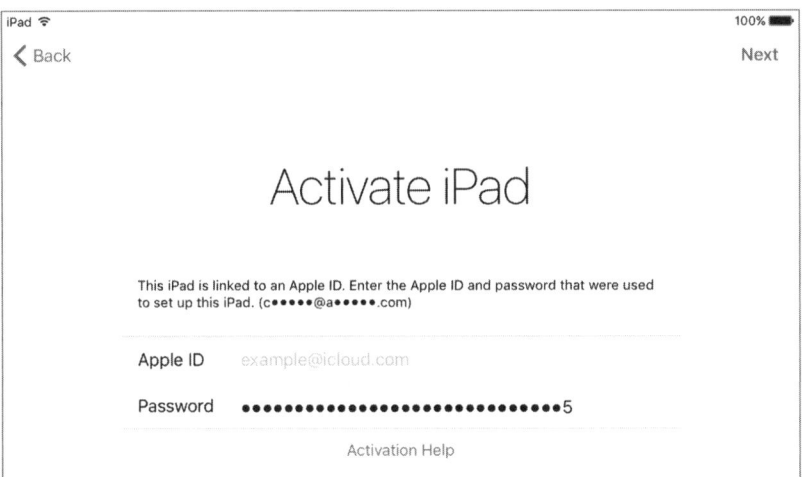

NOTE ▶ The Activation Lock bypass code is re-created with a new code every time a supervised iOS device is reactivated. In other words, using the bypass code will result in a new bypass code being generated.

TIP ▶ The Activation Lock bypass code is case-sensitive. It's easy to make a mistake entering the Activation Lock bypass code. Consider using the Clear Activation Lock task, as described in the next section.

Clear Activation Lock Task

The other option is to clear the Activation Lock remotely via the Profile Manager administration portal. To clear Activation Lock, simply select a device, device group, user, or user group, and then from the Action (gear icon) menu, choose the Clear Activation Lock task.

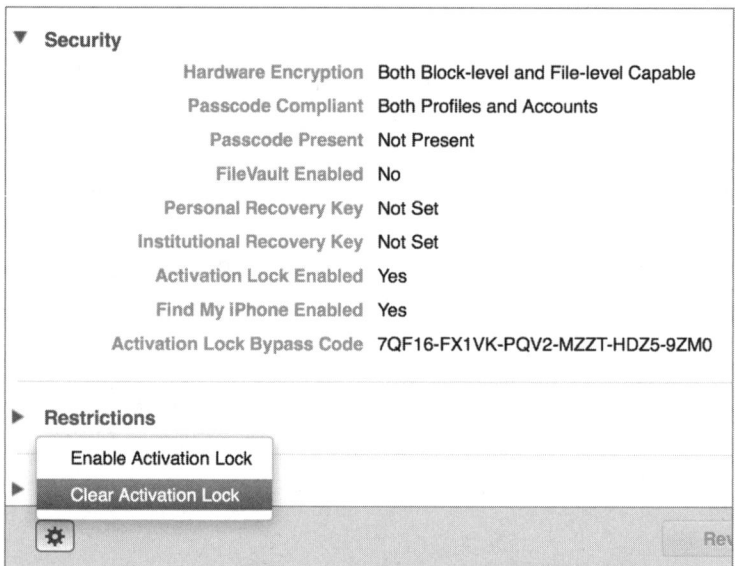

Keep in mind that if you select a user or user group, you will be clearing Activation Lock only for devices associated with the selected users. The Clear Activation Lock task will send a message to Apple's activation servers to clear Activation Lock.

After you clear the device's Activation Lock, the user may still be stuck at the Setup Assistant Activation Lock screen. In this case, the user needs to simply navigate to the previous Setup Assistant screen and then continue. This will force the device to requery Apple's activation servers and should result in an unlocked device.

Exercise 9.1
Observe Activation Lock on an Unsupervised Device

▶ **Prerequisites**

- Exercise 4.1, "Prepare Your Mac to Install OS X Server for El Capitan"
- Exercise 4.2, "Install OS X Server for El Capitan"
- Exercise 4.3, "Configure OS X Server for El Capitan"
- Exercise 7.1, "Enable Device Management"
- iCloud must be available in the country associated with your Apple ID. Refer to www.apple.com/legal/internet-services/icloud/ww/.

Challenge
Observe that Activation Lock is enabled on an unsupervised iOS device if you turn on Find My Device, even if the device is enrolled in your MDM service.

- Enroll in your server's Profile manager service as a user.
- Sign in to iCloud and turn on Find My iPad (this exercise uses "Find My iPad"; this name may vary by device).
- Send a Wipe task to that device.
- Observe that Activation Lock was turned on.

Considerations
To successfully complete this exercise, your iOS device needs to be unsupervised. Enroll using the user portal instead of the Device Enrollment Program (DEP).

Solution

Erase All Content and Settings
If your iOS device is at the Welcome screen, skip to the next section.

1 On your iOS device, if necessary, slide at the "slide to unlock" screen.

2 If necessary, enter the passcode.

3 Open Settings.

4 Navigate to General > Reset.

5 Tap Erase All Content and Settings.

6 If your iOS device has a passcode, enter the passcode.

7 In the confirmation dialog, tap Erase.

8 In the extra confirmation dialog, tap Erase.

Wait while the iOS device erases all content and settings.

Prepare Your iOS Device with Setup Assistant
Set up your iOS device without entering an Apple ID.

1 Slide at the "slide to set up" screen.

2 Tap your language.

3 Tap your country or region.

4 Tap your Wi-Fi network. In an instructor-led environment, this may be Classroom Wireless.

5 Enter the Wi-Fi password, and then tap Join.

   In an instructor-led environment, the password may be student!.

6 Tap Enable Location Services.

7 If you see the Touch ID screen, tap Set Up Touch ID Later, and then tap Continue.

8 At the Create a Passcode screen, for the purposes of this exercise, tap Passcode Options, tap Don't Add Passcode, and then tap Continue.

   NOTE ▶ In production it is best practice to have a passcode for your iOS device.

9 At the Apps & Data screen, tap Set Up as New iPad (this screen may vary by device).

10 At the Apple ID screen, tap "Don't have an Apple ID or forgot it."

11 At the next Apple ID screen, tap Set Up Later in Settings.

12 In the confirmation dialog, tap Don't Use.

13 Read the terms and conditions, tap Agree, and then, if necessary, tap Agree to confirm.

14 If you see the Siri screen, tap Turn On Siri.

15 At the Diagnostics screen, tap Send to Apple.

16 At the App Analytics screen, tap Share with App Developers.

17 At the Welcome screen, tap Get Started.

Enroll with Your MDM

1 On your iOS device, in Safari, open the user portal (https://servern.local/mydevices, where *n* is your student number).

2 If you see the message "Cannot Verify Server Identity," tap Continue.

3 In the Please Log In window, enter the following credentials, and tap Log In:

▶ User Name: sue
▶ Password: net

4 Tap Enroll.

5 Tap Install, tap Install again, and then tap Trust.

6 Tap Done.

7 If necessary, navigate to General > Device Management, and view the Remote Management profile to verify you are enrolled with your MDM.

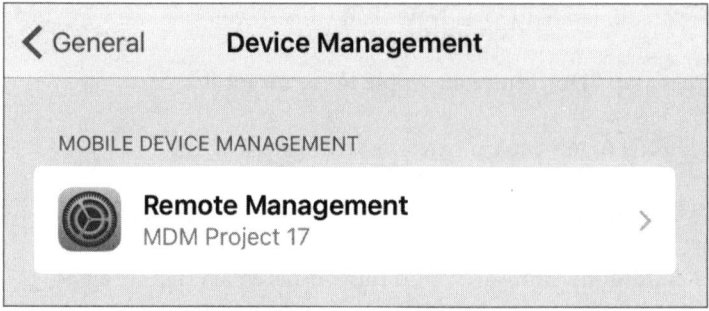

8 On your server Mac, in Safari, open the Profile Manager administration portal (https://servern.local/profilemanager, where *n* is your student number), and then authenticate with local administrator credentials.

9 In the Profile Manager administration portal sidebar, select Devices.

10 Select the iOS device you just enrolled as Sue Wu, and if necessary, click the About tab.

Observe that the device is not supervised.

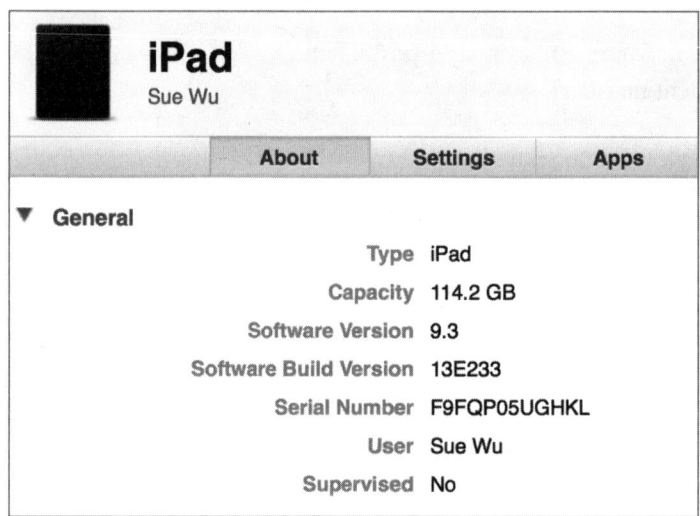

11 Click the disclosure triangle next to Security, and observe that Activation Lock and Find My iPhone are not turned on.

```
▼ Security
        Hardware Encryption  Both Block-level and File-level Capable
         Passcode Compliant  Both Profiles and Accounts
            Passcode Present  Not Present
      Activation Lock Enabled  No
        Find My iPhone Enabled  No
```

Enable Activation Lock on Your iOS Device

1. On your iOS device, if necessary, slide at the "slide to unlock" screen.

2. If necessary, enter the passcode.

3. Navigate to Settings > iCloud.

4. Enter your client testing Apple ID credentials, and tap Sign In.

5. If you have two-step verification turned on for the Apple ID, choose a device to receive a verification code, tap Send, and then enter the four-digit verification code.

6. If you are presented with a Merge with iCloud screen, tap Don't Merge.

7. If necessary, at the Terms and Conditions screen, tap Agree, and then tap Agree again.

8. At the Find My iPad Enabled screen, tap OK.

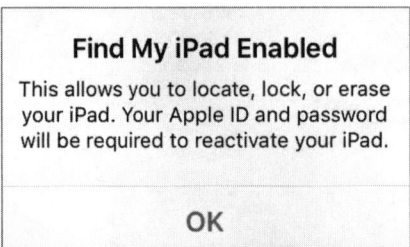

9 Observe that in the iCloud settings list, Find My iPad is On.

10 On your server Mac, if necessary, open the Profile Manager administration portal, and in the sidebar, select Devices.

11 If necessary, select the iOS device where you just turned on Find My iPad, and click the disclosure triangle next to Security.

12 Click the action (gear) menu, and select Update Info.

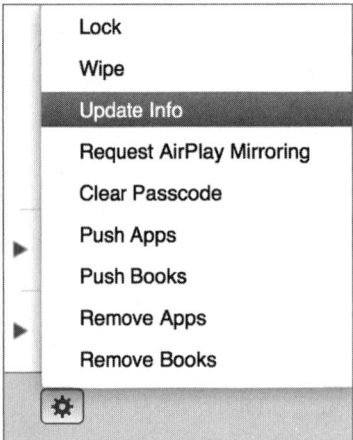

13 At the Update Info confirmation dialog, click Update Info.

14 Observe that Activation Lock and Find My iPhone are enabled.

```
▼ Security
        Hardware Encryption   Both Block-level and File-level Capable
         Passcode Compliant   Both Profiles and Accounts
           Passcode Present   Not Present
      Activation Lock Enabled Yes
       Find My iPhone Enabled Yes
```

Wipe the iOS Device

1 Click the Action (gear icon) menu, and choose Wipe.

2 In the Wipe confirmation dialog, click Wipe.

3 After the wipe task completes, select the placeholder for the iPad you just wiped, and click the Remove (–) button.

4 In the confirmation dialog, click Remove Placeholder.

Set Up the Device Using Your Apple ID Credentials

1 Slide at the "slide to set up" screen.

2 Tap your language.

3 Tap your country or region.

4 Tap your Wi-Fi network. In an instructor-led environment, this may be Classroom Wireless.

5 Enter the Wi-Fi password, and then tap Join.

   In an instructor-led environment, the password may be student!.

   Note that at this point you are prompted for the Apple ID credentials you used to turn on Find My iPad, so Activation Lock is turned on.

6 Enter your client testing Apple ID credentials.

> **Activate iPad**
>
> This iPad is linked to an Apple ID. Enter the Apple ID and password that were used to set up this iPad. (c●●●●●@k●●●●●.com)
>
> Apple ID clienttestingappleid@karneboge.com
>
> Password ●●●●●●●●●●●●●
>
> Activation Help

7   Tap Next.

Because you successfully entered the Apple ID credentials that you used to turn on Activation Lock, you were able to successfully clear Activation Lock from the iOS device.

8   Tap Enable Location Services.

9   If you see the Touch ID screen, tap Set Up Touch ID Later, and then tap Continue.

10 At the Create a Passcode screen, for the purposes of this exercise, tap Passcode Options, tap Don't Add Passcode, and then tap Continue.

> **NOTE** ▸ In production it is best practice to have a passcode for your iOS device.

11 At the Apps & Data screen, tap Set Up as New iPad (this screen may vary by device).

12 At the Apple ID screen, tap "Don't have an Apple ID or forgot it."

13 At the next Apple ID screen, tap Set Up Later in Settings.

14 In the confirmation dialog, tap Don't Use.

15 Read the terms and conditions, tap Agree, and then, if necessary, tap Agree to confirm.

16 If you see the Siri screen, tap Turn On Siri.

17 At the Diagnostics screen, tap Send to Apple.

18 At the App Analytics screen, tap Share with App Developers.

19 At the Welcome screen, tap Get Started.

In this exercise, you successfully enrolled in your server's MDM service using an iPad that was not supervised. Then, you turned on Find My iPad and observed that even though you were enrolled in MDM management, Activation Lock was still turned on.

Finally, you observed the effects of Activation Lock by setting up your iOS device and unlocking it with your Apple ID credentials.

Exercise 9.2
Control Activation Lock on a Supervised Device

▶ **Prerequisites**

- Exercise 4.1, "Prepare Your Mac to Install OS X Server for El Capitan"
- Exercise 4.2, "Install OS X Server for El Capitan"
- Exercise 4.3, "Configure OS X Server for El Capitan"
- Exercise 7.1, "Enable Device Management"
- Exercise 8.2, "Configure Profile Manager for the Device Enrollment Program"
- iCloud must be available in the country associated with your Apple ID. Refer to www.apple.com/legal/internet-services/icloud/ww/.

Challenge
Demonstrate that a supervised iOS device cannot have Activation Lock turned on unless your MDM solution allows Activation Lock. By default, Profile Manager does not allow Activation Lock, and your supervised device does not have Activation Lock turned on:

- Enroll and supervise an iOS device over the air as a user using the DEP.
- Sign in to iCloud, and turn on Find My iPad.
- Observe that Activation Lock was not turned on.
- Send a Wipe task to that device.

When you use the device Setup Assistant, Activation Lock will not be turned on, so you will not need to provide your Apple ID credentials to activate the iOS device.

Then, configure the DEP Devices group in your server's Profile Manager service to Allow Activation Lock on any supervised iOS device. Repeat the process from the beginning of the exercise:

- Enroll and supervise an iOS device over the air as a user using the DEP.
- Sign in to iCloud, and turn on Find My iPad.
- Observe that Activation Lock was turned on.
- Send a Wipe task to the device.

This time, when you run through the device Setup Assistant, you will be challenged for your Apple ID credentials (which proves that Activation Lock is turned on), but instead of your Apple ID credentials, use the Activation Lock bypass code to bypass the Activation screen on a freshly wiped iOS device.

Considerations

In order to supervise your iOS device, prepare your device using the DEP.

For the second part of the exercise, configure the enrollment settings for the DEP Devices group to allow the following options:

- Supervised devices: Allow Activation Lock
- Allow Activation Lock only if Bypass Code is available

    NOTE ▶ Settings for the DEP Devices group do not apply to member devices that are enrolled via an enrollment profile; they apply only to member devices that are enrolled with user credentials and associated with a user. Devices need to be members of the group prior to turning on Find My Device. If doing this with Setup Assistant, use a placeholder record.

Solution

Assign the Device to Your MDM Server

1   Use your server computer to log in to the Apple Deployment Programs site in Safari (https://deploy.apple.com) using your DEP administrator account with two-step verification.

2   In the sidebar, select Device Enrollment Program, and then select Manage Devices.

3   For step 1, select Choose Devices By: Serial Number.

4   Enter the serial number of your iOS device (the iOS device must be eligible for DEP).

    To identify the serial number, look at the back of the iOS device, or if your iOS device is on and accessible, go to Settings > General > About.

5   For step 2, Choose Action, leave the pop-up menu at Assign to Server.

6   Click the Choose MDM Server pop-up menu, and choose your server.

7   Click OK.

8   In the Assignment Complete pane, click OK.

Adjust the Enrollment Settings and Add the New DEP Placeholder Record to the DEP Devices Group

1   If you do not have a Safari tab or window open to your Profile Manager administration portal, on your server Mac, in Safari, open https://servern.local/profilemanager (where *n* is your student number), and then authenticate with your server's local administrator credentials.

2   In the Profile Manager sidebar, select Devices.

3   At the bottom of the Devices section, click the Refresh button.

4   Confirm that there is a new placeholder record for the iOS device you just assigned to your server. The name of the placeholder will vary based on the type of iOS device you assigned to your MDM server in the Apple Deployment Programs site.

5   In the Profile Manager sidebar, select Device Groups, and then select DEP Devices.

6   Click the Settings tab.

7   Under Enrollment Settings, scroll down to Setup Assistant Options, and select Apple ID. Do not adjust the Activation Lock Settings at this time.

```
iOS and OS X
☑ Location Services
☐ Set Up as New or Restore
☑ Apple ID
☐ Terms and Conditions
☐ App Analytics
```

8   Click the Add (+) button, and choose Add Devices.

9   For the iOS device you just assigned to your MDM server, click Add.

10 Click Done.

11 Click Save.

Erase All Content and Settings
If your iOS device is at the Welcome screen, skip to the next section.

1   On your iOS device, if necessary, slide at the "slide to unlock" screen.

2   If necessary, enter the passcode.

3   Open Settings.

4   Navigate to General > Reset.

5   Tap Erase All Content and Settings.

6   If your iOS device has a passcode, enter the passcode.

7   In the confirmation dialog, tap Erase.

8   In the extra confirmation dialog, tap Erase.

Wait while the iOS device erases all content and settings.

Enroll with Your MDM Using the DEP and Enable Find My iPad During the Device Setup Assistant

1   On your iOS device, slide at the "slide to set up" screen.

2   Tap your language.

3   Tap your country or region.

4   Tap your Wi-Fi network. In an instructor-led environment, this may be Classroom Wireless.

5   If necessary, enter the Wi-Fi password, and then tap Join.

    In an instructor-led environment, the password may be student!.

6   At the Location Services screen, tap Enable Location Services.

7   At the Configuration screen, tap Next.

8   Enter credentials for a network user (Username: sue, Password: net).

9   Tap Next, and wait while your device enrolls with your organization and applies any applicable configuration profiles.

10 At the Apple ID screen, tap Sign In with Your Apple ID.

11 Enter your client testing Apple ID credentials, and tap Next.

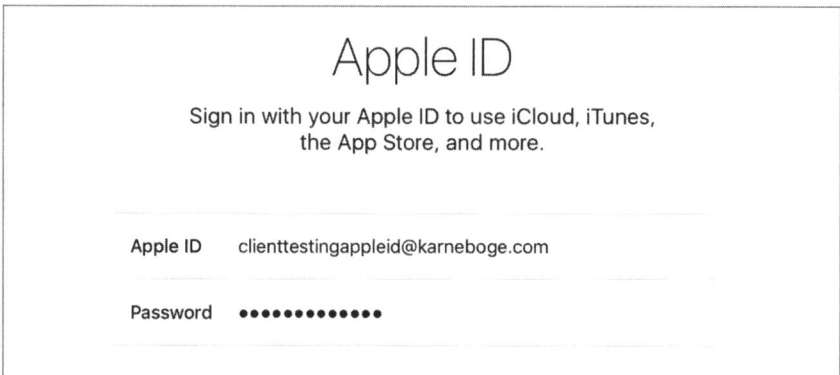

12 If you have two-step authentication turned on for the Apple ID, choose a device to receive a verification code, tap Send, and then enter the four-digit verification code.

13 At the Terms and Conditions screen, tap Agree.

Your iOS device will use your Apple ID to sign in to iCloud and will turn on Find My iPad.

14 At the Welcome screen, tap Get Started.

Send the Wipe Task to the Device

1 On your server Mac, in Safari, open https://server*n*.local/profilemanager (where *n* is your student number), and then authenticate with local administrator credentials.

2 In the Profile Manager administration portal sidebar, select Devices.

3 Select the iOS device you just supervised and enrolled as Sue Wu.

4 Click the About tab.

5 Click the Action (gear icon) menu, and choose Update Info.

6 In the Update Info confirmation dialog, click Update Info.

7 Wait for the Update Info task to complete. You can watch the count of current active tasks in Active Tasks in the Profile Manager administration portal sidebar.

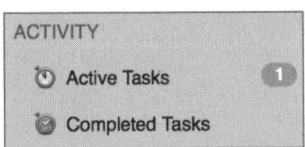

8 Tap the Security disclosure triangle to reveal more information.

9 Confirm that Activation Lock Enabled is set to No.

If Activation Lock Enabled is set to Yes, click the Settings tab, and confirm that any Allow Activation Lock checkboxes under "Supervised DEP devices" and "Supervised devices" are not selected; repeat this for any device groups that your iOS device may be a member of and for any user groups that Sue Wu is a member of. Repeat this again for the everyone group as well as Sue Wu's user record.

▼ Security	
Hardware Encryption	Both Block-level and File-level Capable
Passcode Compliant	Both Profiles and Accounts
Passcode Present	Not Present
Activation Lock Enabled	No
Find My iPhone Enabled	Yes

10 Click the Action pop-up menu, and choose Wipe.

11 In the Wipe confirmation dialog, click Wipe.

Allow Activation Lock

1 In the Profile Manager administration portal sidebar, select Device Groups.

2 Select the DEP Devices group.

3 If necessary, click the Settings tab.

4 Under Enrollment Settings, select the checkbox Allow Activation Lock under "Supervised devices."

5 The other checkbox is automatically selected; leave selected "Allow Activation Lock only if Bypass Code is available."

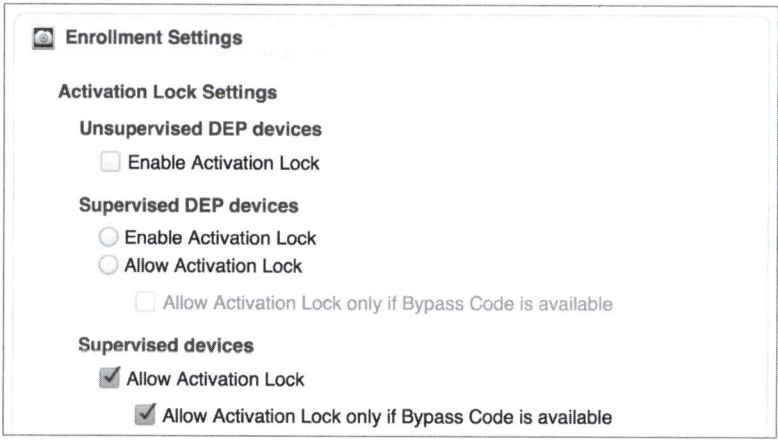

6 Click Save.

Enroll with Your MDM Using the DEP and Enable Find My iPad During the Device Setup Assistant

1. On your iOS device, slide at the "slide to set up" screen.

2. Tap your language.

3. Tap your country or region.

4. Tap your Wi-Fi network. In an instructor-led environment, this may be Classroom Wireless.

5. If necessary, enter the Wi-Fi password, and then tap Join.

    In an instructor-led environment, the password may be student!.

6. At the Location Services screen, tap Enable Location Services.

7. At the Configuration screen, tap Next.

8. Enter credentials for a network user (Username: sue, Password: net).

9. Tap Next, and wait while your device enrolls with your organization and applies any applicable configuration profiles.

10. At the Apple ID screen, tap Sign In with Your Apple ID.

11. Enter your client testing Apple ID credentials, and tap Next.

12. If you have two-step authentication turned on for the Apple ID, choose a device to receive a verification code, tap Send, and then enter the four-digit verification code.

13. At the Terms and Conditions screen, tap Agree.

    Your iOS device will use your Apple ID to sign in to iCloud and will turn on Find My iPad.

14. At the Welcome screen, tap Get Started.

Gather the Activation Lock Bypass Code

1. In the Profile Manager administration portal sidebar, select Devices.

2. Select the iOS device you just supervised and enrolled as Sue Wu.

3   If necessary, click the About tab.

4   If necessary, click the Security disclosure triangle to reveal more information.

5   Note that both Activation Lock Enabled and Find My iPhone are set to No.

    This is outdated information, so you will update the information next.

6   Click the Action (gear) pop-up menu, and choose Update Info.

7   At the Update Info confirmation dialog, click Update Info.

8   Wait for the Update Info task to complete.

    Note that both Activation Lock Enabled and Find My iPhone changed from No to Yes.

9   If both Activation Lock Enabled and Find My iPhone do not display the status of Yes, Update Info again.

▼ Security	
Hardware Encryption	Both Block-level and File-level Capable
Passcode Compliant	Both Profiles and Accounts
Passcode Present	Not Present
Activation Lock Enabled	Yes
Find My iPhone Enabled	Yes
Activation Lock Bypass Code	TEE8V-UA8Q1-9UUL-Q715-AJ7L-PLW2

Wipe the iOS Device

1   Click the Action (gear icon) menu, and choose Wipe.

2   In the Wipe confirmation dialog, click Wipe.

    Because you need the Activation Lock bypass code, do not remove the placeholder.

Set Up the Device Using the Activation Lock Bypass Code

1   On your iOS device, slide at the "slide to set up" screen.

2   Tap your language.

3   Tap your country or region.

4   Tap your Wi-Fi network. In an instructor-led environment, this may be Classroom Wireless.

5   If necessary, enter the Wi-Fi password, and then tap Join.

    In an instructor-led environment, the password may be student!.

    Note that at this point you are prompted for the Apple ID credentials you used to enroll with Find My iPad, so Activation Lock is activated.

6   Leave the Apple ID field blank.

7   Enter the Activation Lock bypass code, including the dashes, in the Password field.

    The Activation Lock bypass code is case sensitive.

8   Tap Next.

9   At the Location Services screen, tap Enable Location Services.

    If you see the Configuration screen, congratulations, you successfully used the Activation Lock bypass code!

10 At the Configuration screen, tap Next.

11 Enter credentials for a network user (Username: sue, Password: net).

12 Tap Next, and wait while your device enrolls with your organization and applies any applicable configuration profiles.

13 At the Apple ID screen, tap "Don't have an Apple ID or forgot it."

14 At the next Apple ID screen, tap Set Up Later in Settings.

15 In the confirmation dialog, tap Don't Use.

16 At the Welcome screen, tap Get Started.

Unassign the iOS Device

Remove the iOS device from being assigned to your MDM server.

1 If your Apple Deployment Programs session in Safari has timed out, use your server computer to log in to the Apple Deployment Programs site in Safari (https://deploy.apple.com) using your DEP administrator account with two-step verification.

2 Select Device Enrollment Program in the sidebar.

3 Click in the Search for Serial Number field.

4 Enter the iOS device's serial number in the Search field.

5 Press Return to search.

6 Click the Assigned To pop-up menu, and then choose Unassigned.

7 Click Reassign to unassign your iOS device.

Unenroll Your iOS Device and Remove the Placeholder

1 In the Profile Manager administration portal sidebar, if necessary, select Devices, and then select the iOS device assigned to Sue Wu.

2 Click the Remove (–) button, and then click Unenroll.

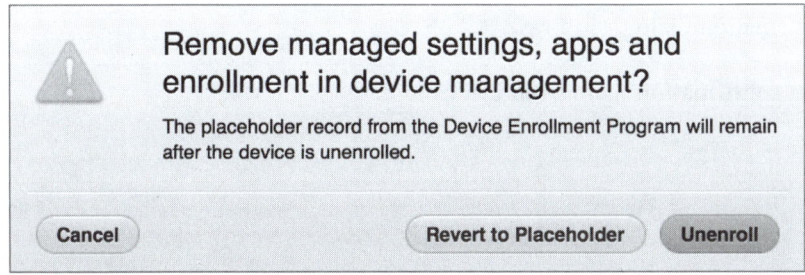

3 At the bottom of the Devices section, click the Refresh button.

4 Select the placeholder record, click the Remove (–) button, and then click Remove.

   NOTE ▶ Before removing a placeholder record in a production environment, always make sure Activation Lock is no longer turned on, as removing the placeholder record will also purge the Activation Lock bypass code.

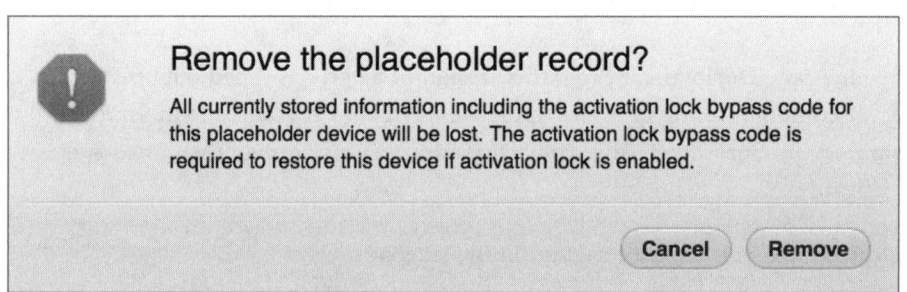

5 Close the Profile Manager administration portal window.

Erase All Content and Settings

1 On your iOS device, if necessary, slide at the "slide to unlock" screen.

2 If necessary, enter the passcode.

3 Open Settings.

4 Navigate to General > Reset.

5 Tap Erase All Content and Settings.

6 If your iOS device has a passcode, enter the passcode.

7 In the confirmation dialog, tap Erase.

8 In the extra confirmation dialog, tap Erase.

In this exercise, you used the DEP to supervise and enroll an iOS device with your Profile Manager server and turned on Find My iPad. In this exercise, you confirmed that when you wiped this iOS device, Activation Lock was not turned on, because you had not adjusted Activation Lock settings to be allowed in the Profile Manager administration portal.

Then you configured the DEP Devices group to allow Activation Lock for any supervised iOS device that is enrolled in your Profile Manager service. You repeated the process of wiping an enrolled supervised iOS device that had Find My iPad turned on, you confirmed Activation Lock was enabled in the Profile Manager administration portal, and you used the Activation Lock bypass code when you were prompted for the Apple ID credentials that activated Find My iPad.

Lesson 10
VPP-Managed Apps and Books

The popularity of Apple devices is largely made possible courtesy of a huge library of available apps that greatly extend the capabilities of iOS and OS X. After all, users are interested in running apps, not operating systems.

For iOS, the vast majority of apps are available only on the App Store, and for OS X many titles are now available on the App Store. Certainly, all current versions of popular Apple software titles are available only from the App Store, including software that is considered standard issue for Apple devices, such as Pages, Numbers, and Keynote. Further, the easiest way to distribute purchased books to Apple devices is through the iBooks Store.

In this lesson, you will learn how organizations can manage and deploy apps and books sourced from Apple stores. The primary focus of this lesson is the Apple Volume Purchase Program, which allows organizations to purchase apps and books in bulk. You will see how to purchase items for your organization from VPP and then manage the deployment of these items using Profile Manager (of course, other Mobile Device Management [MDM] systems can use the same underlying concepts).

> **NOTE** ▶ If your school is enrolled in Apple School Manager, you can use Apple School Manager to purchase apps and books. See https://help.apple.com/schoolmanager for more details.

GOALS

▶ Understand workflows for deploying apps and books sourced from Apple stores

▶ Purchase apps and books for your institution via the Volume Purchase Program (VPP)

▶ Deploy VPP apps and books to users over the air using Profile Manager

▶ Deploy VPP apps directly to Apple devices over the air using Profile Manager

Reference 10.1
Volume Purchase Program Essentials

Historically, software for computing devices has been licensed by individual software developers. Unfortunately, bulk licensing varies greatly between different developers, as does managing deployments of the software.

Managing and deploying apps and books from Apple stores is quite different from traditional licensing models. Early versions of the Apple Volume Purchase Program didn't quite meet the needs of all organizations, but with updates to the program, it now provides a licensing model that works for most organizations. And with device-based app assignment for iOS 9 or later devices and El Capitan or later computers, the story gets even better.

A single source for licensing content is a significant convenience for organizations. Just think, VPP is a single unified source for licensing apps and books from hundreds of thousands of different vendors and publishers. You can certainly argue that administrators face a learning curve when working with VPP, but no other licensing model provides the breadth of products found in the Apple stores.

This section provides an overview of Apple stores and VPP. You will learn how VPP licensing is architected, and you will also find out how to purchase items on behalf of your organization so you can later deploy them to iOS and OS X devices.

What's New

One of the most exciting announcements (at least for those of us who administer Apple devices) that came out of the 2015 Apple Worldwide Developer Conference (WWDC) was that you could assign VPP apps to iOS 9 and El Capitan devices without requiring an Apple ID. Device-based app assignment greatly simplifies many deployment scenarios, but keep in mind that it's available only for iOS 9 or later and El Capitan or later.

People were also happy to hear that with iOS 9 or later and El Capitan or later organizations have the ability to assign VPP apps to users or devices in any country where the app is available (as opposed to needing to create one VPP administrator account per country).

Another new feature of iOS 9 and later and OS X El Capitan and later is the ability for the MDM to limit access to the App Store yet still allow an MDM to push apps, app updates, and system updates.

Apple Stores Overview and Licensing

Apps for both iOS and OS X devices are available from the App Store. On both platforms you'll find the App Store app, which is used for purchasing, downloading, installing, and updating apps on the device. The iTunes app, available on both OS X and Windows, can also be used to acquire iOS apps for syncing to locally attached iOS devices.

Digital publications or books for both iOS and OS X are available from the iBooks Store. Again, on both platforms you'll find the iBooks app, which is used for purchasing, downloading, installing, and updating books on the device. The iBooks app is also used for viewing digital publications or books and organizing this content regardless of the source. In other words, the iBooks app also provides storage and access to digital documents such as PDFs or ePub documents.

NOTE ▶ There are countless other sources for digital content on Apple devices, including other sources from Apple like the iTunes U and Podcasts apps. However, this lesson's focus is helping organizations manage purchased items sourced from Apple stores; thus, it focuses on managing content licensed for organizations through VPP.

Putting aside MDM device-based app assignment for the moment, when a user visits the App Store and the iBooks Store, she must authenticate with her Apple ID. This is because apps and books from Apple stores are licensed to users or, more specifically, their Apple IDs (except of course for VPP apps purchased by an organization for managed distribution and assigned to a device).

This fundamental licensing rule causes much confusion for many traditional IT administrators, but understand that this licensing rule allows for a significant advantage to the Apple platform. If you assign an app to a user and he authenticates with his Apple ID, he can install items he owns on multiple devices, which makes the Apple licensing model flexible for users with multiple Apple devices. He can use the app on organization-owned devices and also install it on any devices that he owns, even if he doesn't bring them into work.

> **MORE INFO** ▶ This guide provides only a general overview of the Apple stores' licensing model. If you want to know more about the model, please feel free to read the terms and conditions at www.apple.com/legal/internet-services/itunes/.

VPP Licensing Overview

Understanding that items purchased on the Apple stores belong to Apple IDs is important to understanding how VPP works. Again, VPP is a program that allows organizations to purchase apps and books from the Apple stores in bulk. VPP has its own specific licensing terms that apply to organizational ownership.

> **MORE INFO** ▶ This guide provides only a general overview of the VPP licensing model, with a focus on businesses. If you want to know more about the model, you will be presented with the terms and conditions when you enroll in the program at https://deploy.apple.com (for businesses) or https://school.apple.com (for schools). You'll also find a link to the VPP terms and conditions at the bottom of the VPP store.

VPP currently offers two licensing models for items purchased on behalf of an organization: legacy redeemable codes and VPP Managed Distribution.

Legacy VPP Redemption Codes

The original incarnation of VPP allowed organizations to purchase redemption codes in bulk. Although this option is still available, it presents an unacceptable licensing model for most organizations.

Specifically, the only method to deploy redemption codes over the air requires that the code is "consumed" by an Apple ID. For example, if you gave a redemption code to one of your users, she would apply it to her Apple ID, which effectively transfers item ownership from the organization to the user. In other words, the organization just gifted an item to the user.

Giving up licensed items is unacceptable for many organizations and may even be illegal for certain organizations, such as public schools, that are not legally allowed to transfer assets to employees or students. Unfortunately, this situation led to deployment workflows where administrators had to keep track of "institutional" Apple IDs, where each organization-owned device had its own Apple ID, or users were granted only temporary or shared access to an Apple ID that "belonged" to the organization. This type of workflow not only is a pain to manage (because it's not what Apple designed for) but also technically violates the Apple license agreement for Apple ID usage.

At this point, the only popular valid workflow for VPP redemption codes is to use them for supervised devices managed via the legacy Apple Configurator. This legacy workflow is specifically designed for shared iOS devices where the user never authenticates with a personal Apple ID to the device's App Store; instead, an institutional Apple ID is used to authenticate app installations via legacy Apple Configurator. This institutional Apple ID is used in conjunction with VPP redemption codes to allow legacy Apple Configurator to install purchased apps directly to locally attached supervised iOS devices. Importantly, the act of unsupervising an iOS device will return the VPP codes to legacy Apple Configurator for use by another device.

For shared-use iOS devices with iOS 9 or later, consider using managed distribution instead of redeemable codes.

> **MORE INFO** ▶ Deploying VPP redemption codes via legacy Apple Configurator is covered in the previous edition of this guide, *Managing Apple Devices, Second Edition: Deploying and Maintaining iOS 8 and OS X Yosemite Devices* in Lesson 11, "Apple Configurator: App Management."

VPP Managed Distribution

Apple has added a second, more palatable licensing option for items acquired via VPP, called Managed Distribution, which solves many of the problems inherent with legacy redeemable codes.

With VPP Managed Distribution, you can use a compatible MDM service to automatically assign organizationally owned VPP book licenses to users and groups and to assign organizationally owned VPP app licenses to users, groups, devices, and device groups. You can assign VPP books to users and groups; you can never revoke VPP books once you've assigned them. You can revoke VPP app licenses after you've assigned them.

In addition, when you install apps via your MDM service, those apps are considered managed apps, which allows for greater administrative control over those apps. See Lesson 16, "Managing Access," to learn more about controlling access to documents with managed apps and accounts.

> **NOTE ▶** When assigning a VPP app to a user or group using Profile Manager, you must choose an assignment mode of Apple ID or Device. Even though a user must provide her Apple ID credentials in order to take advantage of an app assigned with the assignment mode of Apple ID, you as an administrator do not have access to the Apple ID account name that the user provides.

VPP Managed Distribution is limited to the following:

- iOS 7 or later or OS X Mavericks v10.9 or later for VPP Managed Distribution to a user or group (a user must provide her Apple ID to participate)
- iOS 9 or later or OS X El Capitan v10.11 or later for the additional functionality of VPP Managed Distribution of apps to a device without providing an Apple ID on the device

	Managed Distribution of VPP Books	Managed Distribution of VPP Apps to Users and Groups	Managed Distribution of VPP Apps to Devices and Device Groups
iOS 6 and earlier; OS X 10.8 and earlier	No	No	No
iOS 7 to iOS 8; OS X 10.9 to 10.10	Yes	Yes	No
iOS 9 or later; OS X 10.11 or later	Yes	Yes	Yes

With Profile Manager in Server 5, you can assign VPP apps to the following:

- Devices
- Device groups
- Users
- Groups

There are up to two additional choices in the Profile Manager administration portal when assigning VPP apps:

- Assignment Mode—When assigning VPP apps to users and groups, you can choose Device or Apple ID. When assigning VPP apps to devices or device groups, you don't see the Assignment Mode choice, but you are implicitly using the assignment mode of Device. Each device that you assign the app to uses one license; each user you assign the app to uses one license (and a user can install an app on many devices they control).
- Installation Mode—The Automatic option installs the app automatically if possible. Manual means that the user can use the App Store to install the app, or an administrator can send the Push Apps task.

	Assignment Mode	Available Installation Modes
Assign VPP Apps to Device or Device Group	(Device)	Automatic/Manual
Assign VPP Apps to User or Group	Device	Automatic/Manual
Assign VPP Apps to User or Group	Apple ID	Manual

The following table illustrates the possibilities for how VPP apps are installed for users and devices that are already enrolled with Profile Manager, depending on the Assignment Mode and Installation Mode choices (other MDMs may use different terms and have different behavior).

Effects of Assignment Mode and Installation Mode on Assigning VPP Managed Distribution Apps				
Device Type	Supervision State	Assignment Mode	Installation Mode	Result
iOS device with iOS 9 or later	Not supervised	Device	Automatic	User prompted to allow app to be installed
iOS device with iOS 9 or later	Not supervised	Device	Manual	Administrator must push app, then user is prompted to allow app to be installed
iOS device with iOS 9 or later	Not supervised	Apple ID	Manual	App added to user's Purchased list in the App Store; Administrator can push app, then user is prompted to allow app to be installed
iOS device with iOS 9 or later	Supervised	Device	Automatic	App installed without user intervention
iOS device with iOS 9 or later	Supervised	Device	Manual	Administrator must push app, then user is prompted to allow app to be installed
iOS device with iOS 9 or later	Supervised	Apple ID	Manual	App added to user's Purchased list in the App Store; Administrator can push app, then user is prompted to allow app to be installed
Mac with OS X 10.11 or later	N/A	Device	Automatic	App installed without user intervention
Mac with OS X 10.11 or later	N/A	Device	Manual	Administrator must push app, then user is prompted to allow app to be installed
Mac with OS X 10.11 or later	N/A	Apple ID	Manual	App added to user's Purchased list in the Mac App Store; Administrator can push app, then user is prompted to allow app to be installed

How do you decide which VPP Managed Distribution model is appropriate for your organization? It comes back to your ownership and use model (and you may have multiple models):

- For organization-owned personalized devices, as well as user-owned devices, consider assigning VPP Managed Distribution apps to users with the assignment mode of Apple ID so users can take advantage of the apps on other devices they use.
- For organization-owned shared devices, you'd want to assign VPP Managed Distribution apps to devices.
- Keep in mind that if you use an assignment mode of Device, each time you assign an app to a device, it uses a license. If your users have multiple devices, this can have an impact on the number of copies of each app you need to purchase; for apps with a high cost, this can add up quickly.

Most importantly, with either model of VPP Managed Distribution of apps, the organization always retains ownership of purchased apps. After you assign an app, you can later revoke the assignment and reassign the app. The organization always "owns" the app license.

However, the same isn't true for book licenses deployed via VPP Managed Distribution; once you assign a book to a user's Apple ID, it is given to the user. The assumption is that once a user reads a book, it's "consumed" by the user, whereas apps provide long-term use that can be transferred to other users.

Another advantage to VPP Managed Distribution is that it's all controlled over the air via your MDM service. MDM services that are compatible with VPP Managed Distribution will communicate with both Apple's VPP servers and your managed devices to coordinate the assignment and installation of purchased items.

From a user's perspective, one advantage of VPP Managed Distribution to an Apple ID is that users can continue to use their own Apple IDs. With VPP Managed Distribution to an Apple ID, there is no need to manage the Apple IDs that items are assigned to. In fact, there is currently no method for an administrator to find out which Apple ID a user has entered to claim assigned apps and books.

Although this process may sound unconventional to a traditional IT administrator, its design intentionally favors the convenience of the user. After all, a user may come into your organization owning thousands of dollars worth of apps and books. Why prevent this user from accessing their own assets?

Instead, with VPP Managed Distribution, you can temporarily assign organizationally owned apps to the user's Apple ID and then revoke them later if the user leaves.

Finally, recognize that the VPP Managed Distribution to Apple ID workflow doesn't fit well for deployments of shared Apple devices. This is because on both iOS and OS X, only one Apple ID can be signed in to automatically receive VPP app and book assignments. If users share devices, which Apple ID should be used? Use VPP Managed Distribution of apps to a device instead.

> **NOTE** ▶ Items installed via VPP assignment are downloaded from Apple directly to your devices, which can consume a tremendous amount of bandwidth, unless you have configured local Apple caching servers. Lesson 5, "Caching Service," covers the Caching service.

Managed Apps and Books

When you use an MDM service to install an app (a VPP Managed Distribution app or an in-house enterprise iOS app) or book (a VPP Managed Distribution book or an in-house book), that app or book is considered managed. There are a few methods to automatically download and install VPP Managed Distribution apps over the air:

- ▶ Assign an app to an enrolled computer or supervised iOS device (or device group) with Installation Mode set to Automatic

- Assign an app to a user or group that is associated with an enrolled computer or an iOS device that is enrolled and supervised
- Send the Push Apps task via an MDM service

Managed installation requires that the device is enrolled in an MDM service, but it allows for greater administrative control over installed apps and books.

An MDM service can exert the following extra control over managed apps:

- Specify whether managed apps and the data associated with managed apps are removed from an iOS device if a user or an administrator unenrolls the device from the MDM service
- Specify whether data from managed apps can be included when a device is backed up to iTunes or to iCloud (to prevent the data from being restored to another potentially unmanaged device)
- Convert unmanaged apps (apps that are installed by a user instead of by an MDM service) to managed apps without losing user data (at the time of this writing, Profile Manager does not implement this control)

Additional features for managed apps for devices with iOS 7 or later include the ability for app developers to identify configuration settings that can be set after the app is installed as a managed app and to specify settings that can be read using an MDM service.

Additional features for managed apps for devices with iOS 8 or later include the ability to specify managed domains in Safari (documents downloaded from Safari managed domains are considered managed sources) and the ability to restrict managed apps from storing data in iCloud while preserving the ability for unmanaged apps to store data in iCloud.

For iOS 8 or later, you can use an MDM service to distribute books; these books are then considered managed books. Managed books can include the following:

- iBooks store books you've purchased via VPP
- PDF documents
- Documents in eBook format
- Documents in iBooks format, such as documents you create with iBooks Author

You can use your MDM service to update managed books, prevent them from being opened in unmanaged apps or unmanaged accounts, and prevent in-house managed books from being backed up. When you assign an in-house book to a user or iOS device (you cannot assign an in-house book to a Mac computer, and you can assign VPP books only to users), that managed book appears on an iOS device only if both of the following are true:

- The device is enrolled with your MDM service
- The device is assigned to the user in your MDM service

These features help an organization keep organizational information from being inadvertently used in inappropriate ways.

Once you assign a book that you purchase via the VPP to a user, you cannot revoke that assignment, nor can you reassign that purchased book.

> **MORE INFO** ▶ The additional complexity and ability of managed apps warrants separate coverage; please see Lesson 16, "Managing Access."

Reference 10.2
VPP Service Enrollment and Administration

> **NOTE** ▶ If you've already enrolled your educational institution in the VPP or the Device Enrollment Program (DEP), you can use the agent account that you used to enroll with the VPP or the DEP to upgrade to Apple School Manager. See https://help.apple.com/schoolmanager for more details.

VPP is one of the services offered as part of the Apple Deployment Programs (for businesses) and as part of Apple School Manager (for schools). Another one of these programs, the DEP (for businesses), is detailed in Lesson 8, "Out-of-the-Box Management via Apple Programs for Device Enrollment." These programs have similar technical and organizational requirements for enrollment. If your organization has yet to enroll in either of these programs, they can do so following the instructions outlined in the exercises of Lesson 8.

> **MORE INFO** ▶ If your organization isn't able to take advantage of the DEP service because of regional limitations, you should know that the VPP is available in more regions than the DEP service. You can find out whether the VPP is available in your region by visiting https://deploy.apple.com/enroll/selectcountry.

VPP Service Enrollment

> **NOTE** ▶ This section covers information and procedures for businesses; see https://help.apple.com/schoolmanager for details about Apple School Manager.

The person in your organization who enrolls into the Apple Deployment Programs is known as the *program agent*. If the program agent for your organization has already completed the enrollment process for the DEP service, as covered in the previous lesson, he can enroll for the VPP in just a matter of minutes.

> **NOTE** ▶ If the program agent wants to use the same Apple ID for both the VPP and the DEP, he must complete the enrollment for one of the two programs first. Once the enrollment is complete for one of the programs, he should sign in to the Apple Deployment Programs site first and then enroll into the other program. If he attempts to enroll into another program from the start page before signing in, he will have to enroll with a different Apple ID.

To verify your organization's VPP status, the program agent needs to sign in to the Apple Deployment Programs site at https://deploy.apple.com. The "Welcome back" screen will show the current status of the organization's enrollments in the Apple Deployment Programs.

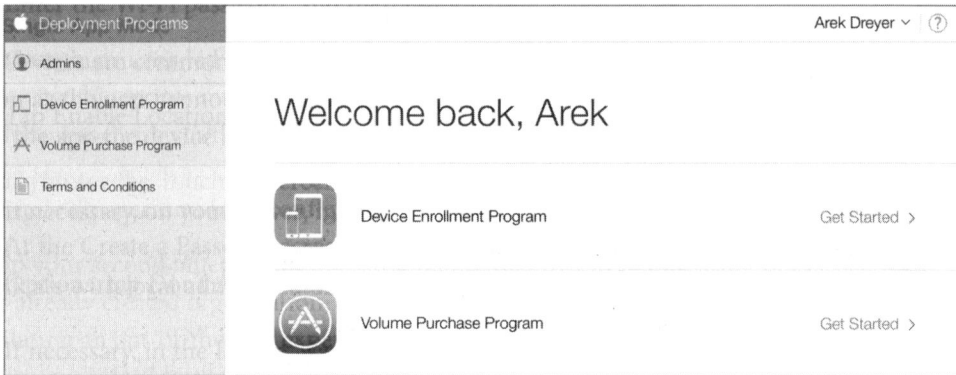

If the blue link adjacent to Volume Purchase Program reads "Get Started," your organization is already enrolled for VPP. At this point, the program agent can sign in to the VPP store or grant administrative access to other users by clicking the Admins link to the left.

However, if the blue link adjacent to Volume Purchase Program reads "Enroll," the program agent will need to complete the VPP enrollment process. Verifying the organization information and completing the VPP enrollment takes just a few minutes.

Once enrolled, the program agent can be the sole administrator for both the VPP and the DEP service. Alternatively, for larger organizations, the program agent can create additional administrators and delegate administration to them. When the program agent is signed in to the Apple Deployment Programs site, he can delegate administrative access by clicking the Admins link, then clicking Add Admin Account. Managing administrators is also covered in Lesson 8, "Out-of-the-Box Management via Apple Programs for Device Enrollment."

VPP Website

At the time of this writing, there are two areas of the VPP website (https://vpp.itunes.apple.com/) for managing VPP purchases: the Education Store and the Business Store.

With the VPP for business, you can purchase App Store, Mac App Store, and iBooks Store apps and books. If you coordinate with third-party developers, you can purchase custom business to business (B2B) apps for iOS that are built specifically for your business; these can be free or paid. For each B2B app, the third-party developer adds your VPP account to its authorized purchasers list, so only authorized personnel can see and purchase the B2B app. The security of the data in a B2B app is the responsibility of the developer; you should confirm that the third-party developer adheres to best practices for in-app authorization and encryption.

Although it's outside the scope of this guide, app developers can offer educational organizations discounts when items are purchased in bulk (20 or more).

If your organization is a business, you can navigate to the VPP store from the Apple Deployment Programs site by clicking the Volume Purchase Program link to the left. This link will automatically take you to the correct VPP store sign-in page, but you will have to authenticate with your credentials again.

TIP ▶ To avoid authenticating twice to manage VPP purchases, bookmark the VPP sign-in page instead of the Apple Deployment Programs page.

VPP Account Management

NOTE ▶ This section information about procedures for businesses; see https://help.apple.com/schoolmanager for details about Apple School Manager.

Once signed in to the VPP store, at the top right you'll see your Apple ID; clicking it reveals a pop-up menu with VPP account management options.

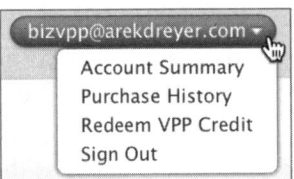

From the VPP account pop-up menu, you can view or manage your VPP:

- Account Summary—On the Account Summary page, you can download the VPP server token for integrating with your MDM service, view your purchase history, redeem VPP credits, view your VPP credit redemption history, and edit your direct payment and billing information.
- Purchase History—This is a direct link to view the history of VPP purchases and license credits.
- Redeem VPP Credit—This is a direct link to enter VPP credit codes that will add funds to your VPP account.
- Sign Out—Use this to sign out of the VPP store.

Reference 10.3
Integrate VPP with Profile Manager

In this section, you will see how to use VPP Managed Distribution with Apple's Profile Manager service. That being said, the core technologies behind VPP Managed Distribution remain the same even between different MDM service implementations. Thus, even if your organization chooses to use another MDM service, the concepts covered in this guide still apply.

> **NOTE** ▶ This section covers information and procedures for businesses; see https://help.apple.com/schoolmanager for details about Apple School Manager.

> **MORE INFO** ▶ You'll find detailed step-by-step instructions for using VPP Managed Distribution with Profile Manager in the exercises later in this lesson.

Assuming your organization's VPP account is active and you have access to the VPP store, there are four general steps for integrating VPP Managed Distribution with your MDM service:

1. Install the VPP service token in your MDM service. This step is required only one time for each server configured. However, the VPP server token must be replaced annually by repeating the same process used to install the server token.
2. Purchase app and book licenses for Managed Distribution via the VPP store. It's likely that you will return to the VPP store on occasion to make new purchases and verify license usage.

3. From your MDM service, assign VPP apps and books to your users. As you add more VPP licenses and as users come and go, it's likely that you'll be regularly returning to your MDM service to verify and manage VPP assignments.

4. From your MDM service, invite users to participate in your organization's VPP. The user needs to accept the invitation only once to join your organization's VPP Managed Distribution.

MDM Service VPP Integration

Essentially, VPP Managed Distribution is a mechanism that can assign apps and books to a user's Apple ID. Most of the mechanics that make VPP Managed Distribution work are on Apple's servers. Profile Manager, or any other MDM solution that supports VPP Managed Distribution, simply acts as an interface for managing your organization's app and book assignments.

Also, it's important to recognize that VPP Managed Distribution does not rely on device management. In fact, devices don't have to be enrolled at all to take advantage of VPP Managed Distribution. For example, devices owned by the user may never be enrolled in your MDM service, but as long as the users accept your invitation to VPP Managed Distribution, you can assign apps and books to their Apple IDs.

In theory, you could even use a separate MDM service entirely for managing devices. For example, you may find it beneficial to manage your Apple devices with a third-party MDM service that provides better integration with your network infrastructure. Unfortunately, some third-party MDM services may not support VPP Managed Distribution. This isn't a problem, though, because you can use Profile Manager to only manage app and book assignments while still using a third-party MDM to manage devices.

You do gain a few benefits from using a single MDM service for both device management and VPP Managed Distribution. Specifically, you can send VPP invitations to enrolled Apple devices via the APNs, and you can assign items to enrolled devices with iOS 9 or later or OS X 10.11 or later. Also, you can collect inventory information from managed devices to verify whether they have indeed installed the apps you have assigned.

Profile Manager VPP Integration

To integrate an MDM service with your organization's VPP account, you need to download a server token from the VPP store and install it in the MDM service. Start by signing in to the VPP store, and from the Apple ID pop-up menu, choose Account Summary.

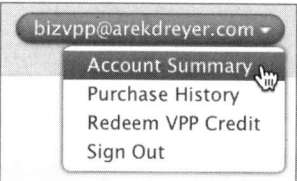

On the Account Summary page, click the Download Token link to the right. The VPP server token takes only a few moments to download. Look for it in the default download folder; it should have a name like "sToken for *AppleID*.vpptoken," where *AppleID* is the account you signed in with.

In the Server app, select the Profile Manager service, and select the "Distribute apps and books from the Volume Purchase Program" checkbox. This will open a dialog prompting you to import the VPP server token.

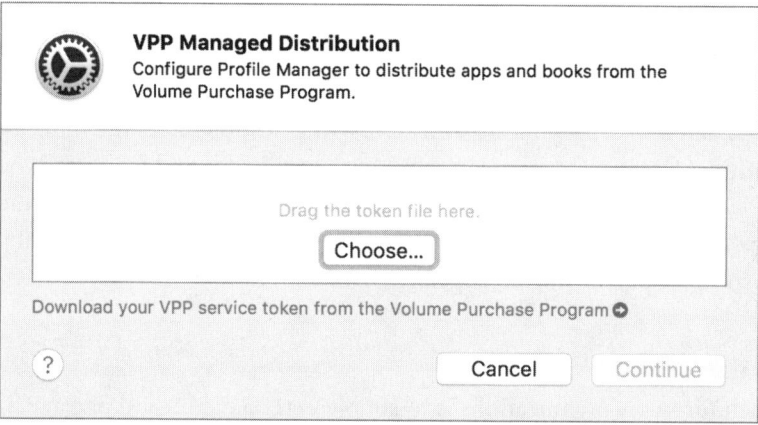

Drag the VPP server token into the VPP Managed Distribution dialog, or click Choose to select the VPP server token from an Open dialog. Once you have selected the token, click Continue, and then click Done. At this point, Profile Manager should have all it needs to access your organization's VPP assets.

> **NOTE** ▶ The VPP server token must be replaced annually by repeating the same process used to install the server token.

NOTE ▶ When you add a VPP server token to Profile Manager, it will automatically "reset" all assignments in the associated VPP account if it was configured for another server. In other words, if you were testing another MDM service with VPP, when you add the VPP server token to Profile Manager, it will revoke all apps that were assigned by the previous MDM service.

NOTE ▶ Profile Manager supports only a single VPP account configuration. If you have a more complex organization with multiple VPP accounts or a need to segregate VPP licenses, you should consider a third-party MDM service capable of handling more complex VPP configurations.

Reference 10.4
Purchasing VPP Apps and Books

NOTE ▶ This section covers information and procedures for businesses; see https://help.apple.com/schoolmanager for details about Apple School Manager.

Purchasing free apps and books for your organization's VPP account costs the same as it does in iTunes: nothing. However, if you plan to purchase paid apps and books for your organization's VPP account, you'll have to start, as expected, with some form of payment. More specifically, you'll need credit, in the form of either direct credit card or PayPal payment or, for more complex purchasing arrangements, VPP credit.

Direct VPP Payment

The easiest approach for many organizations is to simply enter a credit card or PayPal account for direct VPP payment processing. To enter or verify VPP payment information, start by signing in to the VPP store, and from the Apple ID pop-up menu, choose Account Summary. At the bottom of the Account Summary page, click the Edit Payment Information button to manage your organization's credit card and billing information.

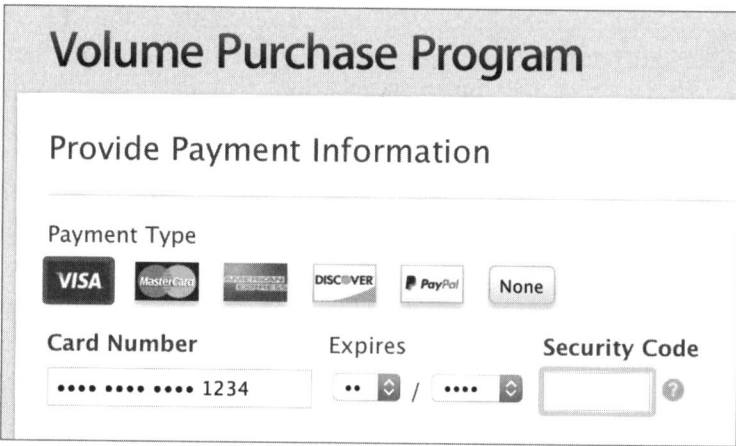

Once Apple has verified your organization's payment and billing information here, you can make VPP purchases directly in the VPP store without any further complications.

VPP Credit

For more complex payment arrangements and refunds, organizations acquire VPP credit. At the top of the VPP store, you'll see your organization's information along with your VPP credit total on the far right ($0.00 in the following figure).

You gain VPP credit through nondirect purchases and refunds. For example, your organization may have a purchase order arrangement with Apple. In this case, your organization would purchase VPP credits with a purchase order via your regular Apple sales contact. During the purchase, the email address for the VPP administrator is required.

Once the purchase order is processed, a temporary (30-day) VPP program credit code is generated. A VPP administrator can get this code by signing in with an Apple ID to the VPP program credit store at https://volumepurchaseprogramcredit.apple.com. This site will list all the organization's VPP credit purchases and refunds along with any VPP credit codes that are ready to be applied to that VPP account.

The VPP credit code needs to be entered in the VPP store to add credit to the VPP account. To enter VPP credit codes, start by signing in to the VPP store, and from the Apple ID pop-up menu, choose Redeem VPP Credit. Once the VPP credit code is validated, the credits will be applied to the VPP account and can then be used for VPP purchases.

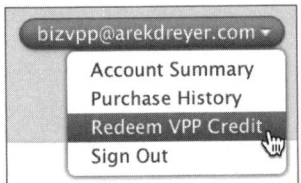

You can also gain VPP credits and licenses through refunds and migrations. You can request support for VPP, including requests for credit refunds and migrations, by clicking the Contact Support link at the bottom of the VPP store.

As an example, you can migrate existing VPP redemption codes to Managed Distribution licenses. Also, every time your organization purchases new Apple devices, you can request VPP licenses for managing the software included with the device. At the time of this writing, every purchase of every Apple device now includes iMovie, GarageBand, Pages, Numbers, and Keynote. Make sure to request licenses for these items every time your organization purchases new Apple devices.

> **MORE INFO** ▶ For more information about requesting VPP licenses in these cases, see Apple Support article HT202863, "Migrate from redemption codes to managed distribution with the Volume Purchase Program"; article HT202953, "Request iOS apps through the Volume Purchase Program"; and article HT203022, "Request Mac apps through the Volume Purchase Program."

VPP Purchases

Despite the potential complexity of enrolling in VPP and applying VPP credits to your account, once these initial steps are complete, making purchases in the VPP store is quick and easy. The VPP store home page features a large search field, and you can specify a type of media for your search from the pop-up menu.

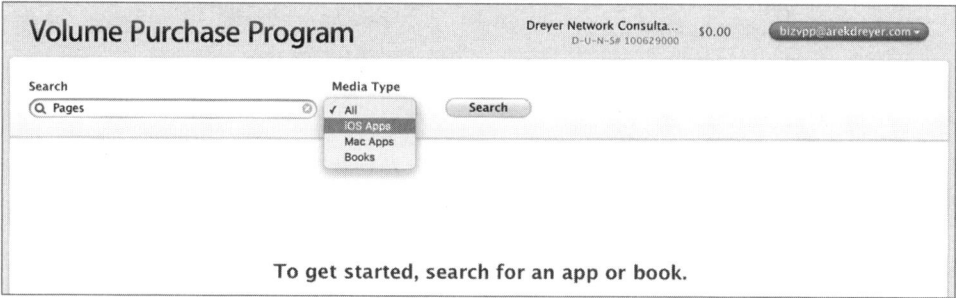

TIP ▶ If you don't see the VPP search bar, you need to navigate back to the VPP home page by clicking the VPP Home link near the top left of the VPP store.

Once you have identified the app or book you want to purchase, select the title to go to the Purchase Details screen. From this screen, you will specify the quantity of licenses you want to purchase and the distribution type.

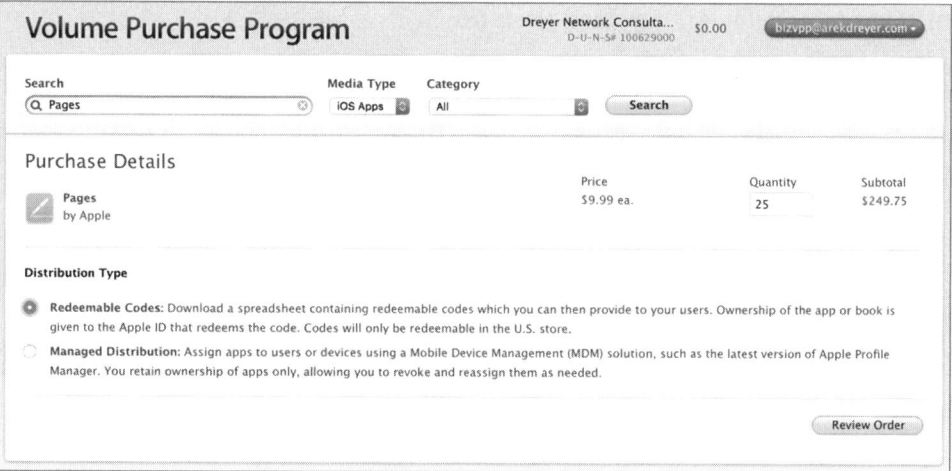

You can request redeemable codes only for paid apps and books. When you use the VPP to purchase free apps and books, the only distribution type available is Managed Distribution.

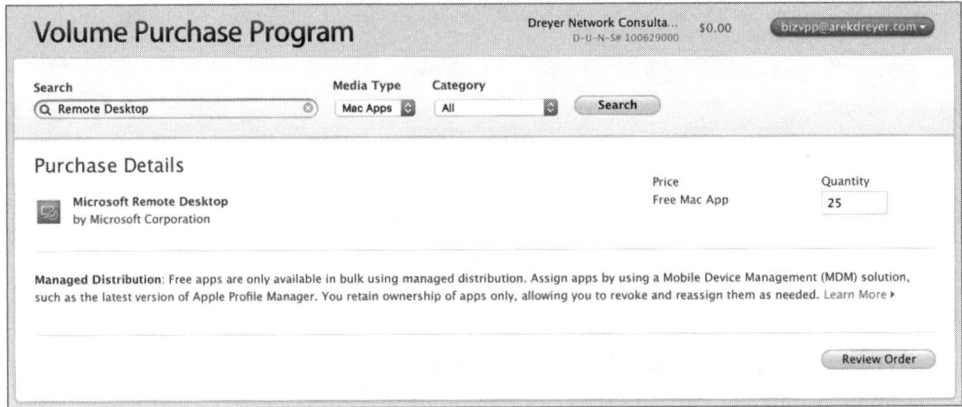

"Purchasing" free items in VPP may seem strange, but this is how you can make sure your users have access to the items they need from your organization. From a technical perspective, your MDM service needs licenses for every item it's going to deploy to your users, even free items. In other words, if you need to deploy free apps and books via your MDM service, you must "purchase" these free items as well.

> **MORE INFO** ▶ You can enter a quantity of up to 10,000 when purchasing items. However, the more licensees you request, the longer it will take for the VPP service to generate the required license codes.

> **MORE INFO** ▶ Because free items are, well, free, even if you revoke an item from a user's Apple ID to reclaim the license, the user's Apple ID will still own a copy of the free item.

Clicking the Review Order button doesn't yet process the order. Instead, you will be presented with an Order Summary screen allowing you to verify the order before you click the Place Order button to commit.

Depending on the quantity of your order, generating the licenses may take several minutes or longer. You can verify the order status from the Purchase History page in the VPP store. Once you see the words "Managed Licenses" or "Download Codes," your purchases are ready.

> **TIP** ▶ If you have requested thousands of licensees, generating your request may take several hours. In this case, you should work on something else, like other VPP purchases, and wait for an email from the VPP service letting you know when the licenses are ready.

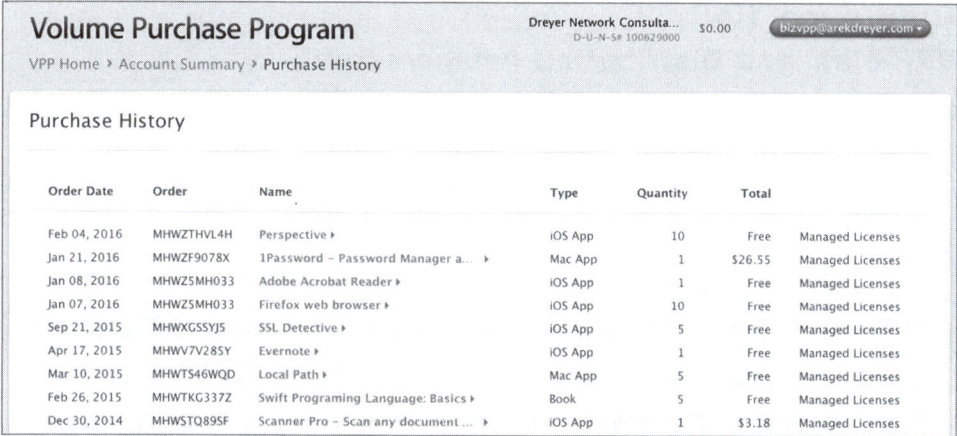

The Managed Distribution items will appear automatically in your VPP service, as covered next in this lesson. If you're using redemption codes, you can download them by clicking the Download Codes button.

VPP Purchases in Profile Manager

You can verify your VPP Managed Distribution purchases by opening the Profile Manager store and selecting Apps or Books from the Library. Any purchases made in the VPP store for Managed Distribution should automatically appear in the Profile Manager once the licenses are generated by the VPP service. Further, as you assign apps and books to users, you can return here to verify Available and Purchased totals.

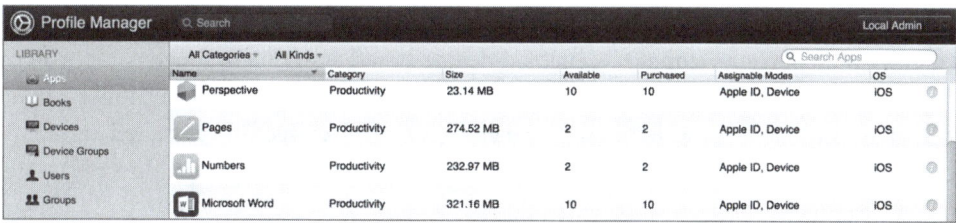

TIP In the Profile Manager Apps and Books lists you can find out more information about a specific item by clicking the small information (lowercase *i* in a circle) button to the far right of the item. You can also navigate directly to the VPP web portal by clicking the Get More Apps link at the bottom of the Apps list.

Reference 10.5
VPP Managed Distribution Assignments

Once Profile Manager recognizes your VPP Managed Distribution purchases, you can assign apps and books to your users and assign apps to your devices. Again, like other user-based configuration in Profile Manager, you can assign apps and books to individual users or to groups of users, and now for iOS 9 or later and OS X El Capitan or later, you can assign VPP Managed Distribution apps to devices and device groups as well.

You can assign apps and books after inviting users to VPP Managed Distribution as well, but it's recommended that you make as many assignments as you can prior to inviting users. There are two reasons for this. First, it's a bit more complicated for the VPP system to process individual assignments after users are enrolled in VPP Managed Distribution. In other words, the VPP system is less prone to delays when assignments are made before users are invited. Second, it will be an odd experience for your users if they are invited to your organization's VPP Managed Distribution only to find there is nothing there for them. In short, it makes for a better user experience when you assign VPP Managed Distribution items before inviting users.

Assigning VPP Apps and Books

To assign VPP Managed Distribution purchases in Profile Manager, you can select a user, user group, device, or device group, and then click the Apps or Books tab. Clicking the Add (+) button at the bottom of the Apps or Books list will bring up a dialog, allowing you to assign VPP purchases to the selected user, user group, device, or device group.

Selecting a user or group (but not a device or device group) offers the Assignment Mode column; if an app's developer has enabled device-based assignment for that app, you can choose between assigning each app to an Apple ID or to a device. If you choose Apple ID, Installation Mode is set to Manual (supervised iOS devices get apps installed automatically; otherwise, users must use the App Store to install apps you assign this way).

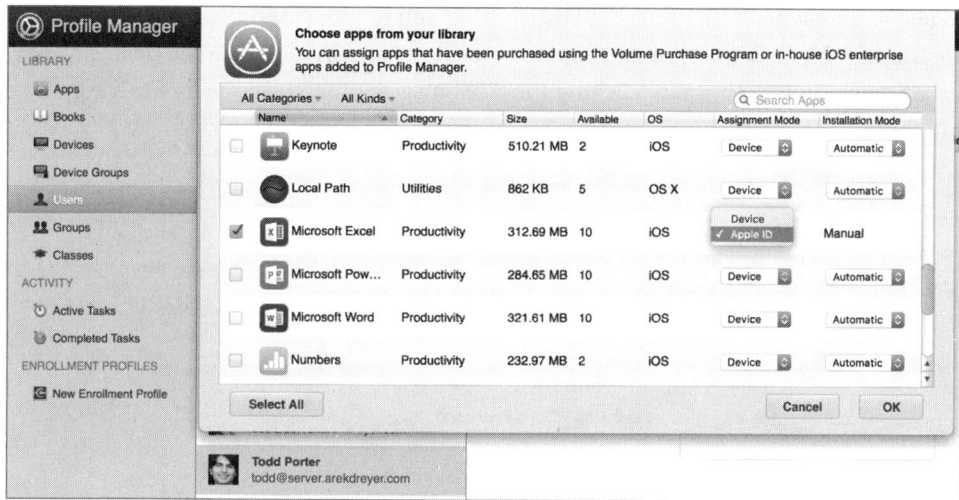

When adding apps for a device or device group, you will not see the Assignment Mode column (the Apple ID Assignment Mode option is available only for users and groups). For each app, you can choose an Installation Mode setting of either Automatic (in which case the app gets installed automatically) or Manual (in which case an MDM administrator must install the app).

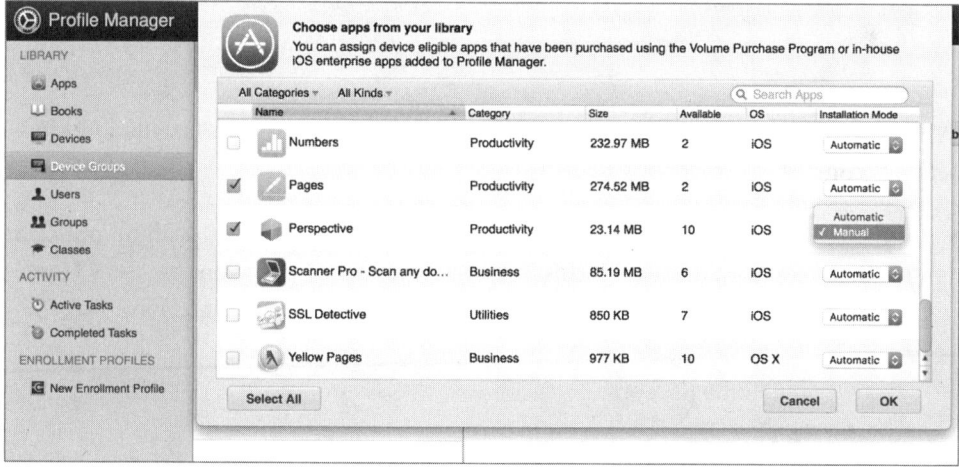

After you click OK to dismiss the dialog, make sure to click Save in Profile Manager to apply the changes.

When you assign a VPP Managed Distribution app to a device or device group, with Installation Mode set to Manual, you can install the app by selecting the device or device group, clicking the Apps tab, clicking the Action (gear) menu, choosing Push Apps, selecting the apps to push, and then clicking OK.

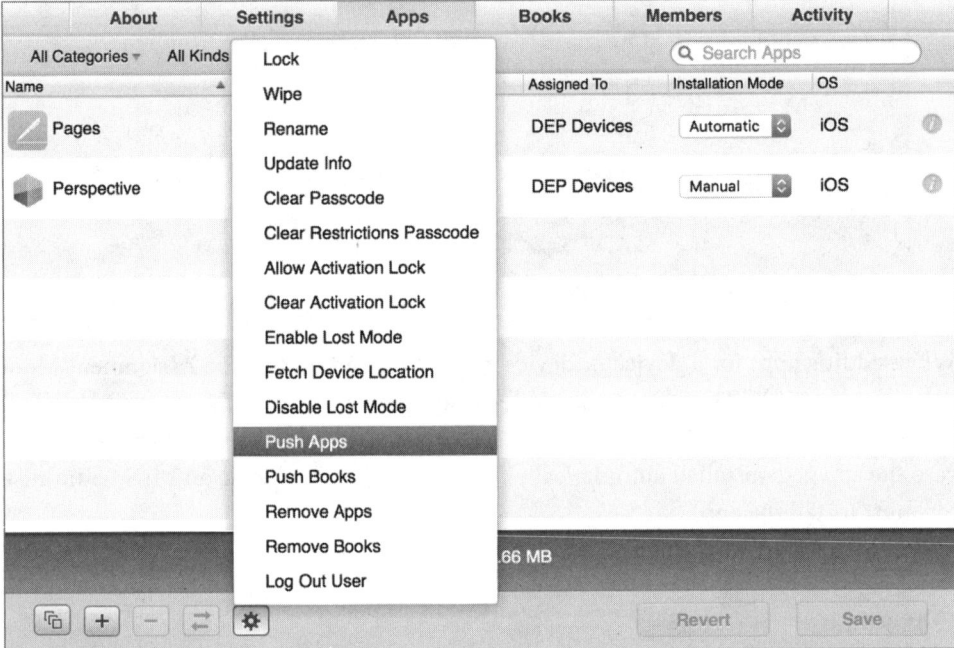

When you assign a VPP Managed Distribution app to a device with Installation Mode offset to Automatic, the following happens:

▶ If the iOS device is supervised, the app is automatically installed without notice or intervention from the user. If this causes new items to appear on the user's Home screen for the first time, the user sees a message about editing the Home screen.

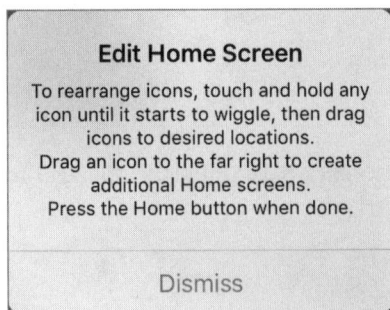

▶ If device is not a supervised iOS device, the user gets a prompt about installing the app.

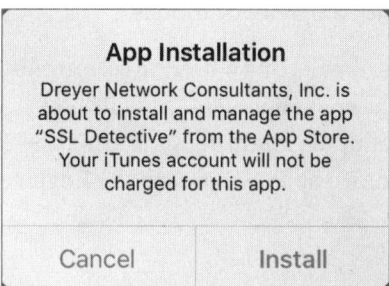

NOTE ▶ You need to turn on VPP Managed Distribution for user groups before you can assign VPP apps or books to the group. In the Profile Manager web interface, select the user group, click the About tab, and then select the Enable VPP Managed Distribution Services checkbox.

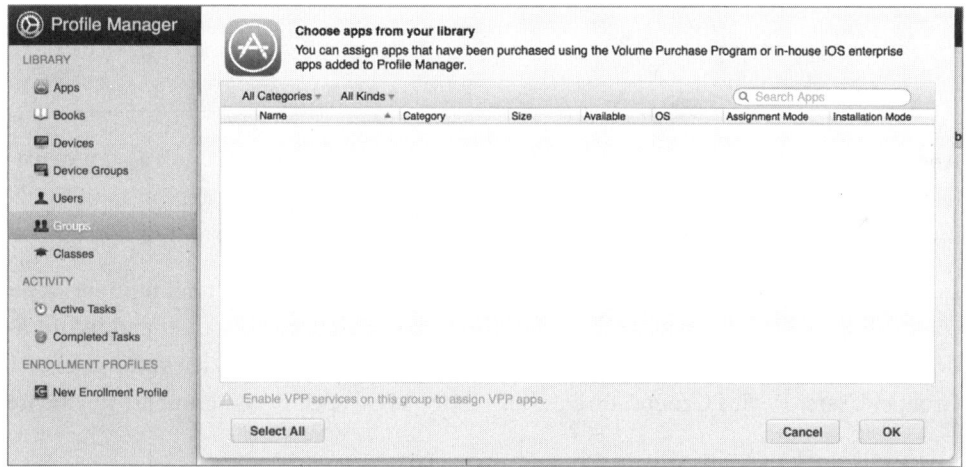

NOTE ▶ VPP assignments are on a first-come, first-served basis. If you don't have enough copies of an app or book for the number you have assigned, the items are assigned in chronological order based on when the user accepted the VPP Managed Distribution enrollment.

If you assign VPP Managed Distribution apps via Apple ID and selected users are already enrolled in VPP Managed Distribution, their accounts should receive the items within a few moments. However, if you have selected a user or user group where members have yet to enroll, Profile Manager will immediately set aside the appropriate number of licenses for those users. Once those users enroll into VPP Managed Distribution, as covered later in this lesson, they will see their assigned items in the App Store or iBooks.

In Profile Manager, you can verify VPP assignments by selecting a user or user group and then clicking the Apps or Books tab. Viewing a user's assignment list will show both user-assigned and user group–assigned items. Notice in the following screenshot the user Barbara has an app assigned to her user account and two apps assigned to the Engineering group she belongs to:

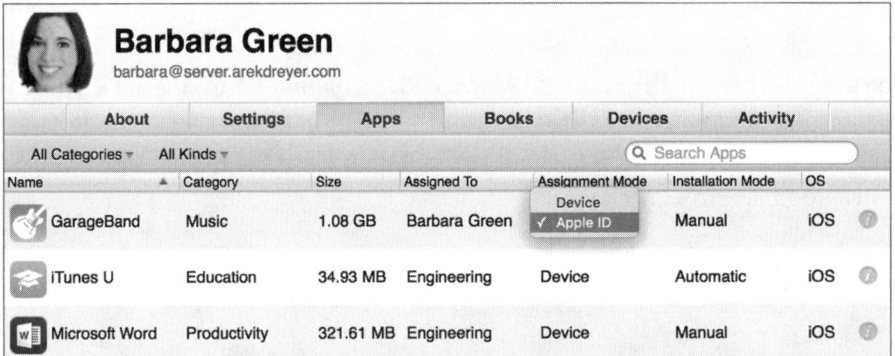

Another method in Profile Manager allows you to manage app and book assignments from the item's point of view. You can view the details for a specific app or book by clicking the small information button (lowercase *i* in a circle) to the far right of the item.

In the VPP app or book detailed information page, you can see the total number of purchased and available licenses in the top-right corner. Below you'll see general information about the item and then below that the Assignment list. In this list you can click the Groups, Users, Device Groups, or Devices tab to reveal specific assignments for the item.

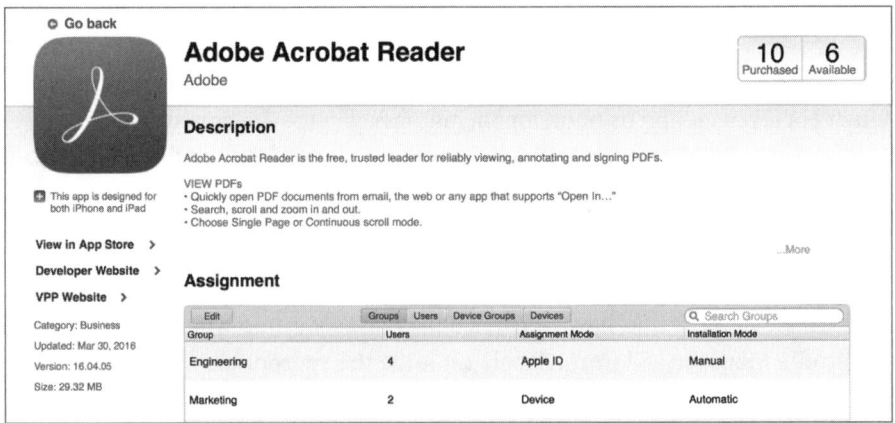

Finally, clicking the Edit button at the top left of the Assignment list will allow you to manage the assignment of this item.

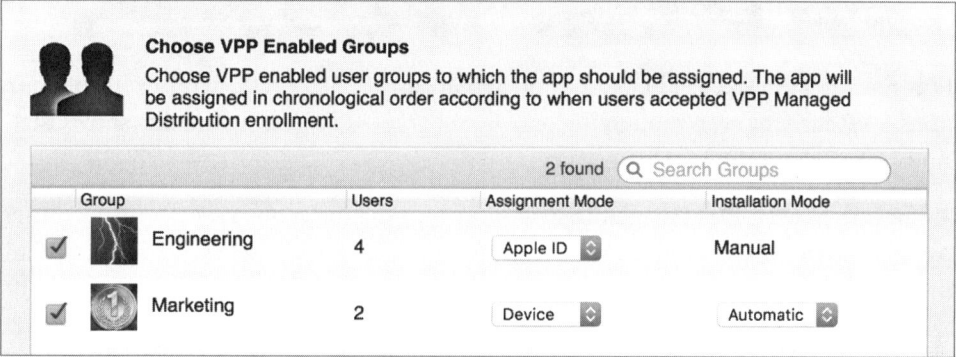

Revoking VPP-Assigned Apps

Making adjustments to VPP Managed Distribution assignments in Profile Manager is as easy as using the buttons at the bottom of the user or user group Apps and Books lists.

Note that clicking Add (+) will bring up the dialog shown earlier but as a convenience will show only those VPP items that have not yet been assigned to the user. The Remove (–) button is used to revoke and unassign the selected app. If you need to select and revoke all apps, you can click the Select All button (stacked boxes icon) and then the Remove (–) button. The Change Modes button (two arrows icon) allows you to change the Installation Mode and Assignment Mode options. Again, when you're done managing app assignments, make sure to click Save in Profile Manager to apply the changes.

> **NOTE ▶** If the Remove (–) button isn't available in Profile Manager, the app you're trying to revoke is assigned to a different user group. Refer to the Apps list to find the specific group the app is currently assigned to.

After removing VPP Managed Distribution app assignments via Apple ID, the user should receive a push notice that the apps are no longer assigned to his Apple ID. Take note that free apps will still remain in the user's purchases and will not be removed from the user's devices, as a default.

Fear not, all VPP Managed Distribution app licenses are still returned to your organization's VPP account even though the user is still granted access. Again, this shows that Apple cares about the user experience.

As for purchased VPP Managed Distribution apps that have been revoked from a user's Apple ID, they will be immediately removed from the user's purchases, but as a default, they will not be removed from the user's iOS devices for some time. This is to prevent the accidental removal of app data on iOS devices. Again, it's another example of Apple caring about the user experience.

At a minimum, the user will have 30 days to purchase the app on his own, but this is an option set independently by each app developer. In theory, an app could remain on the device forever if the developer did not set a time frame for removal. Even if the app sits on the device forever, it will still not be in his purchase list and will not be allowed to update or install on another device until the user purchases the app.

Reference 10.6
VPP Managed Distribution User Enrollment

To accept book assignments and VPP Managed Distribution apps assigned to Apple ID, a user's Apple ID must be enrolled into VPP Managed Distribution. The user begins the enrollment process by opening a specially crafted uniform resource locator (URL) that will automatically redirect to the App Store. Profile Manager can automatically generate these URLs and send them via an email message to the user or a push notification to the user's managed devices. A user needs to accept your VPP invitation only once to be enrolled into your organization's VPP Managed Distribution.

Sending VPP Invitations

As with all user-based features in Profile Manager, you can choose to send VPP invitations by user or by user groups. If Profile Manager is to send email messages to your users, each user must have an email address associated with her account in your directory service. On the other hand, if Profile Manager is to send a push notification to the user's devices, she must be in possession of an enrolled device that is associated with the user's account.

NOTE ▶ Ideally your directory service user records will include email addresses. In Profile Manager you can tell whether this is the case by the user's full email address appearing just below the user's real name. If not, you can manually enter addresses in Profile Manager when sending VPP invitations via email.

NOTE ▶ Profile Manager sends email messages via the standard Simple Mail Transfer Protocol (SMTP) over Transmission Control Protocol (TCP) port 25. If this standard port is blocked or your email service doesn't accept unauthenticated SMTP, then you will need to configure an SMTP relay as covered by Apple Support article HT202962, "OS X Server: Sending email invitations, notifications and alerts when an SMTP relay is required."

To send an individual user a VPP invitation in Profile Manager, select the user from the Users list, and on the About tab you'll find the VPP Managed Distribution settings. Depending on whether the user has an email address or enrolled devices, you will see specific buttons for sending invitations. For example, as you can see in the following screenshot, Barbara has a known email address and an enrolled device:

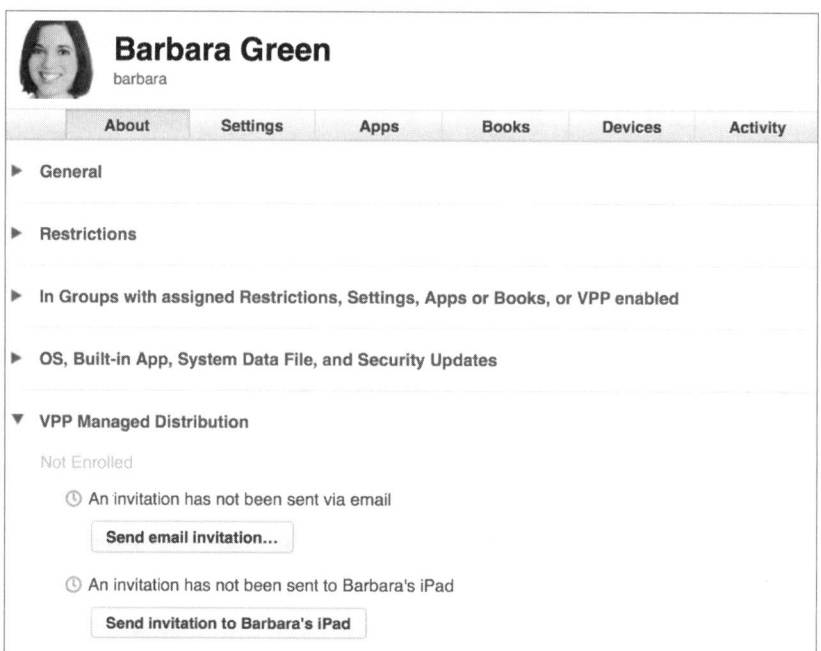

To send a group of users VPP invitations in Profile Manager, select the group from the User Groups list, and on the About tab you'll find similar VPP Managed Distribution settings. You must first select Enable VPP Managed Distribution Services for the group to make the invitation options appear. From the Invite pop-up menu, you can choose to send invitations to users not previously invited or to users not enrolled. The latter option is required if you want to send repeat invitations.

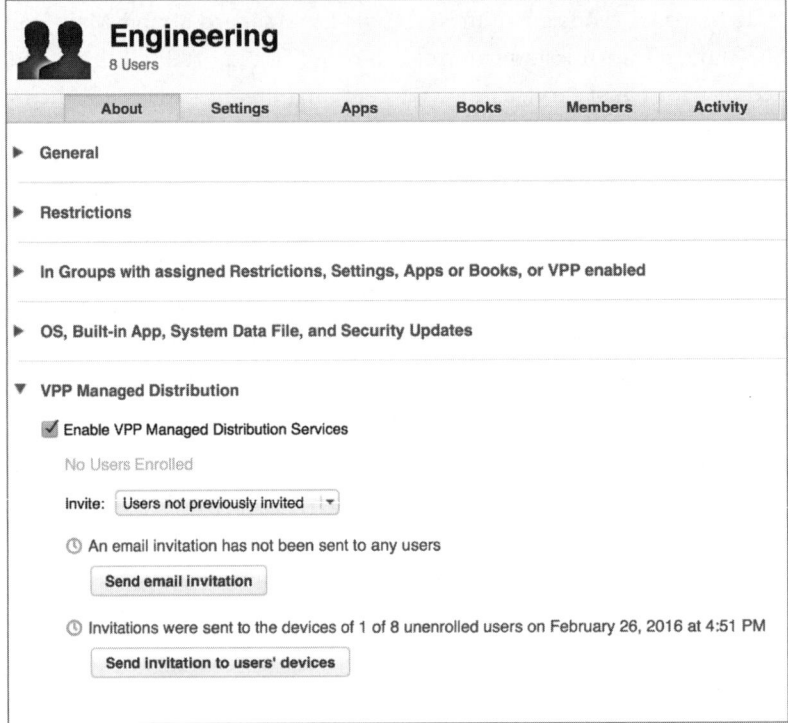

The potentially varied nature of a user's account and associated devices can make sending invitations a bit messy. For example, some users may be lacking an email address, while others are lacking enrolled devices. Note that you can invite a person even if she does not participate in your MDM service, as long as there is an account in a directory service that your MDM service is bound to (so you can select her user account) and you have an email address for her. The previous screenshot shows a variety of invitation statuses. Fortunately, Profile Manager does a commendable job of keeping things straight. Further, you can always send multiple invitations to users who have not yet enrolled.

> **NOTE ▶** Use caution when sending group-based VPP invitations via push to OS X Mavericks and iOS 7 devices. These previous system versions don't handle receiving the VPP push during an inopportune time, like when the user is still working through Setup Assistant.

Accepting VPP Invitations

The VPP invitation message will include a brief description and an obvious button to start the enrollment process. Not shown in the following screenshots is the email message, which features an obvious Sign In button.

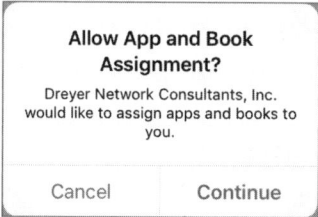
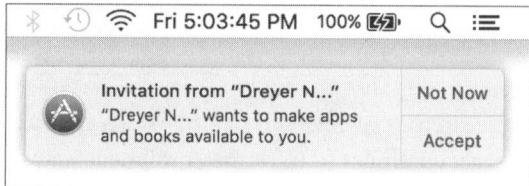

For the URL in the message to work properly when the user clicks it, she must be on an Apple device that meets the minimum requirements for enrolling in VPP Managed Distribution. Specifically, she must be on an iOS device running iOS 7.1 or later or on an OS X computer running OS X 10.9 or later.

Clicking the link will redirect to the App Store, where the user will be prompted to authenticate with an Apple ID and agree to the VPP Managed Distribution terms and conditions. A user needs to sign in and agree only once to complete the enrollment. At this point, not only is the user signed in to the App Store with her Apple ID, her account is also now enrolled to receive app and book assignments from your VPP Managed Distribution.

Verifying VPP Enrollment

In the Profile Manager administration portal, you can return to the user or user group and click the About tab to verify the status of VPP Managed Distribution enrollment. The following figure is for a user:

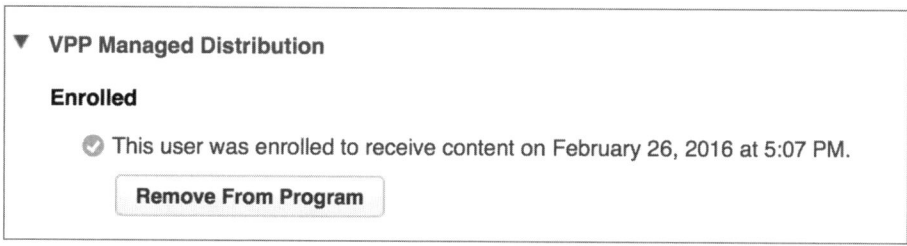

The following figure is for a group:

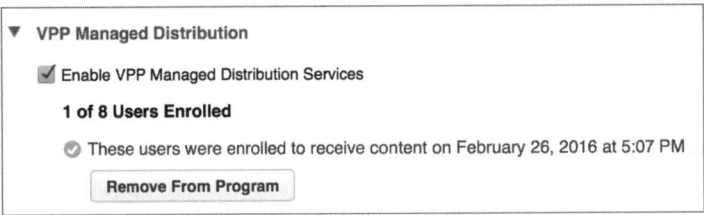

As you can see in the previous screenshot, which shows the enrollment status of a user group, Profile Manager continues to track the enrollment status for individuals within the group.

Note that you are not allowed to see what Apple ID the user chose to enroll with. This is by design because the user is allowed to enter whatever Apple ID is best for her needs. Again, the point is that a user needs only a single Apple ID to access personal items *and* organizational items.

The only additional VPP enrollment reporting is limited to managed devices with iOS 8 or later. On these devices, you can confirm that the user has indeed signed in to iTunes on the device with the Apple ID enrolled in VPP Managed Distribution. In Profile Manager, select a device, and then select the About tab; in the Details section you'll find the Signed in to iTunes and VPP User attributes.

TIP ▶ You may need to update the inventory information in Profile Manager to verify VPP user information. You can do this by selecting the Update Info task from the Action (gear icon) menu at the bottom of the Profile Manager interface.

Remove VPP Managed Distribution Apps

To prevent the accidental loss of data on an iOS device, the Profile Manager service will not remove an app unless you explicitly send the Remove Apps task or unless the user or an administrator unenrolls the device from the MDM service, in which case managed apps and their data are removed. While viewing the Apps tab for a user, group, iOS device, or device group, you can click the Action (gear) menu and choose Remove Apps.

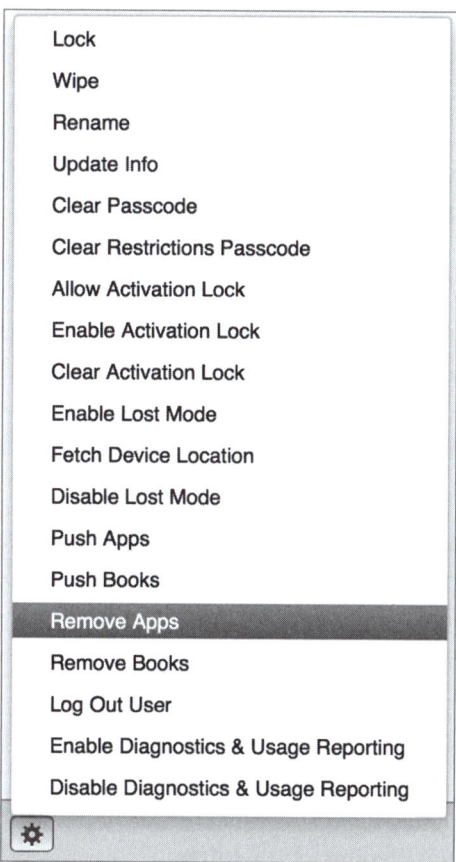

Finally, select the managed apps to remove, and then click OK.

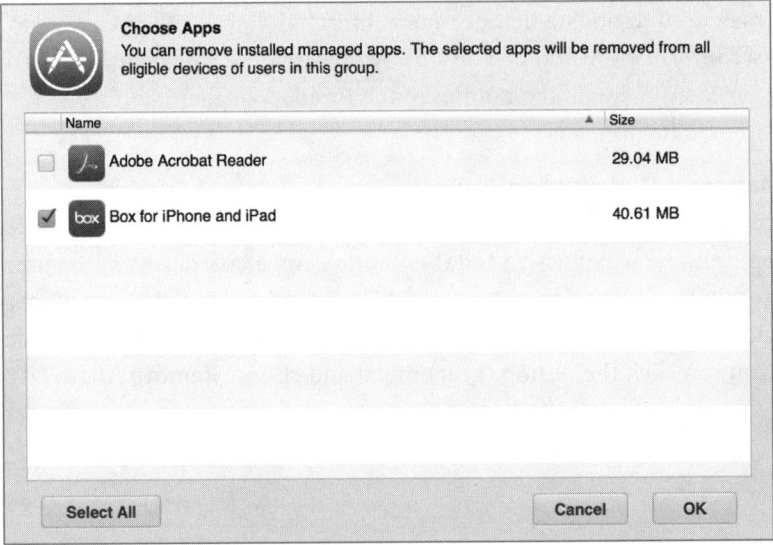

It doesn't matter if an enrolled iOS device is supervised or not; when it receives the Remove Apps command, it will remove the specified apps.

Remove VPP Managed Distribution

Ultimately, if for some reason you don't trust this user or she should otherwise no longer need organizational items, you can always remove her from the program. You can also remove an entire group of users. As shown in previous screenshots, clicking the Remove From Program button will remove the selected user or user group from VPP Managed Distribution.

The current version of Profile Manager will also automatically revoke any VPP-assigned apps when you remove a user or user group from VPP Managed Distribution. Thus, users should receive notification that previously assigned VPP apps are no longer available to their accounts, as described previously in this lesson.

Although removing a user or user group from VPP Managed Distribution will revoke the app licenses, it doesn't remove the user or user group app assignments in Profile Manager. In other words, after removing a user or user group from VPP Managed Distribution, you will also need to remove the user or user group's app assignments. Only then will the revoked VPP app licenses become available for assigning to other users.

> **NOTE ▶** At the time of this writing, if you revoke an app that you assigned to a device and then unenroll the device, the licenses do not return immediately.

Reference 10.7
Installing VPP Managed Distribution Apps and Books Assigned via Apple ID

In this section, you will see how a user enrolled in VPP Managed Distribution can install apps and books assigned to her Apple ID.

Manually Install VPP Apps and Books

The default user experience when receiving VPP apps and books assigned via Apple ID may not be entirely automatic.

This is because the default settings are to only install purchases made directly by the user on the device. In other words, as a default, only if a user makes a purchase on the device will the App Store and iBooks automatically download and install the item. Thus, the default behavior for VPP apps and books assigned via Apple ID is for the user to manually choose the items from his Purchases list.

> **TIP** ▸ If the user's Purchases list isn't updating with the VPP Managed Distribution items assigned via Apple ID, have the user sign out with his Apple ID and then back in. Remember, on iOS, the Apple ID is authenticated in the Settings app > iTunes & App Store, while on OS X it's authenticated in the Mac App Store and iBooks apps separately.

In this case, if a user in VPP Managed Distribution opens the App Store, she will see the VPP Managed Distribution apps assigned via Apple ID in her Purchases list along with any other apps the user may have purchased. Clicking the Free button or download (cloud with an arrow) button will install the app.

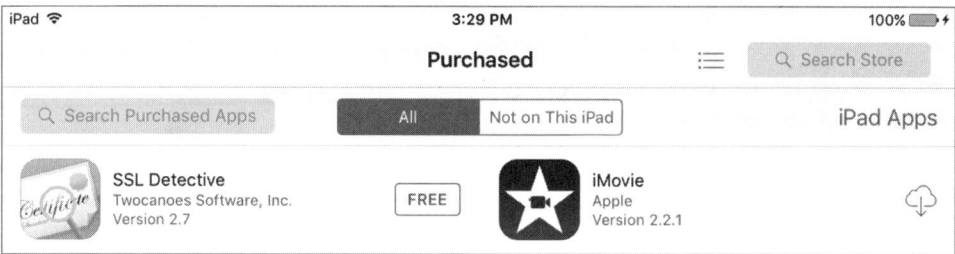

> **NOTE** ▸ A user enrolled in VPP Managed Distribution can also take advantage of items shared via iCloud Family Sharing. However, items assigned via VPP Managed Distribution are not available to the other users in iCloud Family Sharing.

As for iBooks, a user in VPP Managed Distribution will see his VPP-assigned books in both his Library and Purchases lists along with any other books he may have purchased. Again, clicking the Free button or download button will install the book.

NOTE ▶ The iBooks app is not included with iOS 7 and must be installed separately. Obviously, if a device is lacking the iBooks app, it will not be able to access VPP-assigned books.

NOTE ▶ Apps and books installed by the user or automatically downloaded via local settings are not considered "managed." Managed app and book settings are applied only to apps and books installed via an MDM service; see Lesson 16, "Managing Access" for more information.

Exercise 10.1
Configure Profile Manager for the Volume Purchase Program

▶ **Prerequisites**

- ▶ Exercise 4.1, "Prepare Your Mac to Install OS X Server for El Capitan"
- ▶ Exercise 4.2, "Install OS X Server for El Capitan"
- ▶ Exercise 4.3, "Configure OS X Server for El Capitan"
- ▶ Exercise 6.1, "Turn On Profile Manager"
- ▶ Exercise 7.1, "Enable Device Management"
- ▶ Exercise 8.1, "Enroll with the Apple Deployment Programs (Optional)"

Challenge

Configure Profile Manager to distribute apps and books from the Volume Purchase Program (VPP). Provide a new email address for an Apple ID through the Apple Deployment Programs (ADP) site, which this guide refers to as your VPP administrator account.

Considerations

This process requires you to use the Server app, the ADP site, and the VPP store.

> **WARNING** ▶ Do not use a VPP token if it is already in use by a production MDM server. When you create a new VPP administrator account and download the token associated with that new Apple ID, this does not affect your production server.

Solution

Create a VPP Administrator Account (Optional)

If you did not enroll with the Apple Deployment Programs in Exercise 8.1 or already have a VPP administrator account created, skip ahead to the section "Log In with Your VPP Administrator Account."

1   On your server, in Safari, if you are already logged in to the Apple Deployment Programs site with your Device Enrollment Program administrator account, click your name in the upper-right corner of the Safari window, and then choose Sign Out.

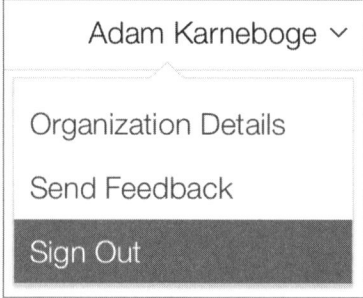

2   Log in to the Apple Deployment Programs site in Safari (https://deploy.apple.com) using your Apple Deployment Programs agent account with two-step verification.

3   In the sidebar, select Admins.

4   Click Add Admin Account.

5   Select the Volume Purchase Program checkbox.

6   Enter a valid first name and last name.

7   In the Work E-mail field, enter an email address for use as your VPP administrator account.

    NOTE ▶ Like your ADP agent and DEP administrator accounts, the email address you choose for your VPP administrator account must not already be in use as an Apple ID or as a secondary email address associated to an Apple ID and cannot be used to log in to the iTunes Store or any other Apple service.

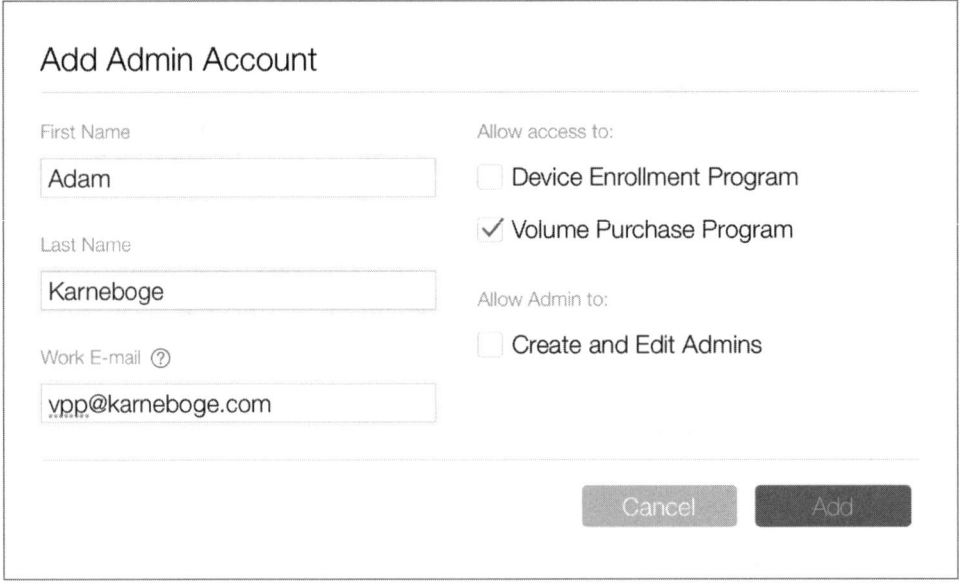

8   Click Add.

9   Review the list of Apple Deployment Programs agents and administrators.

10 Click your name in the upper-right corner, and then choose Sign Out.

Activate Your VPP Administrator Account (Optional)

1. Check your email for your VPP administrator account, and open the mail message with the subject "Join Apple Deployment Programs."

2. Select the temporary password, and press Command-C to copy the text.

3. Click Sign In, which opens the Apple ID site.

4. Enter the credentials for the VPP administrator account you just created, enter the temporary password, and then press Return.

5. Press Command-V to enter the temporary password in the current password field.

6. Enter a new password in the new password and confirm password fields.

   NOTE ▶ Use a secure password you will remember.

7. Click Update. The Apple ID site will now ask you to verify your new VPP administrator Apple ID.

8. Click Continue to send a verification email. You will see an area to enter a six-digit verification code.

9. Check the email client that receives mail for the VPP administrator Apple ID.

10. In the confirmation email you receive from Apple, there will be a six-digit verification code.

11. Enter the six-digit verification code, and click Verify.

12. Enter a birthday, choose three security questions, and then click Update.

    The Apple ID webpage informs you, "Apple ID Updated Successfully."

13. Click Continue.

14. Close the Safari window.

Log In with Your VPP Administrator Account

1   In Safari, open the Apple Deployment Programs site (https://deploy.apple.com).

2   Enter your VPP administrator account credentials, and click Sign In.

3   In the sidebar, click Volume Purchase Program, which takes you to the VPP store for your type of program (Business or Education).

4   Enter your VPP administrator account credentials, and click Sign In.

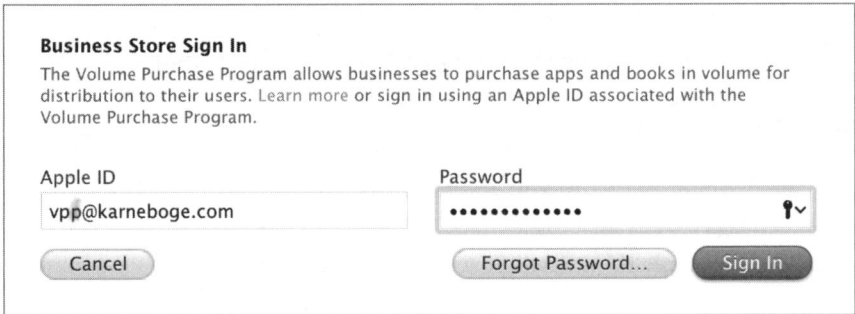

5   If Safari asks to save this password, click Never for This Website.

6   If you see the message that your Apple ID has not yet been used with the VPP store, click Continue.

7   If necessary, read the terms and conditions, select the checkbox that you have read and agree to the VPP terms and conditions, and then click Agree.

8   In the upper-right corner of the Safari window, click the pop-up menu, and choose Account Summary.

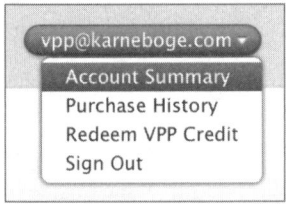

9   Click Download Token.

   This downloads the token to your Downloads folder.

Edit Your Payment Information

Since you're already at your VPP account summary page, enter your payment information now so you don't have to later. While a payment type (credit/debit card) is not required, you must provide a billing name (with title) and address before you can order any software, even if it is free.

VPP Managed Distribution requires a license to be purchased for every app that you will assign, whether it costs money or not.

1   Click Edit Payment Information.

2   Although you can use VPP without purchasing apps, these exercises require you to purchase licenses for at least two free apps.

   Enter valid payment information (including specifying your title under Billing Address), and then click Done. You can select None for Payment Type if you intend to purchase only free apps.

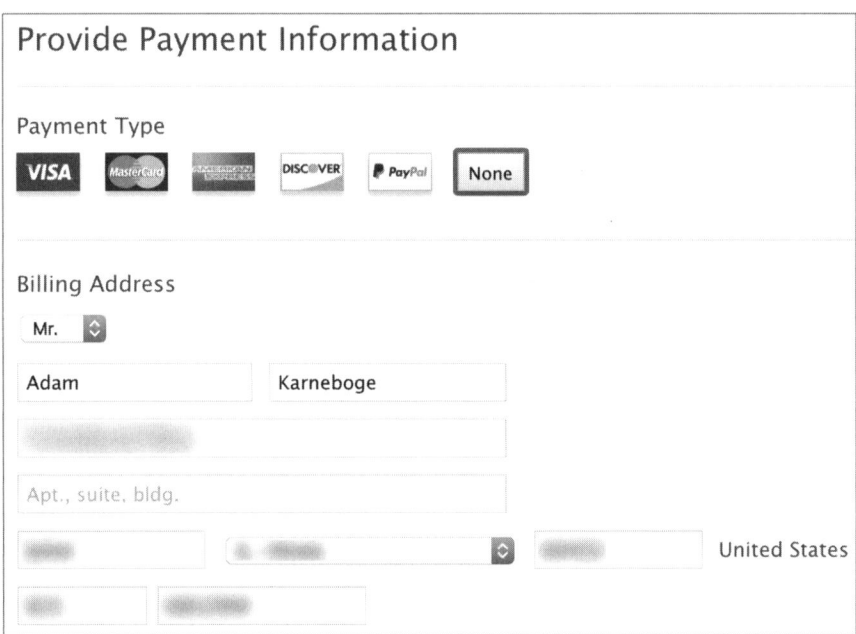

3   If you did enter a payment type other than None and Safari asks if you want it to remember this credit card, click Never for this Card.

4   Close the Safari window.

Configure for the VPP

1. Open the Server app, and connect to your server if necessary.

2. In the Server app sidebar, select Profile Manager.

3. Select the "Distribute apps and books from the Volume Purchase Program" checkbox.

4. Click Choose.

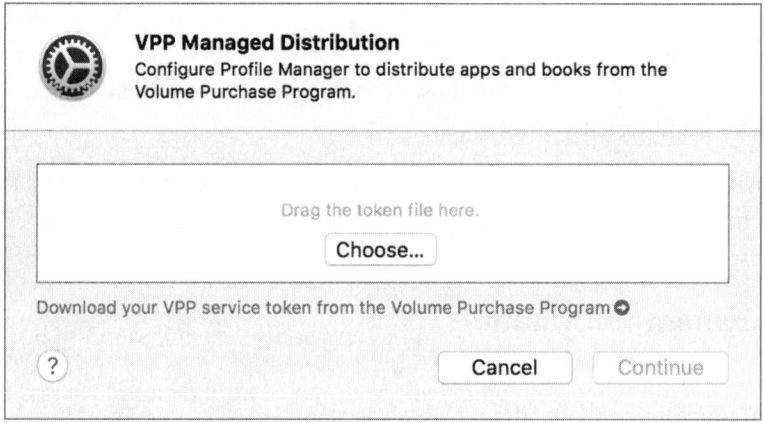

5. In the sidebar, select Downloads.

6. Select your token. It is a file that ends with the suffix "vpptoken."

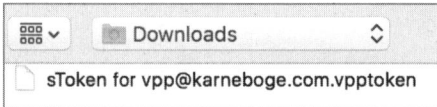

7. Click Choose.

8. At the VPP Managed Distribution pane, with the sToken information displayed, click Continue.

    If you see a message that your VPP account is already in use and you are sure that your VPP account is not in use by any active server, click Continue; otherwise, click Cancel.

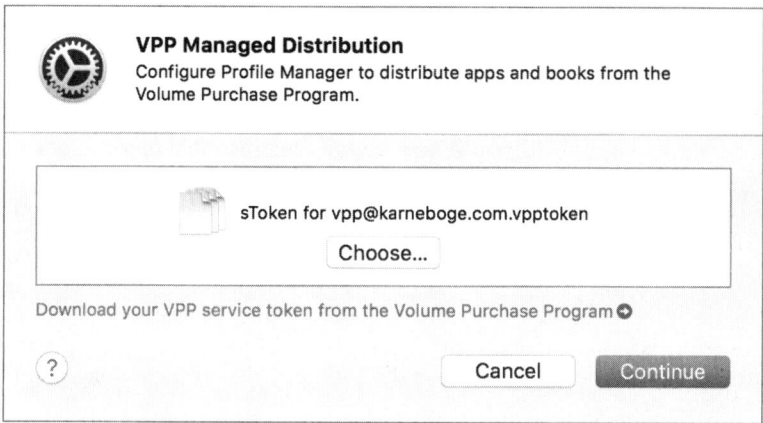

9 Click Done.

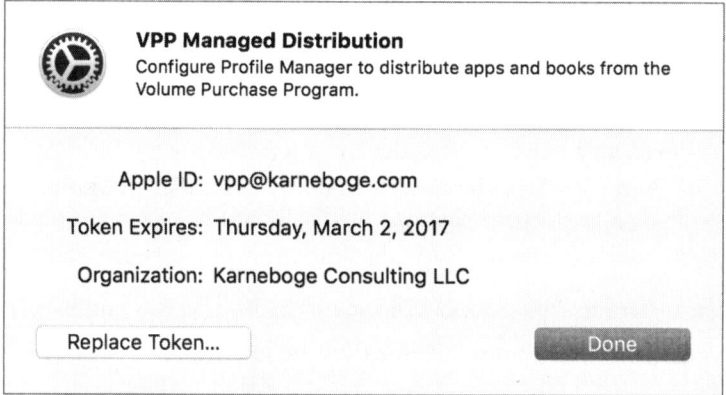

10 Quit the Server app.

In this exercise, you provided an email for an Apple ID that is specifically for administering the VPP, you downloaded the token for managed distribution, and you used that token to integrate your Profile Manager service with VPP managed distribution services.

Exercise 10.2
Purchase and Assign Licensed Apps to Devices

> **Prerequisite**
>
> ▸ Exercise 10.1, "Configure Profile Manager for the Volume Purchase Program"

Challenge

Use your VPP administrator account to purchase the following items for managed distribution:

- Free app for iOS
- Free or paid app for iOS
- Free app for Mac
- Free book (to be used in a later exercise)

Add a DEP-eligible iOS device to a newly created device group, and assign the apps to the group (iOS VPP Devices). Add your Mac computer to a newly created device group, and assign the Mac app to the group (Mac VPP Devices).

Considerations

You can purchase any items you want, but this guide uses the following:

- SSL Detective (Quantity: 5)
- Swype or The Calculator Free (Quantity: 3) (at the time of writing, Swype is $0.99 USD in the U.S. store)
- iBooks Author for Mac (Quantity: 5)
- Self Publishing Using iBooks Author by JAMF Software (Quantity: 5)

Solution

Purchase a Free App for iOS

1   On your server Mac, in Safari, open the Profile Manager administration portal (https://server*n*.local/profilemanager, where *n* is your student number), authenticate with local administrator credentials, and then in the Profile Manager sidebar, select Apps.

2 If there are any apps listed, click Get More Apps in the lower-right corner of the Profile Manager administration portal window.

   Otherwise, click Volume Purchase Program.

3 Click the link for the appropriate VPP store (Business or Education) for your organization.

4 If necessary, enter your VPP administrator account credentials, and then click Sign In.

5 Click the Media Type pop-up menu, and choose iOS Apps.

6 In the Search field, enter SSL Detective.

7 Click Search.

8 Select SSL Detective.

9 Scroll down and inspect the details of this app, which include screenshots, ratings, and reviews.

10 Scroll back up, and confirm that the Price column displays Free iOS App.

11 In the Quantity field, enter 5.

12 Click Review Order.

13 Review the order details.

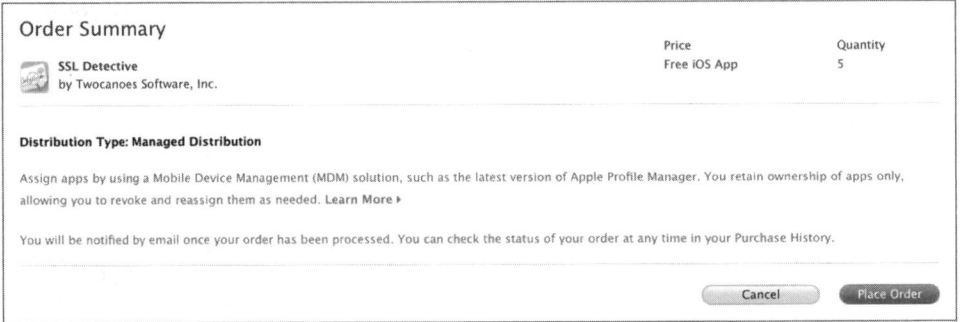

14 Click Place Order.

Purchase a Free or Paid iOS App

1 In the Search field, enter the name of a free or paid app.

This exercise uses Swype because it is only 99 cents (in the U.S. store) at the time of writing, but you can use any app you like. If you want to purchase a free app instead, you can choose The Calculator Free.

2 Click the Media Type pop-up menu, and choose iOS Apps.

3 Click Search.

4 Review the search results.

5 Click the app.

6 In the Quantity field, enter a number. This exercises uses 3, but you could specify as low a number as 1.

Confirm that the subtotal amount is what you expect it to be.

TIP ▶ Many developers, including Apple, give half-price prices on their apps for VPP orders over 20 licenses. If you plan to do large deployments, always attempt to purchase at least 20 licenses at a time.

7 If purchasing a paid app, for Distribution Type, select Managed Distribution.

8   Click Review Order.

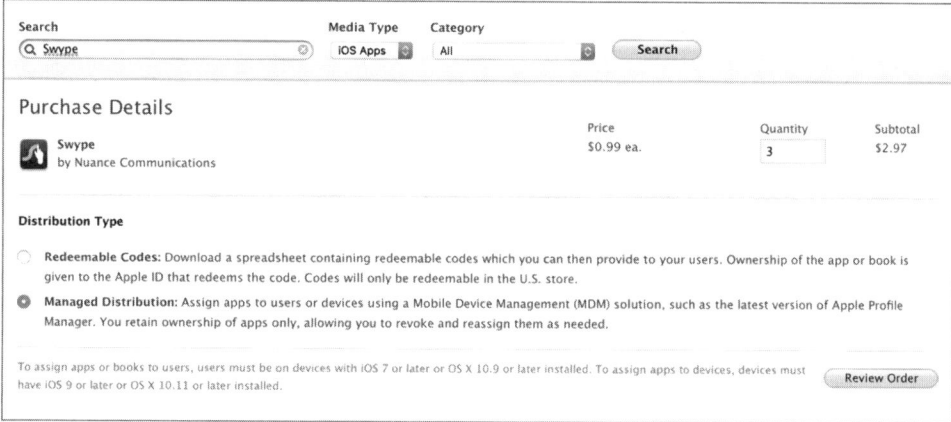

9   Confirm the details of the order one last time, and then click Place Order.

10 Enter your VPP administrator account credentials if necessary, and then click Buy. Review the information about your order.

Purchase a Free Book

1   In the Search field, enter Self Publishing Using iBooks Author.

2   Click the Media Type pop-up menu, and choose Books.

3   Click Search.

4   Select the Self Publishing Using iBooks Author item from JAMF University Press.

5   Enter 5 in the Quantity field.

6   Click Review Order.

7   Click Place Order.

422 VPP-Managed Apps and Books

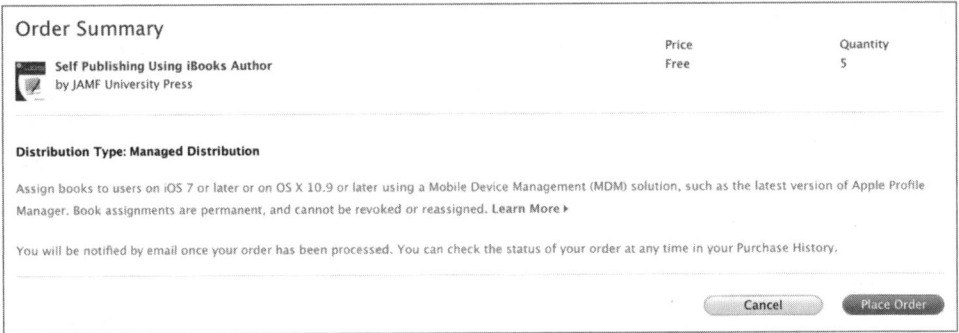

Your order is complete. You will assign this book in a later exercise.

Purchase a Free Mac App

1. In the Search field, enter iBooks Author.

2. Click the Media Type pop-up menu, and choose Mac Apps.

3. Click Search.

4. Click the iBooks Author item from Apple.

5. Enter 5 in the Quantity field.

6. Click Review Order.

7. Click Place Order.

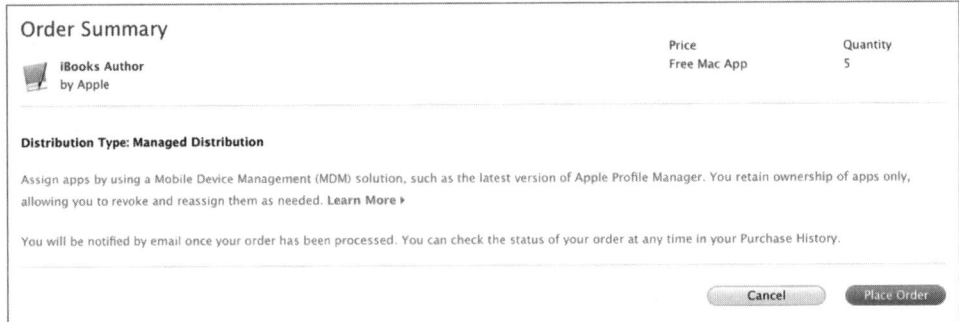

Your order is complete.

Confirm That the Books and Apps Are Listed in Profile Manager

1 In the Profile Manager administration portal sidebar, select Apps.

2 Confirm that the apps you purchased are listed.

   NOTE ▶ How quickly purchases appear in your MDM server varies by quantity and other factors. In this exercise, it make take several minutes for all of your purchases to appear. You may also need to refresh the Profile Manager administration portal or restart the Profile Manager service.

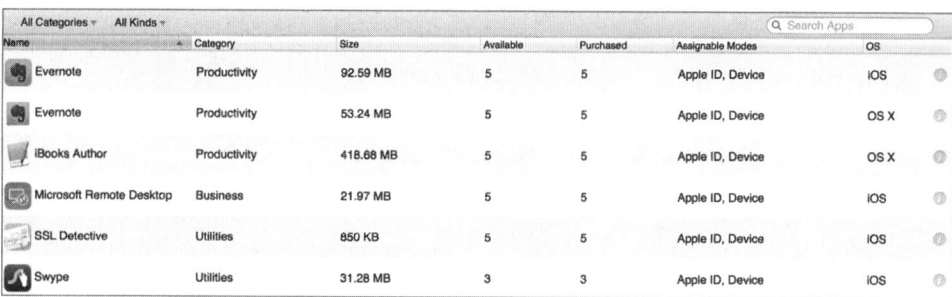

3 In the sidebar, select Books.

4 Confirm that the book you purchased is listed. This book will be used in a later exercise.

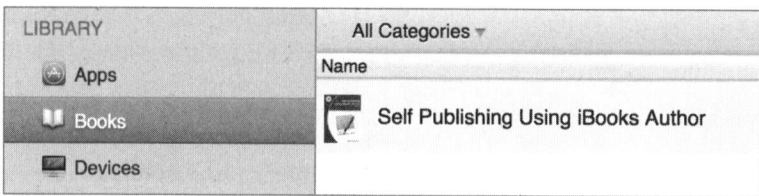

Assign Your iOS Device to the MDM Server

1 Use your server computer to log in to the Apple Deployment Programs site in Safari (https://deploy.apple.com) using your DEP administrator account with two-step verification.

2 In the sidebar, select Device Enrollment Program, and then select Manage Devices.

3 For step 1, select Choose Devices By: Serial Number.

4   Enter the serial number of your iOS device (the iOS device must be eligible for the DEP).

    To identify the serial number, look at the back of the iOS device, or if your iOS device is on and accessible, navigate to Settings > General > About.

5   For step 2, Choose Action, leave the pop-up menu at Assign to Server.

6   Click the Choose MDM Server pop-up menu, and choose your server.

7   Click OK.

8   In the Assignment Complete pane, click OK.

9   Click your name in the upper-right corner, and then choose Sign Out.

Create a Device Group and Add Your iOS Device Placeholder

1   If necessary, open a new Safari window (Command-N), open the Profile Manager administration portal (https://servern.local/profilemanager, where *n* is your student number), and then authenticate with your server's local administrator credentials.

2   In the Profile Manager sidebar, select Devices.

3   At the bottom of the Devices section, click the Refresh button, and confirm that there is a new placeholder record for the iOS device you just assigned to your server.

4   In the Profile Manager sidebar, select Device Groups.

5   If you do not yet have any device groups, click Add Device Group.

    If you already have device groups, click the Add (+) button at the bottom of the Device Groups column in the Profile Manager window.

6   Replace the default name, New Device Group, with a more descriptive name, such as iOS VPP Devices.

7   Click the Add (+) button, and choose Add Devices.

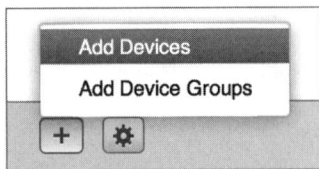

8 For the iOS device you just assigned to your MDM server, click Add.

9 Click Done.

10 Click the Settings tab.

11 Select the checkbox Prompt User To Enroll Device.

12 Select the checkbox "Do not allow user to skip enrollment step."

13 Select the checkbox "Prevent unenrollment."

14 Leave the checkbox selected for Allow Pairing with a Mac, and leave the checkbox deselected for Configure as Shared iPad.

15 Deselect "Require credentials for enrollment."

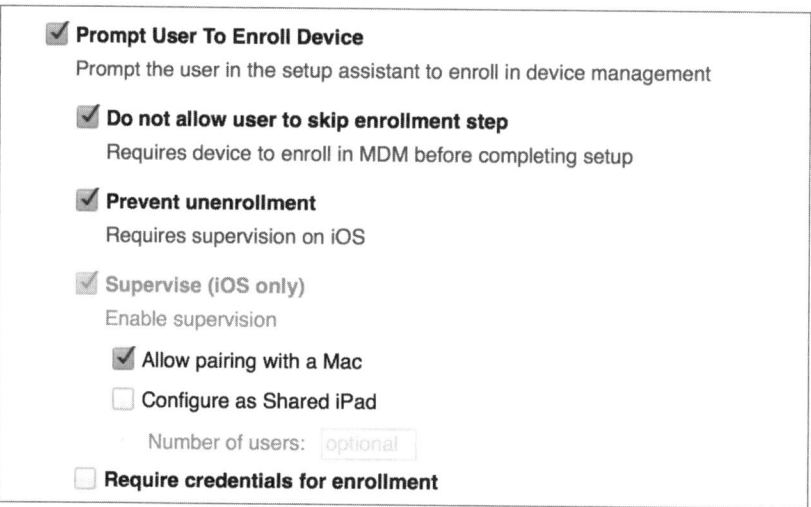

16 Scroll to the Setup Assistant Options section. In the iOS and OS X section, leave Location Services selected, and deselect the other four options. In the iOS section, deselect each checkbox. You will be creating a separate group for Mac computers, so it is not necessary to adjust the OS X Setup Assistant options.

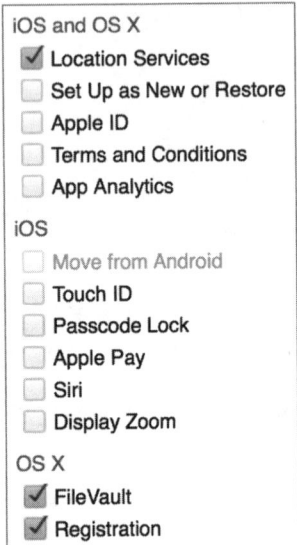

17 Click Save.

Add a Mac Computer Placeholder and Create a Device Group

1 While still viewing the Profile Manager administration portal, in the sidebar, select Devices.

2 Click the Add (+) button, and select Add Placeholder.

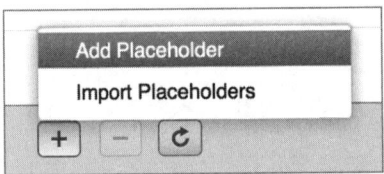

3 In the Add Device pane, leave Device Type as iOS/OSX, and enter the name client*n* (where *n* is your student number).

4 Enter the serial number of your client Mac.

Different Mac computers have their serial number located in different places. If your Mac computer is on and accessible, navigate to the Apple Menu > About This Mac.

5 Click Add. A placeholder should now be visible in the Devices list.

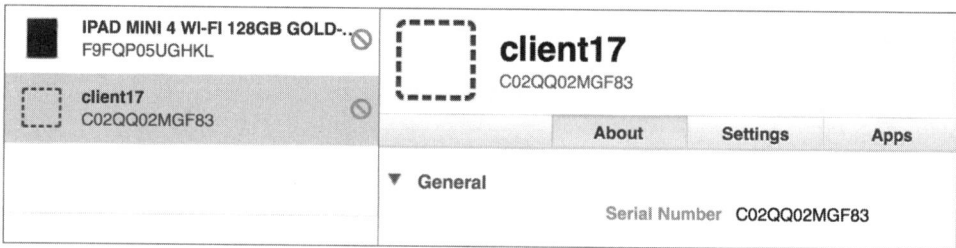

6 In the Profile Manager sidebar, select Device Groups.

7 Click the Add (+) button at the bottom of the Device Groups column in the Profile Manager window.

8 Replace the default name, New Device Group, with a more descriptive name, such as Mac VPP Devices.

9 Click the Add (+) button, and choose Add Devices.

10 For the Mac computer named "client17", click Add.

11 Click Done.

12 Click Save.

Assign Apps

1 While still viewing the Mac VPP Devices group, click the Apps tab.

2 Click Add (+).

3 Select iBooks Author.

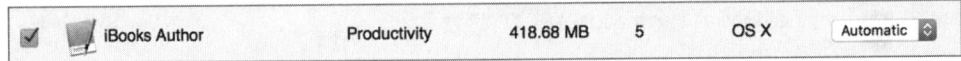

4 Click OK.

5 Leave Installation Mode at Automatic, and click Save.

6 Select the iOS VPP Devices group, and click the Apps tab.

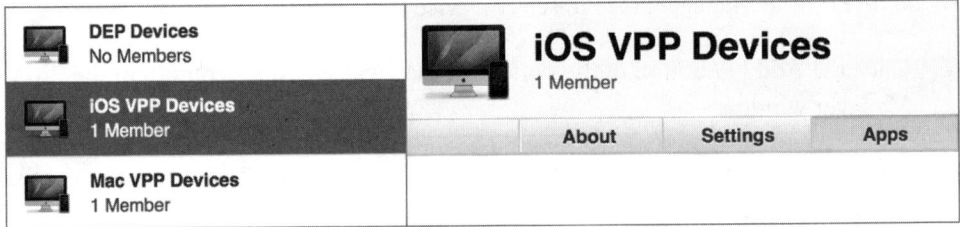

7 Click Add (+).

8 Select SSL Detective.

9 Click OK.

10 Leave Installation Mode at Automatic, and click Save.

In this exercise, you used the VPP store to purchase a free app and a paid app for iOS, a free Mac app, and a free book for later use. You then assigned your iOS device to your MDM server using the ADP site. Finally, you created two device groups and assigned the apps you purchased to both your iOS device and a placeholder for your client Mac.

Exercise 10.3
Deploy Licensed Apps to Devices

▶ **Prerequisite**

▶ Exercise 10.1, "Configure Profile Manager for the Volume Purchase Program"

▶ Exercise 10.2, "Purchase and Assign Licensed Apps to Devices"

Challenge

Enroll your iOS device using the Device Enrollment Program, and observe the automatic deployment of an app upon enrollment. Enroll your client Mac computer using the user portal, and observe the automatic deployment of an app.

Considerations

Because the previous exercise used device assignment, you do not need to associate your device to a user or enter an Apple ID for device-based VPP app deployment to succeed.

Solution

Erase All Content and Settings

If your iOS device is at the Welcome screen, skip to the next section.

1   Press the Home button.

2   Open Settings.

3   Navigate to General > Reset.

4   Tap Erase All Content and Settings.

5   If your iOS device has a passcode, enter the passcode.

6   In the confirmation dialog, tap Erase.

7   In the extra confirmation dialog, tap Erase.

Wait while the iOS device erases all content and settings.

Enroll the iOS Device with the Setup Assistant and Observe Automatic App Installation

1   Slide at the "slide to set up" screen.

2   Tap your language.

3   Tap your country or region.

4 Tap your Wi-Fi network. In an instructor-led environment, this may be Classroom Wireless.

5 If necessary, enter the Wi-Fi password, and then tap Join.

In an instructor-led environment, the password may be student!.

6 At the Location Services screen, tap Enable Location Services.

7 At the Configuration screen, tap Next.

You deselected "Require credentials for enrollment" for the iOS VPP Devices group, so enrollment proceeds without user credentials.

8 At the Welcome screen, tap Get Started.

9 In the Profile Manager sidebar, click Active Tasks, and quickly observe the active task on your server as SSL Detective is automatically installed on your iOS device.

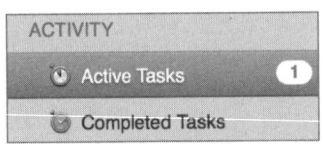

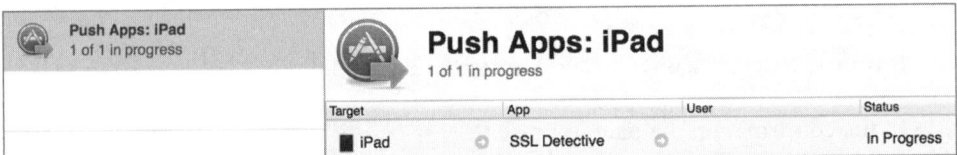

If the task proceeds too quickly, in the Profile Manager sidebar, click Completed Tasks, and look for the Push Apps: iPad task with the text "1 succeeded" underneath.

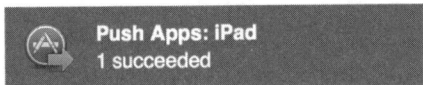

10 If necessary, dismiss the Edit Home Screen notification.

11 If necessary, slide on your iOS device to verify that the SSL Detective app was installed.

Enroll Your Client Mac Computer with the User Portal, and Observe Automatic App Installation

1   On your client Mac computer, in Safari, open the user portal (https://server*n*.local/mydevices, where *n* is your student number).

2   If you see the message "Safari can't verify the identity of the website "server*n*.local" (where *n* is your student number), click Continue.

3   Log out if necessary; then In the Please Log In window, enter the following credentials, and click Log In:

▶   User Name: enrico
▶   Password: net

4   If you are asked "Would you like to save this password?" click Never for This Website.

5   Click Enroll.

    The profile will be downloaded, and System Preferences will automatically open.

6   Click Continue, and then click Install.

7   Enter the local administrator password, and click OK.

8   Quit System Preferences and Safari.

9. On your server, in the Profile Manager sidebar, click Completed Tasks and look for the Push Apps: client*n* (where *n* is your student number) task with the text "1 succeeded" underneath.

   It may take a few minutes for the task to complete. In this case, look for the task under Active Tasks.

   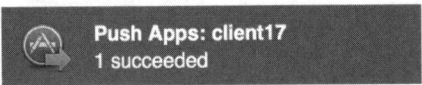

10. Click Launchpad in the Dock, and observe that iBooks Author is installed and available.

11. If iBooks Author does not appear in Launchpad, from the menu bar, choose Go > Applications.

12. If necessary, scroll and observe that iBooks Author is installed and available.

In this exercise, you enrolled both your iOS device and your client Mac and observed that automatic installation of apps succeeded automatically.

Exercise 10.4
Assign Apps and Books to Users and Invite Participants for VPP Managed Distribution

> **Prerequisite**
>
> ▸ Exercise 10.1, "Configure Profile Manager for the Volume Purchase Program"
>
> ▸ Exercise 10.2, "Purchase and Assign Licensed Apps to Devices"
>
> ▸ Exercise 10.3, "Deploy Licensed Apps to Devices"

Challenge

Assign an app and a book to a group of users (Engineering). Invite a member of the invited group (Lucy Sanchez is a member of the Engineering group) to participate in the Volume Purchase Program.

When you accept the invitation, provide your client testing Apple ID credentials (although you could use any Apple ID).

Use the Profile Manager administration portal to confirm that the user accepted the invitation.

Associate Lucy Sanchez with your iOS device, and install the app and book.

Use the Home Screen Layout payload to configure the Home screen on your iOS device.

Considerations

Inviting a user to enroll in VPP can be done via either push notification or email. However, since Lucy Sanchez will not be associated with the iOS device at this point in the exercise, you will need to use an email invitation for Lucy Sanchez to successfully enroll in VPP managed distribution.

Although you could use a configuration profile to expedite the setup of Mail for Lucy Sanchez, to keep the requirements for this exercise as simple as possible, just set up Mail for Lucy Sanchez manually.

If your server uses a fully qualified domain name (FQDN) instead of a Bonjour .local name, use your server's FQDN instead of its Bonjour name for Mail.

Solution

Enable VPP Managed Distribution Services

1. If necessary, use your server to log into the Profile Manager administration portal (https://server*n*.local/profilemanager, where *n* is your student number), and then authenticate with your server's local administrator credentials.

2. In the Profile Manager sidebar, select Groups.

3. Select Engineering.

4   If necessary, click the About tab.

5   Scroll and select the checkbox Enable VPP Managed Distribution Services.

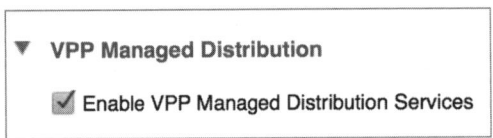

6   Click Save.

    NOTE ▶ Do not send any invitations until you assign apps and books in the next section.

Assign Apps

1   While still viewing the Engineering group, click the Apps tab.

2   Click Add (+).

3   Select Swype (or the other free or paid app you purchased).

4   In the Assignment Mode pop-up menu, select Apple ID.

Note the warning about how apps will be assigned in chronological order according to when users accepted VPP Managed Distribution enrollment. This warning appears when you do not have enough copies of an app for all the members in the group.

5   Click OK.

6   Review the list of apps you are about to assign to members of the Engineering group.

7   Click Save.

Assign Books

1. In the Profile Manager administration portal, for the Engineering group, click the Books tab.

2. Click Add (+).

3. Select the one book listed.

   Books can be assigned only to users, so there is no option to assign to a device.

   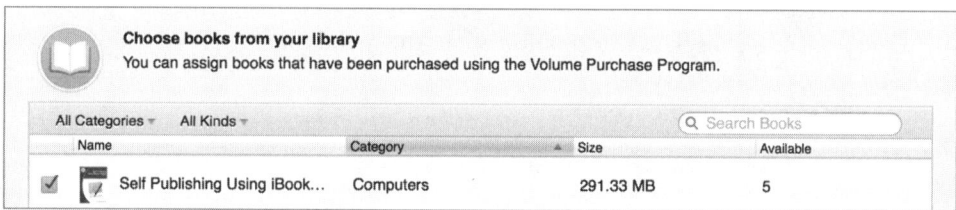

4. Click OK.

5. Click Save.

Send the Email Invitation

1. If necessary, in the Profile Manager administration portal sidebar, select Groups.

2. If necessary, select Engineering.

3. Click the About tab.

4. Scroll to the VPP Managed Distribution section.

   Remember that you used the Server app to configure the Mail service and to specify a user's email address. If necessary, review the procedure from Exercise 4.3, "Configure OS X Server for El Capitan."

5. Click "Send email invitation."

   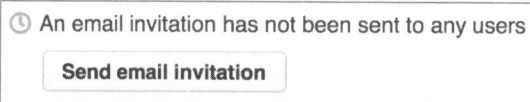

6   In the confirmation dialog, click Send.

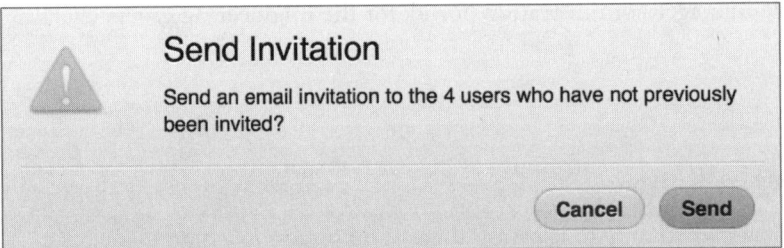

Profile Manager displays information about the invitation.

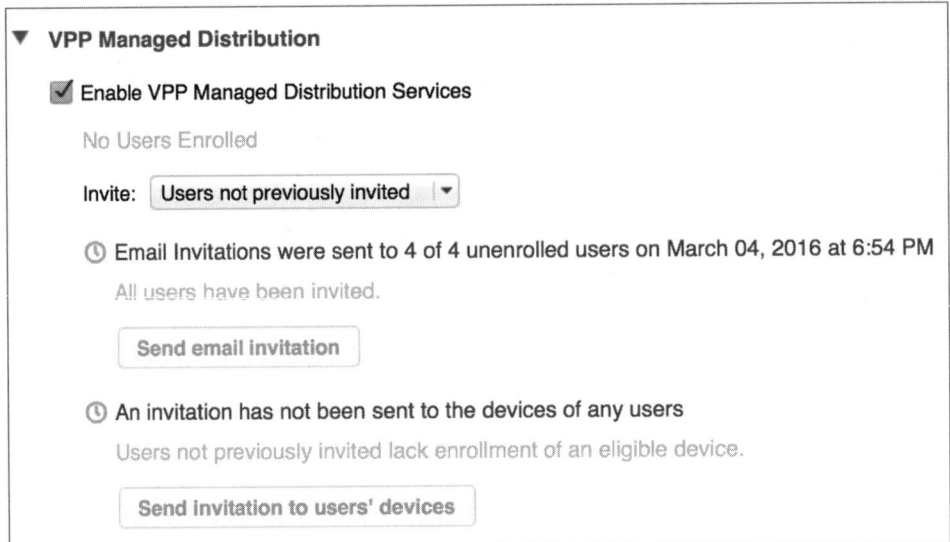

Configure Mail for the Network User on Your iOS Device

> **NOTE** ▶ If your server uses a fully qualified domain name instead of a Bonjour .local name, use your server's FQDN instead of its Bonjour name for Mail; your iOS device settings will look different than the figures in this section.

1   On your iOS device, slide at the "slide to unlock" screen, and open Mail.

2   At the Welcome to Mail screen, tap Other.

3 Enter the following information:

- Name: Lucy Sanchez
- Email: lucy@server*n*.local (where *n* is your student number)
- Password: net
- Description: This is automatically entered.

Cancel	New Account	Next
Name	Lucy Sanchez	
Email	lucy@server17.local	
Password	•••	
Description	Server17	

4 Tap Next.

5 In the New Account pane, enter the following information:

- Incoming Mail Server:
- Host Name: server*n*.local (where *n* is your student number)
- User Name: lucy
- Password: net will be automatically entered.
- Outgoing Mail Server:
- Host Name: server*n*.local (where *n* is your student number)
- User Name: lucy
- Password: net

6 Tap Next.

7 If necessary, each time you see the Cannot Verify Server Identity dialog, tap Continue.

8 In the IMAP pane, tap Save.

Allow VPP Access to Your iTunes Account

1. If necessary, tap Inbox in the upper-left corner to display your inbox.

2. Tap the message from your MDM.

3. In the body of the message, tap Sign In.

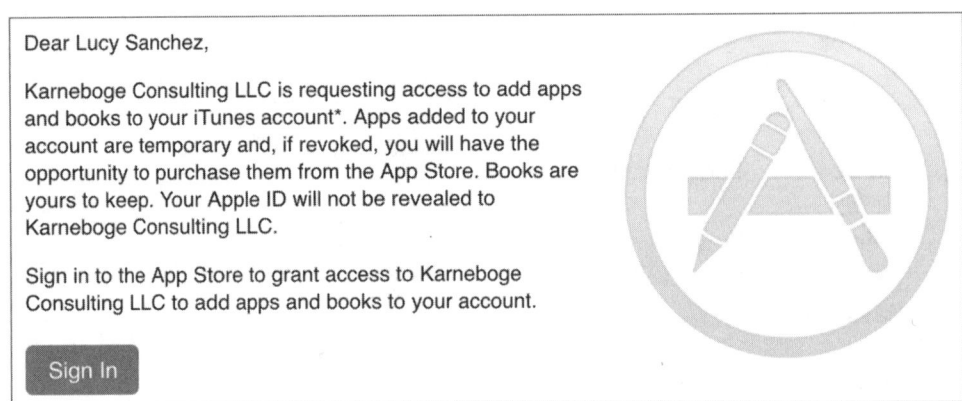

4. Safari opens.

    If necessary, in the Cannot Verify Server Identity dialog, tap Continue.

5. In the Please Log In pane, enter the credentials for Lucy Sanchez (User Name: lucy, Password: net).

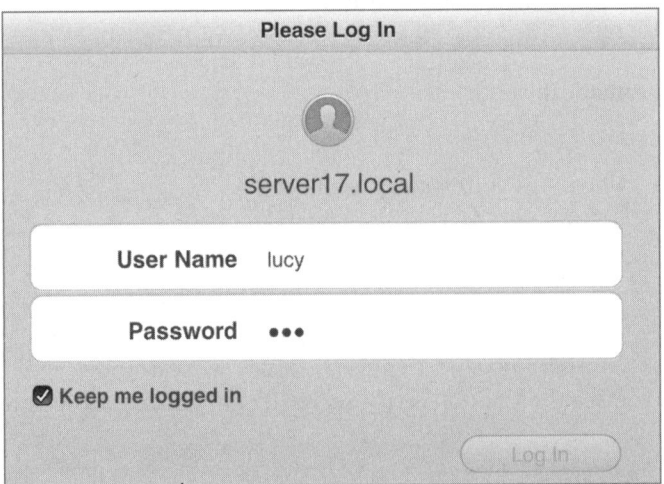

6 Tap Log in.

7 In the Open this Page in App Store dialog, tap Open.

8 In the Sign-In to associate account dialog, tap Sign In.

9 Tap Use Existing Apple ID.

10 Enter your client testing Apple ID credentials.

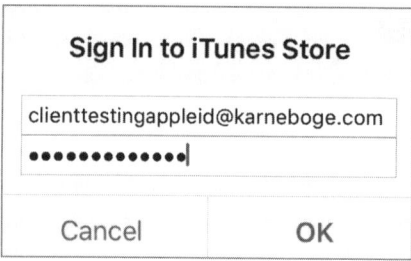

11 Tap OK.

12 Read the terms and conditions.

13 Scroll to the bottom to access additional pages, tap Agree, and then in the confirmation dialog, tap Agree.

14 In the Allow Assignment pane, tap OK.

15 Your iOS device is open at the App Store.

   If you have an iPad, tap Purchased at the bottom of the screen.

   If you have an iPhone or iPod touch, tap Updates at the bottom of the screen, and then tap Purchased.

16 Confirm that no items are displayed.

   You haven't purchased any iOS items with this client testing Apple ID yet, and while you have previously assigned apps to Lucy Sanchez, you have not yet associated your iOS device to this user.

17 If you see the dialog about downloading Apple Apps, tap Not Now.

Confirm the Invitation in the Profile Manager Administration Portal

1 In the Profile Manager administration portal sidebar, select Users.

2 At the bottom of the column of Users, click Refresh to update the information.

3 Select Lucy Sanchez, and then click the About tab.

4 Scroll down, and inspect the VPP Managed Distribution section for Lucy Sanchez.

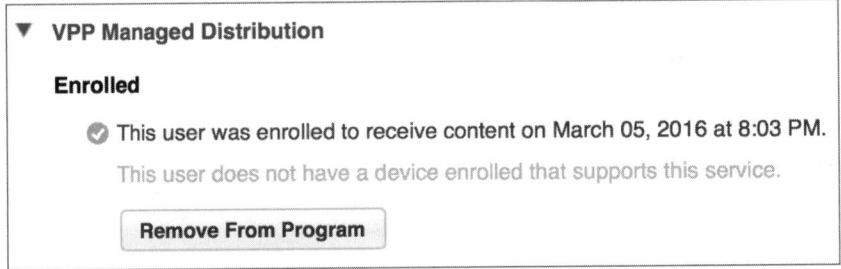

Associate the Network User with Your Enrolled iOS Device

In Exercise 10.3, "Deploy Licensed Apps to Devices," to emphasize device assignment, you enrolled your iOS device using the DEP but did not provide user credentials. For user-assigned apps to install, you need to have a device associated with your user.

1 While still viewing the user Lucy Sanchez, click the Devices tab.

2 Click Add (+), and select Add Devices.

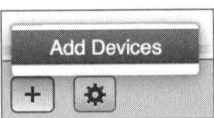

3 Click Add next to your iOS device, and then click Done.

4 Click Save.

   Observe that your iOS device is now associated with Lucy Sanchez.

5 In the Profile Manager sidebar, select Completed Tasks.

6   Observe that the VPP book that was assigned to Lucy was automatically deployed to your iOS device.

Tasks do not show in Completed Tasks until they have Succeeded. The automatic push of the book may take a few minutes.

Install User Assigned Apps on Your iOS Device

1   On your iOS device, slide at the "slide to unlock" screen, and if necessary, open the App Store.

2   Your iOS device is open at the App Store.

   If you have an iPad, tap Purchased at the bottom of the screen.

   If you have an iPhone or iPod touch, tap Updates at the bottom of the screen, and then tap Purchased.

3   Confirm that Swype (or the free or paid app you assigned to Lucy Sanchez) is now available to be installed.

   NOTE ▶ It may take several minutes for the app to appear in your purchases list.

   Note that you as an administrator of the Profile Manager service do not have any indication as to which Apple ID the user provided. This is by design.

4   Press the home button and then open the App Store.

5   If you have an iPad, tap Purchased at the bottom of the screen.

   If you have an iPhone or iPod touch, tap Updates at the bottom of the screen, and then tap Purchased.

6 Confirm that the apps you recently assigned appear.

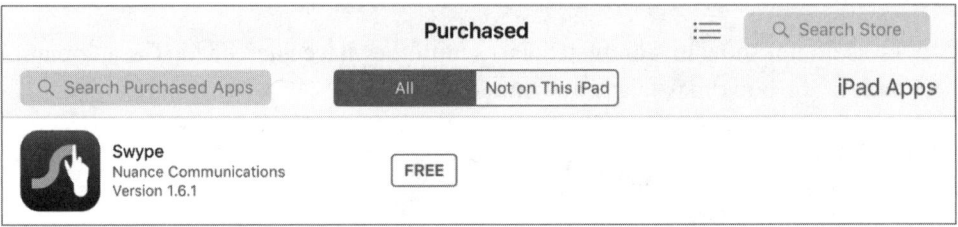

7 For each purchased item, tap Free, and then tap Install App.

If the App Store displays a Download (looks like a cloud with an arrow) icon instead of a Free button, tap the Download icon.

8 Tap the Home button, swipe to the second Home screen if necessary, and confirm that the apps start downloading.

View the Book on Your iOS Device

1 On your iOS device, open iBooks.

2 If you see the Sync iBooks dialog, tap Don't Sync.

3 If necessary, tap My Books in the lower-left corner of the screen.

4 Confirm that the book you assigned appears on the bookshelf. This book was automatically pushed when you associated Lucy Sanchez to the iOS device.

Manage the Home Screen of Your iOS Device

1   If necessary, open the Profile Manager administration portal, and log in with local administrator credentials.

2   In the Profile Manager sidebar, select Devices.

3   Select the iOS device that is enrolled and associated with Lucy Sanchez.

4   Click the Settings tab.

5   In the Settings for iPad (or your iOS device name) section, click Edit to begin creating a profile.

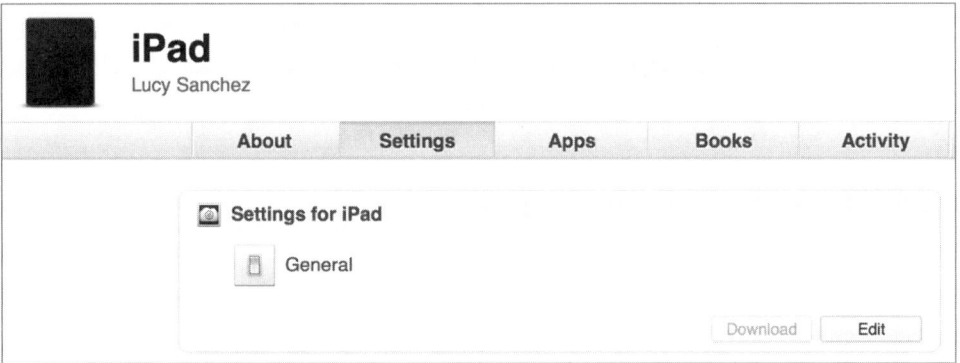

6   In the Description field for the General payload, enter descriptive text such as Home Screen Layout.

7   In the Security pull-down menu, select With Authorization, and in the Authorization Password field, type profilepw.

    This will require that the profile can be removed only by a person with the password, likely an administrator.

8   In the payload sidebar, scroll and select the Home Screen Layout payload, and click Configure.

    This payload allows an administrator the ability to manage how apps are arranged and displayed on the Home screen and Dock on an iOS device.

9   In the Dock field, click Add (+).

10 Click "<click to edit app name>" twice, and type Safari.

    Wait a few moments. Profile Manager will search the App Store not only for currently known Apple-installed apps but any apps currently in the App Store containing that name.

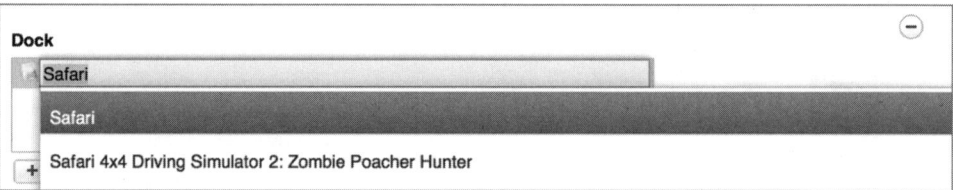

11 Select Safari.

12 In the Page 1 field, click Add (+), and then select Add Folder.

13 Click the folder name twice, type MDM Project *n* Apps (where *n* is your student number), and press Return.

14 In the Page 1 – MDM Project *n* Apps field (where *n* is your student number), click Add (+), double-click to add SSL Detective, and then press Return.

15 In the Page 1 – MDM Project *n* Apps field (where *n* is your student number), click Add (+), double-click to add Swype (or whichever free or paid app you chose), and then press Return.

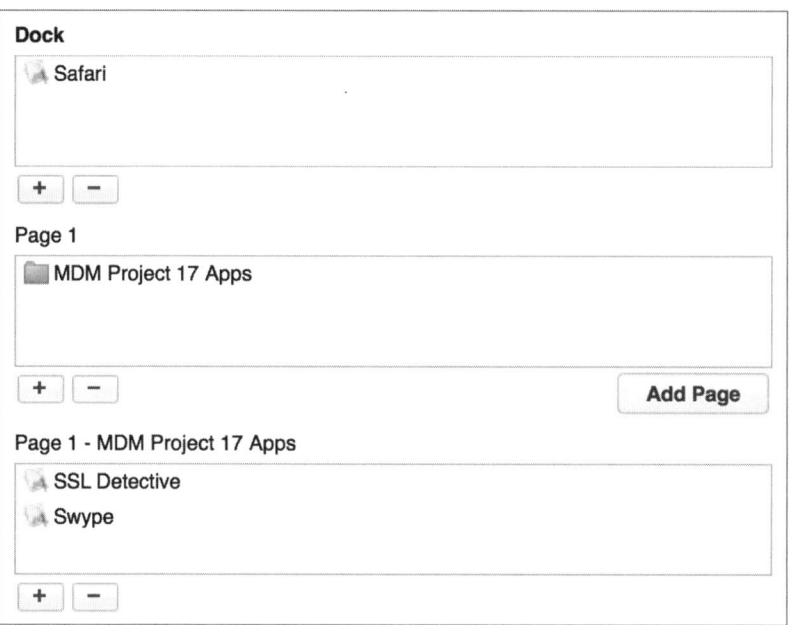

16 Click OK.

17 Click Save, and review that there is an active task sending the new configuration profile to your iOS device.

18 On your iOS device, inspect the results. There should be a folder on the front page, and the only app in the Dock should be Safari.

Restrict App Usage

The iOS Restrictions payload in Profile Manager allows you to adjust which apps are available for use on an iOS device.

1 While still in the Profile Manager administration portal, in the settings for Lucy Sanchez's iOS device, click Edit.

2 In the payload sidebar, under iOS select Restrictions.

3 Click Configure.

4 Click the Apps tab, and scroll to the Restrict App Usage section.

   Observe that restricting app usage is limited to supervised iOS devices.

5 Under the pop-up menu, select Allow Some Apps Only.

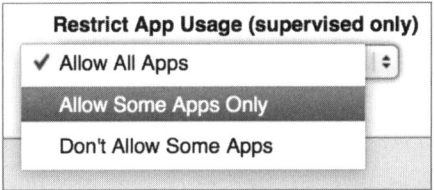

6 Click Add (+).

7 Click "<click to edit app name>" twice, and type Safari.

8 Repeat step 7 for Swype (or the other free or paid app you purchased) and SSL Detective.

9 Click OK.

10 Click Save.

   Observe that the restrictions payload has been added to the configuration profile for your iOS device.

11 On your iOS device, inspect the results. There should be a folder on the front page containing Swype (or the other free or paid app you purchased) and SSL Detective, and the only app in the Dock should be Safari.

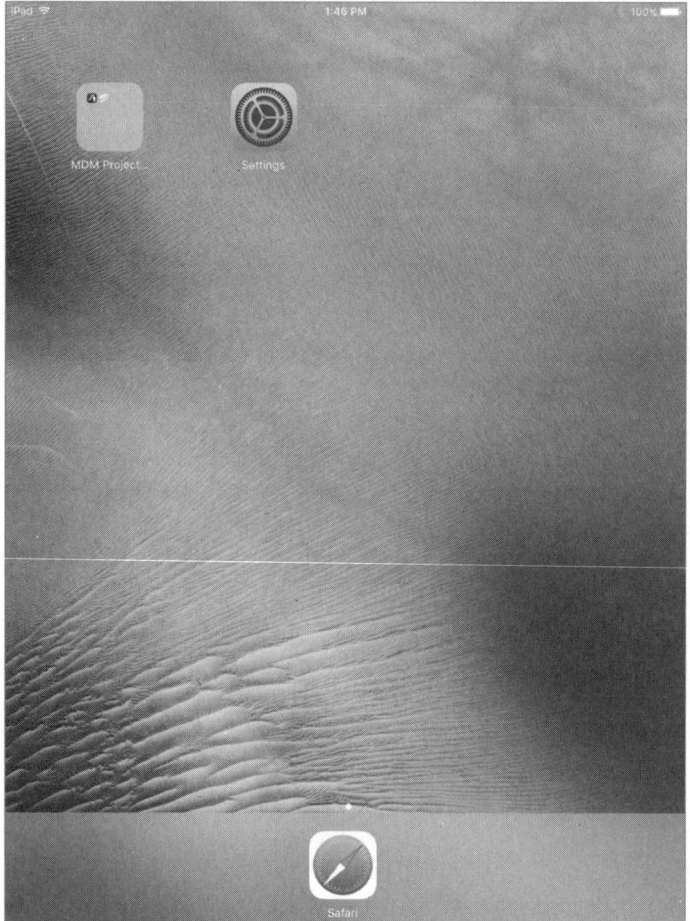

Observe that Settings is also available, even though you did not add it to your approved list. Settings will always be available, regardless of whether it is in your approved or disapproved list. If your iOS device is an iPhone, you will also see the Phone app.

In this exercise, you invited a group to participate in VPP managed distribution services and assigned an app and a book to that group (and by association the users in that group). On your iOS device, you used Mail to accept the invitation, authenticated to the Profile

Manager service with network user credentials, and then provided Apple ID credentials. As an administrator, you used the Profile Manager administration portal to confirm that the invitation was accepted and the user successfully enrolled in VPP managed distribution. You used the App Store to install the apps that were made available to you through VPP managed distribution services. You also used iBooks to confirm access to the book that was assigned to you. Finally, you created a configuration profile containing the Home Screen Layout and Restrictions (iOS) payloads (both new in Profile Manager in Server 5.1) to manage the look of the Home screen and restrict app usage on your iOS device.

Exercise 10.5
Inspect the Effects of App Assignment and Remove VPP Managed Distribution Services

▶ **Prerequisite**

- ▶ Exercise 10.1, "Configure Profile Manager for the Volume Purchase Program"
- ▶ Exercise 10.2, "Purchase and Assign Licensed Apps to Devices"
- ▶ Exercise 10.3, "Deploy Licensed Apps to Devices"
- ▶ Exercise 10.4, "Assign Apps and Books to Users and Invite Participants for VPP Managed Distribution"

Challenge

Inspect the availability of the apps and books that were assigned to your devices and to your network user.

Remove the Engineering group from VPP managed distribution services, and then unassign the apps from the group.

Remove the Home Screen Layout configuration profile, and unassign the apps from the iOS VPP Apps and Mac VPP Apps device group.

Inspect how this changes the number of available apps and books.

Unenroll your client Mac and your iOS device, unassign your iOS device from the DEP, remove the remaining placeholders, and wipe your iOS device.

Considerations

Removing the group from VPP managed distribution services revokes the apps that have been assigned, but the apps are still assigned to the group.

Once you assign a book through VPP managed distribution, your organization cannot reclaim that book.

Solution

Inspect Apps and Books Availability

1. On your server Mac, in the Profile Manager administration portal sidebar, select Apps.

2. Confirm that each item has the expected number in the Available and Purchased columns.

   You purchased five copies of SSL Detective, and you assigned the app to the iOS Devices group, which contains only one iOS device, so there are four copies available.

   You purchased five copies of iBooks Author and assigned it to the Mac VPP Devices group, so there are four copies available.

   You purchased three copies of Swype (or a free app), and you assigned the app to the Engineering group, which has four members, so there are no copies of Swype available.

Name	Category	Size	Available	Purchased
Evernote	Productivity	92.59 MB	5	5
Evernote	Productivity	53.24 MB	5	5
iBooks Author	Productivity	418.68 MB	4	5
Microsoft Remote Desktop	Business	21.97 MB	5	5
SSL Detective	Utilities	850 KB	4	5
Swype	Utilities	31.28 MB	0	3

3. For the app SSL Detective, click Assignment Info (the letter *i* in italics on the right) to view information about its assignment.

4   Click the Device Groups tab (in Assignment Info), and observe that the app was assigned to all devices in that group.

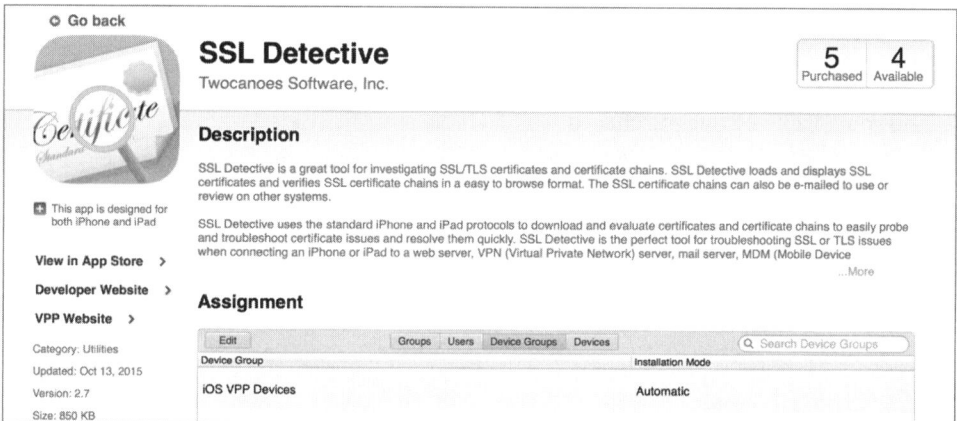

5   Click "Go back."

6   For the app Swype, click Assignment Info (the letter *i* in italics on the right) to view information about its assignment.

7   Click the Groups tab, and confirm that the Engineering group is listed, with its four members. Observe that Assignment Mode is Apple ID, indicating that the app was assigned to Users.

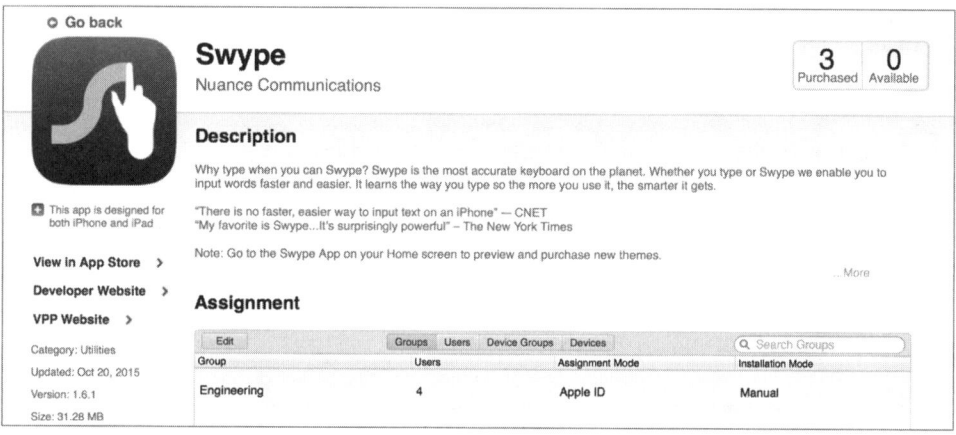

8   Click "Go back."

9 In the Profile Manager sidebar, select Books.

10 Confirm that the item has the expected number in the Available and Purchased columns.

Books are different from apps; only one user downloaded the book, so there are still four available of five purchased.

11 In the Profile Manager sidebar, select Users.

12 Select Lucy Sanchez.

13 Click the Apps tab.

14 Confirm that the user-assigned app is listed.

Note that the app is assigned to the Engineering group and that the assignment mode is Apple ID.

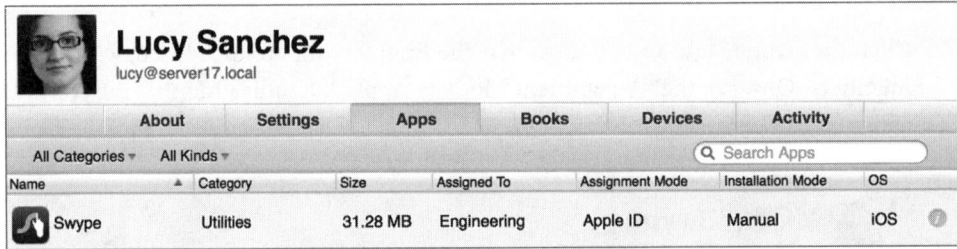

15 Click the Books tab, and confirm that the assigned book is listed.

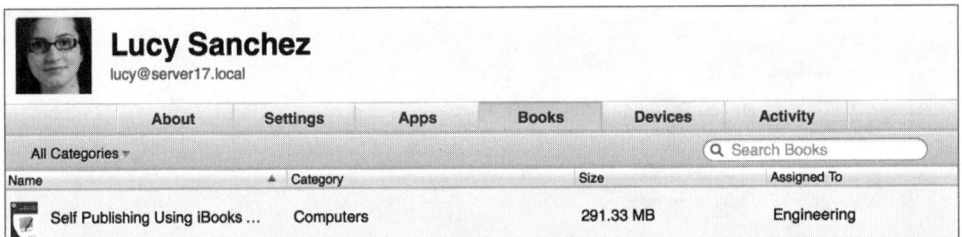

Remove Engineering from VPP Managed Distribution

1 In the Profile Manager administration portal sidebar, select Groups, select Engineering, and then, if necessary, click the About tab.

   NOTE ▶ The Remove From Program button does not have a confirmation dialog.

2 Click Remove From Program.

   You can optionally refresh Safari for confirmation that Engineering was removed from VPP Managed Distribution.

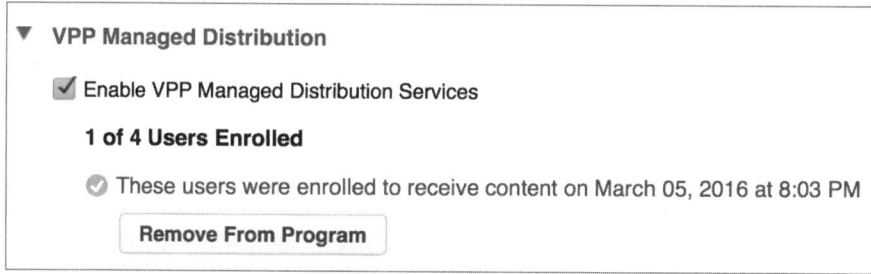

   NOTE ▶ The book you assigned is permanently assigned to the Apple ID you specified when you accepted the invitation to the VPP managed distribution program.

The VPP apps are no longer assigned to the Apple ID you specified when you accepted the invitation to the VPP managed distribution program.

Eventually (it could take up to a day), your iOS device will receive a notification banner for each app no longer assigned to you. For the purposes of this exercise, you will wipe your iOS device at the end of this exercise, and you may not see these notifications. Of course, you could choose to wait for the notifications to appear before continuing with the exercises.

If your iOS device is at the Lock screen, the notifications appear as banners.

If your iOS device is not at the Lock screen, iOS displays a banner at the top of the screen for each app that is no longer assigned to you. Because banners go away automatically, you might miss them. To review your notifications, you can swipe down from the top of the screen to view Notification Center and then tap Notifications.

After you tap a banner notification that an app is no longer assigned to you, Safari automatically opens a page about VPP.

Remove the Home Screen Layout and Restrictions (iOS) Configuration Profile

1. In the Profile Manager administration portal sidebar, select Devices, select your iOS device, and select Settings.

2. Under Settings for iPad, click Remove (–).

3. In the confirmation dialog, click Remove All Settings.

4. Click Save.

Unassign Apps

Even though you removed Engineering from VPP managed distribution services, you still have apps assigned to the group. Unassign them so you can reassign them later if necessary.

1. In the Profile Manager administration portal sidebar, select Groups, select Engineering, and then click the Apps tab.

2. Select Swype (or the free app you purchased).

3. Click Remove (–), and then click Save.

4. In the Profile Manager sidebar, select Device Groups, select iOS VPP Devices, and then click the Apps tab.

5. Select SSL Detective.

6. Click Remove (–), and then click Save.

7. Repeat steps 4–6 for the Mac VPP Devices group.

Inspect Available App Licenses

1. In the Profile Manager Administration portal sidebar, select Apps.

2. Confirm that each item has the expected number in the Available and Purchased columns, as shown in the following figure:

Name	Category	Size	Available	Purchased
Evernote	Productivity	92.59 MB	5	5
Evernote	Productivity	53.24 MB	5	5
iBooks Author	Productivity	418.68 MB	5	5
Microsoft Remote Desktop	Business	21.97 MB	5	5
SSL Detective	Utilities	850 KB	5	5
Swype	Utilities	31.28 MB	3	3

If not all of your licenses are returned, refresh your session with the Profile Manager administration portal, or turn the Profile Manager service off and then on.

Inspect Books

1   In the sidebar, select Books.

2   Confirm that the number in the Available column did not increase; a book is permanently assigned.

Disassociate Lucy Sanchez from Your iOS Device

1   In the Profile Manager administration portal sidebar, select Users, select Lucy Sanchez, and select Devices.

2   Click Remove (x) to remove your iOS device.

3   Click Save.

Unassign the iOS Device
Remove the iOS device from being assigned to your MDM server.

1   Use your server computer to log in to the Apple Deployment Programs site in Safari (https://deploy.apple.com) using your DEP administrator account with two-step verification.

2   Select Device Enrollment Program in the sidebar.

3 Click in the Search for Serial Number field.

4 Enter the iOS device's serial number in the Search field.

5 Press Return to search.

6 Click the Assigned To pop-up menu, and then choose Unassigned.

7 Click Reassign to unassign your iOS device.

Unenroll Your iOS Device and Your Client Mac and Remove the Placeholders

1 In the Profile Manager administration portal sidebar, select Devices, and then select your iOS device.

2 Click the Remove (–) button, and then click Unenroll.

3 At the bottom of the Devices section, click the Refresh button.

4 Select the placeholder record, click the Remove (–) button, and then click Remove.

5 Select your client Mac, client*n* (where *n* is your student number, click the Remove (–) button, and then click Unenroll.

6 Select the placeholder record, click the Remove (–) button, and then click Remove Placeholder.

7 Close the Profile Manager administration portal window.

Erase All Content and Settings

1 On your iOS device, if necessary, slide at the "slide to unlock" screen.

2 If necessary, enter the passcode.

3 Open Settings.

4 Navigate to General > Reset.

5 Tap Erase All Content and Settings.

6 If your iOS device has a passcode, enter the passcode.

7   In the confirmation dialog, tap Erase.

8   In the extra confirmation dialog, tap Erase.

In this exercise, you demonstrated that Profile Manager keeps track of how many copies of each item were purchased and how many are available to be assigned to other devices and users.

You removed the Engineering group from VPP Managed Distribution services, removed the Home Screen Layout configuration profile, unassigned apps, and inspected the licenses afterward. You disassociated Lucy Sanchez from your iOS device and unassigned it from your MDM server in the ADP site so it will not enroll using the DEP on its next setup. You unenrolled your iOS device and client Mac and removed the respective placeholders. Finally, you wiped your iOS device.

Lesson 11
In-House Apps and Books

The ability for customers to create their own custom apps for iOS and OS X is a huge factor in the success of Apple devices in organizations both large and small. For a variety of reasons, though, deploying custom in-house apps (also known as enterprise apps) via the App Store is not the best solution. For example, many in-house apps are relevant to an organization's specific needs only and should not be made available to the public via the App Store.

Instead, many organizations will deploy their custom in-house apps directly to managed Apple devices. Similarly, in-house documentation can be deployed directly to your managed Apple devices without involving third-party services.

In this lesson, you will explore workflows for deploying in-house apps and books to both iOS and OS X devices. Specific instruction will also be included in this lesson for any in-house deployment methods supported by Profile Manager.

GOALS

▶ Understand workflows for deploying apps and books sourced to your own organization and other non–Volume Purchase Program (VPP) sources

▶ Deploy in-house apps to iOS and OS X devices with Profile Manager

▶ Deploy in-house books to iOS devices with Profile Manager

Reference 11.1
Deploy In-House Apps and Books

With respect to deploying apps and books to Apple devices, the term *in-house* simply means any item that isn't acquired via an Apple store. Because you or your organization source in-house items, they don't require that the user enter an Apple ID to be installed on managed devices. Also, you can remove both in-house apps and books from managed iOS devices when needed.

As long as the in-house apps and books are properly created, iOS will accept in-house apps and books, and OS X will accept in-house apps. This section covers the general processes for both acquiring and deploying your items directly to managed Apple devices without involving an Apple store.

Acquire In-House iOS Apps

iOS apps are created by developers using OS X computers via the Xcode app, which is available only from the Mac App Store. While anyone can get Xcode for free and start to develop iOS apps, a developer must join an Apple Developer Program to test and deploy custom in-house apps on iOS devices.

A variety of different Apple Developer Program memberships are available, but the ability to build iOS apps that can be deployed to an unlimited number of managed devices is limited to the Apple Developer Enterprise Program. Membership in the Apple Developer Enterprise Program requires an annual subscription fee of $299 USD (see https://developer.apple.com/support/purchase-activation/) and is available only to companies or organizations with a D-U-N-S number.

> **MORE INFO** ▶ You can find out more about the Apple Developer Program membership programs from the official website, https://developer.apple.com/programs/.

The processes required to build an iOS app are well beyond the scope of this guide. Indeed, iOS app deployment is its own profession that can take years to master. The focus of this guide is how to deploy the in-house iOS app once it's created.

> **MORE INFO** ▶ Search for "Create in-house apps" at https://help.apple.com/deployment/ios/ for more information about the process of creating in-house apps, including rebuilding your app to keep a valid enterprise distribution certificate associated with your app.

The final output of the iOS app creation process is the generation of an iOS app bundle file, which uses the .ipa file type designation. This file contains all the assets necessary for the app to run on your iOS devices. iOS in-house apps built by Xcode for iOS 8 or later require only a single properly created .ipa file for deployment.

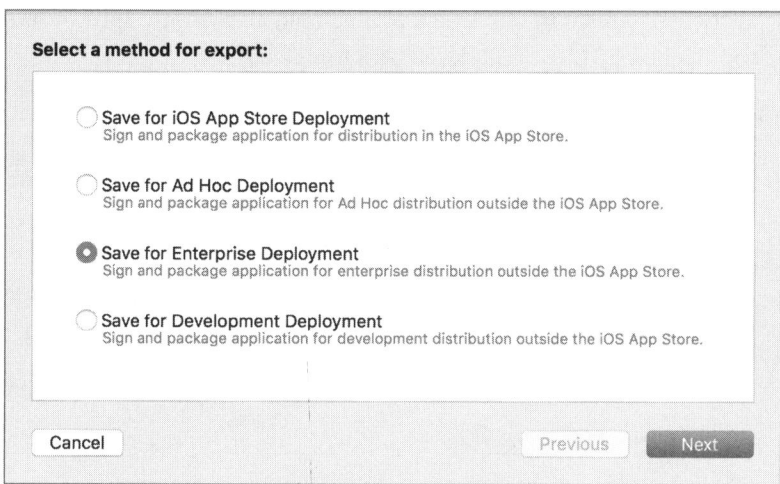

Once you have acquired an .ipa file from the development process, you can then deploy it to managed iOS devices using the methods described later in this lesson.

Intersphere.ipa

NOTE ▶ Prior to iOS 8, a separate provisioning profile needed to be installed on iOS devices to allow enterprise iOS apps to open. As long as the app is built for iOS 8 or later, Xcode will automatically include the enterprise provisioning information inside the .ipa file.

Acquire In-House OS X Apps

Developers using the Xcode app can also create custom OS X apps. Although Xcode is free, to test and deploy custom in-house apps on OS X computers that have the default Gatekeeper security settings, a developer must join an Apple Developer Program.

NOTE ▶ You do not need to join the Apple Developer Enterprise Program to sign and distribute apps for OS X; the Apple Developer Enterprise Program is for building and distributing in-house iOS apps.

Gatekeeper is a security mechanism in OS X that, as a default, allows only apps from the Mac App Store or apps signed by identified developers to open.

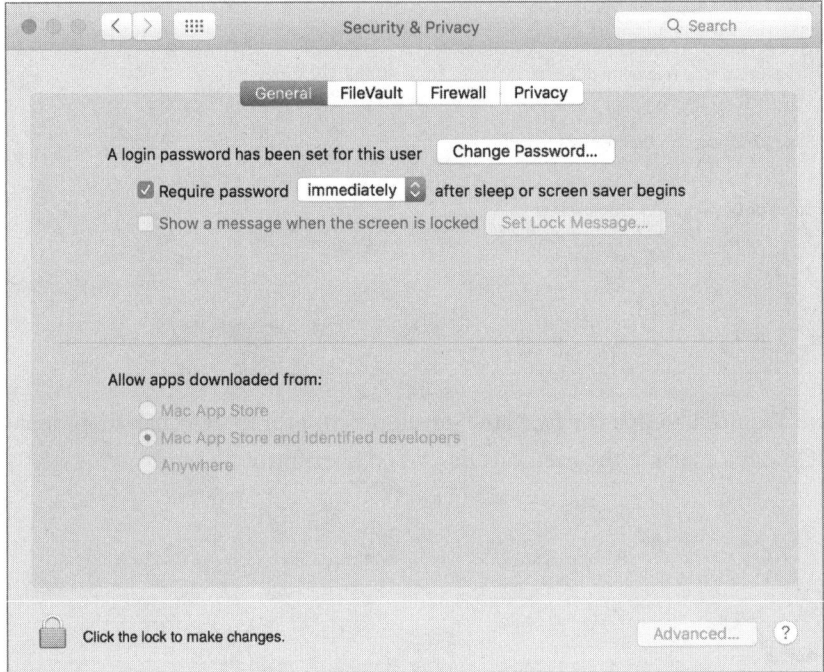

This default Gatekeeper behavior can be overridden by a local administrator or changed to a less-restrictive setting using the local Security & Privacy preference. An installed configuration profile can also allow for less or more restrictive Gatekeeper settings.

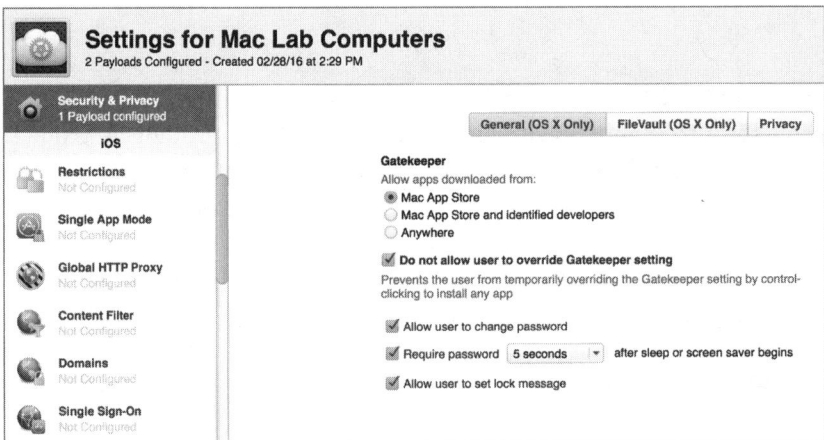

However, it's a security risk to weaken Gatekeeper's default behavior. Further, app signing guarantees the integrity of your custom-built OS X app.

Rather than weaken Gatekeeper's default behavior, you should use Xcode to build in-house OS X apps and sign them with Developer ID. To sign your app with Developer ID, you or your company needs to join the Apple Developer Program, which requires an annual subscription fee of $99 USD (of course, if your organization is already in the Apple Enterprise Developer Program, it does not need to also join the Apple Developer Program).

The final output of the OS X app creation process is the generation of an OS X app bundle, which uses the .app file type designation. This bundle contains all the assets necessary for the app to run on your OS X computers. Assuming the OS X app was signed with your developer certificate in Xcode, it will not require any modification of the default Gatekeeper settings on OS X. Once you have acquired an .app bundle from the development process, you can then deploy it to managed OS X computers using the methods described later in this lesson.

Process It.app

MORE INFO ▶ See https://help.apple.com/deployment/osx/; search for "Create in-house apps" for more information.

Another source for custom in-house OS X apps is to build your own using OS X's built-in automation tools Automator and AppleScript. Both Automator and AppleScript allow you to build custom workflows that are capable of completing almost any task on OS X. These automation tools accomplish this by having the ability to control other apps already installed on an OS X system. Again, building Automator and AppleScript apps is well beyond the scope of this guide, but when used properly, these tools will generate an app bundle ready for deployment.

MORE INFO ▶ You can find out more about Automator and AppleScript from the Mac OS X Automation website, https://macosxautomation.com/.

Acquire In-House Books

The default app on both iOS and OS X for storing and opening in-house books is iBooks. Also, with both iOS 8 and OS X Yosemite, the iBooks application is now included with the system software. iBooks supports several document types:

- PDF—By far the most common document type supported by iBooks, PDF has become a widespread document standard. Originally created by Adobe, PDFs are created from many sources, including any app capable of printing on an Apple device. One difference between iOS and OS X is that attempting to open a PDF in iBooks on OS X will instead open the PDF in the Preview app by default.

- EPUB—The standard file type used by many e-book vendors, EPUB files can also be created from many sources. Although EPUB is a free and open file format, creating EPUB files is limited to apps specifically designed to support the format. For example, Pages can export documents as EPUB, but Keynote cannot.

- iBooks Author file—Files created by the iBooks Author app are recognized by the file type extension of .ibooks. This proprietary format is an extension of the EPUB file type that adds support for additional capabilities such as support for multitouch and complex mathematical equation formatting. The iBooks Author app is available for free, but only on the Mac App Store.

MORE INFO ▶ You can find out more about iBooks Author from https://www.apple.com/ibooks-author/.

Similar to app creation, the creation of in-house books or documents is well beyond the scope of this guide. However, because iBooks has support for such popular file types, it shouldn't be hard for your organization to produce or acquire the necessary files to deploy.

Workflows for Deploying In-House Apps and Books to iOS Devices

You have a variety of methods to choose from when deploying in-house iOS apps (.ipa) or in-house books (.pdf, .epub, or .ibooks) to iOS devices:

- iTunes—In-house iOS apps and books can be manually added to the iTunes Library on a PC and then synced to connected iOS devices. This workflow is valid only if the user syncs to an iTunes library on a regular basis. Even then, the user will have to manually add the in-house items (and any updates) to the iTunes library. In short, this method doesn't scale well because it relies on heavy user involvement.

▶ Apple Configurator 2—If your preparation workflow takes advantage of Apple Configurator 2 for iOS device setup, you might want to consider deploying in-house iOS apps via Apple Configurator 2 as well. Covered in Lesson 14, "Apple Configurator 2: App and Document Management," deploying an in house iOS app with Apple Configurator 2 is similar to deploying a free iOS app from the App Store.

▶ Direct Web Download—Properly constructed webpages can host in-house iOS apps and books that users can download to their iOS device. Building a webpage to host in-house iOS apps is beyond the scope of this guide, but you can find information about the process from the Apple iOS deployment guide, https://help.apple.com/deployment/ios/; search for "Install in-house apps wirelessly." On the other hand, books can be hosted from any standard web page without any special formatting. Alternately, you can take advantage of the OS X Server Wiki service to host books, as covered in Lesson 21, "Configuring the Wiki Service," in *Apple Pro Training Series: OS X Server 5.0 Essentials: Using and Supporting OS X Server on El Capitan* (Peachpit, 2016).

▶ MDM—One method to automatically push in-house apps and books remotely to iOS devices is via a Mobile Device Management (MDM) service. Furthermore, even for in-house apps and books, installing apps and books via MDM is the only method that results in "managed" apps and books. Administrators have a variety of additional restrictions that can be placed on apps and books that are managed, including the ability to wirelessly remove the items. These additional management features and the sheer scalability of MDM-based installation make it the most popular option. In fact, the remaining sections in this lesson specifically detail using Profile Manager to push in-house apps and books to managed devices.

Workflows for Deploying In-House Apps to OS X Computers

OS X has allowed for the installation of custom OS X apps since its inception, well before contemporary management tools like MDM. However, iBooks is a relatively recent development. As such, the specific steps required for deploying OS X apps (.app) compared to deploying books (.pdf, .epub, or .ibooks) on OS X varies quite a bit between deployment methods:

▶ File System—Users can simply open OS X apps and books from any file system the Mac can attach to. There is no requirement in OS X to "install" apps. They can open from any attached source, including both local drives and mounted network shares. However, user interaction would be required to copy the app or book content to the computer's local drive.

▶ Apple Remote Desktop—This Apple management app, also known as ARD, allows administrators to copy any file to remote OS X computers en masse. With ARD, in-house apps can be copied directly into the /Applications folder, effectively installing the app. On the other hand, while ARD can copy books to OS X computers, those files must be imported into iBooks, which is a separate step that ARD cannot directly automate. Using ARD to manage OS X is beyond the scope of this guide, but you can find out more at the Apple website, https://www.apple.com/remotedesktop/.

▶ Direct Web Download—For many years OS X apps and books have been deployed via websites. However, on OS X, the default behavior for web downloads is to save them to the ~/Downloads folder. Further, OS X app bundles must be contained inside a .zip or .dmg archive to be hosted on a web server. Thus, deploying in-house OS X apps and books from a website requires a great deal of user interaction to extract and install the items.

▶ MDM—OS X Yosemite introduced the ability for an MDM service to automatically assign both in-house OS X apps and in-house books to users of OS X computers. Unfortunately, Profile Manager has limited support of the management of in-house items for OS X. Specifically, Profile Manager can only push in-house OS X apps and has no ability to remove in-house OS X apps. Further, Profile Manager has no support for the management of in-house books to OS X computers. If you require greater control over the deployment of in-house OS X apps and books, then you should consider a third-party MDM, Mobile Content Management (MCM), or Mobile Application Management (MAM) service.

TIP Technically, you can deploy any single-bundle OS X app via MDM, including those created by third parties. For example, Profile Manager can push Google Chrome.app to managed OS X devices.

Table 11.1 summarizes the ability to assign and deploy VPP Managed Distribution apps and books, in-house apps, and in-house books to users and user groups and to devices that are enrolled with your MDM service.

Table 11.1 Assignment Capabilities

Assign To	In-House App	In-House Book	VPP App	VPP Book
User or user group	Yes	Yes	Yes	Yes
iOS device	Yes	Yes	iOS 9 or later	No
Mac computer	Yes	No	OS X El Capitan or later	No

Reference 11.2
Manage In-House Apps and Books via Profile Manager

As covered previously, when deploying in-house apps and books via Profile Manager, the capabilities and workflows vary between managed iOS and OS X devices.

MORE INFO ▶ Detailed step-by-step instructions for deploying in-house apps and books with Profile Manager are presented in the exercises later in this lesson.

In-House Apps and Books in the Profile Manager Library

Before you can push in-house apps and books to Apple devices using Profile Manager, the items must be uploaded to the Profile Manager Library. In the Profile Manager web portal, selecting either Apps or Books in the Library list will reveal items that can be pushed to manage devices.

As covered in Lesson 10, "VPP-Managed Apps and Books," items from VPP Managed Distribution will automatically appear in the Profile Manager Library. To add your own in-house items, simply click the Add (+) button at the bottom of the Apps or Books list, and then select the item to upload. Profile Manager will accept any of the in-house app or book file formats covered previously in this lesson.

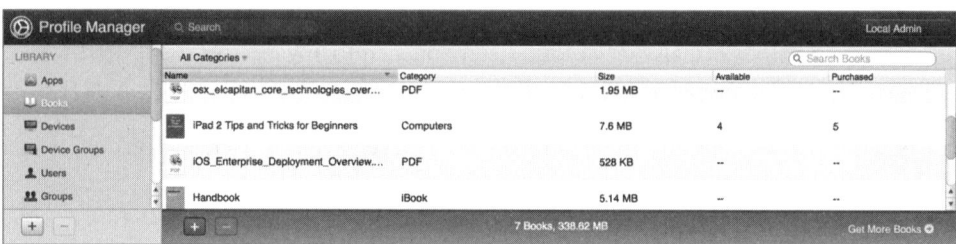

Once added to Profile Manager, in-house items are easily identified in the Library by their specific category designation. For example, in-house apps are automatically categorized as Enterprise, and in-house books are categorized by their file type: PDF, EPUB, or iBooks. You'll also notice that in-house items have no Available or Purchased numbers because there are no licensing limitations to items that you create in-house.

In-house apps and books are also unique in that they can be removed by selecting the item in Profile Manager and then clicking the Remove (–) button. Removing an in-house item from the Profile Manager Library will also remove items from any managed iOS devices the items were installed to.

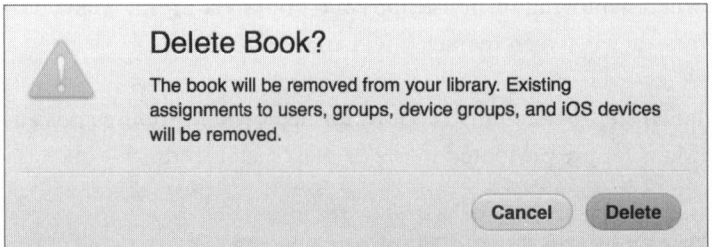

Manage In-House Apps and Books for iOS Devices

Profile Manager can automatically push in-house iOS apps and books to any managed iOS 8 or later device. Profile Manager can also automatically remove in-house items previously pushed to iOS devices. In-house apps and books are managed similarly to iOS configuration settings in Profile Manager. In other words, you can associate in-house iOS apps and books to a user, user group, device, or device group, and Profile Manager will automatically push the items to the appropriate iOS devices.

> **MORE INFO** ▶ As covered in Lesson 7, "Mobile Device Management," Profile Manager can automatically push management settings to individual devices or device groups. Settings can also be automatically pushed to any devices associated with a user in Profile Manager.

To assign in-house apps and books in Profile Manager, select a user, user group, device, or device group in the Library, and then click the Apps or Books tab.

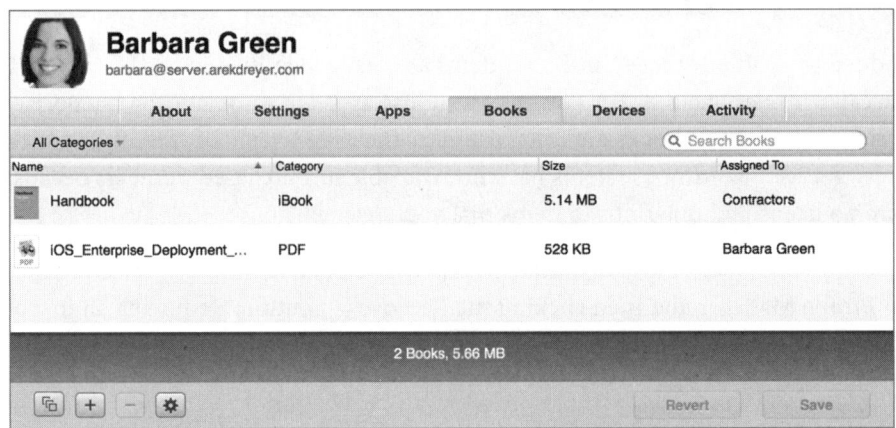

Clicking the Add (+) button at the bottom of the Apps or Books list will bring up a dialog allowing you to assign in-house items to the users or devices selected in the Library.

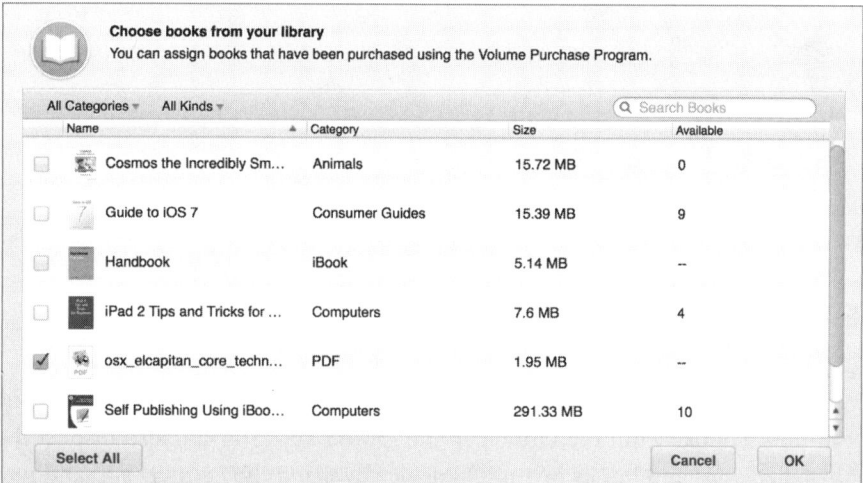

Conversely, you can remove a previously assigned in-house app or book by selecting the item and then clicking the Remove (–) button. As always, after you click OK to dismiss the dialog, make sure to click Save in Profile Manager to apply the changes.

After saving changes, Profile Manager should automatically push or remove any in-house apps or books for the appropriate iOS devices. If for some reason the in-house apps and books aren't automatically pushed or removed in a timely manner, you can use the Update Info task in an attempt to force managed iOS devices to respond. To do this, choose Update Info from the Action (gear icon) menu.

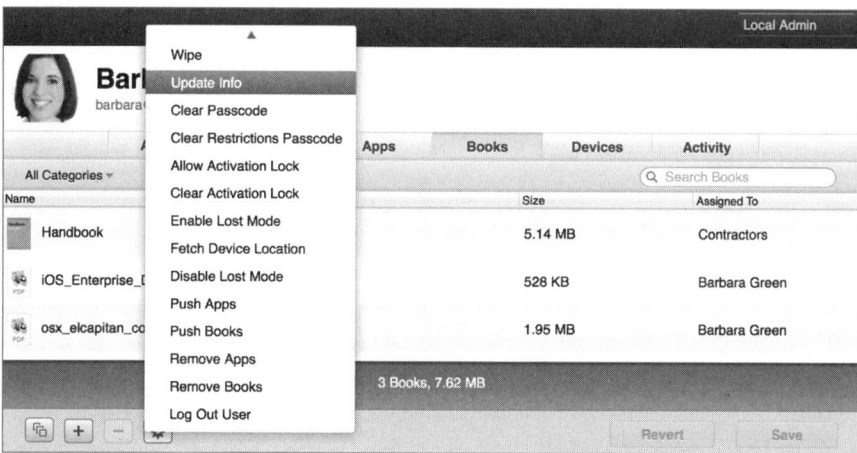

In-house apps and books will install automatically on iOS devices that are supervised. Unsupervised devices will prompt the user via notification to accept the pushed in-house items.

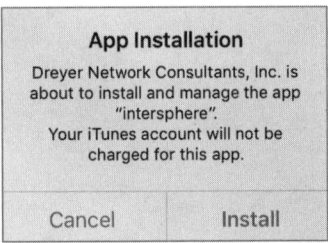

NOTE ▶ Installing in-house apps and books does not require that an Apple ID is signed in to the device.

You can verify the installation of in-house iOS apps from the device's Home screen and can verify in-house books from the Library in the iBooks app. You can also inspect the full list of installed apps and books on an iOS device by using the Settings app and navigating to General > Device Management > Remote Management.

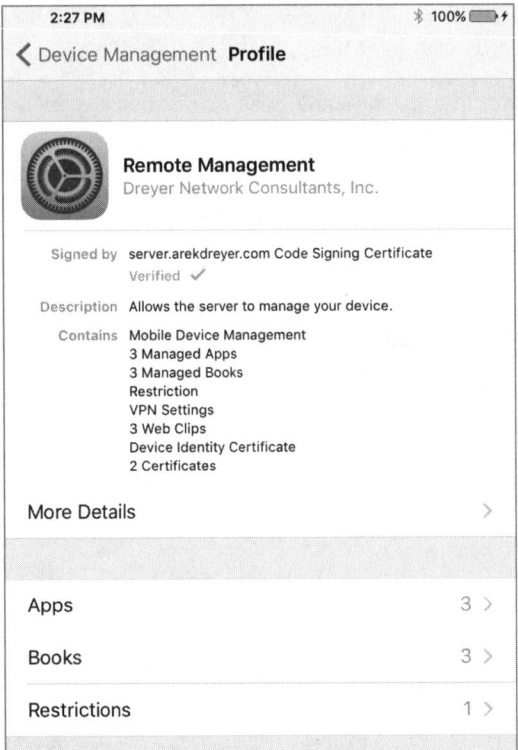

Tapping Apps lists in-house apps and VPP Managed Distribution apps. Tapping Books lists in-house books only.

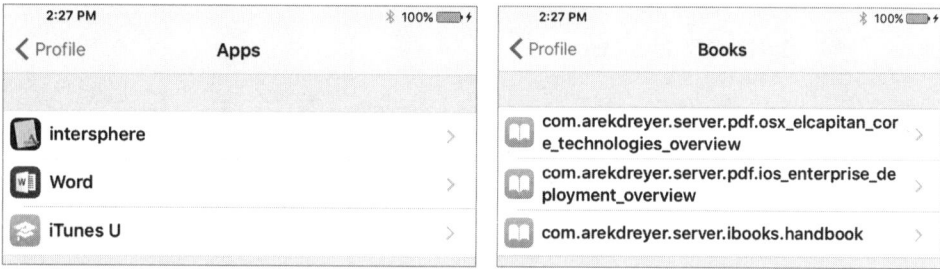

TIP ▶ Unless you restrict the removal of apps (an option available only via MDM on supervised iOS devices), the user will be allowed to delete your in-house apps.

When a user first opens an in-house app that was installed via MDM, the user will not be prompted to trust your Developer ID, as long as the iOS device is using iOS 9 or later; otherwise, for iOS 8 and earlier, the user must tap the Trust button to allow any of your in-house iOS apps to open on the device (this will happen only once per developer ID, but once the user trusts a developer ID, all other iOS apps from the developer are allowed).

MORE INFO ▶ If you use Apple Configurator 2 to install an in-house app, when a user opens the app, she will see an "Untrusted Enterprise Developer" message, including the information that "Until this developer has been trusted, their enterprise apps will not be available for use," even if the device is supervised.

Push In-House Apps to OS X Computers

Profile Manager is quite limited when it comes to deploying in-house OS X apps to OS X computers. When you assign an in-house app to an enrolled OS X computer with an Assignment Mode of Device and an Installation Mode of Automatic, the in-house app will automatically be installed. However, if you assign an in-house app with an Assignment Mode of Apple ID or an Installation Mode of Manual, you need to initiate a push of the in-house OS X app to install it.

Profile Manager doesn't track the assignment of in-house OS X apps to users or devices in the Library like it does with in-house iOS apps.

Assuming the in-house OS X app has been uploaded to Profile Manager, as covered previously in this lesson, the process to push an in-house app to OS X computers is easy. Simply select a user, group, device, or device group from the Library, and then choose the

Push Apps task from the Action (gear icon) menu at the bottom of the Profile Manager web portal.

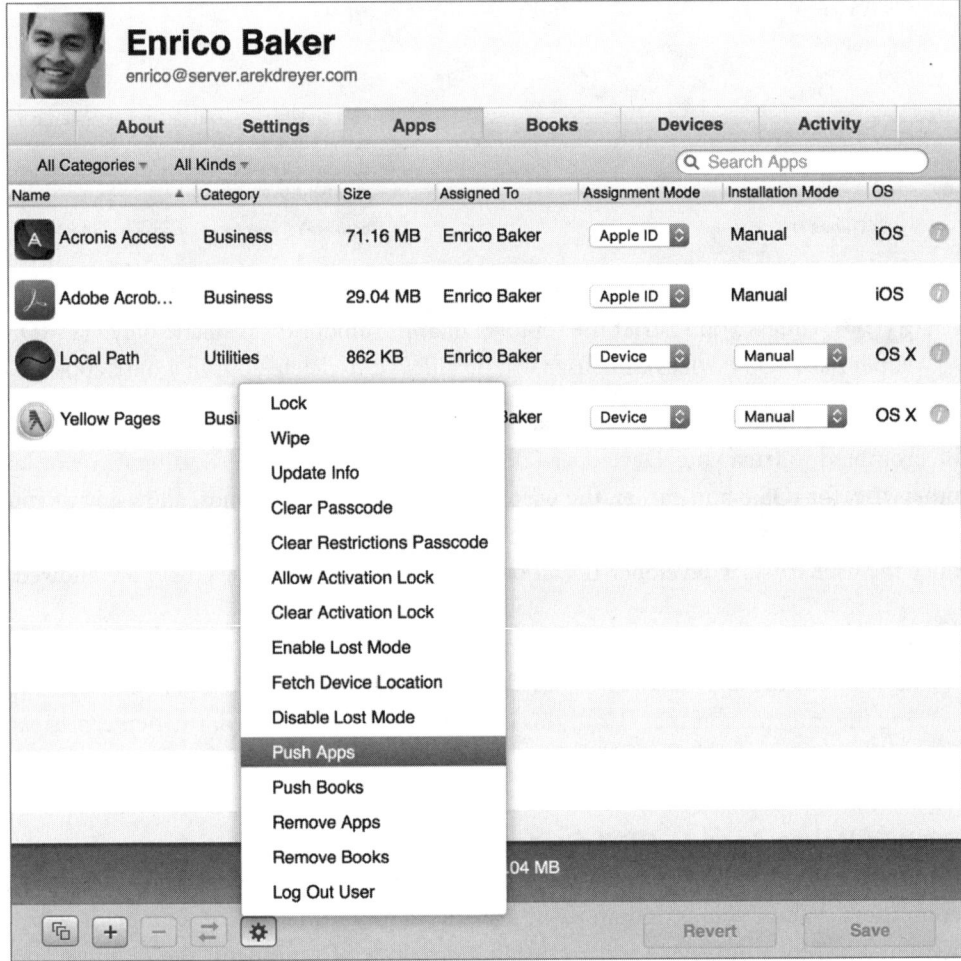

You will be prompted to select the in-house OS X apps that you want to deploy.

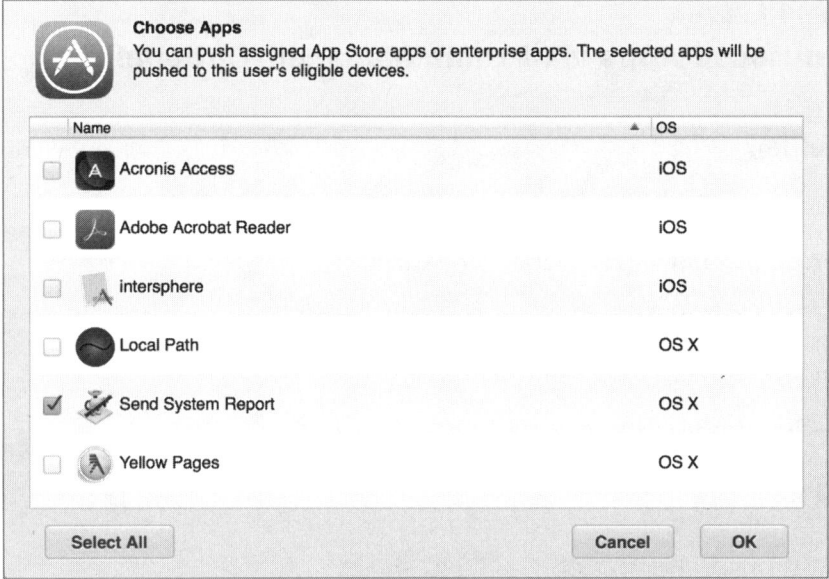

NOTE ▶ If you select a user or group in the Profile Manager Library, only OS X computers that are currently associated with the selected users will receive the pushed in-house app.

While the app is downloading to the computer, if the Launchpad icon is visible in the Dock, a download progress bar appears under the Launchpad icon in the Dock.

Once the installation task is completed on the selected OS X computers, the in-house OS X apps you pushed can be found in the computer's /Applications folder. As a convenience, any new apps are automatically added to Launchpad, and if the Launchpad icon is in the user's Dock, the icon will bounce, indicating that new apps are available.

As covered previously in this lesson, assuming the deployed OS X app was created properly, the default Gatekeeper settings should allow the app to open without any additional user confirmation. Finally, it's important to recognize that once in-house OS X apps are installed, any local administrator on the OS X computer can move or delete the app. If you need to prevent the removal of in-house OS X apps, you need to restrict users to accounts that do not have local administrator access.

Exercise 11.1
Deploy In-House Apps via Profile Manager (Optional)

> **Prerequisites**
> - Exercise 4.1, "Prepare Your Mac to Install OS X Server for El Capitan"
> - Exercise 4.2, "Install OS X Server for El Capitan"
> - Exercise 4.3, "Configure OS X Server for El Capitan"
> - Exercise 6.1, "Turn On Profile Manager"
> - Exercise 7.1, "Enable Device Management"
> - An in-house enterprise iOS app

Challenge

Enroll an iOS device with your server's Profile Manager service as network user Carl Dunn, a member of the Marketing group. Enroll your client Mac with your server's Profile Manager service.

Deploy an in-house iOS enterprise app to a managed device. Inspect the Remote Management profile before and after.

Deploy an in-house OS X app to a managed Mac.

If your organization is not enrolled with the iOS Developer Enterprise Program, you cannot generate your own in-house enterprise iOS app; simply read along with the exercise until the section "Enroll Your Client Mac," and then start performing the steps.

Considerations

The user portal is an effective way of enrolling devices with your MDM server. A user can enroll multiple devices using their credentials.

Solution

Erase All Content and Settings

If your iOS device is at the Welcome screen, skip to the next section.

1   On your iOS device, if necessary, slide at the "slide to unlock" screen.

2   If necessary, enter the passcode.

3   Open Settings.

4   Navigate to General > Reset.

5   Tap Erase All Content and Settings.

6   If your iOS device has a passcode, enter the passcode.

7   In the confirmation dialog, tap Erase.

8   In the extra confirmation dialog, tap Erase.

Wait while the iOS device erases all content and settings.

Prepare Your iOS Device with Setup Assistant

1   Slide at the "slide to set up" screen.

2   Tap your language.

3   Tap your country or region.

4   Tap your Wi-Fi network. In an instructor-led environment, this may be Classroom Wireless.

5   Enter the Wi-Fi password, and then tap Join.

   In an instructor-led environment, the password may be student!.

6   Tap Enable Location Services.

7   If you see the Touch ID screen, tap Set Up Touch ID Later, and then tap Continue.

8   At the Create a Passcode screen, for the purposes of this exercise, tap Passcode Options, tap Don't Add Passcode, and then tap Continue.

   NOTE ▶ In production it is best practice to have a passcode for your iOS device.

9   At the Apps & Data screen, tap Set Up as New iPad (this screen may vary by device).

10 At the Apple ID screen, tap "Don't have an Apple ID or forgot it."

11 At the next Apple ID screen, tap Set Up Later in Settings.

12 In the confirmation dialog, tap Don't Use.

13 Read the terms and conditions, and tap Agree to confirm.

14 If you see the Siri screen, tap Turn On Siri.

15 At the Diagnostics screen, tap Send to Apple.

16 At the App Analytics screen, tap Share with App Developers.

17 At the Welcome screen, tap Get Started.

Enroll Your iOS Device

1   On your iOS device, in Safari, open the user portal (https://server*n*.local/mydevices, where *n* is your student number).

2   If you see the message "Cannot Verify Server Identity," tap Continue.

3   In the Please Log In window, enter the following credentials:

   ▶ User Name: carl
   ▶ Password: net

4   Deselect the "Keep me logged in" checkbox.

5   Tap Log In.

Exercise 11.1 Deploy In-House Apps via Profile Manager (Optional) 477

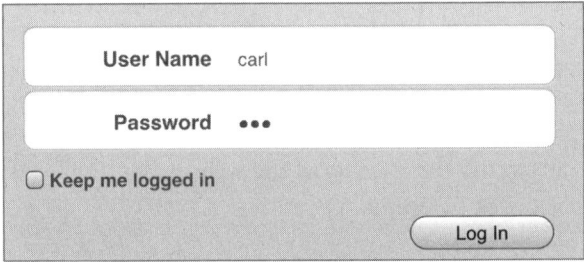

6   If the user portal displays the Profiles tab, tap the Devices tab.

7   Tap Enroll.

8   Tap Install, tap Install again, and then tap Trust.

9   At the "Profile Installed" message, tap Done.

10 Wait a few moments for the user portal devices page to update. This may take up to 30 seconds. Optionally, you can choose to refresh the user portal.

11 Confirm that information about your iOS device, including its serial number, is displayed.

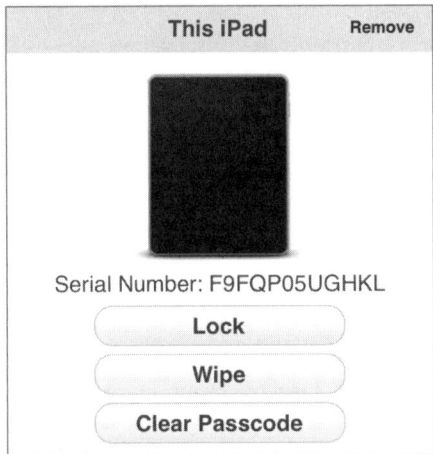

12 Tap Logout.

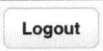

Enroll Your Client Mac

1. On your client Mac, in Safari, open the user portal (https://server*n*.local/mydevices, where *n* is your student number).

2. If you see the message "Safari can't verify the identity of the website 'server*n*.local'" (where *n* is your student number), click Continue.

3. Deselect the checkbox "Keep me logged in."

4. Provide the following credentials:
   - User Name: carl
   - Password: net

5. Click Log In.

6. If you are asked "Would you like to save this password?" click Never for This Website.

7. If the user portal displays the Profiles tab, click the Devices tab.

8. In the This Mac section, click Enroll.

9. Profiles preferences automatically opens.

   Click Continue, click Install, provide local administrator credentials, and click OK.

10. Quit System Preferences.

11. Wait a few moments for the user portal devices page to update. This may take up to 30 seconds. Optionally, you can choose to refresh the user portal.

12 Click Logout.

13 Close the Safari window.

Add an In-House iOS Enterprise App

1 On your server Mac, if you don't already have a connection open to your Profile Manager administration portal, then in Safari, open https://server*n*.local/profilemanager, where *n* is your student number, and authenticate with local administrator credentials.

2 In the Profile Manager administration portal sidebar, select Apps.

> **NOTE ▶** If your organization is not enrolled with the iOS Developer Enterprise Program, you do not have access to an in-house iOS enterprise app, so you can only read along with this exercise; you can continue performing the steps of this exercise at the section "Enroll Your Client Mac."

3 Click Add (+).

4 In the dialog that appears, select your in-house enterprise app.

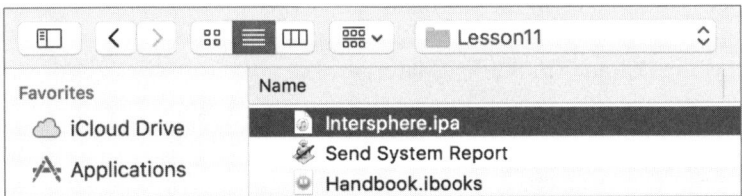

5 Click Choose.

6 Confirm that the new app appears in the list of apps.

480 In-House Apps and Books

7 Click All Categories, and then choose Enterprise.

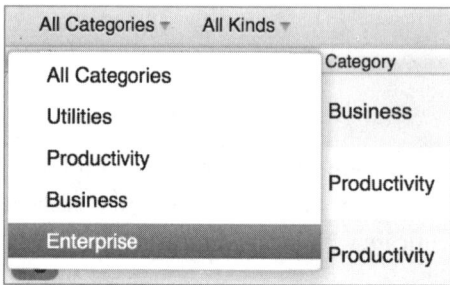

8 Confirm that only your enterprise app appears in the list.

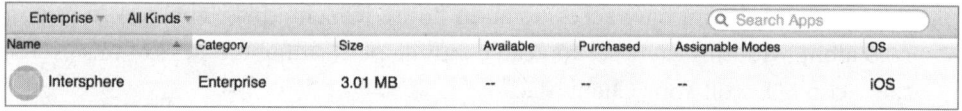

Add an OS X Enterprise App

1 If necessary, in the Profile Manager administration portal sidebar, select Apps.

2 Click Add (+).

3 In the dialog, select Documents in the sidebar.

4 Navigate to the Lesson11 folder in StudentMaterials.

5 Select the Send System Report app.

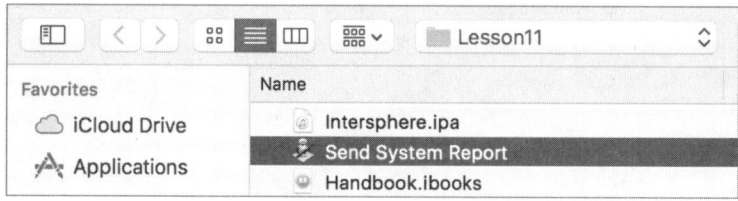

6 Click Choose.

7   Confirm that the new app appears in the list of apps.

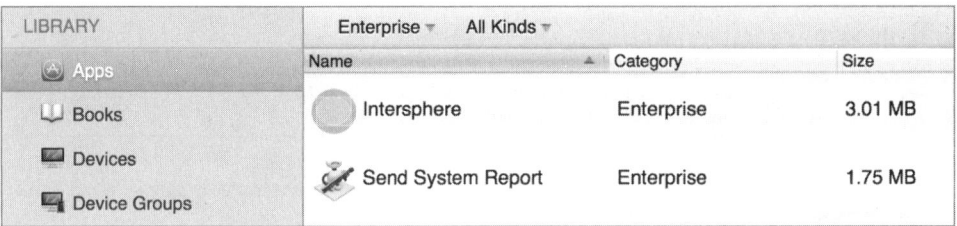

8   Click your in-house enterprise app, and then choose All Categories.

9   Confirm that all apps appear again.

Assign the In-House iOS Enterprise App to a Device

1   In the Profile Manager administration portal sidebar, select Devices.

2   Select your iOS device.

3   Click the Apps tab.

4   Confirm that the Apps tab displays the text "No Apps."

5   Click Add (+).

6   Click All Categories, and then choose Enterprise.

Note that the in-house enterprise app has an installation mode of Automatic, which is not changeable. This means the app will be automatically pushed to the device when you save.

7   Select the checkbox for the in-house iOS enterprise app.

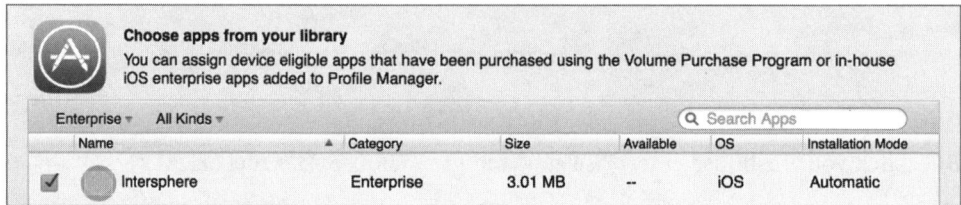

8   Click OK. Do not click Save at this point.

Examine Remote Management Profile Before Saving and Install the In-House iOS Enterprise App

1   On your iOS device, open Settings > General > Device Management.

2   Tap the Remote Management profile.

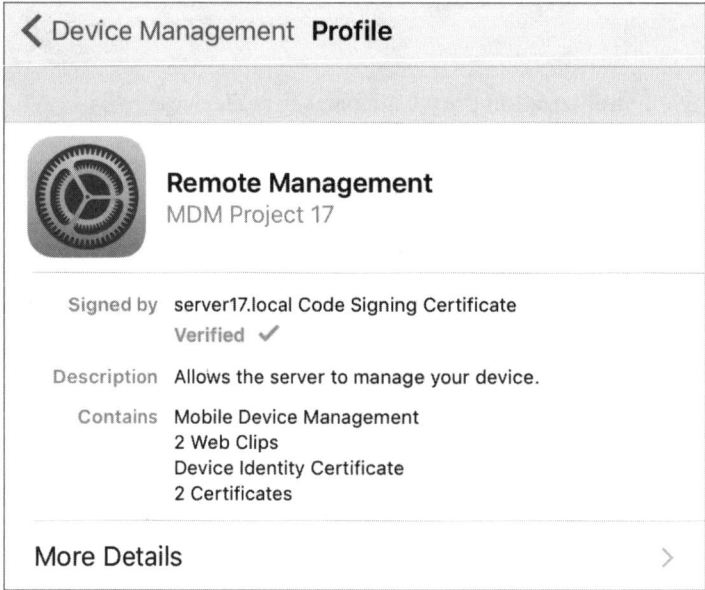

Note that there is no information listed about apps yet.

1 Press the Home button.

2 On your server in the Profile Manager administration portal, click Save.

3 On your iOS device, in the App Installation notification, tap Install.

   A notification is displayed because this iOS device is not currently supervised. Had it been enrolled using the DEP with Supervision enabled or supervised with Apple Configurator 2 prior to enrollment, app installation would take place without notification and user intervention.

4 If you see the Edit Home Screen notification, tap Dismiss.

5 Observe how the iOS enterprise app is automatically pushed to and installed on your iOS device.

Inspect the Remote Management Profile Again

1 On your iOS device, open Settings > General > Device Management.

2 Tap the Remote Management profile.

3   Note that the Contains field has Managed App listed, which was not there before; additionally, there is an Apps section with more information available for one app.

4   Press the Home button.

Push the OS X Enterprise App to a Group

1   In the Profile Manager administration portal sidebar, select Groups.

2   Select the Marketing group, and then click the Apps tab.

3   Click the Action (gear icon) menu, and choose Push Apps.

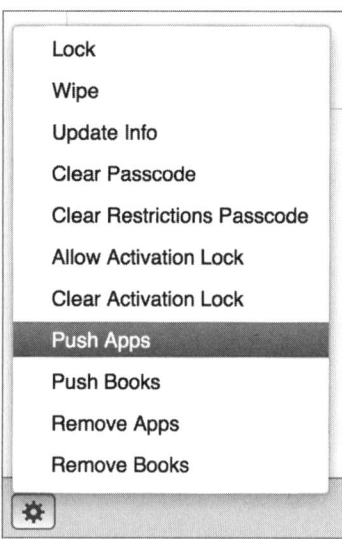

4 Select the checkbox for the in-house OS X app. In this example, we are using Send System Report.

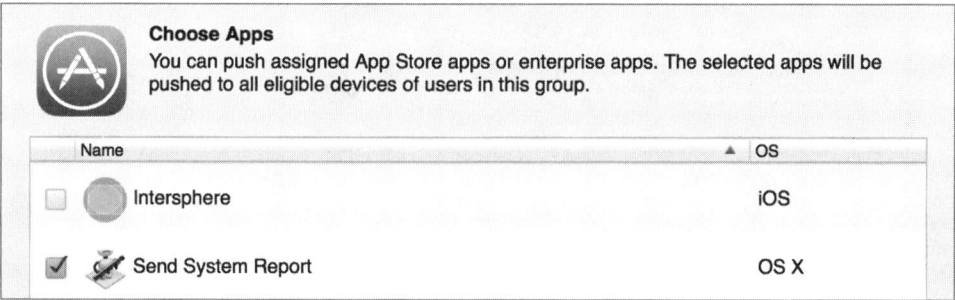

5 Click OK.

Run the OS X App on Your Client Mac

After you click OK in the Profile Manager administration portal on your client Mac, a progress bar appears under the Launchpad icon in the Dock while the app is installed.

1 On your client Mac, after the progress bar disappears and the Launchpad icon bounces once, click Launchpad in the Dock.

2 Select the in-house OS X app that was just installed.

3 Click OK in the dialog.

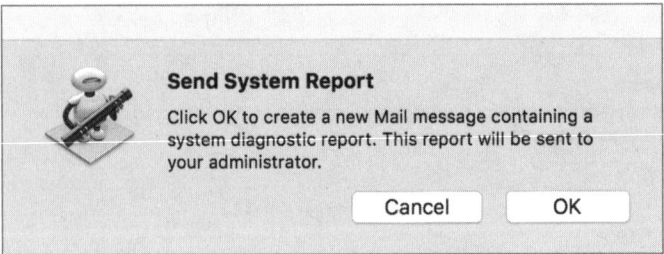

4 Click the gear in the status menu to view the status of the app's progress.

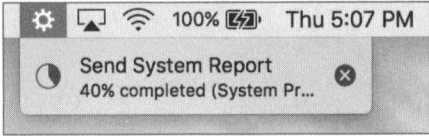

5 Once the message is ready to send, an attachment appears at the bottom of the message.

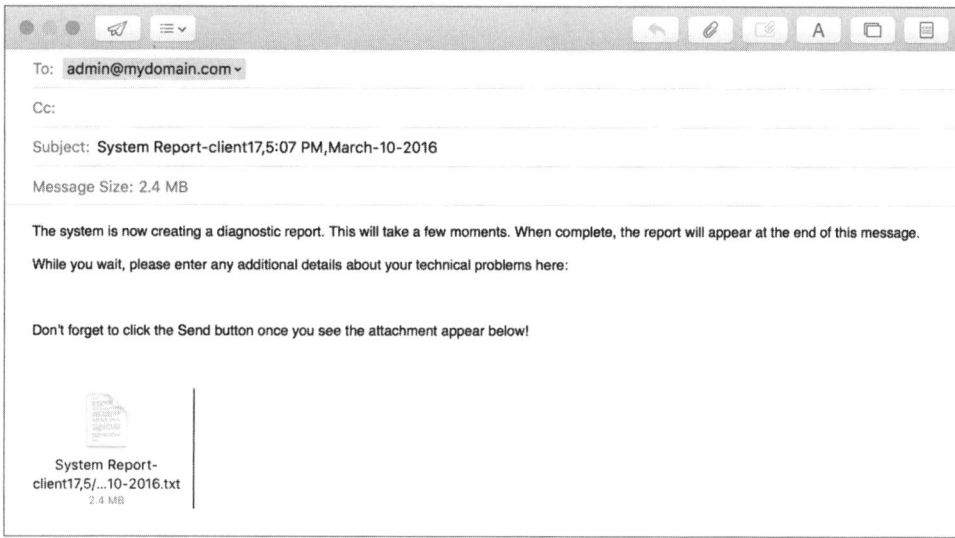

6 Close the Mail message without sending it, and then when prompted, click Don't Save.

7 Quit Mail.

Remove the In-House Enterprise iOS App

1 In the Profile Manager administration portal sidebar, select Apps.

2 Click All Categories, and then choose the in-house iOS enterprise app.

3 Select the in-house iOS enterprise app.

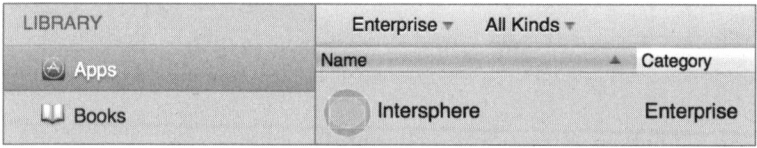

4 Click Delete (–).

5 In the confirmation dialog, click Delete.

While the assignment of your iOS enterprise app to your iOS device has been removed, the app will not be removed from the device until it is no longer enrolled.

Unenroll Your iOS Device and Remove the Placeholder

1   In the Profile Manager administration portal sidebar, select Devices, and then select your iOS device.

2   Click the Remove (–) button, and then click Unenroll.

3   Select the placeholder record, click the Remove (–) button, and then click Remove Placeholder.

Confirm the In-House iOS Enterprise App Is Deleted

1   On your iOS device, confirm that the in-house iOS enterprise app is no longer available.

Unenroll Your Client Mac and Remove the Placeholder

1   In the Profile Manager administration portal sidebar, select Devices, and then select your client Mac.

2   Click the Remove (–) button, and then click Unenroll.

3   Select the placeholder record, click the Remove (–) button, and then click Remove Placeholder.

4   Close the Profile Manager administration portal window.

In this exercise, you enrolled your iOS device and client Mac with your Profile Manager service. You added an in-house iOS enterprise app and an enterprise OS X app. You assigned the iOS enterprise app to your iOS device and demonstrated automatic install. You assigned the OS X enterprise app to the Marketing group and pushed the app. You examined the Remote Management profile on your iOS device before and after pushing the in-house enterprise iOS app. You removed the in-house iOS enterprise app and unenrolled your iOS device, which removed the app. Finally, you unenrolled your client Mac.

Exercise 11.2
Deploy In-House Books via Profile Manager

▶ **Prerequisites**

- ▶ Exercise 4.1, "Prepare Your Mac to install OS X Server for El Capitan"
- ▶ Exercise 4.2, "Install OS X Server for El Capitan"
- ▶ Exercise 4.3, "Configure OS X Server for El Capitan"
- ▶ Exercise 6.1, "Turn On Profile Manager"
- ▶ Exercise 7.1, "Enable Device Management"

Challenge
Deploy an in-house book to your iOS device, and then remove it.

Considerations
This exercise uses a file in the student materials that was exported from iBooks Author to a file in iBooks format; however, you can use any file in PDF, EPUB, or iBooks format as an in-house book.

Solution

Enroll Your iOS Device

1 If necessary, on your iOS device, in Safari, open the user portal (https://servern.local/mydevices, where *n* is your student number).

2. If you see the message "Cannot Verify Server Identity," tap Continue.

3. In the Please Log In window, enter the following credentials:
   - User Name: carl
   - Password: net

4. Deselect the "Keep me logged in" checkbox.

5. Tap Log In.

6. If the user portal displays the Profiles tab, tap the Devices tab.

7. Tap Enroll.

8. Tap Install, tap Install again, and then tap Trust.

9. At the "Profile Installed" message, tap Done.

10. Wait a few moments for the user portal devices page to update. This may take up to 30 seconds. Optionally, you can choose to refresh the user portal.

11. Confirm that information about your iOS device, including its serial number, is displayed.

Add the In-House Book

1. On your server Mac, if you don't already have a connection open to your Profile Manager administration portal, then in Safari, open https://server*n*.local/profilemanager (where *n* is your student number), and authenticate with local administrator credentials.

2. In the Profile Manager administration portal sidebar, select Books.

3. Click Add (+).

4. In the sidebar, select Documents.

5. Navigate to the StudentMaterials/Lesson11/ folder.

6. Select the Handbook.ibooks file.

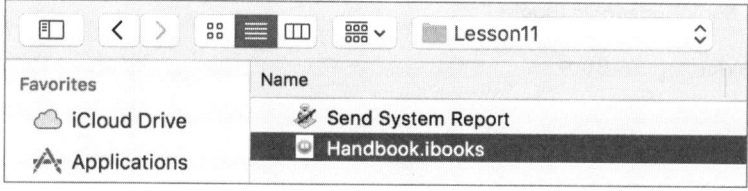

7 Click Choose.

8 Confirm that the book is listed.

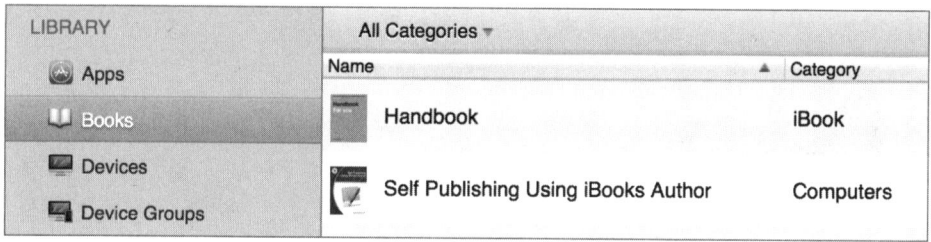

Assign the In-House Book

1 In the Profile Manager administration portal sidebar, select Groups.

2 Select Marketing.

3 Click the Books tab.

4 Click Add (+).

5 Select the in-house book you recently added.

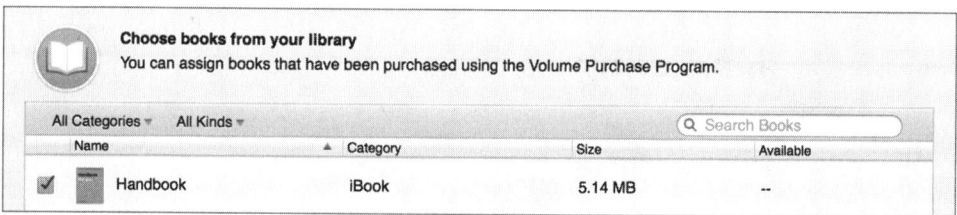

6 Click OK.

7 Click Save.

Confirm the In-House Book Appears in iBooks

1   On your iOS device, open iBooks.

2   If you see the Sign In Required message, tap Not Now.

3   Tap My Books.

4   Confirm that the new in-house book appears.

5   Tap the in-house book to open it.

Unassign the In-House Book

1   In the Profile Manager administration portal sidebar, while still viewing the Marketing group's Books tab, select the in-house book.

2 Click Remove (–).

3 Click Save.

Unenroll Your iOS Device and Remove the Placeholder

1 In the Profile Manager administration portal sidebar, select Devices, and then select your iOS device.

2 Click the Remove (–) button, and then click Unenroll.

3 Select the placeholder record, click the Remove (–) button, and then click Remove Placeholder.

4 Close the Profile Manager administration portal window.

Confirm the In-House Book Is Removed in iBooks

1 On your iOS device, while still viewing the in-house book in iBooks, wait until the in-house book closes and iBooks displays the bookshelf without the in-house book on the shelf.

Erase All Content and Settings

1 On your iOS device, if necessary, slide at the "slide to unlock" screen.

2 If necessary, enter the passcode.

3   Open Settings.

4   Navigate to General > Reset.

5   Tap Erase All Content and Settings.

6   If your iOS device has a passcode, enter the passcode.

7   In the confirmation dialog, tap Erase.

8   In the extra confirmation dialog, tap Erase.

In this exercise, you added an in-house book to your Profile Manager service. You added that book to a group and confirmed that it was automatically added to iBooks on an iOS device associated with a member of the group. You removed the book assignment from the group. Finally, you unenrolled your iOS device and saw that the book was removed from the iOS device.

Lesson 12
Apple Configurator 2: Planning and Setup

Apple Configurator 2 is a free app for OS X 10.11.1 or later that serves as a starting and restarting point for many shared-use iOS deployments.

This app can also be used to provide ongoing management for iOS devices, but it's generally much less flexible than a Mobile Device Management (MDM) service because to modify an iOS device using Apple Configurator 2, it must be physically connected to a Mac computer running Apple Configurator 2.

That being said, Apple Configurator 2 specializes in the initial deployment tasks required to prepare an iOS device for organizational use. Whether you are deploying new iOS devices or redeploying existing devices, an Apple Configurator 2 workflow can ensure that all your devices will have a uniform configuration when users receive them.

GOALS

▶ Understand the benefits and limitations of Apple Configurator 2

▶ Install and set up Apple Configurator 2

Even if you plan to use an MDM service for many administrative tasks, you will still need to complete the initial setup and enroll all your devices. In this case, you can use an Apple Configurator 2 workflow to automate the setup and enrollment process for organization-owned shared devices, thus saving administrators countless hours preparing new iOS devices or re-preparing previously used devices.

This lesson starts with an introduction to the capabilities of Apple Configurator 2. You will also install Apple Configurator 2 and explore its various main components and preference settings. Ultimately, this lesson serves as a foundation for later Apple Configurator 2–based lessons in this guide.

> **MORE INFO** ▶ Preparing iOS devices with Apple Configurator 2 is covered in Lesson 13, "Apple Configurator 2: Preparing, Configuring, and Managing iOS Devices." Installing apps and documents with Apple Configurator 2 is covered in Lesson 14, "Apple Configurator 2: App and Document Management." For the latest information about Apple Configurator 2, see https://help.apple.com/configurator/.

Reference 12.1
About Apple Configurator 2

Like the legacy Apple Configurator, you can use Apple Configurator 2 to help you quickly set up and maintain iOS devices, including the following:

- Simplify account setup
- Configure organizational policies
- Distribute apps and documents
- Apply restrictions
- Supervise organization-owned devices, which enables extra administrative functionality
- Modify wallpaper and lock screen appearance

Compared with legacy Apple Configurator, the new Apple Configurator 2 offers the following improvements:

- Create and edit blueprints with custom configuration workflows that you can quickly apply to many iOS devices
- Share the supervision identity among multiple Mac computers so you can configure the same supervised iOS device on more than one Mac computer with Apple Configurator 2
- View the log for an iOS device to help in troubleshooting
- Quickly create configuration profiles
- Use iCloud to share profiles among multiple Mac computers with Apple Configurator 2
- Distribute documents via apps that support it
- Create and apply tags to blueprints and iOS devices to organize them into groups
- Save a device's unlock token, which you can use to unlock the device in case a user forgets the passcode for his supervised device
- Clear a device's passcode and restrictions passcode
- Rename a device, including using a token to represent the following characteristics of a device: number, serial, type, capacity, port, and station
- Revive a device that is stuck in recovery mode, has been partially configured, or has missing supervision information, including attempting to recover data on the device
- Install automation tools, which include the command-line tool cfgutil, which you can use in shell scripts to automate configuration and Apple Configurator 2 actions for

the Automator app, which you can use to create workflows and distribute them to people who will use them to configure devices

▶ Install VPP Managed Distribution apps, apps purchased with an Apple ID, and iOS in-house enterprise apps

▶ Sign configuration profiles

▶ View Apple Configurator 2 activity by choosing Window > Activity

Apple Configurator 2.2 or later adds the following features:

▶ Modify the Home Screen layout of apps and folders

▶ Integrate with Bretford PowerSync+ carts and stations, including using the slot number when renaming devices

Apple Configurator 2.2 or later adds the following features that require iOS 9.3 or later:

▶ Configure OS X Server and Google accounts

▶ Specify domains to allow save and AutoFill passwords in Safari

▶ Allow Mail Drop for Exchange or Mail accounts

▶ Set and enforce a Lock screen message ("If lost, return to" and Asset tag) (supervised only)

▶ Configure Notification settings (supervised only)

▶ Set restrictions (supervised only) for Apple Music, Radio, and Notifications Modification

▶ Set restrictions (supervised only) to specify which apps to show or hide on the Home screen

▶ Set restrictions for iCloud Photo Library and Screen View in the Classroom app

The following legacy features from Apple Configurator are no longer available with Apple Configurator 2:

▶ The Assign feature, with its ability to check out an iOS device to a user and then check in that device, copying all the files the user created back to the Apple Configurator workstation, is no longer available for Apple Configurator 2. However, you can choose Actions > Add > Documents to place documents on iOS devices and choose Actions > Export > Documents to export documents from iOS devices to a folder on the Mac running Apple Configurator 2.

- The Prepare and Refresh modes, which continuously configure all iOS devices that Apple Configurator sees over USB (and which caused some administrators to accidentally wipe a personal iOS device that might have been low on charge) are gone for Apple Configurator 2; you must actively select an iOS device (or group of iOS devices) and explicitly initiate an action such as prepare, update, or apply a blueprint, or you can use command-line tools for automation.
- The ability to automatically refresh a supervised iOS device that Apple Configurator sees over USB is not available for Apple Configurator 2, unless you use command-line tools.
- The ability to assign apps using VPP redemption codes is not available for Apple Configurator 2; you must use VPP Managed Distribution instead.
- The ability to manage iOS devices with iOS 6 or earlier is not available for Apple Configurator 2 (but you can use Apple Configurator 2 to update devices with the latest versions of iOS 5 and iOS 6 to the latest available version of iOS).

Reference 12.2
Apple Configurator 2 Planning

This section provides a general introduction of Apple Configurator 2 and also delves into several logistical considerations when using it to deploy large numbers of devices.

Apple Configurator 2 Prepare and Supervise

The primary function of Apple Configurator 2 is to prepare iOS devices en masse so they are configured similarly. The act of preparing an iOS device with Apple Configurator 2 also allows you to supervise the device. In fact, Apple Configurator 2 is one of only two methods for supervising an iOS device, the other being using one of the Apple programs for device enrollment, namely, the Device Enrollment Program (DEP) (for businesses) or Apple School Manager (for schools).

As covered previously, administrators have much greater control over supervised devices—so much more control that one of the primary decisions to be made when planning a deployment is whether you will need to supervise iOS devices.

In other words, if your deployment needs require that iOS devices be supervised, then the beginning of your preparation workflow must start with either Apple Configurator 2 or one of the Apple programs for device enrollment (the DEP or Apple School Manager). Further, if you are in a situation where the DEP or Apple School Manager services are unavailable to you, then your only solution for preparing supervised iOS devices is Apple Configurator 2.

However, to complete preparation of iOS devices with Apple Configurator 2, they must be physically connected via universal serial bus (USB) to an OS X computer running Apple Configurator 2. This physical requirement of using Apple Configurator 2 may lead to considerable logistical hurdles in your deployment plans.

Apple Configurator 2 Logistical Considerations

A single OS X computer running Apple Configurator 2 can certainly be used to prepare dozens of iOS devices. However, the laws of physics get in the way of this single Mac workflow once you begin to scale up. Obviously, if you have a large number of iOS devices to configure, you must consider the logistical issues that arise when you need to physically connect all those devices via USB to a single OS X computer running Apple Configurator 2.

One way to speed things up is to use high-power USB hubs or carts that support multiple simultaneous device syncing and charging. When shopping for such a device, expect to spend a bit more for a USB hub with enough power to start up and charge iOS devices with potentially drained batteries. Lesser hubs don't provide enough power and thus can't start up iOS devices that are turned off or low on charge.

MORE INFO ▶ Apple recommends only USB hubs or carts that are part of the MFi program. Accessories that are part of this program go through testing and certification to ensure their compatibility with Apple devices. You can find out more at https://developer.apple.com/programs/mfi/.

Another option is to use multiple separate Apple Configurator 2 sync stations. Each station would have its own OS X computer connected to a USB hub or cart. This may be necessary if groups of devices are separated by a great distance. It may also be a necessity if supervised devices are going to be updated on a regular basis with Apple Configurator 2.

Some workflows involve updating as often as every night when the devices are stored for the evening. This is a popular option for shared iOS devices when used in conjunction with a syncing and charging storage cart. In this case, you would need an OS X computer running Apple Configurator 2 on every cart or at least within a few feet of multiple carts for the USB cable to reach.

Apple Configurator 2 Backup and Migration

Apple Configurator 2 stores some management information on the Mac computer's local system volume. If a Mac computer running Apple Configurator 2 were lost or the system volume were otherwise unrecoverable, the information used by Apple Configurator 2 would be gone with it.

This scenario would be merely an inconvenience if you used Apple Configurator 2 only to prepare unsupervised devices. However, if you plan to supervise iOS devices using Apple Configurator 2, you should absolutely have a plan to back up and restore the Mac system volume should the need arise.

The backup is critical because the process of supervising a device using Apple Configurator 2 creates a trust between the computer running Apple Configurator 2 and the device. Once an iOS device is supervised, it cannot be supervised by another system unless it's completely erased and reset or that other Mac has access to the supervision identity. The Apple Configurator 2 supervision information is stored on the Mac computer's local system volume. Thus, if that Mac computer is lost or its system volume is otherwise unrecoverable, the supervised devices cannot be managed by another Apple Configurator 2 system that does not have access to the supervision identity until the supervised devices are erased and reset.

The free backup software built in to OS X, Time Machine, fully supports backing up systems running Apple Configurator 2. Time Machine also features single-click setup of the backup. Simply plug an external drive into an OS X computer, and it will automatically prompt you to set up Time Machine.

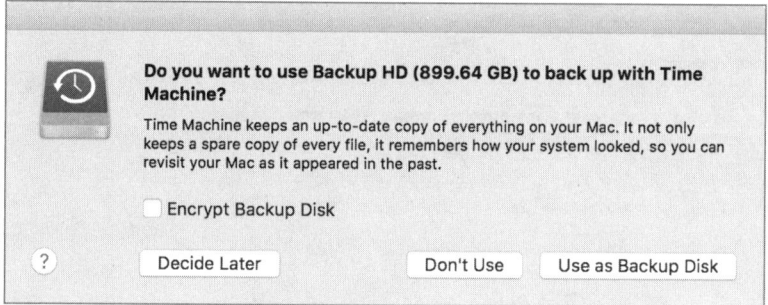

Encrypting your Time Machine backup drives is strongly suggested, especially when they contain mission-critical information such as the trust settings for Apple Configurator 2. If someone were to steal an unencrypted backup of your Apple Configurator 2 system, they could easily restore the backup to another Mac computer. Thus, your supervised devices would trust the imposter Apple Configurator 2 system as if it were the original.

> **MORE INFO** ▸ You can find out more about choosing an encrypted backup disk from Apple Support article PH21940, "OS X El Capitan: Choose a backup disk and set encryption options."

These are some locations that Apple Configurator 2 uses to store information:

- ~/Library/Group Containers/K36BKF7T3D.group.com.apple.configurator/—Most files, including firmware, preferences, logs, and blueprints
- ~/Library/Keychains—The certificate used in the Supervision identity
- /private/var/db/lockdown—Device pairing information

Make sure these locations are not excluded from your backup.

Apple Configurator 2 uses a new model for managing devices that does not use a database to store device configurations, profiles, apps, documents, or other media. If you used a legacy version of Apple Configurator, choose Apple Configurator 2 > Migration Assistant to migrate from Apple Configurator to Apple Configurator 2. The Apple Configurator Migration Assistant walks you through several steps to migrate the relevant configurations, files, and settings.

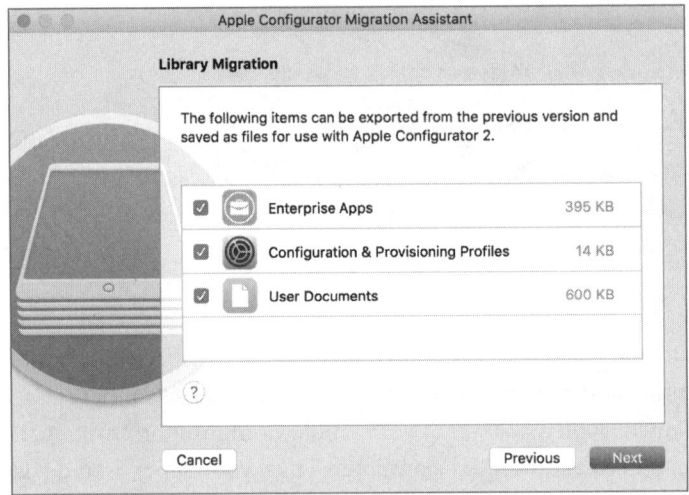

TIP You can manually copy firmware that was downloaded by the legacy version of Apple Configurator by copying the contents of ~/Library/Containers/com.apple.configurator/Data/Library/Caches/com.apple.configurator/Firmware/ to ~/Library/Group Containers/K36BKF7T3D.group.com.apple.configurator/Library/Caches/Firmware/.

Prepare Devices Limitations

For any Apple Configurator 2 feature to work, iOS devices must be allowed to *pair* (or attach) with the computer running Apple Configurator 2. Because pairing can be locked out for an existing iOS device, you may come across devices that Apple Configurator 2 cannot prepare. Further, many Apple Configurator 2 preparation workflows must first erase and reset the iOS device. For example, Apple Configurator 2 must first erase and reset any iOS device you want to supervise.

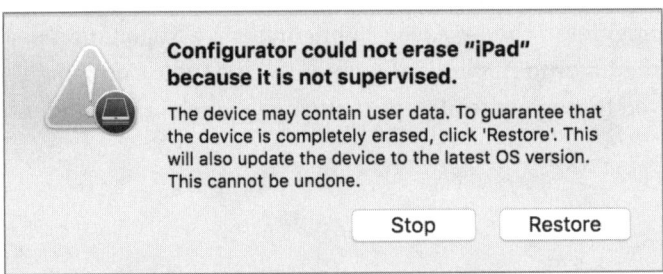

The requirement to unlock pairing or possibly erase an iOS device to manage it may seem like an inconvenience to an administrator, but to do otherwise would be a huge security risk. Imagine if someone could temporarily steal your personal iPhone and then, without you knowing, supervise and manage the device before returning it to you. These Apple Configurator 2 prepare restrictions are in place to protect personal iOS devices from being surreptitiously supervised and managed by unauthorized users.

Several specific situations can prevent Apple Configurator 2 from being able to prepare an iOS device:

▶ Supervised by another Mac with pairing disabled—If an iOS device is already supervised and managed by another Mac running Apple Configurator 2, the device can be optionally locked out from pairing. If this is the case, the device won't pair to any other computer. To remedy this situation, you can erase the device, you can export the organization and supervision identity from the Mac that supervised the device and then import those on another Mac with Apple Configurator 2 and try again, or you can supervise the device again with pairing allowed.

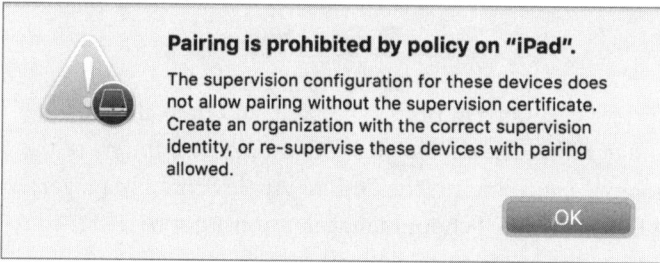

▶ Locked devices that don't trust your Mac—Even if an iOS device is allowed to pair with other computers, if the device is locked, it will not be allowed to pair with new untrusted computers. To make this device available for Apple Configurator 2 preparation, you must unlock the device and then tap the Trust button to allow the device to pair with the Mac running Apple Configurator 2. Apple Configurator 2 can collect the name, model, state, UDID (the device ID), and ECID (a 64-bit identifier unique to the processor in each iOS device) for a connected iOS device even if it does not trust the Mac running Apple Configurator 2.

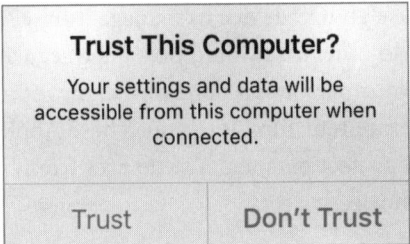

- If you select an iOS device, choose Actions > Prepare, and choose Configuration: Automated Enrollment. The device must be enrolled in one of the Apple programs for device enrollment (the DEP or Apple School Manager) and assigned to a server; otherwise, the preparation will fail.

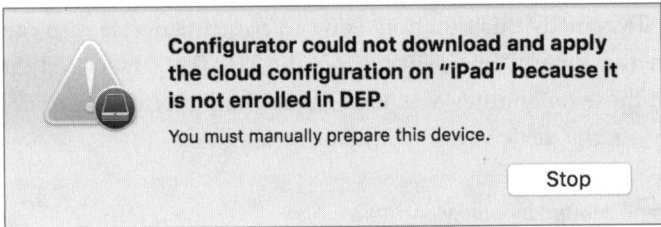

- If you select an iOS device, choose Actions > Prepare, and then choose Configuration: Manual. Either the device must not be enrolled in one of the Apple programs for device enrollment (the DEP or Apple School Manager) or, if it is enrolled in the DEP or Apple School Manager, it must not be assigned to an MDM server; otherwise, the preparation will fail.

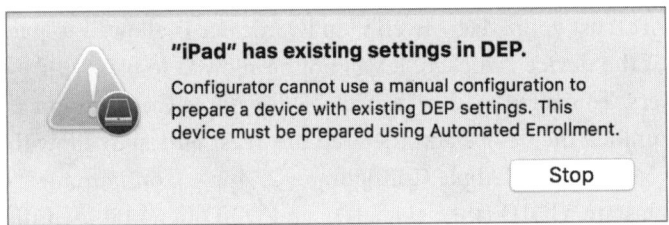

MORE INFO ▸ Managing Apple programs for device enrollment is covered in Lesson 8, "Out-of-the-Box Management via Apple Programs for Device Enrollment."

▶ iCloud Find My Device enabled or Activation Lock enabled—If a user has signed in to iCloud and turned on the Find My Device feature, Activation Lock is probably turned on. Find My Device or Activation Lock will prevent erasing and resetting the iOS device. To make this device available for Apple Configurator 2 preparation, Find My Device must be turned off, and Activation Lock must be removed.

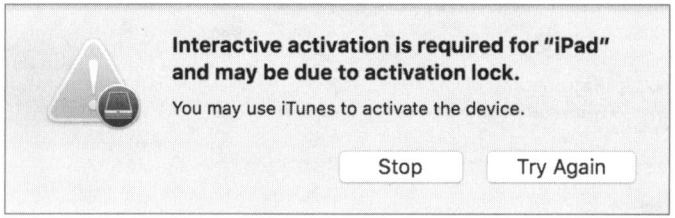

MORE INFO ▶ Managing Activation Lock is covered in Lesson 9, "Activation Lock Management."

▶ Unresponsive devices—iOS devices that are otherwise unresponsive aren't reachable by Apple Configurator 2. First, make sure that any USB hub you're using is capable of providing enough charge to wake a device with a drained battery. You can also try to revive the device by plugging it into a regular Apple charger. If the device is still unresponsive, it should be evaluated for repair by a qualified service technician.

▶ Other scenarios—If an iOS device has been partially configured, is missing information such as supervision identity, or is stuck in recovery mode, you can select the device and then choose Actions > Advanced > Revive Device.

Reference 12.3
Apple Configurator 2 Installation and Setup

This section outlines the steps involved with the initial installation and setup of Apple Configurator 2.

MORE INFO ▶ You'll find detailed step-by-step instructions for installing Apple Configurator 2 in the exercises later in this lesson.

Apple Configurator 2 Installation

Apple Configurator 2 is available for free in the Mac App Store. You should use an administrative Apple ID that does not have a credit card associated with it. A simple search for *configurator* in the Mac App Store should return it as the first item.

As of this writing, the current version of Apple Configurator 2 (2.2) is compatible with any Mac computer capable of running OS X v10.11.4 or later. Make sure the Mac computer has iTunes 12.3.3 or later; otherwise, you'll see a message telling you to update iTunes.

> **TIP** OS X, Apple Configurator 2, and iTunes can all be updated automatically via the Mac App Store software update mechanism. Apple always recommends that you use the latest available versions of the system and apps.

Apple Configurator 2 Views

When you first open Apple Configurator 2, after accepting the license agreement, you'll see a Welcome message, with a "Take a quick tour" link and a Get Started button. If you click the tour link, view the contents, close the Quick Tour window, and then click Get Started, you will see the device browser, which consists of the following:

- Default toolbar, including the Search field
- Favorites bar, including All Devices, Supervised, Unsupervised, and Recovery
- All connected iOS devices

In the previous figure, the red badge displayed with an iPad indicates that it has an iOS update available.

The View button allows you to change between an icon view of your devices or blueprints and a detailed list, as well as select how the items are sorted.

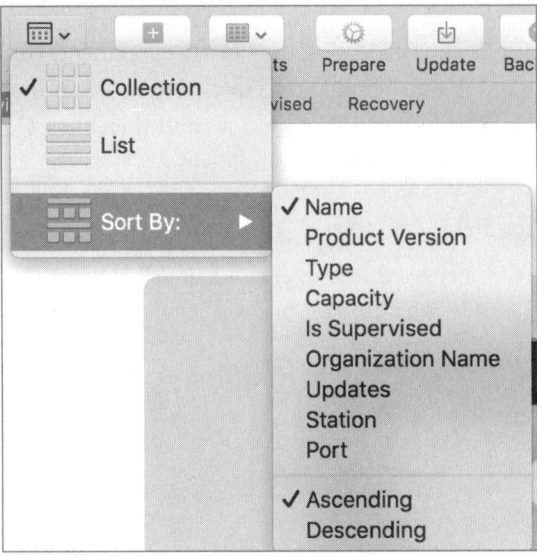

You can use the Add button to add apps from your purchase history (for a personal Apple ID for free apps or an Apple ID associated with your VPP account) or from your Mac, documents for apps that support iTunes file sharing, or profiles.

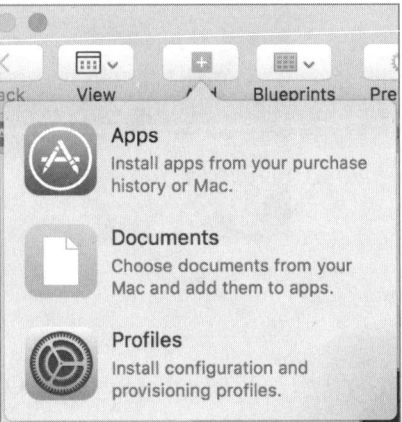

When you click the Blueprints button, the menu contains any blueprints you have, and the bottom of the menu is Edit Blueprints, which changes the main window from All Devices to a blueprint browser and editor. Don't forget to click Done to exit the blueprint editor and return to the device browser.

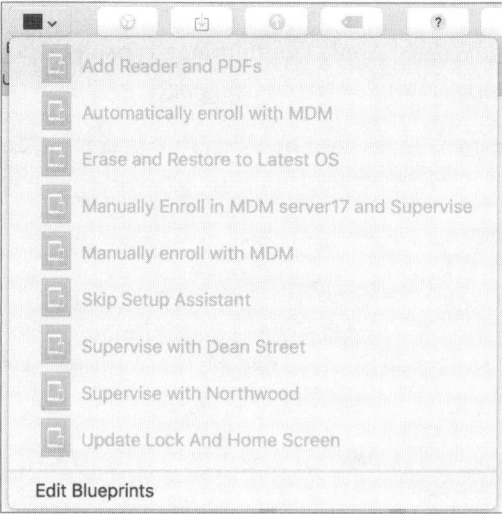

The Prepare button is available in the default toolbar. With one or more iOS devices selected, you can click the Prepare button to supervise, enroll in an MDM server, or configure the Setup Assistant experience.

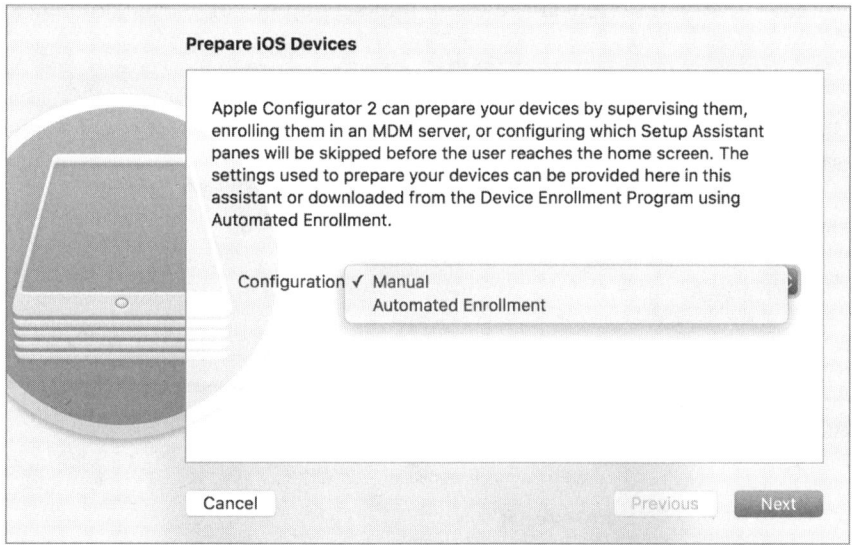

The Update button installs an update for iOS for a device if one is available.

The Back Up button creates a backup of the device, but if you've been using workflows that rely on using backups and restores with legacy Apple Configurator, consider whether you can use the new features of Apple Configurator 2 to avoid using backups and restores.

The Tag button assigns tags to selected devices. To create a new tag, simply enter it, and then press Return to create the tag.

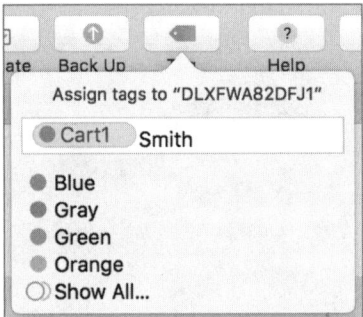

And of course, the Help button opens Help for Apple Configurator 2, which is continually updated. Do not forget this resource.

One more thing: The Actions > Advanced menu offers a number of useful commands.

Apple Configurator 2 Preferences

Before you start using Apple Configurator 2 to prepare and manage devices, you should take a quick look at the Apple Configurator 2 preferences. You can access these settings by choosing Apple Configurator 2 > Preferences from the menu or by pressing Control-, (comma). The following screenshots illustrate Apple Configurator 2 preferences with sample settings.

The General tab addresses completion and warning sounds, allows you to reset warning dialogs, and configures whether the device window is always displayed when you first open Apple Configurator 2.

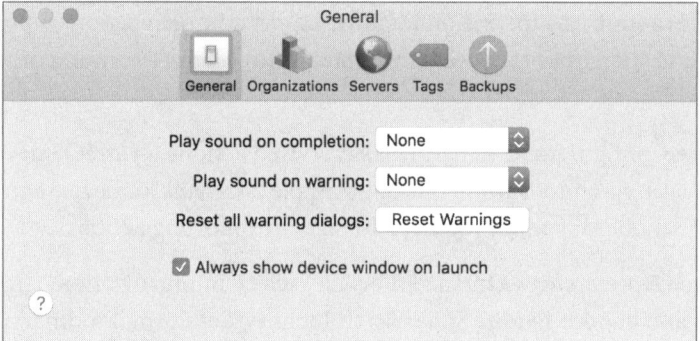

Use the Organizations tab to create and edit multiple organizations and supervision identities. An organization contains contact information and a supervision identity. A supervision identity contains a public key infrastructure (PKI) certificate (which contains an identity and a private key) that's used to securely establish a relationship between Apple Configurator 2 and an iOS device.

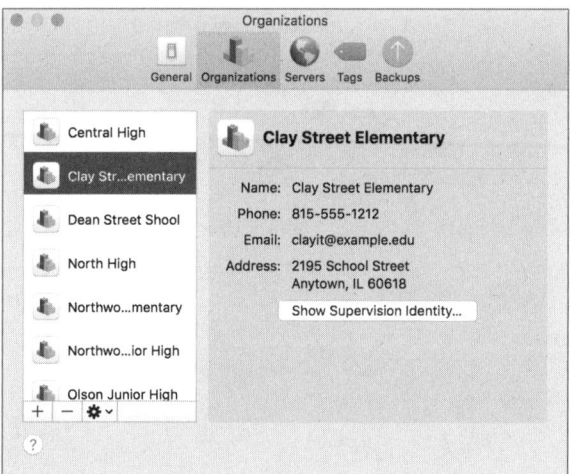

When you create an organization, either you must allow Apple Configurator 2 to generate a new supervision identity or you must choose an existing supervision identity. The combination of the organization and its supervision identity allows you to use Apple Configurator 2 to supervise devices that are not assigned an MDM server via one of the Apple programs for device enrollment (the DEP or Apple School Manager).

With the legacy Apple Configurator, you could update settings for a supervised iOS device only by using Apple Configurator on the Mac computer that supervised the device. However, with Apple Configurator 2, you can update settings for supervised iOS devices using multiple Mac computers running Apple Configurator 2 by configuring a unified supervision identity. To configure a unified supervision identity, export an organization, export its supervision identity, and then import those into Apple Configurator 2 running on the other Mac computers.

Additionally, to use Apple Configurator 2 to perform supervised actions on an iOS device enrolled with Profile Manager via a profile from one of the Apple programs for device enrollment (the DEP or Apple School Manager), you need to take the following actions.

In the Apple Configurator 2 preferences Organizations tab, select an organization, click the Action (gear) menu, and choose Export Supervision Identity. Set Format to Encrypted PKCS12 (.p12), name the file, specify a location to save it to, and then click Save.

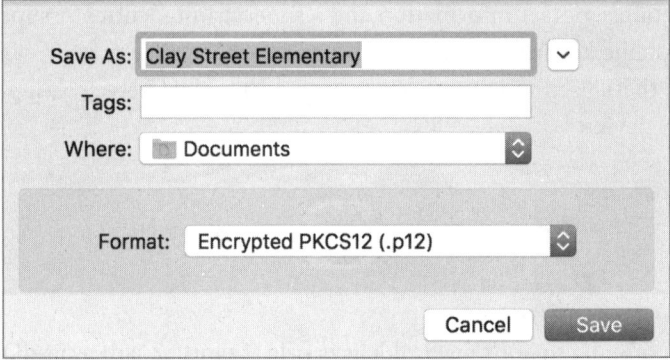

Enter and verify a password to protect the security of the supervision identity, and then click OK. Copy the .p12 file to your server.

In the Server app, open the Profile Manager pane. Click Configure beneath "Enroll devices using the Device Enrollment Program," select the checkbox "Use Apple Configurator to configure enrolled devices," click the pop-up menu and choose Import, drag the supervision identity (via its .p12 file) into the pane, and then click Import. In the Server app, the Device Enrollment pane displays information about the supervision identity; finally, click Done.

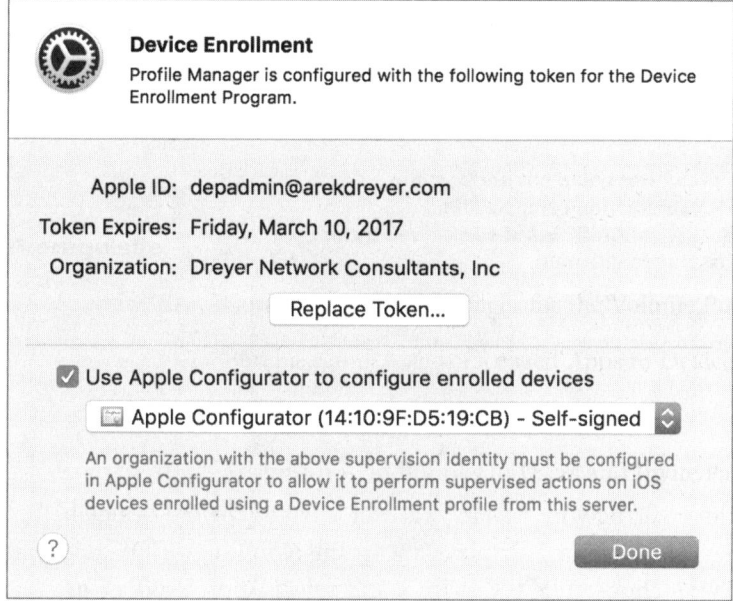

MORE INFO ▶ Alternatively, you could use Keychain Access on your server to export the default supervision identity (for example, the server.arekdreyer.com certificate signed by the OD intermediate CA) and import it with Keychain Access on Mac computers running Apple Configurator 2. When you see the message that com.apple.configurator.xpc.DeviceService.xpc wants to sign using the key "privateKey" in your keychain, click Allow, and then click Allow again when the message appears for a second time.

If you do not select the option "Use Apple Configurator to configure enrolled devices," then when you connect a Mac computer running Apple Configurator 2 to an iOS device that has been assigned to and enrolled with your Profile Manager service via one of the Apple programs for device enrollment (the DEP or Apple School Manager) and you have configured the device to be supervised, the following happens:

▶ If the option "Allow pairing with a Mac" was selected for the device before it enrolled, the device prompts with a Trust This Computer? dialog. If you tap Trust, you can use Apple Configurator 2 to configure the device, but if you attempt to take actions that require supervision (such as Start Single App Mode), Apple Configurator 2 displays a dialog that it cannot perform the action because the device is not supervised by an existing organization.

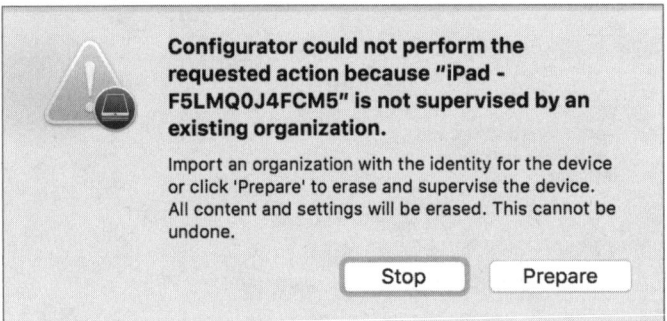

▶ If the option "Allow pairing with a Mac" was not selected for the device before it enrolled, Apple Configurator 2 displays a warning icon for the iOS device; if you select the device, choose File > Get Info, and select Apps, Profiles, or Console in the sidebar, you'll see the message that pairing is prohibited by policy on the device, including "The supervision configuration for these devices does not allow pairing without the supervision certificate. Create an organization with the correct supervision identity, or re-supervise these devices with pairing allowed."

NOTE ▶ If you use Apple Configurator 2 on the same Mac computer that hosts your Profile Manager service, Apple Configurator 2 has access to the default supervision identity, and you can use Apple Configurator 2 to perform supervised actions on iOS devices that have enrolled with your Profile Manager service via one of the Apple programs for device enrollment.

Use the Servers tab to specify one or more servers to use for MDM.

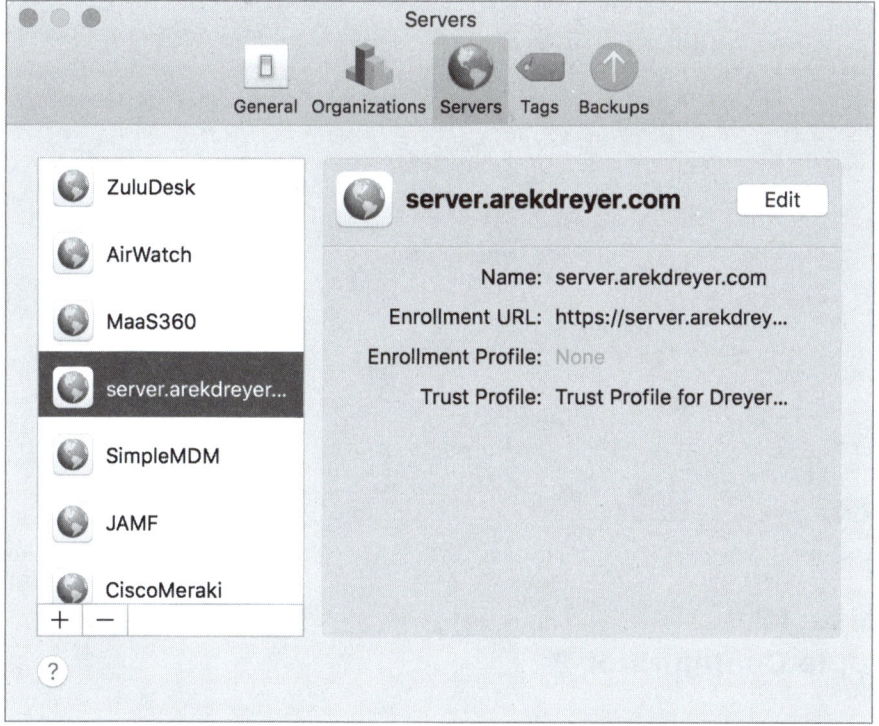

MORE INFO ▶ See Exercise 12.1, "Get Apple Configurator 2," for more information about using the Edit button to inspect the information related to a server.

Use the Tags tab to create and edit tags to apply to iOS devices and blueprints to help you organize.

The Backups tab displays information about the backups you've made of iOS devices. If you use iTunes to make a backup of your personal iOS device, do not be surprised when that backup appears here. You can search for backups and delete the ones you no longer need.

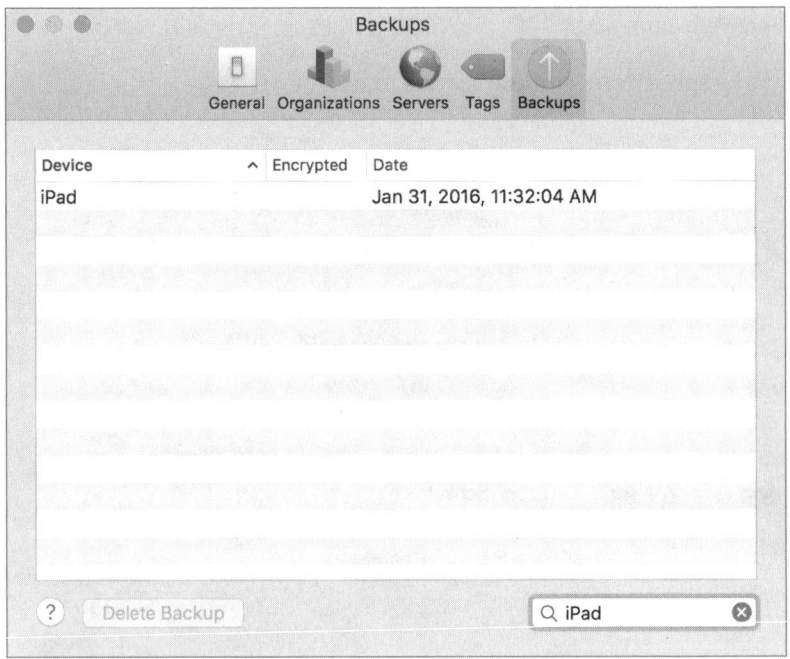

Exercise 12.1
Get Apple Configurator 2

▶ **Prerequisites**

- ▶ Exercise 2.2, "Create Apple IDs"
- ▶ Exercise 4.1, "Prepare Your Mac to Install OS X Server for El Capitan"
- ▶ Exercise 7.1, "Enable Device Management"

Challenge

Use the Mac App Store to purchase and install Apple Configurator 2. Open Apple Configurator 2, and inspect and modify Apple Configurator 2 Preferences. Create an organization, and inspect the automatically created certificate for supervision. Define a MDM server. Install the Apple Configurator 2 command-line tool.

Considerations

To keep the setup simple, the figures in this exercise assume that you install Apple Configurator 2 on your client Mac, which has been used for other purposes during these exercises. In a production environment, it is recommended to use a Mac that is dedicated to Apple Configurator 2.

Solution

Install Apple Configurator 2

1 On your client Mac, from the Apple menu, choose App Store.

2 If you are not already logged in to the App Store, choose Store > Sign In.

3 Enter your administrator Apple ID credentials, and click Sign In.

4 Enter Apple Configurator 2 in the search field in the upper-right corner of the App Store, and press Return.

5 In the search results, click Apple Configurator 2.

6 If you haven't yet purchased it, click Get.

7 Click Install App.

8 If necessary, sign in again with your Apple ID credentials.

9 If you see the "Require a password when making purchases on this computer" pane, click Require After 15 Minutes.

Run Apple Configurator 2 for the First Time

1   After the Install button changes to Open, click Open.

2   Read the license agreement, and then click Accept.

3   In the Dock, Control-click Apple Configurator 2, and in the shortcut menu, choose Options > Keep in Dock.

Examine Apple Configurator 2 Preferences

1   From the menu bar, choose Apple Configurator 2 > Preferences.

2   In the Preferences toolbar, click the General tab if it is not already selected.

3   For "Play sound on completion," choose Glass, or another sound of your liking.

4   For "Play sound on warning," choose Blow, or another sound of your liking.

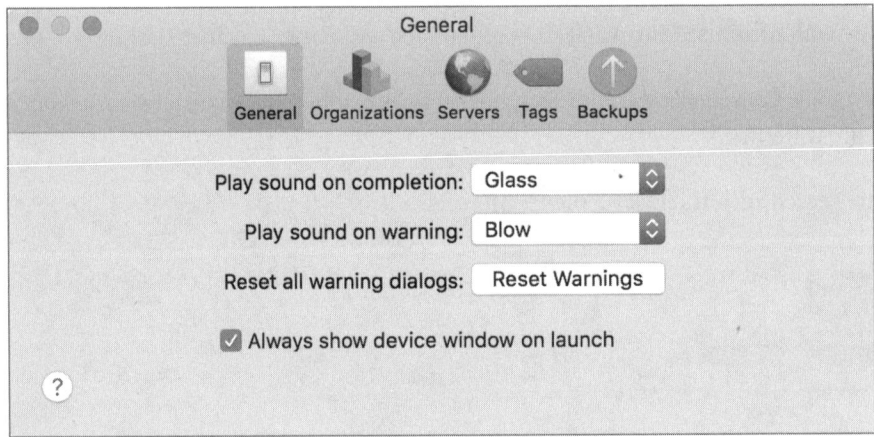

5   In the Preferences toolbar, click Tags.

   Like the Finder's Tags feature, Tags allow you to assign an identifier to one or more iOS devices.

6   Click Backups. There are no backups at this time.

   Backups from iTunes will be displayed here, as well as any backups you create with Apple Configurator 2.

Create an Organization

Organizations allow Apple Configurator 2 to supervise devices that are not in the Device Enrollment Program (DEP) and can be shared among other Apple Configurator 2 stations and Profile Manager for a unified supervision identity.

1   In the Preferences toolbar, click Organizations.

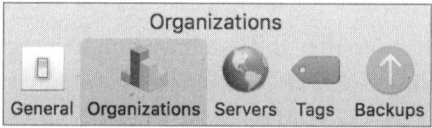

2   Click Add (+).

3   Click Next.

4   At the Create an Organization screen, enter Configurator Project n, replacing *n* with your student number.

5   For the remaining fields, enter information of your liking.

   NOTE ▸ In a production environment, this information should be accurate and reflect your organization, as it will be used to create a supervision identity.

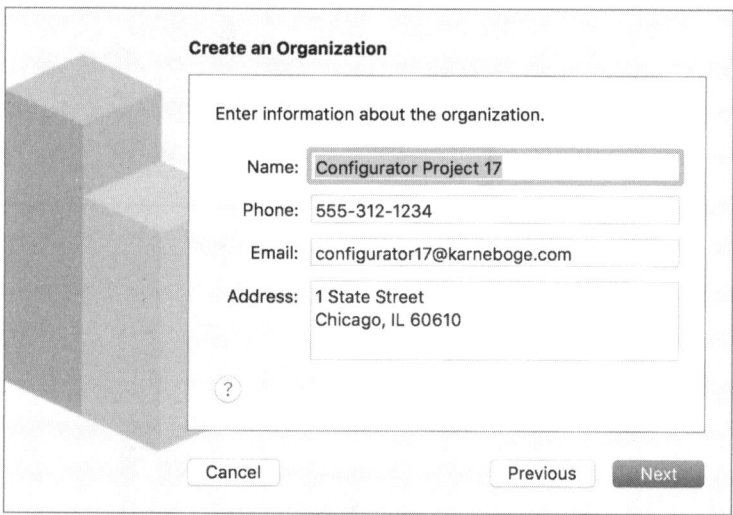

6 Click Next.

7 If you are prompted for your administrator credentials, provide them, and then click Update Settings. Otherwise, if your Mac computer already has a supervision identity (for example, if your Mac is running OS X Server and is configured as an Open Directory Master), select "Generate a new supervision identity," click Done, enter your administrator credentials, and then click Update Settings.

Your resulting organization will be displayed. Note that you can have multiple organizations, and you can import or export organizations from other Apple Configurator 2 workstations.

Inspect the Apple Configurator 2 Certificate

1 While still in the Apple Configurator 2 Preferences window, in the Preferences toolbar, click Organizations if necessary.

2 Select your organization.

3 Click Show Supervision Identity.

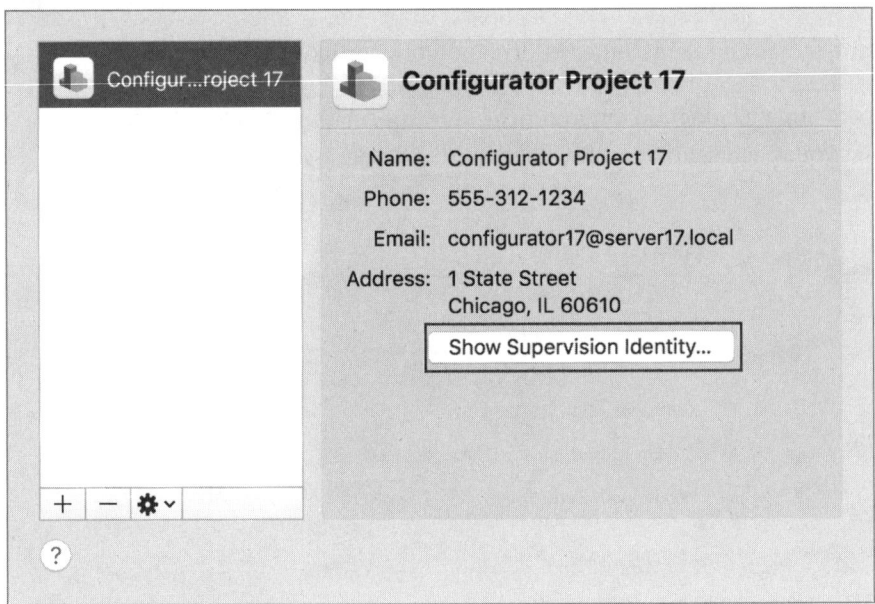

4 In the certificate pane, next to Details, click the disclosure triangle.

Note that the certificate contains the organization that you created in the previous section.

5   Scroll to examine the other information, and then click OK.

    NOTE ▶ You could also view the supervision identity certificate, as well as the public and private keys, using Keychain Access.

For each organization, Apple Configurator 2 automatically creates the certificate (and its public/private key pair) and places it in the login keychain of the currently logged-in user. This certificate is used to supervise iOS devices. Be sure to back up this certificate; Time Machine is a supported method of backing up the Mac you use with Apple Configurator 2. See the earlier section "Apple Configurator 2 Planning" for more information.

Define an MDM Server

In the later exercises, you will be simulating an out-of-the-box enrollment experience during Setup Assistant on an iOS device using the MDM server you define here.

1   While still in the Apple Configurator 2 Preferences window, in the Preferences toolbar, click Servers.

2   Click Add (+).

3   Click Next.

4   In the Define an MDM Server window, in the Name field, enter the name of your MDM server (MDM Project *n*, where *n* is your student number).

5   In the Hostname or URL field, modify the URL, replacing the myserver.local portion with server*n*.local and replacing *n* with your student number.

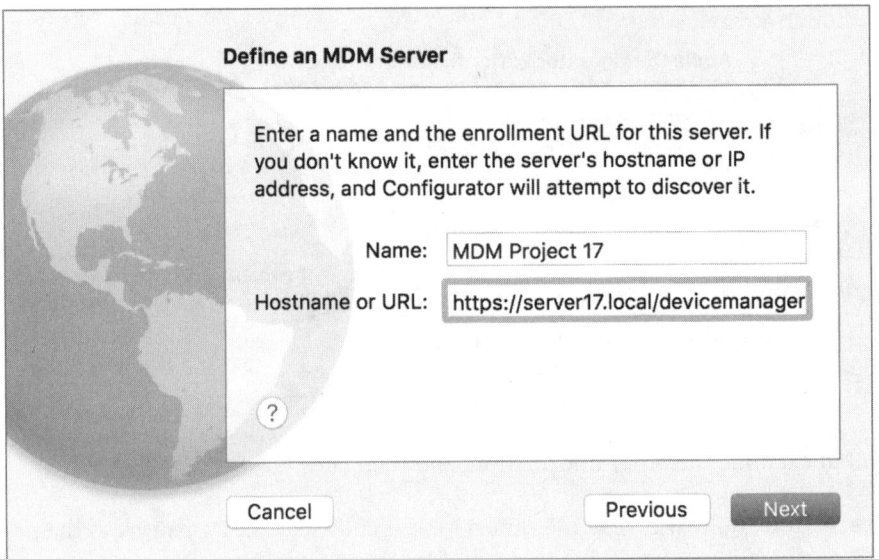

NOTE ▶ The URL predefined in this window is the default enrollment URL for Profile Manager. Other MDM solutions often have different enrollment URLs. Consult your MDM vendor's documentation for the exact enrollment URL. It is critical that this URL be correct, as enrollment will fail if it is not.

6   Click Next. You will not be enrolling any Apple TV devices in the subsequent exercises, so you do not need to provide Enrollment and Trust Profiles.

7   Click Next, and in the MDM Project *n* (where *n* is your student number) server window, click Edit.

Observe the trust certificates, as well as the Trust Profile. These were obtained from your MDM server while defining the server in Apple Configurator 2.

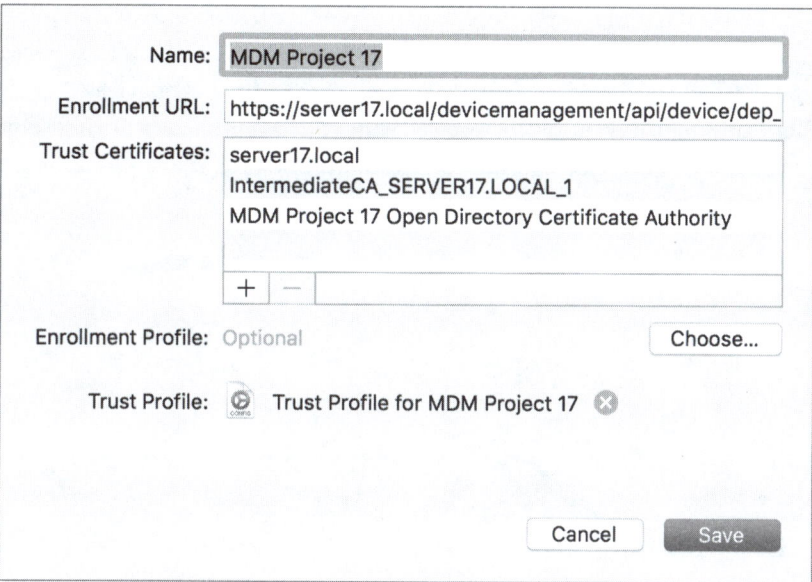

8 Click Save, and then close the Preferences window.

Install the Apple Configurator 2 Command-Line Tool

1 From the menu bar, choose Apple Configurator 2 > Install Automation Tools.

2 Click Install.

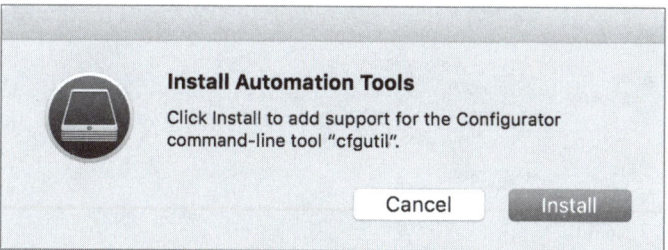

3 Provide your administrator credentials, and click Add Helper.

The command-line tool cfgutil is added to Apple Configurator 2, and a symbolic link is placed in /usr/local/bin/. For more information, see the **cfgutil** man page.

In this exercise, you used the Mac App Store to get Apple Configurator 2. You modified Apple Configurator 2 Preferences, created an organization that will be used to supervise iOS devices, and defined your Profile Manager server, which will allow devices that are not in the DEP to automatically enroll themselves with your MDM server during setup. Finally, you installed the Apple Configurator 2 command-line tool, cfgutil, which you can use for further automation.

Lesson 13

Apple Configurator 2: Preparing, Configuring, and Managing iOS Devices

This lesson builds on the previous lesson, which provided an introduction to Apple Configurator 2. The goal of these lessons is to let you experience different Apple Configurator 2 workflows to find out which methods best fit your needs.

Remember that Apple Configurator 2 and Apple programs for device enrollment (the Device Enrollment Program [DEP] for businesses and Apple School Manager for schools) are the only two methods to apply supervision, which proves ownership of the device and allows a set of features and restrictions that are not available otherwise.

For devices that require a less heavy-handed management, using Apple Configurator 2 with supervision turned off may be the best approach. The most obvious examples are devices that are personally owned or to be used exclusively by a single individual.

Further, for unsupervised devices, it's likely that they will interact with Apple Configurator 2 only for initial preparation and enrollment into a Mobile Device Management (MDM) service. After that, it's assumed that all future management will be via MDM services, again benefiting deployments where a single individual will carry the device.

GOALS

▶ Create and edit configuration profiles

▶ Prepare iOS devices

▶ Create and edit blueprints

▶ Organize devices

▶ Use backups

▶ Automate device management

If your deployment requirements need to take full advantage of all the available management options, you will need to supervise your iOS devices. In this case, obvious examples include shared devices or devices being used in circumstances that require greater control, such as primary education environments.

Reference 13.1
Use Configuration Profiles

In this section, you will explore how Apple Configurator 2 can be used to create, edit, and install profiles.

Create and Edit Profiles

Apple Configurator 2 offers a full interface for creating and editing profiles for iOS devices. The interface mimics creating and editing profiles in Profile Manager, so refer to Lesson 6, "Configuration and Profiles," for more information about profile content.

> **NOTE ▶** Although you can export configuration profiles created in Apple Configurator 2, these profiles are designed to be installed exclusively on iOS devices and are not supported to be installed on OS X computers. As covered in Lesson 6, "Configuration and Profiles," Profile Manager provides an interface for creating profiles that are compatible with both OS X and iOS.

To create a new profile, choose File > New Profile (or press Command-N). Enter a name in the Name field; this will be visible to the user on the device. Apple Configurator 2 automatically assigns the profile a unique identifier.

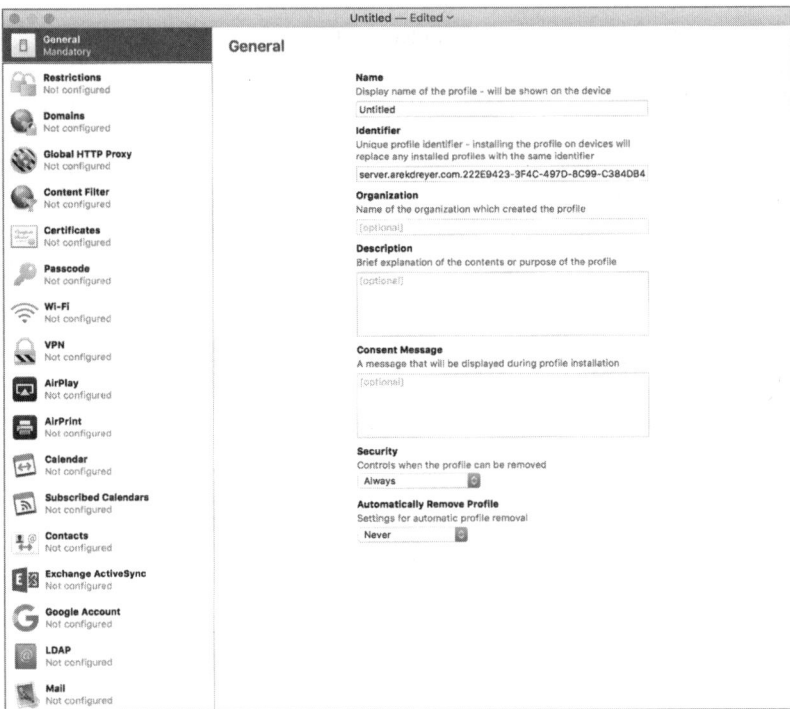

To save the profile, choose File > Save (or press Command-S). You may find it convenient to log in to iCloud on multiple Apple Configurator 2 workstations with an organizational Apple ID that's dedicated to Apple Configurator 2; in this case, in the save dialog, click the Where pop-up menu and choose Configurator — iCloud. In the Save As field, enter a descriptive name for the configuration profile, and then click Save.

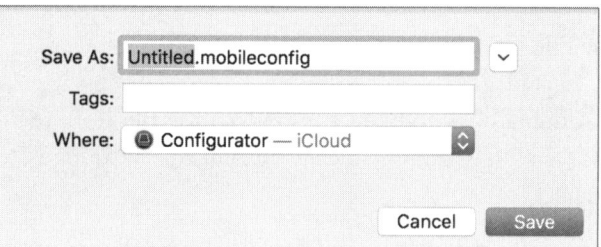

It's possible to sign your profile with a signing identity to help ensure that the contents of the profile are intact and have not been maliciously modified; if the contents of a signed profile are modified, the signature is no longer valid, the profile is no longer valid, and it cannot be installed. To sign a profile, choose File > Sign Profile, click the Signing Identity pop-up menu, choose a signing identity, and then click Sign.

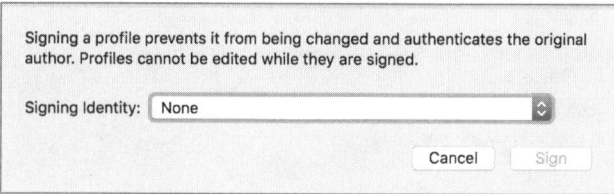

MORE INFO ▶ If you do not sign a profile, it will appear as Unsigned. If you sign a profile and choose an identity that was automatically generated by Apple Configurator 2, the profile will appear as Unverified, but you can still add it to devices. If you choose an Apple Developer ID identity, the profile will appear as Verified. To find out more about obtaining an Apple Developer ID identity, see https://developer.apple.com/.

You cannot modify a signed profile.

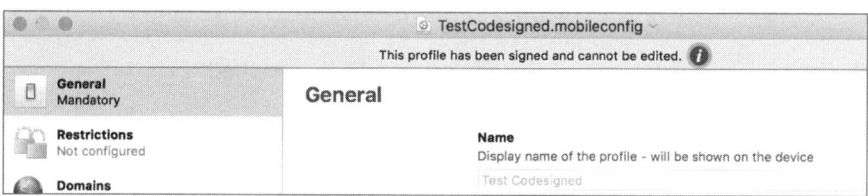

However, it's simple to unsign a profile; choose File > Unsign Profile. After you make your desired edits, you can choose File > Sign Profile to sign it again.

> **NOTE ▶** The legacy version of Apple Configurator cannot sign profiles, nor can it modify imported profiles that are code signed or profiles that contain MDM enrollment information.

To edit an existing profile, choose File > Open, or choose File > Open Recent.

> **TIP ▶** In the Finder, if you double-click to open a .mobileconfig file from the Configurator folder in iCloud Drive, it will automatically open in Apple Configurator 2 instead of with Profiles preferences.

Install Profiles

Once you've created a profile, you can install it on devices.

For devices that you've supervised, you can add a profile without interacting on the device, even if it is still at Setup Assistant. Select one or more devices, choose Actions > Add > Profiles, select the profile to add, and then click Add.

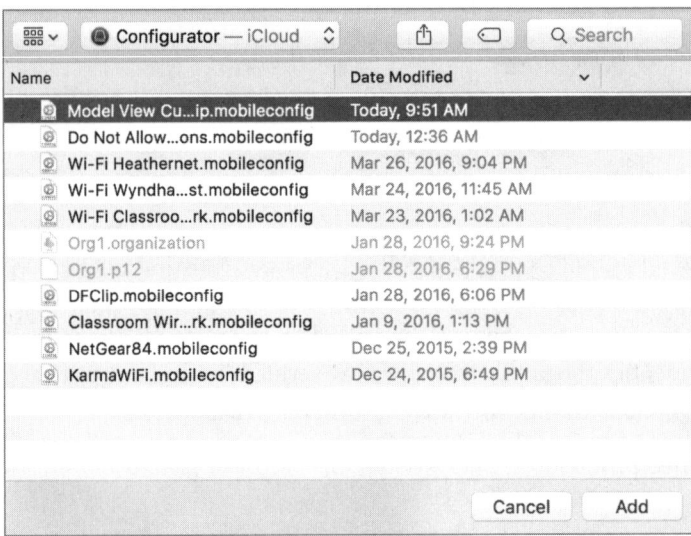

For devices that are supervised, the profile is automatically installed.

For devices not supervised, you must use the device to accept the installation of the profile.

NOTE ► If you have not completed Setup Assistant on your unsupervised iOS device, you will not be presented with the option to tap Install on the device to accept the installation of the profile, so the profile will not be installed.

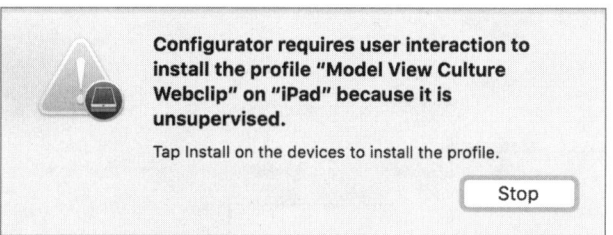

On the device, start the process of installing the profile by tapping Install.

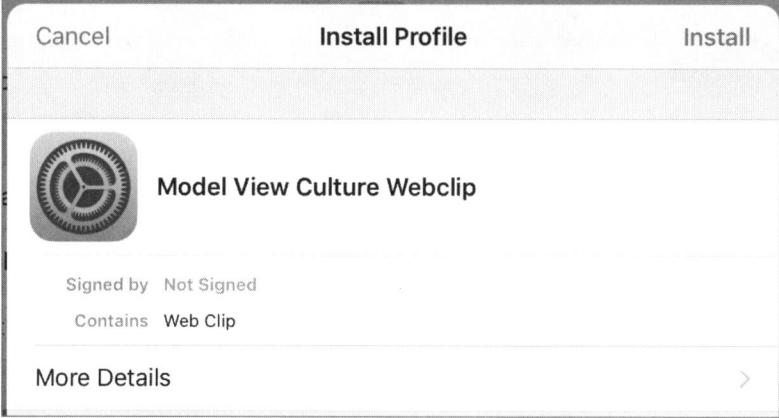

Next, if the profile is not signed, tap Install at the warning. Then at the Tap Install dialog, tap Install. Finally, at the Profile Installed message, tap Done.

This process may seem like a lot of hassle, but it's required to guarantee the security of personal iOS devices. As such, this workflow is a valid method to provide additional configuration for personal devices that have already been set up.

Configuration profiles and enrollment profiles installed via Apple Configurator 2 can be removed by the user. This applies to both supervised and unsupervised iOS devices. At the time of this writing, the only method to force a device to remain enrolled in an MDM service is via one of the Apple programs for device enrollment (the DEP for businesses and Apple School Manager for schools). This program is detailed in Lesson 8, "Out-of-the-Box Management via Apple Programs for Device Enrollment."

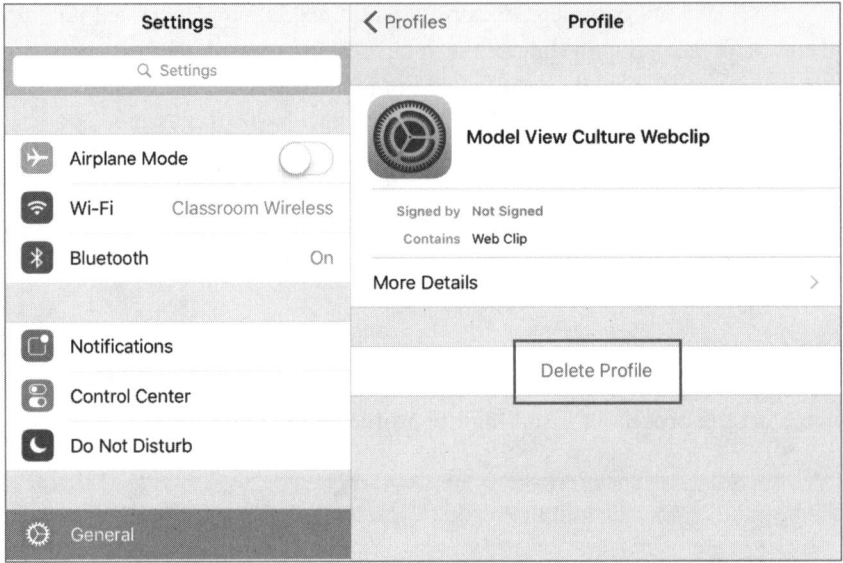

Reference 13.2
Prepare iOS Devices

You can use Apple Configurator 2 to help enroll devices into your MDM with the action named Prepare. In addition to helping you set up and enroll your device, the Prepare action also allows you to supervise a device. It's so commonly used that the Prepare button is in the toolbar.

A popular alternative to fully configuring an iOS device during preparation is to allow the user to complete iOS Setup Assistant but to customize the experience to meet your organizational requirements. This process allows you to provide a mostly "out-of-the-box" experience for the user because he would be the first person to set up the device. Apple Configurator 2 workflows that allow the user to complete iOS Setup Assistant are most often used when devices are used by individual users and aren't shared.

Keep in mind that preparing an iOS device with Apple Configurator 2 allows administrators to fully manage the device prior to the user setting it up. So, even if the user is allowed to experience iOS Setup Assistant, you may have already used Apple Configurator 2 to supervise the device and install custom profiles and apps.

Customizing iOS Setup Assistant can also be a huge time-saver if you plan to take advantage of user-based management. For example, instead of installing an anonymous MDM enrollment profile, you can customize iOS Setup Assistant to include user-authenticated MDM enrollment. In this case, because the user is completing the enrollment during setup, the MDM service will automatically associate the user with the device. This not only updates your device inventory but also allows the MDM service to automatically push down user-based profiles along with device-based profiles.

> **TIP** ▶ If for some reason you are unable to use one of the Apple programs for device enrollment (the DEP or Apple School Manager), the alternative is to use an Apple Configurator 2 workflow that customizes iOS Setup Assistant to include MDM enrollment.

When you use Apple Configurator 2 to restore or prepare an iOS device, it may have to download an iOS system file (a file ending in the suffix .ipsw). Each iOS system is usually from 1–2 GB in size. However, keep in mind that different models of iOS device will require different versions of the iOS system software. At the time of this writing, there are dozens of different device-specific builds of the iOS system software.

> **TIP** ▶ If you have multiple Apple Configurator 2 Mac systems to get up and running with iOS software updates, having a local Apple Caching server will save you a tremendous amount of time downloading the updates. The Caching service is covered in Lesson 5, "Caching Service."

After you click Prepare, you have to decide whether to use Automated Enrollment or Manual enrollment.

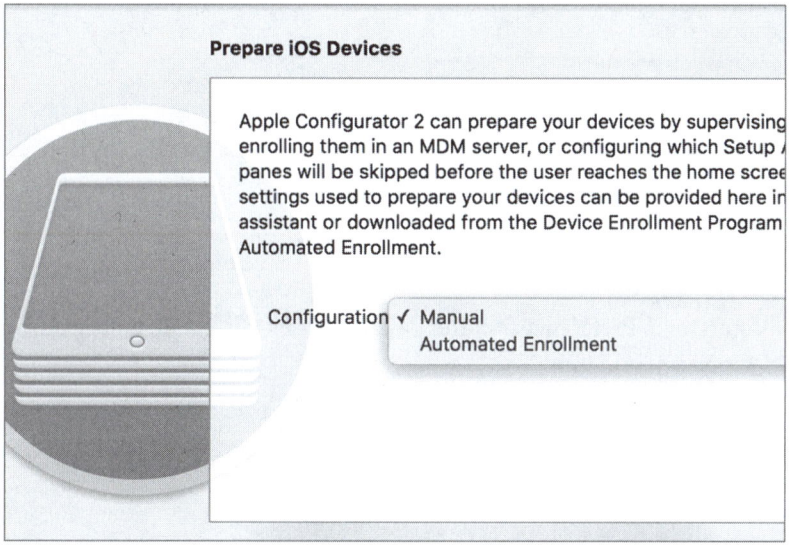

Prepare Using Manual

For devices that are not enrolled in one of the Apple programs for device enrollment (the DEP or Apple School Manager) you must choose Manual.

NOTE ▶ You can also use Manual for devices that are enrolled in one of programs for Apple device enrollment, if they are not assigned an MDM server.

You need some initial preparation before you start the prepare process and choose Manual:

▶ In the Profile Manager administration portal, select a user or a group, click the About tab, select the option "Allow enrollment during Setup Assistant for devices configured using Apple Configurator," and then click Save. It's convenient to modify this setting for the Everyone group.

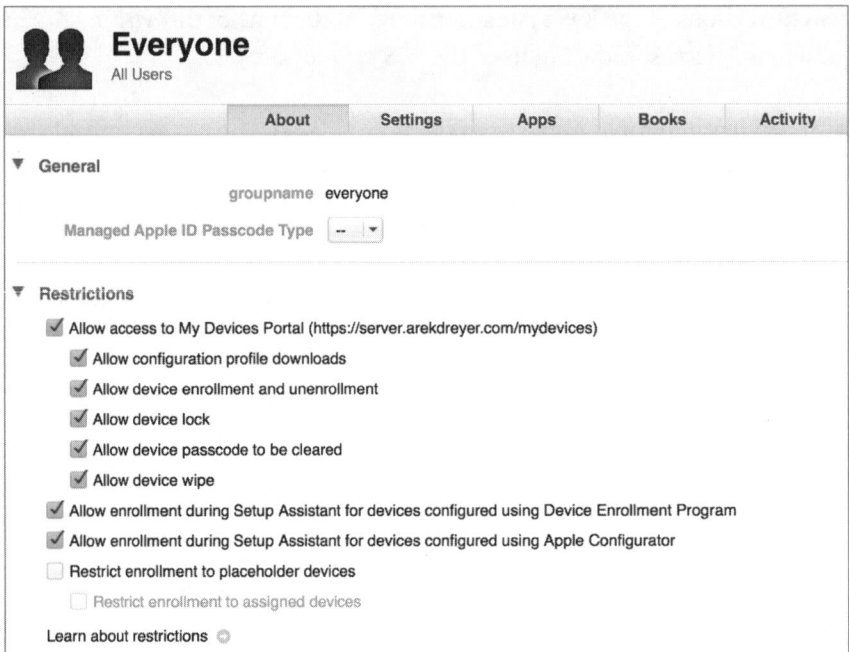

▶ In Apple Configurator 2 Preferences, in the Organizations tab, create an organization along with its supervision identity.

▶ In Apple Configurator 2 Preferences, in the Servers tab, create a server, which includes its enrollment URL, any certificates required to trust the MDM service, and an optional enrollment profile.

In the Enroll in MDM Server pane, specify an MDM server or choose Do Not Enroll in MDM. Whereas devices that are enrolled in one of the Apple programs for device enrollment have their MDM server specified in the appropriate program portal, you have to specify one or more MDM servers in the Apple Configurator 2 preferences, in the Servers tab.

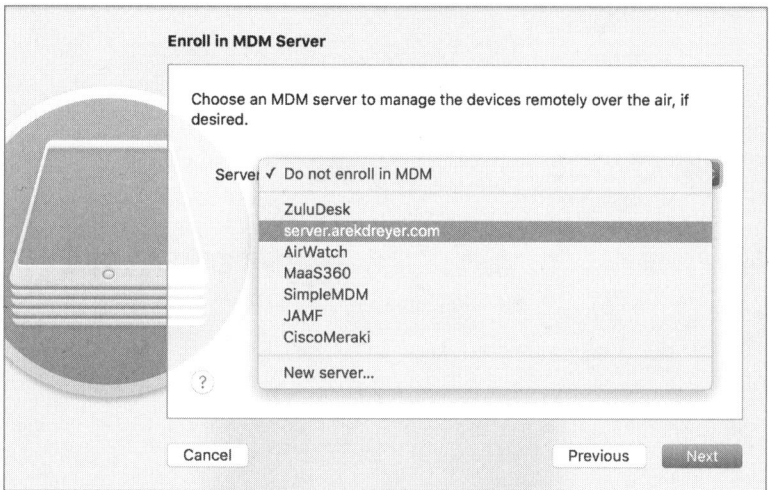

Choose whether to supervise the device. If you choose to supervise the device, you can also choose whether to allow the device to pair with other computers. If you do not supervise a device, you cannot prevent it from pairing.

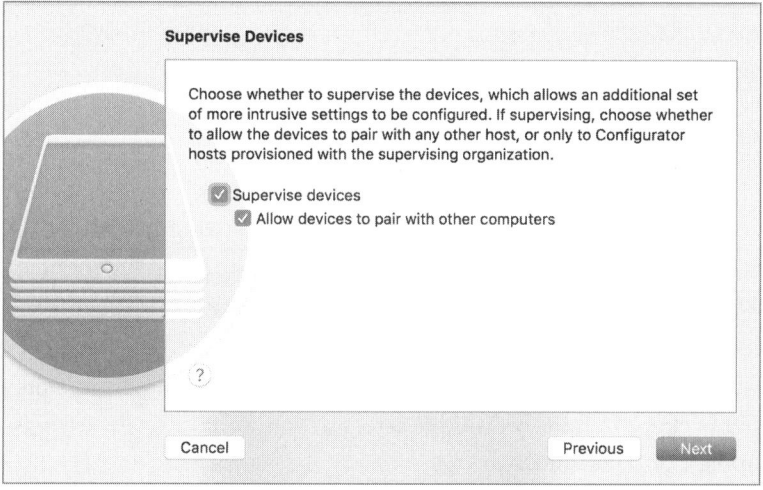

At the Assign to Organization pane, if you chose to supervise devices in the Supervise Devices pane, you must choose an organization to use for supervision. To add, import, export, and remove organizations, choose Apple Configurator 2 > Preferences, and then click the Organizations tab. If you chose to not supervise devices in the Supervise Devices pane, you can also choose None in the pop-up menu here.

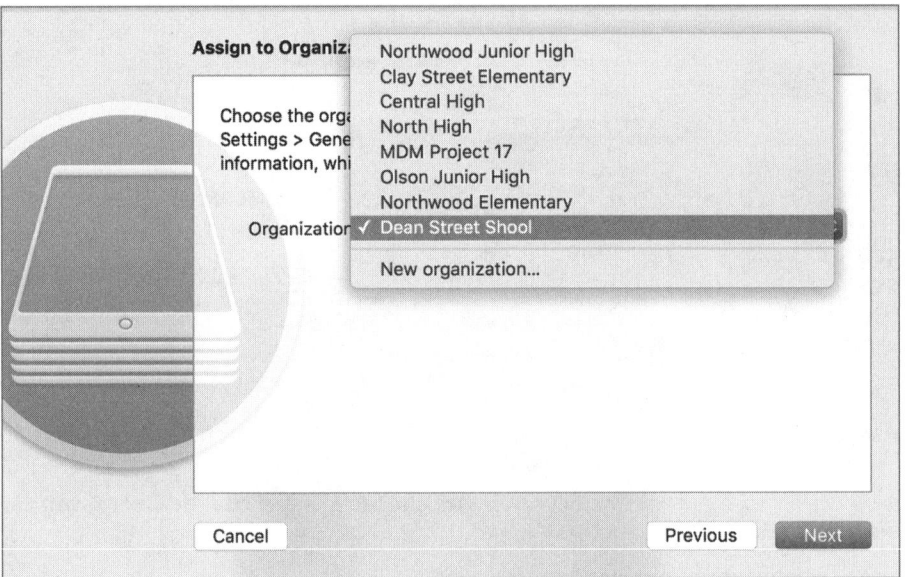

The final pane before the Prepare button becomes available is the Configure iOS Setup Assistant pane. When iOS Setup Assistant is prepared via Apple Configurator 2, you can skip the following screens:

- Language
- Region
- Location Services—If you skip this screen, the more private setting to disable Location Services will be the default, and the time zone will be set to that of Cupertino, CA. After setup, a user can use Settings > General > Date & Time to change the zone.
- Set Up—If you skip this screen, the user will not be allowed to restore from a previous iTunes or iCloud backup. Definitely skip this screen if you want to retain settings deployed via Apple Configurator 2.

- Apple ID—If you skip this screen, the user will not be prompted to sign in with their Apple ID. After setup, the user can still sign in to Apple services from the Settings app (unless you chose to install a profile restricting account modifications), but this makes configuration more difficult for the user. In other words, if you plan to allow the user to access iCloud or take advantage of managed VPP assignments to users and groups, you shouldn't skip this step.
- Zoom—If you skip this screen, the user can turn on Zoom after setup.
- Siri—If you skip this screen, the more private setting to disable Siri speech recognition will be the default.
- Diagnostics—If you skip this screen, the more private setting to turn off automatic diagnostics reporting to Apple and app analytics reporting to app developers will be the default.
- Passcode—If you skip this screen, the user will not be prompted to set a device passcode. After setup, the user can still set a passcode from the Settings app or be prompted to set a passcode via a profile requirement. Users should be encouraged to set a passcode to protect their information, so skipping this step is not recommended.

    TIP ▶ Keep in mind, if you're worried that users may forget their device passcodes, they can always be reset at a moment's notice via a push from an MDM service.

- Touch ID—If you skip this screen, the user will not be prompted to configure Touch ID. After setup, the user can still configure Touch ID from the Settings app (unless you chose to install a profile restricting account modifications), but this makes configuration more difficult for the user. Again, for nonshared devices, users should be encouraged to protect their information, so skipping this step is not recommended.
- Apple Pay—If you skip this screen, the user will not be prompted to set up Apple Pay. After setup, the user can still set up Apple Pay from the Settings app (unless you chose to install a profile restricting account modifications).

    NOTE ▶ To set up Apple Pay, the user must first sign in to her iCloud account. Further, Apple Pay is most secure if the user has set up Touch ID. In other words, if you're going to show Apple Pay during Setup Assistant, you should also show the Apple ID and Touch ID screens.

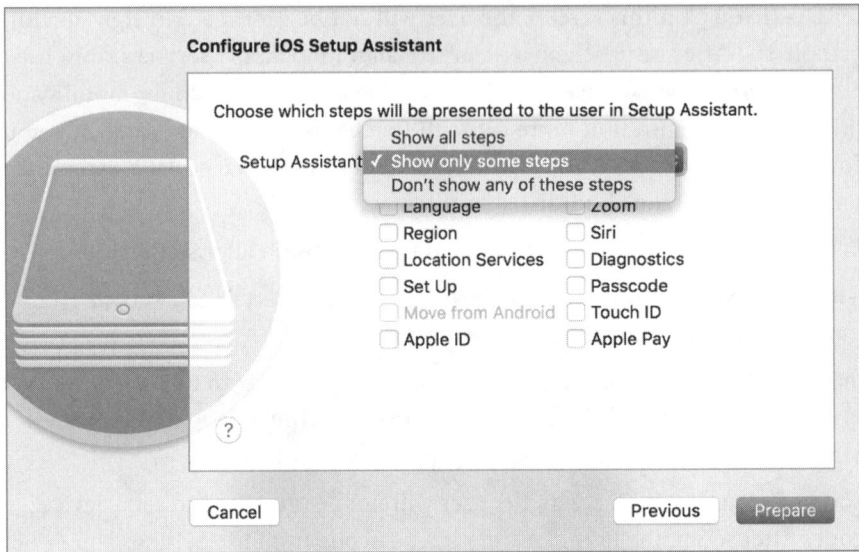

After the Prepare process is complete, you can distribute the device to the user. At Setup Assistant, the user must do the following:

- Choose and join a Wi-Fi network (unless the device has cellular service or Ethernet access via an Apple USB Camera Adapter that is connected to an Ethernet adapter)
- Read and agree to the terms and conditions
- Interact with the elements of Setup Assistant that are specified in the MDM record

Prepare Using Automated Enrollment

For devices that are enrolled in one of the Apple programs for device enrollment (the DEP or Apple School Manager), you can choose either Automated Enrollment or Manual.

Before choosing Automated Enrollment, ensure that the device is assigned an MDM server. The following figure illustrates that you can verify that a particular device is assigned to an MDM server in the DEP portal.

Additionally, and this is a step that many people new to the process forget, ensure that your MDM server is configured to prompt the device to enroll. You can configure this for a device or a device group that the device belongs to.

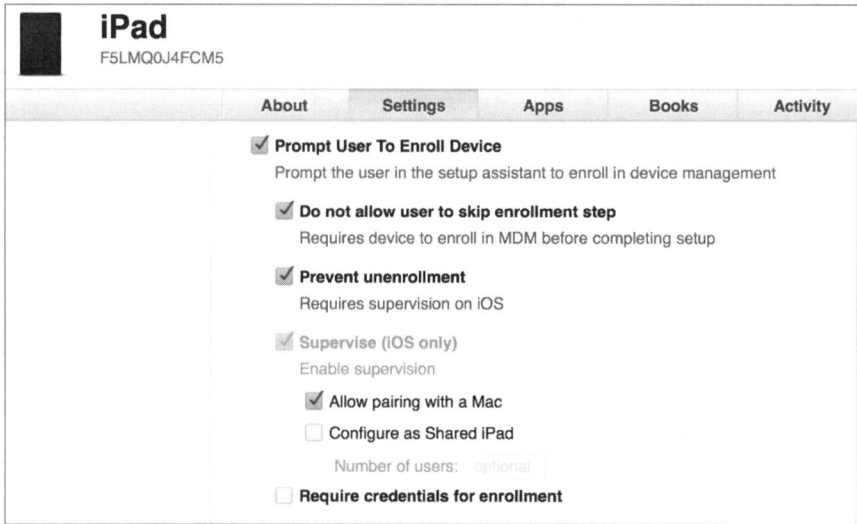

You can specify the options that are hidden from the user in Setup Assistant.

> **NOTE ▶** At the time of writing, you must deselect the checkbox for that option to hide it in Setup Assistant, which is contrary to the description of Setup Assistant Options.

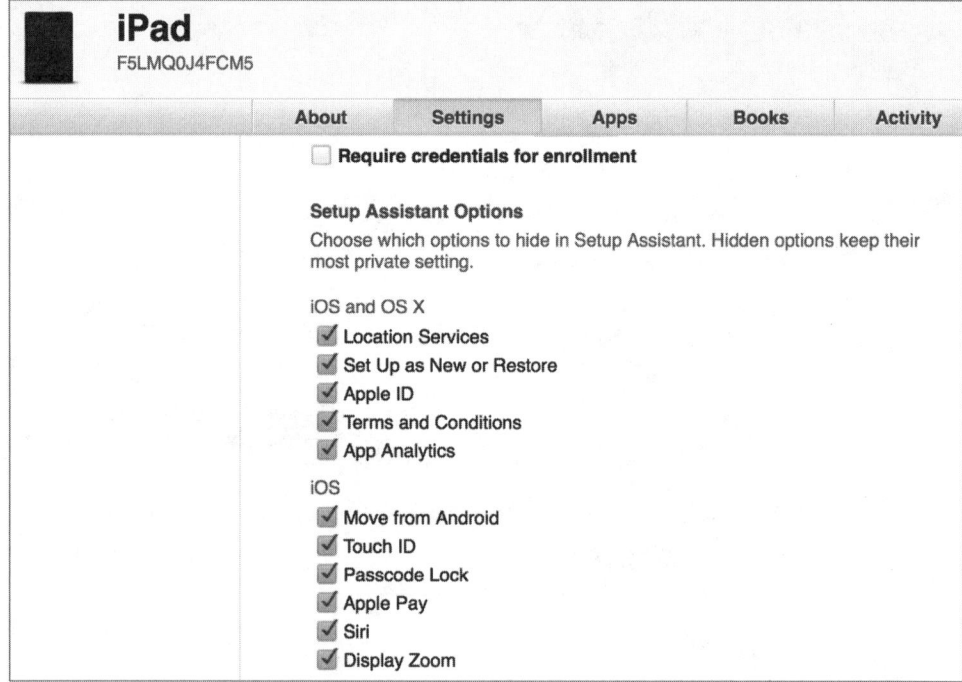

After you choose Automated Enrollment in the Prepare iOS Devices pane and then click Next, there are only a few steps left.

In the Automated Enrollment Profile pane, specify a configuration profile that contains only a Wi-Fi payload (of course, it must also have a General payload); if this profile contains other payloads, the preparation will fail with a message that "This profile can only be installed on a Supervised device." Just make sure to turn on the Auto Join option in the Wi-Fi settings of the profile to force the iOS device to automatically join the wireless network. Otherwise, the preparation will fail with a message about a network error. If you don't have such a configuration profile handy, just press Command-N to create a new configuration profile.

> **NOTE** ▶ This configuration profile does not remain on the device after it is enrolled in your MDM.

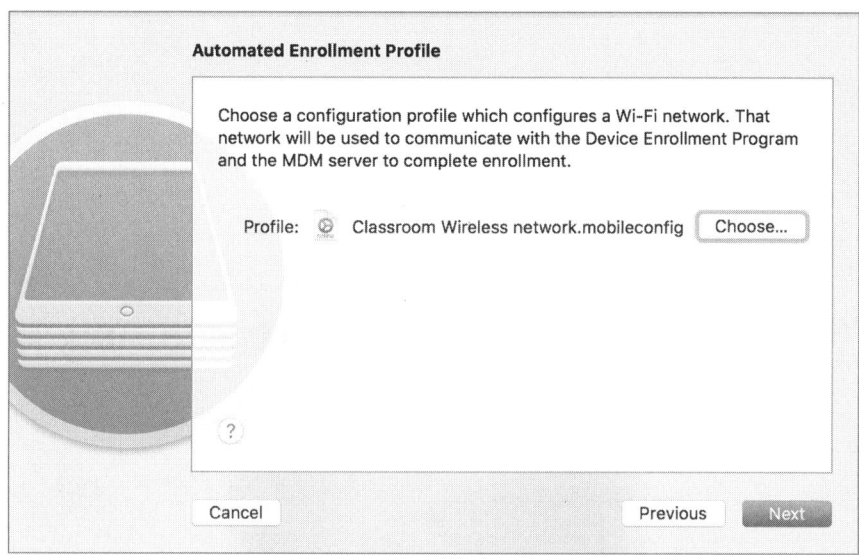

In the Automated Enrollment Credentials pane, you can provide credentials for enrolling with the MDM. If your MDM service doesn't require the device to provide credentials, then you can leave these fields blank, and the device will be enrolled but not associated with any particular user. If Profile Manager is the MDM, for example, you can later assign an enrolled device to a user.

▶ Click Prepare.

After the prepare is complete, it is ready for you to distribute to the user.

If you chose to hide all Setup Assistant options, the user will not even see Setup Assistant; the device will be enrolled and ready to use.

The following figure is an overview of the choices you'll make after you click Prepare:

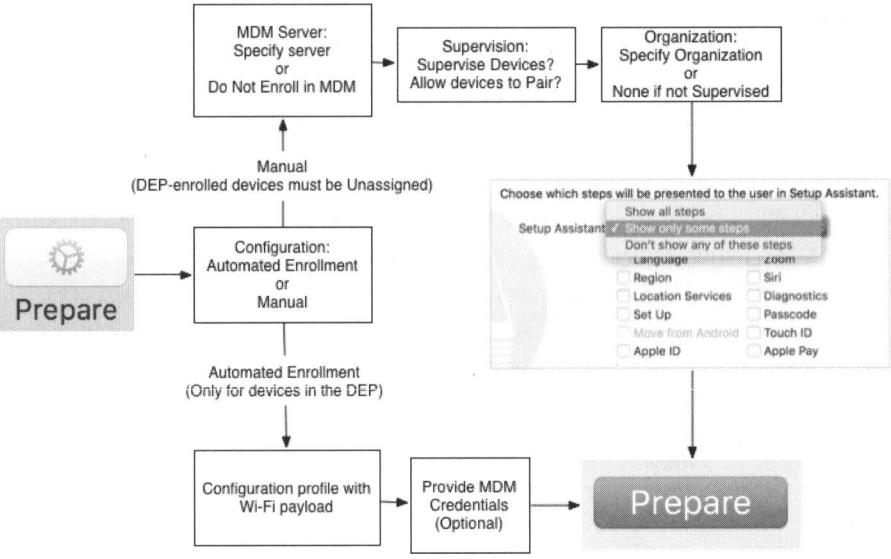

Verify Setup Assistant Customizations
Once you have defined your prepare options and iOS Setup Assistant customizations, verify enrollment functionality by preparing a device with Apple Configurator 2 and working through Setup Assistant. If you have defined user-based enrollment settings (in Profile Manager, this option is "Require credentials for enrollment"), a screen appears during setup requiring that you authenticate with a user to enroll.

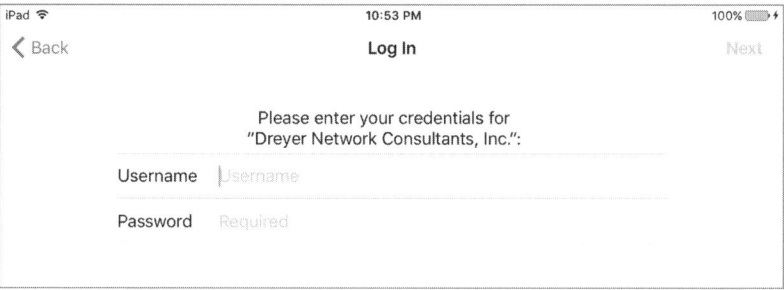

NOTE ▶ If you're having trouble successfully enrolling iOS devices during Setup Assistant, keep in mind that certain settings on your MDM service can prevent this ability. The default behavior of Profile Manager is to allow all users the ability to enroll any number of devices when configured during Setup Assistant. However, there are restrictions available in Profile Manager and other third-party MDM services that can prevent or limit user access to enrollment.

After Setup Assistant is complete, the device should immediately start receiving any pushed profiles, apps, or books as defined by the MDM service. You can also verify the setup and enrollment configuration in the Settings app by navigating to General > Device Management. There you will find the Remote Management configuration created during the Setup Assistant user enrollment.

With this workflow, be aware that users may be allowed to skip the iOS Setup Assistant enrollment, including with the following:

▶ Devices not enrolled in one of the Apple programs for device enrollment

▶ Devices enrolled in one of the Apple programs for device enrollment but not assigned to a server

▶ Devices enrolled in one of the Apple programs for device enrollment but not configured with a device or device group record that prompts the user to enroll

Further, even if users do complete the enrollment, unless the device was enrolled with the Automatic Enrollment option, they can always remove the Remote Management configuration from the Settings app. The only way to enforce device enrollment is via one of the Apple programs for device enrollment, as covered in Lesson 8, "Out-of-the Box Management via Apple Programs for Device Enrollment."

Prepare Apple TV Devices

To make Apple TV devices available as resources to your users, consider enrolling them in your MDM. Preparing an Apple TV device is similar to preparing any other kind of Apple TV. Apple TV supports Wi-Fi and Certificate payload settings only.

Connect your Apple TV to your Mac via a USB-C cable for Apple TV (fourth generation) or a Micro-USB cable for Apple TV (second or third generation), and then click Prepare.

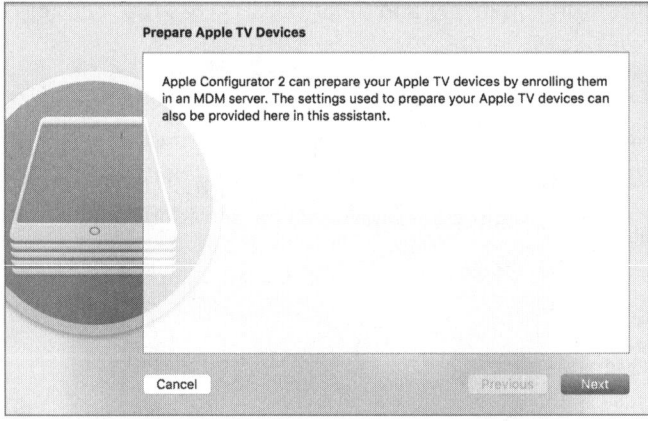

Similar to Manual enrollment, choose an MDM server, or choose to not enroll.

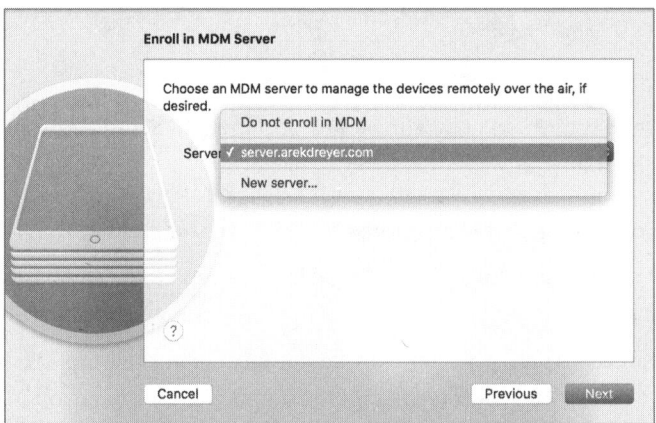

Unlike Manual enrollment, when enrolling an Apple TV, you need to provide an enrollment profile.

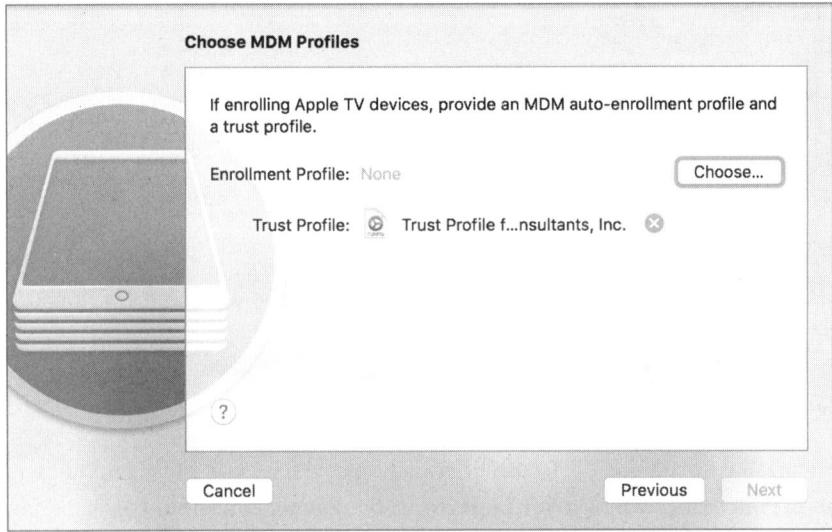

NOTE ▶ If you supply an enrollment profile when you define the server in Apple Configurator 2 preferences, you will not see this pane.

One workflow for this is to use Profile Manager a create a device group named "Apple TV," create an enrollment profile, name it "Apple TV Enrollment," and automatically add devices that use that enrollment profile to the Apple TV device group. Finally, click the Download button so you can specify that enrollment profile in Apple Configurator 2.

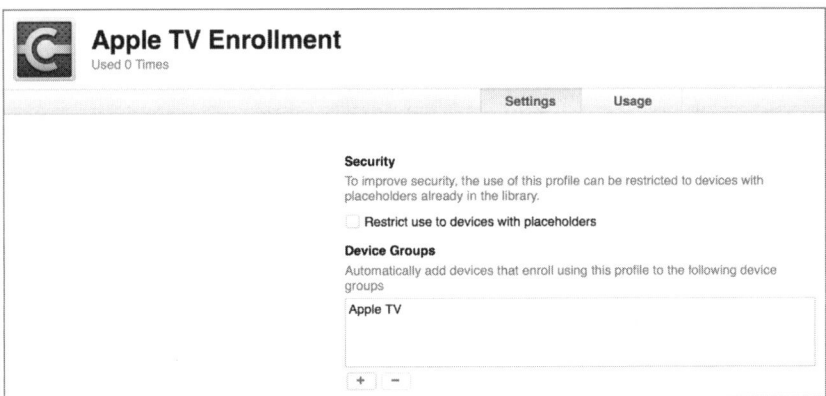

After you've chosen the enrollment profile, click Next.

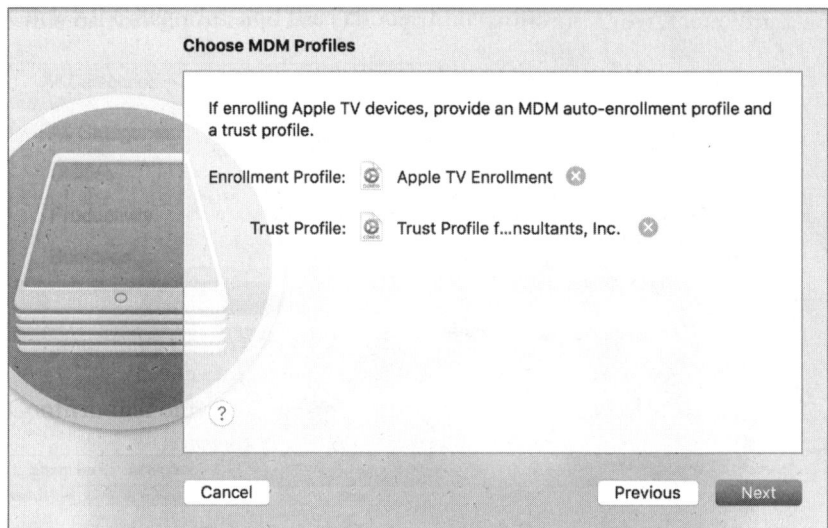

Choose a network for the Apple TV to use; if you choose Wi-Fi, you must provide a configuration profile that contains a Wi-Fi payload. Of course, you should already have one handy from preparing other iOS devices. If you choose Ethernet, the profile field disappears.

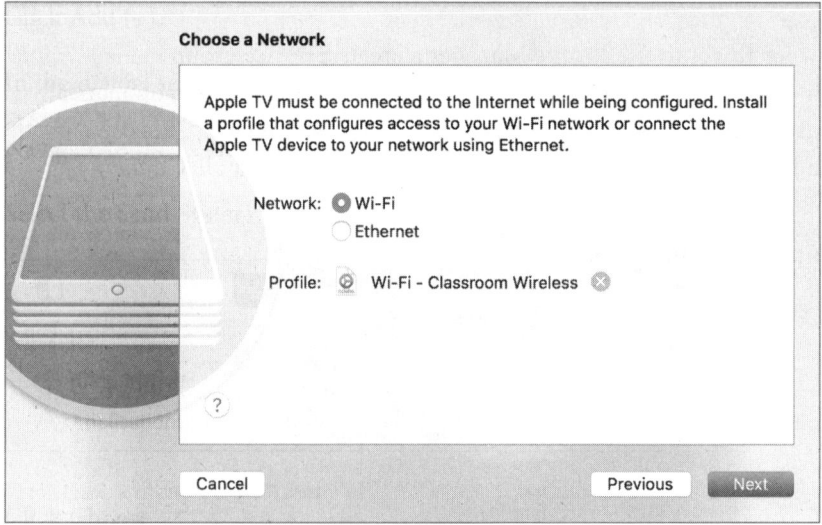

Finally, you will choose a language (at the time of this writing this might be a pop-up menu with no content; if so, don't bother clicking it) and privacy settings; then you can click Prepare.

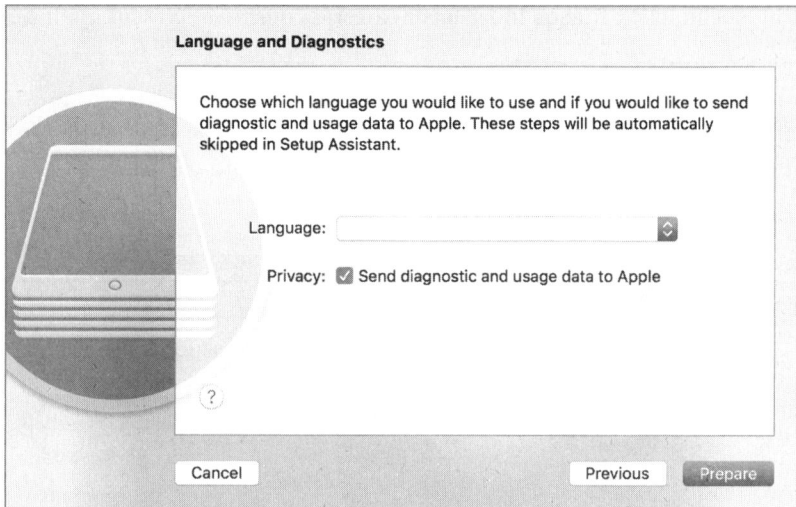

The Prepare action is pretty powerful, but you can make it even more powerful by applying the Prepare action to a blueprint that adds more functionality.

Reference 13.3
Create and Use Blueprints

Blueprints allow you to apply a predefined set of actions to a device or set of devices. Most of the things you can do with Apple Configurator 2 to an iOS device, you can do to a blueprint (you can't add documents to blueprints). When you have a blueprint ready, you can select one or more iOS devices, choose Actions > Apply, and then choose your blueprint.

If you have a number of complex workflows, it's possible to apply more than one blueprint on a group of iOS devices. For example, one workflow might use a set of blueprints to handle naming a group of iOS devices and another blueprint to enroll the devices in MDM.

To create your first blueprint, choose File > New Blueprint, edit the name of the blueprint, and then press Return to save the name change. Great, you have a blueprint, so now it's time to edit it. Double-click your blueprint, or choose File > Get Info.

Just like when you edit an iOS device, you can add apps and profiles and take actions such as modifying the formula for the device name, the wallpaper, and the apps in the Home Screen layout. Remember that the things you do to a blueprint don't actually do anything until you apply them to one or more iOS devices. This includes the buttons in the toolbar such as Prepare, Update, Back Up, as well as actions not in the toolbar, such as Actions > Restore from Backup and Actions > Advanced > Start Single App Mode.

While editing a blueprint, click Info in the sidebar to get an overview of what the blueprint does.

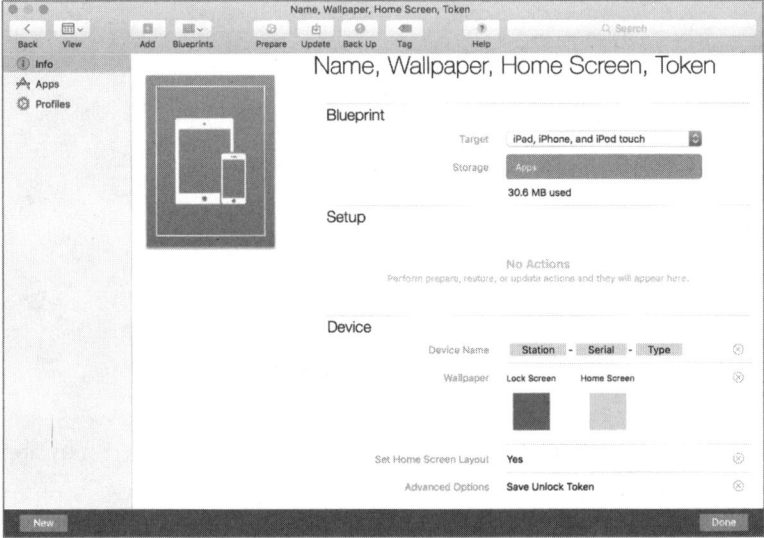

To stop editing a blueprint, click Done in the lower-right corner, or click Back in the upper-left corner. You don't need to save your changes; your changes are automatically saved as you work.

To apply a blueprint to one or more devices, select the devices, click the Blueprint button in the toolbar, and then choose the blueprint.

Reference 13.4
Organize Devices

You can apply tags to iOS devices and then use those tags to display only the devices with the tags you specify. Tagging and categorizing your iOS devices into device groups helps you locate and manage devices that require similar configuration.

Apply and Create Tags

Select one or more devices, and then click Tag in the toolbar.

Start entering text, and then press Tab to make what you type a tag. If it's not already a tag, the outline of a circle appears to the left of the tag (like "Cart2" in the following figure). If it's already a tag, that circle is solid. In addition to entering text, you can just select an existing tag. Choose Show All to show all the tags. When you're done creating and applying tags, press Return to save the changes.

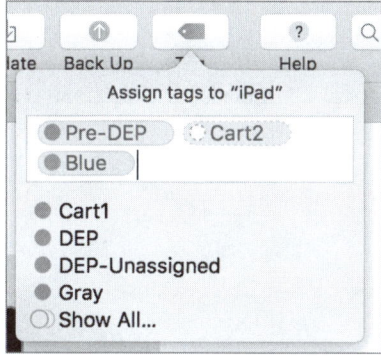

TIP You can edit the collection of tags that are available to assign by choosing Apple Configurator 2 > Preferences and then selecting Tags.

Search for Devices

The Search field is in the upper-right corner of the Apple Configurator 2 main window. Enter your tags in the Search field.

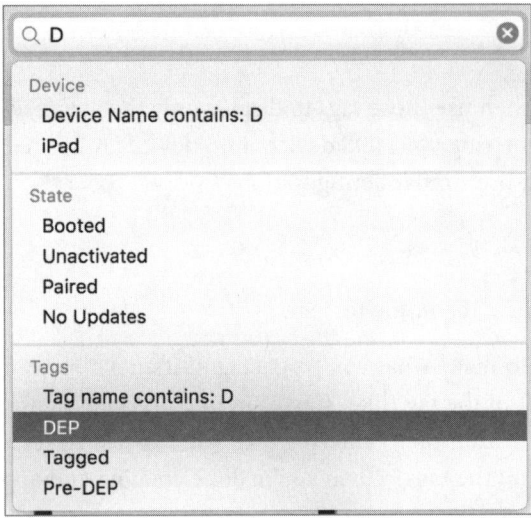

Note in the previous figure that you can search for devices based on tags as well as other characteristics, including the following:

- State: Activated, Booted, No Updates, Paired, Recovery, Supervised, Unactivated, Unpaired, Unsupervised, and Updates available
- Device name contains
- App name contains
- Profiles name contains
- iOS version contains

In the following figure, the devices that meet the criteria are displayed (with the tags Pre-DEP and Blue and a state of Activated).

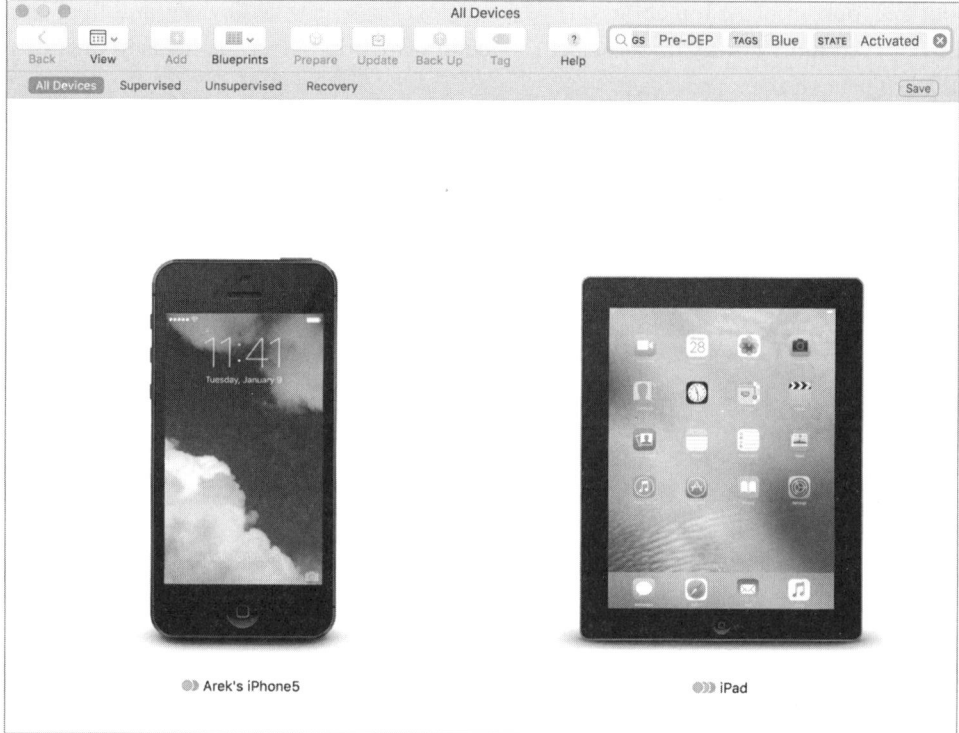

If you have a search combination that you can use again, click Save, and name it, and it will be added next to the default favorites group (by default this consists of All Devices, Supervised, Unsupervised, and Recovery).

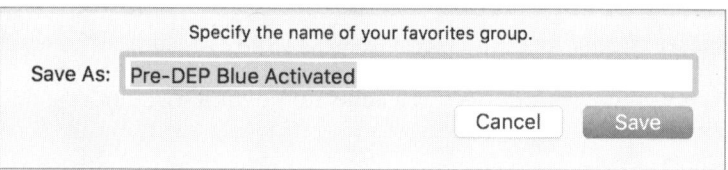

When you no longer need a favorites group, simply drag it from the toolbar and it disappears in a puff of smoke.

View or Export Device Information

To view information about a single device, select it and choose File > Get Info (or press Command-I).

But to export information about one or more devices, select the devices, and then choose Actions > Export > Info. If you select Device Information, select the fields to include in the export, and then click Save.

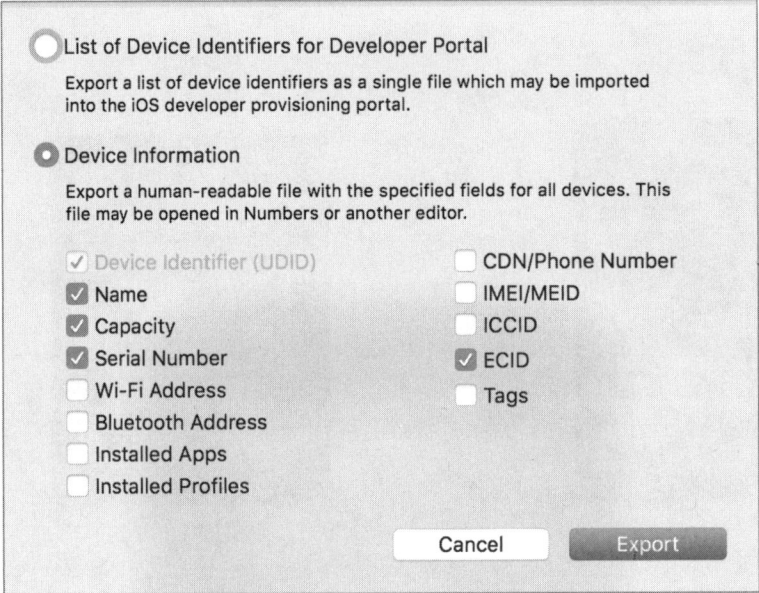

Provide a filename, location to save, and a format (CSV [comma separated values] or property list), and then click Save.

Sort Devices

Apple Configurator 2 offers flexibility in the way it allows you to view and sort devices.

You can change between viewing your devices as a collection or as a list.

No matter what view you select, you can choose the category that Apple Configurator 2 uses to sort the devices.

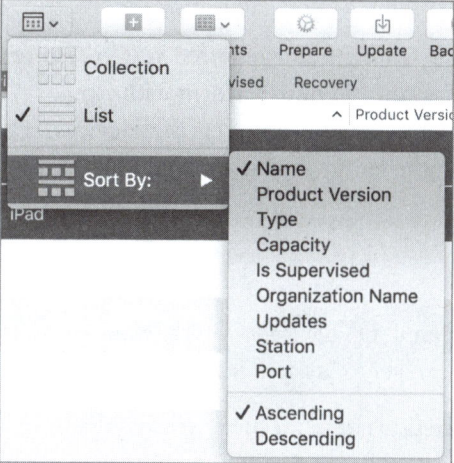

Reference 13.5 Back Up and Restore iOS Devices

Even though Apple Configurator 2 offers a lot more functionality than the legacy version of Apple Configurator to prepare devices before you distribute them to users, there are still a few reasons to restore devices from backup:

▸ Prepopulate apps with data, documents, and configuration

▸ Set a Restrictions Passcode (so that users cannot create a Restrictions Passcode before you specify one) but not a device passcode

> **TIP** After an iOS device is enrolled with your MDM service, you can deselect "Allow modifying restrictions," but only if the device is supervised.

For institution-owned personalized devices, it's best to allow the user to experience Setup Assistant. Resist the temptation to lock down everything possible; encourage your users to use their own Apple IDs, unless of course you have a good reason to do otherwise.

For institution-owned shared devices that are enrolled in one of the Apple programs for device enrollment (the DEP for business or Apple School Manager for schools), you can perform the prepare action with Automatic configuration, resulting in devices that completely skip Setup Assistant and are enrolled with your MDM service. Then the MDM service can apply a configuration profile to enforce a passcode requirement, among other configurations and restrictions.

> **MORE INFO** ▶ The legacy version of Apple Configurator required you to restore from backup to accomplish many tasks that you can now perform with Apple Configurator 2, including configuring a lock screen for unsupervised devices, setting the Home screen background, configuring the Home screen app and folder layout, and adding app documents.

Backup and Restore Introduction

The ability to restore the backup of a fully prepared iOS device to multiple devices in Apple Configurator 2 is the closest an administrator can get to "system imaging" an iOS device.

The concept of "system imaging" an iOS device is exciting for many seasoned administrators because it's a workflow they have probably been using for years to deploy PCs and Mac computers. However, it's simply not the same thing. Traditional system imaging techniques access the entire system volume, making a bit-for-bit copy of a configured system relatively straightforward.

Unfortunately, this simply isn't possible with iOS because of the security architecture of its design. iOS device storage is broken up into multiple partitions that each serve a different purpose, and in many cases these partitions are encrypted in such a way that they can be decrypted only on the original device. Creating a uniform image of an entire iOS device that can be restored to another device is not possible. Therefore, the closest you can get to "imaging" an iOS device is to restore the content of a backup to multiple devices.

However, there are a few things that you can accomplish with Apple Configurator 2 only via a restore of a backup, including the following:

- ▶ Preconfigure Restrictions (in Settings > Restrictions)
- ▶ Preconfigure the Restrictions Passcode (an encrypted backup is required)
- ▶ Preconfigure the answers to some of the screens of Setup Assistant (such as enable Siri and enable sending diagnostics and usage data)
- ▶ Prepopulate apps with documents and data (especially for apps that do not use iTunes document sharing)

MORE INFO ▶ You can find a more thorough list of iOS backup content in Apple Support article HT204136, "About backups in iCloud and iTunes."

Backup and Restore Limitations

There are many limitations and caveats when restoring a backup via Apple Configurator 2. For starters, understand that iOS backups do not contain any parts of the iOS system or apps. iOS backups are designed to save only documents and configuration information. (Backing up the iOS system and apps doesn't make much sense because you can always download them again for free from Apple's servers.)

NOTE ▶ See Apple Support document HT205199, "Preserve documents created with assigned apps and iOS 9," for information about how versions of iOS 9 prior to iOS 9.3 do not restore app data when a device is re-installed, so users of those iOS versions should store their documents using iCloud Drive or a similar service.

NOTE ▶ iOS backups do not include content that is synced via iTunes. This not only includes apps but also includes music, pictures, and movies. The exception to this is items still stored in the Camera Roll that have not yet been synced.

Another new feature of Apple Configurator 2 over the legacy Apple Configurator is that Apple Configurator 2 can create encrypted iOS backups. Unencrypted iOS backups cannot restore the keychain or any other saved secrets to a different iOS device, so if you use unecrypted backups, you can get interesting results. For example, if you make an unencrypted backup of an iOS device that has Restrictions turned on and is locked with a Restrictions Passcode, when you restore that unencrypted backup to a different iOS device, the Restriction settings are intact but the Restriction Passcode is missing, and the user will be prompted to set a four-digit Restrictions Passcode. To preserve the Restrictions Passcode, restore from an encrypted backup.

To save secrets (passcodes, Wi-Fi passwords, account authentication, Restrictions Passcode) to be restored to multiple iOS devices, you have to make an encrypted backup of the device: You select a device, choose Actions > Advanced > Enable Encrypted Backups, enter a password, and then click Set Password.

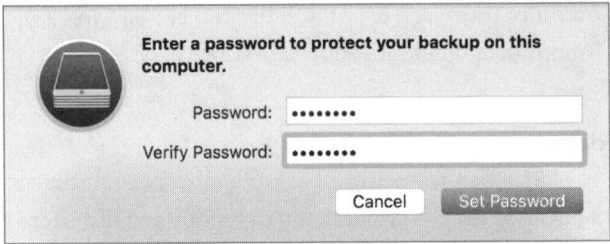

NOTE ▶ Select a secure password and remember it. There is no option to save this password in your keychain. You can open Keychain Access and then choose File > New Secure Note to manually create a secure note with this password.

Also, certain types of data are device specific. Even if the data is saved to the backup, when restored to another iOS device, it can't be decrypted. A relevant example is configuration profiles. Even though they are backed up, they are stored in a device-specific manner and will not appear when restored to a different iOS device.

Beyond system data, you must also consider that app data can be an issue when restored between different iOS devices. App developers may store the app data using methods that prevent it from being portable between iOS devices. Unfortunately, the only way to tell whether a specific app's data can be restored between different iOS devices is to test.

In fact, given the number of ways an iOS backup might not work when restored between devices, thorough testing is required. Specifically, if you plan to use Apple Configurator 2 to restore an iOS backup, you need to test the workflow between two different iOS devices. Configure and back up from one device, and then restore to another. Only then can you verify what will actually work in practice.

NOTE ▶ iOS backups are not compatible among different families of iOS devices. For example, an iPad backup cannot be restored to an iPhone.

NOTE ▶ iOS backups may not be compatible across different major versions of iOS. For best results, always back up and restore to iOS devices using the same iOS version.

NOTE ▶ You cannot make a backup of an iOS device that has not completed Setup Assistant.

You cannot use Apple Configurator 2 to restore a device into a state of being supervised; the legacy Apple Configurator workflow of supervising a device, making a backup of the supervised device, then restoring from the backup of the supervised device is not available for Apple Configurator 2.

Create iOS Backups for Restore

When setting up the template iOS device to be backed up for restore, make sure to complete and test all the settings in Apple Configurator 2 on the template iOS device.

Once you have prepared a template iOS device and it's ready for backup, connect it via USB to a Mac running Apple Configurator 2. Select the device. Remember that if you want an encrypted backup, you must choose Actions > Advanced > Enable Encrypted Backups. Then choose Back Up from the toolbar (or choose Actions > Back Up).

When complete, Apple Configurator 2 will automatically store the backup data in an appropriate location, with the name of the device. You can view the list of backups along with their encryption status and date, in the Backups tab after choosing Apple Configurator 2 > Preferences. If there is a backup you no longer need, you can select it and click Delete Backup.

Restore from an iOS Backup

Select one or more connected iOS devices, and then choose Actions > Restore from Backup.

> **TIP** The Restore command is different from the Restore from Backup command. The Restore command not only erases all content and settings but also restores the latest available version of iOS for that device. The Restore from Backup command restores a backup to the device.

Select the appropriate backup, and then click Restore.

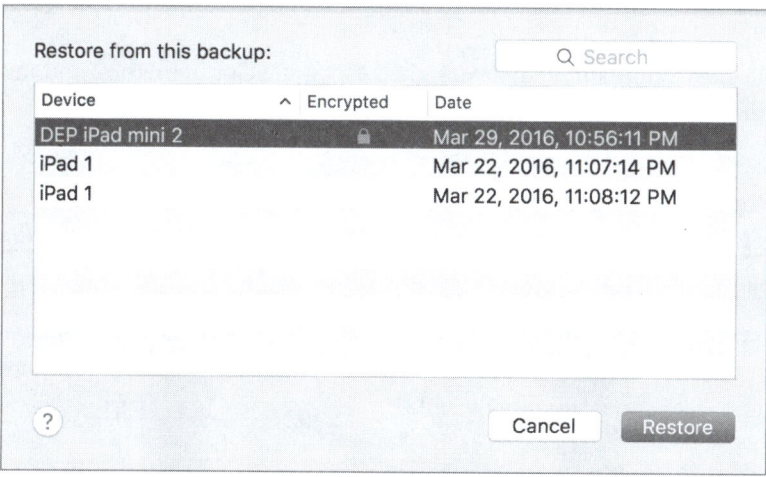

If the backup is encrypted, provide the password used for that backup, and then click Restore Backup.

Reference 13.6
Automate Device Management

You can use Automator and the command-line utility cfgutil to harness the power of Apple Configurator, including sharing workflows with nonadministrative staff without needing to train them to use Apple Configurator.

Install Apple Configurator Automation Tools
On your computer running Apple Configurator 2, choose Apple Configurator 2 > Install Automation Tools, and then at confirmation dialog, click Confirm.

This automatically adds Automator actions designed for Apple Configurator 2 and installs the cfgutil command-line utility.

Use Apple Configurator 2 Automator Actions
Automator comes preinstalled with OS X, right in the /Applications folder. Use Spotlight to open Automator, select Workflow, and click Choose.

The actions that have the Apple Configurator 2 icon are automatically available in Automator after you install Apple Configurator 2. In the Search field, enter configurator so the Apple Configurator 2 actions are more visible.

Reference 13.6 Automate Device Management 557

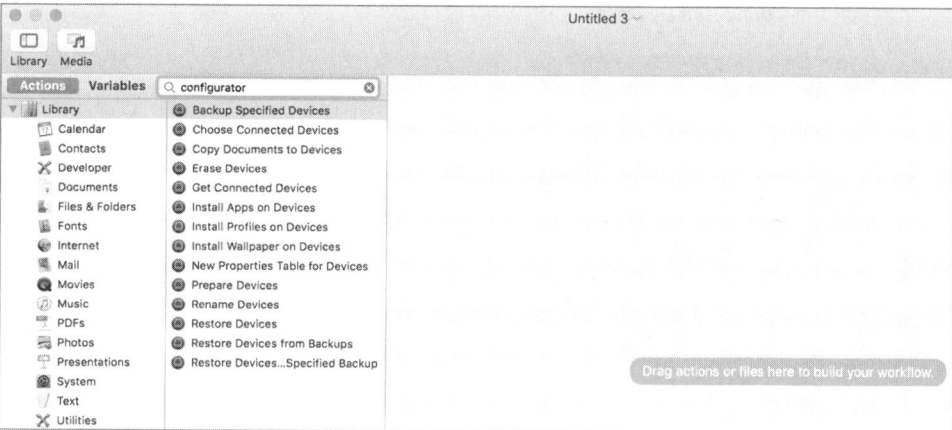

Drag actions to the right to add the action to the workflow.

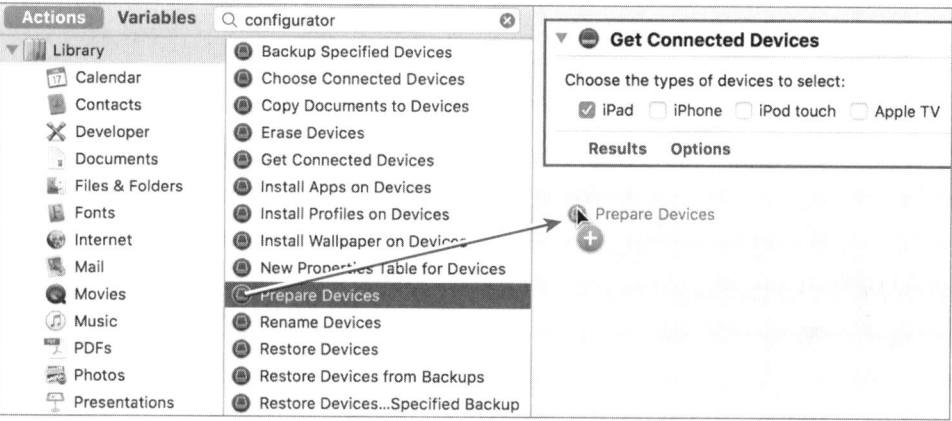

Some actions require you to manually enter information, rather than choose it from a pop-up menu.

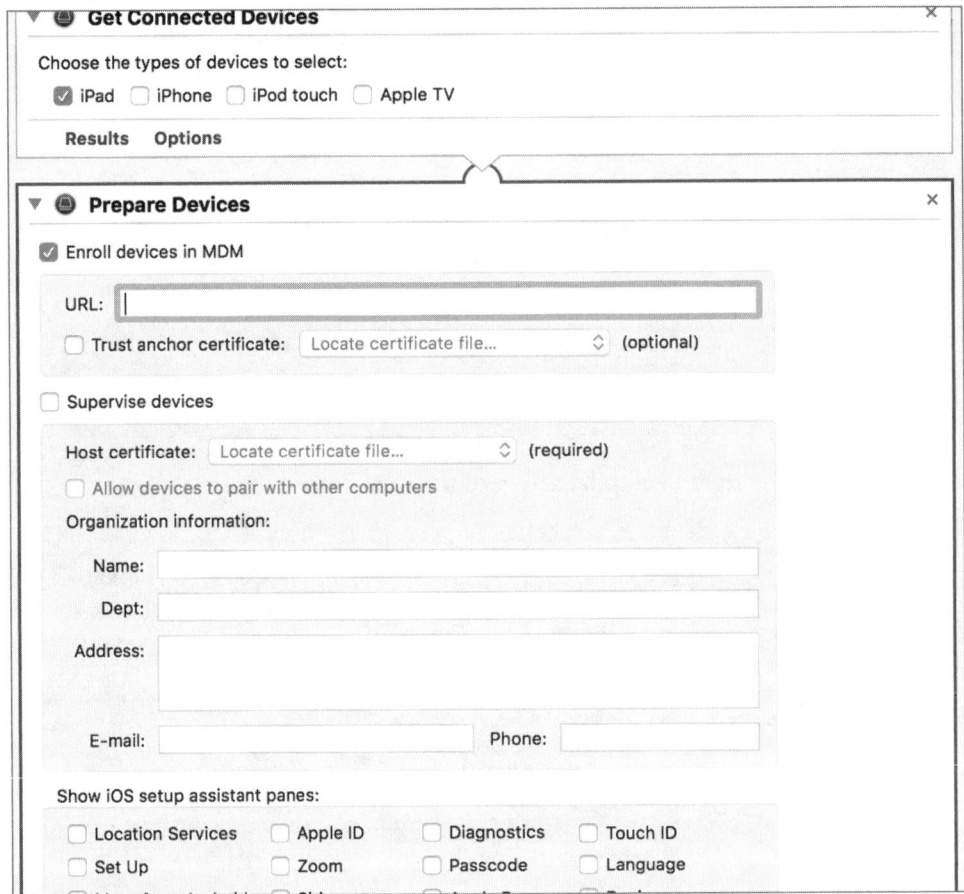

When you run the workflow, the actions are run sequentially, starting with the action at the top of the workflow list.

> **MORE INFO** ▶ See https://configautomation.com/ for more information about using Automator with Apple Configurator 2, including examples of using Xcode to create new Automator actions specifically for use with Apple Configurator 2.

Export Apple Configurator 2 Automator Actions

Here's where Automator becomes even more useful: You can save your workflow as a standalone app, which you can distribute to other people in your organization. Choose File > Save, navigate to your desired location on disk, assign a relevant name, click the File Format pop-up menu and choose Application, and then click Save.

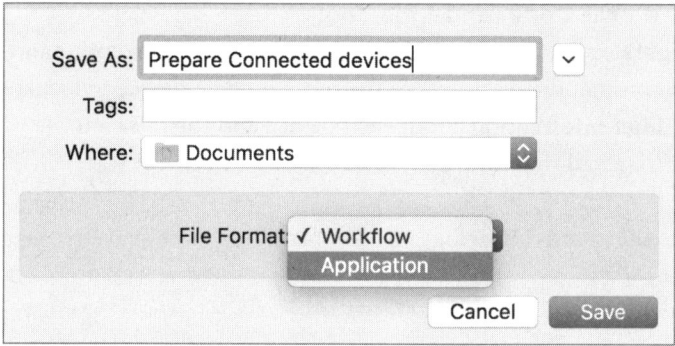

After you distribute the app, another person can open the app to run the workflow.

Cart2.app

If you make this app available on the Internet or an internal web service for download, you need to take extra steps to allow this app to be run on another Mac that has the default Gatekeeper security settings, which is "Allow apps downloaded from: Mac App Store and identified developers." Sign the app with an Apple Developer ID Application identity. Choose File > Export, click the Code Sign pop-up menu, choose your Developer ID Application identity, and then click Save.

> **MORE INFO** ▶ To find out more about Gatekeeper, see Reference 16.3, "Understand Application Security," in *Apple Pro Training Series: OS X Support Essentials 10.11: Supporting and Troubleshooting OS X El Capitan*, and see Apple Support article HT202491, "OS X: About Gatekeeper."

> **NOTE** ▶ To find out more about obtaining an Apple Developer ID identity, see https://developer.apple.com/.

> **NOTE** ▶ If you manually copy this app to another Mac in your organization via AirDrop or a removable disk like a flash drive, Gatekeeper will not object.

Use the Apple Configurator 2 Command-Line Tool

Installing the Apple Configurator 2 automation tools also installs the cfgutil command-line tool, which you can use in command-line scripts to further automate device management. An example script could gather information about each device and then use another command-line tool called curl to upload that information to a web service.

> **TIP** When using cfgutil in a script, refer to its full path; it is located at /usr/local/bin/cfgutil.

Exercise 13.1
Create Configuration Profiles with Apple Configurator 2

▶ **Prerequisite**

▶ Exercise 2.1, "Configure Your Client Mac"

▶ Exercise 12.1, "Get Apple Configurator 2"

Challenge

Use Apple Configurator 2 to create two configuration profiles. One should be a simple configuration profile that autojoins iOS devices to the classroom Wi-Fi network or a Wi-Fi network of your choosing.

The other configuration profile should be applied to iOS devices that will be used in a shared-use environment. Disable FaceTime and Game Center, enforce a passcode policy, and define a Lock screen message.

These two configuration profiles should be saved to the desktop of the client Mac for use in later exercises.

Considerations

Like with Profile Manager and other MDM solutions, creating configuration profiles with Apple Configurator 2 means you can apply settings to many devices at one time.

Configuration profiles can contain one or many payloads.

Many configuration profile payloads and their respective settings will take effect only on supervised devices. If applied to an unsupervised iOS device, the settings listed as (supervised only) will be ignored.

Solution

Create a Configuration Profile Using the Wi-Fi Payload

1   On your client Mac, if necessary, open Apple Configurator 2.

2   Choose File > New Profile.

3   In the Name field for the General payload, enter Wi-Fi Profile.

    NOTE ► Like with profiles made using Profile Manager or other MDM solutions, the General payload is always mandatory.

4   In the Description field, enter descriptive text, such as Joins the iOS device to the Wi-Fi network.

5   For Security, select With Authorization, and enter the password profilepw.

    NOTE ► In a production environment, it is always best practice to use a strong password.

6   Leave all the other settings at their defaults.

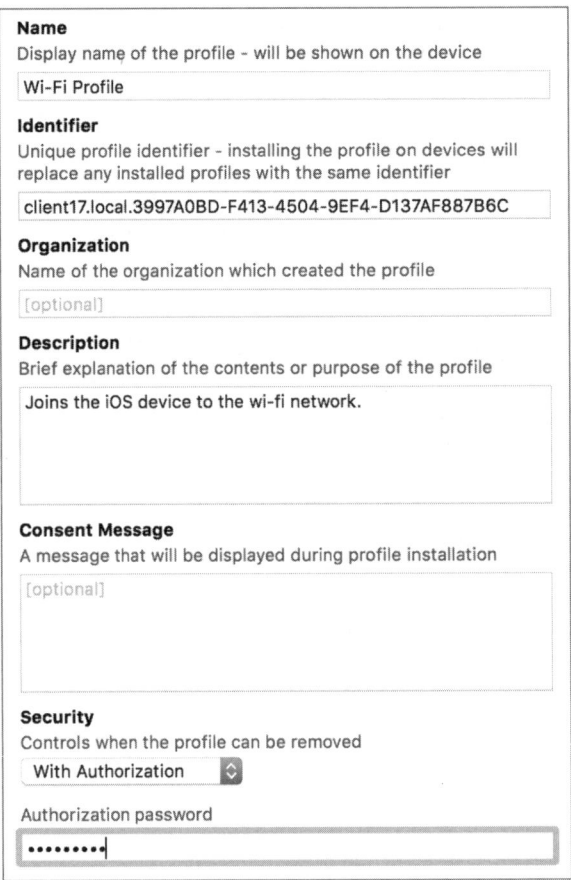

7   In the payload sidebar, choose Wi-Fi, and then click Configure.

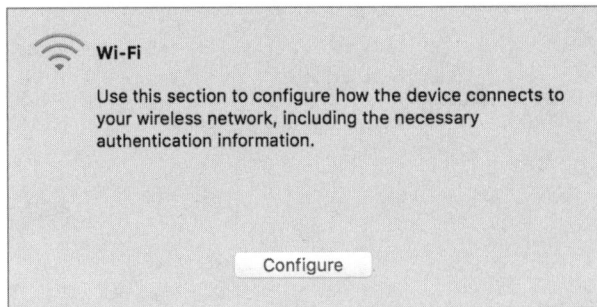

8   Enter the name of your Wi-Fi network in the SSID field. In an instructor-led environment, this may be Classroom Wireless.

Note the red arrow next to the SSID field and the dimmed [required] text in the field. Both of these will appear in any configuration profile fields when they are mandatory.

9   Under Security Type, select WPA/WPA2 Personal.

10 Enter the password. In an instructor-led environment, this may be student!.

11 Choose File > Save. Leave the name as Wi-Fi Profile, and select Desktop from the Where pop-up menu.

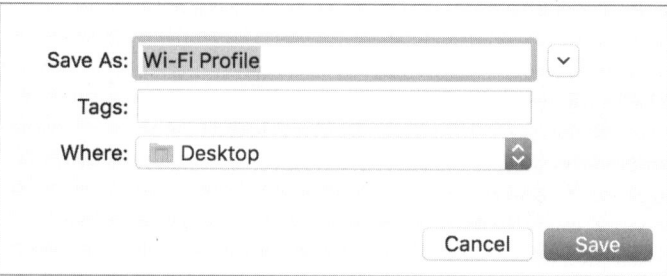

12 Click Save.

13 Close the Wi-Fi Profile window.

Create a Complex Configuration Profile for iOS Device Management

1 Choose File > New Profile.

2 In the Name field for the General payload, enter AC2 Project *n* Management, where *n* is your student number.

3 For Security, select With Authorization, and enter the password profilepw.

4 Leave all the other settings at their defaults.

5 In the payload sidebar, select Restrictions, and click Configure.

6 Under Functionality, deselect Allow FaceTime and Allow iMessage (supervised only).

Observe that the Allow iMessage restriction will take effect only on supervised iOS devices. Many restrictions require supervision. It is best practice to always supervise organization-owned iOS devices.

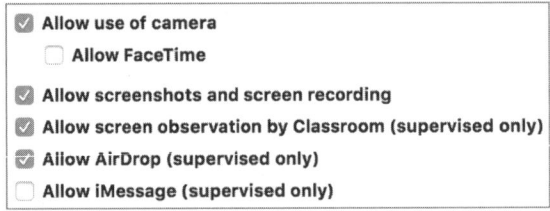

7 Click the Apps tab, and deselect "Allow use of Game Center (supervised only)."

8 Click the Passcode payload, and click Configure.

9 For "Minimum passcode length," select 6, and leave all the other settings at their defaults.

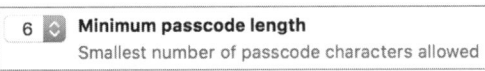

10 In the payload sidebar, scroll to Lock Screen Message, and then click Configure.

Observe that the entire Lock Screen Message payload will take effect only on supervised devices.

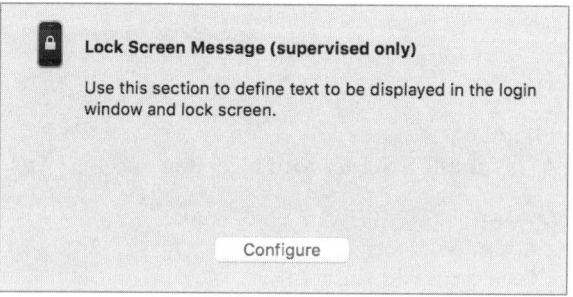

11 In the "If Lost, Return to…" Message field, enter information such as Adam Karneboge at adam@karneboge.com or your name, email, and/or phone number.

12 Under Asset Tag information, for demonstration purposes, enter text such as Asset 00001.

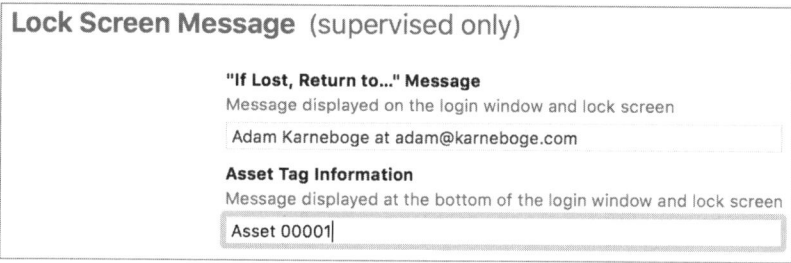

13 In the payload sidebar, scroll and observe that Lock Screen Message, Passcode, and Restrictions all say 1 Payload Configured.

14 Choose File > Save. Change the name to something descriptive such as Restrictions Passcode Lock Screen, denoting the payloads configured, and select Desktop from the Where pop-up menu.

15 Click Save.

16 Close the Restrictions Passcode Lock Screen configuration profile window.

In this exercise, you created two configuration profiles. One contained only the Wi-Fi payload and can be used to join your iOS device to a Wi-Fi network. The other profile contained multiple payloads that may often be used for an iOS device deployed in a shared-use environment, such as a cart in an educational organization.

Exercise 13.2
Prepare an iOS Device Using Automated Enrollment via the DEP

> **Prerequisite**
> - Exercise 4.1, "Prepare Your Mac for OS X Server for El Capitan"
> - Exercise 4.2, "Install OS X Server for El Capitan"
> - Exercise 4.3, "Configure OS X Server for El Capitan"
> - Exercise 6.2, "Create, Download, and Install Profiles for Users and Groups"
> - Exercise 7.1, "Enable Device Management"
> - Exercise 8.1, "Enroll with Apple Deployment Programs"
> - Exercise 8.2, "Configure Profile Manager for the Device Enrollment Program"
> - Exercise 12.1, "Get Apple Configurator 2"
> - Exercise 13.1, "Create Configuration Profiles with Apple Configurator 2"

Challenge

Assign your iOS device to your MDM server in the Apple Deployment Programs site. Configure the enrollment settings for the device, and then prepare it using the Prepare action in Apple Configurator 2. Use automated enrollment, and enroll the device via the DEP using credentials of a member of a group with web clips. Inspect the effects of this exercise.

Considerations

While you are performing this exercise on only one iOS device, Apple Configurator 2 can perform the Prepare action on as many devices as you can physically connect using USB.

Solution

Assign the iOS Device to Your MDM Server

Before using automated enrollment via Apple Configurator 2's Prepare action, you need to assign the iOS device to your MDM server using the Apple Deployment Programs site.

1. Use your server computer to log in to the Apple Deployment Programs site in Safari (https://deploy.apple.com) using your DEP administrator account with two-step verification.

2. In the sidebar, select Device Enrollment Program, and then select Manage Devices.

3. For Step 1, select Choose Devices By: Serial Number.

4. Enter the serial number of your iOS device (the iOS device must be eligible for the DEP).

   To identify the serial number, look at the back of the iOS device, or if your iOS device is on and accessible, choose Settings > General > About.

5. For Step 2, Choose Action, leave the pop-up menu at Assign to Server.

6. Click the Choose MDM Server pop-up menu, and choose your server.

7. Click OK.

8. In the Assignment Complete pane, click OK.

Adjust the Enrollment Settings, and Add the New DEP Placeholder Record to the DEP Devices Group

1. On your server Mac, in Safari, open the Profile Manager administration portal (https://server*n*.local/profilemanager, where *n* is your student number), and then authenticate with your server's local administrator credentials.

2. In the Profile Manager sidebar, select Devices.

3. At the bottom of the Devices section, click the Refresh button.

4. Confirm that there is a new placeholder record for the iOS device you just assigned to your server. The name of the placeholder will vary based on the type of iOS device you assigned to your MDM server in the Apple Deployment Programs site.

5. In the Profile Manager sidebar, select Device Groups, and then select DEP Devices.

6. Click the Settings tab.

7. If necessary, under Enrollment Settings, scroll down to Setup Assistant Options, and deselect Apple ID.

8   Click the Add (+) button, and choose Add Devices.

9   For the iOS device you just assigned to your MDM server, click Add.

10 Click Done.

11 Click Save.

Erase All Content and Settings

If your iOS device is at the Welcome screen, skip to the next section.

1   On your iOS device, if necessary, slide at the "slide to unlock" screen.

2   If necessary, enter the passcode.

3   Open Settings.

4   Navigate to General > Reset.

5   Tap Erase All Content and Settings.

6   If your iOS device has a passcode, enter the passcode.

7   In the confirmation dialog, tap Erase.

8   In the extra confirmation dialog, tap Erase.

Wait while the iOS device erases all content and settings.

Use the Prepare Action

The Prepare action is unique to Apple Configurator 2 and allows you to quickly prepare one or many iOS devices at one time. It can also be added to a blueprint for a more powerful workflow, as demonstrated in Exercise 13.3, "Create and Apply Blueprints." However, in this exercise, you will use it without a blueprint.

1 On your client Mac, if necessary, open Apple Configurator 2.

2 Click Get Started.

3 Connect your iOS device to your client Mac using the appropriate cable for your device.

Your iOS device should appear in the Apple Configurator 2 All Devices window with an image of it at the Setup Assistant screen.

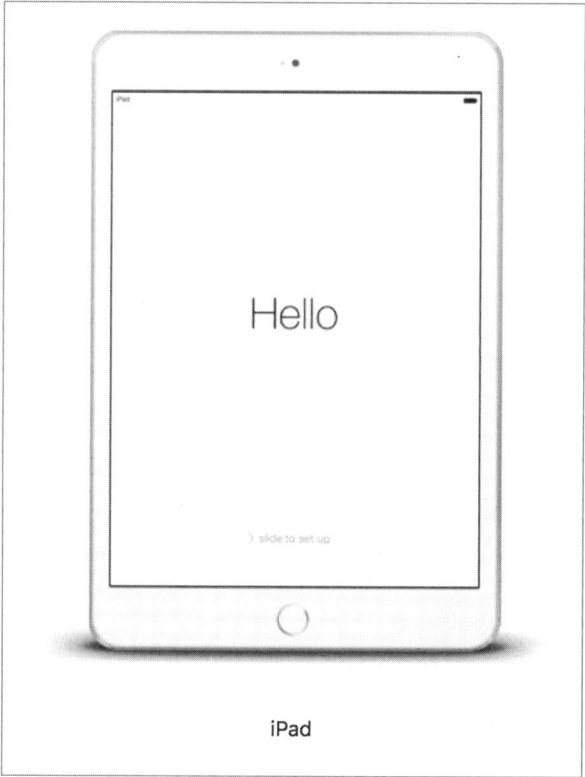

4 Select your iOS device, and click the Prepare action in the toolbar.

5 For Configuration, select Automated Enrollment, and then click Next.

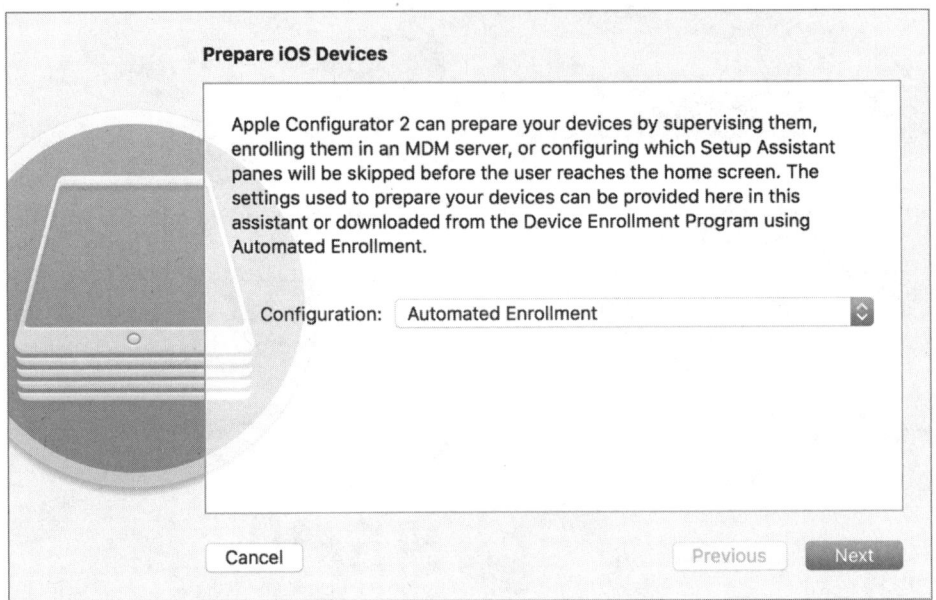

6 In the Automated Enrollment Profile window, click Choose. Select Wi-Fi Profile that you created in the previous exercise, and then click Open.

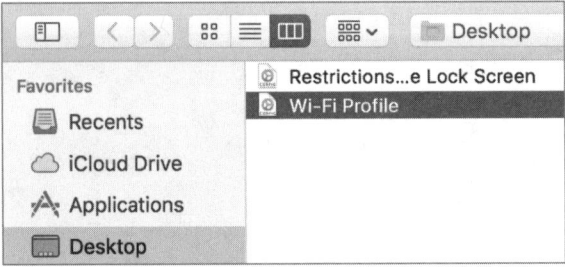

As automated enrollment uses the Device Enrollment Program (DEP) to enroll with your MDM server, the iOS device must automatically be online for Apple Configurator 2 to prepare your device successfully.

7 Click Next.

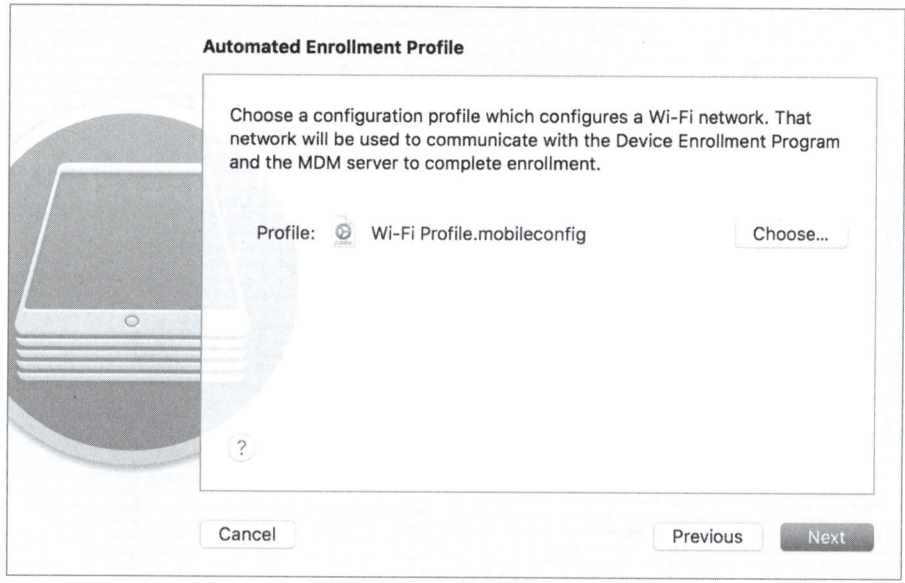

8   In the Automated Enrollment Credentials window, enter the following credentials, and click Prepare:

▶ User Name: todd

▶ Password: net

It is important to remember that the Enrollment settings for the DEP Devices group on your MDM server require credentials for enrollment. It is equally important to note that in the scenario that multiple devices were selected and prepared using this action, all the devices will be associated with the user todd, which may not be optimal. For the purposes of this exercise, you will continue down this path.

9   Apple Configurator 2 will go through a series of steps that will enroll your device using the DEP with your MDM server, supervise it wirelessly, and take it past the setup screen automatically.

10 Apple Configurator 2 will show an image representative of your iOS device at the Home screen.

Observe the Effects of the Prepare Action Using Automated Enrollment

As Apple Configurator 2 prepared your iOS device using the DEP, it also supervised the device over the air and enrolled it with your MDM server using a user that is a member of a group with some settings. This can be powerful for mass deployments using USB hubs or carts. Let's observe the effects of this action.

1 On your iOS device, slide at the "slide to set up screen," and tap Enable Location Services.

2 Press the Sleep/Wake button on your iOS device to return it to the lock screen.

3 On your iOS device, press the Home button, and observe the text on the Lock screen, noting that the iPad is managed by your organization.

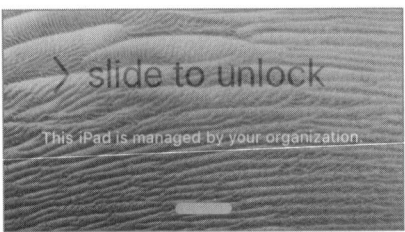

4 Slide at the "slide to unlock" screen, and observe the two web clips that are present on the second screen.

    Todd Porter is a member of the Marketing group, which has a configuration profile using the Web Clips payload on your MDM server.

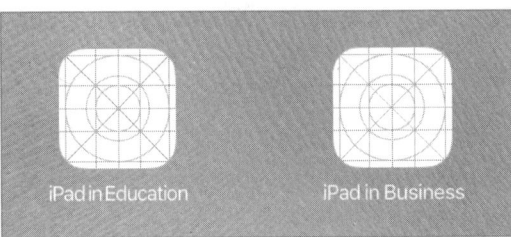

5 Navigate to Settings > General > Profiles & Device Management. Notice that both Remote Management and Wi-Fi Profile are present.

6 Tap Remote Management. Observe the two web clips in the Contains section.

7 Tap Profile, and then tap Wi-Fi Profile.

The Wi-Fi profile was installed by Apple Configurator 2; thus, it is not part of the settings contained in the Remote Management profile as you saw previously.

8 Tap Delete Profile.

You are prompted for a password. This is because you defined a password for this profile in Exercise 13.1, "Create Configurator Profiles with Apple Configurator 2."

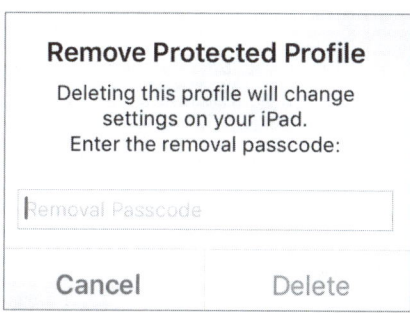

9 Tap Cancel, and then tap Back.

10 Tap General, and then scroll and tap About.

11 Notice the message under the device name reinforcing that the device is supervised by your organization.

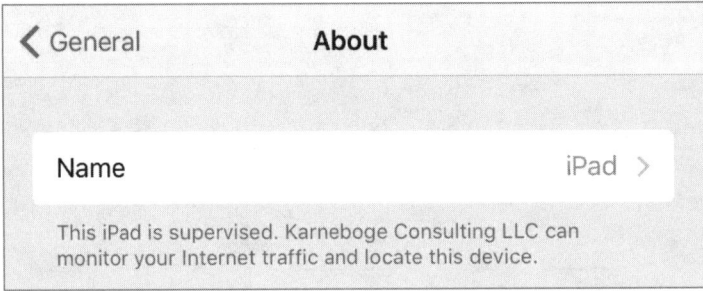

Unassign the iOS Device

Remove the iOS device from being assigned to your MDM server.

1 Use your server computer to log in to the Apple Deployment Programs site in Safari (https://deploy.apple.com) using your DEP administrator account with two-step verification.

2 Select Device Enrollment Program in the sidebar.

3 Click in the Search for Serial Number field.

4 Enter the iOS device's serial number in the Search field.

5 Press Return to search.

6 Click the Assigned To pop-up menu, and then choose Unassigned.

7 Click Reassign to unassign your iOS device.

Unenroll Your iOS Device and Remove the Placeholder

1 In the Profile Manager administration portal sidebar, select Devices, and then select your iOS device.

2   Click the Remove (–) button, and then click Unenroll.

3   At the bottom of the Devices section, click the Refresh button.

4   Select the placeholder record, click the Remove (–) button, and then click Remove.

5   Close the Profile Manager administration portal window.

Erase All Content and Settings

1   On your iOS device, if necessary, slide at the "slide to unlock" screen.

2   If necessary, enter the passcode.

3   Open Settings.

4   Navigate to General > Reset.

5   Tap Erase All Content and Settings.

6   If your iOS device has a passcode, enter the passcode.

7   In the confirmation dialog, tap Erase.

8   In the extra confirmation dialog, tap Erase.

In this exercise, you assigned your device to your MDM server and added it to the DEP Devices group. You ensured that the iPad was wiped, and then you prepared it using Apple Configurator 2's Prepare action. You set the Prepare action to use automated enrollment and prepared the device using Todd Porter's credentials. During the course of these steps, Apple Configurator 2 used the DEP to enroll the iOS device with your MDM server and associated the device with Todd Porter. It also supervised the device. It is important to understand that while this action was done to only one iOS device, you could have performed it on many iOS devices with ease.

You inspected the effects of this action and then unassigned the iOS device from your MDM server, unenrolled it from your MDM server, and wiped it for use in the following exercises.

Exercise 13.3
Create and Apply Blueprints

▶ **Prerequisite**

- ▶ Exercise 4.1, "Prepare Your Mac for OS X Server for El Capitan"
- ▶ Exercise 4.2, "Install OS X Server for El Capitan"
- ▶ Exercise 4.3, "Configure OS X Server for El Capitan"
- ▶ Exercise 6.2, "Create, Download, and Install Profiles for Users and Groups"
- ▶ Exercise 7.1, "Enable Device Management"
- ▶ Exercise 8.1, "Enroll with Apple Deployment Programs"
- ▶ Exercise 8.2, "Configure Profile Manager for the Device Enrollment Program"
- ▶ Exercise 12.1, "Get Apple Configurator 2"
- ▶ Exercise 13.1, "Create Configuration Profiles with Apple Configurator 2"

Challenge

Create two blueprints in Apple Configurator 2. In the first blueprint, use the Prepare action to supervise your iOS device with your organization, but do not enroll with an MDM server. Apply a custom tag, a custom device name, a custom Home screen layout, a custom wallpaper, and both configuration profiles created in Exercise 13.1.

Set up your second blueprint in the same manner as your first blueprint. Supervise with your already created organization, and enroll with your already defined MDM server simulating an out-of-the-box experience. Demonstrate MDM Lost Mode, a feature that requires an MDM server and a supervised iOS device.

Considerations

While you are applying blueprints to only one iOS device, the power of Apple Configurator 2's blueprints can be realized when applying them to as many devices as you can physically connect using USB.

While creating blueprints, your iOS device does not need to be connected to the computer running Apple Configurator 2.

Solution

Erase All Content and Settings

If your iOS device is at the Welcome screen, skip to the next section.

1   Press the Home button.

2   Open Settings.

3   Navigate to General > Reset.

4   Tap Erase All Content and Settings.

5   If your iOS device has a passcode, enter the passcode.

6   In the confirmation dialog, tap Erase.

7   In the extra confirmation dialog, tap Erase.

Wait while the iOS device erases all content and settings.

Create and Configure a Blueprint

When creating Blueprints, your iOS device does not need to be connected to the computer running Apple Configurator 2.

1   If necessary, open Apple Configurator 2 on your client Mac.

2   In the toolbar, click Blueprints, and choose Edit Blueprints.

3   In the All Blueprints window, click New. Name your blueprint Configurator n-1, where n is your student number.

4 Double-click your new blueprint. Set the target for the type of iOS device you are working with.

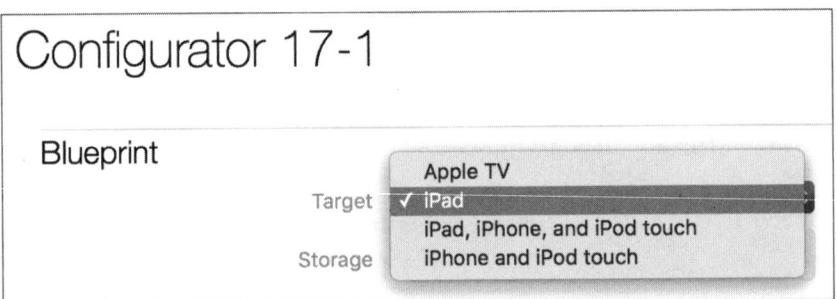

5 In the toolbar, click Tag. Type Supervised with Management to create a custom tag, and press Return.

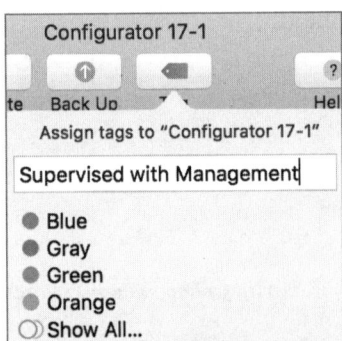

Observe how the tag is added to the Device section of the blueprint.

6   Choose Actions > Modify > Device Name. Enter a name for your iPad.

7   In the "Rename device" pane, click Add (+), and choose Number.

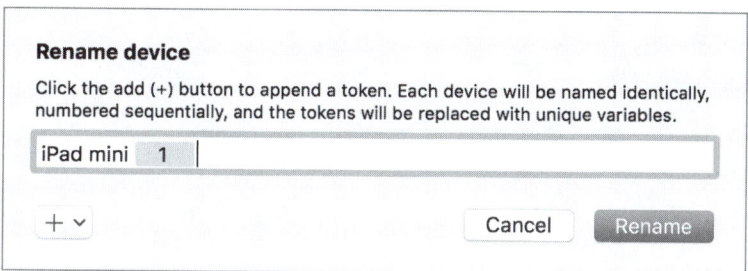

8   Click Rename.

9   Choose Actions > Modify > Wallpapers. For the Lock screen, click Choose Image.

10 From the Lesson13 folder in StudentMaterials, select background.png.

11 Repeat steps 9 and 10 for the Home screen.

12 Click Custom Text. Click Add (+), and select Device Name.

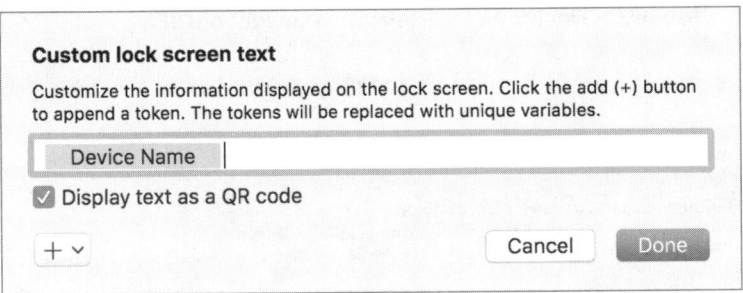

13 Select "Display text as a QR code," and then click Done.

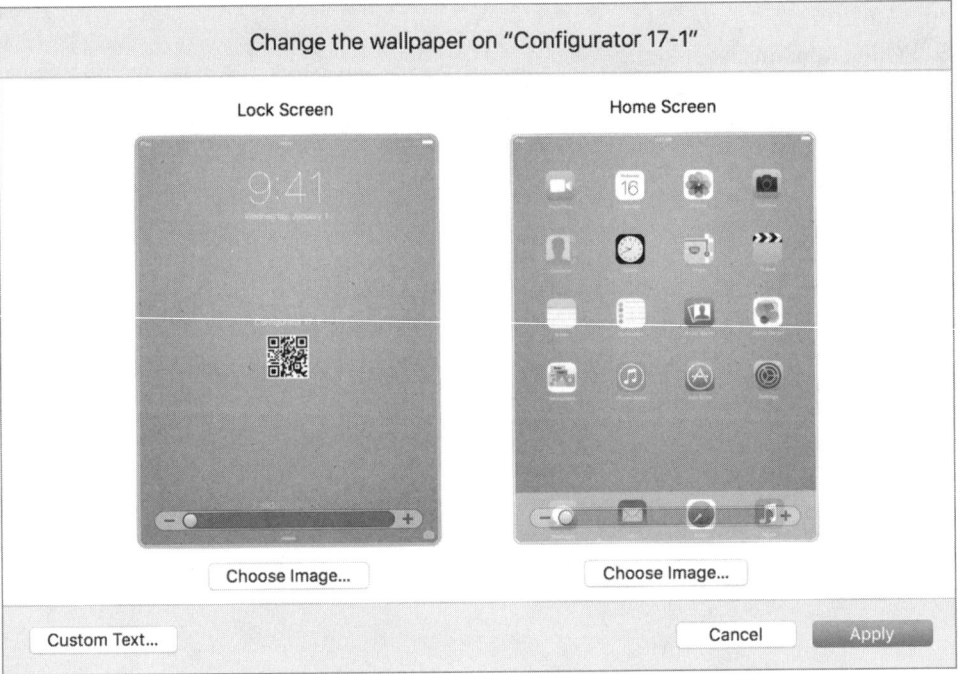

14 Click Apply.

15 Choose Actions > Modify > Home Screen Layout.

16 Configure the Home screen to your liking, and then click Apply.

17 In the Blueprint sidebar, select Profiles.

18 Click Add Profiles, and then choose the two configuration profiles you created in Exercise 13.1.

> **NOTE ▶** In OS X, you can use the Command and Shift keys in different ways to select multiple files at a time.

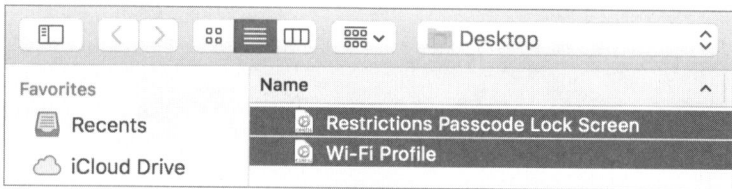

Observe that you have added two profiles to the blueprint.

19 In the sidebar, select Info, and observe that the blueprint now contains a profile in storage.

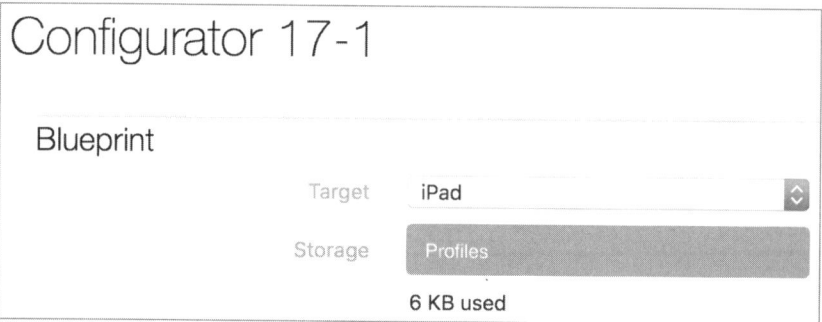

20 While still configuring your blueprint, in the toolbar, click Prepare.

21 For Configuration, select Manual, and then click Next.

22 For Server, select "Do not enroll in MDM," and click Next.

23 In the Supervise Devices pane, select "Supervise devices," and if necessary, select "Allow devices to pair with other computers."

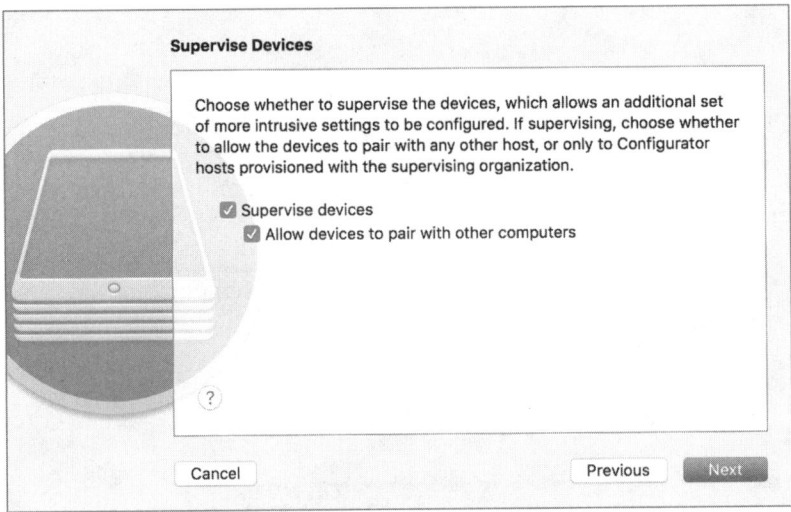

24 Click Next.

25 In the Assign to Organization pane, leave your organization selected, and then click Next.

26 In the Configure iOS Setup Assistant pane, choose "Show only some steps," and then select Location Services.

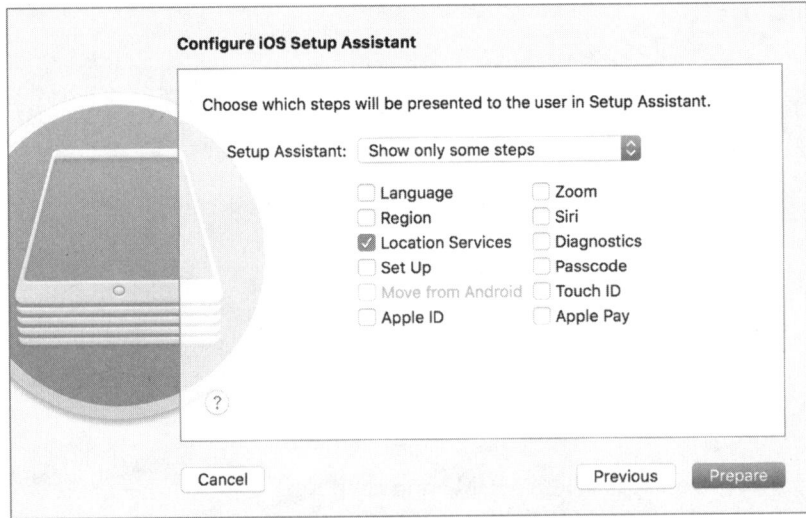

27 Click Prepare, and note how the action is added to your blueprint.

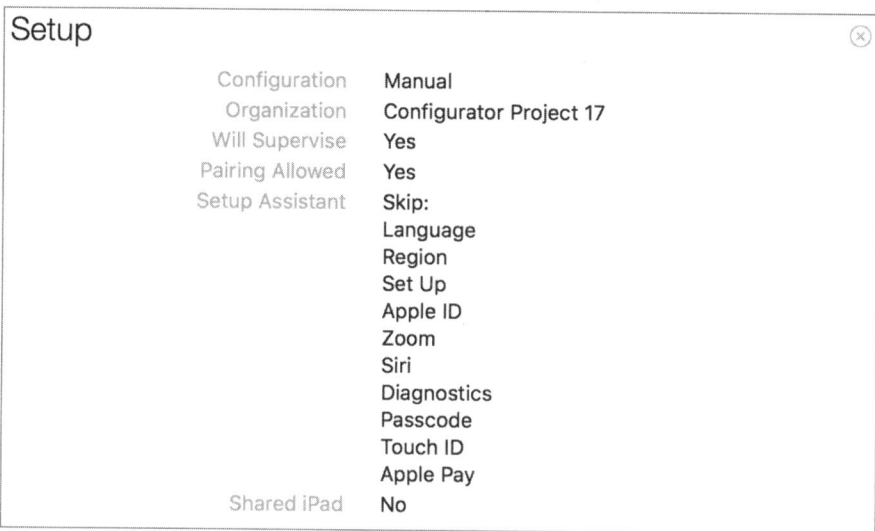

28 Scroll to observe your blueprint's configuration, and then click Done.

Apply the Blueprint to Your iOS Device

Once a blueprint is created, you can apply it to one or many iOS devices.

1 If necessary, connect your iOS device to your client Mac using the appropriate cable for your device.

2 Select your iOS device, click Blueprints in the toolbar, and choose your Configurator *n*-1 Blueprint (where *n* is your student number).

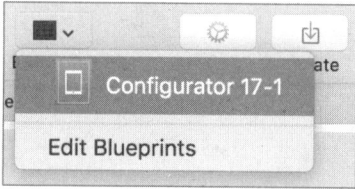

3 When prompted to apply your blueprint, click Apply.

Apple Configurator 2 will go through a series of steps to prepare the device according to your blueprint's specifications.

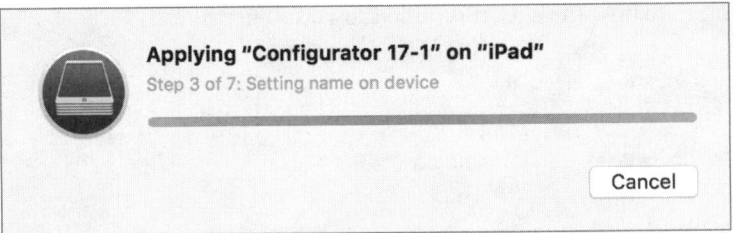

Observe how Apple Configurator 2's All Devices screen changes to display the custom Home Screen Layout profile you defined.

4   In Apple Configurator 2, double-click your iOS device.

Note the information about the iPad and that it is now supervised. Observe that you could install additional profiles as well as apps and change any of the settings you defined earlier. Additionally, you are able to view the console for a live view of the log on your iOS device when it is connected using the appropriate cable for your device.

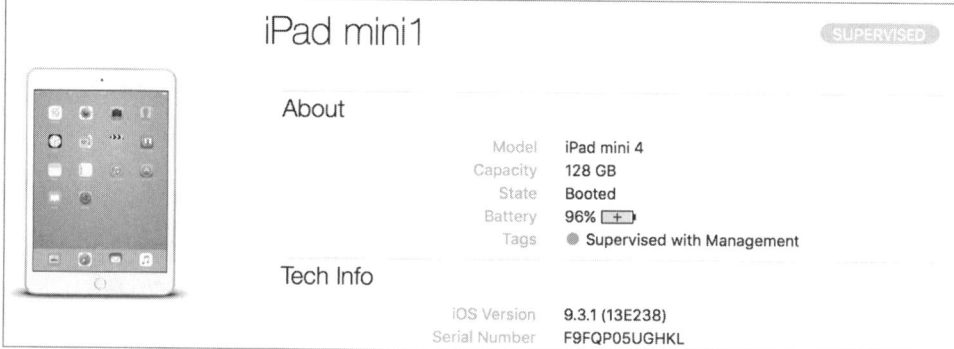

5 Click Back (<).

6 On your iOS device, slide at the "slide to set up" screen.

7 As the Wi-Fi network was already defined by the Wi-Fi Configuration Profile you made, tap Next.

8 At the Location Services screen, tap Enable Location Services.

9 Read the terms and conditions, tap Agree, and tap Agree again.

10 At the Welcome to iPad screen, tap Get Started.

In the AC2 Project *n* Management configuration profile (where *n* is your student number), you turned on the passcode payload and set the minimum passcode length at six characters. Thus, the iOS device prompts you to set a passcode.

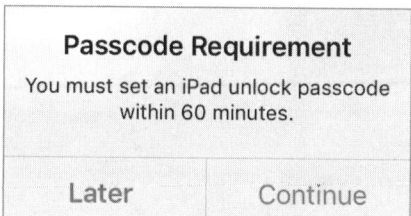

11 If the Passcode Requirement notification does not remain on the home screen, press the Sleep/Wake button, and then slide at the slide to unlock screen.

12 At the Passcode Requirement notification, tap Continue.

13 Enter 123456 as the passcode, and tap Continue. Then, reenter your new passcode, and tap Save.

14 Navigate to Settings > General > About.

Observe that this iPad is supervised by the organization you created in Apple Configurator 2 (Configurator Project *n*, where *n* is your student number).

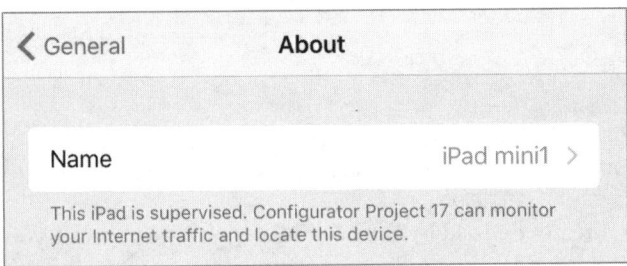

15 Tap General, and scroll to Profiles. Review the two profiles that exist.

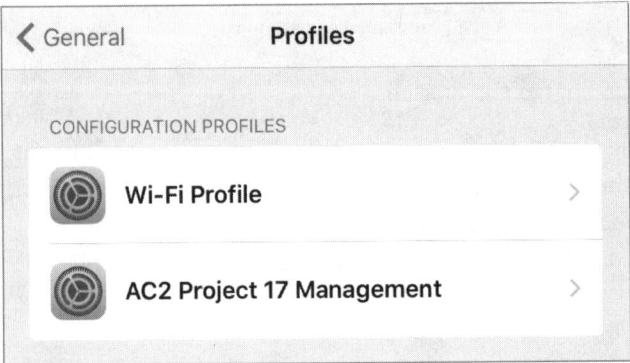

16 Tap AC2 Project *n* Management (where *n* is your student number).

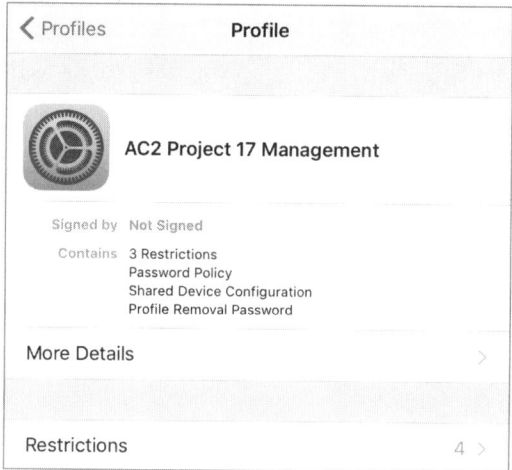

17 Press the Home button.

Observe the custom Home screen layout and custom wallpaper that you defined. Note that FaceTime, Messages, and Game Center are not displayed on the Home screen, as they are restricted.

18 Click the Sleep/Wake button, and then press the Home button.

Observe the custom Lock screen. It contains the device name you defined, as well as the QR code for ease of inventory collection. It is also noted that the device is supervised and your Lock screen message is displayed.

Erase All Content and Settings Using Apple Configurator 2

You have repeatedly wiped your iPad locally on the device or with your MDM server during the exercises in this guide. Using Apple Configurator, you are able to wipe one or many iOS devices at a time.

1 If necessary, connect your iOS device to your client Mac using the appropriate cable for your device.

2 On your client Mac, in Apple Configurator 2, ensure that your iOS device is selected.

3 Choose Actions > Advanced > Erase All Content and Settings.

4 In the following pane, click Erase.

Apple Configurator 2 will unsupervised and wipe the device.

Duplicate a Blueprint and Modify the Prepare Action

Blueprints can be duplicated to avoid repeating many steps and can be easily modified for different configurations. For this Blueprint, you will add a tag and modify the Prepare action to simulate an out-of-the-box experience for a device that is not in the Device Enrollment Program.

1 In the Apple Configurator 2 toolbar, click Blueprints, and then Edit Blueprints.

2 Control-click the Configurator *n*-1 blueprint (where *n* is your student number), and then select Duplicate.

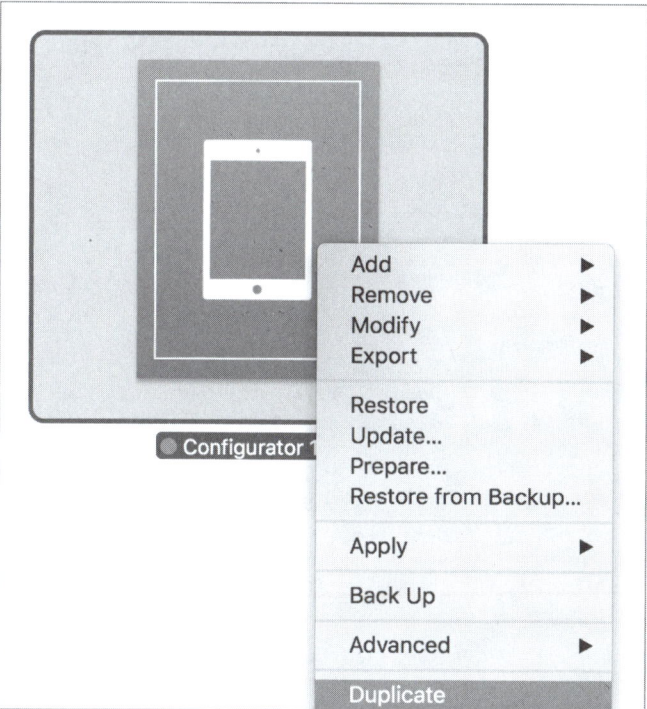

3 Single-click the name of the duplicated blueprint.

4 Name the duplicated blueprint Configurator *n*-2 (where *n* is your student number), and then press Return.

5 Double-click the Configurator *n*-2 blueprint (where *n* is your student number).

6 Choose Apple Configurator 2 > Preferences, and in the Preferences toolbar, click Tags.

7 Click Add (+)

8 Name the new tag Enrolled.

9 Click Change Color, and choose a color of your liking.

10 Press Return.

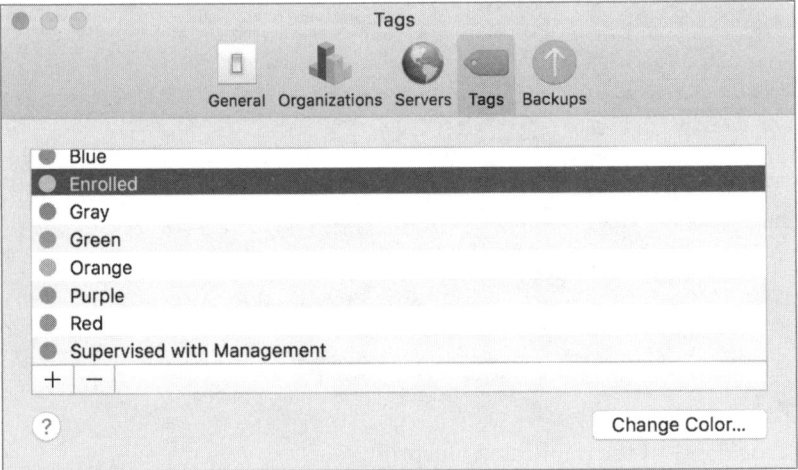

11 Close the Preferences window, and then in the toolbar, click Tag.

12 Click the Enrolled Tag to add it, and then press Return.

Observe that the blueprint now has two tags indicating its configuration.

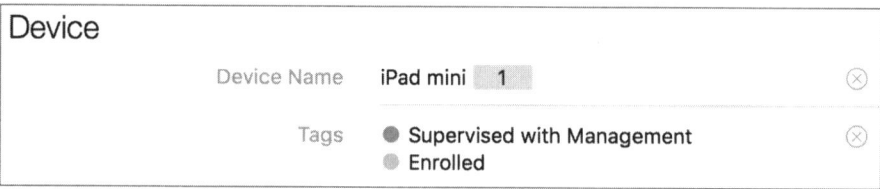

13 In the toolbar, click Prepare.

14 For Configuration, select Manual, and then click Next.

15 For Server, select MDM Project *n* (where *n* is your student number), and click Next.

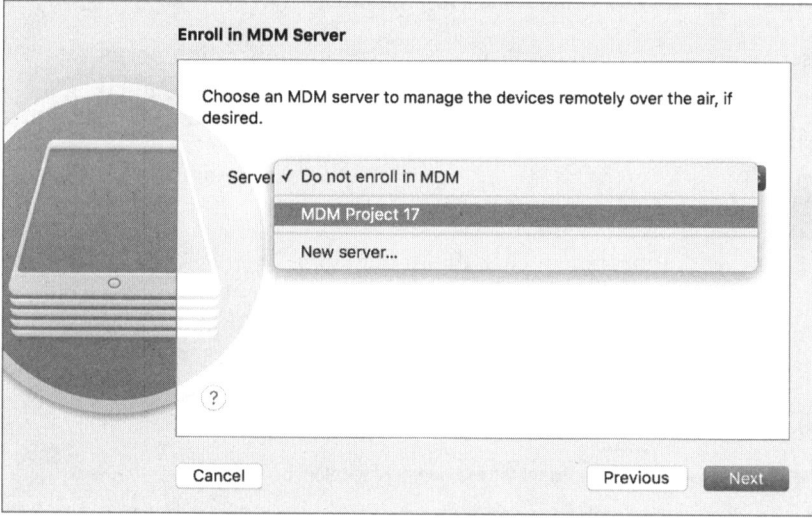

16 In the Supervise Devices pane, select "Supervise devices," and if necessary, select "Allow devices to pair with other computers."

17 Click Next.

18 In the Assign to Organization pane, leave your organization selected, and then click Next.

19 In the Configure iOS Setup Assistant pane, choose "Show only some steps," and then select Location Services.

20 Click Prepare, and note how the action is added to your blueprint.

21 Scroll to observe your blueprint's configuration and the modified Prepare action.

Note the MDM server URL.

Setup		
	Configuration	Manual
	Organization	Configurator Project 17
	MDM Server	https://server17.local/devicemanagement/api/device/dep_mdm_enroll
	Will Supervise	Yes

22 Click Done.

Allow Enrollment During Setup Assistant for the Everyone Group

1 On your server, in Safari, open the Profile Manager administration portal (https://server*n*.local/profilemanager, where *n* is your student number), and then authenticate with local administrator credentials.

2 Select Groups.

3 Select Everyone, and, if necessary, click the About tab.

4 Select the checkbox "Allow enrollment during Setup Assistant for devices configured using Apple Configurator."

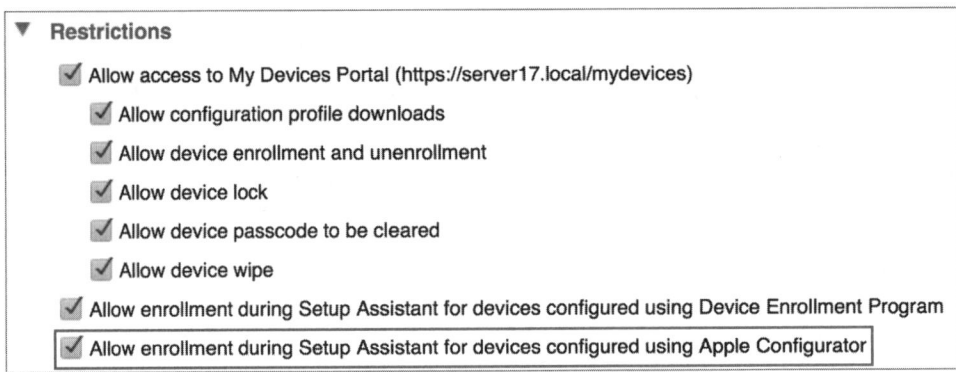

5 Click Save.

Apply the Blueprint to Your iOS Device

1   If necessary, connect your iOS device to your client Mac using the appropriate cable for your device.

2   Control-click your iOS device, and choose Apply > Configurator *n*-2 (where *n* is your student number) from the shortcut menu.

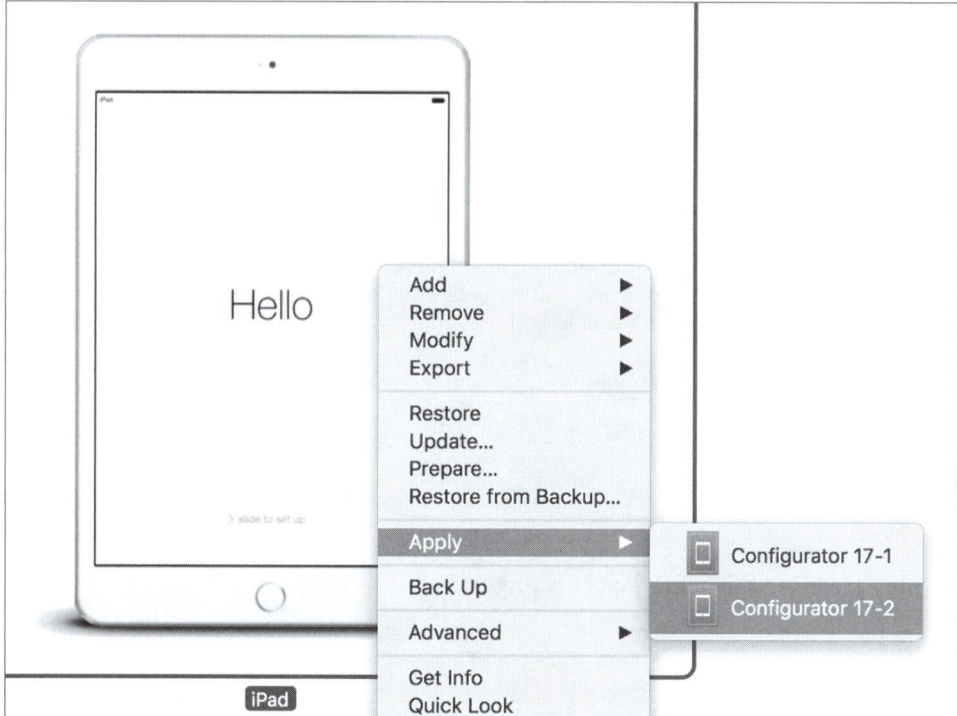

3   Click Apply.

    Apple Configurator 2 will go through a series of steps to prepare the device according to your blueprint's specifications. Observe that your iOS device now has two tags.

4   On your iOS device, slide at the "slide to set up" screen.

5   As the Wi-Fi network was already defined by Wi-Fi Configuration Profile that you made, tap Next.

6. At the Location Services screen, tap Enable Location Services.

7. At the Configuration screen, tap About Configuration.

   Observe the information about the organization you created in Exercise 12.1.

8. Tap Done, and then tap "Apply configuration."

9. Tap Next. Your iOS device will begin to enroll with your MDM server.

10. At the Log In screen, enter the following credentials, and click Next:
    - User Name: todd
    - Password: net

11 Read the terms and conditions, tap Agree, and tap "Agree again."

12 At the Welcome to iPad screen, tap Get Started.

13 At the Passcode Requirement notification, tap Continue.

If the Passcode Requirement notification does not remain on the Home screen, press the Sleep/Wake button, and then slide at the "slide to unlock" screen.

14 Enter 123456 as the passcode, and tap Continue. Then, reenter your new passcode, and tap Save.

As your device is associated with Todd Porter, who is a member of the Marketing group, two web clips are present on the device.

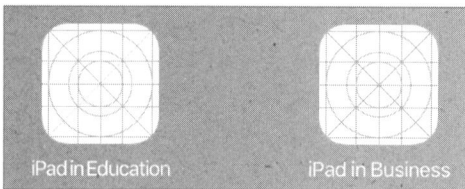

15 Navigate to Settings > General > Profiles & Device Management.

There is now a Remote Management profile from your MDM server, as well as two configuration profiles from Apple Configurator 2.

16 Inspect each of the three profiles.

Even though you did not use the Device Enrollment Program to enroll the iOS device, it is still supervised using the supervision identity from Apple Configurator 2 and enrolled in your MDM server in the same fashion. You simulated an out-of-the-box experience. This can be a powerful method to employ on iOS devices that are not eligible for enrollment using the DEP.

Turn On MDM Lost Mode

A powerful new feature of Profile Manager in Server 5.1 and iOS 9.3 is the ability to turn on MDM lost mode and remotely lock an iOS device, while visually tracking its current location. This can be done to any iOS device that is supervised, whether it is supervised by an organization in Apple Configurator 2 or via the Device Enrollment Program.

1. On your server, in the Profile Manager administration portal, select Devices from the sidebar, and then select the iOS device you just enrolled.

2. From the Action (gear) menu, choose Enable Lost Mode.

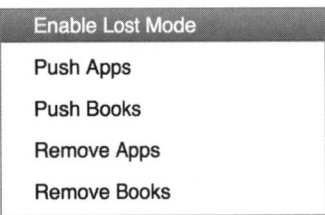

3. For the Lock Screen Message, enter This iPad is owned by Configurator Project *n* (where *n* is your student number).

4. Enter a phone number.

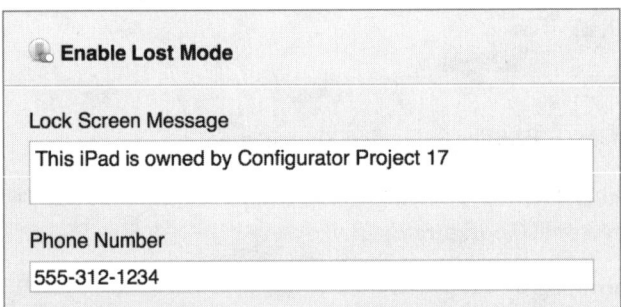

5. Click Enable Lost Mode.

6. Press the Home button on your iOS device, and observe the Lost iPad notification.

7   In the Profile Manager administration portal, from the Action (gear) menu, select Fetch Device Location, and then in the confirmation dialog, click Fetch Device Location.

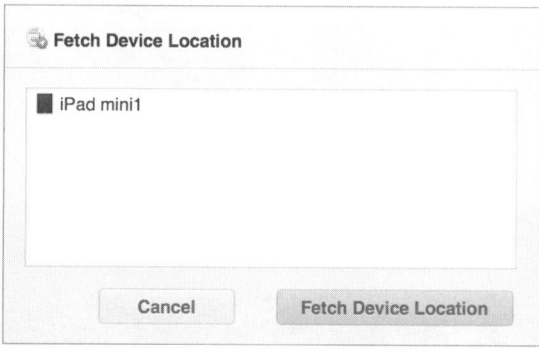

8 In your device information, click the disclosure triangle next to Details.

   Review the information. Lost Mode Enabled reads Yes, and the location is displayed.

9 Click the arrow next to Show in Maps.

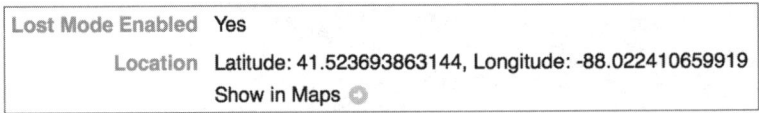

10 At the "Maps would like to use your current location" dialog, click Allow.

   The Maps application opens and displays the current location of the device.

11 Quit Maps, and in the Profile Manager administration portal, while your iOS device is still selected, click the Action (gear) menu, and select Disable Lost Mode.

12 In the Disable Lost Mode confirmation dialog, click Disable Lost Mode.

13 Press the Home button on your iOS device, and observe the notification on the screen that Lost Mode was turned on and the location of the device was fetched.

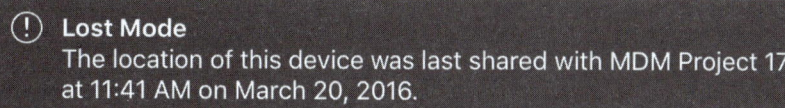

Wipe the iOS Device

1 On your server, in the Profile Manager administration portal, select Devices from the sidebar.

2 Select your iOS device, click the Action (gear) menu, and choose Wipe.

3 In the Wipe confirmation dialog, click Wipe.

4 Select the placeholder for the iPad you just wiped, and click the Remove (–) button.

5 In the confirmation dialog, click Remove.

In this exercise, you created a blueprint and configured it to supervise your iOS device but not enroll it with an MDM server. You demonstrated actions such as tags, wallpapers, and Home screen layout. You added configuration profiles and applied the blueprint to your iOS device. You then inspected the effects of this blueprint.

You then duplicated your first blueprint, added a different tag, and modified the Prepare action to enroll with your MDM server and simulate an out-of-the-box experience. You applied the blueprint, and because your device is enrolled with your MDM server and supervised, you demonstrated MDM Lost Mode. Finally, you sent the wipe task from the MDM server to your iOS device and removed the placeholder.

Exercise 13.4
Back Up and Restore an iOS Device

▶ **Prerequisite**

▶ Exercise 13.3, "Create and Apply Blueprints"

Challenge

Apply a blueprint that will prepare a fresh iOS device. Customize the device with the actions in the blueprint and some photos to simulate user data.

Create a backup of the iOS device with Apple Configurator 2, restore it, and confirm that your settings and photos were restored.

Considerations

Once you apply the blueprint to the iOS device, take some photos. You can instead add some screen captures to your saved photos; simultaneously press the Sleep/Wake and Home buttons, and the screen capture will be saved to the Photos app. When you connect an iOS device with photos in the Camera Roll to a Mac computer, Photos automatically opens. You can change this behavior in the upper-right corner of the Import tab in the Photos application on your Mac computer.

Solution

Apply the Blueprint to Your iOS Device

Once a blueprint is created, you can apply it to one or many iOS devices.

1   If necessary, connect your iOS device to your client Mac using the appropriate cable for your device.

2   Select your iOS device, and in the toolbar, choose your Configurator n-1 Blueprint (where n is your student number).

3   When prompted to apply your blueprint, click Apply.

   Apple Configurator 2 will go through a series of steps to prepare the device according to your blueprint's specifications.

4   On your iOS device, slide at the "slide to set up" screen.

5   As the Wi-Fi network was already defined by Wi-Fi Configuration Profile that you made, tap Next.

6   At the Location Services screen, tap Enable Location Services.

7   Read the terms and conditions, tap Agree, and tap Agree again.

8   At the Welcome to iPad screen, tap Get Started.

In the AC2 Project *n* Management configuration profile (where *n* is your student number), you turned on the passcode payload and set the minimum passcode length at six characters. Thus, the iOS device prompts you to set a passcode.

9   At the Passcode Requirement notification, tap Later.

Add Some Photos

1   On your iOS device, open Camera.

2   At the Allow Camera to access your location notification, click Allow.

3   Take some photos. You can disconnect your iOS device from your client Mac if necessary.

4   Press the Home button.

5   Take a screen capture by simultaneously pressing the Sleep/Wake and Home buttons.

6   Open Photos.

7   If necessary, tap Photos at the bottom of the screen, and confirm that the photos and the screen capture are there.

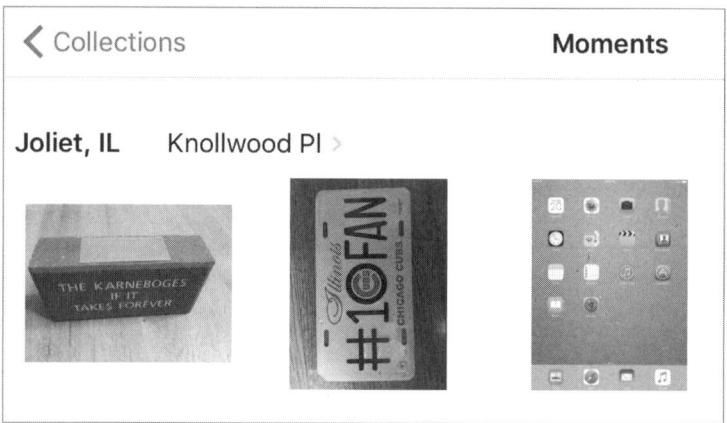

Create a Backup of the iOS Device with Apple Configurator 2

1 If necessary, connect your iOS device to your client Mac using the appropriate cable for your device.

2 Select your iOS device, and in the toolbar, click Back Up.

As your iOS device contains very little data, the backup will proceed rather quickly.

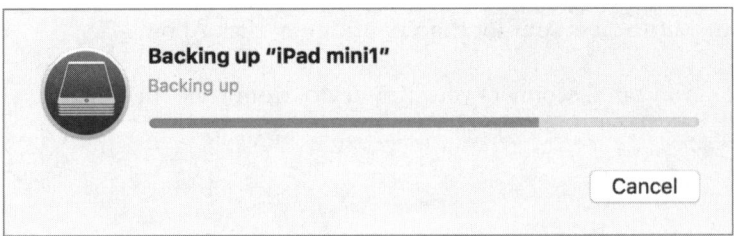

3 Choose Apple Configurator 2 > Preferences, and then click Backups in the toolbar.

Observe that the backup you just created is present. If it is not, quit Apple Configurator 2, and reopen the application.

NOTE ▶ It is best practice to encrypt your device backups.

4 Close the Preferences window.

Restore Your iOS Device from Backup

1 Select your iOS device, and choose Actions > Advanced > Erase All Content and Settings.

2 In the confirmation dialog, click Erase.

3   If you're in a classroom environment, temporarily swap iOS devices with a neighbor.

    If you are performing these exercises independently, you can restore to another iOS device if both devices are the same model, or you can just restore to the original iOS device.

4   If the iOS device is not already connected to your client Mac running Apple Configurator 2, connect it now.

5   Select your iOS device, and then choose Actions > Restore from Backup.

6   Select the backup you created earlier in this exercise, and click Restore.

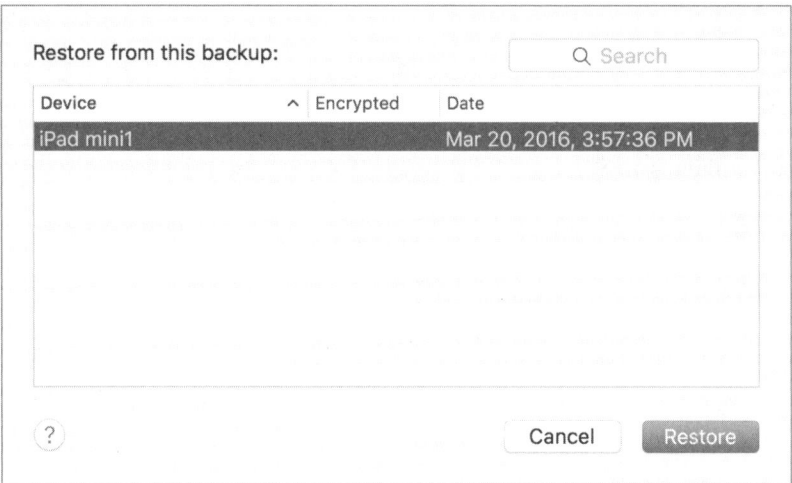

7   Wait while Apple Configurator 2 restores the backup, and the iOS device restarts.

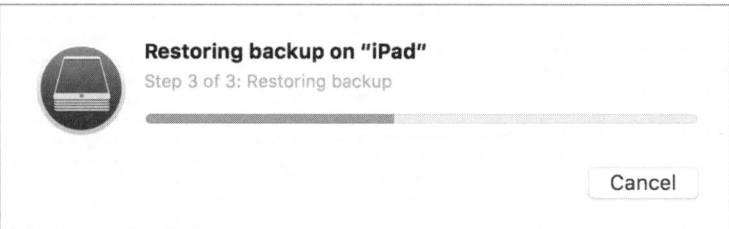

8   Slide at the "slide to set up" screen.

9   At the Update Completed screen, tap Continue.

10 At the Location Services screen, tap Enable Location Services.

11 At the Welcome to iPad screen, tap Get Started.

12 At the Passcode Requirement notification, tap Later.

13 Tap Photos, and ensure that the photos you took earlier are present.

Erase All Content and Settings

1 On your iOS device, if necessary, slide at the "slide to unlock" screen.

2 If necessary, enter the passcode.

3 Open Settings.

4 Navigate to General > Reset.

5 Tap Erase All Content and Settings.

6 If your iOS device has a passcode, enter the passcode.

7 In the confirmation dialog, tap Erase.

8 In the extra confirmation dialog, tap Erase.

In this exercise, you used Apple Configurator 2 to apply a blueprint, take some photos, make a backup of a customized iOS device, and restore from a backup.

Lesson 14
Apple Configurator 2: App and Document Management

This final Apple Configurator 2–focused lesson builds on the previous two lessons in this guide. At this point, it's assumed you've explored how to prepare and manage iOS devices using Apple Configurator 2. Here you will focus on using Apple Configurator 2 to distribute apps and documents to iOS devices connected over USB. You will also learn how to take advantage of single app mode to lock a supervised iOS device to a specific app.

For most workflows, the ideal situation is to use your MDM to distribute apps and books. However, there are some situations for which an MDM is not available.

However, while you can use Profile Manager to push enterprise docs, Profile Manager does not offer the ability to distribute documents to apps, nor does it offer the ability to export documents from apps on iOS devices for viewing and editing on a Mac.

That being said, the document handling abilities of Apple Configurator 2 require a physical USB connection and are limited by the bandwidth of USB. Adding a multigigabyte file to a cart of 30 iOS devices or exporting similarly sized files from that many iOS devices will take a considerable amount of time. It may make more sense to use another Mobile Content Management (MCM) system and use Apple Configurator 2's app and document management capabilities for testing and training purposes.

GOALS

► Understand the different methods to deploy apps locally to iOS devices with Apple Configurator 2

► Explore methods to update apps deployed via Apple Configurator 2

► Add documents to iOS devices and then export them

► Lock an iOS device to a single app using single app mode

Reference 14.1
Considerations for Managing Apps with Apple Configurator 2

Apple Configurator 2 provides the only supported method to deploy App Store–sourced iOS apps via a local universal serial bus (USB) connection to multiple iOS devices. An administrator may also choose to deploy iOS apps remotely via a Mobile Device Management (MDM) service, but this may not be the best solution in certain environments.

For example, if your Wi-Fi infrastructure isn't as robust as you'd like it to be for deploying apps over the air, deploying your initial set of iOS apps during device preparation via Apple Configurator 2 may be quicker. In other cases, your deployment could be so small that it doesn't warrant an MDM service. Whatever the usage case may be, in this section you will explore how Apple Configurator 2 can install iOS apps.

> **NOTE** ▶ If you plan to deploy apps with Apple Configurator 2, you need to make sure the Mac computer has iTunes 12.3 or later for downloading iOS app resources.

Apple Configurator and Apple IDs

Apple IDs come into play several different ways when you're using Apple Configurator 2. One general rule is that organizational Apple IDs used for managing Apple Deployment Programs, such as the Device Enrollment Program (DEP), the Volume Purchase Program (VPP), and Apple School Manager, cannot be used in the App Store, Mac App Store, or iTunes to make purchases.

If you're used to using the legacy version of Apple Configurator, there are some new options with Apple Configurator 2, and you no longer need to authenticate your Mac computer in iTunes. However, you cannot use Apple Configurator 2 to distribute VPP apps that use redemption codes; you need to migrate those apps to use managed distribution.

> **MORE INFO** ▶ See Apple Support article HT202863, "Migrate from redemption codes to managed distribution with the Volume Purchase Program," for more information about migrating from redemption codes to managed distribution.

Consider the following Apple ID authorizations that occur when using Apple Configurator 2:

- ▶ Mac App Store—Using an organizational Apple ID at the Mac App Store to install and update Apple Configurator 2 is one option. This Apple ID doesn't need to be associated with any of the other Apple IDs used for iOS deployment purposes. A common solution is to create a separate organizational Apple ID for each Mac that will run Apple Configurator 2.

MORE INFO ▶ The Apple ID you plan to use for installing iOS apps via Apple Configurator does not need to have a credit card associated with it. In fact, not having any credit card information saved is better if the Apple ID is known by multiple people. You can find out more from Apple Support article HT204034, "Create an iTunes Store, App Store, or iBooks Store account without a credit card or other payment method."

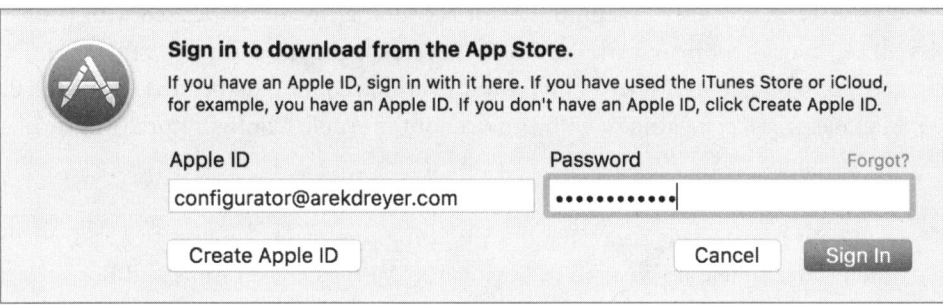

▶ VPP—If you have more than a few Mac computers running Apple Configurator 2, rather than creating several organizational Apple IDs for downloading Apple Configurator 2, consider enrolling those Mac computers in your MDM service, purchasing multiple copies of Apple Configurator 2 with the VPP administrator account that is associated with your MDM, and then assigning Apple Configurator 2 to your Mac computers with the installation mode of Automatic so it is automatically installed.

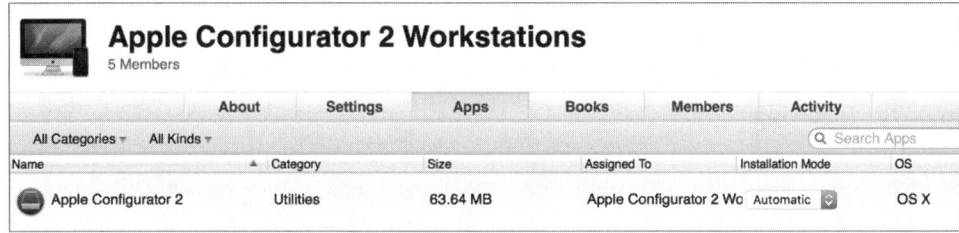

▶ Personal Apple ID—You can sign in with a personal Apple ID to deploy any app in that Apple ID's purchased history. This is not a commonly used feature, because you must also enter this Apple ID in the iTunes & App Store settings on each iOS device to open apps distributed with this personal Apple ID method.

> **NOTE** ▶ Use caution when deploying iOS apps that are temporarily free, such as those on a special promotion, in Apple Configurator 2. If that app returns to requiring payment, you may not be able to re-deploy the app in the future without purchasing the app.

- VPP administrator account—You can sign in with a VPP administrator account to deploy any app that you purchased with that VPP account. You should use your VPP agent account to create a separate VPP administrator account for use with Apple Configurator 2.

> **WARNING** ▶ If your VPP administrator account is already associated with your MDM, consult with your MDM vendor before logging in with that VPP administrator account. For example, if the VPP administrator account is associated with your Profile Manager service, logging in with this account in Apple Configurator 2 will revoke all app assignments.

> **MORE INFO** ▶ Details regarding the VPP program, including how to acquire VPP redemption codes, are covered in Lesson 10, "VPP-Managed Apps and Books."

> **TIP** As a reminder, if you have multiple Apple Configurator 2 Mac systems to get up and running with multiple large iOS apps, having a local Apple caching server will save you a tremendous amount of Internet bandwidth and time downloading iOS apps. The Caching service is covered in Lesson 5, "Caching Service."

Reference 14.2
Manage Apps and Documents via Apple Configurator 2

As long as you have a USB connection to an iOS device, you can use Apple Configurator 2 to do the following:

- Use a VPP account to assign, install, and remove VPP apps from the App Store
- Use a personal Apple ID account to install and remove apps from the App Store
- Install and remove apps that have already been downloaded via iTunes on your Mac
- Install and remove in-house enterprise iOS apps
- Update iOS and apps
- Add documents to iOS devices, for apps that support iTunes document sharing

▶ Export documents from iOS devices to your Mac for later review or archiving, for apps that support iTunes document sharing

▶ Lock an iOS device to a single app

Manage Apps with Personal Apple ID

Adding apps with a personal Apple ID is one option for adding apps; it's not appropriate for most situations, but this guide covers this option for completeness. You can use a personal Apple ID to install apps from the App Store on multiple iOS devices, but you need to enter the credentials for that personal Apple ID on each iOS device to open the app or to update the app from the device. Additionally, you should review the terms and conditions for installing an app from the App Store on multiple iOS devices before implementing this option.

Choose Store > Sign In, provide the personal Apple ID credentials, and then click Sign In.

Once you're logged in with the personal Apple ID, choose one or more devices or blueprints, and then choose Actions > Add > Apps. Apple Configurator 2 displays the list of apps available, based on the purchase history for that personal Apple ID. You can use the pop-up menu to change the type of apps displayed, toggle between icon and list view, use the Search field, and click a column header to change the sort order. Select one or more apps, and then click Add.

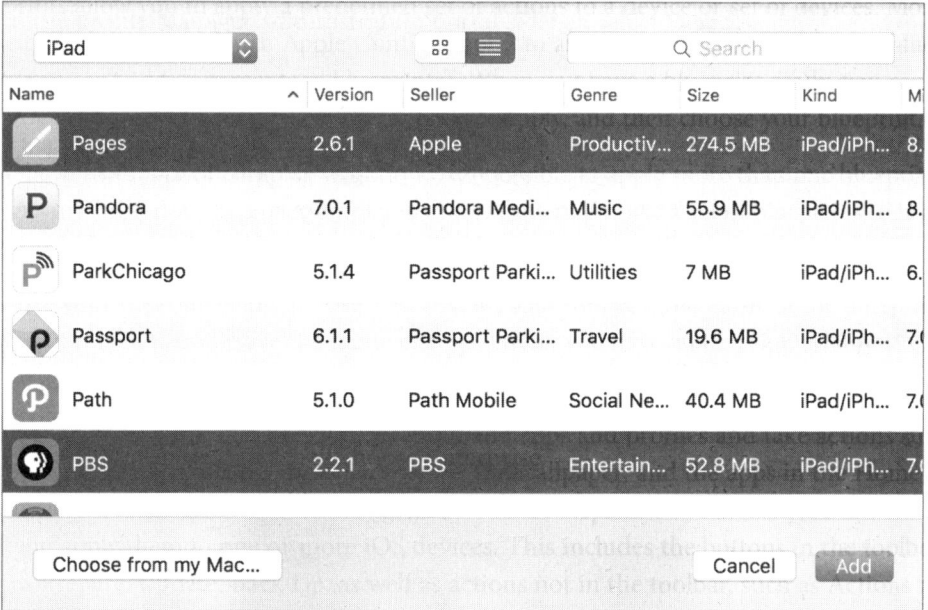

Alternatively, if you already downloaded apps using iTunes, you can click the "Choose from my Mac" button. The default location is in the iTunes Mobile Applications folder, which is buried inside the iTunes music library. The default location is ~/Music/iTunes/iTunes Media/Mobile Applications, but it might also be ~/Music/iTunes/iTunes Music/Mobile Applications if your home folder has been used with previous versions of iTunes.

> **TIP** You can select multiple iOS apps to import by using the Shift-click or Command-click keyboard shortcut.

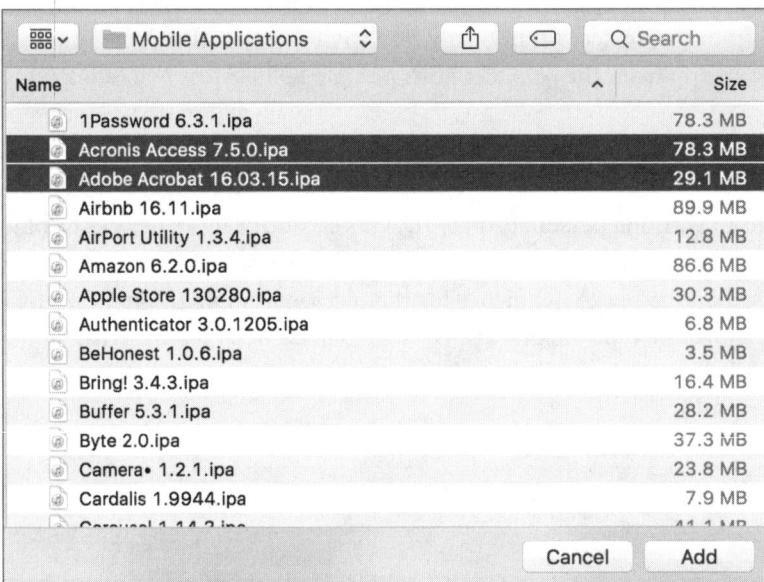

Apple Configurator 2 downloads the apps from the App Store (using the Caching service if one is available) and then transfers the apps to the device.

If the personal Apple ID is not already stored in Settings > iTunes & App Store on the device, the first time a user opens one of these transferred apps on the iOS device, she will be prompted for the Apple ID credentials.

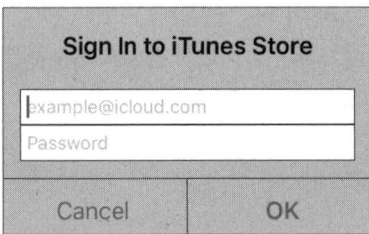

Having personal Apple ID credentials stored on multiple iOS devices may be appropriate for some workflows, but in most cases it is probably much more appropriate to use a VPP administrator account to add App Store apps than it is to use a personal Apple ID.

You can choose Store > Log Out to log out in preparation for the next section.

Manage Apps with VPP Apple ID

You can use Apple Configurator 2 to distribute VPP apps, but you should not use the same VPP administrator account that you use with your MDM solution. Instead, create a new VPP administrator account for use with Apple Configurator 2, and make separate purchases with this VPP administrator account for use with Apple Configurator 2.

> **MORE INFO** ▶ See Reference 10.2, "VPP Service Enrollment and Administration," for more information about creating a VPP administrator account.

Choose Store > Sign In, provide the credentials for the VPP administrator account that is dedicated for use with Apple Configurator 2, and then click Sign In.

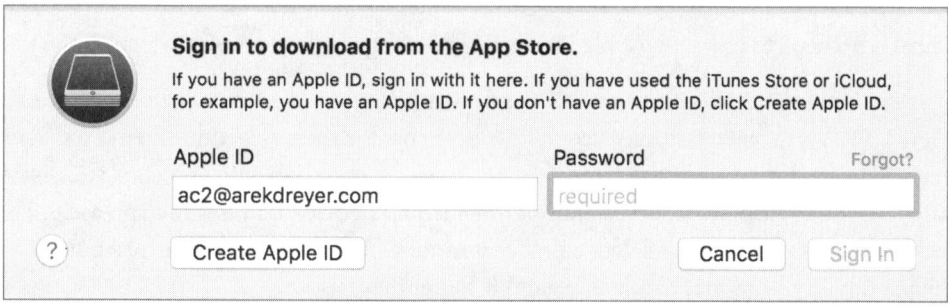

Next, choose one or more devices or blueprints, and then choose Actions > Add > Apps. You can use the pop-up menu to change the type of apps displayed, toggle between icon and list views, and use the Search field. If you are in the list view, you can click a column header to change the sort order (note that the Copies Available column is a visual indication that you are viewing VPP apps instead of personal Apple ID apps). Select one or more apps, and then click Add.

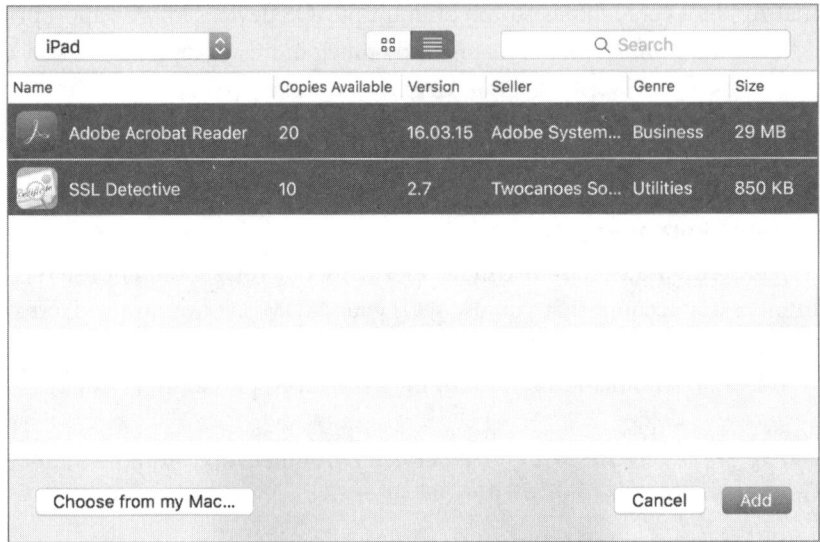

Apple Configurator 2 then assigns the apps to the devices, downloads the apps from the App Store (using the Caching service if one is available), and then transfers the apps to the device.

There is no need to have any Apple ID stored in Settings > iTunes & App Store on the device.

If you're still logged in with your VPP administrator account, you can choose Window > View VPP Assignments. It may take a few moments for the correct number of available licenses to be displayed. If the pane is in list view, for each app, you can click the disclosure triangle to display the serial number of each iOS device that has the app assigned to it. Furthermore, you can select a device and then click the Revoke License button to revoke the license so you can later assign it to another device.

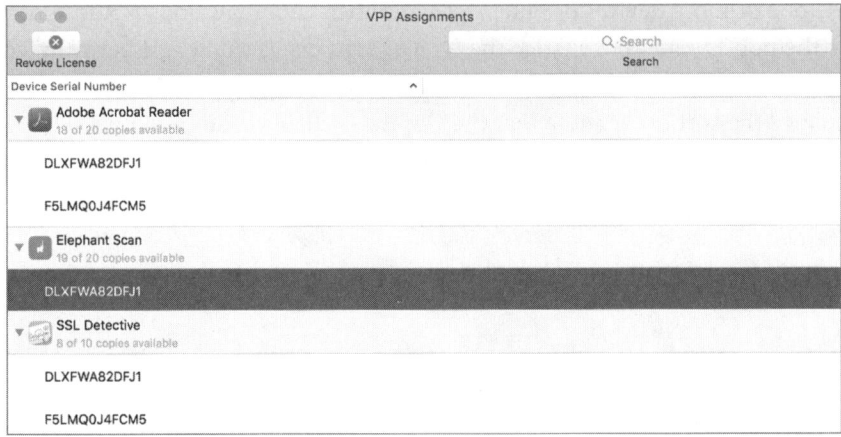

Revoking an app doesn't remove the app from the device; to remove the app, you must choose Actions > Remove > Apps, select the app, and then click Remove Apps.

Add In-House Enterprise Apps
If you have in-house enterprise apps, you just need the .ipa file available on your Mac computer.

After you click Add Apps, click the "Choose from my Mac" button.

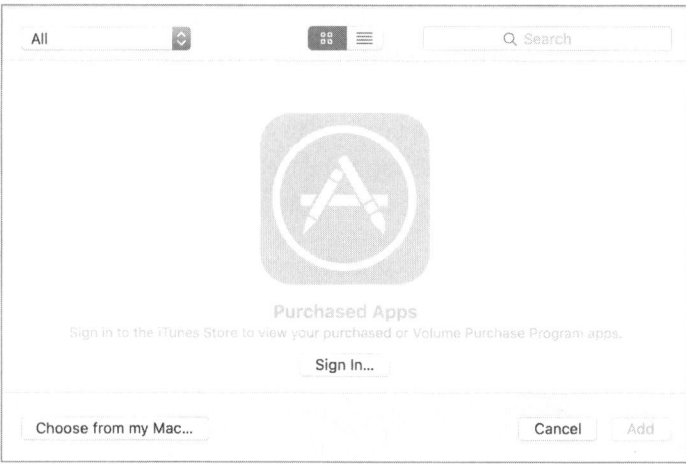

Navigate to the place where your in-house enterprise app or apps are stored, select the apps, and then click Add.

If you use Apple Configurator 2 to install an in-house enterprise iOS app on an iOS device (rather than using MDM to install the app on the device), when a user opens the app, she will see a message that the developer is not trusted.

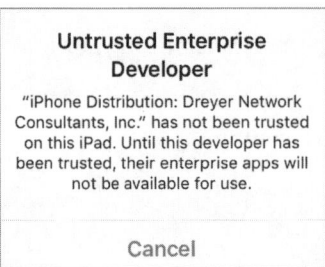

In this scenario, to successfully open the app, she needs to first open Settings > Device Management, tap the device management profile, tap the developer in the Enterprise App section, and trust the developer.

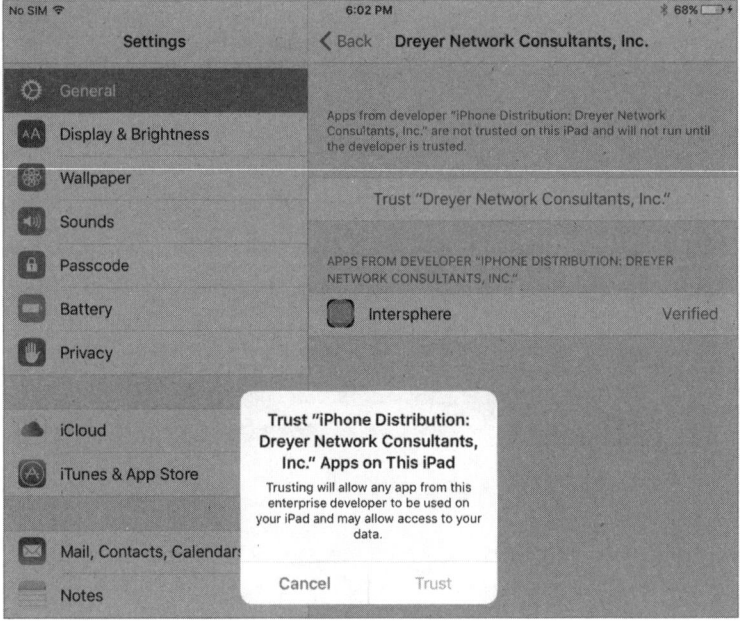

TIP When you use MDM to install an in-house enterprise app on an iOS device, users do not need to explicitly trust the app author. However, if you use Apple Configurator 2 to install an in-house enterprise app on that same iOS device, a user must explicitly trust the app author, even if the in-house enterprise app distributed by MDM is from the same author.

View Apps

To view the apps on an iOS device, select the device, choose File > Get Info, and then select Apps in the sidebar. In the following figure, SSL Detective has a VPP banner to indicate that the app is assigned to the device but not installed on the device. You cannot tell from the icons, but in this example, Adobe Acrobat Reader was assigned and installed via Apple Configurator 2, SSL Detective was assigned via MDM, and the United Airlines app was installed by the user from the App Store.

Remove Apps

To remove any app, even an app that was not assigned and installed by Apple Configurator 2, select the devices or blueprints, choose File > Get Info, and then click Apps in the sidebar. Select the apps to remove, and then choose Edit > Delete. At the confirmation window, click Remove.

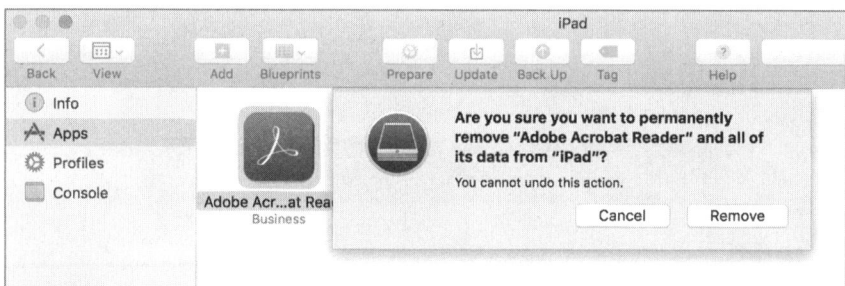

NOTE ▶ Removing an app also removes all data and documents associated with the app from the iOS device.

Add Documents

If an app supports iTunes file sharing, you can use Apple Configurator 2 to assign a document to that app.

MORE INFO ▶ See Apple Support article HT201301, "About File Sharing on iPhone, iPad, and iPod touch," for more information about iTunes file sharing.

Select one or more devices, choose Actions > Add > Documents, select a supported app, and then click Choose.

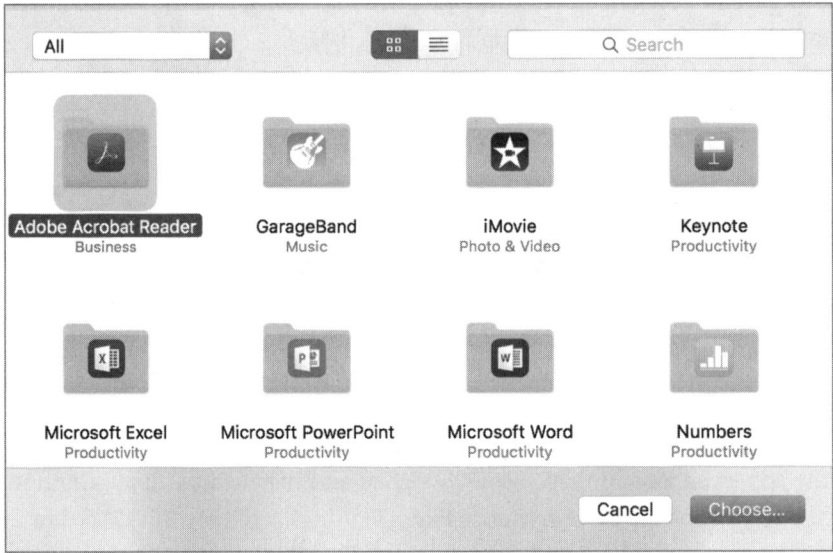

Navigate to and select the documents to add, and then click Add.

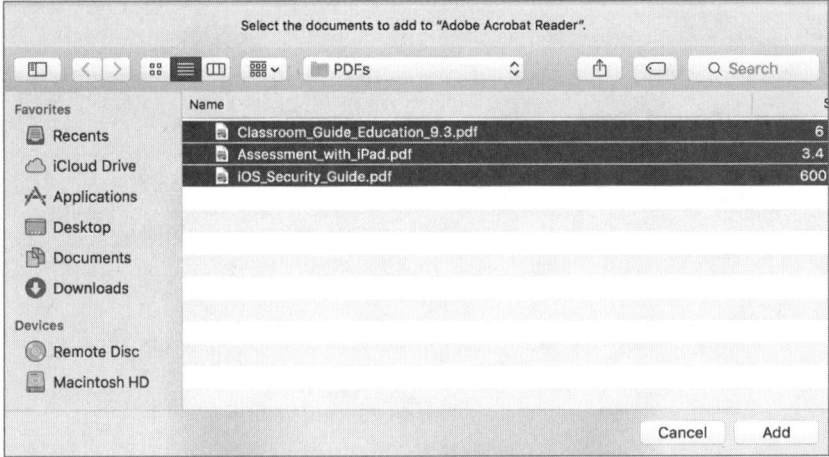

After the transfer is complete, when you open the app, the documents are available for that app.

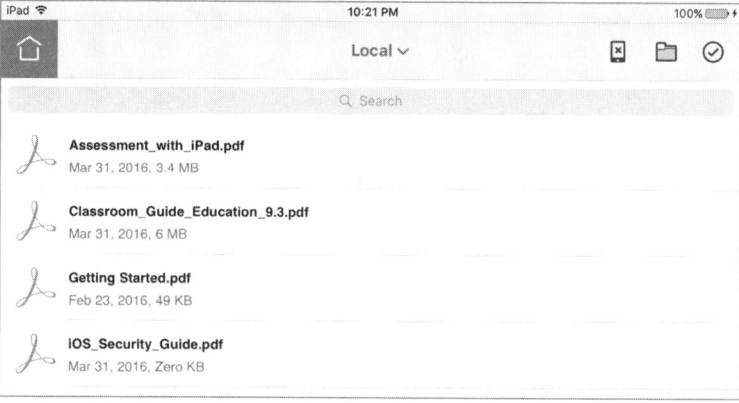

Export Documents

If an app supports iTunes document sharing, you can use Apple Configurator 2 to export documents from that app to your Mac. Select the device or devices, and choose Actions > Export > Documents. Select the apps that are associated with the documents you want to export. If you are in the list view, you can use the disclosure triangles to display the name and kind of documents associated with each app. After you select the apps or documents to export, click Choose.

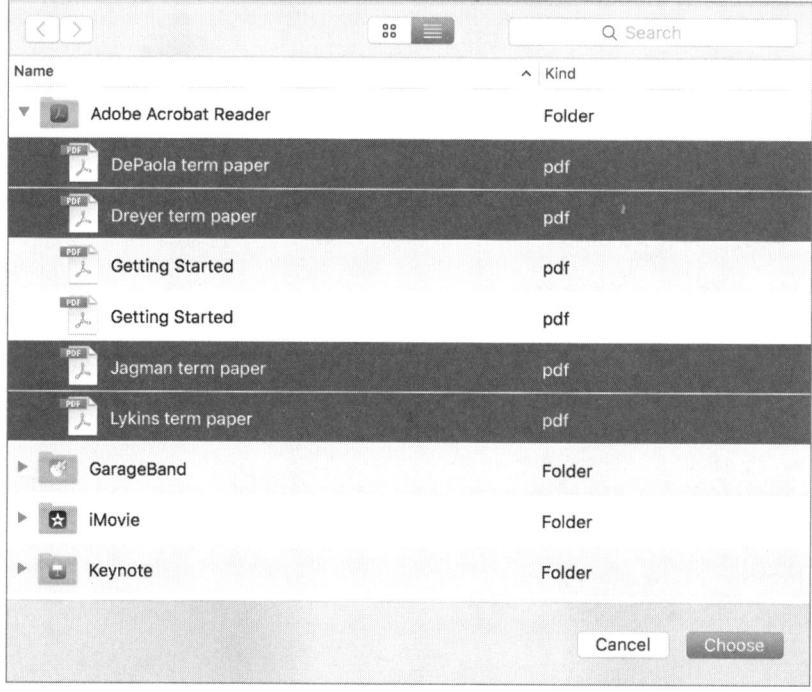

Then select the location for the exported documents. Each document will be in a folder, whose name is made from the name of the app, followed by the name of the device in parentheses.

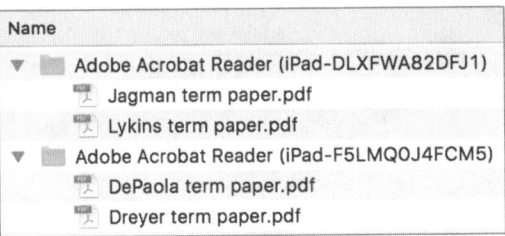

Reference 14.3
Update Apps Deployed via Apple Configurator 2

You may find that immediately after you deploy an app with Apple Configurator 2, an update will be available. Luckily, it's easy to see when an app is available, and it's easy to update.

Update Apps via Apple Configurator

When a device displays a red badge in the device browser window, that means an iOS update, an app update, or both are available. In the following figure, there are three updates available for the device:

To see what is ready for an update, double-click the device, or choose File > Get Info. While Info is selected in the left column, note that there is an Update button in the iOS version section. This available update explains the number 1 next to Info in the left column.

In the left column, the Apps category is marked as having two available updates; when you select Apps, the apps that have updates available are marked.

To update the device, click Update in the toolbar.

The dialog indicates what will be updated; click Update.

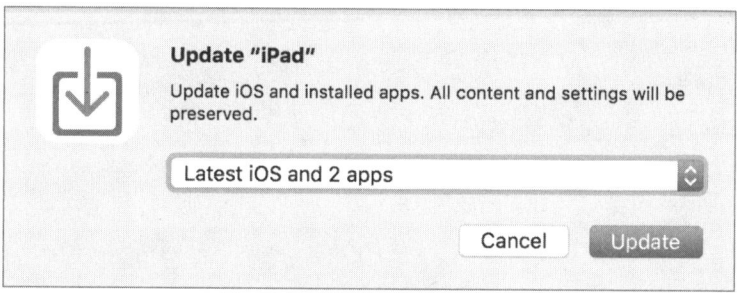

Update Apps via iOS Software Update

The far easier solution for most environments is to have iOS automatically update apps via the built-in software update mechanism. Once configured, this solution is fully automatic and almost never needs to interrupt the user or administrators.

> **TIP** As a reminder, having a local Apple caching server will save you a tremendous amount of Internet bandwidth and time updating iOS apps over the air. The Caching service is covered in Lesson 5, "Caching Service."

As convenient as the iOS software update mechanism is, it isn't without its caveats. First is the potential issue of turning on iOS software updates. Wi-Fi–only iOS devices will have this setting turned on as a default. However, if an iOS device includes cellular capability, as a default the iOS software update preference will be turned off. A potential solution when preparing these devices is to turn on iOS software updates on a template iOS device and then save and restore a backup to the others.

Even if you have the service turned on, someone still has to authenticate once with an Apple ID to allow the App Store to download updates. Unfortunately, this setting cannot be restored from a backup because it contains secrets (the Apple ID authentication). Thus, to turn on automatic updates, an administrator will have to authenticate with an Apple ID in the App Store or via iTunes & App Store in the Settings app. Configuring this in the Settings app is preferred because you can also verify whether automatic updates are turned on.

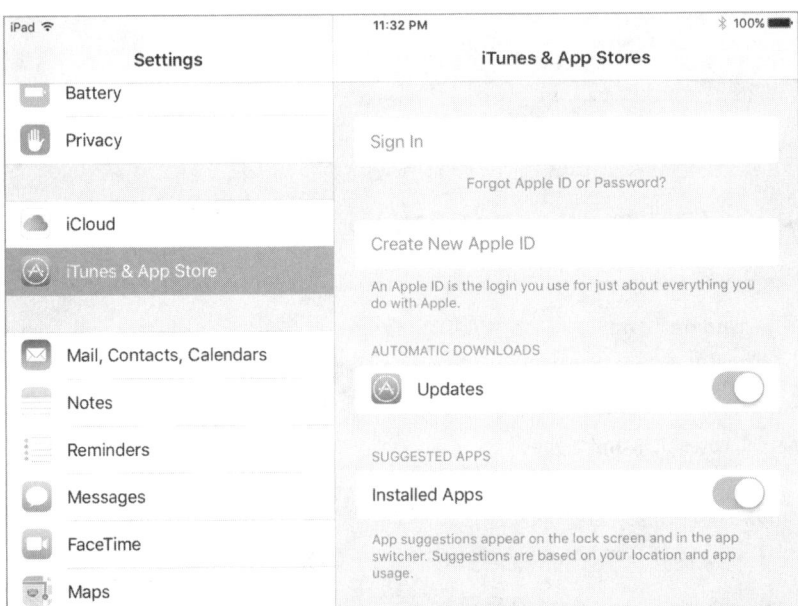

This leads us to the second problem: Which Apple ID? As covered previously, iOS apps installed with a personal Apple ID via Apple Configurator 2 will belong to that personal Apple ID. Thus, if a user or the system attempts to update these apps on the iOS device, he will need to be signed in with that same Apple ID.

Even if you do sign in with that personal Apple ID, this prevents the user from using his own Apple ID in the App Store. This is probably not an issue for shared iOS devices, especially if the workflow involves using the same Apple ID for all the devices in the same cart or physical area.

However, for deployments where the iOS devices are used primarily by individual users, requiring a shared Apple ID for App Store access is not ideal. Again, if your iOS devices are going to be primarily used by individual users, you're better off deploying all iOS apps using VPP-managed deployment (as covered in Lesson 10, "VPP-Managed Apps and Books") instead of Apple Configurator 2.

Reference 14.4
Single App Mode

Ever wonder how the iPads placed around the Apple Store that show prices are locked into a specific app? Single app mode is the answer. This mode can be engaged on supervised iOS devices locally via Apple Configurator 2 or over the air via an MDM service. In this section, you will explore how to put an iOS device into single app mode from both Apple Configurator 2 and Profile Manager.

Single App Mode via Apple Configurator 2

The Supervise view of Apple Configurator 2 allows you to lock iOS devices to a specific app. However, it's important to remember that supervised iOS devices are tied to the supervision identity that Apple Configurator 2 used to prepare the device. Thus, an instance of Apple Configurator 2 can manage single app mode only for iOS devices if it has the appropriate supervision identity.

To lock iOS devices to a specific app, select the devices, choose Actions > Advanced > Start Single App Mode, and then select an app from the Lock to App pop-up menu.

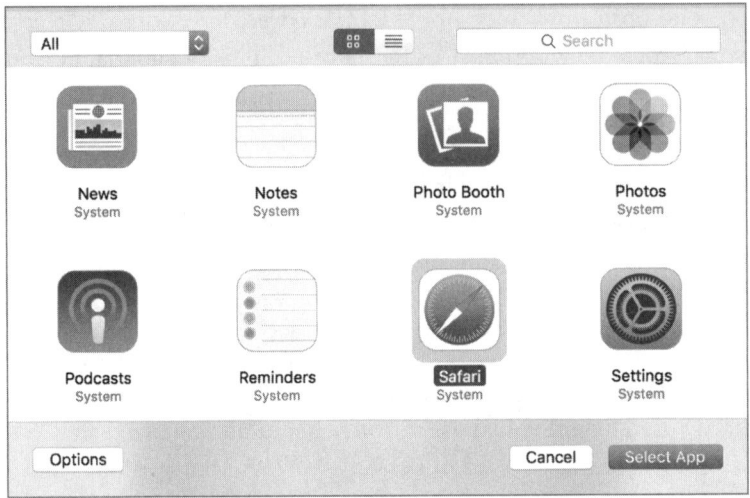

NOTE ▶ Only apps that are installed on at least one of the selected iOS devices appear in the pop-up menu. If you select an app that is not installed on one of the selected iOS devices, that device will display the following message and prevent any apps from opening until you stop single app mode: "Guided Access app unavailable. Please contact your administrator."

If your app-locked iOS devices require further restrictions, click the Options button. In the single app mode settings dialog, you can severely limit the device. While these additional options may seem excessively restrictive, in some environments this is the desired result. For example, if a device is to act as an always-on kiosk, turning off all the physical buttons may be best.

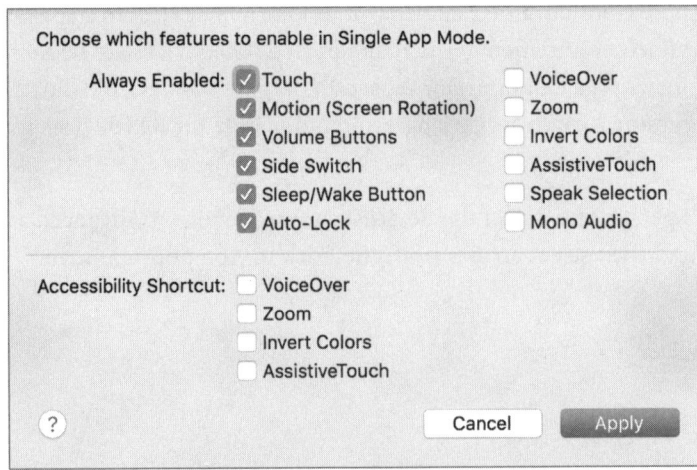

Once you have made your single app mode selections, click the Select App button at the bottom of Apple Configurator 2 to begin applying the settings to the supervised iOS devices. Any other iOS app will be paused on the devices, and the selected app will automatically open. The user will not be allowed to open another app or use any of the features you have turned off as defined by the single app mode settings.

To turn off single app mode, ensure that the iOS devices are connected to the Mac running Apple Configurator 2, select them, and then choose Actions > Advanced > Stop Single App Mode.

TIP Stopping single app mode will not close the app because this might interrupt the user's work.

Single App Mode via Profile Manager

As long as an iOS device is supervised via Apple Configurator 2 or one of the Apple programs for device enrollment (the DEP for businesses and Apple School Manager for schools), it can also be locked to an app over the air via an MDM service. In Profile Manager, the single app mode settings can pushed automatically via device or device group settings profile. Specifically, in the Profile Manager web interface, you can edit a device or device group's settings to include a single app mode payload. Be default, only built-in apps and apps that you have added using iOS restrictions will appear in the Lock to App pop-up menu; according to Help, "Additional apps show up in this list, if they've been added using the iOS restrictions settings."

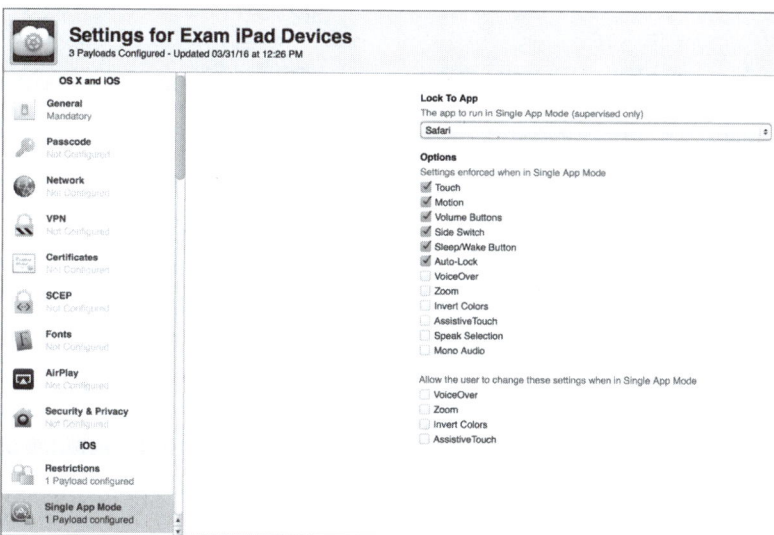

As you can see in the previous screenshot, the Single App Mode setting is in the iOS section of the sidebar; single app mode is available only to iOS devices. Further, single app mode settings in Profile Manger are identical to those found in Apple Configurator 2. The obvious advantage here is that changes made to single app mode for the selected devices are pushed to the devices over the air mere moments after you click the Save button in Profile Manager.

Rather than repeatedly modifying a configuration profile to change whether a device or device group is in single app mode, consider creating a device group with a configuration profile that specifies an app for single app mode. Then use that group's Membership tab to add and remove devices and device groups.

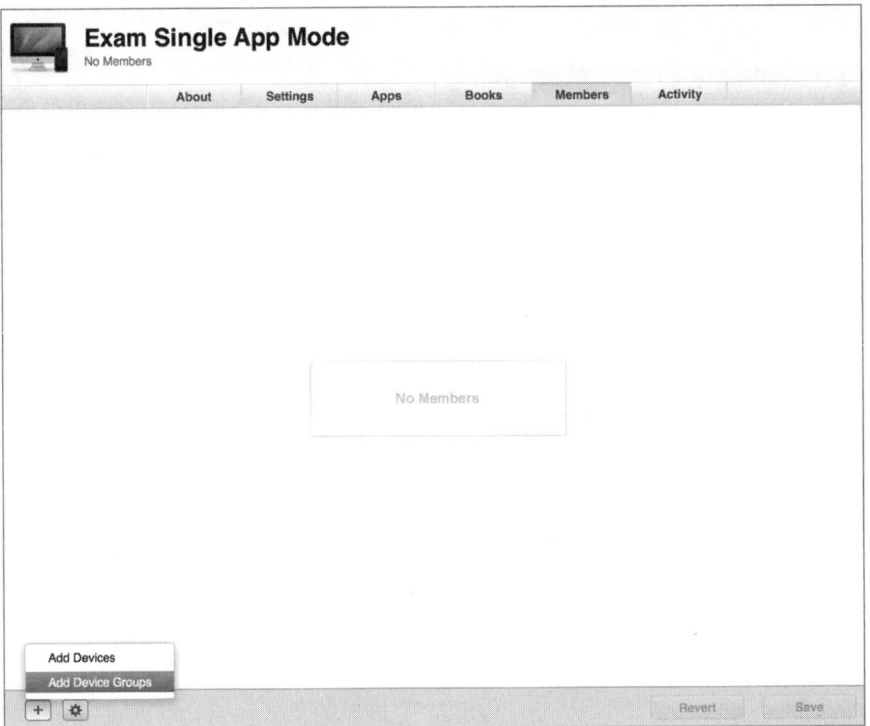

NOTE ▶ If your deployment would benefit from frequent single app mode changes (in a classroom environment, for example), then you may want to consider using the new Classroom app from Apple, or a third-party MDM solution, to provide a better interface for managing single app mode. For example, the Casper Suite includes the Casper Focus iOS app that allows teachers to quickly and easily manage single app mode for a group of devices in a classroom.

Exercise 14.1
Distribute Volume Purchase Program Apps via Apple Configurator 2

▶ **Prerequisites**

- ▶ Exercise 10.1, "Configure Profile Manager for the Volume Purchase Program"
- ▶ Exercise 10.2, "Purchase and Assign Licensed Apps to Devices"
- ▶ Exercise 12.1, "Get Apple Configurator 2"
- ▶ Exercise 13.1, "Create Configuration Profiles with Apple Configurator 2"
- ▶ Exercise 13.3, "Create and Apply Blueprints"

Challenge

Use your Volume Purchase Program (VPP) administrator credentials to sign in to Apple Configurator 2. Duplicate a blueprint used for MDM enrollment. Remove management via Apple Configurator 2 and set the Wi-Fi profile to expire. Add apps to the blueprint. Prepare your iOS device using the blueprint to distribute licenses of free apps to an iOS device. Create a folder with your apps using the Home Screen Layout payload from your MDM, and inspect the results.

Considerations

While apps can be distributed using a personal Apple ID, for more than one device, a VPP account is needed to be in compliance with many license agreements. Always read the license agreement for an app before distributing it.

As you learned in Chapter 10, "VPP-Managed Apps and Books," you need as many licenses as devices you intend to distribute the app on.

Unlike with previous versions of Apple Configurator, you do not need to preload apps on the computer running Apple Configurator 2, nor do you need to create a separate ID for app acquisition and distribution. Apple Configurator 2 downloads and distributes the apps as needed.

For best performance, with large app distribution loads, a caching server running on the Apple Configurator 2 computer is best practice.

Solution

Sign In to Apple Configurator 2 Using Your VPP Administrator Account

In previous exercises, you created a VPP administrator account and purchased licenses for two apps. You will use the same account in this exercise. Much like Profile Manager and other MDM solutions, Apple Configurator 2 is fully integrated with the Volume Purchase Program.

1   If necessary, open Apple Configurator 2 on your client Mac.

2   Choose Store > Sign In.

3   In the "Sign in to download from the App Store" pane, sign in using your VPP administrator Apple ID, which you created in Exercise 10.1.

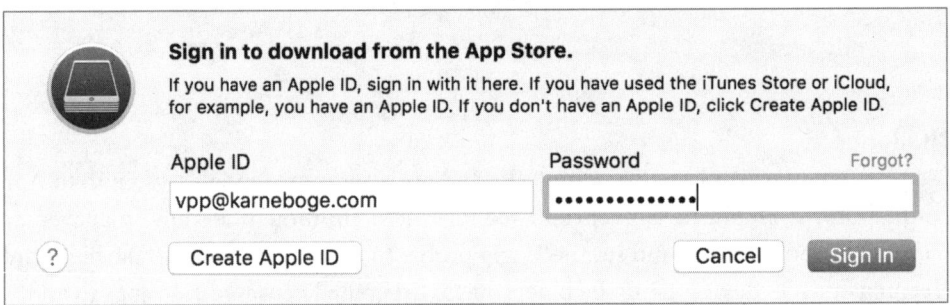

4   Click Sign In.

5   If you see a warning that your VPP account is already in use by your server, click Enable.

    As you are no longer assigning VPP apps from your server, you can click Enable.

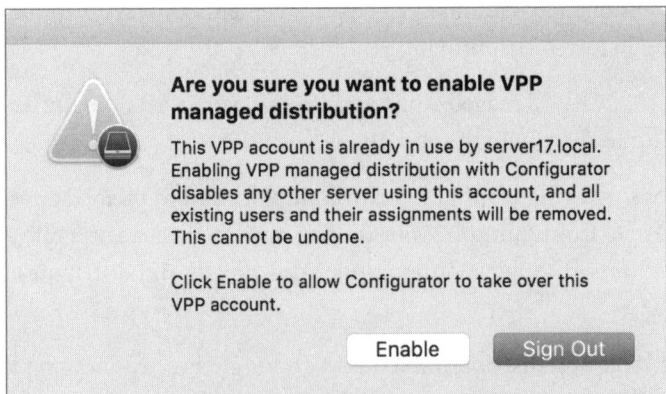

WARNING ▶ In a production environment, you should never click Enable in this dialog. At the time of this writing, VPP tokens cannot be shared among MDM servers or between a MDM server and an instance of Apple Configurator 2. Clicking Enable in a production environment will cause all apps that are assigned by that MDM to be revoked.

6   If you are asked to verify your identity using two-step verification, click Continue, enter the verification code, and click Verify.

7   The Store menu should now read Sign Out, indicating that you are signed in to the App Store. Do not choose Sign Out.

Duplicate a Blueprint and Remove Management

While you could easily add apps to an existing blueprint that contains all the management you need, you will create a new blueprint for the purposes of loading a base set of apps using VPP Managed Distribution and remove the management from this blueprint. Many organizations have devices that are not eligible for the DEP. These organizations will load a base set of apps, supervise their devices, enroll with the MDM using Apple Configurator 2, and then load additional apps and ongoing management from the MDM. This exercise simulates this workflow.

1   In the Apple Configurator 2 toolbar, click Blueprints, and then click Edit Blueprints.

2   Control-click the Configurator *n*-2 blueprint (where *n* is your student number), and then select Duplicate.

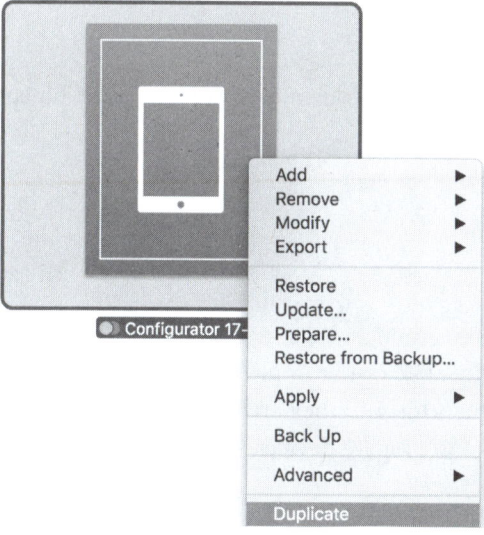

3 Single-click the name of the duplicated blueprint.

4 Name the duplicated blueprint Configurator *n*-3 (where *n* is your student number), and then press Return.

5 Double-click the Configurator *n*-3 blueprint (where *n* is your student number).

6 Choose Apple Configurator 2 > Preferences, and in the Preferences toolbar, click Tags.

7 Click Add (+)

8 Name the new tag Apps.

9 Click Change Color, and choose a color of your liking.

10 Close the Colors window, and then press Return.

11 Click Add (+).

12 Name the new tag Supervised.

13 Click Change Color, and choose a color of your liking.

14 Close the Colors window, and press Return.

15 Close the Preferences window, and then in the toolbar, click Tag.

16 Remove the Supervised with Management tag, add your two new tags, and then press Return.

17 Click outside of the tags window, and then scroll down to observe that the blueprint now has three tags indicating its configuration.

NOTE ▶ The purpose of tags is to easily group and distinguish groups of devices from each other regardless of the device state or the Apple Configurator 2 station you are using. Tags are an addition to a blueprint, and they are applied to and live on the device itself when the blueprint is used to prepare devices.

18 Click Remove (X) in all three areas to remove Device Name, Wallpaper, and Set Home Screen Layout.

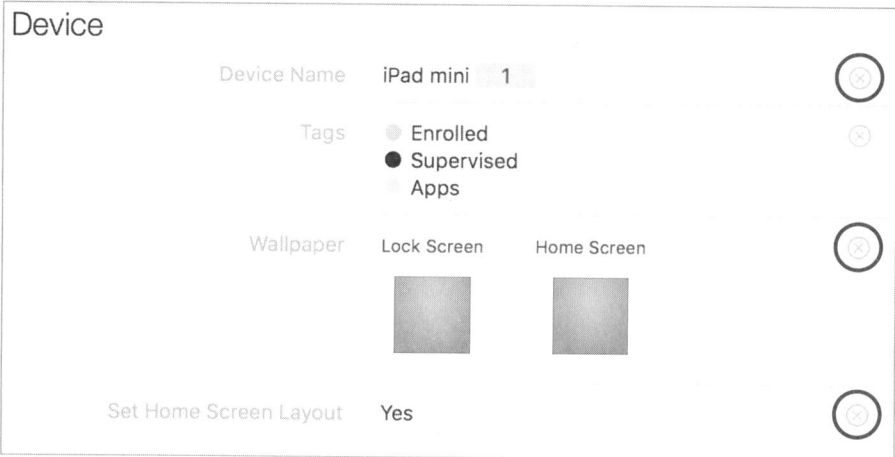

Create an Expiring Wi-Fi Profile and Remove the Existing Profiles

Often, for ease of enrollment, organizations will create a temporary enrollment network with less security (no password or a WPA2 password) and set up a Wi-Fi profile with that network that expires at a later time. The organization then provides management from the MDM that joins the devices to the secure corporate network.

1 Choose File > New Profile.

2 In the Name field for the General payload, enter Wi-Fi Expiring.

3 For Automatically Remove Profile, select After Interval, and enter 0 days 1 hours.

4 Leave all the other settings at their defaults.

5 In the payload sidebar, chose Wi-Fi, and then select Configure.

6 Enter the name of your Wi-Fi network in the SSID field. In an instructor-led environment, this may be Classroom Wireless.

7 Under Security Type, select WPA/WPA2 Personal.

8 Enter the password. In an instructor-led environment, this may be student!.

9 Choose File > Save. Leave the name as Wi-Fi Expiring Profile, and select Desktop from the Where pop-up menu.

10 Click Save.

11 Close the Wi-Fi Expiring Profile window.

12 In the Blueprint sidebar, click Profiles.

13 Select both existing profiles, and press Delete. Then in the confirmation dialog, click Remove.

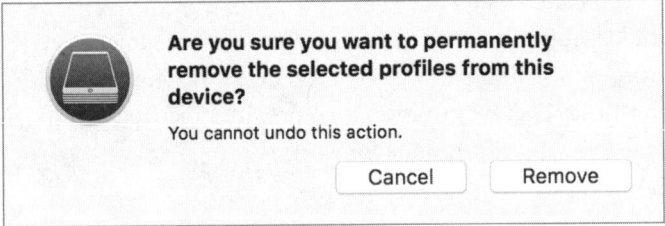

14 Click Add Profiles, and then select Desktop.

15 Select the Wi-Fi Expiring profile, and click Add.

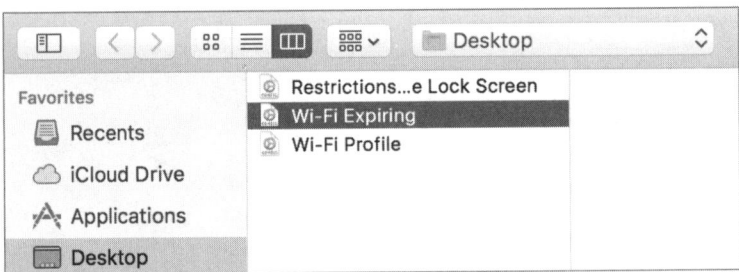

Your blueprint should have only the Wi-Fi Expiring profile present.

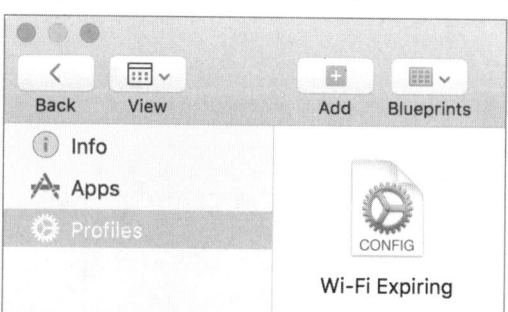

Add Apps to a Blueprint

Apps can be added to one or more devices in several ways. For mass deployment, however, it is best practice to add them to a blueprint so that the same configuration can be applied to multiple iOS devices.

1 In the Blueprint sidebar, click Apps.

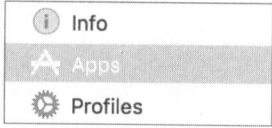

2 Click Add Apps.

Observe that you are using VPP Managed Distribution, as apps display the number of copies available beneath the name of the app.

3   Command-click SSL Detective and the additional free or paid app that you purchased in Exercise 10.2. Ensure both apps are highlighted.

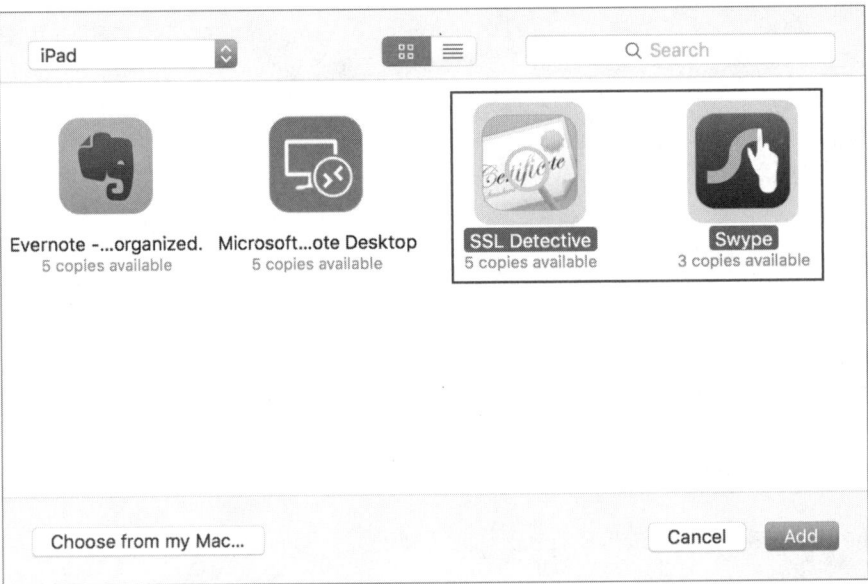

4   Click Add. You will see a progress bar for a short period, and the apps will be added to the blueprint.

NOTE ▶ The apps were not actually downloaded from the App Store at this point. They are merely added to the blueprint and will be downloaded on demand when you prepare a device. It is best practice to have a caching server running on the Apple Configurator 2 computer for best performance.

5   In the Blueprint sidebar, click Info.

Review that the blueprint now contains Apps and Profiles in Storage.

6   Click Done.

Erase All Content and Settings

If your iOS device is at the Welcome screen, skip to the next section.

1   On your iOS device, if necessary, slide at the "slide to unlock" screen.

2   If necessary, enter the passcode.

3   Open Settings.

4   Navigate to General > Reset.

5   Tap Erase All Content and Settings.

6   If your iOS device has a passcode, enter the passcode.

7   In the confirmation dialog, tap Erase.

8   In the extra confirmation dialog, tap Erase.

Wait while the iOS device erases all content and settings.

Apply the Blueprint to Your iOS Device

1   If necessary, connect your iOS device to your client Mac using the appropriate cable for your device.

2   Select your iOS device, select Blueprints from the toolbar, and then select Configurator *n*-3 (where *n* is your student number).

3   In the notification pane, click Apply.

4   Watch as Apple Configurator 2 prepares the device and deploys the configuration and apps.

    Note that Apple Configurator 2 downloads the apps needed on demand.

    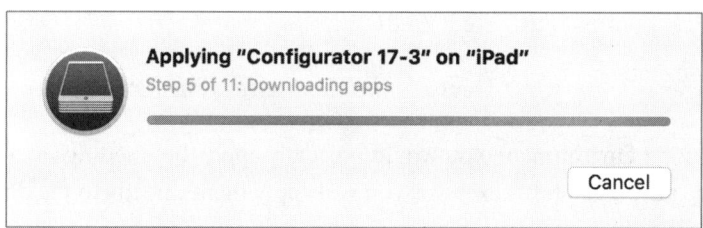

5   On your iOS device, slide at the "slide to set up" screen.

6   As the Wi-Fi network was already defined by the Wi-Fi Configuration Profile you made, tap Next.

7   At the Location Services screen, tap Enable Location Services.

8   At the Configuration screen, tap Apply Configuration, and then tap Next.

9   At the Log In screen, enter the following credentials, and tap Next:

▶ User Name: todd

▶ Password: net

10 Read the terms and conditions, tap Agree, and tap Agree again.

11 At the Welcome to iPad screen, tap Get Started.

12 If you see the Passcode Requirement notification, tap Later.

13 Slide to the second page of the Home screen, and observe that both apps were installed.

Manage the Network and Home Screen Layout Payloads for the Marketing Group

It is best practice to do any ongoing management from a MDM server.

1   On your server, in Safari, open the Profile Manager administration portal (https://servern.local/profilemanager, where *n* is your student number), and then authenticate with local administrator credentials.

2   In the Profile Manager sidebar, select Devices, and then select your iOS device.

   NOTE ▶ In a production environment, you would normally apply these settings to a device group. For the purposes of this exercise, you will apply them directly to the device.

3   Click the Settings tab.

4   Under Settings for iPad, click Edit.

5   In the General payload, for Security, select With Authorization, and enter the password profilepw.

6   In the payload sidebar, choose Network, and then click Configure.

7   Enter the name of your Wi-Fi network in the SSID field. In an instructor-led environment, this may be Classroom Wireless.

8   Under Security Type, select WPA/WPA2 Personal.

9   Enter the password. In an instructor-led environment, this may be student!.

10 In the payload sidebar, scroll and select the Home Screen Layout payload, and click Configure.

11 In the Page 1 field, click Add (+), and then select Add Folder.

12 Click twice on the Folder Name, type VPP Apps, and then press Return.

13 In the Page 1 – VPP Apps field, click Add (+), and add SSL Detective.

14 In the Page 1 – VPP Apps field, click Add (+), and add Swype, or whichever free or paid app you chose in Exercise 10.2.

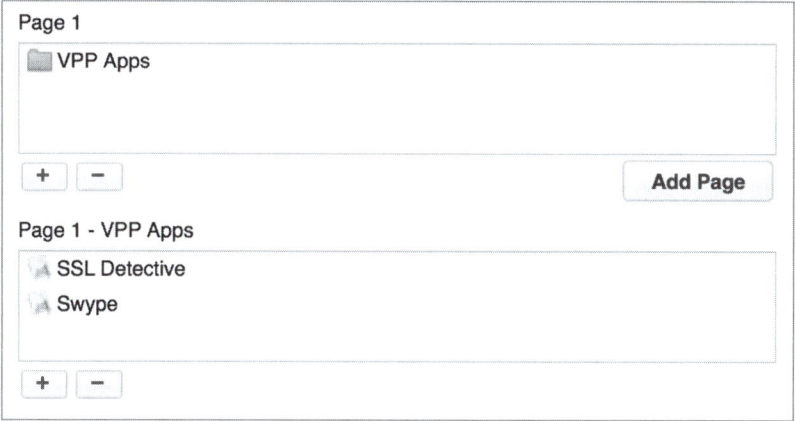

15 Click OK.

16 Click Save. The settings from the MDM should automatically push to the iOS device.

Inspect the Management on the iOS Device

1 On your iOS device, view the Home screen. As we did not specify any items for the Dock, it is blank. There is a VPP Apps folder.

2 Tap VPP Apps. The apps you installed appear in the folder.

3 Navigate to Settings > General > Profiles & Device Management.

The Wi-Fi Expiring profile came from Apple Configurator 2 and will expire and remove itself after one hour.

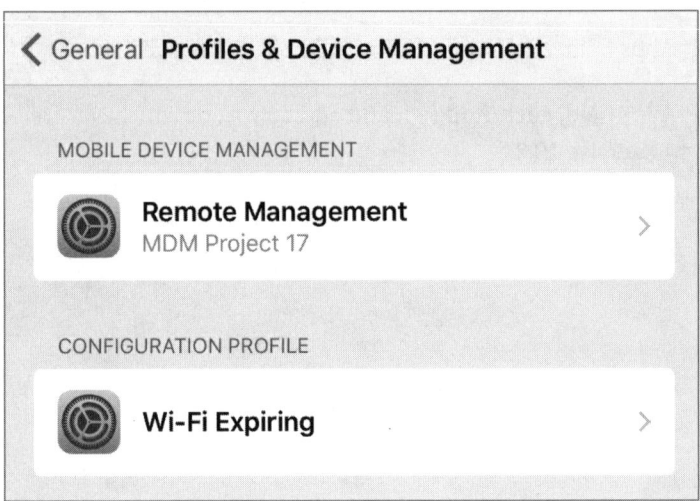

4 Tap Remote Management. Observe the payloads that the profile contains.

Exercise 14.1 Distribute Volume Purchase Program Apps via Apple Configurator 2   **637**

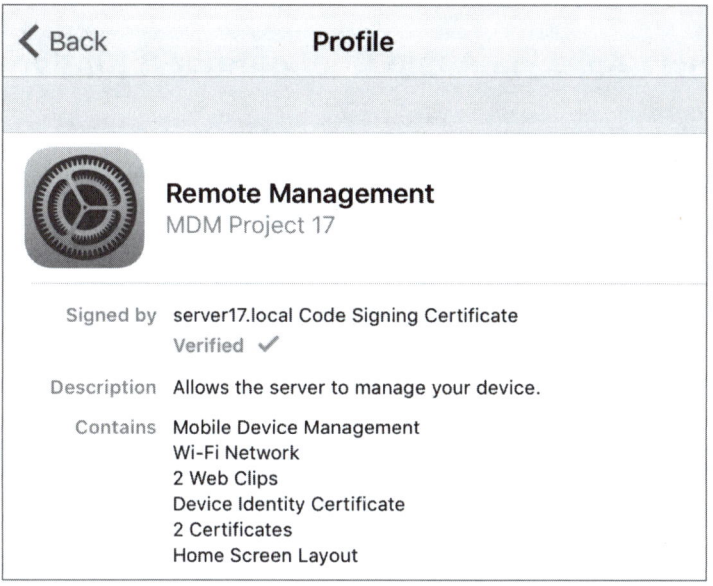

5   If necessary, on your server, in the Profile Manager sidebar, select Devices, and then select your iOS device.

6   If necessary, click Settings, and then under Settings for iPad, click Edit.

7   Scroll and select Home Screen Layout. Click Remove (–).

8   Click Remove All Settings.

9   Click Save.

10 On your iOS device, press the Home button.

Observe how Home Screen Layout returns to its default layout.

In this exercise, you signed in to Apple Configurator 2 with your VPP administrator account. You duplicated an existing blueprint, added two tags, and removed the existing actions. You then created a Wi-Fi profile that expires after one hour and removed the configuration profile with restrictions. You added VPP apps to a blueprint and then applied the blueprint to the iOS device. Finally, you created permanent Wi-Fi and Home Screen Layout payloads from the MDM server and inspected the results on your iOS device.

Exercise 14.2
Distribute In-House Apps via Apple Configurator 2 (Optional)

> **Prerequisites**
>
> ► Exercise 14.1, "Distribute Volume Purchase Program Apps via Apple Configurator 2"

Challenge
Load an in-house enterprise app on your iOS device. Use the Single App Mode payload on your MDM server. Clean up your MDM server and erase all content and settings on your iOS Device.

Considerations
Apps are best distributed using a blueprint. For the purposes of this exercise, however, you will add an app directly to the existing app load of your iOS device.

Solution

Add an In-House App from Your Mac Computer to Your iOS Device

1   If necessary, open Apple Configurator 2 on your client Mac.

2   Double-click your iOS device, and in the sidebar, choose Apps.

    Observe the two existing VPP apps.

3   In the toolbar, click Add (+), and click Apps.

4   Click Choose from my Mac, and navigate to the Lesson11 folder in StudentMaterials.

5   Select the in-house iOS enterprise app, and click Add.

Observe that the in-house iOS enterprise app is now in the apps window, and that the app is immediately added to the device.

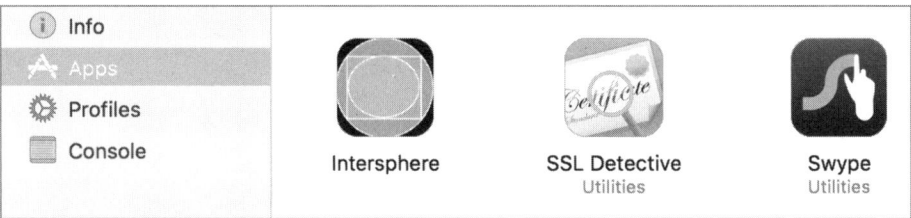

6   On your iOS device, press the Home button, and then slide and observe that the in-house iOS enterprise app is loaded on the device.

7   Navigate to Settings > General > Profiles & Device Management.

8   Tap the profile for the in-house iOS enterprise app.

9   Tap Trust for the organization that signed the in-house iOS enterprise app, and then in the notification, tap Trust.

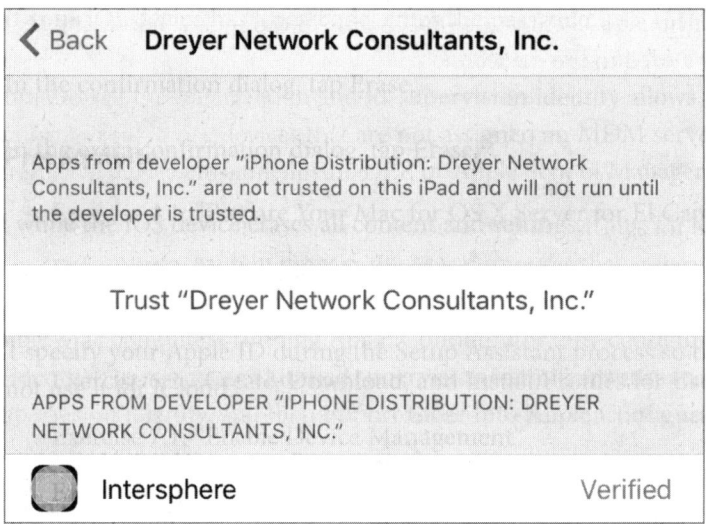

10 Press the Home button, slide if necessary, and tap the in-house iOS enterprise app.

The in-house iOS enterprise app will open.

11 Press the Home button to return to the Home screen.

Use Single App Mode

iOS devices are commonly used in kiosk scenarios in stores or in testing scenarios in education as the user cannot leave the app or use the iOS device for any other function other than the app the device is locked to.

1 If necessary, on your server, in Safari, open the Profile Manager administration portal (https://server*n*.local/profilemanager, where *n* is your student number), and then authenticate with local administrator credentials.

2 If necessary, in the Profile Manager sidebar, select Devices, and then select your iOS device.

3 Click the Action (gear) menu, and select Update Info.

4 In the confirmation dialog, click Update Info.

5   If necessary, click the Settings tab.

6   Under Settings for iPad, click Edit.

7   In the payload sidebar, click Single App Mode.

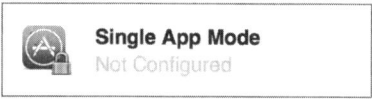

8   Click Configure

9   Under the Lock to App menu, select the in-house iOS enterprise app.

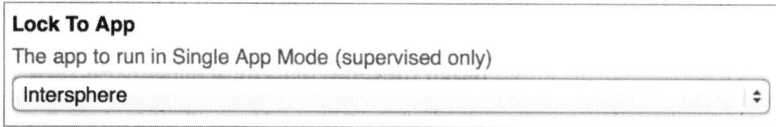

10   Leave all the other settings at their defaults.

11   Click OK.

12   Click Save.

     The setting will be pushed to your iOS device. On your iOS device, all apps will disappear, and the in-house iOS enterprise app will open.

13   On your iOS device, press the Home button.

     Note that you are not able to leave the app.

Clean Up

1   On your server, in the Profile Manager sidebar, click Devices, and select your iOS device.

2   Click Remove (–), and click Unenroll.

3   Remove the placeholder by clicking Remove (–) again.

4   In the confirmation dialog, click Remove.

5   On your client Mac, in Apple Configurator 2, choose Window > VPP Assignments.

    Observe that the two apps you have assigned have used licenses.

    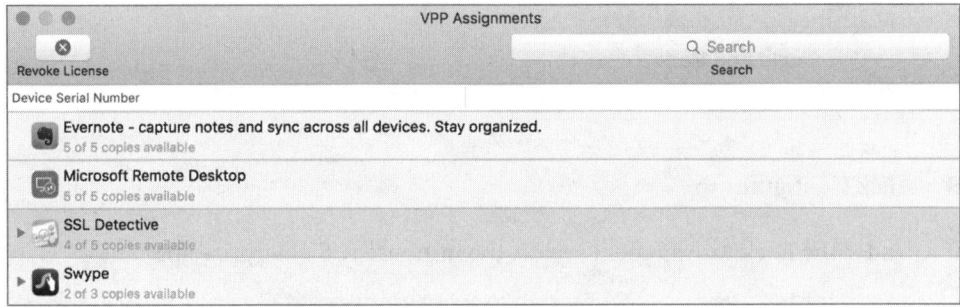

6   Click the disclosure triangle, and note how the license is associated with the serial number of your iOS device.

7   Click SSL Detective, and click Revoke License.

8   In the confirmation dialog, click Revoke.

    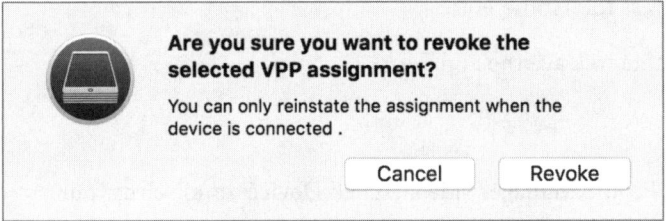

9   Repeat steps 7 and 8 for the other app you assigned.

10 Close the VPP Assignments window.

11 Click Back (<) in the toolbar.

Erase All Content and Settings Using Apple Configurator 2

1   On your client Mac, in Apple Configurator 2, ensure that your iOS device is selected.

2   Choose Actions > Advanced > Erase All Content and Settings.

3   In the following pane, click Erase.

   Apple Configurator 2 will unsupervise and wipe the device.

In this exercise, you deployed an in-house enterprise app to your iOS device. You used the Single App Mode payload on your MDM server to lock the device to the enterprise app. Finally, you revoked VPP licenses.

Lesson 15

User Data and Services

Beyond all other aspects of their Apple device experience, users care most about their content. After all, the user-created content brings meaning to the apps and functionality of these devices.

GOAL

▶ Consider solutions for sharing and backing up user content

As an administrator, your job doesn't stop at simply preparing and managing devices. Successful Apple deployments also rely heavily on tools and methods that allow users to easily consume, create, and share content. Further, as an administrator, you should make sure users are doing what they need to prepare for the worst-case scenario, the complete loss of an Apple device. In the first part of this lesson, you will explore solutions for sharing and protecting user content on iOS and OS X devices.

Reference 15.1
User Content Considerations

This section covers tools and methods used for sharing and backing up user content on Apple devices. Where appropriate, solutions that support both platforms will be highlighted. It's important to recognize that at this point, iOS and OS X still offer quite different solutions for managing user content, even as each platform is informed by the strengths of the other. Apple has worked hard to unify some of these methods, but some insurmountable differences still exist between the two systems in specific areas such as traditional file-sharing and backup solutions.

Traditional Sharing and Storage Options

OS X has a long history of providing a flexible file system that allows for nearly unlimited options for managing content. On the other hand, Apple designed iOS with simplicity in mind, and with simplicity comes limited choices for managing content when using traditional file-sharing techniques.

The following are some traditional storage options available to iOS devices:

▶ **Locally attached drives**—iOS is quite limited in this respect. Every iOS device includes a universal serial bus (USB) adapter, but it's used only for syncing and charging. Apple also offers the USB Camera Adapter and the SD Card Camera Reader for iOS devices, but these adapters just provide read-only access for camera storage.

> **TIP** ▶ The iOS Apple USB Camera Adapter does allow for other USB devices such as keyboards, audio-input devices, hubs, Ethernet adapters, and bar code scanners, but it does not support any storage devices outside of digital cameras. See Apple Support article HT202034, "Use Apple USB camera adapters with other USB devices," for more information.

▶ **Network file sharing with OS X Server**—OS X Server 5 on OS X El Capitan introduced features to the File Sharing service that make it easier to share files with devices with iOS 9. On your iOS device with iOS 9 or later, tap Settings > Mail, Contacts, Calendars > Add Account > Other > Add OS X Server account. In the Server app, edit the properties for a shared folder, and in the Access section, select the iOS checkbox. Additionally, in the main File Sharing pane, you can select the checkbox "Create personal folders when users connect on iOS."

> **MORE INFO** ▶ See Reference 11.2, "Creating Share Points," in *OS X Server 5.0 Essentials: Apple Pro Training Series: Using and Supporting OS X Server on El Capitan* for more information about sharing files for iOS using OS X Server.

▶ **Network file sharing**—As a default, iOS is quite limited in this respect. Some apps, such as Keynote, Numbers, and Pages, are designed specifically to take advantage of built-in iOS WebDAV file sharing, as covered later in this lesson. Support for other file-sharing protocols, such as Apple Filing Protocol (AFP) and Server Message Block (SMB), is possible only when using third-party iOS apps and services.

▶ **Collaboration services**—iOS offers good support for sharing content via email, messaging, wiki, and calendaring services that support attachments. Although file attachments aren't the best way to share a lot of items, collaboration services are easily the most widely compatible methods for people to share files.

> **MORE INFO** ▶ See Lesson 20, Lesson 21, Lesson 22, and Lesson 24 in *OS X Server 5.0 Essentials: Apple Pro Training Series: Using and Supporting OS X Server on El Capitan* for more information about the collaborative services in OS X Server.

▶ Ad hoc services—Apple has created several ad hoc sharing options for iOS devices. AirDrop allows iOS 7 or later devices to share files within local wireless range. With iOS 8, AirDrop was updated to support file sharing with OS X Yosemite and later as well. For media content, AirPlay allows compatible iOS devices to stream playback over AirPlay devices, such as Apple TV. However, AirPlay streaming is only temporary, and it doesn't fully share content to other devices.

MORE INFO ▶ For more information about using AirDrop with iOS devices, see Apple Support article HT204144, "Share content with AirDrop from your iPhone, iPad, or iPod touch."

TIP ▶ Software available from third parties will add AirPlay compatibility to unsupported devices—for example, to allow a Mac or PC to behave as an AirPlay destination. Solutions for adding AirPlay support include AirServer and Reflector.

The following are some traditional storage options available to OS X computers:

▶ Locally attached drives—This is one area where OS X is much more flexible than iOS. Odds are if you can physically connect the storage device to your Mac, it will probably just work. OS X does have limited write capability for NTFS volumes, but this can be resolved with freely available software drivers. Ultimately, the inclusion of the Finder app in OS X allows users to move and copy files to any location.

▶ Network file sharing—Again, OS X offers great flexibility for sharing files via traditional file-sharing protocols. Odds are if you have access to a file-sharing service, it will use one of the protocols supported by OS X. Common file-sharing protocols are SMB, AFP, WebDAV, and File Transfer Protocol (FTP).

▶ Collaboration services—OS X also offers good support for sharing content via email, messaging, wiki, and calendaring services that support attachments. Again, though file attachments aren't the best way to share a lot of items, collaboration services are available to almost every user on every device.

▶ Ad hoc services—In addition to AirDrop and AirPlay support, OS X offers good support for ad hoc file sharing with Bluetooth-enabled devices. Again, AirDrop was upgraded in iOS 8 and OS X Yosemite to allow ad hoc sharing between both platforms.

MORE INFO ▶ For more information about using AirDrop with OS X computers, see Apple Support article HT203106, "Use AirDrop to send content from your Mac."

Internet Sharing and Storage Options

In the last few years, Internet and cloud services have followed a popularity trajectory similar to that of mobile devices. This is no wonder because the two go hand in hand to provide a highly mobile solution to the content problem. After all, if your device can go anywhere, the content you want should be available everywhere.

Apple has pretty much unified built-in support for Internet-based services between iOS and OS X. Both systems can be configured to use Internet service accounts for Apple iCloud, Microsoft Exchange, Google, Twitter, Facebook, LinkedIn, Yahoo, AOL, Vimeo, and Flickr, along with other common network service protocols including those hosted from a system running OS X Server.

In iOS, you'll find the account sign-in and settings for Internet services split in the Settings app. Some are in the Mail, Contacts, Calendars settings, and some are listed separately, such as for Twitter, Facebook, Flickr, and Vimeo.

MORE INFO ▶ The Internet services that appear may vary according to your region. See Apple Support article HT202605, "Sign in to social networks like Facebook and Twitter on your iPhone, iPad, and iPod touch," for more information about setting your language or adding a Chinese-language keyboard to reveal more options.

On OS X, you'll find account sign-in and settings for all these services in the appropriately named Internet Accounts system preference.

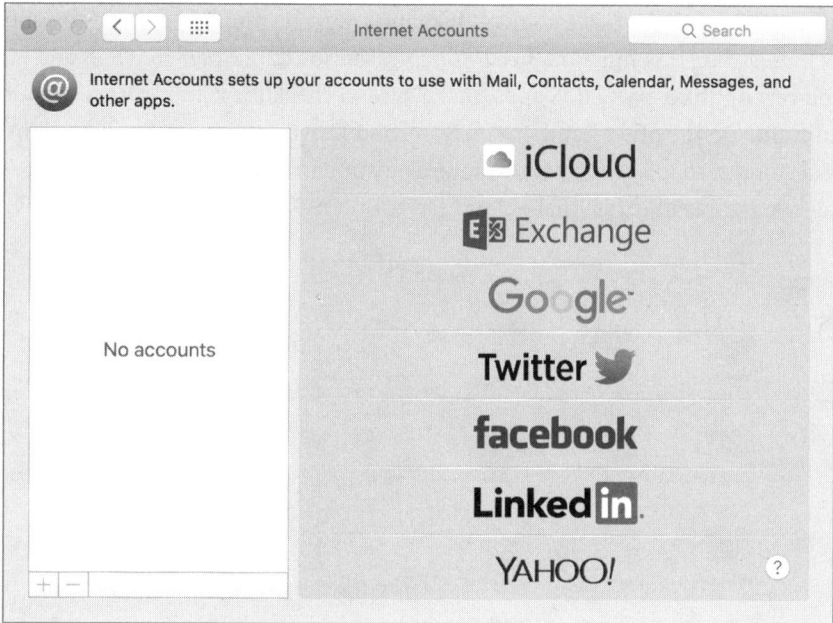

NOTE ▶ The services that appear in the Internet Accounts pane may vary according to your region. For example, you can open System Preferences, open Keyboard preferences, add a Chinese input source, and then open Internet Accounts preferences to reveal more options.

Beyond the built-in Internet services, both iOS and OS X support other third-party Internet storage services with the installation of appropriate apps. For example, popular Internet storage solutions such as Dropbox, Google Drive, Microsoft OneDrive, and Box all have free iOS and OS X apps that allow for service access.

The availability of a visible system in OS X allows users to save and access just about any file with a third-party Internet storage service. On the other hand, iOS lacks a visible file system, so apps must be properly created to access items from a third-party Internet storage service.

Fortunately, iOS 8 introduced the ability for third parties to create Share and Document Provider App Extensions, thus allowing any properly created app to directly access a third-party Internet storage service. For example, with the Dropbox iOS app installed, the Pages iOS app can save directly to Dropbox via the Sharing panel.

iCloud Drive

Of Internet storage services, Apple's iCloud Drive, introduced along with iOS 8 and OS X Yosemite, features the deepest integration throughout the systems by allowing any app (from both Apple and third parties) to save content. iOS apps must be properly created to support iCloud Drive, but adding this functionality is much easier for developers in iOS 8 and later. Even so, if you rely on third-party iOS apps, make sure to check for iCloud Drive support before you commit. On the other hand, in OS X, iCloud Drive appears in the file system like any other local storage, so OS X apps don't require any updating to support iCloud Drive. The following two figures illustrate that iCloud Drive on OS X and iOS appear similarly:

Users who have created a new iCloud account with iOS 8 and later or OS X Yosemite and later will automatically have iCloud Drive enabled when they sign in to iCloud. However, existing iCloud accounts need to be upgraded to support iCloud Drive. When an existing iCloud account signs in to a device with iOS 8 and later or OS X Yosemite and later for the first time, the user is asked to upgrade to iCloud Drive. This most often happens during the Setup Assistant process, but it can also be initiated from the iCloud settings.

> **MORE INFO** ► You can find out more about iCloud drive from the Apple website, https://www.apple.com/icloud/icloud-drive/.

iOS iTunes Syncing

One mechanism that brings iOS and OS X together is iTunes sync functionality. Originally, iOS devices were heavily dependent on iTunes for access to nearly all forms of content. As iOS has matured, its dependence on syncing to a PC via iTunes has shrunk to the point where it's not necessary for a great number of users and uses.

That being said, iOS devices still maintain a syncing functionality with iTunes that, depending on the need, may still be quite useful. First, understand that any items synced via iTunes are often not part of an iOS backup. This serves a dual purpose to minimize iOS backup size and to access the items in iTunes for the PC as well. The assumption is that large media files, such as music and movies, can be played back in iTunes for the PC and don't change much, so they are synced via iTunes instead of being part of an iOS backup.

> **NOTE** ► An exception to the lack of media in iOS backups are media items created by an iOS app. For example, media in the Camera Roll of the Camera app will be included in an iOS backup.

Second, if you or your users have a great deal of media to transfer to an iOS device for offline use, iTunes sync is still the best method. As you can see from the following screenshot, iTunes can be used to sync apps, ringtones, music, movies, TV shows, books (and other things read by iBooks such as PDFs), and photos. iTunes can also sync other items, including audiobooks, iTunes U content, Safari bookmarks, contacts, calendars, and notes. Finally, iTunes can be used to sync some documents between iOS apps and the PC running iTunes, though this is dependent on support from each specific iOS app.

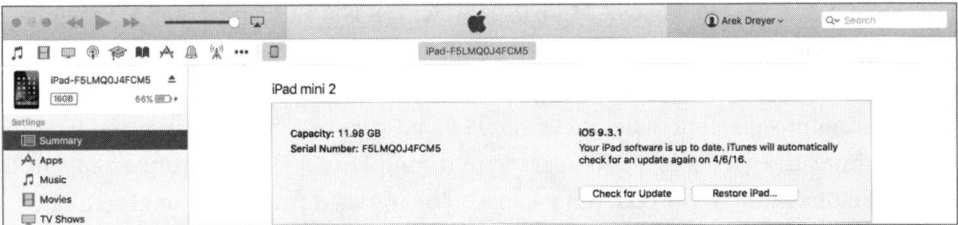

iOS Backup Solutions

The only supported systemwide backup solution for iOS is the one Apple built in to the system. iTunes and iCloud are the two iOS backup destinations. iTunes allows for local fast backups over both USB and local Wi-Fi, whereas iCloud backup performance is dependent on your Internet connection speed. Once enabled, iOS will attempt to keep the backup content fresh by automatically backing up on a regular basis as long as the device is on Wi-Fi, plugged in for charging, and locked.

An iTunes iOS backup contains basically everything that isn't the system or installed apps or isn't synced via iTunes. Further, encrypted iTunes iOS backups will include the keychain, which contains secrets such as user names and passwords. Both enabling and restoring iTunes iOS backups are managed by the iTunes app from the attached PC.

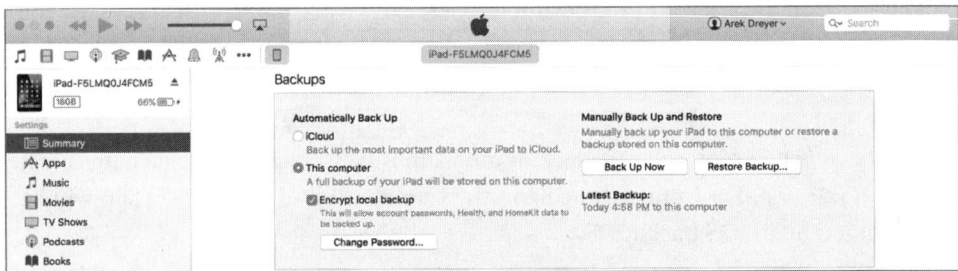

MORE INFO ▶ You can find out more about the content of iTunes iOS backups in Apple Support article HT204136, "About backups in iCloud and iTunes."

An iCloud iOS backup is similar to an iTunes backup except it excludes anything also stored in iCloud. The assumption is that items already stored in iCloud don't need to be backed up again to iCloud. You turn on iCloud iOS backups in Settings > iCloud > iCloud Backup, and you can restore iCloud iOS backups only during the iOS Setup Assistant process.

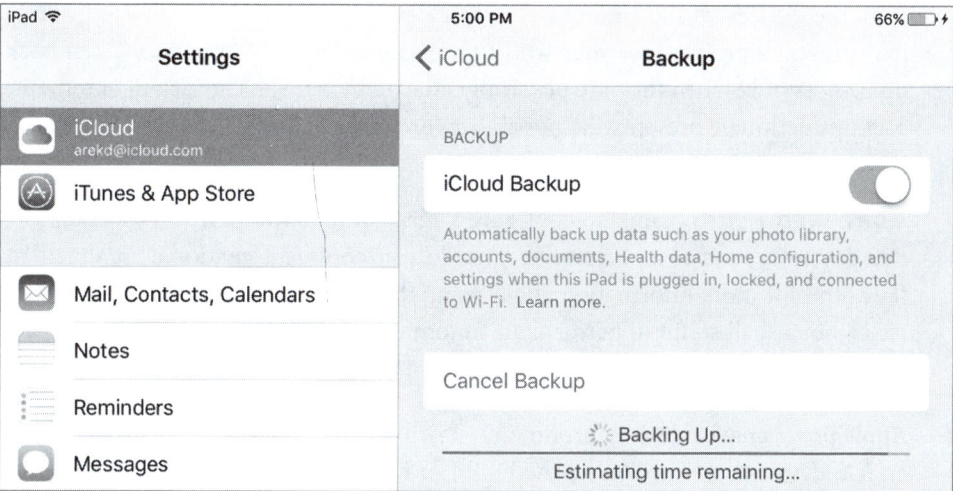

MORE INFO ▶ You can find out more about the content of iCloud iOS backups in Apple Support article PH12519, "iCloud: iCloud storage and backup overview."

iOS Restoration Workflows

From a management perspective, restoring an iOS backup presents two main problems: iOS devices allow for restoration only during the iOS Setup Assistant process, and restoring an iOS backup to a different device will not restore any installed profiles, thus negating management settings.

Given these iOS restoration limitations, consider how this works with your iOS management workflow:

▶ User self-enrolled device—In this case, the restoration workflow is similar to a normal personal device. Simply restore to the new iOS device as normal, through either iTunes or iCloud. Then enroll the new device as you would any other self-enrolled device.

▶ Unsupervised Apple Configurator 2 device—In this case, the restoration workflow is similar to a normal personal device. The only difference is that after the new iOS device has been restored, it can't be prepared with Apple Configurator 2. Instead, you can use Apple Configurator 2 to manually install any necessary profiles.

▶ Supervised Apple Configurator 2 device—Restoring an iOS backup via iTunes or iCloud to a different device will not maintain supervision. In this case, the only possible workflow to perform a restore and maintain supervision is to back up from the old device and restore to the new device via Apple Configurator 2. This may present a problem for your workflow because Apple Configurator 2 can back up devices only when they are physically attached via USB. The lack of automatic backups definitely presents the possibility for a user to lose data if the old iOS device is permanently lost.

> **MORE INFO** ▶ It's possible to configure a Mac computer to perform a backup of an iOS device as soon as it is connected. See https://configautomation.com/attach-workflow.html for more information about using the **cfgutil** command-line tool to automatically run a shell script to perform an Automator workflow (such as Backup Specified Devices) any time an iOS device is connected to a Mac computer.

- Apple programs for device enrollment—With iOS 8 or later, restoring a backup to an iOS device that's enrolled in the DEP (for business) or Apple School Manager (for schools) with managed Setup Assistant works properly only as long as the Set Up as New or Restore option is allowed. During Setup Assistant, the user will be allowed to start the restore process (from iCloud or from iTunes) before the device is enrolled. Immediately after the restore is complete, the device will automatically restart, and then Setup Assistant will continue with any required enrollment steps.

If your management workflow is incompatible with restoring from an iOS backup, you need to consider alternate solutions for saving user data. In many ways, iCloud or third-party Internet storage services can negate the need for backing up iOS devices.

Even if your organization doesn't allow iCloud, as an administrator, users will look to you for guidance about how to keep their content safe. Thus, before your users become heavily dependent on iOS devices for mission-critical work, you need to find a method to back up or save this information in case an iOS device is lost or damaged beyond repair.

OS X Backup Solutions

Again, because of the more flexible nature of OS X, an administrator has a wide variety of choices for backing up and restoring OS X computers. Apple's Time Machine is a robust and easy-to-use solution that provides a near-full system backup of OS X computers. The only items left out of a Time Machine backup are basically temporary or items in the Trash.

Time Machine can be set to back up to a locally attached drive with just one click. You can also connect to network backup destinations and manage Time Machine from the Time Machine system preference.

TIP ▶ Because Time Machine can back up an entire OS X system, you are strongly encouraged to turn on encryption for Time Machine backup destinations.

Time Machine supports locally attached drives, Apple AirPort Time Capsule Wi-Fi routers with storage, and OS X Server computers providing the Time Machine service. Although backing up over Wi-Fi is much more convenient, one downside of Time Machine is its high overhead. A single AirPort Time Capsule or OS X Server computer providing the Time Machine service will quickly fill up when backing up more than a few OS X devices.

Also, from a management perspective, Time Machine lacks in almost every way when compared to a backup solution designed to meet the needs of an organization. Even when providing the Time Machine service via OS X Server, there is no centralized management for any of the backup settings except for the option to limit each backup to a size you specify.

The general lack of enterprise features makes Time Machine less than ideal for many organizations, but for others this isn't such a big deal. Time Machine is still a reliable backup solution that can be used by nearly anyone, so it may still have a place in your organization.

After all, Time Machine's greatest strength is its flexibility when restoring from a backup. Full systems can be restored using OS X Recovery. User accounts can be restored during Setup Assistant or with the Migration Assistant app. Individual items can be restored from the Time Machine Finder interface.

Thus, to recover from a completely lost OS X system, you can simply restore the entire system. However, similar to iOS, a fully restored system on a different Mac computer will have to be reenrolled into your MDM service. Alternatively, you can prepare a new system using your existing deployment workflow and then restore only the user's home folder.

Managing Backups

If a user makes a backup of a device that contains organizational data, she can restore the backup to another device, including the organizational data. Your organization may decide to restrict backups to prevent users from restoring organizational data to devices that are not managed by the organization.

With Profile Manager as an example MDM, the following restrictions available for managed iOS devices can help you manage backups:

▶ Allow iCloud backup—Deselect this option to disallow users from using iCloud to make a backup of an iOS device (allowed by default).

▶ Allow backup of enterprise books—Deselect this option to disallow users from backing up enterprise books that are installed via MDM (allowed by default).

▶ Force encrypted backups—Select this option to force the user of the device to set a password for making backups, to protect the backup from being used by unauthorized users (not forced by default).

▶ Allow pairing with non-Configurator hosts (supervised only)—This option (not shown in the following screenshot) is allowed by default; deselect to prevent a user from using iTunes to make a backup of the device (this also prevents a user from using Image Capture with the device). You can also prevent pairing when you use Apple Configurator or Apple Configurator 2 to supervise an iOS device.

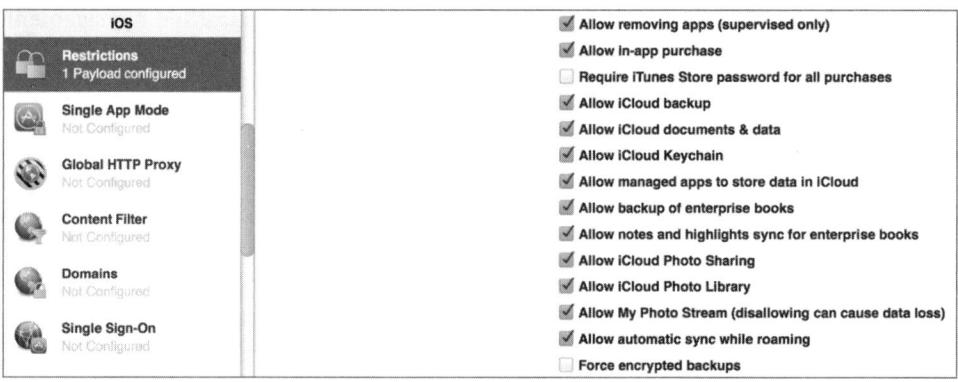

Additionally, for OS X, you can use Profile Manager to disable access to Time Machine preferences to prevent users from setting up a new Time Machine backup disk. This will not prevent users from copying files manually or from installing another backup solution.

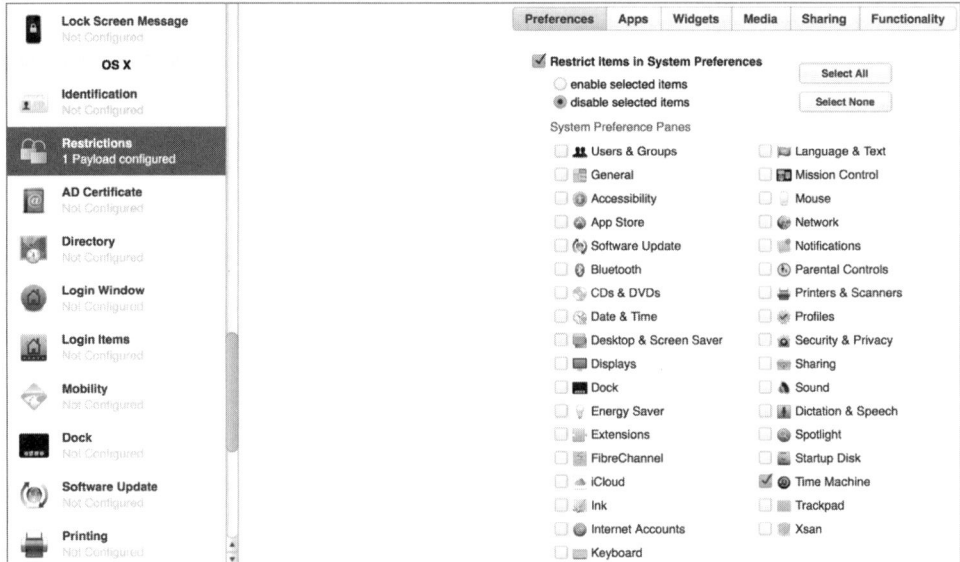

NOTE ▶ If a Time Machine destination disk is already defined, restricting access to Time Machine preferences does not prevent Time Machine backups from running.

Lesson 16
Managing Access

While most administrators are concerned with providing access for their users to save and share files, for some organizations preventing this access is more important. Over the years, Apple has increased the number of ways an administrator can use profiles to restrict access to content and services.

This lesson explores profile-based restrictions that can be set for limiting access to apps, services, sharing, storage, and backup on both iOS and OS X devices. This lesson's primary focus is to show you how to take advantage of Managed Open In to control sharing of organizationally owned content on iOS devices. The latter half of this lesson briefly discusses general restrictions settings.

GOALS

▶ Prevent users from sharing organizationally owned content with Managed Open In

▶ Explore management settings that can limit access to apps and services

Reference 16.1
Managed Open In

Introduced with iOS 7, Managed Open In is a set of restrictions allowing administrators to give users access to sharing services while still restricting organizationally owned content. The Managed Open In restrictions specifically limit document sharing between managed and unmanaged apps and accounts on iOS devices. However, to take advantage of Managed Open In, administrators must first configure managed apps and accounts on iOS devices.

> **MORE INFO** ▶ Managing app assignments with Profile Manager is covered in Lesson 10, "VPP-Managed Apps and Books," and Lesson 11, "In-House Apps and Books."

A managed account is a service account that is configured via a profile installed from an MDM service. For example, in Profile Manager you can create profiles that will automatically configure traditional mail, Exchange settings, and for iOS 9 and later, Google Account settings. In this case, these accounts configured via a Profile Manager profile are considered managed.

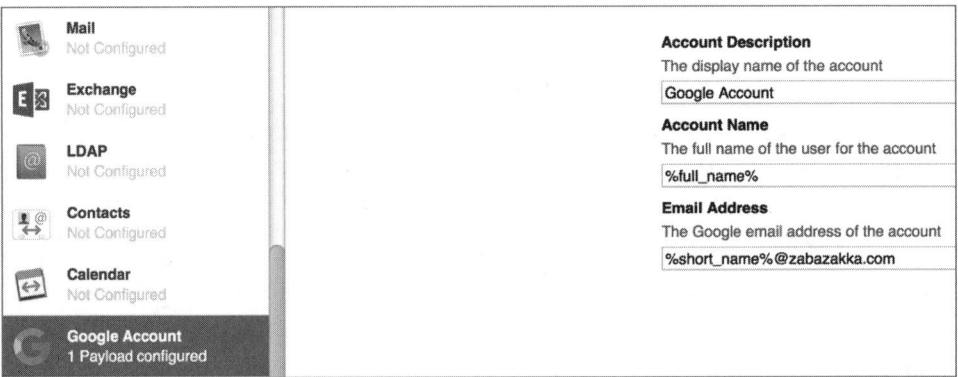

MORE INFO ▶ Deploying configuration profiles with Profile Manager is covered in Lesson 7, "Mobile Device Management."

The distinction between managed apps and accounts and unmanaged apps and accounts allows the system to distinguish between organizational items and personal items. The assumption is that managed apps and accounts will always be automatically provided via the MDM service and that unmanaged apps and accounts will always be manually configured via the user. This lays the foundation for Managed Open In.

For iOS 8 and older, if a user manually installs an app or manually configures an account you want managed, the user will have to first remove the item so that Profile Manager can then push down the "managed" version. A new feature for iOS 9 is the ability for an MDM to manage an app that was already installed. However, at the time of this writing, Profile Manager does not appear to support this feature. If your MDM does not support making previously installed apps managed and if your organizational security relies on Managed Open In, your workflow plan will have to include steps for remediating unmanaged apps and accounts.

NOTE ▶ Profile Manager has limited inventory reporting that makes it difficult to locate unmanaged items that should be managed. If this type of security reporting is important to your organization, then you should consider a third-party MDM service with better security reporting.

Configuring Managed Open In

Two settings nestled in the middle of the iOS restrictions list in Profile Manager can be used to turn on Managed Open In:

▶ Allow documents from managed sources in unmanaged destinations—Disallowing this option will prevent users from copying or moving documents from your organizational apps and accounts to their personal apps and accounts. In other words, disallowing this will prevent outbound sharing.

▶ Allow documents from unmanaged sources in managed destinations—Disallowing this option will prevent users from copying or moving documents from their personal apps and accounts into your organizational apps and accounts. In other words, disallowing this will prevent inbound sharing.

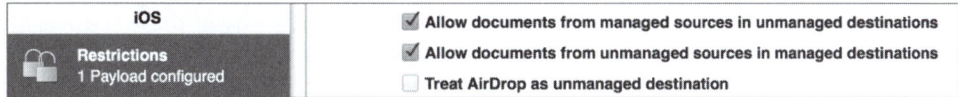

For devices with iOS 8 and later, an MDM service can prevent unmanaged third-party keyboards from appearing over managed apps; in Profile Manager you must deselect "Allow documents from managed sources in unmanaged destinations" for this third-party keyboard restriction to take effect.

A new feature for iOS 9 is the ability to treat AirDrop as an unmanaged destination to prevent sharing organizational information over AirDrop.

> **MORE INFO** ▶ Understanding the full Managed Open In workflow without actually doing all the steps is difficult. In this case, you are strongly encouraged to complete Exercise 16.1, "Manage Open In," to fully understand the workflow necessary to make this feature possible.

Reference 16.2
Limit Access to Content and Services

This section explores profile-based restrictions that can be set for limiting general access to sharing, storage, and backup services on both iOS and OS X devices.

> **MORE INFO** ▶ Detailed step-by-step instructions for deploying profile-based restrictions via Profile Manager are presented in the exercises later in this lesson.

iOS Restrictions to Limit Content and Services

One of the conduits for sharing files with iOS devices is via the universal serial bus (USB) sync and charge cable included with every iOS device. The act of sharing information by connecting an iOS device to a Mac or PC is known as *pairing*. Administrators can prevent a supervised iOS device from pairing by locking out this ability entirely.

> **MORE INFO** ▶ Pair locking can be turned on via Apple Configurator as covered in Lesson 13, "Apple Configurator 2: Preparing, Configuring, and Managing iOS Devices," or via management by the Device Enrollment Program (DEP) (for businesses) or Apple School Manager (for schools) as covered in Lesson 8, "Out-of-the-Box Management via Apple Programs for Device Enrollment."

For more granular control of access to content and services on iOS devices, you can create and deploy configuration profiles. In Profile Manager, the majority of these settings are found in the iOS Restrictions payload.

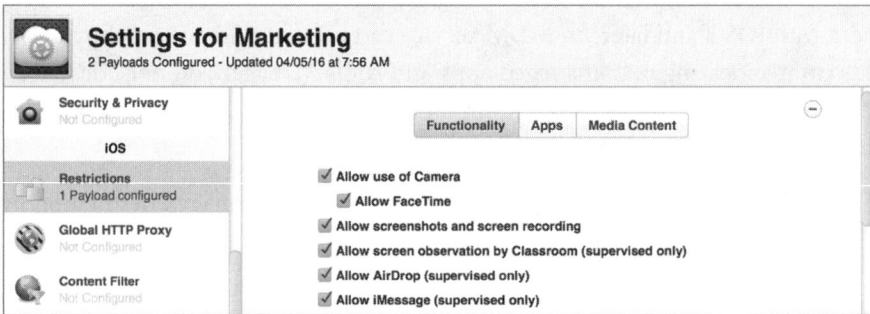

Options for limiting access to content and services on iOS include the following:

- Disallow use of the camera
- Disallow use of the FaceTime app
- Disallow taking screenshots and screen recording
- Disallow screen observation by the Classroom app (supervised only)
- Disallow AirDrop (supervised)
- Disallow iMessage (supervised only)
- Disallow Apple Music (supervised only)
- Disallow Radio (supervised only)
- Disallow voice dialing while device is locked
- Disallow Siri

- Disallow Siri while device is locked
- Disable Siri profanity filter (supervised only)
- Disallow user-generated content in Siri (supervised only)
- Disallow access to iBooks Store (supervised only)
- Disallow installing apps using Apple Configurator and iTunes
- Disallow installing apps and App Store (supervised only), thus preventing the installation of all nonapproved file-sharing apps
- Disallow automatic app downloads (supervised only), thus preventing the installation of all nonapproved file-sharing apps that were purchased on another iOS device with the same Apple ID
- Disallow removing apps (supervised only)
- Disallow in-app purchases
- Require iTunes Store password for all purchases
- Disallow iCloud backup
- Disallow iCloud documents & data
- Disallow iCloud Keychain
- Disallow managed apps to store data in iCloud, thus preventing the data from being restored on another iOS device
- Disallow backup of enterprise books, thus preventing the books from being restored on another iOS device
- Disallow notes and highlights sync for enterprise books
- Disallow iCloud Photo Sharing
- Disallow iCloud Photo Library
- Disallow My Photo Stream (disallowing can cause data loss)
- Disallow automatic sync while roaming
- Force encrypted backups (to iTunes)
- Force limited ad tracking
- Disallow the ability to Erase All Content and Settings (or wipe) from the Settings app (supervised only)
- Disallow users from accepting untrusted TLS certificates
- Disallow automatic updates to certificate trust settings
- Disallow trusting new enterprise app authors

- Disallow the installation of other configuration profiles (supervised only)
- Disallow modifying account settings, thus disabling the ability to add unmanaged accounts and services (supervised only)
- Disallow modifying cellular data app settings (supervised only)
- Disallow modifying device name (supervised only)
- Disallow modifying Find My Friends settings (supervised only)
- Disallow modifying notifications settings (supervised only)
- Disallow modifying passcode (supervised only)
- Disallow modifying Touch ID fingerprints (supervised only)
- Disallow modifying restrictions (supervised only)
- Disallow modifying Wallpaper (supervised only)
- Disallow Handoff
- Disallow Spotlight Suggestions
- Disallow Touch ID to unlock device
- Force Apple Watch wrist detection
- Disallow pairing with Apple Watch (supervised only)
- Require passcode on first AirPlay pairing
- Disallow predictive keyboard (supervised only)
- Disallow keyboard shortcuts (supervised only)
- Disallow auto correction (supervised only)
- Disallow spell check (supervised only)
- Disallow Wallet notifications in Lock screen
- Disallow Show Control Center in Lock screen
- Disallow Show Notification Center in Lock screen
- Disallow Show Today view in Lock screen
- Force all network connections to go through a global Hypertext Transfer Protocol (HTTP) proxy, allowing administrators to block access to specific Internet services
- Filter content; choose between Limit Adult Content, Specific Websites Only, or specify and configure a third-party filtering plug-in
- Allow only specific URLs
- Disallow specific URLs

OS X Restrictions to Limit Content and Services

Another system can easily access the storage inside many Mac computers via Target Disk Mode. Alternatively, a motivated person could simply disassemble a Mac to gain access to its internal storage. Both situations are easily resolved by turning on FileVault. This feature of OS X will encrypt the system volume, thus requiring authenticated access to the system drive. Turning on FileVault effectively prevents unauthorized access to a Mac computer's system drive.

> **MORE INFO** ▶ Details about managing FileVault on OS X are beyond the scope of this guide. For more information, please refer to Lesson 10, "Manage FileVault," in *Apple Training Pro Series: OS X Support Essentials 10.11: Supporting and Troubleshooting OS X El Capitan* (Peachpit Press, 2016).

For more granular control of access to content and services on OS X computers, you can create and deploy configuration profiles. In Profile Manager, most of these settings are in the OS X Restrictions payload.

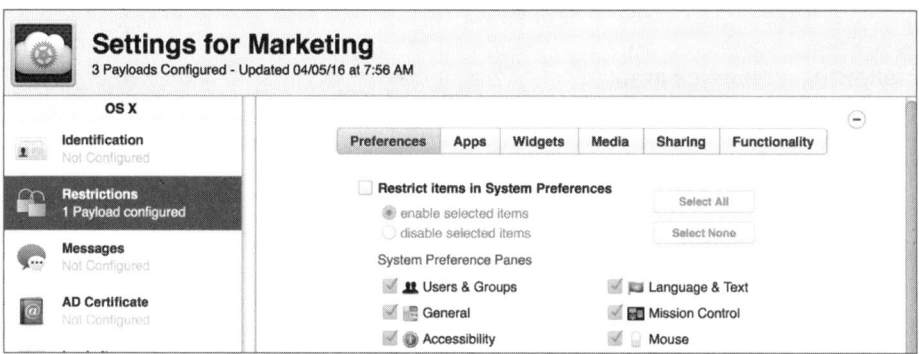

Options for limiting access to content and services on OS X include the following:

- Disallow access to specific System Preference panes, thus disabling the ability to add new local users, additional Internet accounts and services, and additional Time Machine backup destinations
- Restrict which apps are allowed to launch, by allowing specific apps to launch, allowing apps to launch from specific folders, and disallowing apps from launching from specific folders
- Restrict App Store to MDM installed apps and software updates, thus preventing any nonapproved apps
- Disallow access to physical media, including external disks and optical discs

- Disallow AirDrop
- Disallow specific Internet Accounts services, thus allowing for granular control of adding Internet or cloud-sharing services
- Lock the desktop picture to a specific local file or the default desktop
- Disallow specific services from appearing in the share menu
- Disallow use of Camera, iCloud documents & data, iCloud password for local accounts, and Spotlight Suggestions

iOS Restrictions for Apps

For all iOS devices, you can do the following:

- Disallow use of iTunes Store
- Disallow use of Safari, or if you allow Safari, you can disable AutoFill, force fraud warning, disable JavaScript, and block pop-ups, and, for cookies, handle cookies by choosing from the following: Always Block, Allow from Current Websites Only, Allow from Websites I Visit, and Always Allow

The following options are available only for supervised devices:

- Disallow use of News (supervised only)
- Disallow use of Podcasts (supervised only)
- Disallow use of Game Center (supervised only), including disallow multiplayer gaming and disallow adding Game Center friends

In the iOS restrictions settings, in the Apps tab, under Restrict App Usage, you can take advantage of a feature new to iOS 9 and choose the following for supervised devices:

- Allow All Apps
- Allow Some Apps Only (you must specify the list of allowed apps)
- Don't Allow Some Apps (you must specify the list of disallowed apps)

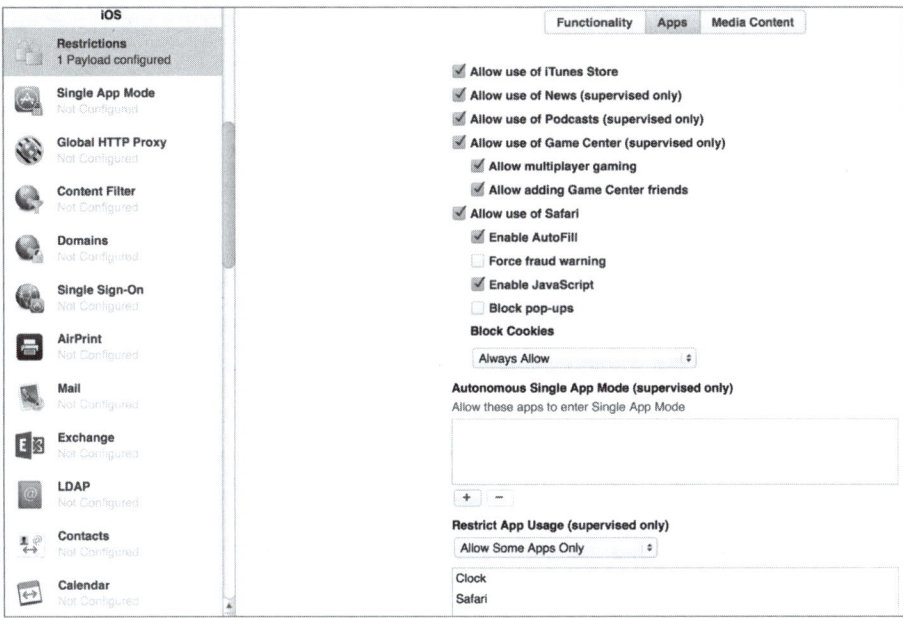

Exercise 16.1
Manage Open In

▶ **Prerequisites**

- Exercise 4.3, "Configure OS X Server for El Capitan"
- Exercise 7.1, "Enable Device Management"
- Exercise 10.2, "Purchase and Assign Licensed Apps to Devices"
- An iOS device with iOS 9.3 or later

Challenge

Create a configuration profile for the group Workgroup that includes Mail account configuration settings for network users of your server.

Start with a freshly wiped iOS device, but do not enter an Apple ID during the device Setup Assistant.

Open the App Store, and download a free app that can read PDF documents that will be considered unmanaged:

▶ Adobe Acrobat

Additionally, iBooks comes preinstalled on all iOS 9 devices; because this app is not installed via MDM, it is also considered unmanaged.

Acquire your Volume Purchase Program (VPP) token from the VPP Store and configure Profile Manager for the VPP.

Enroll your iOS device with your server's Profile Manager service as the user Maria Miller. Most Mail settings are provided by the configuration profile; the only thing you need to provide on your iOS device is the network user's password.

Assign and observe Profile Manager automatically push two free apps that can read PDF documents:

▶ Foxit PDF (by Foxit Corporation)
▶ FileManager (by TapMedia Ltd.)

Because you installed these apps while the device was under management, they will be considered managed.

On your server, use the supplied custom app from the StudentMaterials folder to send a PDF document to Maria Miller. On your iOS device, open the PDF document in Mail and then show that you can open it in all four apps that can read PDF documents.

After you've established a baseline for opening documents, move on to managing Open In. Edit the Workgroup configuration profile to disallow the following options for iOS:

▶ Allow documents from managed sources in unmanaged destinations
▶ Allow documents from unmanaged sources in managed destinations

To generate a new document from a managed source, send Maria Miller a new PDF. Demonstrate that you cannot open a document from a managed source (this new PDF file) in unmanaged destinations (Adobe Acrobat and iBooks).

Demonstrate that you cannot use the unmanaged apps to send that first PDF file via the managed Mail account. Finally, demonstrate that you can use the managed apps to send the second PDF file via the Managed Mail account.

Considerations

Use your client testing Apple ID to get a free copy of Adobe Acrobat for this exercise.

Use variable substitution in the Mail payload of a configuration profile to provide the user's full name, email address, and short name. When the user opens Mail on her iOS device, she needs to provide only her password.

Solution

Configure Mail for Workgroup

NOTE ▸ If your server uses a fully qualified domain name (FQDN) instead of a Bonjour .local name, use your server's FQDN instead of its Bonjour name for mail; your iOS device settings will look different from the figures in this section.

1 On your server Mac, in Safari, open the Profile Manager administration portal (https://servern.local/profilemanager, where *n* is your student number), and then authenticate with local administrator credentials.

2 In the Profile Manager administration portal sidebar, select Groups.

3 Select Workgroup.

4 Click the Settings tab.

5 Click Edit.

6 In the sidebar, select Mail.

7 Click Configure.

8 Enter the following information:

▸ Account Description: Server *n* Mail (where *n* is your student number)

▸ User Display Name: %full_name%

▸ Email Address: %email%

9 Deselect the checkbox "Allow user to move messages from this account."

Account Description
The display name of the account (e.g. "Company Mail Account")
Server 17 Mail

Account Type
The protocol for accessing the account
IMAP Path Prefix: optional

User Display Name
The display name of the user (e.g. "John Appleseed")
%full_name%

Email Address
The address of the account (e.g. "john@example.com")
%email%

☐ Allow user to move messages from this account
Messages can be moved out of this account into another

10 On the Incoming Mail tab, enter the following information:

- Mail Server and Port: server*n*.local (where *n* is your student number)
- Port: Leave this set to 993.
- User Name: %short_name%

11 Leave the other settings at their defaults.

12 Click the Outgoing Mail tab.

13 Enter the following information:

- Mail Server and Port: server*n*.local (where *n* is your student number)
- Port: Leave this set to 587.
- User Name: %short_name%

14 Select the checkbox "Outgoing password same as incoming."

15 Leave the other settings at their defaults.

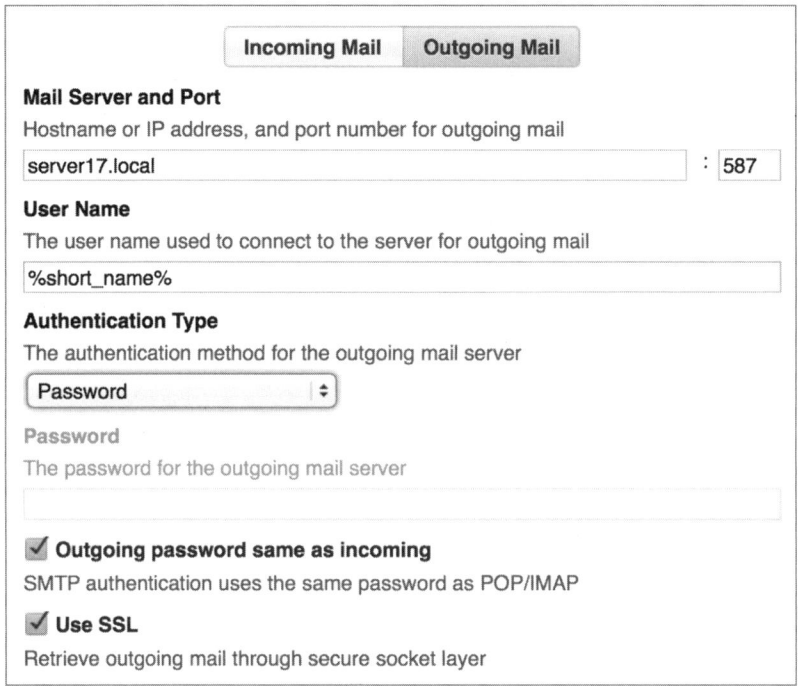

16 Click OK.

17 Click Save.

Review that Workgroup now has mail settings configured.

NOTE ▶ Workgroup is a default group set up by promoting your server to an Open Directory master. All users created or imported into Open Directory will automatically become members.

Erase All Content and Settings

If your iOS device is at the Welcome screen, skip to the next section.

1 Press the Home button.

2 Open Settings.

3 Navigate to General > Reset.

4 Tap Erase All Content and Settings.

5   If your iOS device has a passcode, enter the passcode.

6   In the confirmation dialog, tap Erase.

7   In the extra confirmation dialog, tap Erase.

Wait while the iOS device erases all content and settings.

Use the Device Setup Assistant Without an Apple ID
Don't specify your Apple ID during the Setup Assistant process so that Setup Assistant will not use it for iCloud.

1   Slide at the "slide to set up" screen.

2   Tap your language.

3   Tap your country or region.

4   Tap your Wi-Fi network. In an instructor-led environment, this may be Classroom Wireless.

5   Enter the Wi-Fi password, and then tap Join.

    In an instructor-led environment, the password may be student!.

6   Tap Enable Location Services.

7   If you see the Touch ID screen, tap Set Up Touch ID Later, and then tap Continue.

8   At the Create a Passcode screen, for the purposes of this exercise, tap Passcode Options, tap Don't Add Passcode, and then tap Continue.

    NOTE ▶ In production it is best practice to have a passcode for your iOS device.

9   At the Apps & Data screen, tap Set Up as New iPad (this screen may vary by device).

10 At the Apple ID screen, tap "Don't have an Apple ID or forgot it."

11 At the next Apple ID screen, tap Set Up Later in Settings.

12 In the confirmation dialog, tap Don't Use.

13 Read the terms and conditions, and tap Agree to confirm.

14 If you see the Siri screen, tap Turn On Siri.

15 At the Diagnostics screen, tap Send to Apple.

16 At the App Analytics screen, tap Share with App Developers.

17 At the Welcome screen, tap Get Started.

Use the App Store to Install an App That Can Read PDF Documents

1 On your iOS device, open the App Store.

2 If your iOS device is an iPod touch or an iPhone, tap Search, and then tap Purchased.

   If your iOS device is an iPad, tap Purchased.

3 Tap Sign In.

4 Tap Use Existing Apple ID.

5 Enter your client testing Apple ID credentials, and then tap OK.

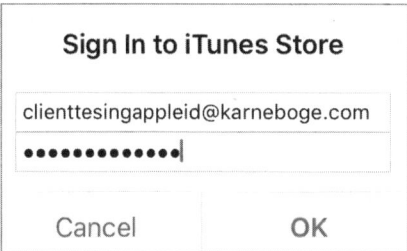

6 Tap Explore.

7 In the "Allow App Store to access your location" dialog, tap Allow.

8 If your iOS device is an iPod touch or an iPhone, tap Search.

9 In the Search field, enter Adobe Acrobat Reader, and then tap Search.

10 For the Adobe Acrobat Reader item, tap Get, and then tap Install.

11 If you are asked to Sign In with your Apple ID credentials again, enter the password for your Apple ID, and tap Continue.

12 At the Require password for additional purchases on this device dialog, tap Require After 15 Minutes.

Adobe Acrobat Reader starts to download.

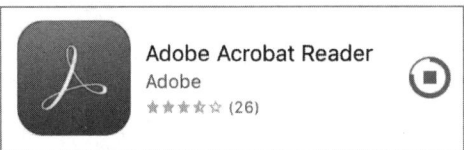

Acquire Your VPP Token and Configure for the Volume Purchase Program

Though you configured your server for the Volume Purchase Program (VPP) in previous exercises, you used the VPP token in the just-completed Apple Configurator 2 exercises. Thus, you need to re-configure your server to use the Volume Purchased Program to distribute apps and books using Profile Manager.

1 On your server, in Safari, open the Apple Deployment Programs site (https://deploy.apple.com).

2 Enter your VPP administrator account credentials, and click Sign In.

3 In the sidebar, click Volume Purchase Program, which takes you to the VPP store for your type of program (Business or Education).

4 Enter your VPP administrator account credentials, and click Sign In.

5 If Safari asks to save this password, click Never for This Website.

6 In the upper-right corner of the Safari window, click the pop-up menu, and choose Account Summary.

7 Click Download Token.

This downloads the token to your Downloads folder.

8 Open the Server app, and connect to your server if necessary.

9 In the Server app sidebar, select Profile Manager.

10 Select the "Distribute apps and books from the Volume Purchase Program" checkbox.

   WARNING ▶ As of the time of this writing, VPP tokens cannot be shared among MDM servers or between an MDM server and an instance of Apple Configurator 2. Selecting this in a production environment will cause all apps that are assigned by Apple Configurator 2 to be revoked.

11 Click Choose.

12 In the sidebar, select Downloads.

13 Select your token. It is a file that ends with the suffix vpptoken.

14 Click Choose.

15 At the VPP Managed Distribution pane, with the sToken information displayed, click Continue.

   If you see a message that your VPP account is already in use and you are sure that your VPP account is not in use by any active server or Apple Configurator 2 computer, click Continue; otherwise, click Cancel.

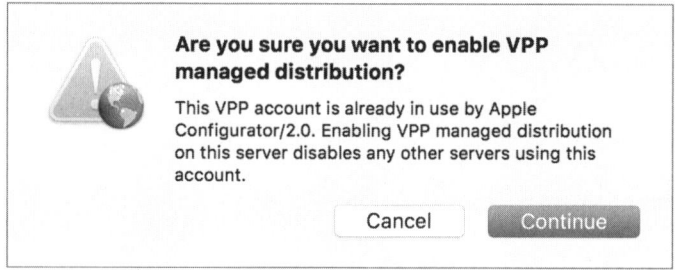

16 Click Done.

Enroll Your iOS Device as Maria Miller

1 On your iOS device, press the Home button, and open Safari to the user portal (http://servern.local/mydevices, where *n* is your student number).

2 In the Cannot Verify Server Identity dialog, tap Continue.

3 In the User Name field, enter maria.

4   In the Password field, enter net.

5   Deselect the "Keep me logged in" checkbox.

6   Tap Log In.

7   If necessary, tap the Devices tab, and then for your iOS device, tap Enroll.

8   In the Install Profile dialog, tap Install.

9   At the warning, tap Install.

10 In the trust dialog, tap Trust.

11 In the Profile Installed dialog, tap Done.

12 Press the Home button, and then open Settings.

    Settings should automatically display Settings > General > Device Management.

13 Tap Remote Management.

14 Confirm that the profile includes Email Account settings.

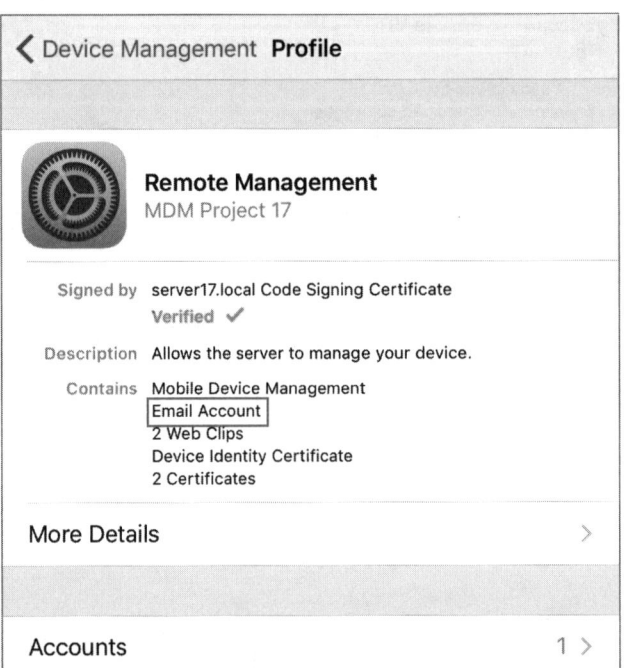

Use the VPP to Get Two Apps That Can Read PDF Documents

1 On your server Mac, if you do not already have the Profile Manager administration portal open, then in Safari, open https://servern.local/profilemanager (where *n* is your student number), and authenticate with local administrator credentials.

2 Select Apps in the Profile Manager administration portal sidebar.

3 In the lower-right corner, click Get More Apps.

4 Click the link for the appropriate store for your organization.

5 Provide your VPP administrator account credentials if necessary, and click Sign In.

6 Enter Foxit PDF in the search field.

7 Click the Media Type pop-up menu, and choose iOS Apps.

8 Click Search.

9 Click the Foxit PDF item developed by Foxit Corporation.

10 Enter 5 in the Quantity field.

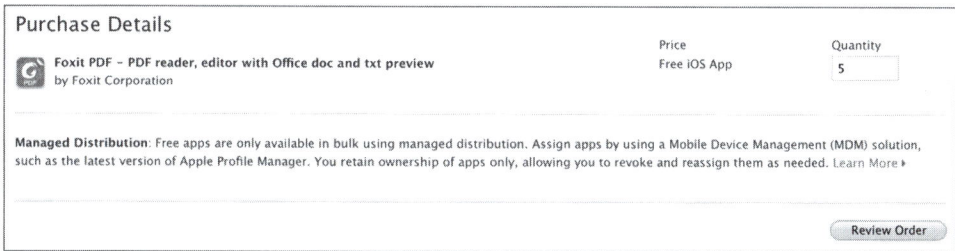

11 Click Review Order.

12 Confirm the details of the order, and then click Place Order.

13 In the Search field, enter File Manager.

14 Click the Media Type pop-up menu, and choose iOS Apps.

15 Click Search.

16 Select the File Manager (FREE) item developed by TapMedia, Ltd.

17 Enter 5 in the Quantity field.

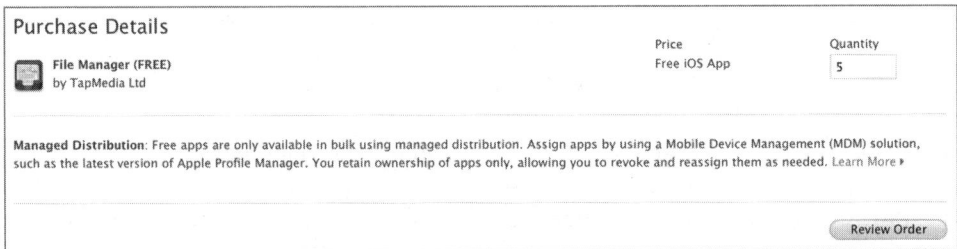

18 Click Review Order.

19 Confirm the details of the order, and then click Place Order.

20 Close the Safari window that displays the VPP store page.

21 In the Profile Manager administration portal page that displays Apps, confirm that Foxit PDF and File Manager are both listed.

It may take some time for the purchase of the free apps to be processed. You can press Command-R to refresh the Profile Manager administration portal.

Assign and Install Two Managed VPP Apps That Can Read PDF Documents

1 In the Profile Manager administration portal sidebar, select Users.

2 Select Maria Miller.

3 Click the Apps tab for Maria Miller.

4 Click Add (+).

5 Select the checkbox for File Manager.

6 Select the checkbox for Foxit PDF.

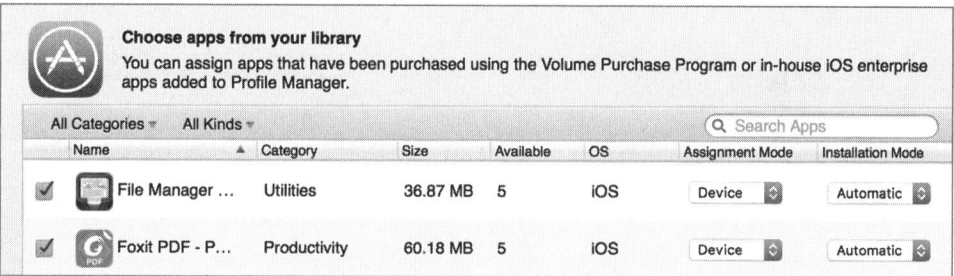

7 Leave Assignment Mode at Device and Installation Mode at Automatic.

8 Click OK to close the "Choose apps from your library" pane.

9 Review the list of VPP apps you are about to assign and install.

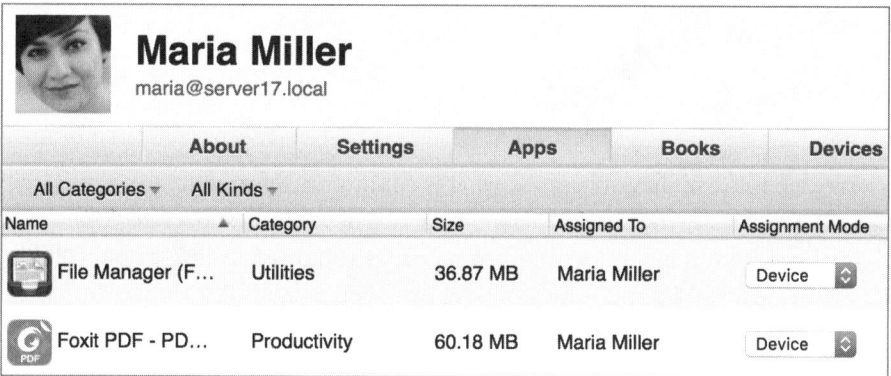

10 Click Save.

11 Observe there is an active task in the Profile Manager sidebar.

This task is automatically pushing File Manager (FREE) and Foxit PDF to your iOS device that is associated with Maria Miller.

12 On your iOS device, at the App Installation notification for Foxit PDF, tap Install.

13 At the App Installation notification for File Manager (FREE), tap Install.

14 At the Edit Home Screen notification, click Dismiss.

15 Both File Manager and Foxit PDF should now be installed on your iOS device.

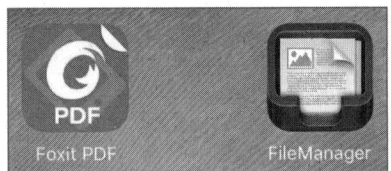

In previous exercises, you have observed what is commonly referred to as *silent install* of apps on your iOS device. In those exercises, your iOS device was supervised. As it is not supervised at this point, the user will be prompted, as you discovered. As you will see, you can have an unsupervised device and still have managed apps.

Mail Maria Miller a PDF Document Before You Restrict Open In

1 On your server Mac, click the Finder in the Dock.

2 Choose Go > Documents; in the Documents folder, open StudentMaterials, and then open the Lesson16 folder.

3 Open the Send PDF Document app.

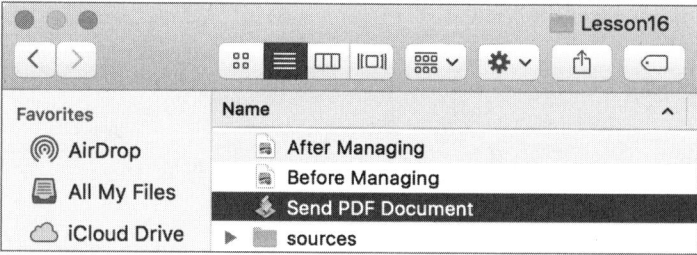

4 In the dialog, click "I have not managed Open In yet."

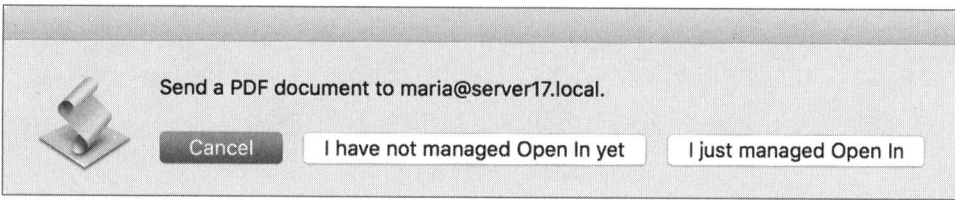

5 In the dialog, click OK.

Attempt to Open the PDF Document from Mail in All Four Apps

1 On your iOS device, open Mail.

2 In the Password Required dialog, enter the password for your server's network account for Maria Miller (net), and then tap OK.

3 At the upper-left corner of the screen, tap Inbox.

4 Tap the new message to read it.

5   Tap the attached PDF document to view it.

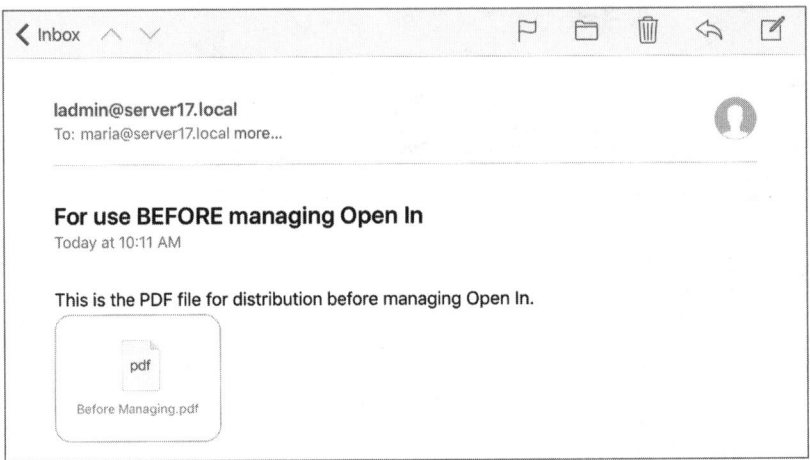

6   Tap the document to reveal more options.

7   Tap Share (square with an arrow).

8   Confirm that iBooks and Adobe Acrobat are available choices.

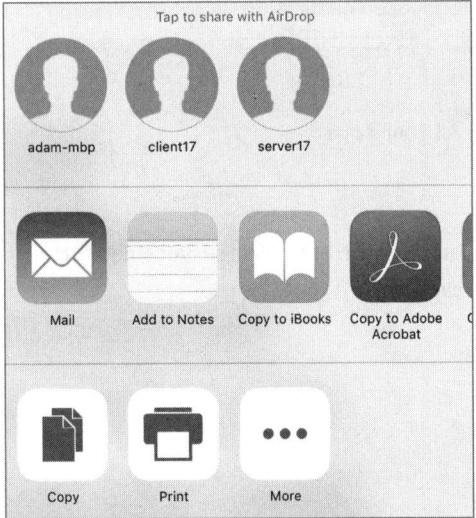

9   Swipe to reveal more Share choices.

    Confirm that FileManager and Foxit PDF are also choices.

10 Swipe back to reveal iBooks as a choice, and then tap Copy to iBooks.

11 If you see a Welcome to iBooks dialog, tap OK.

12 If you see a Sync iBooks dialog, tap Sync.

13 Confirm that you can read the document in iBooks.

    The word *Library* in the upper-left corner of the screen is an indication that you are using iBooks.

14 Press the Home button, and then open Mail.

15 Tap Open In, and then tap Copy to Adobe Acrobat.

16 Swipe through the introductory screens, and then tap Continue.

17 Confirm that you can read the document in Adobe Acrobat.

18. Press the Home button, and then open Mail.

19. Tap Share, and then tap Copy to Foxit PDF.

20. In the Help Us Improve dialog, tap Allow.

21. Confirm that you can read the document in Foxit PDF.

22. Press the Home button, and then open Mail.

23. Tap Share, and then tap Copy to FileManager.

24. Confirm that you see the document.

25. Tap the document to confirm that you can read its contents.

26 On your iOS device, press the Home button.

You just confirmed that you can copy the document to all four apps, and now it's time for you to manage Open In.

Manage Open In Settings

1 On your server Mac, in the Profile Manager administration portal sidebar, select Groups.

2 Select Workgroup.

3 Click the Settings tab.

4 For Settings for Workgroup, click Edit.

5 In the sidebar, scroll to the iOS section, and then select Restrictions.

6 Click Configure.

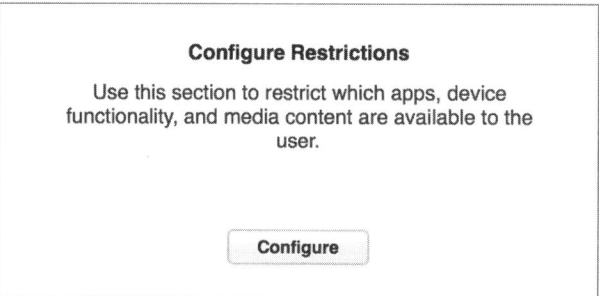

7 Click the Functionality tab if it is not already selected.

8 Deselect the checkbox "Allow documents from managed sources in unmanaged destinations."

9 Deselect the checkbox "Allow documents from unmanaged sources in managed destinations."

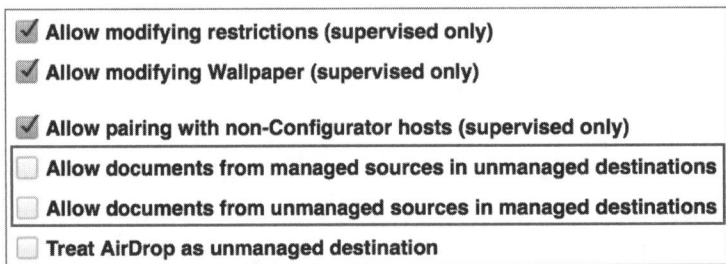

10 Click OK.

11 Confirm that Settings for Workgroup displays an icon for the Restrictions settings.

12 Click Save.

13 Keep the Profile Manager administration portal window open.

Mail the Second PDF Document

1 On your server Mac, click the Finder in the Dock.

2 If you do not already have the Lesson16 folder open, choose Go > Documents; then in the Documents folder, open StudentMaterials, and then open the Lesson16 folder.

3 Open the Send PDF Document app.

4 Click "I just managed Open In."

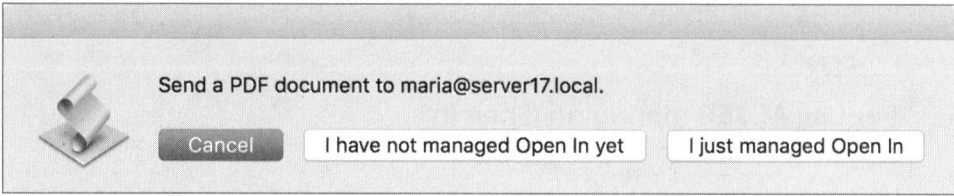

5 In the confirmation dialog, click OK.

Attempt to Open the Second PDF Document from Mail in All Four Apps

Remember that in the previous section, you have not yet managed Open In, so you should be able to open the PDF document in all four apps that can open PDF documents. Each of these apps adds the document to its internal collection of documents after you open the document, so it will be available even after you start managing Open In.

Because you updated the configuration profile for Workgroup, which contains settings for Mail, you will be prompted to enter your password again.

1 On your iOS device, open Mail.

2 If Mail still displays the Before Managing.pdf document, tap the document to reveal more options, tap Done in the upper-left corner, and then tap Inbox.

3 Even though the inbox appears empty, swipe down in the inbox in order to refresh the contents.

   This causes the password dialog to appear.

4 When you see the Password Required dialog, enter the password net, and then tap OK.

5 Open the new message.

6 Tap the PDF document that is attached.

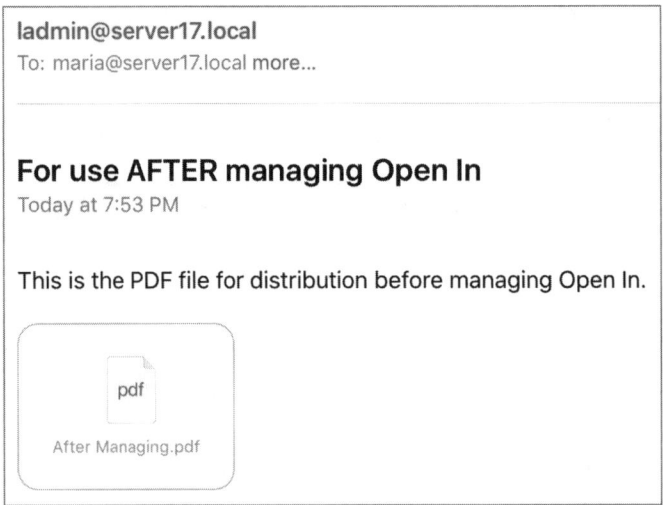

7 Tap the document to reveal more options.

8 In the upper-right corner of the screen, tap Share (square with an arrow).

9 Confirm that only the managed apps that can read PDF documents (Mail, Foxit PDF, and FileManager) are available.

Confirm that Adobe Acrobat and iBooks are not available in the Open In list of apps.

10 Tap Copy to Foxit PDF.

11 Confirm that you can read the document in Foxit PDF.

12 Press the Home button, and then open Mail.

13 Tap Share (square with an arrow), and then tap Copy to File Manager.

14 If File Manager is already displaying the contents of the Before Managing.pdf file, tap the document, and then tap Documents in the upper-left corner to return to the list of documents.

15 Confirm that you can see the new document (After Managing.pdf).

16 Tap After Managing.pdf, and confirm that you can read its contents.

Attempt to Send a Document from an Unmanaged App via a Managed Mail Account

Because you used a configuration profile to configure your Mail settings, your mail account is considered a managed account. You should not be able to send a document from an unmanaged app via your managed Mail account.

Remember that you installed Adobe Acrobat from the App Store, and iBooks came preinstalled with iOS 9, so they are considered unmanaged apps.

1   On your iOS device, press the Home button, and then open Adobe Acrobat.

    Adobe Acrobat should still display the Before Managing.pdf file.

2   In the lower-right corner of the screen, tap the Share (square with an arrow) icon.

3 In the lower-right corner of the screen, tap Share File.

4 Tap Share Flattened Copy.

5 Tap Mail.

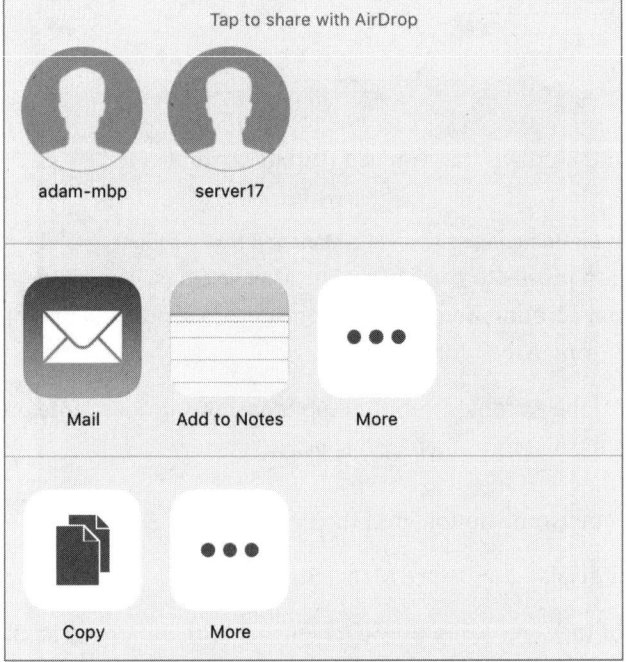

You do not see an error message, but you are unable to share this document from an unmanaged source (Adobe Acrobat) with a managed destination (Mail).

Open a Document in an Unmanaged App from an Unmanaged Source

1   While still viewing the document in Adobe Acrobat, tap the Share (square with an arrow) icon.

2   Tap Open In.

3   Tap Copy to iBooks.

4   Confirm that you can read the document in iBooks.

Send a Document from a Managed App via a Managed Mail Account

Because you used a configuration profile to configure your Mail settings, your mail account is considered a managed account.

Remember that the VPP apps Foxit PDF and FileManager were automatically installed by your MDM server, so they are considered managed apps. iBooks was preinstalled, so it is considered an unmanaged app.

1   On your iOS device, press the Home button, and then open FileManager.

2   While viewing the After Managing.pdf document, tap the Share icon.

3   Tap Share.

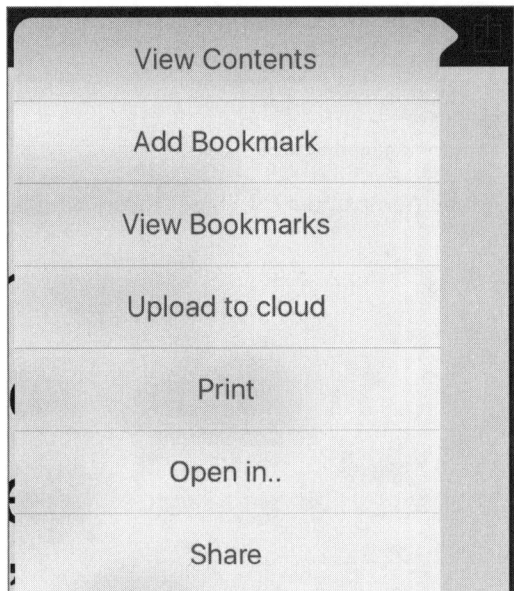

4 Tap Email.

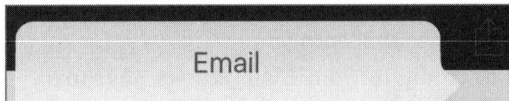

5 Confirm that a new message appears with the document attached.

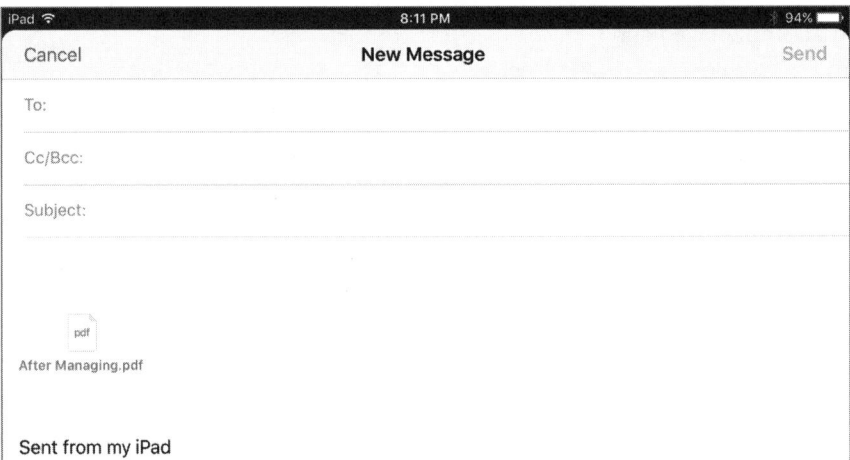

6 Tap Cancel, and then tap Delete Draft; for the purposes of this exercise, do not actually send the message.

In this exercise, you used a configuration profile to manage Open In. Specifically, you disallowed the following:

▶ Allow documents from managed sources in unmanaged destinations
▶ Allow documents from unmanaged sources in managed destinations

You demonstrated that, from a managed Mail account, you cannot open a document in an unmanaged app (in this exercise, Adobe Acrobat and iBooks). You also demonstrated that from a managed app (in this exercise, Foxit PDF and File Manager), you can send a document via a managed Mail account.

Exercise 16.2
Restrict Access to Services via Profile

▶ **Prerequisite**

▶ Exercise 16.1, "Manage Open In"

Challenge
Edit Workgroup's configuration profile with restrictions:

▶ For OS X, select the option "Require admin password to install or update apps."

Demonstrate the previous items with the following restriction:

▶ On OS X, a standard (nonadministrator) user cannot install apps with the Mac App Store without providing administrator user credentials.

Remove the restrictions.

Considerations

If your server uses an FQDN instead of a Bonjour .local name, use your server's FQDN instead of its Bonjour name for mail.

In Exercise 16.1, "Manage Open In," on your iOS device, you used your client testing Apple ID to install Adobe Acrobat.

Solution

Create a Standard Local Account on Your Client Mac

> **NOTE** ▶ You can use any name you like for this local account; the exercise is written with Chris Johnson as an example.

1 On your client Mac, open System Preferences, and then choose View > Users & Groups.

2 Click the lock in the lower-left corner, next to "Click the lock to make changes."

3 Enter local administrator credentials, and click Unlock.

4 Click Add (+).

5 Leave the New Account pop-up menu at Standard.

6 Enter the following information:

- Full Name: Chris Johnson
- Account Name: chris
- Password and verify: chrispw

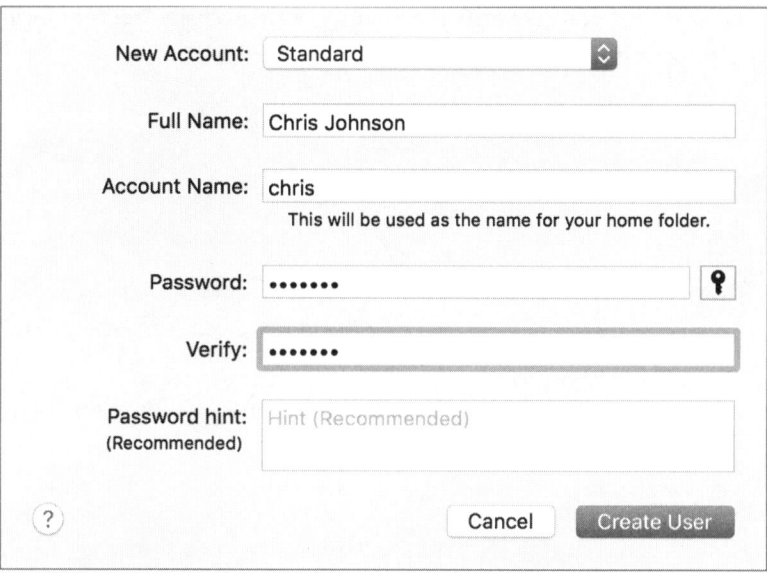

7 Click Create User.

8 Wait until the new user appears in the column of users, and then press Command-Q to quit System Preferences.

9 From the Apple menu, choose Log Out Local Admin, and then in the confirmation dialog, click Log Out.

Log In on Your Mac Client Computer

1 On your client Mac, in the login window, click Chris Johnson.

2 Enter chrispw, and then press Return to log in.

3 At the Sign in with Your Apple ID screen, select "Don't sign in," click Continue, and click Skip to confirm that you want to skip signing in with an Apple ID.

Enroll Your Client Mac

1 On your client Mac computer, in Safari, open the user portal (https://server*n*.local/mydevices, where *n* is your student number).

2   If you see the message "Safari can't verify the identity of the website "server*n*.local" (where *n* is your student number), click Continue.

3   In the Please Log In window, enter the following credentials:

▶   **User Name:** maria

▶   **Password:** net

4   Deselect the "Keep me logged in" checkbox.

5   Click Log In.

6   If you see the message "Would you like to save this password?" dialog, click Never for This Website.

7   If necessary, click the Devices tab.

8   Under This Mac, click Enroll.

9   Click Continue.

10 Click Install.

11 Enter the local administrator credentials (**Username:** ladmin, **Password:** ladminpw), and click OK.

12 Confirm that the Remote Management profile for your server appears.

13 Press Command-Q to quit System Preferences.

14 Close the Safari window that is open to the My Devices page.

Configure Restrictions for Your Client Mac

1   On your server computer, in the Profile Manager administration portal sidebar, select Devices; then select your client computer, and click Settings.

2   In the Settings section for your client computer, click Edit.

3   In the sidebar, scroll to the OS X section, and select Restrictions.

4   Click Configure.

5   Click the Apps tab.

6   Select the "Require admin password to install or update apps" checkbox.

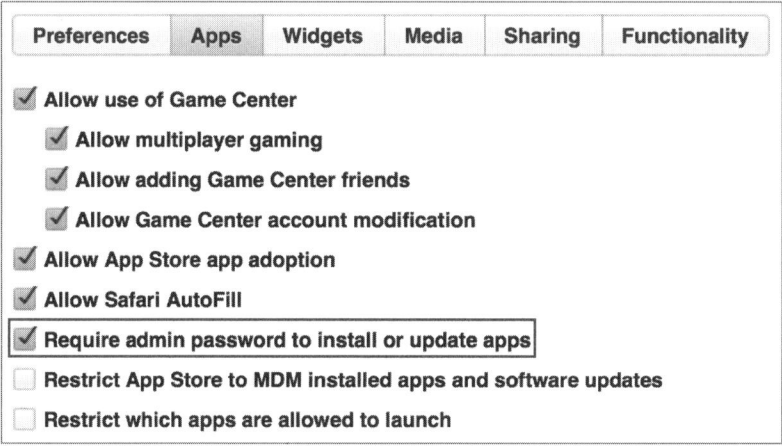

7   Click OK.

8   Click Save.

Attempt to Install OS X Apps

You can choose any additional free app you like; this exercise uses Beacon Scan from Twocanoes Software, Inc., as an example.

1   On your client Mac, open the App Store.

2   Choose Store > Sign In.

3   Enter your client testing Apple ID credentials, and then click Sign In.

4   In the Search field, enter Beacon Scan, and then press Return.

5   For Beacon Scan, click Get.

6   Click Install App.

7   Sign in again with your Apple ID credentials.

8   At the "Require a password when making purchases on this computer" dialog, click Require After 15 Minutes.

9   In the dialog asking for administrator credentials, click Cancel.

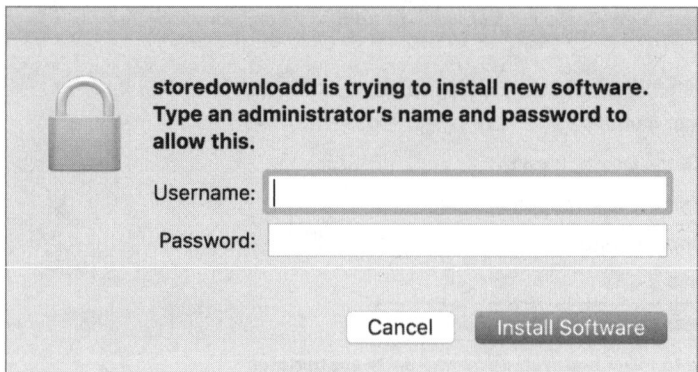

10 At the notice that the app failed to download, click OK.

Purchase a New Free OS X App for VPP Managed Distribution

You can choose any free app you like; this exercise uses Local Path from Twocanoes Software, Inc., as an example.

1   In the Profile Manager administration portal sidebar, select Apps.

2   In the lower-right corner, click Get More Apps.

3   In the Volume Purchase Program page, click the link for the store appropriate for your organization.

4 Enter your VPP administrator account credentials, and then click Sign In.

5 In the Search field, enter Local Path.

6 Click the Media Type pop-up menu, and choose Mac Apps.

7 Click Search.

8 Select Local Path by developer Twocanoes Software, Inc.

9 In the Quantity field, enter 5.

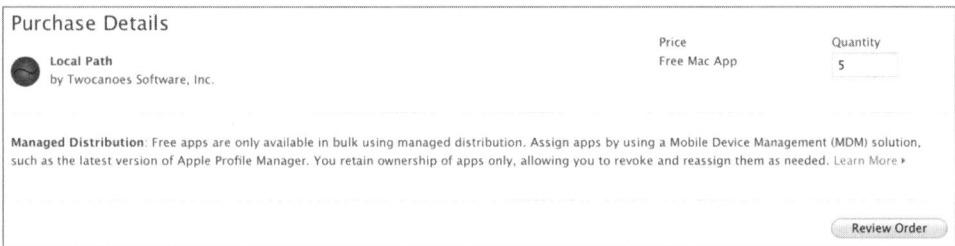

10 Click Review Order.

11 Review your order, and then click Place Order.

12 In the upper-right corner, click your VPP account, and then choose Sign Out.

13 Close the Volume Purchase Program window.

Assign and Install the New Free OS X App to Maria Miller

1 In the Profile Manager administration portal sidebar, select Users, and select Maria Miller.

2 Click the Apps tab, and then click Add (+).

3 Select Local Path.

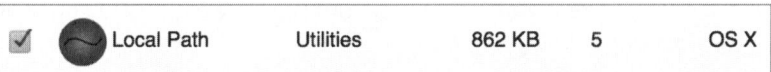

4 Click OK.

5 Click Save.

6 Open Launchpad from the Dock.

   Observe that Local Path is successfully installed on your client Mac.

Remove OS X Restrictions

1 On your server Mac, in the Profile Manager administration portal sidebar, select Devices, select your client computer, and if necessary, click the Settings tab.

2 In the settings for your client computer, click Edit.

3 In the sidebar, in the OS X section, select Restrictions.

4 Click Remove (–) in the upper-right corner.

5 Click OK, and then in the confirmation dialog, click Remove All Settings.

6 Click Save.

Install an OS X App

1 On your client Mac computer, if you do not have the App Store open at the Purchased tab, open the App Store, and then click the Purchased tab.

2 For Beacon Scan (the app that you purchased and attempted to install), click Install.

3 Confirm that the app is installed.

4 Quit the App Store.

In this exercise, you configured a profile for a device with settings for OS X restrictions by selecting the option "Require admin password to install or update apps"; with this configuration profile installed, a standard local user cannot install an item from the Mac App Store without providing administrator user credentials. However, a VPP app assigned from an MDM server is installed successfully.

Lesson 17
Develop a Management Plan

Planning is the most important step in your Apple deployment process; judicious planning always pays off later. The primary goal of system administration, after all, is to efficiently maintain a computing environment that meets an organization's requirements and its users' needs. The amount of time you dedicate to planning will no doubt be less than the amount of time you'll spend fixing a problem that has been replicated on all your Apple devices.

As you've seen in this guide, many management technologies and techniques are available, and plans are as varied as the organizations that use them. No single management plan works in all situations.

Considering all the technologies and features discussed in this guide, you may feel overwhelmed with the possibilities. The goal of this lesson, indeed the goal of this guide, is to help you develop a plan for managing your organization's Apple devices.

GOALS

▸ Define requirements for your organization's deployment

▸ Consider third-party management solutions

▸ Develop a management plan

Reference 17.1
Define Requirements

You can certainly start by identifying specific technical solutions and then create a plan around those solutions. However, this bottom-up approach yields inflexible solutions because you've already chosen the answers before you've considered the problem as a whole. Instead, this guide encourages a top-down approach, first identifying the primary requirements that will influence your management plan.

Planning Methodology

When considering the deployment and management of Apple devices, two "meta" choices will affect all aspects of your plan. First, who owns the devices: the individual or the organization? Second, are these devices used primarily by a single person or shared between multiple people?

The answers to these two fundamental questions lead us to what Apple considers the three primary deployment scenarios:

- User-owned device—This scenario reflects a workflow where the user personally owns the Apple device but administrators need to allow access to organizational assets and services. Other common terms used to describe this scenario include "bring your own device" (BYOD) in enterprise environments and "student-owned device" in education environments.

- Organization-owned, personally enabled device—This scenario reflects a workflow where the organization owns the Apple device and it's used by an individual user only. Other common terms used to describe this scenario include "corporate-owned personal device" in enterprise environments and "one-to-one device" in education environments.

- Organization-owned, nonpersonalized device—This scenario reflects a workflow where the organization owns the Apple device and it's shared by multiple users. Other common terms used to describe this scenario include "single-use device" or "kiosk device" in enterprise environments and "shared device" or "cart device" in education environments.

Your organization may quite possibly use all three types of deployment scenarios based on its needs. For example, in a primary education environment, the faculty and staff devices are likely managed as organization-owned, personally enabled devices, while the student devices are managed as organization-owned, nonpersonalized devices.

Once you focus on planning for a specific deployment scenario, there are a few main concepts to consider. You'll find that no matter the size or scope, all management plans consist of one or more of the following concepts:

- Logistics and infrastructure
- Usage management
- System deployment
- Item management
- Ongoing maintenance

Logistics and Infrastructure

How are you going to physically deliver the devices to your users or get them onto their desks or into the lab? And delivery is just one part of the physical management. You must also consider your deployment's load on your infrastructure and its physical security and consider the replacement or disposal of your existing system.

General logistics and infrastructure concepts are covered in Lesson 2, "Apple Management Concepts," and Lesson 3, "Infrastructure Considerations." Logistics and infrastructure concepts specific to implementing OS X Server are covered in Lesson 4, "OS X Server 5 on El Capitan."

Usage Management

Once your systems have been deployed, how will you maintain a secure and consistent user environment that lets users access the resources they need? Your organization's management is likely responsible for creating a policy that defines users' access to computing resources. The enforcement of these usage policies must be implemented as part of your management plan.

Usage management issues can be addressed by the technologies and techniques covered in Lesson 6, "Configuration and Profiles," and Lesson 7, "Mobile Device Management," as well as Lesson 16, "Managing Access."

System Deployment

How will you ensure that all your devices have uniform configurations? This concept is what most administrators think of when deployment is mentioned. After all, maintaining a uniform computing environment across all your systems is the best way to ensure that things run smoothly.

Beyond this, what individual configuration needs to occur on each device after they have all received identical configuration? Although maintaining system uniformity is a primary deployment goal, some settings must be unique to each device. For example, each device must be individually enrolled into a Mobile Device Management (MDM) service. The challenge is to deploy these unique settings on multiple devices as efficiently as possible.

System deployment issues can be addressed by the technologies and techniques covered in in Lesson 8, "Out-of-the-Box Management via Apple Programs for Device Enrollment," as well as Lessons 12 through 14, covering the use of Apple Configurator 2.

Item Management

In some instances, deploying individual files, folders, or software items, such as an app or book, to your devices may be all you need to do. How will you efficiently deploy these items to all your devices? A variety of techniques can help you accomplish this task.

Also, how will users save and track the items they create? Mobile devices can be easily lost or damaged and need replacement. How will your users' data be recovered in this case? Again, a variety of products exist to help users keep their data safe.

Item management issues can be addressed by the technologies and techniques covered in Lesson 10, "VPP-Managed Apps and Books," and Lesson 11, "In-House Apps and Books," as well as in Lesson 15, "User Data and Services."

Ongoing Maintenance

How will you efficiently make administrative changes and monitor activity on all your devices? How will you ensure that licensed items, such as apps and books, are properly accounted for on all your devices? How will you keep the software on all your devices up to date? Solutions that allow you to perform these tasks quickly on multiple devices simultaneously are a necessity for maintaining your deployed systems.

Ongoing maintenance issues can be addressed by the technologies and techniques covered throughout this guide. Specific solutions include the Apple Caching service covered in Lesson 5, "Caching Service," and MDM services covered in Lesson 7, "Mobile Device Management."

Reference 17.2
Consider Third-Party Solutions

Although Apple provides tools for many system management functions for most medium-sized to large deployments, the Apple tools are not always the most appropriate choice. IT administrators are often frustrated by the lack of certain "enterprise-grade" features in Apple's management tools. What they don't realize is that Apple's goal is to provide only the foundational technologies and baseline solutions required to address a customer's needs. Any "missing" features can be provided by third parties, which are better equipped for creating specialized solutions for advanced customer needs.

This approach is common for Apple solutions. For example, Apple provides the software drivers for interfacing with digital cameras and basic photo-editing software with the Photos app, but advanced users require more robust tools so they purchase products such as

Adobe Photoshop. The same is true for the needs of IT administrators; Apple provides the core functionality and basic solutions, but third parties specialize in advanced solutions.

This combination of foundational technologies from Apple and advanced solutions from third parties benefits IT administrators and users alike because an organization has the ability to choose the best solution possible. Indeed, beyond all the technologies and techniques covered in this guide, even more advanced solutions are provided by third-party developers.

> **MORE INFO** ▶ Search for "Considerations for choosing an MDM solution" at https://help.apple.com/deployment/osx/ and https://help.apple.com/deployment/ios/ for more information.

Third-Party Management Features

Third-party solutions for managing Apple devices are far too numerous to be covered by any single guide. Instead, this lesson provides guidance for considering third-party Apple management solutions by discussing specific technologies or features you should look for, such as the following:

- Platform agnostic—From both a server and client perspective, Apple technologies are obviously designed specifically to support Apple computers and devices. Some third-party solutions support multiple platforms in terms of both server architecture and client operating systems.

- Scalable—Profile Manager is a single-server solution that simply doesn't scale compared to some other MDM solutions. Both the number of "actions" and the total number of managed devices affect MDM service performance. For example, an MDM service that manages only 100 devices but with an administrator who is constantly making changes would require higher performance than an MDM service that mostly sits idle managing 500 devices. If you find the performance of a single Profile Manager instance lacking, then you should consider a management solution that can scale. Scalable management solutions often use a cluster of servers behind a load balancer to provide better performance for large organizations and fault tolerance should an individual server become inactive.

- Infrastructure integration—Third-party management solutions can provide better integration with other parts of your infrastructure. For example, many network solutions vendors now offer MDM services as part of their network management systems. This type of integration is especially important if your organization requires the use of advanced network security methods or advanced directory service integration.

- ▶ Inventory requirements—Third-party management solutions can provide much more robust inventory collection and analysis. Some can even integrate with other management solutions to provide a unified inventory for organizations with different computing platforms.
- ▶ Advanced deployment—If your organization needs to deploy and update non-Apple-supplied software or highly customized configurations, you should consider a third-party solution. Items in this category represent the most common need for a third-party management solution. For example, Profile Manager provides no means to deploy and update the Adobe Creative Suite or Microsoft Office for OS X.
- ▶ Self-service options—Profile Manager provides only basic MDM service task functionality from the user web portal. If your organization wants to give users more choices about managing their own devices, consider a third-party management solution that offers more advanced self-servicing options. For example, some solutions allow administrators to define their own "store" of custom apps, books, and configuration items that users can choose from on their own.
- ▶ Education focus—The Classroom app and Apple School Manager provide a great foundation for educational organizations. Third-party solutions provide additional functionality for teaching and learning environments, such as facilitating sharing of educational materials or managing student testing.
- ▶ Administrative flexibility—Profile Manager provides only a single level of administrative control. In short, if you're a server administrator, you have access to all the administrative functions and devices in Profile Manager. Other management solutions allow for more granular control of managed devices and management features. If you are part of a larger organization where multiple administrators require access to manage devices, you should consider a management solution that allows for more flexibility.

Exercise 17.1
Develop a Management Plan

Challenge
Considering the technologies and features covered by this guide, craft a management plan for your organization's Apple devices.

Considerations

Ideally, you will have read all the previous reference sections and completed all the previous exercises before attempting to create a deployment plan.

Further, you should experiment with your own workflows to see what works best for your organization's needs.

Solution

Try to complete as much of the following template as possible. It covers many aspects of a complete management solution. You may not have an immediate answer for all questions, but at least taking the time to consider answers for each question is a good brainstorming technique.

Also, when planning for Apple devices, start by framing the answers around an Apple deployment scenario. As covered earlier, they are individual personal device, institutional personal device, and institutional shared device. You will find that each question that follows probably has a completely different answer based on the deployment scenario you're planning for. In fact, if you plan to use multiple deployment scenarios, you should consider going through this list separately for each type of scenario.

Logistics and Infrastructure

Physical Logistics

Are there Apple services that you cannot take advantage of in your country or region?

Will your new equipment work within your current power infrastructure?

Will there be any high-density situations that require more power or cooling, such as charging stations or computer labs?

What is the physical workflow plan from delivery by courier to user deployment?

For new devices, what will you do with the packaging material?

While the devices are being prepared for deployment, where will they be securely stored?

Will you be implementing any permanent hardware security measures such as carts or security locks for the devices?

Do you require inventory labels to be generated and applied?

For new devices, will you be using a protective cover or case? When is the item installed on the device or given to the user?

Network Infrastructure

Do you have enough wired Ethernet connections to facilitate your new equipment?

Does your wireless infrastructure support the planned density of your new Apple deployment?

Are there enough DHCP-assignable addresses available on each local network? In many environments, a single person may very well have three or more devices each requiring a unique IP address.

Is your wireless infrastructure available in all the areas required by your organization?

What security mechanisms will you use to protect access to your wireless infrastructure? How can devices be automatically configured for access?

Will there be a "Guest" or "Enrollment" wireless network to allow for new or unmanaged devices?

Will there be any situations where network subnetting must be properly configured for Bonjour discovery?

Will an upgrade to Internet bandwidth be required to facilitate Apple Store item installations, updates, and Internet storage services?

What network services will your Apple devices require access to? Examples include directory services, email and calendaring, file services, and print services.

Does your network block or proxy outbound access to Apple services?

Does your network block or proxy access to your management servers?

Do your clients need to be able to access your management servers from outside your network? What network services must be changed to accommodate this? Examples include firewall, Domain Name System (DNS), and Secure Sockets Layer (SSL) certificate configuration.

Are there any additional network security services that your Apple devices need to integrate with? Examples include proxy and filtering services, virtual private network (VPN) access, and 802.1X network authentication.

Training and Professional Development

How will you provide initial and ongoing training for your help-desk staff?

How will you provide initial and ongoing training and professional development for your end users?

How will you gather feedback from your users about whether your deployment is meeting their needs?

Usage Management

Apple ID Planning

How do you plan to make sure each user in your organization who needs an Apple ID has one?

Are there any students in your organization younger than 13 years old for whom your organization must create Managed Apple IDs?

Will students in your organization at least 13 years and older be using personal Apple IDs, or will you be creating Managed Apple IDs for them?

Which institutional Apple IDs need to be created?

- Apple ID for acquiring and updating OS X Server and setting up APN services
- Apple ID for Apple Deployment Programs program agent/Apple ID for Apple School Manager administrator
- Apple IDs for Device Enrollment Program administrators/Managed Apple IDs for Apple School Manager managers
- Apple IDs for Volume Purchase Program administrators
- Apple IDs for Enterprise Developer facilitators
- Apple IDs for GSX Program facilitators

Usage Policy

Does your organization have up-to-date usage policies? If not, what are you waiting for?

How do you plan to distribute usage policy documentation or agreements to your users?

Are there specific device usage policies you plan to enforce via management settings?

Are there specific network usage policies you plan to enforce via management settings?

Do you plan to further limit usage by imposing additional restrictions?

Will you be integrating with a directory service? If so, what configuration is necessary?

Who will be allowed to have full administrator access on OS X computers?

Will profiles be downloaded manually or pushed automatically?

Will profiles be defined by user, user group, device, or device group?

System Deployment

Do any of your management needs require MDM service enrollment?

If you need to enroll iOS devices, how will this be accomplished? Options include user-based enrollment, Apple Configurator 2, or Apple Programs for Device Enrollment such as the Device Enrollment Program (for business) or Apple School Manager (for schools).

If you need to enroll OS X devices, how will this be accomplished? Options include user-based enrollment, NetInstall, or the Device Enrollment Program.

Do any of your management needs require iOS device supervision?

If you need to supervise iOS devices, how will this be accomplished? Apple Configurator 2 or the Device Enrollment Program?

If you're considering user-based enrollment, should any Setup Assistant steps be skipped?

If you're considering Apple Configurator 2, what profiles and apps can be installed during iOS device preparation?

What post-preparation issues need to be solved in your situation? Examples include signing in to network or cloud services and syncing user items.

Are you going to migrate user data from an older device to new devices? What method will you use? How long do you anticipate this process will take per device?

Do you need to assign specific names to devices?

Item Management

How do you plan to install new apps on iOS devices?

How do you plan to install new apps on OS X computers?

How do you plan to install new books to Apple devices?

Will iOS devices need to sync media to and from computer systems?

Are users going to be allowed access to Internet services? How will they configure access to these services? Is additional software required?

Are users going to be allowed access to local storage solutions? Examples include wiki and file sharing.

How are users going to back up important information from their iOS device?

How are users going to back up important information from their OS X computers?

Do you need to restrict the movement of organizational information on iOS devices to prevent unauthorized sharing (via Managed Open In)?

Ongoing Maintenance

Software Updates

How often will your devices update Apple system software?

How often will your devices update other Apple-sourced apps?

Given the number of items installed and updated from Apple's servers, how many caching servers would be helpful in your environment?

What method will you use to handle additions and third-party updates?

When will system deployment components be reviewed/updated?

When will client settings (managed or otherwise) be reviewed/updated?

Service and Support Options

What is the plan to handle daily support queries?

Will you be taking advantage of any recovery solutions, such as Apple's Find My Device? When will this service be turned on? What Apple ID will be used to turn on this service?

Will your iOS devices be updated to version 9.3.x, and will your MDM be capable of recovering devices using Apple's newly introduced MDM Lost Mode?

If a device needs to be physically repaired or replaced, what is the plan?

What turnaround time is required for repairs? Will you carry spare accessories or devices?

Will your organization need additional AppleCare warranty services?

Will your organization obtain third-party theft or damage insurance for computers and devices?

Could your organization take advantage of the Self-Service program to manage service and repairs locally?

How do you plan to dispose of or recycle old computers?

Index

Numbers
802.1X, securing data in transit, 78

A
Access management
- iOS app restrictions, 666–667
- with Managed Open In, 659–661, 667–693
- restricting to services via profile, 693–700
- sharing/storage in iOS, 662–664
- sharing/storage in OS X, 665–666
- testing OS X Server access and reachability, 105–106

Accounts
- activating DEP administrator account, 316
- activating VPP administrator account, 413
- allowing VPP access to iTunes account, 438–439
- configuring fresh OS X install on server, 120–121
- creating local administrator account, 45
- creating/verifying ADP agent account, 307–312
- creating/verifying DEP administrator account, 314–315, 317–318
- creating VPP administrator account, 411–412
- defining enrollment settings for assignments, 298–299
- logging in with VPP administrator account, 414
- managing VPP accounts, 386–387

Activation Lock
- allowing, 365–366
- behavior, 342–343
- bypass code, 366–369
- clearing with Profile Manager, 349–350
- defining assignment enrollment settings, 296
- Find My Device and, 340–341
- iCloud services and, 31–33
- impact on administration, 339–340
- iOS device preparation limitations in Apple Configurator 2, 505
- managing, 343–344
- overview of, 339
- on supervised device, 359–371
- turning on, 344–348
- on unsupervised device, 351–359

Active Directory, securing data in transit, 80

Activity Monitor, examining Caching service, 160–161

Ad hoc services, as traditional iOS and OS X sharing option, 647

Administration portal, Profile Manager, 176

Administrative tasks, Profile Manager, 239–242

Administrators
- activating DEP administrator account, 316
- activating VPP administrator account, 413
- authenticating, 418
- configuring fresh OS X install on server, 120
- creating DEP administrator account, 314–315
- creating local administrator account, 45
- creating new administrator account, 46–47, 122–123
- creating/verifying administrator Apple ID, 53–55, 58–61
- creating VPP administrator account, 411–412
- defining assignment enrollment settings, 299
- downloading profiles, 187–188
- impact of Activation Lock on, 339–340
- logging in with VPP administrator account, 414
- managing DEP administrators, 279–282
- mandatory skill requirements for book lessons, 8
- third-party management solutions and, 706
- verifying DEP administrator account, 317–318

ADP (Apple Deployment Program)
- creating/verifying program agent account, 307–312
- DEP service. *See* DEP (Device Enrollment Program)
- program agent, 384
- using Apple IDs, 606
- verifying Apple IDs, 23
- VPP service. *See* VPP (Volume Purchase Program)

AFP (Apple Filing Protocol), 72

AirDrop
- ad hoc sharing for iOS devices, 647
- downloading student materials, 128
- prevent sharing organizational information over, 661
- securing data in transit, 80

Airplane mode, turning on/off, 98

AirPlay, 69, 647

Amsys plc, installing/running Services Test app, 96

APNs (Apple Push Notification service)
- Activation Lock using, 345
- automatically pushing profiles, 244
- confirming connectivity to, 91–93
- device management requirements, 220
- enabling, 134–135

713

Index

inspecting pushed profiles, 244–247
network service availability and, 74
pushing configurations and tasks, 216–218
securing data in transit, 80–81

App Store
adding apps with VPP Apple ID, 611–613
attempting install on restricted client Mac, 697–698
creating/verifying administrator Apple ID, 53–55
creating/verifying client Apple ID, 56–58
downloading Apple Configurator 2, 517
downloading apps from, 167
installing app that can read PDFs, 673–674
installing OS X apps, 700
purchasing apps and books, 385
purchasing OS X Server, 131–132
testing Caching service, 159
updating iOS apps, 620
updating software, 49, 127
VPP and, 37, 375–376

Apple Configurator 2
Activation Lock behavior and, 343
backup and migration, 500–502
combining DEP or Apple School Manager with, 275
comparing versions of, 496–498
Console app, 162
creating an organization, 519–520
defining assignment enrollment settings, 296
defining MDM server, 521–523
deploying in-house apps and books to iOS devices, 465
erasing/resetting iOS devices, 341
examining preferences, 518
inspecting organization certificate, 520–521
inspecting profile documents, 172–173
installing, 506, 517
installing command-line tool, 523–524
institutional use of Apple IDs, 25
limitations on device preparation, 502–505
logistical considerations, 499–500
overview of, 495
performing initial configuration, 87
preferences, 511–516

preparing and supervising iOS devices, 498–499
redemption codes for purchased apps, 37–38
restoring/managing iOS workflows, 653–654
running for first time, 518
supervising devices, 15
views, 507–510

Apple Configurator 2, managing apps/documents
adding apps, 609–611
adding documents, 615–617
adding in-house enterprise apps, 613–614
Apple IDs and, 606–608
distributing in-house apps, 638–643
distributing VPP apps. See VPP (Volume Purchase Program), distributing apps
exporting documents, 617–618
managing apps with VPP Apple ID, 611–613
overview of, 605
removing apps, 615
single app mode, 621–624
updating apps, 618–621
viewing apps, 615

Apple Configurator 2, managing iOS devices
automating, 556–560
backing up/restoring, 551–555, 599–604
creating configuration profiles, 560–565
creating/using blueprints, 545–546, 576–599
organizing devices by groups, 547–551
overview of, 525
preparing. See Preparing iOS devices, Apple Configurator 2
using configuration profiles, 526–530

Apple Deployment Program. See ADP (Apple Deployment Program)
Apple Developer ID, 527, 559
Apple Developer Program, 25, 461
Apple Device Enrollment program. See Enrollment
Apple devices, introduction to guide
exercise setup, 4–8
learning methodology, 2–3
lesson structure, 3–4

online documentation, 8
prerequisites, 1–2
Apple Filing Protocol (AFP), 72
Apple IDs
activating DEP administrator account, 316
adding apps with personal ID, 609–611
adding apps with VPP, 611–613
Apple Configurator 2 and, 606–608
creating, 19–20
creating two, 52–53
creating/verifying administrator ID, 53–55
creating/verifying ADP agent account, 308–312
creating/verifying client ID, 56–58
DEP service enrollment and, 278–279
deploying, 39–41
developing management plan for, 709
institutional use of, 25
licensing and, 375–376
managing, 20–22
mandatory requirement for completing book lessons, 5
overview of, 17–19
setting up iCloud, 26–28
setting up iOS device, 357–359
Setup Assistant and, 535
sharing, 23–24
updating iOS apps and, 620–621
using same ID for VPP and DEP, 384
using Setup Assistant without, 672–673
verifying, 22–23
verifying access administrator access, 58–61
verifying DEP administrator account, 317–318
Apple Pay, 535
Apple Push Notification service. See APNs (Apple Push Notification service)
Apple Remote Desktop, 465–466
Apple School Manager
Activation Lock and, 348
assignment placeholders, 292–293
configuring assignments, 292
creating Apple IDs, 24
creating device groups, 293–294
defining assignment enrollment settings, 295–299

Index

enrollment limitations, 302–303
forcing continued enrollment in MDM service, 529
institutional use of Apple IDs, 25
overview of, 38–39, 274–276
preparing iOS devices via automated enrollment, 536–540
restoring/managing iOS workflows, 654
rules for Apple IDs, 606
supervising devices, 498
verifying functionality, 299–302
Apple store, 20
Apple TV
    Caching service support, 147–148
    planning subnets, 69–70
    preparing, 542–545
Apple USB Camera Adapter, 646
Apple websites, 20
AppleCare support, 88–89
Apps
    assigning, 396–401, 427–428, 434
    assigning/installing free OS X, 699–700
    attempting to install on restricted client Mac, 697–698
    attempting to send document from unmanaged, 689–691
    available from Apple stores, 375
    confirming listing in Profile Manager, 423
    deleting/reinstalling, 168–169
    deploying, 428–432
    inspecting availability, 450–452
    inspecting available licenses, 454–455
    installing on iOS device, 441–442
    iOS restrictions, 666–667
    managed apps, 226, 381–383
    Managed Distribution, 378
    Managed Open In and, 660–661
    managing. *See* Apple Configurator 2, managing apps/documents
    manually installing, 409–410
    MDM features, 216
    purchasing, 390
    purchasing free app for iOS device, 418–420
    purchasing free app for OS X computer, 422
    purchasing free OS X app for VPP managed distribution, 698–699
    purchasing paid app for iOS device, 420–421
    removing Managed Distribution apps, 407–408
    restricting use, 446–449
    revoking assigned, 401–402
    sending document from managed, 691–693
    unassigning, 454
Apps, in-house
    acquiring, 464
    adding enterprise, 479–481, 613–614
    assigning enterprise, 481–482
    deploying, 459, 464–466
    deploying with Profile Manager, 474–475
    distributing via Apple Configurator 2, 638–643
    enrolling, 476–478
    examining Remote Management profile before saving/installing, 482–484
    managing, 468–471
    preparing devices for, 475–476
    pushing, 471–473, 484–485
    removing, 487–488
    running on client Mac, 485–487
    unenrolling, 488–489
    uploading to Profile Manager library, 467–468
Architecture
    Caching service, 147
    MDM, 215–216
Assets, recording asset information, 86
Assignment
    apps, 396–401, 427–428, 434
    books, 396–401, 435
    configuring, 292
    creating device groups from, 293–294
    defining enrollment settings for, 295–299
    of DEP devices, 288
    of devices to MDM service, 326–327
    in-house apps, 466
    in-house books, 466, 491
    in-house enterprise app, 481–482
    installing assigned apps on iOS device, 441–442
    iOS devices to MDM service, 423–424
    placeholders, 292–293
    revoking assigned apps, 401–402

unassigning apps, 454
unassigning in-house books, 492–493
unassigning iOS devices, 334, 369, 455–456
Assignment Mode, VPP, 379, 396–397
Authentication
    securing data in transit, 78
    verifying Apple IDs, 23
    Wi-Fi, 69
Automated enrollment
    effects of Prepare action, 572–574
    preparing iOS device via DEP, 566–572
    preparing iOS devices via Apple Configurator 2, 536–540
Automated management, Apple Configurator 2
    exporting Automator actions, 558–559
    installing Automation Tools, 556
    using Automator actions, 556–558
    using cfgutil command, 560
Automatic discovery, Caching service, 149
Automatic Login, 47
Automator
    exporting actions, 558–559
    installing, 556
    using actions, 556–558

B

Backups
    backing up iOS devices, 652–653
    backing up OS X computers, 654–656
    to iCloud, 62–63
    managing, 656–657
    media lacking in iOS, 651
    before recycling or disposal, 87
    requirements for OS X services, 103
    restoration workflows, 653–654
    restoring iOS devices, 551–555, 602
    supervising, 500–502
Bandwidth, for network infrastructure, 67
BIND (Berkeley Internet Name Domain), 156–157
Blueprints, creating/applying
    allowing enrollment for Everyone group, 592
    applying to supervised iOS device, 600–601
    applying to your iOS device, 583–588, 593–595

Index

challenges in, 576
considerations, 576–577
creating and configuring, 577–583
distributing VPP apps, 627–629, 631–634
duplicating and modifying Prepare action, 589–592
Erase All Content and Settings, 577, 588–589
overview of, 545–546
turning on MDM lost mode, 595–599
wiping iOS device, 599
Bonjour, 69
Books
assigning, 396–401, 435
availability from Apple stores, 375
confirming list of purchased, 423
inspecting, 455
inspecting availability, 450–452
installing, 409–410
managed, 381–383
Managed Distribution, 378
purchasing, 390, 421–422
viewing on iOS device, 442–443
Books, in-house
acquiring, 464
adding, 490–491
assigning, 491
confirming on iOS device, 492
deploying, 459, 464–466
deploying with Profile Manager, 489
enrolling, 489–490
managing, 468–471
removing, 493–494
unassigning, 492–493
unenrolling, 493
uploading to Profile Manager library, 467–468
Brownouts, power, 83
Browsers
configuring Safari to open to Apple Support, 263–264
DEP service requirements, 277
BYOD ("bring your own device"), 39
Bypass code, Activation Lock, 349–350, 366–369

C

Cables, Apple TV, 542
CacheWarmer, 163
Caching service
architecture of, 147
automatic discovery, 149
with complex networks, 151–152
configuration options, 157–158
confirming registration with Apple, 166
downloading apps, 167
editing permissions, 153–157
examining with Activity Monitor, 160–163
finding suspected issues, 160
iCloud data, 30
monitoring, 158–159
as OS X service, 100
on private network, 149–151
requirements, 147–149
setting up, 152
testing, 159–160
turning on/verifying, 165
updating iOS apps over the air via, 620
verifying, 167–170
Caching Service pane, 167–168
CalDAV, 71
Calendars, 71, 142
CAs (certificate authorities)
issues with untrusted certificates, 111–112
OD (Open Directory), 180
purchasing code-signing certificate, 174
signing certificate with Open Directory CA, 109–111
signing certificate with widely trusted CA, 112–114
verifying certificates, 107–108
Certificate-signing request (CSR), 112–114
Certificates
configuring OS X Server, 107–109
importing certificate identity, 114–115
issues with untrusted certificates, 111–112
securing data in transit, 79
securing transmission, 107
signing with Open Directory CA, 109–111
signing with widely trusted CA, 112–114
cfgutil, 523–524, 560
Chain of trust, 108, 111
CIDR (Classless Inter-Domain Routing), 155
Classroom app, 624
Classroom feature, 11
Clients
configuration profile, 196–198
configuring. *See* OS X clients, configuring
configuring server on, 143–145
creating standard local account, 694–695
enrolling, 476–479
enrolling in VPP, 431–432
enrolling using user portal, 254–256
removing from management, 268–269
restricting access to services, 693–700
running OS X apps, 485–487
unenrolling, 488–489
verifying Caching service, 169–170
Cloud services. *See also* iCloud, 72–73
Code signing
comparing signed and unsigned profiles, 207
configuring Profile Manager for, 206–207
inspecting profiles, 205–206
installing signed profiles, 210–211
installing unsigned modified profiles, 212–213
installing unsigned profiles, 208–210
profiles, 174–176
turning on, 180
Collaboration services, 646–647
Command-line tool, 523–524, 560
Computer accounts. *See also* Accounts, 45, 120–121
Computer name
server network considerations, 104
specifying, 47–48, 123–124
Configuration profiles
adding passcode to, 263
adding to blueprint, 580
applying blueprint to iOS device, 586–587
comparing signed and unsigned profiles, 207–208
configuring Profile Manager for signing, 206–207
confirming, 262
creating/editing, 526–527
creating for groups, 201–202, 261–262
creating for users, 194–195
creating with Apple Configurator 2, 560–565
default, 178–179
downloading, 196–200

Index 717

downloading/installing updated, 203–204
editing payload of, 184–185
inspecting unsigned profiles, 205–206
installing signed and unsigned profiles, 210–213
installing with Apple Configurator 2, 528–530
limiting access to content/services on iOS devices, 662–664
MDM features, 216
modifying signed and unsigned profiles, 208–212
preparing iOS devices via automated enrollment, 538–539
removing, 200, 204, 529–530
removing from downloads folder, 271
restoring backups, 554
restricting service access, 693–700
signing/unsigning, 527–528
types of profiles, 172
updating, 202–203
Connectivity, telnet confirming, 91–93
Console, Apple Configurator, 162, 166
Contacts, 71, 142
Cooling infrastructure, 85–86
Credentials. *See also* Apple IDs
applying blueprints, 594
Automated Enrollment, 539
clearing Activation Lock, 349
creating/verifying ADP agent account, 309–311
defining assignment enrollment settings, 296
logging into VPP administrator account, 414
preparing iOS devices, 331
setting up iOS device, 357–359
Credit card payment, 607
CSR (certificate-signing request), 112–114
Customers, Apple focus on experience of. *See also* Users, 10

D

Data
backing up, 87
restoring, 554
secure erase, 88
securing data at rest, 76–77

securing data in transit, 78–81
Datagram Transport Layer Security (DTLS), 79
Delivery
Profile Manager and, 184
receiving, 86
DEP (Device Enrollment Program). *See also* Enrollment
activating administrator account, 316
Activation Lock and, 348
adding administrator account, 314–315
adding MDM server, 319
adding placeholder to device group, 327–328, 361–362, 567–568
adding public key to MDM server on DEP site, 321
adding servers, 283–286
allowing Activation Lock, 365–366
assigning devices, 288, 326–327, 567
assignment placeholders, 292–293
configuring assignments, 292
configuring Profile Manager for, 318
confirming device enrollment, 337
creating device groups for DEP placeholder records, 323–325
creating device groups from assignments, 293–294
creating/managing device enrollment, 329–330
creating/verifying ADP agent account, 307–312
defining assignment enrollment settings, 295–299
deploying organization-owned devices, 40
enrolling in, 312–313
enrollment limitations, 302–303
exporting server's public key, 320
forcing device to remain enrolled, 529
inspecting configuration profiles, 332–334
institutional use of Apple IDs, 25
integrating with Profile Manager, 282–283
managing DEP administrators, 279–282
managing devices, 288–292
managing servers, 286–287

overview of, 35–37, 274–276
preparing device using automated enrollment, 566–575
preparing devices with Apple Configurator 2, 536–540
preparing devices with Setup Assistant, 330–332, 336
Profile Manager support, 176
removing devices assigned to MDM server, 574
removing placeholders, 335
restoring/managing iOS workflows, 654
rules for Apple IDs, 606
service enrollment, 278–279
service requirements, 276–278
steamlining enrollment, 219
supervising devices, 15
supervision of devices, 498
unassigning devices, 334
verifying administrator account, 317–318
verifying functionality, 299–302
wiping devices, 335
Deployment
DEP and, 35–37
of equipment to user or location, 87
in-house apps and books, 459, 464–466
in-house apps with Profile Manager, 474–475
in-house books with Profile Manager, 489
managing with MDM, 258–259
options, 35
scenarios, 38–41
third-party management solutions and advanced, 706
VPP and, 37–38
Device Enrollment Program. *See* DEP (Device Enrollment Program)
Device Information, exporting in Apple Configurator 2, 550
Device placeholders. *See* Placeholders
DHCP (Dynamic Host Control Protocol)
configuring fresh OS X install, 120
configuring network interfaces, 126
mandatory requirements for completing book lessons, 7
server network considerations, 103
Digital signatures, verifying certificates, 107
Directory Services, 70
Disposal/recycling, devices, 87–88

DNS (Domain Name System)
    availability of Internet services, 74–75
    Caching service and, 151
    configuring network interfaces, 126
    confirming connectivity to APNs, 92
    confirming PTR records, 116–119
    server network considerations, 104–105
Documents. *See also* Apple Configurator 2, managing apps/documents, 172–174
Downloading profiles
    as administrator, 187–188
    for client Mac, 196–198
    for iOS device, 198–200
    updating, 203–204
    as user, 188–189
DTLS (Datagram Transport Layer Security), 79
Duplicating blueprints, 589–592, 627–629
Dynamic Host Control Protocol. *See* DHCP (Dynamic Host Control Protocol)

E

EAS (Exchange ActiveSync), 71, 81
Editing
    blueprints, 545–546, 577–583
    configuration profiles, 527–528
    duplicating blueprint, 589–592
    tags, 547
El Capitan
    configuring for OS X client, 42–43
    configuring for OS X Server, 133–134
    verifying server hardware requirements, 101–102
Email
    adding alternative address, 59–61
    encouraging user enrollment in MDM, 223
    network service integration, 71
    sending VPP invitations, 403, 435–436
EMM (Enterprise Mobility Management). *See also* MDM (Mobile Device Management), 263
Encryption
    of backups, 553, 555
    securing data at rest, 77
    securing iCloud, 29

Energy Saver, system preferences, 103
Enrollment
    activating DEP administrators, 316
    Activation Lock and, 348
    adding DEP administrators, 314–315
    adding MDM server, 319
    adding placeholder to DEP device group, 327–328, 361–362
    adding public key to MDM server, 321
    adding servers, 283–286
    adjusting settings, 567
    allowing Activation Lock, 365–366
    assigning devices, 288, 326–327
    assignment placeholders, 292–293
    associating network user with enrolled device, 440–441
    of client Macs, 478–479, 695–696
    configuring assignment, 292
    configuring Profile Manager, 318
    confirming enrolled devices, 256–258, 337
    creating device groups, 293–294, 323–325
    creating/managing, 329–330
    creating/verifying ADP agent account, 307–312
    defining assignment settings, 295–299
    in DEP, 276–279, 312–313
    DEP and Apple School Manager and, 274–276
    encouraging users, 223–226
    exporting server's public key, 320
    inspecting device setup profile, 332–334
    integrating DEP with Profile Manager, 282–283
    of iOS devices, 476–477, 489–490, 675–676
    of iOS devices using user portal, 251–254
    of iOS devices with MDM, 353–355, 362–364, 366
    limitations for DEP and Apple School Manager, 302–303
    of Mac computer using user portal, 254–256
    Managed Distribution, 402
    managing DEP administrators, 279–282
    managing DEP devices, 288–292
    managing servers in DEP, 286–287
    in OTA, 250–251
    overview of, 218–219, 273

    preparing iOS devices, 330–332, 336
    process of, 14–15
    removing placeholders, 335
    troubleshooting, 303–305
    unassigning iOS devices, 334
    unenrolling initiated by user, 229–230
    unenrolling iOS devices, 369–370, 488–489, 493
    unenrolling iOS devices from VPP, 456
    unenrolling via OTA, 265–266
    user-initiated, 222
    using Apple Deployment Programs, 305–306
    verifying DEP administrator account, 317–318
    verifying DEP or Apple School Manager functionality, 299–302
    verifying VPP enrollment, 405–406
    via user portal, 226–229
    in VPP, 313–314, 384–385
    wiping iOS devices, 335
Enrollment profiles
    options for enrolling in MDM service, 219
    preparing Apple TV devices, 543
    removing, 529–530
    types of profiles, 172
Enrollment website, 223–224
Enterprise apps
    adding in-house, 479–481, 613–614, 638–640
    assigning, 481–482
    pushing to group, 484–485
Enterprise Mobility Management (EMM). *See also* MDM (Mobile Device Management), 263
Enterprise solutions, AppleCare, 89
ePub
    acquiring digital publications, 375
    acquiring in-house books, 464
    managed books and, 382
Ethernet
    caching server saturating interface, 161
    configuring network interfaces, 125
    configuring OS X on server, 120
    network infrastructure and, 68–69
    requirements for OS X services, 103
    securing data in transit, 78
Everyone group, 592

Index

EWS (Exchange Web Services), 71
Exchange ActiveSync (EAS), 71, 81
Exporting
    Automator actions, 558–559
    device information, 550
    documents from app to Mac, 617–618
Extensible Markup Language (XML), 173–174

F

FaceTime, 80–81
Family sharing, 24
Favorites group, searching for devices, 549
Fetch Device Location, MDM, 597–598
File services, 72
File sharing
    Internet options for, 648–649
    OS X services, 100
    traditional options for, 645–647
File System, deploying apps and books to OS X computer, 465
File Transfer Protocol (FTP), 72
FileVault security, 77
Find My Device
    Activation Lock and, 340–341
    enabling, 356, 366
    iCloud services, 31–33
    recovery solutions, 82
FireWire, 129
Firmware, copying, 502
Folders, iOS, 72
FTP (File Transfer Protocol), 72

G

Gatekeeper security, 461–463, 559
Get Info, Apple Configurator, 549, 615, 619
Gigabit Ethernet. *See also* Ethernet, 103, 161
Groups
    adding placeholder to, 327–328
    allowing enrollment during Setup Assistant, 592
    assigning in-house books, 491
    creating configuration profile for, 201–202, 261–262
    creating for placeholders, 323–325, 424–427
    creating from assignments, 293–294
    creating profiles, 182–183
    creating Wiki page for, 259–261

    importing into server's shared directory node, 138–139
    organizing devices by, 235–236, 547–551
    pushing enterprise app to, 484–485
    removing from Managed Distribution, 453

H

Hardware, OS X Server considerations, 101–103
Heating, ventilation, and air conditioning (HVAC), 86
Help Desk, AppleCare, 89
Home screen, of iOS device
    applying blueprint, 584, 587–588
    configuring blueprint, 579–580
    inspecting device management, 636–637
    overview of, 443–446
    removing layout and restrictions profile, 454
HVAC (heating, ventilation, and air conditioning), 86

I

iBooks Author file, 464
iBooks Store
    acquiring digital publications, 375
    Caching service support, 147–148
    managed books, 382
    purchasing books, 385
    testing Caching service, 159
    VPP and, 37
iCloud
    Activation Lock limiting device preparation, 505
    Activation Lock working in conjunction with, 340
    backing up and managing content, 28–29
    backing up device to, 62–63
    backing up iOS devices, 652–653
    caching personal data, 157
    clearing Activation Lock, 349
    creating Apple IDs, 20
    family sharing and, 33–34
    Find My Device and Activation Lock features, 31–33
    managed distribution and, 382
    network service integration, 72–73
    saving configuration profiles, 527
    securing, 29–30
    setting up, 26–28

iCloud Drive, 72, 650–651
iMessage, 80–81, 223
In-house apps. *See* Apps, in-house
In-house books. *See* Books, in-house
Infrastructure
    cooling, 85–86
    developing management plan, 703, 707–709
    network infrastructure, 67–70
    power infrastructure, 83–84
    third-party management solutions and, 705
Installation Mode, VPP, 379, 398–399
Installation workflows (handling logistics), 86–87
Internet
    DEP service requirements, 277
    iCloud Drive storage service, 650–651
    mandatory requirements for completing book lessons, 6
    network service availability, 74
    planning network infrastructure, 70
    sharing/storage options, 648–649
Internet Accounts, OS X system preferences, 649
Internet Protocol (IP), 74–75
Inventory
    recycling/disposing of, 87
    third-party management solutions and, 706
iOS Apple USB Camera Adapter, 646
iOS devices. *See also* Preparing iOS devices, Apple Configurator 2
    access management. *See* Access management
    adding in-house enterprise apps, 479–480
    adding placeholder to device group, 361–362
    Apple Configurator 2 views, 507–510
    assigning in-house enterprise app to, 481–482
    assigning to MDM service, 326–327
    associating network user with enrolled device, 440–441
    backing up to iCloud, 62–63
    backup solutions, 652–653
    Caching service support, 147–148
    comparing signed and unsigned profiles, 208
    configuring Mail for network user on, 436–437

confirming enrollment, 337
confirming in-house books on, 492
creating/applying blueprints. *See* Blueprints, creating/applying
creating groups for placeholders, 424–426
DEP (Device Enrollment Program), 35–37, 276
deploying in-house apps and books, 464–465
deployment scenarios, 38–41
developing apps for, 460–461
disassociating user from, 455
downloading configuration profile, 198–200
enabling Activation Lock, 355–357
enrolling, 251–254, 353–355, 362–364, 489–490
enrollment limitations for DEP and Apple School Manager, 302–303
erasing content and settings, 341, 351–352, 362, 370
examining Remote Management profile before saving/installing enterprise app, 482–484
iCloud Drive, 650–651
iCloud in managed environments, 26, 29
inspecting setup profile, 332–334
inspecting unsigned configuration profile, 206
installing assigned apps on, 441–442
Internet sharing/storage options, 648–649
iTunes syncing, 651–652
limitations on device preparation by Apple Configurator 2, 502–505
Managed Distribution and, 378
managing backups, 656
managing home screen of, 443–446
managing in-house apps and books, 468–471
overview of, 62
personal folders, 72
physical security, 76
preparing and supervising, 498–499
preparing for Activation Lock, 352–353
preparing for enrollment, 330–332, 336
preparing for in-house apps, 475–476
prerequisites for managing, 1–2
preventing unauthorized access, 340
purchasing free apps, 418–420
purchasing paid apps, 420–421
removing enterprise apps, 487–488
removing from management, 266–268
removing settings, 454
resetting, 63–64, 329–330
restoration workflows, 653–654
setting up, 64–65
storage options for, 646–647
supervising, 16
troubleshooting enrollment, 303–305
turning on Activation Lock, 344–348
unassigning, 334, 369, 455–456
unenrolling, 369–370, 456, 488–489, 493
viewing books on, 442–443
wiping, 335, 357, 364–365
iOS Direct Service Program, 90
IP addresses
    Caching service and, 148–151
    CIDR (Classless Inter-Domain Routing), 155
    configuring network interfaces, 125
    confirming connectivity to APNs, 92
    confirming lack of PTR records, 116
    external access of reachability testing for servers, 105
    mandatory requirements for completing book lessons, 7
    server network considerations, 103–104
IP (Internet Protocol), 74–75
iPads. *See also* iOS devices
    defining enrollment settings for assignments, 296
    enabling Find My iPad, 366
    estimating power needs, 84
    Find My Device and Activation Lock features, 31–33
    Shared iPad feature, 11
iPhones. *See also* iOS devices, 31–33, 84
iPods. *See also* iOS devices, 84
IPv4 addresses. *See* IP addresses
IT (information technology), 10–11

Item management, developing management plan, 704, 710–711
iTunes
    acquiring apps, 375
    Activation Lock behavior and, 342
    adding documents to device via file sharing, 615–617
    allowing VPP access to iTunes account, 438–439
    Caching service support, 147–148, 160
    deploying in-house apps and books to devices, 464
    iOS backup and, 652–653
    managed distribution and, 382
    managing apps with personal Apple ID, 610
    syncing devices, 651–652
    updating apps, 620

K

Kensington security slot, 75
Kerberos, 80
Keychain Access, 513

L

LDAP (Lightweight Directory Access Protocol), 70
Licenses
    inspecting available app licenses, 454–455
    making purchases and, 394
    managing, 24
    reading agreement before distributing app, 625
    VPP and, 376
Lightweight Directory Access Protocol (LDAP), 70
Local administrator accounts. *See also* Accounts, 45, 120
Locally attached drives, storage options, 646–647
Location Services
    applying blueprint to devices, 585, 594, 600
    effects of Prepare action on device using automated enrollment, 572
    restoring device from backup, 603
    Setup Assistant and, 534
Lock screen, 572, 588, 596
Lock Screen Message payload, 564–565
Login, 47, 695
Logistics, developing management plan, 703, 707–709

Index   721

Logs
    examining Caching service, 161–163
    inspecting Push Diagnostics, 95–96
    verifying Caching service, 165, 168–169
Lookup, confirming lack of PTR records, 117
Lost mode, MDM, 595–599

M

Mac App Store
    adding apps with personal Apple ID, 609–611
    authorizations when using Apple Configurator 2, 606–607
    downloading Apple Configurator 2, 506
    purchasing apps and books, 385
    testing Caching service, 159
    VPP and, 37
Mac computers. See OS X computers
Mail service
    attempting to open apps that read PDFs, 681–685, 686–689
    attempting to send document from unmanaged app, 689–691
    configuring for network users, 436–437
    configuring for workgroups, 669–671
    configuring/starting, 139–140
    Open In PDF, 680–681
    sending/receiving test messages, 142
    verifying, 140–141
Maintenance, developing management plan, 704, 711–712
Managed apps and accounts, 659–660
Managed Distribution
    accepting invitations, 405
    assigning apps and books, 396–401
    configuring VPP, 416–417
    confirming invitations, 439
    editing payment information, 415
    enabling, 433–434
    installing apps and books, 409–410
    integrating Profile Manager with VPP, 387–390
    managed apps and books, 381–383
    overview of, 377–381
    removing apps from, 407–408
    removing group from, 453
    revoking assigned apps, 401–402

sending invitations, 402–404, 435–436
uploading items to Profile Manager Library, 467
user enrollment, 402
verifying VPP enrollment, 405–406
verifying VPP purchases, 395
VPP and, 37
Managed Open In
    configuring, 661
    restricting access with, 659–661
    securing data in transit, 81
    workflow, 667–693
Management concepts, Apple
    Apple ID and, 17–19
    Apple School Manager, 38–39
    backing up and managing iCloud content, 28–29
    creating Apple IDs, 19–20
    customer experience and, 10
    DEP and, 35–37
    deployment options scenarios, 35, 38–41
    Find My Device and Activation Lock features, 31–33
    institutional use of Apple IDs, 25
    IT focus at Apple, 10–11
    managing Apple IDs, 20–22
    mobile device management, 14–15
    overview, 9
    profile use, 12–14
    securing iCloud, 29–30
    setting up iCloud, 26–28
    sharing Apple IDs, 23–24
    sharing iCloud service with family, 33–34
    supervising devices, 15–17
    taking advantage of new features, 11
    verifying Apple IDs, 22–23
    VPP and, 37–38
Management plan. See Plan, management
Maps application, lost mode and, 598
MDM (Mobile Device Management)
    adding passcode to configuration profile, 263
    adding public key to server on DEP site, 321
    adding server, 319
    administrative tasks with Profile Manager, 239–242
    Apple Push Notification service, 216–218
    architecture of, 215–216
    assigning devices to, 326–327, 423–424

associating devices with users, 233–235
automatically pushing profiles, 244
comparing Apple Configurator 2 with, 495
configuring Managed Open, 661
configuring Safari to open to Apple Support, 263–264
confirming configuration profile, 262
confirming enrolled devices, 256–258
confirming passcode, 264–265
creating configuration profile for groups, 261–262
creating Wiki page for a group, 259–261
defining server, 521–523
DEP service requirements, 277
deploying apps remotely, 607
deploying in-house apps and books, 465–466
enabling device management, 220–222, 247–249
encouraging user enrollment, 223–226
enrolling Apple TV devices, 542–545
enrolling in, 14–15, 218–219
enrolling in OTA, 250–251
enrolling iOS devices, 251–254, 353–355, 362–364
enrolling OS X computers, 254–256
enrolling via user portal, 226–229
features, 216
importing device lists, 238–239
inspecting automatically pushed profiles, 244–247
inspecting devices, 231–233
inspecting placeholders, 270
installing in-house enterprise app, 614
integrating with VPP service, 388
lost mode, 82–83
managed distribution and, 382–383
managing deployment, 39–40, 258–259
managing devices, 219–220
My Devices user portal tasks, 242
network service availability, 74
organizing device, 243–244
organizing devices by groups, 235–236
overview of, 215

placeholders in Profile Manager, 236–238
preventing removal of enrollment profile, 37
Profile Manager as MDM service, 176
remote locking and wiping, 81–82
removing configuration profiles from downloads folder, 271
removing iOS device from management, 266–268
removing OS X computer from management, 268–269
services using TLS/SSL certificates, 109
turning on lost mode, 595–596
unenrolling, 229–230, 265–266
using Managed Open In, 660

MDM server
adding, 319
adding public key on DEP site, 521–523
assigning device to, 566–567
Automated Enrollment credentials for, 539
defining, 521–523
managing home screen layout payloads, 634–636
preparing iOS devices, 533, 536–537, 566–567
removing iOS devices, 574
VPP tokens cannot be shared among, 627

Memory, 102, 157–158
Micro-USB cable, 542
Migration, with AppleConfigurator 2, 500–502
Mobile Device Management. *See* MDM (Mobile Device Management)
My Devices user portal, 226–229, 242

N

NAT (Network Address Translation), 148–151
NetInstall, OS X services, 100
Network File system (NFS), 72
Network Utility, 116–119
Networks
Caching service and, 149–152
configuring interfaces, 124–126
developing plan for infrastructure, 708
file sharing, 646–647
infrastructure, 67–70

inspecting Push Diagnostics log, 95–96
interface requirements for OS X, 103
mandatory requirements for completing book lessons, 6–7
OS X Server considerations, 103–105
purchasing/running Push Diagnostic app, 93–95
purchasing/running Services Test app, 96–98
pushing network access, 225
service availability, 74–75
service integration, 70–73
telnet for confirming connectivity, 91–93
verifying service availability, 90–91
NFS (Network File system), 72

O

Open Directory
configuring server as Open Directory master, 135–136
creating code-signing certificate, 180
device management requirements, 219–220
issues with untrusted certificates, 111–112
network service integration, 70
signing certificate with Open Directory CA, 109–111
Organizations, Apple Configurator 2, 519–521
OS X clients, configuring
configuring existing system, 46
creating local administrator account, 45
creating new administrator account, 46–47
creating/verifying Apple ID, 56–58
downloading student materials, 50–52
establishing student number, 42–44
overview of, 41–42
specifying computer name, 47–48
turning on remote management, 48–49
updating software, 49
OS X computers
acquiring in-house apps, 461–464

adding in-house app to iOS device, 638–640
adding in-house enterprise apps, 480–481
backup solutions, 654–656
Caching service support, 147–148
comparing signed and unsigned configuration profiles, 207
configuring client computer, 42–43
configuring existing system, 46, 121–123
configuring fresh install of, 119–121
cooling infrastructure, 86
creating device groups for Mac placeholder, 426–427
DEP and, 35–37
deploying in-house apps and books to, 465–466
developing OS X apps, 461–463
downloading configuration profiles, 196–198
enrolling client Macs, 478–479
enrolling in VPP, 431–432
estimating power needs, 84–85
Find My Device and Activation Lock features, 31–33
iCloud and, 26, 29
iCloud Drive, 650–651
inspecting unsigned configuration profile, 205–206
Internet sharing/storage options, 648–649
Managed Distribution, 378
managing backups, 656–657
mandatory requirements for completing book lessons, 5
personal folders, 72
physical security, 76
preparing for use as server, 115
prerequisites for managing iOS devices, 1–2
purchasing free app, 422
pushing enterprise apps to group, 484–485
pushing in-house apps, 471–473
removing from device management, 268–269
restricting access to services, 693–700
running apps on client Macs, 485–487
storage options for, 647
troubleshooting enrollment process, 303–305

unenrolling client Mac, 488–489
verifying Caching service, 169–170
verifying server hardware
   requirements, 101–102
OS X Recovery, 655–656
OS X Server
   benefits of, 99–100
   Caching service requirements, 148
   configuring as Open Directory
      master, 135–136
   configuring existing system on,
      121–123
   configuring for El Capitan,
      133–134
   configuring fresh install on,
      119–121
   configuring network interfaces,
      124–126
   configuring on client computers,
      143–145
   configuring/starting Mail service,
      139–140
   configuring with certificate,
      107–109
   confirming lack of PTR records,
      116–119
   downloading student materials,
      127–129
   enabling APNs, 134–135
   file sharing with, 646
   hardware considerations, 102–103
   importing certificate identity,
      114–115
   importing users and groups into
      shared directory node,
      137–139
   inspecting SSL configuration,
      136–137
   installing, 130–133
   issues with untrusted certificates,
      111–112
   mandatory requirements for
      completing book lessons,
      5–6
   network considerations, 103–105
   preparing Mac computer for, 115
   prerequisites for managing Apple
      devices, 1–2
   securing transmission, 107
   sending/receiving test
      messages, 142
   services, 100
   signing certificates, 109–114
   specifying computer name,
      123–124

testing external access and
   reachability, 105–106
turning on Calendar and Contacts
   services, 142
turning on remote
   management, 124
turning on Wiki service, 143
updating software, 127
verifying hardware requirements,
   101–102
verifying Mail service, 140–141
OTA (over-the-air), 14–15, 177, 250–251

P
Pairing
   allowing with Mac, 514
   device preparation limitations, 503
   preventing supervised devices, 662
Passcode
   adding to configuration
      profile, 263
   applying blueprint to iOS device,
      585–586, 595, 601
   confirming, 264–265
   creating configuration profile, 564
   securing data at rest, 77
   Setup Assistant, 535
Passwords
   authenticating devices, 23
   creating configuration profile,
      561–563, 564
   creating new administrator
      account, 46–47
   creating/verifying administrator
      Apple ID, 53–55
   creating/verifying ADP agent
      account, 308–310
   creating/verifying client Apple
      ID, 57
   managing home screen layout
      payloads for group, 635
   restoring backups, 553–554
   setting up devices, 357–359
Payload, configuration profile,
   185–187, 561
Payment
   creating/verifying administrator
      Apple ID, 54
   creating/verifying client Apple
      ID, 57
   credit option, 391–392
   direct payment option, 390–391
   editing payment information, 415
PayPal, 390

PDFs
   acquiring digital publications, 375
   acquiring in-house books, 464
   managed books and, 382
   print services and, 73
Permissions, Caching service, 153–157
Personal identification numbers
   (PINs), 77
Photos, adding to supervised device, 601
Physical logistics
   cooling infrastructure, 85–86
   developing management plan, 707
   disposal/recycling, 87–88
   estimating power needs, 84–85
   installation workflows (handling
      logistics), 86–87
   overview of, 83
   power infrastructure, 83–84
Physical security, 75–76
PINs (personal identification
   numbers), 77
PKI (public key infrastructure), 79,
   107–108
Placeholders
   adding new record to device
      group, 567–568
   adding to device group, 327–328,
      361–362
   assigning, 292–293
   creating device groups for,
      323–325, 424–427
   importing device lists, 238–239
   inspecting, 270
   in Profile Manager, 236–238
   removing, 335, 369–370,
      488–489, 493
   unenrolling and, 230, 456, 575
Plan, management
   consider third-party solutions,
      704–706
   define requirements, 701–704
   developing, 706–712
   overview of, 701
Ports, 70, 104–105
Power infrastructure, 83–85
Preferences, Apple Configurator 2
   creating backup for supervised
      device, 602
   duplicating device blueprint,
      590, 628
   examining, 518
   overview of, 511–516
   preparing devices for manual
      enrollment, 532–534

Preparing iOS devices, Apple Configurator 2
  Apple TVs, 542–545
  applying to blueprint, 545–546
  automated enrollment, 536–540
  automated enrollment via DEP, 568–574
  configuring blueprint, 580–583
  duplicating blueprint, 589–592
  manual enrollment, 532–536
  overview of, 530–531
  verifying Setup Assistant customizations, 540–542
Print services, 73
Profile Manager
  acquiring public key from, 284–285
  adding passcode to configuration profile, 263
  adding placeholders to device group, 327–328, 567–568
  administrative tasks, 239–242
  Apple Configurator 2 vs., 526
  assigning apps and books, 379, 396–401, 435
  associating devices with users, 233–235
  automatically pushing profiles, 244
  clearing Activation Lock, 349–350
  components of, 176–177
  configuring, 177–178
  configuring for DEP, 318
  configuring for signing configuration profiles, 206–207
  configuring for VPP, 410–411, 416–417
  configuring Managed Open In, 661
  confirming configuration profiles, 262
  confirming enrolled devices, 256–258
  confirming Managed Distribution invitations, 439
  creating configuration profiles for groups, 201–202, 261–262
  creating configuration profiles for users, 194–195
  creating device groups placeholders, 323–325, 424–427
  creating profiles, 181–183
  deploying in-house apps, 474–475
  deploying in-house books, 489
  device management requirements, 219–220
  distributing in-house apps, 640–641
  downloading profiles, 185–189
  editing configuration profile payload, 185–187
  enabling device management, 220–222, 248–249
  enabling Managed Distribution, 433–434
  enrolling iOS devices, 251–254
  enrolling OS X computers, 254–256
  enrolling via user portal, 226–229
  General settings, 184–185
  identifying placeholders, 230
  importing device lists, 238–239
  inspecting app and book availability, 450–452
  inspecting app licenses, 454–455
  inspecting automatically pushed profiles, 244–247
  inspecting devices, 231–233
  inspecting profile documents, 172–173
  integrating with DEP, 282–283
  integrating with VPP, 388–390
  making purchases, 395
  Managed Open In settings, 685–686
  managing Activation Lock, 343–344
  managing backups, 656
  managing devices, 219
  managing in-house apps and books, 468–471
  managing network/home screen layout payloads, 634–636
  organizing device management, 243–244
  organizing devices by groups, 235–236
  OS X services, 100
  placeholders in, 236–238
  preparing Apple TV devices, 543
  preparing iOS devices, 532
  pushing in-house apps, 471–473
  removing Managed Distribution apps, 407–408
  removing placeholders, 335
  restricting access to services, 696–700
  revoking assigned apps, 401–402
  sending VPP invitations, 402–404
  single app mode, 623–624
  turning on, 192–193
  turning on Activation Lock, 344–348
  turning on MDM lost mode, 596–598
  unenrolling, 574–575
  updating configuration profile, 202–203
  uploading in-house apps and books to Profile Manager library, 467–468
  using Managed Open In with, 660
  verifying VPP enrollment, 405–406
  wiping iOS devices, 335, 341
Profile Manager Library, 467–468
Profiles
  cleaning up, 213–214
  code signing, 174–176
  comparing signed and unsigned, 207–208
  components of Profile Manager, 176–177
  configuring Profile Manager service, 177–178
  configuring signing configuration profiles, 206–207
  creating configuration profile, 201–202
  creating for users, 194–195
  default configuration profile, 178–179
  downloading and confirming configuration profile, 196–200
  downloading as administrator, 187–188
  downloading as user, 188–189
  downloading updated configuration profile, 203–204
  editing configuration profile payload, 185–187
  examining Remote Management profile before saving/installing iOS enterprise app, 482–484
  General settings, 184–185
  inspecting profile documents, 172–174
  inspecting setup profile, 332–334
  inspecting unsigned configuration profile, 205–206

Index 725

installing signed and unsigned modified configuration profiles, 210–213
managing via, 12–14
managing Wi-Fi, 628–629
manually installing, 181, 190–191
modifying/installing signed and unsigned configuration profiles, 208–212
removing configuration profile, 200, 204
removing home screen layout and restrictions profile, 454
turning on code signing, 180
turning on Profile Manager, 192–193
types of, 172
understanding, 171
updating configuration profile, 202–203
user and group, 182–183
Profiles & Device Management, 572, 595, 636–637
Program agent, ADP, 307–312, 384
Provisioning profiles, 172
PTR records, DNS, 116–119
Public key infrastructure (PKI), 79, 107–108
Public keys
    acquiring, 284–285
    adding to MDM server, 321
    exporting server's public key, 320
Purchased apps, redemption codes for, 37–38
Push Diagnostic app, 93–96

Q

Queries, MDM device features, 216

R

RAM, effect on caching, 163
Recovery Key, verifying Apple IDs, 23
Recovery solutions, for lost devices, 81–83
Recycling, physical logistics, 87–88
Redemption codes, for purchased apps, 37–38, 376–377, 606
Remote access, configuring server for, 133
Remote Management
    applying blueprint to iOS device, 595
    effects of Prepare action on iOS device, 572–573

examining Remote Management profile before saving/installing enterprise app, 482–484
inspecting on iOS device, 636–637
turning on, 48–49, 124
verifying DEP or Apple School Manager functionality, 301–302
verifying Setup Assistant customizations, 541–542
Replacement parts, self-service, 90
Restore
    from backup, 551–555, 599–604
    iOS workflow, 653–654

S

S/MIME, 29
Safari browser, configuring to open to Apple Support, 263–264
Scalability, of third-party management solutions, 705
School Information System (SIS), 38
Search, for devices in Apple Configurator 2, 547–549
Secure shell (SSH), 80
Secure Sockets Layer. See SSL (Secure Sockets Layer)
Security
    creating configuration profiles, 561–564
    data at rest, 76–77
    data in transit, 78–81
    iCloud, 29–30
    MDM features, 216
    physical, 75–76
    profile, 185
    recovery solutions, 81–83
    theft deterrence, 275
Self-service
    support options, 90
    third-party management solutions and, 706
Server app
    configuring Profile Manager service, 177–178
    configuring server as Open Directory master, 135–136
    configuring server for remote access, 133
    configuring server on client computer, 144–145
    confirming Caching service, 160
    creating Wiki page for a group, 259–261

enabling APNs, 134–135
enabling device management, 248–249
importing users and groups into server's shared directory node, 137–139
inspecting SSL configuration, 136–137
purchasing OS X Server, 131–132
Stats pane, 158–159
turning Caching service on/off, 152
Server Message Block (SMB), 72
Servers
    adding DEP servers, 283–286
    adding MDM server, 319
    adding public key to, 321
    defining with Apple Configurator 2, 521–523
    exporting public key, 320
    managing, 286–287
    removing OS X restrictions, 700
Service logs, 161–163, 165
Service set identifiers (SSIDs), 68
Services. See also by individual services
    developing management plan for, 711–712
    iOS restrictions to limit access to, 662–664
    OS X restrictions to limit access to, 665–666
    OS X Server, 100
    restricting access with profile, 693–700
Services Test app, 96–98
Set Up screen, Setup Assistant, 534
Settings app
    device management and supervision, 12
    inspecting installed profiles, 13
    Internet services in iOS in, 648
    resetting iOS device, 63–64
Setup Assistant
    Activation Lock behavior and, 342
    allowing group enrollment during setup, 592
    configuring blueprint for iOS device, 582–583
    configuring OS X on client, 42–43
    configuring OS X on server, 119–121
    creating Apple IDs, 20
    creating Open Directory master, 110
    defining assignment enrollment settings, 297–299

Diagnostics feature, 535
enabling Find My iPad, 366
enrolling devices with MDM, 362–364
facilitating enrollment, 274–275
installing configuration profiles, 529
preparing iOS devices for enrollment, 330–332, 336
preparing iOS devices for in-house apps, 475–476
preparing iOS devices via automated enrollment, 537, 540
preparing iOS devices via manual enrollment, 534–536
requesting Apple ID, 17–18
restoring/managing iOS workflows, 653–654
setting up iOS device, 64–65
troubleshooting enrollment process, 304–305, 541
using without Apple ID, 672–673
verifying customizations when preparing iOS device, 540–542
verifying DEP or Apple School Manager functionality, 299–302
Shared directory node, 137–139
Shared iPad feature, 11
Sharing
    files. *See* File sharing
    iOS restrictions, 662–664
    OS X restrictions, 665–666
Signed profiles, 527–530
Single app mode
    distributing in-house apps, 640–641
    for iOS device via Apple Configurator 2, 621–623
    for iOS device via Profile Manager, 623–624
    stopping, 623
Single sign-on (SSO), 80
Siri, 535
SIS (School Information System), 38
SMB (Server Message Block), 72
SMTP (Simple Mail Transfer Protocol), 105, 403
Software updates
    configuring client Mac, 49
    developing management plan for, 711

enrollment and, 275
preparing Mac to install OS X Server, 127
updating apps, 620–621
SSH (secure shell), 80
SSIDs (service set identifiers), 68
SSL (Secure Sockets Layer)
    certificates for secure transmission, 107
    inspecting configuration, 136–137
    securing data in transit, 79
SSO (single sign-on), 80
Stats pane, Server app, 158–159
Storage
    Internet options, 648–649
    iOS restrictions, 662–664
    OS X requirements, 103
    OS X restrictions, 665–666
    traditional options, 645–647
Subnets, 69, 104
Supervised iOS devices, 621–623
Supervision
    with Apple Configurator 2, 498–499, 533–534
    backing up and restoring supervised device, 599–604
    backup and migration and, 500–502
    configuring blueprint for iOS device, 582
    creating configuration profile for iOS device, 564
    defining assignment enrollment settings, 296
    of iOS devices, 15–17
    iOS restoration workflows and, 653–654
    modifying Prepare action on iOS device, 591–592
    preparation limitations for iOS devices, 502–505
    remote, 275
Support options
    AppleCare, 88–89
    developing management plan for, 711–712
    overview of, 88
    self-service, 90
Syncing, iOS iTunes, 651–652
System deployment, 703, 710
System imaging, of iOS devices, 551
System Preferences
    configuring network interfaces, 124–126

creating new administrator account, 46–47, 122–123
creating standard local account on client Mac, 694–695
Energy Saver, 103
profiles, 12
setting computer name, 47–48
updating software, 49, 127

T

Tags
    as addition to blueprint, 628
    configuring blueprint for iOS device, 578–579
    duplicating blueprint on iOS device, 590–591
    organizing devices by, 547
    searching for devices by, 547–549
TCP (Transmission Control Protocol), 104–105, 403
Telnet, confirming connectivity, 91–93
Template iOS device, 555, 620
Terminal app, 91–93
Text, 580
Text messaging, 223
Theft deterrence, 275
"Think different," Apple design philosophy, 9
Third-party solutions
    developing management plan with, 704–706
    Internet storage for iOS and OS X, 649
    Share and Document Provider App Extensions for iOS 8, 649
Thunderbolt, 129
Time Machine
    backing up OS X computers, 654–655
    backup and migration and, 500–502
    disabling access to, 657
TLS (Transport Layer Security), 79, 107
Touch ID, Setup Assistant, 77, 535
Training, developing management plan for, 709
Transmission Control Protocol (TCP), 104–105, 403
Transport Layer Security (TLS), 79, 107
Troubleshooting Caching service
    examining log files, 161–163
    examining with Activity Monitor, 160–161

overview of, 159
testing, 159–160
Troubleshooting enrollment
overview of, 303–305
during setup, 541
Trust
creating between DEP and MDM
services, 282
deploying trust profile, 111
types of profiles, 172
TXT records, DNS, 151, 156–157

U

UDP (User Datagram Protocol), 104–105
Unboxing equipment, 86
Uninterruptible power supply (UPS), 103
Unsigned profiles
creating, 528
installing on device, 528–530
Updates
of apps with Apple Configurator 2,
618–619
apps with Software Update,
620–621
developing management plan for
software, 711
of software, 49, 127
UPS (Uninterruptible power supply), 103
Usage management, developing
management plan, 703, 709–710
USB (universal serial bus)
connecting iOS device to OS X
computer, 499–500
distributing to iOS devices via,
606–607
downloading student
materials, 129
preparing Apple TV devices, 542
User data and services
backup solutions, 652–656
iCloud Drive, 650–651
Internet sharing/storage options,
648–649
iTunes syncing, 651–652
managing backups, 656–657
restoration workflows, 653–654
traditional sharing/storage options,
645–647
User Datagram Protocol (UDP), 104–105
User portal
enrolling iOS devices, 251–254
enrolling Mac computers, 254–256,
431–432
enrolling via, 226–229
Profile Manager, 177

removing client Mac from
management, 268–269
removing iOS device from
management, 266–268
tasks, 242
wiping iOS devices, 341
Users
Apple's user centric philosophy, 10
associating devices with, 233–235
creating configuration profile for,
194–195, 261–262
creating profiles, 182–183
disassociating from iOS device, 455
downloading profiles, 188–189
encouraging enrollment in MDM,
223–226
importing into server's shared
directory node, 137–138
unenrolling from MDM, 229–230

V

View VPP Assignments, 612
Views, Apple Configurator 2
of apps on iOS device, 615
getting device information, 549
overview of, 507–510
sorting devices, 550–551
Virtual private networks (VPNs), 78–79
VPNs (virtual private networks), 78–79
VPP (Volume Purchase Program)
accepting Managed Distribution
invitations, 405
account management, 386–387
acquiring tokens/configuring for,
674–675
activating administrator account,
413
adding apps, 611–613
administrator account and MDM,
608
administrator account for Apple
Configurator 2, 626–627
administrator account for
multiple copies of Apple
Configurator 2, 607
administrators, 281
allowing access to iTunes, 438–439
Apple stores and, 375–376
assigning apps, 396–401,
427–428, 434
assigning books, 396–401, 435
assigning devices to MDM service,
423–424
assigning managed apps that read
PDFs, 678–680

associating network user with
enrolled iOS device,
440–441
configuring Mail service for
network user, 436–437
configuring Profile Manager for,
410–411
configuring with Profile Manager,
416–417
confirming listing of purchased
apps and books, 423
confirming Managed Distribution
invitations, 439
creating administrator account,
411–412
creating device groups for
placeholders, 424–427
credit option, 391–392
deploying apps, 428–432, 608
deploying to user-owned
devices, 39
direct payment option, 390–391
disassociating users from iOS
device, 455
editing payment information, 415
enabling Managed Distribution,
433–434
enrolling in, 278, 313–314
erasing content and settings,
456–457
getting apps that read PDFs,
677–678
inspecting app and book
availability, 450–452
inspecting app licenses, 454–455
inspecting books, 455
installing assigned apps, 441–442
institutional use of Apple IDs, 25
integrating with Profile Manager,
387–390
legacy redemption codes, 376–377
licensing and, 376
logging in with administrator
account, 414
making purchases, 392–395
managed apps and books, 381–383
managed deployment, 621
Managed Distribution, 377–381
managing apps with Apple ID,
611–612
managing home screen, 443–446
managing licenses, 24
manually installing apps and
books, 409–410
overview of, 37–38, 373–374

Profile Manager support, 176
purchasing apps and books, 390
purchasing free app for managed
    distribution, 698–699
purchasing free apps, 418–420, 422
purchasing free books, 421–422
purchasing paid app, 420–421
removing group from Managed
    Distribution, 453
removing iOS device settings, 454
removing Managed Distribution
    apps, 407–408
restricting app use, 446–449
revoking assigned apps, 401–402
rules for Apple IDs, 606–608
sending Managed Distribution
    invitations, 402–404,
    435–436
service enrollment, 384–385
unassigning apps, 454
unassigning devices, 455–456
unenrolling devices and removing
    placeholders, 456
verifying enrollment, 405–406
viewing books on iOS device,
    442–443
VPP website, 385–386
VPP (Volume Purchase Program),
    distributing apps
    accepting Managed Distribution
        invitations, 405
    adding apps to blueprint, 631–632
    apply blueprint to iOS device,
        633–634
    challenge/considerations, 625
    confirming Managed Distribution
        invitations, 439
    creating Wi-Fi profile, 629–631
    duplicating blueprints, 627–629
    enabling Managed Distribution,
        433–434
    erasing content and settings, 633
    inspecting iOS device
        management, 636–637
    Managed Distribution, 377–381
    managing network/home screen
        layout payloads, 634–636
    purchasing free app for managed
        distribution, 698–699
    removing group from Managed
        Distribution, 453
    removing Managed Distribution
        apps, 407–408
    sending Managed Distribution
        invitations, 402–404,
        435–436
    sign to Apple Configurator 2,
        626–627

W

Wallpaper, 579, 587
Warranties, 88–89, 90
WebDAV, 72
Wi-Fi
    applying blueprint to iOS device,
        585, 593, 600
    configuring OS X install on
        server, 120
    creating configuration profile,
        561–563
    creating expiring profile, 628–629
    effects of Prepare action using
        automated enrollment,
        572–573
    inspecting iOS device
        management, 636
    managing network/home screen
        layout payloads, 635
    network infrastructure, 68
    preparing iOS devices via
        automated enrollment,
        538–539
    securing data in transit, 78, 80
Wiki service
    creating Wiki page for a group,
        259–261
    overview of, 100
    turning on, 143
Wipe iOS devices, 335, 357, 364–365,
    367, 575, 599
Workgroup, Managed Open In settings,
    685–686
WPA/WPA2, 78

X

Xcode app, 460–463
XML (Extensible Markup Language),
    173–174

Z

Zoom option, Setup Assistant, 535